HOSEA

HOSEA
A COMMENTARY

Gert A. van de Weerd

Hosea: A Commentary
Copyright © 2020 by Gert A. van de Weerd
All rights reserved.

Published in the United States of America by Credo House Publishers,
a division of Credo Communications LLC, Grand Rapids, Michigan
credohousepublishers.com

ISBN: 978-1-62586-178-8

Translation by Eduard van der Maas and Albert Gootjes
Editing by Elizabeth Banks
Composition by Sharon Vanloozenoord

Printed in the United States of America

First English edition

EDITORIAL REVIEWS

Prof. emeritus Dr. Samuel D. Schmitt (Montemorelos University, Mexico):
The two volumes on Daniel and his extended works on such other prophets as Hosea are a responsible search for essentials that underline how promises of Israel's future relate to God's program within the church. A very interesting commentary, which raises new insights.

Prof. emeritus Dr. W. H. Velema (Theological University of Apeldoorn, the Netherlands):
The commentaries of Gert A. van de Weerd stand apart from current mainstream theology. He is so unique that we need a special model to characterize his work.

CONTENTS

Foreword from the Author 8
Preface: 9
      A. The Waiting Room of History   9
      B. Prophecy Is Being Fulfilled   10
      C. The Literal Method   13
      D. The Allegorical Method   15
      E. A Bridge to Judaism   16
      F. Biblical Scholarship   18
      G. Important Points of Departure   19

Introduction 31
      A. Which Text?   31
      B. The Prophet and His Time   32
      C. A Difficult Text   33
      D. How Should We Understand Hosea   34
      E. The Authorship of Hosea   35
      F. Hosea Is Ultimately Eschatology   36
      G. Exegetical Perspectives   38
      H. The Return of Israel   40

Acknowledgments 43

The Commentary on Hosea

Hosea 1	Text	45
	Exegesis	59
Hosea 2	Text	83
	Exegesis	103
Hosea 3	Text	119
	Exegesis	127
Hosea 4	Text	135
	Exegesis	155

Hosea 5	Text	169
	Exegesis	187
Hosea 6	Text	199
	Exegesis	215
Hosea 7	Text	233
	Exegesis	251
Hosea 8	Text	259
	Exegesis	275
Hosea 9	Text	283
	Exegesis	299
Hosea 10	Text	309
	Exegesis	329
Hosea 11	Text	341
	Exegesis	359
Hosea 12	Text	369
	Exegesis	385
Hosea 13	Text	393
	Exegesis	409
Hosea 14	Text	417
	Exegesis	433

Bibliography 445
    General   445
    Other Jewish Sources   451
    The Internet   451
Index Annotations and Excursus 453
About the Author 455

FOREWORD FROM THE AUTHOR

Dear reader,

Hosea is a book that makes the reader fall from one surprise into another (provided the Hebrew text is followed meticulously, which many translations fail to do). It speaks of a passionate love relationship between God and the people of Israel, but also of the grief of God when this relationship is ruptured.

This book of Hosea dramatizes the character of the Almighty. And even though this is done in inadequate human terms (and therefore is limited), it nevertheless reveals sacred things to us.

The book of Hosea is eschatological in nature. It unlocks a surprising amount of information about future events. It talks mainly about the fate of the ten tribes of Israel (the northern nation) and also about their blessed destiny. All these events (to the extent that they are fulfilled to date) seem so perfectly in keeping with history, that God's hand becomes visible on every page of the book.

The prophet Hosea shows himself to be a warm personality. In this he is a type in which (by human measure) something of the character of the Eternal God shows through.

Hosea is a touchingly beautiful book, in which we find words of life. It is therefore rightly called *the second-most beautiful story in the Holy Bible*. The most beautiful remains, of course, the history of Jesus Christ.

In Christ united,

Gert A. van de Weerd

August 2020, Veenendaal, the Netherlands

The Book of HOSEA
Preface

A. The Waiting Room of History

A1. The Lost Ten Tribes
In the book of Hosea, the Almighty resolutely sets aside ten of the twelve tribes (Israel, later called Ephraim after the largest of the ten). He places them in the "waiting room of history." They lose their identity, their special bond with Yahweh, and the knowledge of their ultimate blessed destination. What remains are tribes, families, or peoples who live scattered all over the world. The only thing they have in common is the knowledge that somewhere they have roots in the people of Israel. Sometimes they still preserve some Mosaic practices and/or serve Yahweh, although very imperfectly, and they claim to be descended from the ancient people.

The Ten Tribes have lost almost all knowledge of their high origin. They only know that they are "different." The only one who knows how to find them is God Himself, because it is He who placed them in the waiting room of history. He is also the One who one day will open the door of that waiting room because, prophecy says, that *must* happen!
(See Excursus 7)

A2. God's Holy Name Is at Stake
The downfall of Israel is an intolerable blot on the reputation of the Almighty God. The prophet Ezekiel speaks about this in chapter 36:20–21 (NASB):

> *"When they came to the nations where they went, they profaned My holy name, because it was said of them, 'These are the people of the LORD; yet they have come out of His land.' But I had concern for My holy name, which the house of Israel had profaned among the nations where they went."*

So the people of Israel *must* return to the land of Canaan to take away that reproach. But there is a problem. There are two different groups of people: the Jews (the tribes of Judah, Benjamin and some Levites) and the Israelites (the other ten tribes). The Jews are an easily identifiable people. Since roughly the year 1900 they have begun to return to the promised land. But we know very little about the Ten Tribes. They seem to have disappeared into the mists of history. Ezekiel 37:19 (NASB), however, unmistakably foretells the ultimate return of the Ten Tribes and their reunion with Judah/Benjamin into one people:

> *"Say to them, 'Thus says the Lord GOD, "Behold, I will take the stick of Joseph, which is in the hand of Ephraim, and the tribes of Israel, his companions; and I will put them with it, with the stick of Judah, and make them one stick, and they will be one in My hand."'"*

And Ezekiel 36:24* says (we use a direct translation from the Hebrew text, because of the details):

> *"I will bring you [Israel] forth out of the nations, and I will gather you [Judah] from all countries, and I will bring you [Israel and Judah] back to your own land."*

(*Weerd, Hebrew text translation in *Ezechiël*, vol. 2, 328)

A3. All the Twelve Tribes Will Come Back
The people of Israel were scattered like chaff (Hosea 13:3) and were absorbed into the nations. But they will be made visible (*bring you forth*; see Ezekiel 36:24 above) again in the end times. This process has begun in our time. Today there are people in India, China, and Africa who claim to be descended from Israel. Telugu Jews (Ephraim); Bnei Menashe (Manasseh); Beta Yisrael (Dan); Pathans (various tribes of Israel); Chiang-Min Jews; etc.

In contrast to the Ten Tribes of Israel, it is not necessary to make the Jews—the descendants of the two tribes of Judah and Benjamin—visible. They are easy to find and will be *gathered* from all countries of the world. Nevertheless the Ten Tribes will also return; all the people of Israel will go back to Canaan.
(See Excursus 5)

A4. Hosanna, the King Is Coming!
We, who live now, are witnesses to bewildering events, to a continuous acceleration of the advancement of God's plan of salvation and the fulfillment of all prophecy. This will change the world forever. Neither Washington, Beijing, Brussels, nor Moscow is the center of the world, but Jerusalem, the city of God. A long time ago the psalmist saw this future and sang about it (Psalm 2:4–6 NASB):

> *He who sits in the heavens laughs, the Lord scoffs at them. Then He will speak to them in His anger and terrify them in His fury, saying, "But as for Me, I have installed My King [Jesus] Upon Zion [Jerusalem], My holy mountain."*

B. Prophecy Is Being Fulfilled
Today there is great interest in eschatology—the doctrine concerning the last things—and thus also in biblical prophecies related to the end times. The Revelation of John, once an almost forgotten book of the Bible, is now eagerly read. This has led to a flood of publications. There have probably been more commentaries on Revelation since 1950 than in all preceding centuries. The same applies to a lesser extent to the book of Daniel, especially the second, prophetic part, which bears strong similarities to the Revelation of John.

The prophet Hosea also speaks about the end time. At first glance this would not seem to be the central theme of his prophecy, certainly not if measured by the number of verses dealing with these future events. (Note: a better translation increases this!) However, it certainly is the thrust of his ministry. The demise of Israel is always viewed against the dawn of its future salvation, which finds its crowning in the establishment of the Messianic Kingdom under the kingship of the Messiah. That is the ultimate goal.

The book of Hosea is thus a kind of guide. First of all it states what went wrong between God and His people in the past. It also warns against all sorts of wrong paths the people then took and will continue to take in the future. But again and again its glorious final destiny is held up before the people of Israel: the Messianic Kingdom.

B1. Bible Knowledge Is Increasing
In addition to the interest in biblical prophecy, knowledge of this prophecy also appears on the increase. This is especially true of those prophetic books that have the end times as their theme. However, this phenomenon should not surprise us, for it was foretold long ago in Daniel 12:4:*

> *But you, Daniel, close up these words and seal the scroll until the time of the end. Many will do research and the knowledge will increase."*

And in Daniel 12:8–10:*

8 *As concerns me, I heard it but did not understand it. That is why I asked: my Lord, what results from all this?*
9 *Then he answered: Go, now! Daniel, for the words are shut up and sealed until the time of the end.*
10 *Many will be purified and made blameless and cleansed. But the wicked will continue to do wickedness, and no single wicked one will notice. However, those who are wise will understand.*†

(*Weerd, Aramaic text translation in *Daniël*, vol. 2, 408, 414–17)
(†The true believer will understand prophecy about the end times.)

B2. The Wisdom of the Holy Spirit

The verses in Daniel 12 make it clear that insight into the *end-time prophecy* will be acquired only when that *end time* has arrived (or is near). However, even then *only the wise will understand*—that is, those who possess wisdom in the biblical sense. And the key to this wisdom is given by the Holy Spirit, who can give insight to the believer and will do so when the time is right. Revelation 13:18 (NASB), for example, speaks about this special wisdom:

> *Here is wisdom. Let him who has understanding calculate the number of the beast, for the number is that of a man; and his number is six hundred and sixty-six.*

And another example is Revelation 17:9 (NASB):

> *"Here is the mind which has wisdom. The seven heads are seven mountains on which the woman sits."*

There has been endless speculation about the meaning of the preceding verses, especially about Revelation 13:18. But if we take the Bible seriously, all this is in vain until the Holy Spirit gives *wisdom* to understand these prophecies. Even then, it appears to be reserved for a limited group, namely *the wise*, those who believe and study the prophecy. This special status of believers who understand the prophecies is confirmed in the following Bible texts:

Revelation 1:3 (NASB)
Blessed is <u>he who reads</u>, and <u>those who hear the</u> words of the prophecy.

Revelation 22:6 (NASB)
The Lord, the God of the spirits of the prophets, sent His angel to show to His bond-servants the things which must soon take place.

We find similar expressions in Matthew 24:15, but also in Mark 13:14, where it is written:

Let the reader understand (= the wise)

And in Revelation 2–3, where each of the seven letters to the churches in Asia ends with:

He who has an ear, let him hear what the [Holy] Spirit says to the churches. (NASB)

Only the wise (the true believer) who is focused on listening to God has that *ear*, because only to her or him does the Holy Spirit speak. This illumination by the Holy Spirit is also apparent in 1 Thessalonians 5:4–5 (NASB):

4 *But you, brethren, are not in darkness, that the day would overtake you like a thief;*
5 *for you are all sons of light and sons of day. We are not of night nor of darkness.*

The Old Testament has similar expressions. Thus we find in Zechariah 9:1:*

For those who keep their eye on the Lord and on all the tribes of Israel.

Also in Micah 6:9,† it says:

Then it is wisdom when people see your Name [in it].

In all these texts the prophecy speaks of a specific category of people who acquire insight and *wisdom* at God's time in order to be able to understand the prophecies concerning the end times. This process runs parallel to the increase of evil in the world. That too is a characteristic that can be measured to see if the end times are imminent, as is the growing state of holiness that will then characterize the true believer.

Another example can be found in Daniel 12:10 (NASB):

"Many will be purged, purified and refined, but the wicked will act wickedly; and none of the wicked will understand, but those who have insight will understand."

The true child of God thus becomes more holy in the end times and therefore more averse to evil. Parallel to that phenomenon, the depth of evil increases. Revelation 22:11 (NASB) also speaks of this:

"Let the one who does wrong, still do wrong; and the one who is filthy, still be filthy; and let the one who is righteous, still practice righteousness; and the one who is holy, still keep himself holy."

This process is in operation today! We will see believers gain wisdom and thus insight into biblical prophecy, but both good and evil will also increase and therefore begin to contrast more sharply.

(†Weerd, Hebrew text translation in *Micha*, 293; *Weerd, Hebrew text translation in *Zachariah*, 219)

C. The Literal Method

C1. Dictated by God

The method of biblical interpretation used in this book is called the literal method, which means that the literal meaning of the text is the guideline for exegesis. In the eyes of many, this statement is a "logical way of thinking." Yet sadly, apparently not! Because in theology many suppose a "hidden message" that does not have any direct link with the usual meaning of prophetic words. One reads *church* for *Israel* and believes that the blessings for Israel are transferred to the church. Is there any proof in the Bible for such a change of God's promises? No, absolutely not! And yet the curses remain for Israel—how inconsistent! But doesn't the Almighty hold these two in one hand: curses or blessing for those who follow Him or reject Him?

The literal method of interpretation has consequences for the exegesis of the prophetic word. The apostle Peter makes an important statement in 2 Peter 1:19–21 (NASB):

19 *So we have the prophetic word made more sure, to which you do well to pay attention as to a lamp shining in a dark place, until the day dawns and the morning star arises in your hearts.*
20 *But know this first of all, that no prophecy of Scripture is a matter of one's own interpretation,*

21 *for no prophecy was ever made by an act of human will, but men moved by the Holy Spirit spoke from God.*

According to the apostle Peter, prophecy is thus a word-for-word dictated message from God Himself. This is in contrast to, for example, the historic or poetic books of the Bible like Judges, Nehemiah, and Proverbs—called Ketuvim or Hagiographa. These books are, from a Bible-believing perspective, considered to be inspired by God but not dictated. They therefore lack the absolute authority of the prophetic books.* Since the Almighty is perfect, it logically follows that His message is also perfect.

(*They present a lower level of biblical authority. Thus no dogma should ever be based on Ketuvim writings.)

Our thesis is that originally this message was also much clearer when the Old Testament language (ancient Hebrew) was still being spoken. According to this view, the difficulties in understanding prophecy do not lie with the original text as recorded by the prophet. It was clear, detailed, logical, and methodical.

Unfortunately, the original biblical texts have been lost. What we read today are copies made of handwritten copies, made of handwritten copies, and so forth, made over many centuries. Many scholars therefore judge the reliability of the Bible, and especially that of the Old Testament, as dubious. Fortunately, thanks to important archaeological finds in the past seventy years, this doubt is now no longer necessary. Then again, unbelieving and/or liberal scholars appear to be of a different opinion.

C2. Differences among the Original Texts
The Bible translations, consulted for this Bible commentary to which we refer, show relatively large differences among them. These differences have the following causes:
a. There are differences between the various versions of ancient texts. These are probably the result of inaccurate copying and/or translating. In addition, it is suspected that these differences are "corrections" made by copyists who wanted to clarify the text based on their own viewpoints. (Incidentally, the oldest manuscripts show that Jewish copyists were much more accurate in their work than non-Jewish copyists.)
b. Not every Hebrew word has one fixed meaning. In some cases, it depends upon what the exegete or translator reads in (or into) it. This often leads to small and sometimes even major differences between the various translations.
c. A third cause of the variations among the translations lies in the differences in the doctrinal positions of translators and exegetes which influence their work. It often appears that not the original text but a particular exegesis has been the father of the translation. In other words: It often happens that what one wants to read in a text or, conversely, does not want to read in a text, has strongly colored the translation.

So the influence of a translator on the text is significant. A well-known saying among theologians is: *Every translation is also exegesis*—a very wise word that sets the tone.

C3. Sola Scriptura
The author of this commentary has chosen to understand the Hebrew text to the letter. It will be clear that finding the purest version of the original Hebrew text is therefore of great importance. This is usually the oldest, and thanks to the discovery of many very old manuscripts, great progress has been made in recent decades.

C4. The Literal Method
According to the literal interpretation of the original Hebrew text, the Bible always has the last word and the exegesis needs to be adjusted accordingly. Hence, if there is doubt about

the meaning, we must consistently search for similar texts in the Bible to explain and/or elucidate God's Word from these. This is called "comparing Scripture with Scripture." But if we get stuck, we must decide, if necessary, to accept that there is no reliable explanation for every text.

It is the study of the details that really allows the greatness of the biblical text to shine brightly. The lament of the faithful Jew—that there are seven times seventy interpretations behind each text—does not mean that there are varying possibilities of interpretation in the sense that white might possibly be gray or sometimes even black. It indicates that further study and elaboration on a biblical text will bring to light even more or (more accurately) adds to the interpretation. This in itself is logical, because the Almighty Himself is the author.

C5. Literal Exegesis—The Only Exegetical Method Capable of Proving Itself

It is precisely in the detail of the Hebrew text that such striking similarities with other parts of the Bible appear, both in the same book and in other prophetic books, that only one conclusion is possible: God Himself is the author. To be more clear, there is no method of human origin that can explain how dozens of different writers over a span of more than a thousand years could reach such perfect harmony and detailed agreement without bringing in the existence of God as a further explanation. This is a solid argument which cannot be undone from the unbelieving side. In this the Bible is unique.

C6. The Fingerprint of the Almighty

The deepest meaning of the text and the connections with other parts of the Bible show the contours of the counsel of God (= the plan of God for this world), which is eternal. This means that many facts of salvation history, including the personal actions of important emissaries of God, fit into a recognizable pattern. This is repeated again and again, both in the Old and in the New Testament.

Thus there are clear similarities between the life of Jesus Christ and that of Joseph (the son of the patriarch Jacob) but also between Jesus and Moses. The judgments described in the Revelation of John should also be viewed, for example, in light of the ten plagues that Moses inflicted on Egypt in the name of God (Exodus 7–12), because strong parallels can be observed between the two. We describe this phenomenon with the word *typology*.

God is always the same, and even as every writer can be recognized by his work, God's plan of salvation is also recognizable by His words and deeds. This is how we search for the fingerprint of the Almighty in all salvation facts, hence the great attention to detail.

C7. Prophecy and Logic

All that is good is from God. Anything that is bad or leads to destruction has its source in Satan. This statement can easily be made evident in a list of qualities. For example, *shalom* (well-being, peace, harmony) stands over against chaos, truth over against lie, logic versus disorder, beauty versus decay, peace over against war, reliability versus betrayal, mercy over against cruelty, etc. Of all the qualities mentioned, the first is always from God and always leads to something good—to improvement. The second is from Satan and always leads to something bad—to grief, destruction, or deterioration.

The author wants to apply this simple statement also to the way in which the prophets must be explained. Since 2 Peter 1:19–21 declares prophecy to be God's Word, it is by definition impossible that this message can be confusing and illogical. For then it could not be from God. Only logic is acceptable, and it is found in the literal exegesis.

D. The Allegorical Method

Some Bible-believing interpreters regard Hosea's prophecies as having been, for the most part or even entirely, fulfilled. Where this is clearly not the case, they view it as referring to the church of Jesus Christ or to the salvation after this life. The fact that the content of the prophecy does not correspond to the letter of the Hebrew text, does not seem to be considered an objection. We call this method of explanation the *allegorical exegesis*.

D1. Greek Influence

Western thinking and culture are deeply rooted in the ancient Roman Empire. That was, however, not an original culture, but a mixture of existing cultures. Great military ingenuity and ruthless severity, covered with a sauce of Hellenism (Greek thinking), merged into an almost unbeatable and all-dominating world power. After the decline of the Roman Empire, this culture remained largely intact, although Christian-biblical influences increasingly came to play a role.

The gods of the Romans were clones from the Greek world of gods. Those gods all had very human traits and excelled especially in unreliability. They mainly spoke in riddles or in such a way that the message was always open to more interpretations. This had to be so, because if those gods had spoken clear language, it would soon have become clear that they were human inventions and did not actually exist.

The God of the Old Testament was very trustable. He always spoke clear language that offered no room for doubt. The God whom Jesus Christ spoke about was no different either. However, in the fourth century, Hellenistic thought crept into Christianity. This created *once again* a god who spoke in riddles, even as the oracle of Delphi once did. That god was therefore a familiar image for pagans. So the conversion (in name) to Christianity had now become much easier. This god became widely acceptable and Bible texts could be adapted to fit one's own understanding by means of the allegorical interpretation. But has God indeed changed to such a degree?

D2. The Erroneous Path of Christian Triumphalism

Allegorical interpretation was a child of its time. In AD 324 Constantine the Great triumphed in a civil war for power in the Roman Empire. After he became emperor, the Roman Empire became Christian in name. With that, the prophesied kingdom of God seemed to have arrived. Triumphantly the one-thousand-year kingdom was proclaimed and shortly thereafter was given a firm theological foundation by the church father Augustine. This position was understandable. So much had been suffered. And now it had come about: the Roman Empire had been defeated.

Defeated? Certainly not. The Roman Empire remained powerful and cruel, just as before. But few Christians saw the reality, namely, that the Roman Empire differed greatly from the data provided by the Bible about the future kingdom of God. But isn't that merely a matter of interpretation? In addition, highly regarded theologians such as Origen provided a solution through allegorical interpretation.

Silently the people of Israel were removed from prophecy and replaced by the Christian church. Those troublesome Jews were done. *And* are they not enemies of the Christian faith? *And* was it not written: *"His blood come over us and our children!"* (Matthew 27:25). *And* had not that prophecy clearly been fulfilled?

But the almighty God is unchanging and so is His Word. We should therefore understand it as "clear language." If we do, the text will come to life. Will we then understand everything? Of course not, but it is not a bad thing to acknowledge "I do not know" or "it *may* be this or that." When the time comes, the Holy Spirit will reveal what is still lacking in our understanding.

D3. Allegory in Present-Day Commentaries
The allegorical interpretation is, until the present day, dominant in exegesis. This has also left its mark in the commentaries on the book of Hosea. With this, the possibility of understanding the words of the prophet to the letter disappears. Or to put it another way: if conventional concepts that have a logical and obvious meaning can suddenly mean something entirely different, then a Bible text can be given almost any explanation an exegete wants. Thus any connection with the reality of the written word is severed. Then one can justify every explanation, even the most bizarre, in a simple way. Thus the word of the exegete becomes normative, not God's Word.

The allegorical way of thinking is squarely at odds with Jewish exegesis. This created such a gap between Jews and Christians in the third and fourth centuries AD that a dialogue was hardly possible. Christianity, which was originally regarded as a variant of Judaism, moved away from its roots and became increasingly hostile to the Jews.

Within the Christian church, the allegorical way of thinking has also had a devastating effect, because it opened the door to all kinds of deviant ways of thinking. This resulted in the emergence of many sects that led millions into error until the present day. And they all justify their deviant (allegorical) way of thinking and exegesis from the same Bible.

Now allegory does not necessarily have to be rejected. The Talmud leaves the way open to allegory, provided that it is always preceded by literal exegesis, that is, the literal meaning. The author gladly agrees with this opinion.

So is there a place for interpreting Scripture using allegory? Certainly, provided that it does not replace the literal exegesis. So we can still read Matthew Henry and Spurgeon, both sincere children of God who saw in the ups and downs of Israel the difficult way of the church of the Lord but also of the individual believer. For the continual struggle against evil and the struggle to serve God correctly is a recognizable pattern. In this, the church does not fare any differently than the ancient people of God.

E. A Bridge to Judaism

E1. Anti-Semitism
Christians and Jews have studied the Bible separately for centuries. Their theologies have mutually excluded the other. This led to a great deal of bitterness and enmity. Since the Christian West held power since Constantine the Great became emperor of the Roman Empire, they were able to enforce their viewpoint. This resulted in a hatred, often at ecclesiastical instigation, which we call anti-Semitism.

Since the beginning of the last century, however, there has been a hesitant dialogue between the two parties. The murder of more than six million Jews in World War II accelerated this process. Since the establishment of the state of Israel in 1948, there has been an increasing willingness to listen to each other. This must be so, because we serve the same God. It is unworthy of His great Name if we live in hatred toward each other.

If we try to build a bridge to Judaism, the literal interpretation of Holy Scripture will help. This is not an invention of the author, nor a new method of biblical interpretation. The literal interpretation of the Bible already existed many centuries ago and dominated the dogmatism of the early Christian church.

E2. Which Bible?
The great gap between believing Christians and believing Jews is unnatural and is partly caused by a completely different view of the Bible. The word *Bible* comes from the Greek *biblia* which means *[the] books*. We know an Old and a New Testament, the Jews only the Old. That is their only Bible, which they call *Tanak*. It consists of three groups of books: the law (*Torah*), the prophets (*Nevi'im*) and the writings (*Kethuvim*).

E3. Different Bibles
The view Christians have of the Old Testament is, usually, very different from that of the Jews. The Old Testament is, in the daily life of Christians, a beloved source of stories; for the Jews a holy book. We can classify the various opinions as follows:

E3.a A Thin Bible

For some groups the Bible is, as it is used in practice, no more than the New Testament. Only the psalms have, in addition, gained an important place—not as a source of revelation but as a book that gives support in harsh times and adversity. In the few cases that the Old Testament is quoted, it is limited to those texts that support a passage from the New Testament. This often involves a shocking nonchalance. Texts are wrenched out of context and applied randomly.

E3.b A Selective Bible

A large part of Christianity uses the Old Testament as a supplement to the New Testament. In addition, the Old Testament still provides them with the fascinating stories from the historical books, which have a motivating and corrective function for the believer. The Old Testament is also for them a secondary book.

E3.c *The* Bible

A minority considers the Old Testament as the primary book. A complete whole. That book was finished when the Jewish canon was complete, which took place before the birth of Jesus Christ. Those Christians consider the New Testament as a supplement to the Old Testament.

Conclusion:
The author is of the opinion that the third statement is correct. This view is confirmed by the word of Jesus Christ Himself in Matthew 5:17–18 (NASB):

17 *"Do not think that I came to abolish the Law or the Prophets; I did not come to abolish but to fulfill.*
18 *"For truly I say to you, until heaven and earth pass away, not the smallest letter or stroke shall pass from the Law until all is accomplished."*

So Jesus Christ speaks of a Bible that has been completed. He has come to fulfill that Bible, that is, the Old Testament, what the Jews call *Tanak*. Not to supplement it! Yet the New Testament was written later. Why? Because Jesus was rejected. So He was looking for a new people. That became the church of Christ. To give this a solid scriptural basis, the New Testament had to be written and the Bible was thus expanded.

E4. The Old Testament Is Leading
Only those who hold view E3.c (*The* Bible) build a bridge to Judaism. Those who adhere to the other two are seen by Bible-believing Jews as proclaiming a false doctrine, and that kills any dialogue.

The Old Testament was once a book that was finished; a comprehensive unity in itself. It cannot be explained from the New Testament. It's the other way around, because the New Testament cannot be provided with any logical structure apart from the Old Testament—it has to be explained on the basis of the Old Testament. Therein lies the only foundation for a true exegesis.

The New Testament is not a second Bible. It is only a supplement to the Old Testament, which was at one time a complete whole. No New Testament was needed until the coming of Jesus Christ. Only after the Jews rejected Him did the era of the church of Christ begin. The New Testament filled this need for a supplement.

But, you will say, are then all those references in the Old Testament to Jesus Christ without value? Definitely not. But they have no connection with the name Jesus Christ. Those references speak of the coming Messiah. That this turned out to be the Lord Jesus is knowledge after-the-fact. The Old Testament does not speak about this in terms of Jesus. Rather, it speaks of the coming Messiah and His (earthly) Messianic Kingdom or God's kingdom. If the people of Israel had been worthy, this kingdom would have come, and the New Testament might never have been written.

Note: This does absolutely not mean, that Jesus Christ would then not have suffered for our sins. That had, since time immemorial, been a necessary condition for achieving full reconciliation with God.

(Heschel, *God in Search of Man*; Sherman, *Daniel*, xlvii–lvi; Weerd, *Jesaja*, vol. 2, 11–14)

F. Biblical Scholarship

It is clear as day that many Bible-believing Christians have developed a deep distrust of secular scholarship. This has its roots in a history in which secular scholarship was eager to use its knowledge and efforts to show that the Bible is unreliable. That scholarship was (unfortunately) sometimes right. For the Christian church (not the Bible) often held positions in the past that were contrary to the incontrovertible proofs of scholarship. This did not promote love between the two parties, and this struggle continues to this very day.

F1. New Evidence

Bible-believing Christians usually focus, especially for the above reason, exclusively on Bible research, so that other sources of knowledge are neglected. Understandable as that may be, it is very unfortunate. Even from a secular perspective, it must be admitted that the Bible is much more reliable than people thought. Thus there is increasing evidence today that the books of Moses were indeed written in the time they are dealing with (or at least a part of them). Nor can it be ruled out any more that they may be from the hand of Moses himself.

It has been shown that the description of the Egyptian plagues, and also that of the exodus of the twelve tribes, from Egypt, cannot be regarded as simply a collection of myths and sagas. There are now indications that this may be a very precise description of historical events. This does not mean that scholarship has come to see the ten plagues as miracles of God. Science has found natural causes instead.

Another striking example is the book Daniel, the origins of which were assigned by secular scholarship to the period 200–160 BC. This in contrast to the dating given by the prophet himself. Nowadays there are strong indications that the book is at least one hundred years older than the presumed date and may indeed date back to the period indicated by the book itself. This observation is of great importance, because when we accept the later date, the various predictions of the future, which appear to refer to the near future, appear to have been written *after* they had already taken place—a form of forgery that would be utterly unacceptable in light of the biblical message. But by accepting the earlier dating, there is real prophecy concerning the future!

F2. Better Translations
But there is, of course, also unimpeachable biblical scholarship. We refer specifically to the growing knowledge of the language of the Old Testament, ancient Hebrew, but also to the many ancient scrolls that have been found near the Dead Sea. The study of these has yielded new insights and data concerning the original text. As a result, we now have better translations than in the past. In these newer translations, the prophetic books in particular have become much more readable.

F3. New Media
Also, thanks to the general distribution of the personal computer, the Bible has become available in all sorts of translations to many more people. Original texts, exegesis, and commentaries are also accessible in absolutely perplexing quantities. And as if that is not enough, missing data are almost always available via the internet. A direct result is a huge increase in Bible research, often of a surprisingly high level. In addition, an open discussion about various exegetical issues is being conducted via the internet. This also leads to an enrichment of our knowledge. Thus the prophecy of Daniel is fulfilled in a wonderful way.

G. Important Points of Departure
In studying this Bible book, it is necessary to establish a number of presuppositions as the points of departure on which the exegesis of this book is based. In this way the book of Hosea becomes more readable and understandable.

G1. What we read is usually a translation.
These are based on various source texts. However, every translation is also a form of exegesis. Because the perspective of the translator, or his interpretation of the Hebrew text, will always influence his work. The critical reading of a translation is therefore not only useful but even necessary, especially given the improved Hebrew text available today and the increased knowledge of biblical Hebrew.

G2. We use three translations and the Hebrew text as our basis.
In this commentary we use the Hebrew text as found in the *NIV Interlinear Hebrew-English Old Testament* (NIVIHEOT) as our guide. We also use the NASB (*New American Standard Bible*), the KJV (King James Version) and the NIV (*New International Version*) as examples of traditional translations. It gives the student tools to help draw a comparison between different texts.

G3. The (Hebrew) text has the greatest authority.
It appears that there are often differences among the various Bible translations of Hosea that are in circulation. Sometimes these differences are (implausibly) large. Each of these differences can be discussed exhaustively and (if necessary) refuted. However, this book would no longer be a commentary but rather a refutation of the perspective of a particular exegete. Thus we would wander away from the real message of the prophet as it comes to us from the earliest texts. In this commentary we therefore go first directly to the original text as found in the NIVIHEOT.

G4. Ancient Hebrew is a difficult language.
There is only a limited group of linguistic specialists around the world who have mastered this language so well that they can speak with authority. However, even they still struggle

at times with the Hebrew text. It is only when a number of these specialists join forces, as has happened in the creation of the Hebrew text used in the NIVIHEOT, that this authority reaches the required level.

G5. Some knowledge doesn't make one an authority.
It is a misconception to suppose that if someone has any or even considerable knowledge of ancient Hebrew, he or she is able to present an authoritative translation. It is precisely these individual interpretations of the original text by these types of translator and/or exegetes, that have led to such large differences in translation and exegesis. These have become a great source of confusion.

G6. Reading the original Hebrew or Greek text are no longer essential.
A knowledge of the classical languages is no longer needed. What is needed is a knowledge of the abundantly available literature. There are more than enough study books, interlinear translations (word-for-word translations from the original text) and CD-ROMs, which elucidate all conceivable meanings of the original text. It involves studying with great perseverance for many years. It requires great dedication, but the result is a deepening knowledge of the Bible, which always makes it worth the effort.

Our guiding principle is found in 1 Thessalonians 5:19–21 (NASB):

19 *Do not quench the Spirit;*
20 *do not despise prophetic utterances.*
21 *But examine everything carefully; hold fast to that which is good.*

In this commentary we use the Excursuses to give background information that has assisted us in our exegeses. These address basic historical information and also dogmatic issues that might be controversial.

Excursus 1: The Seven Dispensations

It is inevitable that a short outline of the end times should also be included in this preface. For many Christians, their knowledge of the end times is limited to the fact that Jesus Christ will one day return on the clouds, as foretold in Acts 1:9–11. The how, when, and where, usually remain obscure. The reader, however, must have more data at his disposal if this study is to be done justice. So we briefly cover a number of concepts that have to do with the end times.

1.a The last days
This expression appears several times in the Old Testament. The word *days* does not refer exclusively to a period of twenty-four hours. In the Bible it can refer to an era, a long time, a limited time, as well as to a day of twenty-four hours. In the expression *the last days* the word days refers to an era.

In almost every movement of Christianity there are schemas that divide history into epochs or dispensations. These schemas vary greatly. Most commonly, Christians speak of seven eras (or dispensations):

1. Dispensation of Innocence (from the garden of Eden to the fall)
2. Dispensation of Conscience (from the fall to the flood)
3. Dispensation of Human Rule (from the flood to the Babylonian confusion of tongues)

4. Dispensation of Promise (from Abraham to the exodus from Egypt)
5. Dispensation of Law (from the exodus to the crucifixion of Christ)
6. Dispensation of Grace (from the day of Pentecost to the rapture of the church of Christ)
7. Dispensation of the Kingdom of Christ (from the second coming until the last judgment)

1.b Four different basic Hebrew phrases that refer to the future

1.b1 *In-coming-of-the-days* (Jeremiah 23:20; 30:24; 48:47; 49:39)

This term speaks of more than one day (era) and looks forward to the dispensations that are still future, calculated from the date Jeremiah wrote down his prophecy. Since that took place in the fifth dispensation, Jeremiah thus speaks unmistakably about the two remaining dispensations, the sixth and seventh, which are the dispensation of grace and that of the kingdom of Christ.

1.b2 *In-last-of-the-days* (Isaiah 2:2; Micah 4:1; Hosea 3:5)

This expression speaks of the *last-one*, singular. This is the last age and refers to the seventh dispensation, the kingdom of Christ or the Messianic Kingdom.

1.b3 *In-later-time-of-the-wrath* (Daniel 8:19)

This is probably not a complete era but rather a limited period of time at the end of an era (*later-time-of*), which is characterized here with *wrath* (Hebrew: *revenge*). It is therefore obvious to think of the end of the period of the great tribulation.

1.b4 *In-future-of-the-days* (Daniel 10:14)

This expression is very similar to that of 1.b1 above *(in-coming-of-the-days)* and has probably the same meaning. A second possibility is that these words emphasize the end-time element, that is, the events that occur in roughly the last ten to twenty years before the establishment of the Messianic Kingdom and when Jesus will become king in Jerusalem. In that context it might be possible to read: *in the days that concern the future*. If so, then this text may speak of events that will precede the establishment of the Messianic Kingdom (= the future).

1.c In that day

This term is frequently associated with the expressions we have discussed. This is often correct in terms of content, but not according to the literal sense.

The expression *in that day* is a translation. Literally it reads something like: *on-the-day-this-one*. By this is meant a limited time, which is of great importance in the history of salvation. The phrase *this-one* expresses uniqueness. We could also translate *on-the-day-the-special-one* (= *on that special day*) or, as we find in rabbinical writings, *at the appointed time*. Careful study of all biblical texts where we find this expression teaches us that these texts mainly concern the end time.
(Scherman, xlvii–lvi)

Excursus 2: The End Time

2.a The prelude

The end times, as a period, actually begin a few years before the rapture of the church of Jesus Christ. In those years the Antichrist or man of lawlessness will reveal himself (2 Thessalonians 2:3).

The name antichrist (= against Christ) is a collective name for important people from history who have made life difficult for the church of Christ. It is not incorrect to include figures such as the Roman emperor Nero and Domitian, some popes, Mao Zedong, Stalin, and Hitler in this group. However, if they are rightly ranked under the heading *antichrist*, then each of them has only been *an* antichrist. There will be only one who will be called *the* Antichrist—the last one. The Antichrist will be a world leader who will brilliantly create order in a period that will be characterized by global revolution and chaos, but also by major natural disasters (2 Thessalonians 2:9).

2.b The rapture
Around the time when the Antichrist will come to power, Jesus Christ comes to take away His church. This is an evacuation to protect them from the disasters that will take place. This event shows a striking resemblance to the salvation of Noah and his family (Genesis 6–7; Matthew 24:39). Even as the ark protected them from the flood, which destroyed all humans, the rapture saves the church of Christ from the catastrophic consequences of the coming great tribulation.

The following texts (NASB) speak about this salvation (called *the rapture*); the underlined words are synonyms for the great tribulation.

1 Thessalonians 1:10b:
Jesus, who rescues us from <u>the wrath to come</u>.

1 Thessalonians 5:4–5a:
But you brethren, are not <u>in darkness</u>, that the day would overtake you like a thief; for you are all sons of light and sons of day.

1 Thessalonians 5:5b:
We are not of <u>night nor of darkness</u>.

1 Thessalonians 5:9–10a:
For God has not destined us for <u>wrath</u>, but for obtaining salvation through our Lord Jesus Christ, who died for us.

Revelation 3:10:
"Because you have kept the word of My perseverance, I also will keep you from the <u>hour of testing</u>, that hour which is about to come upon the whole world, to test those who dwell on the earth."

2.c Biblical evidence for the rapture
In 1 Thessalonians 4:15 we find detailed information about the rapture:

For this we say to you by the word of the Lord, that we who are alive and remain until the coming of the Lord, will not precede those who have fallen asleep.

There appears to have been unrest in the congregation of Thessalonica about the question of what will happen to the living members of the church as well as to the deceased ones on the day of the coming of the Lord. The apostle Paul explains this precisely. He says that the living (*we*) will not precede those who died in Christ (*those who have fallen asleep*) in the rapture into heaven. Then 1 Thessalonians 4:16a (NASB) says:

For the Lord Himself will descend from heaven with a shout, with the voice of the archangel and with the trumpet of God.

The coming of Jesus Christ will take place *at a sign* or a command from His Father, God Himself. This will be audible, because a trumpet will sound. Then the Lord Jesus will *descend from heaven* (i.e., He will leave heaven), *and the dead in Christ will rise first.* (1 Thessalonians 4:16b) The sound of the trumpet will raise up all the dead who have *died in Christ*.

Paul continues in 1 Thessalonians 4:17a:

> *Then we who are alive and remain will be caught up together with them in the clouds to meet the Lord in the air.*

Both the dead in Christ who have been resurrected and all then-living believers will ascend up to Jesus Christ, who apparently will be waiting for them in the clouds above.

This text thus does *not* describe the second coming, as many assume. It does not state that Jesus Christ comes to earth, but that the believers go up to Him. This happens in a flash, called here *the twinkling of an eye*. We find this event described in detail in several Scripture passages, including Matthew 24:40–41:

> 40 *"Then there will be two men in the field; one will be taken and one will be left.*
> 41 *"Two women will be grinding at the mill; one will be taken and one will be left."*

The destiny of the believers in Christ who are taken up, is found in 1 Thessalonians 4:17b:

> *And so we shall always be with the Lord.*

That is to say, we will always dwell in the Father's house, the house of God (John 14:2). 1 Thessalonians 5:10 also speaks about this:

> *So that whether we are awake or asleep, we will live together with Him.*

2.d The Antichrist

The disappearance of millions of people from the earth will cause great chaos. The Antichrist will then seize power over part of the world (of which Europe will probably be the basis) and be appointed dictator. This begins a period that our Lord Jesus Christ describes as *a great tribulation* (Matthew 24:21).

Around that same time the Antichrist will make a covenant with the state of Israel and move his seat to Jerusalem. Some expect the rebuilding of the city of Babel as the future capital of the Antichrist. It is possible that an important part of this covenant will involve the rebuilding of the temple. According to many, this is the temple the prophet Ezekiel speaks about in chapters 40–46.

Since many Jews will see the Messiah in the person of the Antichrist, it is very likely that the Antichrist will be a Jew. The church father Irenaeus believed that he would come from the tribe of Dan.

2.e The great tribulation

This period will begin shortly after the rapture of the church of Christ. According to Daniel 9:27 it will last for a one year–week, that is, seven years. After three and a half of the seven years, the Antichrist will unilaterally break the covenant with Israel and establish a statue (a giant idol), that he will require everyone to worship.

This image, called the *abomination of desolation* by the Lord Jesus (Matthew 24:15; Daniel 9:27), will come alive and even speak, according to Revelation 13:15. Anyone who refuses to worship the beast will then be killed.

Especially the orthodox (believing) Jews will refuse to break God's commandment (*You will not bow to them nor serve them* [Exodus 20:5]). They will therefore be killed on a massive scale. The Bible calls this the *time of Jacob's trouble* (Jeremiah 30:7). In the second period of three and a half years of the seven years, the power of the Antichrist on earth will be absolute (Daniel 7:25; 11:36). Then he will also show his true face as a servant of Satan.

Although the church of Christ will have disappeared from the earth, many people will come to faith after the rapture. They will, however, have to fully experience the great tribulation. Matthew 24:22 (NASB) speaks of the persecution of those who remain faithful to God:

> *"Unless those days had been cut short, no life would have been saved; but for the sake of the elect those days will be cut short."*

The books of Daniel and Zechariah and the Revelation of John provide extensive and detailed information concerning the second period of the great tribulation, the battle for Jerusalem, and the establishment of the Messianic Kingdom.

2.f The death of the Antichrist

Shortly before the end of the great tribulation, the Antichrist will come into conflict with a coalition of nations (Daniel 11:40–44). This coalition will raise a great army that will march against the Antichrist. This army will gain the upper hand, and as a result the Antichrist will have to give up Jerusalem.

Jerusalem will then be taken by the coalition army (Zechariah 14:2a) and will be ravaged (Micah 4:11). The largest (unbelieving) part of the inhabitants will then also leave the city (Zechariah 14:2b). They will probably flee into a new valley that will be formed by a great earthquake that will split of the Mount of Olives (Zechariah 14:4–5) and they will find death there (Revelation 11:13).

Shortly thereafter, the coalition army will leave Jerusalem to pursue the retreating army of the Antichrist. In the battle that follows the Antichrist will definitely be defeated. A short time later, he will be killed by a spoken Word of Jesus Christ. Isaiah 11:4b (NASB) testifies:

> *And He [Jesus] will strike the earth with the rod of His mouth, and with the breath of His lips He will slay the wicked [the Antichrist].*

And 2 Thessalonians 2:8–10 (NASB) confirms Isaiah 11:4b

> 8 *Then that lawless one [the Antichrist] will be revealed whom the Lord will slay with the breath of His mouth and bring to an end by the appearance of His coming;*
> 9 *that is, the one whose coming is in accord with the activity of Satan, with all power and signs and false wonders,*
> 10 *and with all the deception of wickedness for those who perish, because they did not receive the love of the truth so as to be saved.*

2.g The return of Christ

When the coalition forces are busy marching against the Antichrist, the Messiah, Jesus Christ, will return to the earth in triumph. According to Zechariah 14:4, He will appear on the Mount of Olives, accompanied by celestial forces (Isaiah 66:15; Zechariah 6:1–8; Matthew 25:31; 2 Thessalonians 1:7b, 10). Next, the Messiah will enter Jerusalem and—together with the remaining believing Jews, also referred to as the *remnant*—will enter into battle with the coalition army (Micah 2:13), which will march against Jerusalem (Zechariah 12:3–9; 14:3).

2.h Armageddon

In the great battle of nations at Armageddon that follows, all enemies of God will be defeated definitively (Zechariah 14:12–15; Micah 4:12–13).

2.i The establishment of the Messianic Kingdom

Then the Messianic Kingdom will be proclaimed. This is also referred to as *the pleasant year (epoch) of the Lord* (Luke 4:19). There will be a world government with Jerusalem as its capital and the Lord Jesus as its king (Daniel 7:27; Ezekiel 37:25; Isaiah 9:6). According to Revelation 20, this blessed kingdom will exist for one thousand years.

The reign of the Messiah will then be expanded to include the whole world by means of the sending out of (in part heavenly) forces, probably under the leadership of the archangels. In that period, the lost Ten Tribes will also play an important role (Zechariah 9:13; 10:7–8).

2.j Additional information

After the Messianic Kingdom has come to an end, the power of Satan will be revived for a short time. After that will come for all God's enemies *the day, burning like an oven* (Malachi 4:1), that is, *the day of judgment*. After the seven dispensations that concern the old earth, human history will close with a period without end, that is the *Day of God*. Then all prophecy will have been fulfilled with the coming of a new heaven and a new earth, where righteousness will dwell (2 Peter 3:12–13; Revelation 21).

2.k When will this take place?

That is not known. The Lord Jesus says that even He does not know (Matthew 24:36), only God the Father knows when that great moment will be. He does give an indication in Matthew 24:34 (NASB), which may allow for a rough approximation:

"Truly I say to you, this generation will not pass away until all these things take place."

The beginning of the period in question, when the countdown to the end time has begun, is set by many at the year of the establishment of the State of Israel. (It will unfortunately not be possible to discuss this in more detail here.) The end, according to the word of Jesus Christ, takes place within a generation after this countdown starts. The question now is: what is a generation and how long is it?

2.l No speculation

We will go a bit further into this matter. This is not motivated by the conviction that the return of Jesus Christ can be accurately predicted, but rather by the many speculations that are spread around.

The duration of a generation is usually calculated on the basis of the average term within which a person gets offspring. For example, if we speak of the third generation, we think usually of a period of fifty to seventy-five years. The duration of one generation, according to the current measure, is therefore for a maximum of twenty-five years. However, the year 1948, when modern Israel was founded, lies now more than seventy years in the past, so it has been shown that this calculation is not applicable. The "escape route" of using the average life-span of man—which is about eighty to eighty-five years—to define a generation has no biblical foundation at all and does not solve anything.

2.m A better measure

Genesis 15:13–16 speaks of *four hundred years being four generations*. With this, a generation is set at one hundred years, which does not correspond to the current life expectancy.

There are, however, two eras that do fit. The period before the flood, when an individual could become almost one thousand years old, and the future era of the Messianic Kingdom. About that blessed kingdom of God, Isaiah 65:20 (NSAB) says:

For the youth will die at the age of one hundred and the one who does not reach the age of one hundred will be thought accursed.

The previous text teaches us that the part of a human life, which we refer to as *youth*, does in that period not end until the age of one hundred. We also read this in the second part of this text; which shows, that persons are only called to account for a sinful way of life, after that period of youth. A kind of "late" bar mitzvah actually. Isaiah 65:22 also says:

For as the lifetime of a tree, so will be the days of My people.

Most likely, the term *trees* is used to indicate olive trees, which grow to one-thousand years old—and so the circle is complete.

The correspondence between the Messianic Kingdom and the period before the flood is striking. In both periods people have a very long life-span. If we apply this data to the statement of Jesus Christ, then the second coming, according to this formula, will take place after 1948, with 2048 as the ultimate

Warning
The author does not want to stand behind this way of calculating—the scriptural basis is too weak and the speculative element too great.

Excursus 3: The Downfall of the Northern Kingdom, Israel

3.a Lost in idolatry
Under King Ahab the worship of God had already become marginalized in the northern kingdom. And after a brief revival under King Jehu, the people of Israel completely sank into idolatry, which they had adopted from the surrounding nations. Thus the nation barely distinguished itself from the gentile nations. The prophet Hosea then pronounced the curse *Lo Ammi* (not My people). This ushered in a series of judgments in which the kingdom of the Ten Tribes, Israel, perished. After that, only Judah remained as the visible bearer of the promise of the messianic age. Israel disappeared from sacred history.

However, the final role of Israel has not played out. The prophecy clearly speaks of a final restoration of the ten tribes of Israel, but that will happen only in the end time when the Messianic Kingdom is established.
(Weerd, *Ezechiël*, vol. 2, 370–72)
(See Excursus 5.)

3.b Samaritans: No bearers of the prophecy
The northern kingdom, Israel, was destroyed as a nation and an identifiable people. This happened as followed: From 733 to 735 BC the Syro-Ephraimite war raged, which was disastrous for Israel. In 734 the Assyrians invaded their country. Parts of Galilee and the entire region of Gilead were lost. At the end of the war, Israel had been reduced to an insignificant country and had become no more than a poor vassal state of Assyria.

Hoshea was the last king of Israel. He was made king by Tiglath-pileser III and paid an annual tribute to him. After Tiglath-pileser died (727), King Hosea stopped paying the taxation and revolted against the new Assyrian king, Shalmaneser V. He asked King So of

Egypt to help him break free of Assyria's power. Then King Shalmaneser marched against Israel. The army of Israel was crushed and King Hosea was captured. The Assyrian army marched through the country, murdering and plundering, and attacked Samaria (2 Kings 17:4–6). In 722 BC the city fell and was utterly destroyed. Thus also the last remaining part of the once-strong realm of Jeroboam II met with doom.

Both wars had taken a heavy toll on human lives. Most of the survivors were deported. Only a small number of people stayed behind in the devastated country. They mingled with foreign peoples who had been transferred by the king of Assyria to the northern part of Canaan (2 Kings 17:24). The descendants from this mix of peoples are called Samaritans. This mixture was never undone, as had happened in Judah under Ezra and Nehemiah. The Samaritans are therefore no longer descendants of Israel and thus also not bearers of the promise. (See 2 Kings 17:24–41.)
(Andersen and Freedman, 32, 35)

3.c A cruel people
The Assyrians were a people entirely focused on military conquest. They were known for their unheard-of cruelty. It is very likely that the final defeat of Israel also meant that almost the entire intelligentsia was killed. Thus the part of the population that could have safeguarded the cultural heritage for the future disappeared.

The people of Israel were now without leadership and were scattered over the great empire. A future restoration as a politically recognizable unit was virtually precluded, and Israel disappeared from history. Those left behind in Canaan mixed with other peoples. Thus the Ten Tribes ceased to be a recognizable identity.

3.d Did Israelites flee to Judah?
Some historians assume that part of the Israelites fled to Judah. They then see the people of Judah after the exile as representing all twelve tribes. That could be the case (and is not illogical), but it probably involved very limited numbers. During the kingship of King Ahaz of Judah there was deep enmity between Judah and Israel, which even degenerated into a war (2 Kings 16). Since Ahaz was an ally of Assyria (the attacker of Israel) during the destruction of Israel, it is unlikely that the Israelites found a safe haven in Judah. The argument that Judah—by the inclusion of large numbers of refugees—also represented Israel, from that time on, will be seen as incorrect and not supported by facts.

3.e Chosen? Temporarily not
After the fall of Israel, the Ten Tribes lost their special status as chosen people. Although their descendants continue to be bearers of the promise, that once again Judah and Israel will be united under a new covenant, in the future Messianic Kingdom (Jeremiah 31:31–33), the descendants of the Ten Tribes have been virtually invisible for a long time. Thus it seems that the status of being *chosen people* no longer applies to that part of Israel. However, that does not detract from the blessed future that awaits them. Before this can happen, their descendants will have to be found first, but that is something that God Himself will bring about. The first sign of that miracle is becoming visible today! (See Excursus 7)

Excursus 4: The Fall of Judah

4.a The exile of Judah
Although the southern kingdom of Judah initially behaved better than Israel, the decay there also took on ever larger dimensions. And more than a hundred years after the fall of Israel, the hour of doom had arrived here also. The seed for ruin was laid by King Ahaz,

who greatly promoted the Baal cult (2 Chronicles 28:3). He even brought human sacrifices, including some of his own children. Thanks to King Hezekiah who succeeded him, a religious revival took place after his death, but that turned out not to be lasting.

Under King Manasseh, Judah fell into abominable idolatry and turned away from God en masse. This king had such a bad influence on his people that he almost extinguished the service of God (2 Kings 21). He profaned the temple of God in Jerusalem by building idol altars and placed a statue of Asherah there. He instituted the sacrificing of people, including some of his own sons. It is said of him (2 Kings 21:9; see also 2 Chronicles 33:10):

> *Manasseh seduced them, so that they did more evil than the nations that the LORD had destroyed before the Israelites.*

That *evil* was so great that it became the downfall of Judah. Even the godly king Josiah could not turn things around; the culpability was too great. However, because of Josiah God postponed the judgment until after his death. (See 2 Kings 22:16–20; 2 Chronicles 34:24–28.)

4.b The Jews kept their identity

King Nebuchadnezzar destroyed the kingdom of Judah in 587 BC. However, the Babylonians took a different approach than the Assyrians. The elite and the well-trained craftsmen (i.e., the upper layer of the population) were not killed but mostly deported.

The displaced population was relocated in large groups elsewhere in the large empire. There they settled more or less as colonists. This saved the culture of the Jewish people. Also, initially, a considerable part of Judah remained in Canaan, the larger part of which later fled to Egypt.

In both Babylon and Egypt large Jewish communities were established and the traditions and the law were maintained, so that they remained Jews, living among pagan peoples. Among them, the promise of the Messianic Kingdom was kept alive. After all, didn't the prophets almost all speak of a blessed future in which David's kingdom would be reestablished? And the first opportunity to bring this about came when the exile ended.

4.c The return of Judah from Babylon

By decree of Cyrus II, the Judean exiles were allowed to return to Canaan and to rebuild the temple. However, only a small part of the exiles responded to the call. According to Ezra 2:64 and Nehemiah 7:66, no more than 42,360 persons did. Most of the people stayed behind in Babylon or Egypt and were therefore disobedient to God.

When the returnees arrived in Canaan, they found the descendants of the remnant of Judah, part of whom had mixed with the pagans. Under Ezra and Nehemiah, Judah was purified from pagan influences. According to Ezra 10:10–12 the whole people of Judah accepted the obligation to comply with the law and to renounce all idolatry. Ezra then forced more than one hundred Jewish families to reject their non-Jewish women. Thus the people were ethnically purified (see Ezra 9–10).

Jerusalem had been totally destroyed, as had been the temple. So they had to start all over again and rebuild everything from the ground up. According to Ezra 3:1–7, the altar was first restored and in 537 BC the rebuilding of the foundations of the temple began. After that, the work stopped for seventeen years. In 520 BC, the Lord sent the prophets Haggai and Zechariah, with instructions for the people to return to the work of rebuilding. This was a success, because a few weeks later the rebuilding was indeed resumed (Haggai 1:12–2:1) and finally completed.

Although there was again a kind of homeland for the Jews, there was in no way a restoration of the status as in the time of King David and Solomon. The country was a plaything for the dominant powers in the Middle East and became independent for only a short time. When the Romans came, this independence was ended.

In AD 70 an attempt was made to shake off the hated yoke of the Romans. This revolt failed miserably and the temple was destroyed again. Once more all forces joined together in revolt, under Bar Kokhba (AD 132–35). That war was also lost. By then, however, the Jewish population was decimated and what remained was expelled from the land of Canaan. Thus all attempts to form a state of its own had come to an end, for many centuries yet to come. But the dream of the Messianic Kingdom remained alive.

In 1948 another attempt was made to see that dream become a reality. Its success does not depend on the efforts of the government of Israel, but it is God's business. All prophecy will be fulfilled in His time.

4.d Different fates
Judah (and Benjamin) also went into exile. However, as already stated, the Jews remained a recognizable people, in contrast to the ten tribes of Israel. It is also probable that they are still God's chosen people today. The knowledge that inexplicably large numbers of Jews are well-known scientists and artists is at least a sign of this possibility.

The Book of HOSEA
Introduction

A. Which Text?

A1. Our Basic Text
The Hebrew text that forms the basis for this commentary comes from NIVIHEOT—the New International Version Interlinear Hebrew-English Old Testament—a word-for-word translation from the Hebrew text that is based on the *Biblia Hebraica Stuttgartensia* (BHS). This in turn has its origin in the Masoretic text of Jacob ben Chajim, also known as the Leningrad Codex B19a. The original of this codex is kept in St. Petersburg (Russia). The BHS is not a static source. Continually, knowledge is added in marginal notes, including new information from the Dead Sea Scrolls.

Example of an interlinear text (Hebrew reads from right to left):

עֲוֹן	וְנִגְלָה	לְיִשְׂרָאֵל	כְּרָפְאִי	עַמִּי:	שְׁבוּת
sin-of	then-he-is-exposed	to-Israel	when-to-heal-me	(7:1) people-of-me	fortune-of

יָבוֹא	וְגַנָּב	שֶׁקֶר	פָעָלוּ	כִּי	שֹׁמְרוֹן	וְרָעוֹת	אֶפְרַיִם
he-breaks-in	and-thief	deceit	they-practice	indeed	Samaria	and-crimes-of	Ephraim

A2. The Authority of the Masoretic Text
Originally, the Leningrad Codex was considered one of the many sources of the Old Testament, certainly not the most important one. With the discovery of the Dead Sea Scrolls, which were found in the period 1947–52, that changed. These scrolls contain large parts of the Old Testament and are many years older than anything that had been discovered before. Some of these scrolls go back to 200 BC or perhaps even further. The texts of the Dead Sea Scrolls were very similar to the Leningrad Codex. This showed that the Jewish copyists had been much more accurate over the centuries than was hitherto assumed and also more accurate than Christian copyists. Since then, the Leningrad Codex has acquired the greatest authority among Bible-believing scholars. It has therefore become the basis for most new Bible translations of the Old Testament.

Incidentally, only a few fragments of the book of Hosea were found among the Dead Sea Scrolls (4QXII).

A3. The Masoretic Text of Aaron ben Moses ben Asher
In ancient times, books were usually written on scrolls of vellum or papyrus. It was not until a few centuries after Christ that books came into vogue. If a book or scroll was worn, or if there was a demand for more copies, the book was copied. Although people worked accurately, errors did occur. A system was then developed to minimize the number of errors and, if possible, to correct them.

The Jewish scholars who took care of the copying and also checked the manuscripts for errors were called *Sopherim* (men of the book) and *Masoretes* (men of the Masora). All the information they collected about errors, interpretations, and the number of letters per book, was included in marginal notes (= masora). Writings from those sources are called Masoretic texts.

The original Hebrew in which by far the largest part of the Old Testament was written, is a language of consonants. For the correct pronunciation one should therefore have a knowledge of the spoken language. This knowledge faded in the last centuries before Christ, because the Jews began to speak Aramaic (and later Greek). They abandoned their mother tongue. Only the rabbis maintained the spoken ancient Hebrew. Concerned that over the centuries they too could lose this knowledge, a system consisting of dots and dashes was developed to indicate in the consonant-only text which vowels should be included and where.

A4. The Leningrad Codex
In the tenth century AD, two wealthy families were engaged in monitoring the basic Hebrew text, the Ben Asher and the Ben Naftali families. The texts of both families were very similar. There were only minor differences. Eventually, a final version of the adapted basic text (called punctuated text) was recorded by the Jewish scholars Ben Buja and Ben Asher. The Leningrad Codex (AD 1008) is a copy of the Masoretic texts of Aaron ben Moses ben Asher and was probably made in Cairo, Egypt. Later it was sold to a resident of Damascus, in Syria. Around 1840–55 it came into the possession of the Russian national library, Saltykov-Shchedrin, in St. Petersburg (formerly Leningrad).

It is ironic (perhaps divine humor) that the main source text for the Bible bears the name of one of the greatest haters of Christianity: Lenin.
(Pfeiffer, Vos, and Rea, 299–303; *Studiebijbel* SBOT 1, *Genesis–Exodus*, 13–16; Vermes, "Hosea"; Zuckerman)

B. The Prophet and His Time

B1. Hosea Ministered in Israel
The prophet Hosea was a contemporary of the prophet Amos and lived in the eighth century BC. He mainly ministered in the northern ten-tribe kingdom of Israel during the reign of Jeroboam II, who ruled from 782 to 753 BC. Under his rule, Israel's power increased significantly and it experienced great economic prosperity. After Jeroboam's death, his son Zechariah succeeded him, but he was assassinated after six months. Then the Northern Kingdom quickly fell into decay. Only thirty-one years after the death of Jeroboam II the kingdom perished when the capital, Samaria, was taken by the Assyrians and utterly destroyed (722 BC).

B2. The Ministry of Hosea
From the text of Hosea 1:1 (*in the days of Uzziah, Jotham, Ahaz, and Hezekiah, kings of Judah*) many exegetes conclude that the prophet began his ministry in the last years of King Uzziah and ended it in the first years of the reign of Hezekiah. This is a period of fifty to sixty years. However, there is no clear indication in the book of Hosea that the prophet experienced the decline of the Northern Kingdom. Nowhere does he speak directly about the turbulent events that began with the death of King Zechariah.

The prophet Hosea speaks about judgments, goals, and future salvation, and he does so in general terms. We never get the impression that a historical report is involved. There is thus no clear connection with the tempestuous events after the reign of Jeroboam II, unless it is in the form of prophecies with general purport about future disasters. It is therefore possible that Hosea died shortly after the coronation of King Zechariah, as some argue.

So nothing can be said with certainty about the period of his ministry. Wood sets it as spanning 753 to 715 BC (thirty-eight years); Stuart speaks of 760 to 722 BC (also thirty-eight years); Keil suggests a period of sixty to sixty-five years; and some Jewish exegetes even speak of seventy years or more. All of these involve assumptions, but adequate substantiation is lacking, so we leave it at that.

B3. Hosea Was Well Educated

On the basis of his language, it is assumed that Hosea had a very good education. We know, however, almost nothing about the prophet Hosea's lineage, where he lived, or what his original profession was. Only the name of his father (Beeri) is mentioned, but that does not bring us much further.

Rabbinical sources say that the father of Hosea (Beeri) is the same as the Beerah mentioned in 1 Chronicles 5:6, who was taken into exile by King Tilgath-Pilneser, the king of Assyria. This Beeri is called a *prince* (or leader) *among the Reubenites*.

B4. Rabbinic Sources

Jewish tradition says that the prophet Hosea was taken into exile and died in Babylon. Before his death he gave instructions to be buried in the Holy Land. Because the road to Canaan was very dangerous, it was agreed to put his body in a coffin, tie it on a camel and then release the camel. He would be buried there where the camel would stop to rest. Tradition says the camel walked unhindered from Babylon to Canaan. He arrived at the cemetery of Safed in Upper Galilee. The inhabitants opened the box and found a letter containing information about Hosea and instructions for his funeral. With great tribute, the prophet was then buried.

(Bromiley, "Hosea," 3–4; Flanders, Crapps, and Smith, 19–24; Jeffrey, 988; McComiskey, 1–3; Rosenberg, vol. 1, xiii; Stuart, xliii; Wolff, xxi–xxiii; Wood, 162–63)

C. A Difficult Text

C1. Hosea: A Poetic Prophet

The book of Hosea contains a poetic structure and a rich vocabulary. The prophet shows himself to be an artist with words. But this has unfortunately led to considerable problems with the translation. For idioms, sayings, and puns are much more difficult to recognize and translate than a text about history or the record of a journey or a historic battle. The translation problems are also reflected in various older translations we have. The differences between them are greater than between the ancient manuscripts of other Bible books.

C2. An Excuse for Textual Freedom

The difficulties with the translation turned out to be an excuse for exegetes to take great liberties. This gave rise to significant differences among contemporary translations and exegeses. In the past forty to fifty years, however, knowledge of ancient Hebrew has increased significantly. Very ancient writings have also been found, and this has resulted in a growing clarity about the correct (original) text and its meaning. Thus many of the arguments used by exegetes/translators to adapt the text to their wishes have disappeared.

The stubbornness with which especially liberal and secular bible scholars defend their old objections is astonishing. Thus many are exposed for what they ultimately are: God's enemies, who want to shut up His Word (often unconsciously) and debilitate it.
(Buss, 38)

D. How Should We Understand Hosea?

D1. Hosea: An Allegory? No!
Most Jewish commentators regard the book of Hosea as an allegory. Many also deny that the prophet Hosea actually entered into a marriage with Gomer (Hosea 1). They see in the prophecy of Hosea an allegory depicting the breach between God and His people. Also among Christians there are many who adhere to the allegorical interpretation, such as Origen and John Calvin, and in more recent times Hengstenberg, Havernick, Hitzig, Keil, and Rosenmuller.

The literal interpretation has been followed by various early church fathers and later by Martin Luther. In our time they include, among others, Delizsch, Kurz, Hofmann, Wellhausen, Cheyne, Boice, and Robertson Smith.

We refrain from entering into the arguments from both sides. In this book we assume that the prophet speaks about reality, just like the other prophets do, and we choose the literal interpretation.
(Bromiley, "Hosea," 3–4)

D2. Doom and Salvation
The book of Hosea focuses on two key points. The first is the downfall of Israel, the kingdom of the Ten Tribes. Over against the message of judgment stands the second key point: the promise of an (as yet very distant) salvation that is realized in the establishment of the Messianic Kingdom. These two are extremes. The salvation is equally as great as the judgment is profound; together they paint a striking contrast.

Hosea is a book of judgment. It is filled with specific prophecies concerning the coming doom of Israel. What is lacking is the prospect in the short term of a conversion that could avert the coming disaster. It was too late for that; the verdict had already been passed; the debt of sin had become too high.

Well, you may say, that is interesting but concerns Israel. This prophecy and its effect lie many centuries behind us. Such an attitude would be a misapprehension, because the society Hosea paints shows remarkable similarities with ours. His analysis of the sins of his time can therefore be broadly transposed to the present. Thus Hosea also takes our measure, and the outcome is not good.

Hosea's prophecy also focuses on the justification of God's judgment over Israel. That is, at the least, remarkable. It is as if the Almighty has a need to justify His actions, although He absolutely does not have to do that in His sovereign omnipotence. However, this need for justification appears to be motivated by love. For if one thing is clear from the book of Hosea, it is the great love of God for His people. Hosea's declaration of love in 2:14–22 speaks volumes in this regard.

The prophet Hosea speaks to a people that will soon disappear into the mists of history. It loses the status of "God's people" and receives a new name: Ephraim. With this, it is finished, for the time being. The Almighty nevertheless still gives them all kinds of instructions which lay the foundation for a salvific turn of their fate in the distant future. Its purpose is the national conversion of the people of Israel to (what is called) the true Israel, which coincides with the establishment of the Messianic Kingdom. However, that radical turn will not come about through their own initiative. The spark is ignited by God Himself (*I will lure her* [Hosea 2:14]).
(See Excursuses 7, 9, 10.)

D3. Illustrative Prophecy

The prophet Hosea is not merely the messenger of doom and salvation. He plays yet another role in his prophetic ministry. For Hosea is instructed to act out part of the divine prophecy. He is commanded to marry an adulteress—a harlot, whom he does not love. Thus his suffering became a type of the suffering of God, because Israel had abandoned Him and served other gods.

In that period the life of Hosea was dark, almost without any perspective. He did not come home to the bosom of a happy family, where a loving wife and children met him with enthusiasm. His family was like the people of Israel—chaotic and a gathering place of negative sentiments. It was a family we would not want to have as neighbors.

D4. A Happy Ending

In the life of Hosea we see remarkable parallels with the suffering of Job. Yet salvation dawns for him also, because in Hosea 3:1 he is told to love his adulterous wife, Gomer. Herein he typifies the enduring love of God for Israel. There is no doubt that God's love will eventually be answered and that the people of Israel will again be the bride of God. We may therefore assume that also for the prophet Hosea there was a prospect of a happy ending.

E. The Authorship of Hosea

E1. Who Wrote the Book

The opinions on the authorship of the book of Hosea vary. Many exegetes isolate certain passages as being *not from the hand of Hosea*. Some rearrange the order of certain chapters and verses (Van de Born and Harper among others). In this way they "correct" the book of Hosea on the basis of the chronology of history (as they see it). Others are of the opinion that little of the book of Hosea is still authentic or from the hand of the prophet Hosea himself. They speak of an *evolutionary process in which the original material of Hosea was transformed and adapted* to the theology of a later period (Harper).

The criticism of the reliability of the text focuses mainly on those passages that speak of the kingdom of the two tribes, Judah; on the references to Deuteronomy; and on the promises of salvation that look forward to the end time. That part of the prophecy, however, is the fingerprint of God's plan of salvation with Israel (the counsel of God) and the backbone of the prophecy. Thus the divine element, which elevates the prophecy above human inventions, is also at stake. The point of view that questions that Hosea is the author, and that the text is reliably preserved according to God's design, is alarming and wrong!
(Bromiley, "Hosea," 3–15; Harper, clix–clxii; Walvoord and Zuck, 1377)

E2. Criticisms of the Book Hosea

The reasons for the criticism of the authorship and/or the rearrangement of certain passages can be reduced to two main causes:

E2.a *Stylistic Differences*

There are stylistic differences between certain passages in the book of Hosea (although there are also exegetes who argue against this). Some therefore conclude that other writers (copyists) have supplemented the book of Hosea. This problem did not exist some centuries ago. Then it was assumed that these differences were due to the simple fact that there were indeed two authors: namely God and Hosea. The prophet Hosea recorded words from God and, if necessary, filled in the less important matters as he saw fit. In the first instance, therefore, there was a word-for-word dictated message from

God, in the second, God-inspired additional prophecy. Today, a significant number of Bible scholars deny that God is the main author and Hosea the coauthor. Therefore they suggest that there are unknown writers who have made additions to the book.

E2.b *Different Hebrew Texts*
Until roughly 1945 to 1950, there were relatively large differences among the various ancient manuscripts that constitute the sources for the book of Hosea. Also, the old Christian source texts were (wrongly) considered to be more important than, for example, the Masoretic texts that came from Jewish sources. Since that time many ancient manuscripts have been found, which turned out to be much older than the oldest manuscripts we previously had. This means that our knowledge about the Hebrew text of the Bible, and especially its reliability, have increased considerably. It is striking that it also has shown that the Masoretic text was purer than had always been thought. The Leningrad Codex has particularly gained a lot of influence. We can therefore present a Bible translation with much greater authority than ever before in the past one thousand years. And look what happens: the prophecy becomes more readable and shows more and more logic and coherence. In this way those who want to understand the literal meaning of the text increasingly have the support of the evidence to uphold the truth of their claims.

E3. Hosea as a Literary Author
The book of Hosea, like the book of Micah, has an unmistakably poetic touch. The Hebrew text is therefore generally praised for its excellent sentence structure. Hosea paints with words and applies varying styles to firmly instill his prophetic message in his audience. Born even calls him a "virtuoso of the word," and that sets the right tone. His large vocabulary suggests that he was of noble birth and received a very thorough education.

Playing with words (paronomasia, or puns), subtle sound associations, and the verbal power of the book add an extra dimension to the message of the prophet. It is unfortunately true that the poetic element is difficult to reflect in a translation. The Hebrew text in the English-language NIVIHEOT still shows something of that poetry. In almost all modern-language translations, however, it has virtually disappeared. In the process, leading to the definitive text, this author has emphatically sought to preserve something of the described literary beauty.
(Born, 19–21)

F. Hosea Is Ultimately Eschatology

F1. The Breach of the Covenant
The prophet Hosea speaks of the breach of the covenant between God and His people (= Israel, the Northern Kingdom, the Ten Tribes), but also of Israel's restoration. Hosea does not discuss the causes of the breach in detail, as Ezekiel does. Hosea puts the history between God and Israel on the canvas in broad strokes, involving the past, the present, and the near and distant future.

In a most revealing way, the prophet speaks about God's emotions, His disappointments, His relentless love, the adultery of Israel, the painful divorce, and the happy reunion of the beloveds (although the latter is still yet to happen).

F2. A Blessed Future
Within eschatology we can speak of general prophecy and of directed prophecy. The Revelation of John, for example, contains end-time prophecy which has a universal meaning

and concerns the entire world. This general aspect is discussed only to a limited extent in Hosea, which mainly focuses on events that specifically concern God's people. The focus lies mainly on the kingdom of the Ten Tribes, Israel.

It is striking that the prophet Hosea, when he speaks eschatologically, usually has the whole people of Israel in view. Like all other prophets, he shows a firm confidence in the restoration of all twelve tribes of Israel and in a blessed future for them—in Canaan, of course, the promised land.

F3. Eschatology

Hosea prophesies about the future and about the purpose God has for the people of Israel—the return to Canaan of all twelve tribes of Israel, after which the Messianic Kingdom will be established. He does so in very clear language. Unfortunately, there are still many Christians who leave no room for a salvific future for Israel and a future Messianic Kingdom. They believe that God's promises to Israel are transferred to the church (without any biblical proof). For them, the book of Hosea is therefore not really something they want to study. However, they cannot ignore Hosea, because there is no doubt that the book does indeed belong in the Bible. Their escape is simple and predictable; they declare the prophecy therefore to be in part only allegorical. The literal meaning of Hosea is set aside and most eschatological sections are taken to refer to history, or transposed to the church of Christ, when it actually concerns the far future of Israel.

I have sometimes wondered how the ancient prophets would have reacted if they had been able to look at this strange form of explanation. It is my firm belief that they would have been stunned by so much misunderstanding and disbelief. For if we reduce the problem of the spiritualization of the prophecy to the naked biblical truth, then the following facts have to be noticed:

F3.a   God swears to Abraham that his descendants will take possession of the land of Canaan forever (Genesis 17:8).
F3.b   The Almighty confirms this oath to Abraham's son Isaac (Genesis 26:3).
F3.c   This oath was reconfirmed also to Isaac's son Jacob (Genesis 35:12).
F3.d   And finally, God's oath is passed on to the sons of Jacob and the two sons of Joseph, Manasseh and Ephraim (Genesis 48–49). With that, the divine promise passed also on to the twelve tribes of Israel and to the tribe of Levi.
F3.e   The divine "sworn oath" that the land of Canaan will come into the possession of the descendants of Abraham *forever* is repeated for each of the sons (tribes) of Jacob and Joseph in Ezekiel 48. There is no doubt whatsoever that this is still unfulfilled prophecy.
F3.f   Yet many Christians explain the prophecies in such a way that this divine promise does not benefit the people of Israel but rather falls to the Christian church as a kind of "spiritual surrogate."
F3.g   Thus we see an inheritance, the beneficiaries of which are known: the descendants of Israel (Jacob)—all twelve tribes. Nevertheless, the Christian church is designated to receive the inheritance (on their own authority!), and Israel—in spite of the sworn oath of God—is left empty-handed.

Where is this found in the Bible? Where did God deny His own oath? *Nowhere!*

F4. The Real Objective Is the Messianic Kingdom

This author is of the opinion that the book of Hosea is primarily eschatological in nature (that is, it primarily concerns the doctrine of the last things). Of course, the prophet denounces the sins of people of Israel and speaks about future judgments that from our perspective have already been fulfilled. However, the prophecy that Hosea proclaims in God's name is always projected onto the ultimate goal: the destiny of the people of Israel in the kingdom of God at the end times. This is still unfulfilled prophecy viewed from a today perspective.

In his prophecy, a prophet looks through time as someone who looks at a mountain range. What is striking, and therefore described, are the mountain peaks. That is, the important moments in God's salvation history. Thus the valleys remain as yet invisible to the prophet, whether they are large (a long period in time) or small (a short one). It may therefore happen that two events, which are described next to each other in the Bible (suggesting successive events), are in fact separated by many years. Many examples of this can be found in the Bible.

F5. The Counsel of God
The prophecy of Hosea shows strong similarities with other prophetic books, especially with Isaiah, Ezekiel, and Zechariah, and to a lesser extent with Amos. This is by no means a coincidence, for the essence of prophecy is that a glimpse of the same counsel of God is granted to several prophets. The prophets look at the future from different perspectives and may also view various parts of that counsel. There is therefore often seeming overlap, especially when it comes to important events in the history of salvation.

G. Exegetical Perspectives

For a manageable overview of the various viewpoints we confine ourselves to the four most common perspectives on the book of Hosea (which incidentally also apply to a number of other prophetic books). They also represent degrees of orthodoxy.

G1. The prophecy is of divine origin, but the text is mutilated.
This view plays an important role among many Bible-believing exegetes. It is argued that at one time there was a reliable text, but that this text was repeatedly copied by slipshod copyists, so that an increasing number of errors has crept in (= text corruption). It is also assumed that some copyists have added words or sentences, or changed them, with the aim of clarifying the text on the basis of their own dogma.

The exegetes in this category (which we will call A-exegetes) regard by and large the majority of the prophecies of Hosea as having already been fulfilled. Others, especially those of an orthodox Calvinistic persuasion and Roman Catholics, still read it as unfulfilled prophecy but usually associate it with the church of Christ. (In this, by and large, Calvinists follow the marginal notes of the Dutch Authorized Version of the Statenbijbel of 1637—which are confirmed in its English equivalent, the King James Version.)

G2. It is unreliable prophecy.
In this option, not only textual corruption is assumed but the original Hebrew text is also criticized. One then seriously doubts whether prophecy has a divine origin or even rejects this possibility. Therefore, human influence is considered to be significant. In commentaries of this kind the author speaks often about legends, stories, and tales as source of the prophecy. His goal is not to unveil the true message of the prophecy, but to write a readable story.

In this view, both the prophet and the sloppy copyist (created by exegetes) play fast and loose with the truth. For example, passages dealing with the end time are often explained as reflecting pious desires and Jewish national feelings that lie outside of reality.

It often happens in the Bible that a prophet makes a prediction which indeed appears fulfilled at a later date. This is rarely taken to be true by these exegetes (which I call B-exegetes). They usually state that the date given in the prophetic book itself is not correct. They then correct the date to the time of, or even after the presumed fulfillment. In this way the incident described becomes a form of historiography and is thus stripped of any divine predictive element. The prophet is accused of predating his book or falsifying the data. This form of fraud is then laconically dismissed as *common practice at that time!* These practices of purported fraud are seen as completely unacceptable from a Bible-believing point of view.

The preceding view therefore seriously undermines the assumption that prophecy has divine authority and that it should therefore be studied carefully. It also degrades prophecy to fallible human work.

G3. Hosea's prophecy is a collection of texts from a variety of sources.
This view believes these texts were then bundled into one document for unknown reasons. This is then called *a collection of writings from various sources* (Ward, xix). The name of a known prophet (in this case Hosea) is attached to give the writing the desired authority. This position, whether or not in combination with perspective G2, is most commonly found in mainline circles today. Although doubt concerning the authority of the prophet has already crept in, the prophecy is still partly taken seriously, although a strong human element is also assumed.

In this option, the prophecy of Hosea will be projected mainly onto the prophet's own time. However, in that case the supposed historical passages do not match the historical facts. In other words: if, for example, five historical events that have demonstrably occurred in the continuous sequence A-B-C-D-E are found in the prophetic book in the sequence B-E-D-A-C, then the reliability of the book comes into serious question. As an explanation for this so-called wrong sequence, one assumes that there have been prophecies from various sources which have been bundled somewhat sloppily by a compiler into a single document.

G4. The prophecy is largely pure and of divine origin.
From this point of view, it is inevitable to decide that the prophet Hosea speaks of a future period—which is indeed his purpose. Then the kingdom of God, or Messianic Kingdom, foretold by many prophets, will become a reality. In this option it is obvious to think of the end times, namely the great tribulation and the establishment of the Messianic Kingdom under the kingship of Jesus Christ. Because only in that period can we find an ultimate fulfillment for Hosea's prophecy, and the details of the prophecy then come fully into their own.

It will be clear that for the Bible-believing Christian only options G1 or G4 is acceptable. But for many from this group, option G4 does not fit in with their dogmas, so on balance there is only one option left. That is the assumption that there is text corruption, so they feel forced to choose option G1.

G5. The Hebrew text becomes purer.
With thesis G1, however, something more is going on. Until recently it was true to a certain extent. It turns out that the various Hebrew texts that were known about seventy years ago show considerable differences. So the conclusion is correct that the transcribers have made mistakes in the past, or have adapted the text to their own understanding. In recent decades, however, the knowledge of the ancient manuscripts has increased considerably and many new ones have been found. The oldest Hebrew Scriptures now date from *before*

the birth of Jesus Christ, an *improvement of more than one thousand years*. Especially the prophetic books have become more comprehensible.

Apart from the fact that we now have older manuscripts, there are also much improved research methods. Mainly thanks to the use of large computer systems, the knowledge of ancient Hebrew has increased considerably. This has yielded so many improvements in the basic text that a reconsideration of existing translations of the prophetic books has become desperately needed.

A striking and wonderful side effect of the increased knowledge of the Bible is that the literal interpretation viewpoint has greatly increased in authority.

G6. Conclusion
With this last observation, option G1, as a proposition, can only be maintained with difficulty and thus remains on balance only option G4. From this only one conclusion can follow: the prophet Hosea speaks, in accordance with his objective, about the ultimate fulfillment of God's salvation, that is, about the end time.

H. The Return of Israel

With the demise of the ten-tribe kingdom—which in that period is called Israel or (later) also Ephraim—this part of God's people disappeared from salvation history. Up to the present day it is unclear where they have gone. There is, however, a beginning of the unveiling of this mystery. We deal with that in Excursus 7.

It is certain that in addition to the two tribes (the Jews), the Ten Tribes will also return to Canaan. This prophecy will come to fulfillment only in the end time. The Bible testifies to this in clear terms. We quote a few texts:

Ezekiel 37:19–28 (NASB):
19 *"Say to them, 'Thus says the Lord GOD, "Behold, I will take the stick of Joseph, which is in the hand of Ephraim, and the tribes of Israel, his companions; and I will put them with it, with the stick of Judah, and make them one stick, and they will be one in My hand.*
20 *"The sticks on which you write will be in your hand before their eyes.*
21 *"Say to them, 'Thus says the Lord GOD, "Behold, I will take the sons of Israel from among the nations where they have gone, and I will gather them from every side and bring them into their own land;*
22 *"and I will make them one nation in the land, on the mountains of Israel; and one king will be king for all of them; and they will no longer be two nations and no longer be divided into two kingdoms.*
23 *"They will no longer defile themselves with their idols, or with their detestable things, or with any of their transgressions; but I will deliver them from all their dwelling places in which they have sinned, and will cleanse them. And they will be My people, and I will be their God.*
24 *"My servant David will be king over them, and they will all have one shepherd; and they will walk in My ordinances and keep My statutes and observe them.*
25 *"They will live on the land that I gave to Jacob My servant, in which your fathers lived; and they will live on it, they, and their sons and their sons' sons, forever; and David My servant will be their prince forever.*
26 *"I will make a covenant of peace with them; it will be an everlasting covenant with them. And I will place them and multiply them, and will set My sanctuary in their midst forever.*

27 *"My dwelling place also will be with them; and I will be their God, and they will be My people.*
28 *"And the nations will know that I am the LORD who sanctifies Israel, when My sanctuary is in their midst forever."'"*

Isaiah 11:12[†]:
> *And He will raise a banner in front of the pagan nations. He will gather those who were rejected from Israel and bring together the scattered of Judah from the four ends of the earth.*

A sharp distinction is drawn here. The *rejected from Israel* are the ten vanished tribes of the northern kingdom, Israel. The *scattered of Judah* are the tribes of Benjamin and Judah (and Levi), whom we now call Jews.

([†]Weerd, Hebrew text translation in *Jesaja*, vol. 1, 391)

Jeremiah 30:18 (NASB):
> *"Thus says the LORD: 'Behold, I will restore the fortunes of the tents of Jacob and have compassion on his dwelling places.'"*

The phrase *tents of Jacob* refers to all twelve tribes.

Jeremiah 31:31–33 (NASB):
31 *"Behold, days are coming," declares the LORD, "when I will make a new covenant with the house of Israel and with the house of Judah,*
32 *"not like the covenant which I made with their fathers in the day I took them by the hand to bring them out of the land of Egypt, My covenant which they broke, although I was a husband to them," declares the LORD.*
33 *"But this is the covenant which I will make with the house of Israel after those days," declares the LORD, "I will put My law within them and on their heart I will write it; and I will be their God, and they shall be My people."*

This speaks again of two identities: *the house of Israel* (the Ten Tribes) and *the house of Judah* (the remaining two tribes and Levi).

Hosea 2:13–14 (English versions: 14–15)[*]
14 *Therefore, see! I will lure her and lead her in the desert. Then I will speak to her heart.*
15 *I will return her vineyards there, and make the valley of Achor a door of hope. Then she will answer [my love] there as in the days of her youth; as on the day when she went out of the land of Egypt.*

([*]Hebrew text translation in pages to follow)

Zechariah 10:7–9 (NASB):
7 *"Ephraim will be like a mighty man, and their heart will be glad as if from wine; indeed, their children will see it and be glad, their heart will rejoice in the LORD.*
8 *"I will whistle for them to gather them together, for I have redeemed them; and they will be as numerous as they were before.*
9 *"When I scatter them among the peoples, they will remember Me in far countries, and they with their children will live and come back."*

ACKNOWLEDGMENTS

Literary Analysis
As said before, we use the NIVIHEOT text as the basis for our translation. In case a textual problem raises, the commentary on the Hebrew text will be preceded by a preliminary or introduction. Next we will study the NIVIHEOT texts more deeply with the help of other sources. After thorough research, we present at the end of each text analysis the corrected version of the text.

After studying the Hebrew text, we begin the exegesis, based on the given translation of the Hebrew text. With each chapter or a particular group of verses an introduction may be given and, if necessary, a short overview of the message of Hosea.

Throughout the book, we have included excursuses to enlighten the reader on general topics that pertain to the background of a prophecy or to address an issue of general dogma.

Annotations, on the other hand, pertain to issues that are specific to the text being addressed.

It is common to reproduce the Hebrew text in our own alphabet. The vocalizing or transliteration of Hebrew words is not standardized. In this commentary we use the spelling of each quoted author.

Sources
In this commentary we use the NIVIHEOT interlinear text. In addition we present three well known translations: the *New American Standard Bible* (NASB), the King James Version (KJV), and the *New International Version* (NIV).

The commentary on the Hebrew text is primary based on Strong's Exhaustive Concordance of the Bible. This is a dictionary of 8672 Hebrew words of great reputation. It is a trustable benchmark in case there are uncertainties concerning the translation of the Hebrew text.

The Letter *Vav*
The Hebrew letter *vav* has a broad sense. We quote Rabbi Moshe Eisemann:
> The prefix ו, *vav*, is an extremely versatile tool of the Hebrew language. Its use is by no means limited to the conjunction "and." Ibn Janach in the Sefer Harikmah isolates no fewer than seventeen instances, in which the Hebrew language uses the ו, *vav*, but where English would require such participles as: so; as; when; with; but, and so on. Thus the translator has considerable freedom of choice and the monotony of a constant repeated "and" can be avoided. On the other hand this flexibility and freedom of choice imposes a great responsibility on him to choose correctly from among the many possible translations.

(Eisemann, xiii)

Untranslatable: ת א
The above Hebrew letters are in general not translated in the NIVIHEOT interlinear text. Instead they use three dots (. . .) in the text line. We also do not pretend we can translate this word and ignore further comment. The strange thing is that the lack of this word does not frustrate the formation of well-written sentence.

HOSEA 1
Hebrew Text Translation

Introduction
The first chapter of Hosea contains many word plays. This literary device is called *paronomasia* and is used to influence the mood of the audience, with the aim of better imprinting the message. Because of the striking cadence of the expressions and the rhymes, they are easily retained in the memory. The disadvantage of this style is that it makes the text harder to understand, because poetic forms frequently suffer in translation. A second disadvantage is that the prophet regularly uses unusual words to arrive at a rhyme or a certain cadence. This too has a negative influence on the quality of the translation, since it becomes much more difficult to use other Scriptures for comparison.

A. Keywords
The book of Hosea contains a number of key words, which cause some difficulties with its translation. These are *Ammi* (= My people), *Lo-Ammi* (= not My people), *Ruchama* (= compassion), *Lo-Ruchama* (= no compassion), *Y^{e}hôvâh* (= YHWH, Yahweh, or I am) and *lo ehyeh* (not I am). They occur in pairs and the positive form (for example, *Ammi*) always stands over against the negative form (*Lo-Ammi*). The preceding words are also regularly used as personal names. It is customary to vocalize the Hebrew word in our own language and we refrain from translating the word.

In the book Hosea, these words also form part of normal sentences where they are used according to their meaning, and then we do have to translate them. However, even where they are used as a personal name, the meaning of the name often plays an important role in the context (and hence in the exegesis). In those cases, the word in question has a double function. If, therefore, a word is used as a personal name in a given context, we do not translate it but give its meaning in parentheses.

The word *Jezreel* (= God sows) holds a special position. There is no *Lo-Jezreel* over against it. It nevertheless falls under the same stylistic form, because the meaning can be negative (God sows judgments, verse 4) and God scatters (also a form of sowing, namely, Israel among the gentile nations), as well as positive (God sows the seed of the Messianic Kingdom, verse 12 and Hosea 2:23).
(Brown, 12)

B. Accurate Translation
There is no great discipline among most exegetes and translators when they translate. Many see in the book of Hosea nothing more than an allegory of which only the main lines are important or—even worse—only as a piece of interesting poetry. For that reason, they concentrate on its literary quality, but leave the real depths of the original text to lie fallow. But it is not so difficult that we cannot make a careful translation using the raw material found in the original Hebrew test. In this exegesis we must take great pains to bring the depths of the original text to light. This will also allow the prophet to speak in great detail.

C. God's Holy Name: YHWH
This is the most commonly used name of God and occurs very frequently in the Old Testament. It is not a name in the normal sense of the word, but is called by scholars *the tetragrammaton* (= the four characters). Usually this is vocalized with the vowels of *adonai*, the

general word for *Lord*, hence *Yahweh*. Most scholars view *to be* or *to become* as its meaning, which is then often reflected in *I am* or *I am who I am* (Exodus 3:14). In English translations we usually find LORD, or sometimes also *God*. However, it is much better to just read *Yahweh*. (Excursus 24)

Verse 1 NASB
The word of the LORD which came to Hosea the son of Beeri, during the days of Uzziah, Jotham, Ahaz and Hezekiah, kings of Judah, and during the days of Jeroboam the son of Joash, king of Israel.

Verse 1 KJV
The word of the LORD that came unto Hosea, the son of Beeri, in the days of Uzziah, Jotham, Ahaz, and Hezekiah, kings of Judah, and in the days of Jeroboam the son of Joash, king of Israel.

Verse 1 NIV
The word of the LORD that came to Hosea son of Beeri during the reigns of Uzziah, Jotham, Ahaz and Hezekiah, kings of Judah, and during the reign of Jeroboam son of Jehoash, king of Israel:

Verse 1 Hebrew Interlinear Text
word-of Yahweh that he-came to Hosea son-of Beeri during-days-of Uzziah Jotam Ahaz Hezekiah kings-of Judah and-during-days-of Jeroboam son-of Joash king-of Israel
The NIVIHEOT translates: *during-days-of.* The Greek text shows: *in the days of.*

We read:
The word of Yahweh came to Hosea, the son of Beeri, in the days of Uzziah, Jotham, Ahaz, and Hezekiah, kings of Judah, and in the days of Jeroboam the son of Joash, king of Israel.

Verse 2 NASB
When the LORD first spoke through Hosea, the LORD said to Hosea, "Go, take to yourself a wife of harlotry and have children of harlotry; for the land commits flagrant harlotry, forsaking the LORD."

Verse 2 KJV
The beginning of the word of the LORD by Hosea. And the LORD said to Hosea, Go, take unto thee a wife of whoredoms and children of whoredoms: for the land hath committed great whoredom, departing from the LORD.

Verse 2 NIV
When the LORD began to speak through Hosea, the LORD said to him: "Go, marry a promiscuous woman and have children with her, for like an adulterous wife this land is guilty of unfaithfulness to the LORD."

Verse 2 Hebrew Interlinear Text
beginning-of he-spoke Yahweh through-Hosea and-he-said Yahweh go to Hosea Go! take! to-yourself wife-of adulteries and-children-of unfaithfulnesses because to-be-guilty-of-adultery she-is-guilty-of-adultery-the-land from-after Yahweh

Verse 2a
beginning-of he-spoke Yahweh through-Hosea

Some interpreters view this sentence as the heading for Hosea 1 and that is certainly possible. But it is not an important point, because it does not change the exegesis in any way.
(Brown, 4; Mays, 21; Reed, 29)

We read: *Yahweh began to speak through Hosea,*

Verse 2b
Go! take! to-yourself wife-of adulteries
The word *laqach* has a very broad meaning. It can indeed mean *to take* but also *to accept* and *to assume*. The context therefore determines the translation. Here we have an order to the prophet Hosea to marry a woman, so *take!* is a good choice.
(Strong's, word 3947; Stuart, 27; Ward, 3)

We read: *go! Take an adulterous woman to yourself*

Verse 2c
and-children-of unfaithfulnesses
These are children born of fornication, so the prophet Hosea is not the father. A. van de Born therefore rightly translates the phrase with the term *bastards* and McComiskey speaks of *adoption*.

Bastard children had little or no rights in Israel. However, it is clear that they are still seen as full-fledged children in Hosea 1. This is only possible with the consent of the prophet Hosea himself. It did not happen at his own request, but at God's command.
(Born, 24; Harper, 206; McComiskey, 15; *NIV Bible Dictionary*, 128; Pfeiffer, Vos, and Rea, 207; Ward, 5)

We read: *and accept children [born] of adultery*

Verse 2d
to-be-guilty-of-adultery she-is-guilty-of-adultery
The word *zanah* is used twice here. Very few translators include this in their text. In the first instance it is a verb of movement that suggests a continual committing of adultery.
(Andersen and Freedman, 169; McComiskey, 17; Strong's, word 2181; Stuart, 23)

We read: *because she has constantly committed adultery*

Verse 2e
from-after Yahweh
The word *achar* has a broad meaning. It can mean *thereafter*, *behind*, *after*, or *to follow* (Deuteronomy 28:14 and 31:16). Literally it says: *From/away* or *behind/following Yahweh*. That is: *leaving Yahweh*. Ward reads: *away from Yahweh*.
(Born, 24; Brown, 6; Strong's, word 310; Stuart, 23; Ward, 3)

We read: *thus Yahweh was left*

The entire sentence:
Yahweh began to speak through Hosea. Then Yahweh said to Hosea, Go! Take an adulterous woman to yourself and accept children born of adultery. For because she has continually committed adultery, the country is guilty of fornication. Thus Yahweh was left.

Verse 3 NASB
So he went and took Gomer the daughter of Diblaim, and she conceived and bore him a son.

Verse 3 KJV
So he went and took Gomer the daughter of Diblaim; which conceived, and bare him a son.

Verse 3 NIV
So he married Gomer daughter of Diblaim, and she conceived and bore him a son.

Verse 3 Hebrew Interlinear Text
so-he-went and-he-married . . . Gomer daughter-of Diblaïm and-she-conceived and-she-bore to-him son
Some translate the word *Diblaïm* and read: *daughter* or *girl of two fig cakes* of *fruit cakes*. We include the second translation in brackets in the text.
(See Annotations 1A)

We read:
Thus he went and married Gomer, the daughter of Diblaim *[daughter of two fruit cakes]*. Then she conceived and bore him a son.

Annotation 1A: Girl of Two Fruit Cakes

In most Bible translations we find in verse 3: *Daughter of Diblaim*. It would also have been possible to translate *girl* or *daughter of two fig/fruit cakes*.

The word *diblayim* is derived from *debelah*, which means compressed, like a cake of dried and compressed figs. But that was also done with other fruits that were easy to dry (and so to store), for example, raisins. The translation *fig cakes* is therefore an interpretation. It is much more logical to read *two fruit cakes*. Strong's gives the meaning as *two cakes*; Brown speaks of *fig cakes*; Harper uses *fig cakes* and *raisin cakes*; and Garrett has *fruit cakes*.

The people of Israel sinned heavily against God by adopting idolatrous worship from the surrounding countries. Especially the service to the Baals and Ishtar, the last of which was worshiped in Babylonia and Assyria as the supreme mother goddess.

Ishtar was known in Sumeria under the name of *Inanna* and among Canaanite peoples as Astarte or Ashtoreth. (She was also called *the bushel of figs Lady*). She was the goddess of sexual love. Her "husband" was the idol Tammuz, of whom, among others, Ezekiel 8:14 speaks. It is certain that at the time of King Jeroboam II the Ishtar cult was widely practiced in Israel.

A fixed part of the Ishtar cult idolatry was temple prostitution. The prostitutes were called *ishtarishu* and they "invited" passersby to participate in the rites. As payment, besides real money, fig cakes were also accepted—the candy bar of that time.

Adultery was strictly forbidden in Israel. But in sinful times people were not too fussy about the law, and temple prostitution became acceptable. During the reign of Jeroboam II, there was also a profound irreligiosity.

Since the meaning of names plays an important role in Hosea, the preceding explanation is very credible. It is also significant that the name *Diblaim* is not found anywhere else in the Bible.

Conclusion:
Gomer was thus probably a temple prostitute and her "services" cost only two fruit cakes. That was a low price and it suggested that Gomer was not very popular, what usually

means "not very attractive." However, there is little support among Bible scholars for this translation. We therefore stay with the traditional reading but also give the alternative text between brackets.

(Andersen and Freedman, 171; Baumgartner, 78; Born, 24; Bromiley, 5; Brown, 6; Buss, 56; Crosius; Easton's Bible Encyclopedia: Diblaim; Garrett, 54; Harper, 211; Keil and Delitzsch, vol. 1, 38; King, 97–101; Mays, 24; Nestle, 233; Riedel, vol. 1, 1–36; Singer, "Diblaim"; Strong's, words 1690, 1691, 2082; Wolff, 16–17)

Verse 4 NASB
And the Lord said to him, "Name him Jezreel; for yet a little while, and I will punish the house of Jehu for the bloodshed of Jezreel, and I will put an end to the kingdom of the house of Israel."

Verse 4 KJV
And the Lord said unto him, Call his name Jezreel; for yet a little while, and I will avenge the blood of Jezreel upon the house of Jehu, and will cause to cease the kingdom of the house of Israel.

Verse 4 NIV
Then the Lord said to Hosea: "Call him Jezreel, because I will soon punish the house of Jehu for the massacre at Jezreel, and I will put an end to the kingdom of Israel."

Verse 4 Hebrew Interlinear Text
then-he-said Yahweh to-him call! name-of-him Jezreel because yet soon and-I-will-punish . . . bloods-of Jezreel on house-of Jehu and-I-will-put-to-end kingdom-of house-of Israel

Verse 4b
call! name-of-him Jezreel
The word *qara* means: *call* (in the sense of *naming*).
Jezreel means *God sows* or *may God sow*.
(Andersen and Freedman, 171; McComiskey, 20; *Studiebijbel* SBOT 12, 26)

We read: **give him the name Jezreel** (*God sows*)

Verse 4c
because yet soon and-I-will-punish
Paqad has a very broad application. It can mean *to name* (Genesis 41:34), *assign* (1 Kings 14:27), *to count* (Exodus 30:12), *to visit* in the sense of *to punish* (Isaiah 10:12), and *to look up* (Genesis 50:24). We prefer the basic meaning and read *and-I-will-visit*.
(McComiskey, 20; Strong's, word 6485; Stuart, 23)

We read: **for yet a little while and I will visit**

Verse 4d
bloods-of Jezreel on house-of Jehu
Most exegetes read *bloodshed-of* here, which we follow.
(Andersen and Freedman, 173; McComiskey, 21)

We read: **the bloodshed of Jezreel upon the house of Jehu**

We read:
And Yahweh said to him, "Give him the name Jezreel [God sows]! For yet a little while and I will visit the bloodshed of Jezreel upon the house of Jehu. Then I will put an end to the kingdom of the house of Israel."

Verse 5 NASB
"On that day I will break the bow of Israel in the valley of Jezreel."

Verse 5 KJV
And it shall come to pass at that day, that I will break the bow of Israel, in the valley of Jezreel.

Verse 5 NIV
"In that day I will destroy Israel's bow in the Valley of Jezreel."

Verse 5 Hebrew Interlinear Text
and-he-will-be in-the-day the-that then-I-will-break . . . bow-of Israel in-valley-of Jezreel

Verse 5a
in-the-day the-that
The KJV usually renders this expression as *at that day*. However, this is a rather weak reflection of the meaning of the Hebrew text, which says literally: *on that day, that one* or *on that day, the special one*. This often indicates an important moment in salvation history.

Rabbinical writings stay closer to the original Hebrew text and speak of *the appointed time*. In this case it involves an important event, namely a campaign of the Assyrians against the northern ten-tribe kingdom of Israel. We read: *on that special day*.
(Sherman, *Daniel*, § VI; Stuart, 30; Weerd, *Daniël*, vol. 2, Weerd, *Ezechiël*, vol. 2, 44–45)
(See Excursus 3.)

We read:
It will also be on that special day that I will break the bow of Israel in the valley of Jezreel.

Verse 6 NASB
*Then she conceived again and gave birth to a daughter. And the L*ORD *said to him, "Name her Lo-ruhamah, for I will no longer have compassion on the house of Israel, that I would ever forgive them."*

Verse 6 KJV
And she conceived again, and bare a daughter. And God said unto him, Call her name Loruhamah: for I will no more have mercy upon the house of Israel; but I will utterly take them away.

Verse 6 NIV
*Gomer conceived again and gave birth to a daughter. Then the L*ORD *said to Hosea, "Call her Lo-Ruhamah (which means 'not loved'), for I will no longer show love to Israel, that I should at all forgive them."*

Verse 6 Hebrew Interlinear Text
and-she-conceived again and-she-bore daughter then-he-said to him call! name-of-her Lo Ruchama for not I-will-continue longer I-will-show-love . . . house-of Israel that to-forgive I-should-forgive to-them

Verse 6a
and-she-conceived again and-she-bore daughter
Some add the name *Gomer*. That's exegeses; it is not so in the Hebrew text.

We read: **again she became pregnant and she gave birth to a daughter**

Verse 6b
then-he-said to him call! name-of-her Lo Ruchama
Opinions on the meaning of *Lo Ruchama* are divided. Some translate *not loved*. Most exegetes read *without mercy* or *without compassion* (see also verse 6c). In this case it is unmistakably a person, so we vocalize the Hebrew basic text, but do put the translation of *Lo Ruchama* in brackets, because it is clear this is an integral part of the exegeses.

We read *give*, imperative, because it is an order from God (*call!*).
(Born, 25; Garrett, 63; Harper, 212; Mays, 285–92; McComiskey, 23)

We read: ***then He said to him: Give her the name Lo-Ruchama*** (*no compassion*)!

Verse 6c
for not I-will-continue longer I-will-show-love . . . house-of Israel
It is fairly rare to translation *racham* as love, as the NIVIHEOT does here (see verse 6b). Most translators and/or exegetes read *compassion*, *love*, or *mercy* here.

The distinction lies in the relationship between the giver of love and the recipient. If the word describes the relationship of a human to the Almighty, it can indeed mean *love* (as is also the case in Psalm 18:1–2). However, if it describes the relationship of God to humanity or a people, there is a huge difference in level and it is more appropriate to use words like *compassion* or *mercy*.
(McComiskey, 24; Reed, 31; Strong's, word 7355)

We read: ***for I will no longer show compassion to the house of Israel***

Verse 6d
that to-forgive I-should-forgive to-them
This is a construction that says that forgiveness (*to-forgive*) was a constant necessity because the people of Israel fell into sin again and again. Born therefore reads: *so that I will always continue to forgive them*. Andersen and Freedman read: *or forgive them at all,* but that is a bit further from the original text.
(Andersen and Freedman, 192–94; Born, 25–26)

We read: ***so that I would always give them forgiveness***

The entire verse:
Again she became pregnant and she gave birth to a daughter. Then He said to him: Give her the name Lo-Ruchama [no compassion]! For I will no longer show compassion to the house of Israel, so that I would always give them forgiveness.

Verse 7 NASB
"*But I will have compassion on the house of Judah and deliver them by the* LORD *their God, and will not deliver them by bow, sword, battle, horses or horsemen.*"

Verse 7 KJV
But I will have mercy upon the house of Judah, and will save them by the LORD *their God, and will not save them by bow, nor by sword, nor by battle, by horses, nor by horsemen.*

Verse 7 NIV
"*Yet I will show love to Judah; and I will save them—not by bow, sword or battle, or by horses and horsemen, but I, the* LORD *their God, will save them.*"

Verse 7 Hebrew Interlinear Text
yet house-of Judah I-will-show-love and-will-save-them by-Yahweh God-of-them but-not I-will-save-them by-bow or-by-sword or-by-battle by-horses and by-horsemen

Verse 7a
yet house-of Judah I-will-show-love
Here too we translate with *compassion* or *mercy*. (See discussion of verse 6c.)
(McComiskey, 24; Reed, 31; Strong's, word 7355)

We read: **but I will show compassion for the house of Judah**

Verse 7b
but-not I-will-save-them by-bow or-by-sword or-by-battle by-horses and-by-horsemen
In the series *bow, sword, horse, and riders*, the word *battle* (or *war*) does not fit. Harper therefore reads *equipment*, but that is not there.

Many translators (for example the NLT and NASB translations) cancel the word. But there is a better solution. If we divide the sentence differently (the words were split at a later date) and connect *battle* with the second part of the sentence, the problem is solved. (Harper, 213, 215; Stuart, 23)

We read: ***but I will not save them by bow or sword, nor by a battle with horses or horsemen***

The entire verse:
But I will show compassion for the house of Judah. Then will I save them by Yahweh their God. But I will not save them by bow or sword, nor by a battle with horses or horsemen.

Verse 8 NASB
When she had weaned Lo-ruhamah, she conceived and gave birth to a son.

Verse 8 KJV
Now when she had weaned Loruhamah, she conceived, and bare a son.

Verse 8 NIV
After she had weaned Lo-Ruhamah, Gomer had another son.

Verse 8 Hebrew Interlinear Text
after-she-weaned . . . Lo Ruchama then-she-conceived and-she-bore son

Verse 8b
then-she-conceived
The *vav* (here translated with *then*) has a broad sense. Since this introduces a third birth, we read *again*.

We read:
After she weaned Lo-Ruchama, she became pregnant again and gave birth to a son.

Verse 9 NASB
And the L*ord**** said, "Name him Lo-ammi, for you are not My people and I am not your God."***

Verse 9 KJV
Then said God, Call his name Loammi: for ye are not my people, and I will not be your God.

Verse 9 NIV
Then the LORD ***said: "Call him Lo-Ammi (which means 'not my people'), for you are not my people and I am not your God.***

Verse 9 Hebrew Interlinear Text
then-he-said call! name-of-him Lo Ammi for you not people-of-me and-I not I-am to-you

Verse 9a
then-he-said call! name-of-him Lo Ammi
The meaning of the name of Gomer's third child is: *Not My people*. We add this between brackets.
(Born, 26; Stuart, 24–25; Reed, 32)

We read: ***He then said: Call him Lo-Ammi*** *[not My people]*!

Verse 9c
and-I not I-am to-you
The Hebrew word *ehyeh* is a variant of the holy name Yahweh (Exodus 3:14). Many translate this word here *God*. But that is not adequate; there is a poetic play on words here. The NIVIHEOT has recognized this and translates *not I-am*. This is a poetic way to say that God will no longer reside in Israel. Thus, the name expresses that God is leaving Israel. The prophecy is not limited to the northern kingdom alone. The ultimate meaning is that God will leave all of Israel (both nations), including the temple in Jerusalem. It is the consequence for breaking the Sinaitic Covenant. This reflects the same contrast as between Ammi and Lo-Ammi and between Ruchama and Lo-Ruchama and therefore we write *I AM* in caps in order to honor the holiness of God's name.
(Andersen and Freedman, 198; Garrett, 70; Mays, 29; McComiskey, 27; Walvoord and Zuck, 1381; Ward, 4; Wolff, 21–22)
(See Excursuses 10, 24.)

We read: ***for you are not My people, and I will no longer be the I AM for you***

The entire verse:
He then said: Call him Lo-Ammi *[not My people]*! ***For you are not My people, and I will no longer be the I AM for you.***

Introduction to Verses 10–12

After verse 9, Hosea suddenly changes the subject and switches to future prophecy. This change has motivated some interpreters and translators to add verses 10–12 to chapter 2. But such a sudden change of subject is not uncommon in the Bible; we find it many times. It is even characteristic of biblical prophecy. Thus, after the darkness of the prophecy of doom, the prospect of the salvific future is kept alive. On the one hand, this is done in order to show the way to a future salvation. On the other hand, it serves as comfort and encouragement for God's people.

Other scholars only add verse 12 to Hosea 2. They believe that the content and structure of verse 12 is in line with verse 1 of Hosea 2 and does not fit in with chapter 1. We cannot go along with this either.

We consider Hosea 1:12 to be a call to repentance. However, it is veiled in a special poetic sentence structure that makes verse 12 somewhat more difficult to fathom. However, the reference to the future, blessed status of God's people is clear. In that sense it is a call to repentance and a clear trumpet call that announces this salutary future.

Verse 10 NASB
Yet the number of the sons of Israel will be like the sand of the sea, which cannot be measured or numbered; and in the place where it is said to them, "You are not My people," it will be said to them, "You are the sons of the living God."

Verse 10 KJV
Yet the number of the children of Israel shall be as the sand of the sea, which cannot be measured nor numbered; and it shall come to pass, that in the place where it was said unto them, Ye are not my people, there it shall be said unto them, Ye are the sons of the living God.

Verse 10 NIV
"Yet the Israelites will be like the sand on the seashore, which cannot be measured or counted. In the place where it was said to them: 'You are not my people,' they will be called 'children of the living God.'"

Verse 10 Hebrew Interlinear Text
yet-he-will-be number-of sons-of Israel like-sand-of the-sea which not he-can-be-measured or-not he-can-be-counted and-he-will-be in-place-of where he-was-said to-them not people-of-me you he-will-be-called to-them sons-of God living-one

We read:
However, the number of the children of Israel will be like the sand of the sea, which cannot be measured, nor can it be counted. It will also happen that, in the place where it was said to them: You are not My people, the name will be given to them: children of the living God!

Verse 11 NASB
And the sons of Judah and the sons of Israel will be gathered together, and they will appoint for themselves one leader, and they will go up from the land, for great will be the day of Jezreel.

Verse 11 KJV
Then shall the children of Judah and the children of Israel be gathered together, and appoint themselves one head, and they shall come up out of the land: for great shall be the day of Jezreel.

Verse 11 NIV
The people of Judah and the people of Israel will come together; they will appoint one leader and will come up out of the land, for great will be the day of Jezreel.

Verse 11 Hebrew Interlinear Text
and-will-be-reunited peoples-of Judah and-peoples-of Israel together and-they-will-appoint for-them leader one and-they-will-come-up out-of the-land for great day-of Jezreel

Verse 11a
and-they-will-be-reunited peoples-of Judah and-peoples-of Israel together
The *vav* (*and*) has a broad meaning. It leads to an event that comes after verse 11.

The NIVIHEOT translates twice with *peoples*. But the word *bên* means *son*, *child*, or *descendant*. Reed speaks of *posterity*. We read *children*, as is also the case in verse 10.
(Owens, 761; Reed, 32)

We read: ***then the children of Judah and the children of Israel will be reunited***

Verse 11b
and-they-will-appoint for-them leader one
The word *rosh* means *head*, sometimes *leader* or *top*. We prefer *head*. It has a messianic meaning, because in ancient Israel there were two leaders (heads): the king and the high priest. Jesus Christ will combine these two in one position (Hebrews 7 and 8; Zechariah 6:13). Kuhnigk rightly calls it *resurrection language*. Stuart reads: *a single leader*.
(Kuhnigk, 8–10; Strong's, word 7218; Stuart, 35; *Studiebijbel* SBOT 12, 30)

We read: ***and they will appoint one head over them***

Verse 11c
and-they-will-come-up out-of-the-land
The meaning of *alah* is *to rise, to ascend, to go up* (Exodus 19:18; Joshua 8:21; and Jeremiah 10:13) or *to exalt*. A translation with *come up* (such as the KJV and NIV) is too far away. The NASB translates *go up*, which is somewhat better.

Literally 11c says *and they will shoot up from the land*, as if they were young grain. Herein we again recognize the two-part unity of land and people, Israel and Canaan (the promised land), which is the sacred soil for the people of Israel.

The sentence opens with *vav*, which leads to an event afterward, so we read: *after*.
(Andersen and Freedman, 203, 208; McComiskey, 28; Strong's, word 5927)

We read: ***after that they will shoot up from the land***

Verse 11d
for great day-of Jezreel
Again, here is a poetic play on words (paronomasia). For the day of Jezreel is the day when God definitively deals with Israel's enemies. That day (or period) also opens the door to the Messianic Kingdom, so it is end-time prophecy. The meaning of Jezreel (*God sows*) refers to that. Because with the downfall of Israel's enemies—which are God's enemies—the seed is sown for the coming kingdom of God.
(McComiskey, 30)

We read: ***for great will be the day of Jezreel*** *[God sows]*

The entire verse:
Then the children of Judah and the children of Israel will be reunited and they will appoint one head over them. Then they will hurry up from the country, because great will be the day of Jezreel *[God sows]*.

Verse 12 Introduction

This verse of Hosea 1 is very controversial. Translators and exegetes propose many variants of the text. However, they all deviate from the original Hebrew text. We refuse to do that, because there must be a very good reason to do so and we couldn't find one.

In principle, this commentary chooses to closely follow the Hebrew text. This allows for few possible adaptations to that text. That is a good thing. In this way we prevent too many of our own fabrications from creeping in. We see in Hosea 1:12 a divine proclamation that concludes the prophecy of salvation in verses 10 and 11. (See introduction to verses 10–12.) (Wolff, 29)

Verse 12 NASB
Say to your brothers, "Ammi," and to your sisters, "Ruhamah."

Verse 12 KJV
Say ye unto your brethren, Ammi; and to your sisters, Ruhamah.

Chapter 2:1 NIV
"Say of your brothers, 'My people,' and of your sisters, 'My loved one.'"

Chapter 2:1 Hebrew Interlinear Text
say! of-brothers-of-you people-of-me and-of-sisters-of-you she-is-loved

Verse 12a
say! of-brothers-of-you
The NIVIHEOT adds an exclamation mark to the word *say!* and thus reads it as an imperative. It involves *calling* or *commanding* (1 Chronicles 21:17) or saying something forcefully; that is *proclaiming* (Psalm 40:9).
(Andersen and Freedman, 212–13; Mays, 30; Strong's, word 559; Wolff, 28–29)

We read: **proclaim to your brothers**

Verse 12b
people-of-me and-of-sisters-of-you she-is-loved
The NIVIHEOT has rightly translated the words *ammi* and *ruchama*. Many interpreters and translators do not and read: *say! of-brothers-of-you Ammi and-of-sisters-of-you Ruchama*. However, when the Hebrew text is vocalized into a proper noun, the core of the prophetic message disappears, because it is implicit in the meaning of both names. We reflect that by translating the names Ammi and Ruchama and including them in parentheses.
(McComiskey, 31; Stuart, 35)

We read: **be My people *[Ammi]*, and your sisters: be merciful *[Ruchama]***

The entire verse:
Proclaim to your brothers: Be My people *[Ammi]*, and to your sisters: Be merciful *[Ruchama]*.

Hosea 1: 1–12—The corrected text:

Verse 1   ***The word of Yahweh came to Hosea, the son of Beeri, in the days of Uzziah, Jotham, Ahaz, and Hezekiah, kings of Judah, and in the days of Jeroboam the son of Joash, king of Israel.***
Verse 2   ***Yahweh began to speak through Hosea. Then Yahweh said to Hosea, Go! Take an adulterous woman to yourself and accept children [born] of adultery. For because she has continually committed adultery, the country is guilty of adultery. Thus Yahweh was left.***
Verse 3   ***Thus he went and married Gomer, the daughter of Diblaim*** *[daughter of two fruit cakes]*. ***Then she conceived and bore him a son.***

Verse 4	*And Yahweh said to him, "Give him the name Jezreel [God sows]! For yet a little while and I will visit the bloodshed of Jezreel upon the house of Jehu. Then I will put an end to the kingdom of the house of Israel."*
Verse 5	*It will also be on that special day that I will break the bow of Israel in the valley of Jezreel.*
Verse 6	*Again she became pregnant and she gave birth to a daughter. Then He said to him: Give her the name Lo-Ruchama [no compassion]! For I will no longer show compassion to the house of Israel, so that I would always give them forgiveness.*
Verse 7	*But I will show compassion for the house of Judah. Then will I save them by Yahweh their God. But I will not save them by bow or sword, nor by a battle with horses or horsemen.*
Verse 8	*After she weaned Lo-Ruchama, she became pregnant again and gave birth to a son.*
Verse 9	*He then said: Call him Lo-Ammi [not My people]! For you are not My people, and I will no longer be the I AM for you.*
Verse 10	*However, the number of the children of Israel will be like the sand of the sea, which cannot be measured, nor can it be counted. It will also happen that, in the place where it was said to them: You are not My people, the name will be given to them: children of the living God!*
Verse 11	*Then the children of Judah and the children of Israel will be reunited and they will appoint one head over them. Then they will hurry up from the country, because great will be the day of Jezreel [God sows].*
Verse 12	*Proclaim to your brothers: Be My people [Ammi], and to your sisters: Be merciful [Ruchama].*

HOSEA 1
Exegesis

Introduction

The prophecy of Hosea begins with a very brief introduction. First, the prophet introduces himself and indicates the approximate time in which he lived. Then he turns to the bizarre story of the forced marriage between the respectable Hosea and a prostitute with a bad reputation: Gomer. Three children are born, which the prophet reports in an almost businesslike tone: *Jezreel*, *Lo-Ruchama*, and *Lo-Ammi*.

The prophet Hosea shows little emotion. Yet there must have been emotion, because Gomer was his wife. This very unusual marriage appears to represent a graphic piece of prophecy. With the birth of the three children God symbolically breaks the Sinaitic Covenant with Israel.

Nevertheless, chapter 1 closes with a remarkable prophecy of salvation, which is just as emphatically positive as the judgment appears to be dark. Thus we read almost in one breath of a high point and a low point in the relationship between God and His people.

A. The People of Israel

Hosea speaks about Israel in verses 1, 5, 6, and 11. That does not address the entire people but solely the Ten Tribes—the Northern Kingdom. After the secession of Judah (and Benjamin) from the union of all twelve tribes, the remaining ten tribes were, legally, heir to the name Israel. Herein lies a cause of possible confusion, since Hosea does not always speak of Israel in a limiting sense. He usually means the Northern Kingdom, but sometimes also all twelve tribes, thus all of Israel. If this is the case, we indicate this in parentheses. (This does not occur in Hosea 1, except for the expression *the children of Israel* in verse 10, which refers to all twelve tribes reunited at the end time!)
(See Annotation 1G; Excursuses 5, 6.)

Verse 1
The word of Yahweh came to Hosea, the son of Beeri, in the days of Uzziah, Jotham, Ahaz, and Hezekiah, kings of Judah, and in the days of Jeroboam the son of Joash, king of Israel.

Verse 1a
The word of Yahweh came to Hosea, the son of Beeri,
The name Hosea means: *[he gives] salvation*. With that, the theme of the book has been set. Of course, the book of Hosea also pays a great deal of attention to the judgments that God calls over the people of Israel. However, these are not an end in and of themselves. The eventual purpose of the book is the ultimate fulfillment of the counsel of God; that is the destiny of Israel and Judah in this world at the end time. Its climax will be the establishment of the Messianic Kingdom and the kingship of Jesus Christ, the Messiah. (For further information about Hosea, see above, Introduction: The Prophet and His Time.)
(Brown, xi; Edelkoort, 176; Kidner, 17)

Verse 1b
in the days of Uzziah, Jotham, Ahaz, and Hezekiah, kings of Judah, and in the days of Jeroboam the son of Joash, king of Israel.

King Uzziah ruled over the southern kingdom of Judah 792/91 to 740/39 BC. Jotham started as regent, because his father, Uzziah, had become leprous. His kingship lasted from 740/39 to 735. He was succeeded by King Ahaz, who ruled from 735 to 716. Then came King Hezekiah, who reigned from 716 to 687. In contrast to the kings of Judah, Hosea mentions only one king of Israel, namely Jeroboam II, who ruled from 787/86 to 747/46 BC.

On the basis of verse 1b, some exegetes conclude that Hosea began his ministry in the last years of King Uzziah and that it ended in the first years of King Hezekiah. This would amount to a time span of thirty to fifty years, or even more.

It is striking that the dates do not run synchronously. The time span of the four Judean kings covers the period from 792 to 687, so a total of 105 years. That of King Jeroboam II of Israel lasted from 782 to 753, that is twenty-nine years.

After this the following kings reigned over Israel: Zechariah, in 753 (six months). He was murdered by Shallum, who was king for only one month. He too was murdered and was succeeded by Menahem, who ruled from 752/51 to 742/41. Then Pekahiah reigned from 742/41 to 740/39. He too was murdered and succeeded by Pekah, who was king from 740/39 to 732/31. And (it becomes monotonous) this king too was murdered. He was succeeded by Hosea, who ruled from 732–724 to the last king, because in 722 the Northern Kingdom, Israel, perished.
(See Introduction: The Prophet and His Time; See below: Alternative Dates)

1b.1 Why all these Judean kings?
It is not clear why only one king of Israel is mentioned and no fewer than four kings of Judah over a period of 105 years. This time span is much longer than the period in which Hosea exercised his prophetic ministry. Four possible explanations are given:

a. Many exegetes assume that Hosea experienced the demise of Israel during his lifetime. The kingdom of Israel perished during the reign of King Ahaz of Judah. The prophet, however, does not speak about him. Some therefore assume that this part of the book of Hosea has been lost or removed by a later editor.

b. A second possibility is that the prophet Hosea did not think it necessary to give a record of the fall of Israel, simply because God did not tell him to. Perhaps Hosea nevertheless mentioned the Judean kings Ahaz and Hezekiah because, in contrast to Israel, under Hezekiah there was a return to God in Judah.

c. A third possibility is that the prophet Hosea died during the reign of King Zechariah. Only a few exegetes consider this option. For if that were the case, Hosea would provide information about the future of Judah (with the names Ahaz and Hezekiah). For many exegetes, especially of a liberal signature, this is not an option since they do not believe that prophets of God can see the future.

d. The house of Jehu was appointed by God Himself. The kings who came after Zechariah were not. In fact, they were not entitled to their kingship, so this may be the reason they are not mentioned. (However, King Zechariah is not mentioned by name, so this is a weak argument.)

Conclusion:
We reject options a and d and have a preference for option c. However, we do not make this choice with great certainty, because argument b cannot be ruled out.
(Bromiley, "Hosea," 1–3; Flanders, Crapps and Smith, 319; Hengstenberg, 166ff.; Keil and Delitzsch, vol. 1, iiff.; King, 30–35; Limburg, 6–7; McComiskey, 1–3; Walvoord and Zuck, 1377)

Alternative Dates
The dates given in the previous discussion are from McComiskey. Others deviate from these. King, for example, gives the following dates for the Kings of Judah: Uzzia 783–742 BC; Jotam 742–735; Achaz 735–715; Hezekiah 715–687. For the kings of Israel: Jeroboam II 786–746 BC; Zechariah 746; Shallum 746; Menahem 745–738; Pekahia 738–737; Pekah 737–732; Hosea 732–724. There are even more variants in circulation. We forgo, however, going into more depth here because it adds nothing essential.

Verse 2

Yahweh began to speak through Hosea. Then Yahweh said to Hosea, Go! Take an adulterous woman to yourself and accept children [born] of fornication. For because she has continually committed adultery, the land is guilty of fornication. Thus Yahweh was forsaken.

The prophecy begins with God's signature. This is not the prophet Hosea speaking, but the Almighty Himself, through the mouth of Hosea. This sets the tone for the book. It is a divine and holy text, which we must not casually criticize.

Verse 2b

Take an adulterous woman to yourself

The prophet Hosea gets a very strange assignment indeed. He must marry a harlot in order to graphically expose the bad relationship between God and Israel. Hosea symbolically represents God; the harlot represents the ten-tribe nation of Israel.

It is not only in Hosea that the relationship between God and Israel is described this way. It is a well-known theme in the Bible. The prophet Ezekiel speaks about it, for example, in chapter 16, verse 15*:

> *"But you trusted in your own beauty and became a prostitute because of your fame, and you lavished your favors on everyone who passed by. For Him it was intended."*

And in Ezekiel 23:2–5†:

2   *"Son of man, there were once two women, daughters of the same mother.*
3   *"They became prostitutes in Egypt—yes, from their childhood they were already involved in prostitution. It was there that her breasts were touched and there her virgin nipples were caressed.*
4   *"Their names were: Ohola, who was the elder, and Oholibah, her sister, and they belonged to me. They also bore me sons and daughters, and their names were: Samaria (Ohola) and Jerusalem (Oholibah).*
5   *"While they still belonged to me, Ohola went into prostitution, for she longed for her lovers, for the warriors of Assyria."*

Ohola, who is a type of the capital Samaria, represents the ten-tribe kingdom of Israel. In the book of Hosea that is Gomer, but both refer to one and the same people.
(Weerd, Hebrew text translation in *Ezechiël*, vol. 1, *361, †611–12)

Many exegetes assume that Gomer became a prostitute only after her marriage. That is not plausible for the following reasons:

1. The text says that Hosea must marry an adulterous woman. That is clear in itself.
2. In Ezekiel 23, Israel is also presented as a harlot—Ohola. The chapter proves that Ohola was already a prostitute in her youth before her marriage with God (Ezekiel 23:3). The

parallels between the book of Hosea and Ezekiel are unmistakable. We do not deal with a capricious God, but with an Almighty God who pursues a steady course. This is why the book of Ezekiel bears authoritatively on the exegesis of this text in Hosea. So we have to assume that Gomer was already a prostitute before she got married.

(Boice, *Minor Prophets*, vol. 1, 15–16; Edelkoort, 176; Kidner, 19; Walvoord and Zuck, 1379; Weerd, *Ezechiël*, vol. 1, 644–46; Wood, 170–72)

Verse 2c
accept children born of fornication
It can hardly be a surprise that a woman who is a prostitute gets pregnant. The possibilities for contraception were limited. What is surprising is that these children must be accepted by the prophet Hosea as his own.

Some exegetes explain verse 2 in such a way that Gomer already had children born of fornication before she married Hosea. The book Hosea gives no further guidance on this.
(Edelkoort, 176; Keil, 29; Walvoord and Zuck, 1380; Wood, 171)

Verse 2d
The country is guilty of adultery
Hosea does not speak of Israel, but of *the land*. That is not a mistake on the part of the prophet. For within the promise to the patriarch Abraham (Genesis 17), which is the foundation of Israel's right to exist, the land (Canaan, the promised land) and people (Israel and Judah) are inextricably linked. This so-called Holy Land of God is infected as with an illness. And this illness is *adultery*.

The land, and with it the people of Israel, is accused of *adultery*. By that term God means that His people have turned away from Him and worshiped other gods. It says *is guilty of.* That suggests a lawsuit, which indeed is coming, in Hosea 2.
(Boice, *Minor* Prophets, vol. 1, 14)

Verse 3
Thus he went and married Gomer, the daughter of Diblaim *[daughter of two fruit cakes]*. ***Then she conceived and bore him a son.***
The meaning of the name *Gomer* is *to achieve* or *to complete*. The meaning of the word probably refers to the completion or termination of the Sinaitic Covenant between God and the people of Israel. The prophet Hosea obeys God and takes a harlot as his wife. There is no indication as to how and where he finds Gomer. The answer may lie in verse 3b.
(Andersen and Freedman, 171; Dahood, 595–97; Wolff, 16)
(See Annotation 1G; Excursus 10.)

Verse 3b:
the daughter of Diblaim *[daughter of two fruit cakes]*
There is nothing in the Bible, nor from other sources, about *Diblaim*. We can therefore conclude that it is an unusual personal name. An alternative translation is *daughter of two fruit cakes*, probably a kind of nickname denoting the price for her services as a prostitute.

As already mentioned in the discussion of the Hebrew text, the meanings of the personal names in the book Hosea play an important role. Therefore, the second translation makes more sense.

Verse 3c
Then she conceived and bore him a son.

Most exegetes assume that Gomer did not become pregnant by the prophet Hosea. The Bible is generally quite clear on this point, as seen here in Ruth 4:13: *"Then Boaz took Ruth and she became his wife and he went in to her."* Here in Hosea we don't have these last words of Ruth 4:13.

The prophet Hosea certainly did not love Gomer. He is told to marry her, not to have intercourse with her, so that may not have happened at all. Verse 2 also speaks of *children born of fornication*, which is quite clear.

Annotation 1B: Temple Prostitution

The people of Israel sinned heavily by taking over perverse idolatry from the surrounding countries. Especially the worship of the Baals and Ishtar. The word Baal is a generic name and means *master*. There were many Baals, such as Baal Melkart, Baal Moloch and Baal Beelzebub. Ishtar was worshiped mainly in Babylonia and Assyria as the supreme mother goddess. An important part of the idol worship of Ishtar was temple prostitution. Fruit cakes (among other things) were used as payment.

Gomer was probably a temple prostitute and her services only cost two fig cakes. That was a low price, which suggests again that Gomer was not very popular, which might mean that she was not very attractive.

It does not state how Hosea found Gomer, which some exegetes find rather strange. If we indeed assume that Gomer was a prostitute in a temple of Ishtar, then it was not so difficult for Hosea to find her. The temples or shrines of Ishtar were public and the sites undoubtedly known. Moreover, this form of idolatry served as a representation of the sins of Israel. So it is not surprising that the prophet Hosea was just looking for a woman there to serve as a role model for the prophecy of divine judgment. For Gomer, the marriage with Hosea was attractive. It gave her a certain status and any children a father.

Sources:
(Andersen and Freedman, 171; Birch, 19–20; Born, 24; Constable, 8; Dee and Schoneveld, vol. 1, 53–54 and vol. 2, 256–57; *Encyclopedia of Western Gods and Goddesses*; Flanders, Crapps, and Smith, 349; Garrett, 52; Harper, 211; Mays, 24; Nissaba, *Goddesses from around the world*; Rowley, 66–97)

Verse 4
And Yahweh said to him, "Give him the name Jezreel [God sows]! For yet a little while and I will visit the bloodshed of Jezreel upon the house of Jehu. Then I will put an end to the kingdom of the house of Israel."

Verse 4b
Give him the name Jezreel [God sows]!
Jezreel is not just an arbitrary name for a newborn child. It is the first pronouncement (judgment) of God on Israel, which is further explained in verse 4c.

There is no doubt that the meaning of the name Jezreel here has an unfavorable undertone. Jezreel was the residence of the Jehu dynasty (2 Kings 9:1–10:1). It was located at the entrance of the Jezreel plain (in northern Canaan, east of Mount Carmel). It was there that a bloodbath was initiated by the newly anointed King Jehu. It led to the death of King Joram of Israel and also of King Ahaziah of Judah (2 Kings 9:16–29).

It was by divine command (2 Kings 9:6–10) that Jehu should kill Queen Jezebel as well

as all male members of the house of Ahab. This laid the foundation for a new beginning under the kingship of Jehu. Perhaps the term God sows (*Jezreel*) has the judgment on the ungodly house of Ahab in view, which also contained the germ of a new beginning. The fact that King Jehu disappointed God does not change that.
(Born, 25; Edelkoort, 177; Kidner, 22)

Verse 4c
I will visit the bloodshed of Jezreel upon the house of Jehu.
Opinions are very divided on the meaning of this sentence. However, it is widely agreed that this refers to the extermination of the house (family) of Ahab and King Joram (2 Kings 9–10)—a directive of God to King Jehu (2 Kings 10:17). So what did Jehu do wrong? He also slaughtered King Ahazia of Judah (2 Kings 9:27) and most of his family (2 Kings 10:13–14). By doing that, he reduced Ahazia's family, descendants of King David, to a few members, which led to the near elimination of the Davidic line by Queen Atalia. With this act Jehu became guilty of *bloodshed*, and therefore his family was also doomed. With the murder of King Zechariah, the son of Jeroboam II, the blood of Jezreel was indeed avenged at the house of Jehu (2 Kings 15:12).
(Annotation 1C)

Verse 4d
Then I will put an end to the kingdom of the house of Israel.
The word *then* introduces the period after King Zechariah (2 Kings 15:8–12). His death ended the Jehu dynasty, and an era began in which internal quarrels tore Israel apart. In this final era, Israel had six kings in thirty-one years (753–722 BC), four of whom were assassinated. In 722 BC the kingdom came to its sad demise, just as the prophet Hosea foretold.

Annotation 1C: The Bloodguilt of King Jehu

1C.1 Jehu was guilty of the murder of David's family.
The Almighty commanded King Jehu to destroy the house of Ahab, but Kind Jehu did not carry that out according to the instructions given him by the prophet of God (2 Kings 9:1–10). On his own initiative he also decided to kill King Ahaziah of Judah (close family of Ahab) and the family members who were traveling with King Ahaziah in Israel (2 Kings 9:27–28 and 10:13–14).

With the death of King Ahaziah and most of his royal family, Jehu laid the foundation for the murder of the royal family still living in Judah. King Ahaziah was descended directly from King David. His lineage is therefore essential for the fulfillment of all messianic prophecy. Ultimately, Jesus Christ, the Messiah, would be born of his lineage. The mother of Ahaziah, Queen Atalia (a daughter of Ahab and Jezebel!), tried to seize power over Judah in the confusion that had arisen after the death of King Ahaziah. She therefore had all the living descendants of King David, whom she could find, killed. Little Joash (the last descendant of King David, 2 Kings 11) barely escaped the massacre.

This attack was a satanic plot. For if Queen Atalia had also killed Joash, the lineage that would lead to Jesus Christ would have ended prematurely! For that reason, Jehu had put a heavy bloodguilt on himself. (See also 2 Kings 8:25–29.)
(Constable, 8; Dee and Schoneveld, vol. 1, 55; Stuart, 29; Walvoord and Zuck, 1380)

1C.2 The bloodguilt was not reconciled.
King Jehu was commanded to exterminate all male members of Ahab's family (2 Kings

9:7–8) *and* to return Israel to God. Bloodguilt arose if someone killed someone else. In this case the justification was that Jehu acted on behalf of God.

However, the goal of killing Ahab's family was to put an end to the wickedness of Israel. The horrible idolatry of the Baals had been imported especially through Queen Jezebel, Ahab's wife. But Jehu failed to return Israel to God. He did put an end to Baal worship, but not to the idolatry at Bethel and Dan, introduced by King Jeroboam. Only the conversion of Israel and the restoration of the worship of God could take away the bloodguilt of Jezreel.
(See Excursus 11.)

Verse 5
It will also be on that special day that I will break the bow of Israel in the valley of Jezreel.
The valley of Jezreel was located in the plain of Jezreel, also called the plain of Megiddo, in the north of Canaan. Many battles have been fought there, such as the victory of Deborah and Barak over the Canaanites (Judges 4–5), Gideon's victory over the Midianites (Judges 6–8), and the defeat of King Saul against the Philistines (1 Samuel 29–31).

We must also seek Armageddon here, where according to Revelation 16:16 the powers of darkness will compete with the hosts of God.

Based on the primary meaning of verse 5, Israel (the ten-tribe kingdom) will suffer a crushing defeat in the valley of Jezreel. That must have been a battle with the Assyrians during the campaign of the Assyrian king, Salmaneser (2 Kings 17:3–5). Through that campaign the power of Israel was finally broken (*that I will break the bow of Israel*). However, the battle itself is not mentioned in the Bible.
(Harper, 20–21; Stuart, 29–30)
(See Excursus 3.)

Verse 6
Again she became pregnant and she gave birth to a daughter. Then He said to him: Give her the name Lo-Ruchama** [no compassion]**! For I will no longer show compassion to the house of Israel, so that I would always grant them forgiveness.
Hosea is not mentioned in the case of this second pregnancy. We will assume therefore that again he was not the father. The second child was born out of fornication, as verse 2 testifies.

It was (and is) highly unusual to give a child a name that has very negative connotations. What if we were to give a child the name Auschwitz or Hiroshima? We have very few examples of this in the Bible (e.g., Ichabod, 1 Samuel 4:21). It is unlikely that Gomer was happy with this name, but the prophet Hosea persisted, because God demanded it from him.
(Birch, 21; Stuart, 31)

Verse 6b
Give her the name Lo-Ruchama** [no compassion]**!
In the last years of King Jeroboam II, Israel's fortunes had taken a turn for the worse. The fat years of economic prosperity were over. The Assyrian empire had meanwhile begun a period of expansion, and that was at the expense of the power of Israel and surrounding states. Militarily, politically, and economically, Israel went rapidly downhill. Jeroboam

II was a strong king, but after him came a series of weak rulers, which increased Israel's problems even further. Israel rapidly entered a period of civil wars, treaties with outside powers, and economic misery. So the people of Israel desperately needed God's compassion. But they refused to repent and to turn to God. On the contrary, Israel continued to fall into heavy sins and thus grieved the Almighty. For a long time, God had let grace take the place of the demand for justice. That came to an end here—enough is enough. The birth of *Lo-Ruchama* (no compassion) is the prophetic sign of this.

Verse 7
But I will show compassion to the house of Judah. Then will I save them by Yahweh their God. But I will not save them by bow or sword, nor by a battle with horses or horsemen.
The fate of the kingdom of Judah was different from the doom of the kingdom of Israel (the ten-tribe kingdom). Judah also sinned heavily, but the decline was not yet as deep as in Israel. Moreover, there arose a kind of revival; an awakening of faith in God under the inspiring leadership of King Hezekiah. Thus Judah is still shown mercy.

Verse 7b
Then will I save them by Yahweh their God
After the downfall of Israel, the kingdom of Judah was the sole bearer of the promise of salvation. That salvation does not come in the form of a glorious victory of the army of Judah, but through the intervention of God Himself. When King Hezekiah was besieged by the army of King Sennacherib of Assyria, God sent an angel of the Lord, who killed 185,000 of the enemy army in one night. That broke the power of Assyria, whose army had destroyed Israel and thus saved Judah (2 Kings 19:35–36).

But this prophecy looks further ahead, because the salvation of Judah under Hezekiah was temporary. Some decades later Judah was destroyed by King Nebuchadnezzar. We also find the ultimate fulfillment of this prophecy in the Messianic Kingdom.
(Constable, 9)
(See Annotation 1D; Excursus 3, 4.)

Annotation 1D: Conditional Prophecy

The theme of Hosea 2 is the complete salvation of Israel, which leads to the establishment of the Messianic Kingdom. The redemption under King Hezekiah, however, was not definitive, as verse 7b certainly suggests. For only a few generations later the kingdom of Judah was overrun by the Babylonians who ravaged the country and utterly destroyed Jerusalem. The survivors were sent into exile and the land was reduced to desolation.

Fulfilled in the Messiah
Did the prophesy fail? Is this prophecy untrustworthy? No way. Here we are faced with conditional prophecy. The complete fulfillment was blocked by the fact that Judah did not really repent. That soon came to light, because under King Manasse it sank deeper in idolatry than ever before. That fact postponed the fulfillment to a much later date. It is thus inevitable that we must look for a second and more definitive fulfillment. And we find it in the person of a small child, Jesus Christ, who was born in Bethlehem Ephrathah.

The promised Messiah came (Luke 2) but was rejected by the Jews. Therefore, he could not become king of Israel. Thus the prophesied salvation had to be postponed again, and it rests still in the waiting room of history. However, the promise was not canceled, as never happens with God's promises. Somewhere in the future this prophecy will be fulfilled—perhaps not far from now! It will be achieved by God Himself and Jesus Christ—not by human intervention—*not . . . by bow or sword, nor by a battle with horses or horsemen.*

Verse 8
After she weaned Lo-Ruchama she became pregnant again and gave birth to a son.
Gomer does not change her sinful behavior. She remains unfaithful to Hosea, since with the third child Hosea's name is not even mentioned again. Hosea was not the father of Lo-Ammi either. The child was born out of fornication (verse 2).

Verse 9
He then said: Call him Lo-Ammi [not My people]! For you are not My people, and I will no longer be I AM for you.
With this prophecy, God breaks the covenant with the ten tribes of Israel. It marks a terrible moment in the history of salvation. This verse also evokes the memory of a prophecy that marked the beginning of the Sinaitic Covenant; Exodus 6:7–8 NASB:

> 7   "Then I will take you for My people, and I will be your God; and you shall know that I am the LORD your God, who brought you out from under the burdens of the Egyptians.
> 8   "I will bring you to the land which I swore to give to Abraham, Isaac, and Jacob, and I will give it to you for a possession; I am the LORD."

Verse 9b
I will no longer be I AM for you.
The God of Israel was called Yahweh, the *I-Am-Who-I-Am*. Now the Sinaitic Covenant is broken and He is no longer the *I AM* for Israel.

This name thus implies the break in the covenant and the destruction of Israel—both countries, notwithstanding that Judah went down many years later. Israel was doomed first and in consequence the Ten Tribes disappeared into the anonymity of the gentile peoples. Tribe by tribe these are: Dan, Asher, Naphtali, Manasseh, Ephraim, Reuben, Simeon, Issachar, Zebulun, and Gad.

Annotation 1E: God's Name Was at Stake

Israel came to grief and was scattered. However, the Ten Tribes will also, like the Jews, return to Canaan. For the downfall of Israel is an intolerable blot on the reputation of God, as Ezekiel 36:20* testifies:

> "They violated My holy name. For it was said of them, These are the people of Yahweh, yet they have left his land."

Israel *must* therefore return to Canaan to take away that defamation.

The Jews (Judah and Benjamin) are well known in the world, but the Ten Tribes have disappeared. Yet Ezekiel 36:24† speaks of two peoples:

> "I will bring you forth from the nations [Israel], and I will gather you from all countries [Judah], and I will bring you back to your own land."

(Weerd, Hebrew text translation in *Ezechiël*, vol. 2, *326, †328)

The fulfillment is imminent.
Israel was scattered like chaff (Hosea 13:3) and swallowed up in the nations. But the Ten Tribes will be made visible again (*bring . . . forth*). That process has started in our time. For there are peoples from India, China, and Africa who say they have descended from the people of Israel: Telugu Jews (Ephraim), Bnei Menashe (Manasseh), Beta Yisrael (Dan), Pathans (various tribes), Chiang-Min Jews. They will all be gathered from all countries of the world. All of Israel goes back to Canaan.

Sources:
(Constable, 10; Kidner, 23; Limburg, 9; Reed, 32; Stuart, 33)
(See Annotation 1G; Excursuses 3, 7, 9, 12.)

Introduction to Verses 10–12

After verse 9, Hosea 1 changes the subject and moves on to future prophecy. It speaks of an unfulfilled, distant future, when the Messianic Kingdom will be established and Jesus Christ will reign as King in Jerusalem.

Changing perspective is characteristic of biblical prophecy. Because despite all the misery of that moment, the beautiful edifice of God's promises remains. Not God, but human failure slows the coming of salvation. We have freedom of choice and therefore a great responsibility for the progress of salvation history. For that reason, God's prophets always draw attention to the ultimate goals of the Almighty. Let us never forget that beyond the horizon of our limited field of vision, there is blessing in store, more blessing than we can imagine. And let us never forget that all of God's promises will be fulfilled: both for the church of Christ and for the whole nation of Israel.
(Ironside, 19)

Which Israel?
A second change is that the name Israel (verse 10) no longer stands exclusively for a part of God's people, namely the ten tribes of the northern kingdom. Verse 10 speaks unmistakably of all twelve tribes, that is, both Israel and Judah (including Benjamin and Levi). They are summed up under their old covenant name: the children of Israel. It is therefore necessary to give some additional explanation about the use of the name Israel in the Bible.

Excursus 5: Israel and Judah

There is a big difference of opinion among exegetes about the meaning of the names Israel and Judah in the prophetic books of the Old Testament. However, our position on this has important consequences for the exegesis of the book of Hosea. We must therefore first provide clarity on this point.

5.a The twelve tribes
The Northern Kingdom consisted of Dan, Asher, Naphtali, Manasseh, Ephraim, Reuben, Simeon, Issachar, Zebulun, and Gad. The Southern Kingdom consisted of the other two tribes, Judah and Benjamin. The tribe of Levi, from which came the Levites and priests, was not assigned any territory but was distributed throughout the land of Canaan. After the temple was built, most priests and Levites lived in and around Jerusalem.

5.b The patriarch Jacob

The history of the name Israel goes back to ancient times, to the patriarch Jacob. He was the son of Isaac, who was the son of Abraham who received the promise that his offspring would grow into a great nation (the promised land). Later, Jacob received a new name—Israel (see Genesis 32:28). That also became the name of the people that descended from the patriarchs, and continues to the present day.

5.c Jacob became Israel

The word Israel has a variable meaning in the Old Testament. First of all, it is the new name for the patriarch Jacob. It shows a changed attitude of God for Jacob, because his new name is a combination of the Hebrew words for *wrestle* and *God*. Modern scholars translate is as: *God struggles*; in the sense of *God is at your side*.

In addition, it is used as the name for all twelve tribes of Israel. Later in history, the ten-tribe (northern) kingdom bears the name Israel, while the remaining two tribes (the southern kingdom) are called Judah. It is precisely at that point that there are great differences among exegetes and many can be quite dogmatic.

In spite of all confusion, the use of the name Israel does not have to create problems. After all, it is possible to determine exactly why different meanings are involved and also what the meaning was at the time of the prophet Hosea.

5.d From Israel, as a whole, to the Northern Kingdom

In the period before the division of the kingdom of Israel into two independent states, Judah and Israel (under King Rehoboam), the names are still as before. At that time the name Israel, if used for the nation, refers to the entire kingdom, so to all twelve tribes. This is apparent, for example, from 1 Samuel 10:20 and following.

The dividing of the kingdom is described in 1 Kings 12. Here too the name Israel refers to all twelve tribes. In 1 Kings 12:23–24 this suddenly changes. There is reference to Judah (with Benjamin) as the one party and Israel (the other ten tribes) as the other part. From that moment on, the name Israel, as a political indication, usually refers to the kingdom of the Ten Tribes. We find the turning point in 1 Kings 12:17 NASB:

> *But as for the sons of Israel who lived in the cities of Judah, Rehoboam reigned over them.*

This text says that there was a part of the *sons of Israel* (whole Israel at that moment), of which Rehoboam became king (Judah). Then the little tribe of Benjamin joined Judah (1 Kings 12:21). They thus left the original kingdom of Israel (the twelve tribes) and then appear to continue as a separate kingdom under the name Judah. In 2 Chronicles 10 we find the same picture. Verses 1, 3, and 16 still speak of Israel as all twelve tribes. King Rehoboam, who was the only legal pretender to the throne (because he descended from King David) is then rejected by the <u>whole people</u> (all twelve tribes, see verse 16). Verse 17 appears to be the same as 1 Kings 12:17. After that event, both the books of 1 and 2 Kings and the book of 2 Chronicles consistently speak of two different nations: Judah and Israel.

5.e Rejected by the whole nation

King Rehoboam was rejected by the whole nation (2 Chronicles 10:16)—all twelve tribes. In fact, he was no longer the king of the *House of Israel*. When Rehoboam took over Judah and Benjamin by force, a new name for the kingdom came into being: *the House of Judah*. The old name was rightly claimed by the ten tribes that remained and chose Jeroboam as king. That is why Ohola, a woman who represents the capital of the ten-tribe kingdom of

Israel—Samaria—is also called the *elder* of the two sisters in Ezekiel 23:4. She (Israel) had the oldest rights.

In spite of the fact that King Rehoboam was rejected by the whole nation, so also by Benjamin and Judah (2 Chronicles 10:16), Rehoboam retained power over these two southern tribes. This was made possible by his strong professional army, that was directly under the command of the king and had no bond with the local population. It was King David who had started building a professional army (2 Samuel 15:18). This army was known under the name Kerethites and Pelethites or Krethi and Plethi. Their first commander was Benaiah (2 Samuel 8:18). King Solomon greatly expanded this army (1 Kings 10:26). It is plausible that in peacetime the army of Israel largely consisted of professional soldiers. These were mainly foreign mercenaries (Krethi = residents of Crete; Plethi = Philistines).

It is very likely that the professional army of King Rehoboam remained loyal to him after the outbreak of the rebellion against his reign. After all, he paid them. The king and his generals decided first and foremost to bring the southern part of the kingdom, including the capital city of Jerusalem, under their control. Rehoboam and his generals had to give up the north, however temporarily. Full control of the country was militarily not feasible at that moment. So Rehoboam became king over the two southern tribes against the will of the tribal chiefs, including those of Judah and Benjamin. Those too had rejected him!

After King Rehoboam returned to Jerusalem, he mobilized all the fighting men of Judah and Benjamin (2 Chronicles 11:1). He decided to march with both the professional army and the conscripts against the remaining ten tribes in order to restore his kingship over all of Israel. It is plausible that he was strong enough to do so, but it was forbidden by God through the prophet Shemaiah (2 Chronicles 11:2–4). Subsequently the situation stabilized, and thus two independent kingdoms emerged.

5.f After the exile
It is not until centuries later, after Israel was carried away by the Assyrians and disappeared, and Judah was taken into the Babylonian captivity, that the name *Israel* is used again of all twelve tribes. This is evident from the books of Ezra and Nehemiah. However, the meaning is then no longer as before. Once again Israel became the name of all twelve tribes, however temporarily.

We must realize that the returned exiles about whom Ezra and Nehemiah write were in fact the nucleus of an *expected massive return of all Jews and Israelites to Canaan*. From that, the kingdom of King David and King Solomon should have risen again. This expectation is reflected in the (scarce) use of the name Israel for all the ten tribes (Ezra 6:16; 7:7; Nehemiah 11:20).

5.g The kingdom of God postponed
The promise about the return concerned all Israel. That is why the division between the two-tribe kingdom and the ten-tribe kingdom and the separate use of the names Judah and Israel does not play a role in the postexilic period. From Zechariah 1:3–6, for example, we learn that this great recovery did not take place. Not only because of the unbelief of the returned exiles, but also because only a small part of the exiles returned. So the majority of the Jews rejected the call of God to go back to Canaan. Consequently, the salvation promises for that moment lapsed and the "restored Israel of the twelve tribes" did not come into being. So the prophesied kingdom of God failed to come about.

Sources:
(Cooper, xxiii; Fisch, 9; Greenberg, vol. 1, 63; Weerd, *Ezechiël*, vol. 1, 70, 406; Weerd, *Micha*, 78–80; Weerd, *Zacharia*, 14–15, 30–32)
(See Annotation 2A.)

Excursus 6: The House of Israel

With *the house of* the Bible usually indicates a family, line, or tribe, depending on the context. When it speaks about *the house of David*, it is clear that it refers to his line. And with *the house of Jacob* (Genesis 46:27) his entire family is meant. If the expression is connected with the name of a country or a particular form of government, then the term *house* has the meaning of a nation of that name or of a kingdom. This also applies to the name *house of Israel*.

6.a The name *Israel* in the prophetic books
The expression *house of Israel* is found in many places in the Bible. There is no doubt that, until the time of the division of Israel, after the death of King Solomon, all twelve tribes are meant. There is disagreement among exegetes about the meaning of this term *after* that event. We therefore have consulted a number of prophets who performed before, during, and after the prophet Hosea.

6.b The prophet Isaiah
We find the expression *house of Israel* in Isaiah 5:7; 8:14; 14:2; 46:3 and 63:7.

Isaiah 5:7	The context shows that this verse is indisputably about the ten-tribe kingdom. The other texts from Isaiah differ from these as follows:
Isaiah 8:14	This is about the future salvation of all Israel. The text therefore is a further elucidation, speaking of *both houses of Israel* to distinguish it from the normal meaning.
Isaiah 14:2	This verse also speaks of all of Israel, but in relation to the past, when both kingdoms were one, and the distant future, when both kingdoms will be one again. The text explicitly states that it also concerns the house of Jacob (all tribes).
Isaiah 46:3	The text speaks of a remnant from all of Israel. That is typical end-time language. Moreover, the text excludes any doubt, because it also mentions that it concerns the house of Jacob (all tribes).
Isaiah 63:7	The term here speaks about the glorious past of Israel when the twelve tribes still formed one people.

6.c The prophet Hosea
We find *house of Israel* in Hosea 1:4; 1:6; 5:1; and 6:10.

In these instances, Hosea speaks of the ten tribes of Israel. But in 1:10–11 and 12:2, the prophet speaks of the distant future and from a much larger perspective; namely the Messianic Kingdom. And then it's always about the entire nation of Israel, as is also clear from the text.

6.d The prophet Amos
We find *house of Israel* in Amos 5:1, 3–4, 25; 6:1, 14; 7:10; and 9:9. The only exception is Amos 5:25. That concerns, however, the exodus from Egypt, and thus the past when all tribes were one.

6.e The prophet Micah
We find *house of Israel* in Micah 1:5; 3:1 and 9. All refer to the ten-tribe kingdom.

6.f The prophet Zechariah
We find *house of Israel* in Zechariah 8:13. Here also the ten-tribe kingdom is referred to.

6.g The prophet Ezekiel
It would go too far to enter into Ezekiel in detail here. However, there is no deviation from the meaning of the name Israel in the context as discussed above.

Conclusion
There is no reason to apply other standards when we study Hosea. We therefore consider the name Israel as representing the Northern Kingdom and Judah, the Southern Kingdom, unless explicitly stated (or apparent from the context) that there is a different meaning. Examples include when Hosea speaks about the past (when the twelve tribes still formed one people) and when the prophecy has the distant future in view (the Messianic Kingdom).
(Cooper, xxiii)

Verse 10
However, the number of the children of Israel will be like the sand of the sea, which cannot be measured, nor can it be counted. It will also happen that, in the place where it was said to them: You are not My people, the name will be given to them: children of the living God!
What is there to explain here? This prophecy stands like a house and cannot be misunderstood. Here is the echo of the old covenant promise to Abraham (Genesis 22:17 NASB):

> *"Indeed I will greatly bless you, and I will greatly multiply your seed as the stars of the heavens and as the sand which is on the seashore; and your seed shall possess the gate of their enemies."*

The clear link between Hosea 1:10 and Genesis 22:17 shows that this prophecy is not limited to the ten tribes but speaks of all of Israel.

Hosea 1:10 is also the fulfillment of an old prophecy that the Almighty gave through His servant Moses to Israel—Deuteronomy 30:1–5 (NASB)

1   *"So it shall be when all of these things have come upon you, the blessing and the curse which I have set before you, and you call them to mind in all nations where the L*ORD *your God has banished you,*
2   *"and you return to the L*ORD *your God and obey Him with all your heart and soul according to all that I command you today, you and your sons,*
3   *"then the L*ORD *your God will restore you from captivity, and have compassion on you, and will gather you again from all the peoples where the L*ORD *your God has scattered you.*
4   *"If your outcasts are at the ends of the earth, from there the L*ORD *your God will gather you, and from there He will bring you back.*
5   *"The L*ORD *your God will bring you into the land which your fathers possessed, and you shall possess it; and He will prosper you and multiply you more than your fathers."*

This prophecy will be wonderfully fulfilled in the last days (the end time).
(Feinberg, *Millennialism*, 120–21; Ironside, chapter 3; Reed, 33; Rosenberg, vol. 1, 8–9; Stuart, 38–39; Walvoord and Zuck, 1381–82)

The Promise Extended
There is no doubt that all the promises described apply to the people of Israel. However, Romans 11:24 teaches us that the church of Christ is grafted upon the noble olive tree (= Israel) and thus may share in part in the blessings for the people of Israel. The apostle Paul explains this further in Romans 9:24–26 (NASB) and quotes the prophet Hosea:

24 *even us, whom He also called, not from among Jews only, but also from among Gentiles.*
25 *As He says also in Hosea,* "I WILL CALL THOSE WHO WERE NOT MY PEOPLE, 'MY PEOPLE,' AND HER WHO WAS NOT BELOVED, 'BELOVED.'"
26 "AND IT SHALL BE THAT IN THE PLACE WHERE IT WAS SAID TO THEM, 'YOU ARE NOT MY PEOPLE,' THERE THEY SHALL BE CALLED SONS OF THE LIVING GOD."

In Paul's words the prophecy is thus extended to converted gentiles—the church of Christ. (See Annotation 6C.)

Verse 11
Then the children of Judah and the children of Israel will be reunited and they will appoint one head over them. Then they will hurry up from the country, because great will be the day of Jezreel [God sows].
The *children of Judah* (the two tribes) will again join the *children of Israel*. That must be because they had seceded (see Excursus 3). Together they will become God's people again in the messianic sense. That is still unfulfilled prophecy.

The prophet Ezekiel confirms this prophecy again in 37:19–22. God speaks so clearly there that we quote the verses in their entirety*:

19 *"Say to them, 'Thus says the sovereign Yahweh: "Behold! I will take the wooden panel of Joseph—which is in the hand of Ephraim—and the tribes of Israel, his companions. Then I will add it to the other—the wooden panel of Judah—and I will make them into one wooden panel. That is how they will become one in My hand."'*
20 *"Then hold the wooden panels on which you wrote with your hand before their eyes.*
21 *"Then say to them, 'Thus speaks the sovereign Yahweh: "Look at Me, who takes the sons of Israel from among the nations—wherever they went—and I will gather them from everywhere and bring them back to their own land.*
22 *"And I will make them one people on the mountains of Israel. Then it will happen that a single king will be king over each of them. Never will it happen that they will once again be two nations, and never again will they be divided into two kingdoms. Never again."'"*

(*Weerd, Hebrew text translation in *Ezechiël*, vol. 2, 357–60)

11.1 Never again—Ezekiel 37:22
This is very clearly spoken. These verses form the core on which the rabbis base the future kingdom of God. All this prophecy will be fulfilled in the Messianic Kingdom, where Jesus Christ, the Messiah, will reign. Let us look forward to that! (Read: 2 Samuel 7:11b–16; Isaiah 9:6–7; Amos 9:11 and Micah 5:2.)
(Andersen and Freedman, 202–03; Boice, *Minor Prophets*, vol. 1, 19; Feinberg, *Minor Prophets*, 20; Rosenberg, vol. 1, 8; Stuart, 40; Wood, 173)

Verse 11b
and they will appoint one head over them
One head, that is Jesus Christ. He will be King of Israel in the end time. The promised Messiah (*David, My servant*, Ezekiel 37:25) will become sole shepherd over them. Thus the two divine offices, king and high priest, as they existed in Israel in the past, are united in one person—Jesus Christ. The prophet Zechariah talks about this in 6:13*:

For He will take possession of His throne and reign on it. He will also be a priest on His throne and harmony will exist between those two ministries.

(Rosenberg, vol. 2, 200; *Weerd, Hebrew text translation in *Zacharia*, 146)

Verse 11d
because great will be the day of Jezreel *[God sows]*
The day of Jezreel is the day of God's wrath in the Bible. That is the day when God deals with His enemies. We often find that theme in the prophets. We quote some texts:

Ezekiel 38:21–23 (NASB)
21 *"I will call for a sword against him [Gog] on all My mountains," declares the Lord GOD. "Every man's sword will be against his brother.*
22 *"With pestilence and with blood I will enter into judgment with him; and I will rain on him and on his troops, and on the many peoples who are with him, a torrential rain, with hailstones, fire and brimstone.*
23 *"I will magnify Myself, sanctify Myself, and make Myself known in the sight of many nations; and they will know that I am the LORD."*

Micah 1:4 (NASB)
The mountains will melt under Him and the valleys will be split, like wax before the fire, like water poured down a steep place.
The coming of the almighty God in His great anger turns out to lead to enormous destruction on earth. The scope of the text is clear. The prophet Micah paints a terrible judgment, an inferno of unprecedented dimensions.

Isaiah 2:19 (NASB)
Men will go into caves of the rocks and into holes of the ground before the terror of the LORD and the splendor of His majesty, when He arises to make the earth tremble.

Isaiah 5:25 (NASB)
On this account the anger of the LORD has burned against His people, and He has stretched out His hand against them and struck them down. And the mountains quaked, and their corpses lay like refuse in the middle of the streets. For all this His anger is not spent, but His hand is still stretched out.

Isaiah 30:27 (NASB)
Behold, the name of the LORD comes from a remote place; Burning is His anger and dense is His smoke; His lips are filled with indignation and His tongue is like a consuming fire;

Isaiah 30:30 (NASB)
And the LORD will cause His voice of authority to be heard, and the descending of His arm to be seen in fierce anger, and in the flame of a consuming fire in cloudburst, downpour and hailstones.

Joel 3:16 (NASB)
The LORD roars from Zion and utters His voice from Jerusalem, and the heavens and the earth tremble. But the LORD is a refuge for His people and a stronghold to the sons of Israel.

Zephaniah 3:8 (NASB)
"My decision is to gather nations, to assemble kingdoms, to pour out on them My indignation, all My burning anger; for all the earth will be devoured by the fire of My zeal."

Zechariah 12:3–4 and 9*
3 *"In that day it will occur that Jerusalem will be an unshakable rock for all nations. And every nation that will take hold on it to wound it shall itself be mortally wounded, in that day, when all the nations of the earth are gathered against her.*

4 *"In that day," says the* LORD, *"I will beat every horse with panic and their riders with madness.*

9 *"And it shall come to pass in that day that I will seek to destroy every people that goes up to Jerusalem."*

(*Weerd, Hebrew text translation in *Zacharia*, 248, 336–37)

Verse 12
Proclaim to your brothers: Be My people *[Ammi]*, and to your sisters: Be merciful *[Ruchama]*.
The prophecy of Hosea 1 closes with an assignment. The salvation of which the prophet Hosea speaks is not something without obligations. It must be proclaimed among the people of Israel that they may repent so that salvation may advance.

Only the assignment for the proclamation is binding. The second part of verse 12 is not in the imperative but has the tone of a loving invitation, as we also find in Hosea 2:13. The great Jewish theologian Rashi paraphrases here, but gives the essence of the message:

Return to My Torah and I will grant forgiveness to your people.

(Rosenberg, vol. 1, 9)

Excursus 7: The Lost Ten Tribes of Israel

The term *lost ten tribes of Israel* does not come from the Bible, which speaks of Israel or Ephraim (after the largest tribe of the ten). There were originally ten tribes plus part of the tribe of Levi. The latter provided the priests and Levites, who lived throughout the northern and southern kingdoms. However, in 2 Chronicles 11:13–15 we read that the priests and Levites left Israel and settled in Judah. So we can just speak of ten tribes.

7.a Where are they? Wild speculations
The fate of the lost ten tribes of Israel has been in the spotlight for many decades and is sometimes the subject of the wildest speculations. Until about 1950 the general opinion was that in the war against the Assyrians, which turned into total defeat with the capture of Samaria in 722 BC, a large part of the people of Israel was massacred. The remaining population was sent into exile by the Assyrians and spread over their enormous empire. The exiles mixed with the local population and disappeared as a recognizable people.

7.b The ethnic distinction of Israel and Judah
Some theologians no longer see any difference between Judah and Israel. They are of the opinion that the current Jewish people are not only descendants of Judah and Benjamin, but also of the other ten tribes. That could be true if we go by human measure. Out of each of the ten tribes, limited numbers have joined the Jews over the centuries. Ezekiel 37:16–17 provides a clarifying statement. From that text it appears that God therefore *no longer* counts these people among Israel but as being part of Judah. They are therefore called *companions* of Judah!

It is also assumed that the distinctions between the twelve tribes have already largely disappeared through intermarriage. And that also seems to be a valid argument. Again, however, we must recognize that as only according to human measure. The Almighty appears to think differently. The prophet Ezekiel is very clear about that.

7.c Prophecy of a return of Israel
The prophecies of, among others, the prophet Ezekiel speak unmistakably about the return

of the ten tribes of Israel in the end times. We cite a number of texts that have been translated directly from the original text.

Ezekiel 34:12b, 13a*
12b *I will save them from every place to which they were scattered; on the day of clouds and thick darkness [= the judgments of the end times].*
13a *And I will bring them forth out of the nations.*

This text speaks about the end time. Since the Jews have been going back to the land of Canaan for decades and the end time has certainly not yet arrived, they cannot be referred to here. The only other possibility is that the text speaks about the ten tribes of Israel. That people is hidden from us, therefore they must be *brought forth*.

Ezekiel 34:16*
I will trace the lost, and I will bring back the scattered.

The Jewish people (Judah and Benjamin) have never been lost. They are still recognizable and familiar today (as was so poignantly clear in the Holocaust). They do not have to be traced, but the people of Israel do.

Ezekiel 36:24*
For I will bring you forth out of the nations, and I will gather you out of all countries and I will bring you back to your own country.

Here too we speak of a people who have merged into the gentile peoples and therefore must first be made "visible."

Ezekiel 37:12*
Therefore, prophesy! Then you will say to them, Thus says the sovereign Yahweh: Behold! I will open your graves, and I will raise you up from your graves, O My people, and I will bring you back to the land of Israel.

A dead people revives. Again, a clear reference to the ten tribes of Israel which have disappeared.

Ezekiel 37:16*
As for you, son of man: Take wooden panels before you and write on the one: For Judah and for the children of Israel who are their companions. Then take another wooden panel and write on it: For Joseph—that is the wooden panel of Ephraim—and all the house of Israel who are his companions.

Ezekiel 37:16 makes a very important statement. It speaks of *Judah* and all of *the children of Israel who are their companions*. Those are the descendants of the other ten tribes. Insofar as they have joined Judah (= the Jews), they are counted among Judah!

The Ten Tribes are called here distinctively *Joseph* and *Ephraim*. Among them are also counted all people from the *whole house of Israel* (including Judah and Benjamin) who belong with them. With that, the absolute distinction between Israel and Judah has been restored.

Ezekiel 37:19*
Then say to them: Thus speaks the sovereign Yahweh: Behold! I will turn the wood panel of Joseph—that is in the hand of Ephraim—and the tribes of Israel, his companions. Then I will add it to the other—the wooden panel of Judah—and I will make them into one wooden panel. That is how they will become one in My hand.

In the time of the end the two nations, Judah and Israel, become one again. That is still unfulfilled prophecy.

Ezekiel 37:21*
Then say to them, Thus says the sovereign Yahweh: Behold Me, who picks up the sons of Israel from among the nations—wherever they went—and I will gather them from everywhere and bring them back to their own land.

Here again the image of a people that has disappeared and that is being tracked by God Himself.

(*Weerd, Hebrew text translation in *Ezechiël*, vol. 2, 277–279, 328, 354, 356, 358–359)

7.d Notable facts coming to light
Since the return of the Jews (Judah, Benjamin, and Levi) the interest in the fate of the other ten tribes has grown considerably. The fact that because of that return a number of prophecies are fulfilled, has convinced Bible-believing researchers that the prophecies about Israel (the former ten-tribe kingdom) should also be taken seriously, since the Bible also speaks about their return. This growing interest has stimulated research and thus all kinds of facts have come to light that are remarkable at the very least.

7.e The ten tribes of Israel slowly becoming visible
Various population groups are mentioned as descendants of Israel or rather, believe themselves to be. Many of these claims are complete nonsense, but not all of them. It is now certain that a number of those population groups are indeed descended from Israel.

Unfortunately, Jews and/or Israelites are not among the most popular population groups in the world, and anti-Semitism is a continually growing evil today. Yet a miraculous phenomenon is being revealed as an increasing number of families, tribes and/or peoples claim that they belong to the lost ten tribes of Israel.

This is not the place to deal exhaustively with all those claims. Besides, I cannot say with any certainty to what extent these claims are well founded. It is a fact, however, that a number of claims are taken seriously and investigated by Jewish authorities. Some of these claims have already been confirmed. This is an important fact in the context of Hosea's prophecy. We cannot ignore that. Therefore, a short description of a number of possible "candidates" is listed below.

7.e1 Lemba Jews
The Lemba live in South Africa and speak Bantu. They claim to be descendants from Israel without mentioning a particular tribe. Genetic research has confirmed this.

7.e2 Bene Ephraim (= children of Ephraim)
These are also called Telugu Jews since they speak Telugu. They live in Andhra Prades, in India, at the delta of the Krishna River. They are so convinced of their origins that they learned Hebrew and converted to Judaism. Since 1981 they have been studied by groups of rabbis, who take their claims increasingly seriously.

7.e3 Bene Manashe (= children of Manasseh)
This is a group of unknown size (some speak of 1 to 2 million), living on the northeast border of Manipur (in India) and in Northern Burma. In Burma they are called the *Lusi*, which means *the ten tribes*. In their songs and prayers we often find the name Manasseh. They are convinced that they belong to the tribe of Manasseh.

A part of the Bene Manashe has converted to Judaism and honors Joseph as their ancestor.

They do not have a written history. However, their tradition speaks of a trip over a red colored sea (Red Sea?) and a cloud column that led them on their wanderings. A high cleric in Israel, Rabbi Eliyahu Avichail, investigated their claims and has been an important supporter ever since.

The Bene Manashe have filed an application with the government of Israel to "return" to the land of Canaan. About one thousand members have already settled in Israel.

7.e4 Beta Israel (= house of Israel)

The dark-colored Falashas (= *foreigners*) are of Ethiopian origin. The total group has about 120,000 members. Although some of them were Christian in name, they have almost all gone over to the Jewish faith. They are already recognized as Jews.

About 90,000 Falashas now live in Israel. Their exact origin is not certain, but there are indications that they are of the tribe of Dan.

7.e5 Igbo Jews

In Nigeria we find another group who claim to be Israelites. They consist of about forty thousand members. They speak Hebrew in addition to their national language. The Igbo tribe claims to have fled fifteen hundred years ago from Arabia. The group consists of several distinct families, who claim to have descended from the tribes of Gad, Zebulun, and Manasseh. They have been adhering for many centuries to religious traditions that correspond to the Jewish ones.

7.e6 The Pashtun

This is a large group with 40–50 million members. They live in Afghanistan, Pakistan and northern Iran. Some of them probably have Israeli ancestors. The old Afghan royal family (the Mahmad Zei family) even claims to descend from Mephiboseth, the son of Jonathan, the son of King Saul (there known as Melek Talut). They probably belong to the tribe of Benjamin (2 Samuel 9).

It is worth noting that several Islamic scholars in past centuries have supported the Pashtun in their claim. They speak in this context about the Bani Yzrael (a corruption of Bene Yisrael = children of Israel) and about Yusef Zai or Yusuf Si (= sons of Joseph). In the Islamic Encyclopedia of Turkey, the following is written: *The Durrani and Galzay tribes have their roots in the Hebrew people.* And: *It is claimed that many others of Afghan origin also originate from the Hebrews.*

Among the Pashtun there are several tribes who have lived in ethnic isolation for an extended period of time and still do so in part. There is a strong resistance among them to marrying outside their own clan or tribe.

A number of tribal names show a strong correspondence with the ten tribes of Israel, such as: Efidi or Ephriti (Ephraim), Rabbani or Rebbani (Ruben), Shinwari (Simeon), Lewani or Levoni (Levi), Daftani (Naphtali), the Gaji or Ghagi (Gad), and Ashurai (Asher). Many Pashtun wear an amulet, with the Hebrew words: *Shema Yisrael* (= Hear Israel), which are standard opening words of pious Jews in their morning and evening prayers. The whole beginning is: *"Hear Israel, the* LORD, *your God is one"* (Deuteronomy 6:4).

Among the Pashtun tribes many Jewish names are found, some more or less corrupted. Unfortunately, there is little written historical material to prove their claim. But there are, however, scrolls with genealogies covering many centuries. These sometimes even go back to their forefathers in Israel.

The Pashtun maintain a large number of Jewish customs and apply circumcision, as prescribed by the Mosaic law, on the eighth day (Muslims do not do this at a fixed age, but it is customary to do so before the thirteenth year of life). The Pashtun do not work or cook on the Sabbath. And in many of their homes we find the star of David.

7.e7 China
In Isaiah 49:12 we find the following, intriguing text, concerning the return of Israel:

> *"Behold, these will come from afar; And lo, these will come from the north and from the west, and these from the land of Sinim."*

This last word, *Sinim*, probably means China. And there also we find strong indications that there are descendants of the people of Israel living there.

7.e8 Chiang-Min Jews
They live in China, on the border with Tibet, and honor a number of religious customs that clearly have Jewish traits. This also applies to the priestly robes they use for their service. They know only one God (which is very unusual in those regions) whom they address as Jawei (= Yahweh).

7.e9 Kaifeng Jews
In the Henan province of China, we find the Kaifeng Jews. Nowadays there is only a small group left, but until the eighteenth century it was a thriving community. In their religion and customs, they have kept the faith of their fathers, and their religion has been known as *The religion that removes the tendon*. In Kaifeng we find a street where for centuries many Kaifeng Jews lived. It is called *The way of the people who teach the Scriptures*.

The written history of the Kaifeng Jews dates back to 1163, when they built a synagogue (the Libai-Si), but it is certain that they had been living in Henan before that. According to tradition, they came in 200 BC from North India to China and are descended from the Jews who were exiled under Ezra (Ezra 9). A small number has been accepted to date as true Jews and have emigrated to Israel.

Sources:
(Avihail and Brin (1978), *Lost Tribes from Assyria*; Berelson, *Tiferet Yisrael Reish Perek Chelek*; Feinberg, *Minor Prophets*, 28; Garlake, *Great Zimbabwe*; Gonen, *To the End of the Earth*; Kaplan, *Beta Israel*; Mikonkie, *The Ten Lost Tribes;* Nova Series, *The Lost Tribes of Israel*; Parfitt, *The Search for a Lost Tribe of Israel*; Shtull, *The Myth of the Lost Tribes*; Weiz, *The Kaifeng Stone Inscriptions*; Wikipedia, Ten Lost Tribes.)

Annotation 1F: The Messianic Kingdom

In Hosea 1:10–11 the prophet speaks about the time of the end. This is a well-known theme and is dominated by the great tribulation and the establishment of a future kingdom of God—the Messianic Kingdom. The Holy Scripture speaks in many places about that future. We give a few.

Zephaniah 3:19–20 (NASB)
19 *"Behold, I am going to deal at that time with all your oppressors. I will save the lame and gather the outcast. And I will turn their shame into praise and renown in all the earth.*
20 *"At that time I will bring you in. Even at the time when I gather you together. Indeed, I will give you renown and praise among all the peoples of the earth, when I restore your fortunes before your eyes,"* says the Lord.

Jeremiah 31:31–33 (NASB)
31 *"Behold, days are coming," declares the* LORD, *"when I will make a new covenant with the house of Israel and with the house of Judah,*
32 *"not like the covenant which I made with their fathers in the day I took them by the hand to bring them out of the land of Egypt, My covenant which they broke, although I was a husband to them," declares the* LORD.
33 *"But this is the covenant which I will make with the house of Israel after those days," declares the* LORD, *"I will put My law within them and on their heart I will write it; and I will be their God, and they shall be My people."*

Jeremiah 33:17–18 (NASB)
17 *"For thus says the* LORD, *'David shall never lack a man to sit on the throne of the house of Israel;*
18 *'and the Levitical priests shall never lack a man before Me to offer burnt offerings, to burn grain offerings and to prepare sacrifices continually.'"*

Isaiah 9:7 (NASB)
There will be no end to the increase of His government or of peace, on the throne of David and over his kingdom, to establish it and to uphold it with justice and righteousness, from then on and forevermore. The zeal of the LORD *of hosts will accomplish this.*

Amos 9:11, 15 (NIV)
"I will restore David's fallen shelter—I will repair its broken walls and restore its ruins—and will rebuild it as it used to be, . . . I will plant Israel in their own land, never again to be uprooted from the land I have given them," says the LORD *your God.*

Annotation 1G: The End of the Sinaitic Covenant

1G.1 The Ten Commandments
The Almighty gave two stone tablets to Moses on Mount Sinai, with ten commandments engraved on them (Exodus 20). These were the basis for a large number of additional commandments that served as a kind of household regulation for the people of Israel. Those laws were aimed at a set-apart society, a holy nation under God's direction. In it the individual was subordinate to the whole. Both believers and unbelievers shared in the blessings that depended in part on the behavior of Israel as a whole. However, even the punishments imposed on the people usually affected both the sinners who caused them and those who had served God properly.

1G.2 The Abrahamic covenant
In the early days—the time of the judges—the nation of Israel consisted of a loose federation of tribes under the kingship of God. They all had the same constitution: the Torah. The country was united under King Saul and King David. After the death of King Solomon the once mighty nation disintegrated. Two new kingdoms arose: Israel and Judah. Despite all its different manifestations, Israel remained primarily a theocracy, of which God was the High King. Each earthly king of Israel more or less functioned as a kind of steward in the name of God.

In the age of the divine nation or theocracy, the prophets were in the service of the people of Israel as a whole. They primarily addressed their message to leaders and/or kings. The prophets formed, together with the high priest, the executive arm of God. They were focused on the preservation of the nation or, when divided, on guiding it back to unity under the kingship of God. Their task was sealed in the Sinaitic Covenant.

1G.3 A new goal: The Messianic Kingdom

By pronouncing *Lo-Ammi* (*not My people*, Hosea 1:9), the Sinaitic Covenant was broken. The original task of the prophets, preserving the nation, was no longer needed. Therefore, God gave the prophets a new goal: Guiding the people of God to a blessed future, what will be realized in the Messianic Kingdom. This future was founded in an earlier covenant, between God and Abraham. It was an everlasting covenant—called Berit Olam—that could not be broken.

1G.4 Back to the Abrahamic covenant

God's people thus fell back on the promise of the Abrahamic covenant. That covenant still stood and promised the following (Genesis 17:7–8 NASB):

7 *"I will establish My covenant between Me and you and your descendants after you throughout their generations for an everlasting covenant, to be God to you and to your descendants after you.*
8 *"I will give to you and to your descendants after you, the land of your sojournings, all the land of Canaan, for an everlasting possession; and I will be their God."*

The goal of the Abrahamic covenant is, that *all the land of Canaan* would be an everlasting *possession* for God's people, Israel, with Him as the highest ruler (*I will be their God*). Well, that was tried for centuries under the Sinaitic Covenant, but failed. But surely the Abrahamic covenant still stands as an unwavering promise for the future.

HOSEA 2
Hebrew Text Translation

Introduction
This is the most beautiful chapter of the book of Hosea and perhaps the most beautiful story of the Old Testament. It is an emotional prophecy in which allegory and reality, but also prose and poetry, merge seamlessly together. The whole forms a beautiful harmonious poem, which is a song of praise to the greatness of Almighty God. Hosea 2 can be seen as a kind of "verbal bridal bouquet." Only in a Bible book such as Solomon's Song of Songs is this highest form of love—the love of God for mankind—sung at a comparable level.

A. Beautiful Poetry
Translating the Bible is not an easy job, and it is even more challenging when poetry is involved. I have done my best to convey this beautiful language, not only to please the reader, but especially in order to offer the maximum view of God's great love.

B. Text Numbering
In commonly used translations two different ways of numbering the verses are used. This is quite confusing. We will use the traditional numbering, initially, but introduce the alternative numbering with the Hebrew text, and continue with this corrected numbering for the balance of the discussion for each verse.

(What is traditionally considered verse 1 of chapter 2 is discussed at the end of chapter 1.)

Verse 2 NASB
"Contend with your mother, contend, for she is not my wife, and I am not her husband; and let her put away her harlotry from her face and her adultery from between her breasts."

Verse 2 KJV
Plead with your mother, plead: for she is not my wife, neither am I her husband: let her therefore put away her whoredoms out of her sight, and her adulteries from between her breasts;

Verse 2 NIV
"Rebuke your mother, rebuke her, for she is not my wife, and I am not her husband. Let her remove the adulterous look from her face and the unfaithfulness from between her breasts."

Verse 2 Hebrew Interlinear Text (= verse 1)
rebuke! to-mother-of-you rebuke! for she not wife-of-me and-I not husband-of-her and-let-her-remove adulteries-of-her from-faces-of-her and-unfaithfulnesses-of-her from-between breasts-of-her

Verse 1a
rebuke! to-mother-of-you rebuke!
The word *rîbū* (from: *rib*) never reflects an appeal to repent, as some suggest. Usually it means *to dispute, to argue, to complain, or to quarrel* (Genesis 26:20; Exodus 21:18;

Judges 21:22; Job 23:6). It often has legal undertones, which is also the case here. So we find *rîḇû* here to read *bring charges*.

The repetition of the word *rîḇū* (*rebuke* or *charge*) indicates great urgency. We prefer to vary and translate the second *rîḇū* as *sue* and add *now*.
(Andersen and Freedman, 214, 219; Born, 27; Garrett, 75; Strong's OT, word 7378; Wolff, 30; Würthwein, 4)

We read: ***press charges against your mother, sue her now!***

Verse 1b
for she not wife-of-me and-I not husband-of-her
Here also we find the word *lo* (*not* my wife, *not* my husband) or my wife/husband no longer. It always stands in contrast to a prior positive status.
(Andersen and Freedman, 221)

We read: ***for she is no longer my wife, and I am no longer her husband.***

Verse 1c
and-let-her-remove adulteries-of-her from-faces-of-her
The word *zenunim* is rare in the Bible. It refers to a kind of whorish behavior. Here we find *zənūnehā* (noun, plural) what suggests showy clothing or makeup.

The Sinaitic Covenant, between God and His people, is compared with marriage in several places in the Bible. If the people of Israel had a relationship with other gods, it was therefore seen as adultery. In this case there is adulterous behavior, as in Ezekiel 23:11 and Nahum 3:4.

The addition of *faces-of-her* indicates that there are signs on the face (e.g., mascara), which make Gomer look like a prostitute. Some speak of *slutty finery*, which is an excellent representation of the Hebrew text.
(Mays, 34; Strong's OT, word 2183; *Studiebijbel* SBOT 12, 32)

We read: ***let her remove that slutty finery from her face***

Verse 1d
and-unfaithfulnesses-of-her from-between breasts-of-her
The word translated here with *unfaithfulnesses* does not occur elsewhere in the Bible. It is derived from the word *naaph* which means *to whore* or *committing adultery*.

Most biblical scholars by far assume that there were flashy marks, amulets, jewelry, and/or tattoos, which belonged to the finery of a professional prostitute of that time. That is a logical conclusion, which also serves the context seamlessly.
(Born, 27; Strong's OT, word 5003 and 5005; Ward, 24)

We read: ***and the signs of her adultery from between her breasts***

The entire text—verse 1:
Press charges against your mother, sue her now! For she is no longer my wife, and I am no longer her husband. Let her remove that slutty finery from her face and the signs of her adultery from between her breasts,

---

Verse 3 NASB
"Or I will strip her naked and expose her as on the day when she was born. I will also make her like a wilderness, make her like desert land and slay her with thirst."

Verse 3 KJV
Lest I strip her naked, and set her as in the day that she was born, and make her as a wilderness, and set her like a dry land, and slay her with thirst.

Verse 3 NIV
"Otherwise I will strip her naked and make her as bare as on the day she was born; I will make her like a desert, turn her into a parched land, and slay her with thirst."

Verse 3 Hebrew Interlinear Text 3 (= verse 2)
otherwise I-will-strip-her naked and-I-will-make-bare-her as-day-of to-be-born-her and-I-will-make-her like-the-desert and-I-will-turn-her into-land-of parched-one and-I-will-slay-her with-the-thirst
In this verse we repeatedly find the Hebrew word *vav* (*and*). There is no need to translate this every time it is used. In English it is more scarcely used.

Verse 2a
otherwise
The word *pen* means *lest*.
(Andersen and Freedman, 225; Brown, 14; McComiskey, 31; Strong's OT, word 6435)

Verse 2b
I-will-strip-her naked
The basic meaning of *pashat* is *to spread out*, but also *to divest of*. It is sometimes translated with *to undress* or *to put off* or *to take off*. It says therefore, *I will undress her*.
(Cheyne, 8; Mays, 34; Strong's OT, word 6584)

We read, 2ab: *lest I undress her naked*

Verse 2c
and-I-will-make-bare-her as-day-of to-be-born-her
The first words of verse 2c have been freely translated by the NIVIHEOT. Literally the Hebrew reads: *and-I-will-have her become* or *I will make her*. The NASB interprets that as, *expose her*, which we will follow.
(Andersen and Freedman, 25; Born, 26; Brown, 14; Strong's OT, word 3322; Stuart, 42)

We read: *(and) I will expose her as on the day she was born*

Verse 2d
and-I-will-make-her like-the-desert
Midbar means *open field* or *wilderness*, which is how many translate it. It refers to a dry steppe that often forms a transition into a desert. That is why it can also be translated *desert*, but that would not be correct. There is no clear reason in this case to deviate from the basic meaning.
(Andersen and Freedman, 225; Strong's OT, word 4057)
(Compare the following translations: BBE, NET, NASB, NRSV, and KJV.)

We read: *I will make her a wilderness*

Verse 2e
and-I-will-turn-her into-land-of parched-one
Here the *vav* (*and*) introduces a further explanation of 2d. We read: *yes*. The word *tsiyah* means *dry* or *parched land*. It can be a desert if the context shows so. In some translations, the meaning of *midbar* and *tsiyah* is at times mixed up. To make things even more difficult, there is a third word that is translated as *desert*. In Jeremiah 50:12 all three are found

together in one verse. We find there: *midbar*, then *tsiyah*, and then *arabah*. Only the last word really means desert.
(Andersen and Freedman, 225: Strong's, word 4057)
(Compare the following translations: BBE, NET, NASB, NRSV, KJV, and NKJV.)

We read: *yes, I will turn her into a parched land*

Verse 2f
and-I-will-slay-her with-the-thirst
The word *and* (vav) leads to the consequence of God's punishments. We read *thus*.

Instead of *killing* (as the vast majority of exegetes translate this), we choose a synonym: *die*.

We read: *I will make her die of thirst*

The entire text—verse 2:
lest I will undress her naked. I will expose her as on the day she was born. I will make her a wilderness; yes, I will turn her into a parched land. I will make her die of thirst.

Verse 4 NASB
"*Also, I will have no compassion on her children, because they are children of harlotry.*"

Verse 4 KJV
And I will not have mercy upon her children; for they be the children of whoredoms.

Verse 4 NIV
"*I will not show my love to her children, because they are the children of adultery.*"

Verse 4 Hebrew Interlinear Text 4 (= verse 3)
and children-of-hers not I-will-show-love because children-of adultery they
Here we find the word *racham*, which means *compassion*, *mercy*, or *grace*, but rarely *love* and when so, it is debated. This is why we deviate from the NIVIHEOT. (See notes on the translation of Hosea 1:6c.)
(Reed, 31; Strong's OT, word 7355)

We read—verse 3:
Furthermore, I will not show her children compassion, for they are children from adultery,

---

Verse 5 NASB
"*For their mother has played the harlot; she who conceived them has acted shamefully. For she said, 'I will go after my lovers, who give me my bread and my water, my wool and my flax, my oil and my drink.'*"

Verse 5 KJV
For their mother hath played the harlot: she that conceived them hath done shamefully: for she said, I will go after my lovers, that give me my bread and my water, my wool and my flax, mine oil and my drink.

Verse 5 NIV
"*Their mother has been unfaithful and has conceived them in disgrace. She said, 'I will*

go after my lovers, who give me my food and my water, my wool and my linen, my oil and my drink.'"

Verse 5 Hebrew Interlinear Text 5 (= verse 4)
indeed she-was-unfaithful mother-of-them she-made-disgraceful conceiving-of-them indeed she-said I-will-go after ones-loving-me ones-giving-of food-of-me and-waters-of-me wool-of-me and-linen-of-me oil-of-me and-drinks-of-me

Verse 4a
indeed she-was-unfaithful mother-of-them she-made-disgraceful
The Hebrew word *ki* usually introduces a causal relationship. The word is very common and has a broad meaning. The correct translation is therefore strongly influenced by the context. The NIVIHEOT reads here *indeed*. That is interpretation and deviates from the vast majority of Bible scholars. We usually find *because, because of, while, though*, and *since* as the usual translations. In this case we prefer *since*.
(Wood, 176; Strong's OT, word 3588)

We read: *since their mother was unfaithful and acted shamefully*

Verse 4b
conceiving-of-them
Sometimes the word *harah* means to be pregnant, but in most cases it means *to become pregnant*.* It describes the moment of conception; the time when God gives life. (See also: *Genesis 4:1, 17; 1 Samuel 1:20; Isaiah 8:3.)
(Strong's OT, word 2029)

We read: *when she conceived them*

Verse 4c
indeed she-said I-will-go after ones-loving-me
The basic meaning of *aheb* is *affection* or *love*. Here we find *məʾahăḇay* It means: *those loving me* or *those who have affection for me*. This can be a deep friendship, love between man and woman, as well as a purely physical affection. The latter plays a main role in the books of both Jeremiah and Ezekiel. That is why we assume that this word also carries that meaning in Hosea. (Incidentally, this is supported by the context, because the text clearly speaks of a prostitute who chases men.)
(Mays, 39; Strong's OT, word 157; Wolff, 34–35)

We read: *for she said: I will go after anyone who wants to make love with me*

The entire text—verse 4:
since their mother was unfaithful and acted shamefully when she conceived them. For she said: I will go after anyone who wants to make love with me, anyone who will give me my food and my water, my wool and my linen, my oil and my drink.
Verse 4a fits much better with verse 3. By adding it to verse 3 the sentence reads much more smoothly. This has been reflected in the final text.

Verse 6 NASB
"Therefore, behold, I will hedge up her way with thorns, and I will build a wall against her so that she cannot find her paths."

Verse 6 KJV
Therefore, behold, I will hedge up thy way with thorns, and make a wall, that she shall not find her paths.

Verse 6 NIV
"Therefore I will block her path with thornbushes; I will wall her in so that she cannot find her way."

Verse 6 Hebrew Interlinear Text 6 (= verse 5)
therefore see I! blocking . . . path-of-her with-the-thornbushes and-I-will-wall-in . . . wall-of-her so-ways-of-her not she-can-find

Verse 5a
therefore see I!
Many translate here with *therefore, see*. That is a rather weak rendering of the Hebrew. Van de Born is more precise and reads *therefore, pay attention*, but he omits *I* (God). Wolff now adds the word to emphasize the text. We stay a bit closer to the Hebrew text.
(Born, 28; Wolff, 30)

We read: ***therefore: see me!***

Verse 5b
blocking . . . path-of-her with-the-thornbushes
I am not very happy with this translation of the NIVIHEOT, because it certainly falls short. The basic meaning of *suk* is *to close in*, *to hedge*, or *to entangle*. The word occurs only twice in the Bible outside of Hosea 2:6. In Job 1:10 it means *to shelter* or *to surround* and in Job 10:11 *to interweave*. The text thus means that the path (= the future) of Gomer (= Israel) will be interwoven with thornbushes, thus with torments or difficulties. We would say: *a path strewn with thorns and thistles*.
(Andersen and Freedman, 236; Mays, 34; Strong's OT, word 7753)

We read: ***who will strew her path with thornbushes***

Verse 5c
and-I-will-wall-in . . . wall-of-her
The word *gadar* means: *to wall in*. It can also mean *wall* (Ecclesiastes 10:8), *fence* (Psalm 62:3) or *hedge* (Psalm 80:12).

The person addressed—Gomer (who represents the people of Israel)—walks on a path (that is the way to the future). We should therefore think of a high thorn hedge, on both sides of a winding road, which obstructs the view.
(Andersen and Freedman, 236–37; Boice, *Minor Prophets*, 24; King, 123; Strong's OT, words 1443, 1447)
(See also: Introduction to Hosea 1.)

We read: ***thus I will hedge her in with a (thorn) hedge***

The entire text—verse 5:
Therefore: see me! Who will strew her path with thornbushes. Thus I will hedge her in with a thorn hedge, so that she can no longer find her way.

Verse 7 NASB
"She will pursue her lovers, but she will not overtake them; and she will seek them, but will not find them. Then she will say, 'I will go back to my first husband, for it was better for me then than now!'"

Verse 7 KJV
And she shall follow after her lovers, but she shall not overtake them; and she shall seek

them, but shall not find them: then shall she say, I will go and return to my first husband; for then was it better with me than now.

Verse 7 NIV
"She will chase after her lovers, but not catch them; she will look for them but not find them. Then she will say, 'I will go back to my husband as at first, for then I was better off than now.'"

Verse 7 Hebrew Interlinear Text (= verse 6)
and-she-will-chase . . . ones-loving-her but-not she-will-catch them indeed-she-will-look-for-them but-not she-will-find then-she-will-say I-will-go and-I-will-go-back to husband-of-me the-first for good for-me then more-than-now

Verse 6a
and-she-will-chase . . . ones-loving-her but-not she-will-catch them
Others speak of: *hunt making*.
(Andersen and Freedman, 238; McComiskey, 35)

We read: *she will chase after her lovers, but not catch them*

Verse 6b
indeed-she-will-look-for-them but-not she-will-find
The first word *indeed* is an interpretation. We find *vav* here, which has a broad meaning. The vast majority of Bible scholars therefore read: *then* or *and*. Others omit the word, because the context does not require it. We follow suit.
(Born, 28)

We read: *she will look for them but not find them*

The entire text—verse 6:
She will chase after her lovers, but not catch them. She will look for them but not find them. Then she will say: I will leave and return to my first husband, for then I was better off than now.

Verse 8 NASB
"For she does not know that it was I who gave her the grain, the new wine and the oil, and lavished on her silver and gold, which they used for Baal."

Verse 8 KJV
For she did not know that I gave her corn, and wine, and oil, and multiplied her silver and gold, which they prepared for Baal.

Verse 8 NIV
"She has not acknowledged that I was the one who gave her the grain, the new wine and oil, who lavished on her the silver and gold—which they used for Baal."

Verse 8 Hebrew Interlinear Text 8 (= verse 7)
and-she not she-acknowledged that I I-gave to-her the-grain and-the-new-wine and-the-oil and-silver I I-lavished on-her and-gold they-used for-the-Baal

Verse 7b
that I I-gave to-her the-grain and-the-new-wine and-the-oil and-silver
Few translators and interpreters include the double *I* in their translation. This is really too bad,

because it is a typical sentence construction with which the great acts of God are emphasized. Born reads: *That it was me*. That is satisfactory, but why not stay even closer to the text? (Born, 29)

We read: ***that I, yes, I gave her the grain and the new wine, and also the oil and silver***

Verse 7c
I I-lavished on-her and-gold they-used for-the-Baal
It is quite striking that the text now switches to the plural. That is of course no coincidence. On the contrary, it is even characteristic of the book of Hosea. The prophet no longer speaks of Gomer, but directly addresses the people of Israel.
(Andersen and Freedman, 243; Cheyne, 50; Mays, 35)

We read: ***yes, I overloaded her with gold, which was used for the Baal.***

The entire text—verse 7:
She did not realize that I, yes, I gave her the grain and the new wine, and also the oil and silver. Yes, I overloaded her with gold, which was used for the Baal.

Verse 9 NASB
"Therefore, I will take back My grain at harvest time and My new wine in its season. I will also take away My wool and My flax given to cover her nakedness."

Verse 9 KJV
Therefore will I return, and take away my corn in the time thereof, and my wine in the season thereof, and will recover my wool and my flax given to cover her nakedness.

Verse 9 NIV
"Therefore I will take away my grain when it ripens and my new wine when it is ready. I will take back my wool and my linen, intended to cover her naked body."

Verse 9 Hebrew Interlinear Text 9 (= verse 8)
therefore I-will-turn and-I-will-take-away grain-of-me when-time-of-him and-new-wine-of-me when-readiness-of-him and-I-will-take-back wool-of-me and-linen-of-me to-cover . . . nakedness-of-her

Verse 8a
therefore I-will-turn
The phrase *I-will-turn* is left out by many exegetes and translators. This is unfortunate and certainly unjustified. Even McComiskey (otherwise a scrupulous scholar) joins in. He only mentions that the text actually says something else but that he cannot fit this into his own exegesis. To solve the problem he ignores the Hebrew text. Others combine *'āšûḇ* (*I-will-turn*) and *lāqaḥtî* (*I-will-take-away*) into one expression and translate it like this: *to take back** or *I will take back again*.† But the text does not say that. We must dig deeper.

The textual problem is clear. Because of the use of *lāqaḥtî* (*I-will-take-away*), to 'translate *'āšûḇ* as *I will turn* creates a kind of repetition or tautology, what is in conflict with the accurate way Hosea writes.

Originally the basic meaning of the root (*shub*) was to move in an opposite direction.‡ Later biblical texts are also known to use it in the sense of *to turn around* or *to turn*, without any explicit direction‡ and sometimes meaning *to repent* or *to refute*.** The theological use of *shub* in the sense of *turn around to God* is debated! It does not automatically imply a return to the point of departure‡; a translation like that needs a strong support of the context and in verse 9a that is not the case; the context suggests even the opposite. In the basic meaning *shub* means *turning away* (that could be *return* or sometimes *subside*, as in Genesis 27:44–45).

Andersen and Freedman therefore read: *I will reverse myself* and also describes it as a *change of attitude*. This expresses exactly what is meant by verse 9. We must therefore translate with *to turn away* or *turning away* (Numbers 25:4; Joshua 22:16; Jeremiah 32:40). We add *from her* for a proper understanding.
(Andersen and Freedman, 244; ‡Botterweck, Ringgren, and Fabry, vol. 14, 464; *Guenther, 63; †Harper, 230; **Koehler and Baumgartner, vol. 2, 1427; McComiskey, 36; Strong's OT, word 7725)

We read: ***Therefore I will turn away [from her]***

Verse 8b
and-I-will-take-away grain-of-me when-time-of-him and-new-wine-of-me
The word *laqach* means *to take*, often with an undertone of *snatching away*,* or *suddenly deliver* somebody or a people (Ezekiel 13:21, 23; 34:10).
(Brown, Driver, and Briggs, word 3947.2b; *Reed, 38; Strong's OT, word 3947)

We read: *and I will take away my grain when it is ripe and the new wine when it is ready*

The entire text—verse 8:
Therefore I will turn away [from her] and I will take away my grain when it is ripe and the new wine when it is ready. I will also take back my wool and my linen, which should cover her nakedness.

Verse 10 NASB
"And then I will uncover her lewdness in the sight of her lovers, and no one will rescue her out of My hand."

Verse 10 KJV
And now will I discover her lewdness in the sight of her lovers, and none shall deliver her out of mine hand.

Verse 10 NIV
"So now I will expose her lewdness before the eyes of her lovers; no one will take her out of my hands."

Verse 10 Hebrew Interlinear Text 10 (= verse 9)
so-now I-will-expose . . . lewdness-of-her before-eyes-of ones-loving-her and-anyone not he-will-take-her from-hand-of-me

Verse 9a
so-now I-will-expose
Galah means *to uncover* or *remove*. A translation with *expose* is a little further away from the Hebrew text. We prefer: *reveal*.
(Strong's OT, word 1540; *Studiebijbel* SBOT 12, 36)

We read: *so now I will reveal*

Verse 9b
. . . lewdness-of-her before-eyes-of ones-loving-her

Nabluth (translated here as *lewdness*) does not appear elsewhere in the Bible. Unfortunately, we are not sure of the meaning, which is why it is translated in various ways. Wolff reads here: *her genitalia*. Others speak—somewhat obliquely—of *shame* or *lasciviousness*.

The word *nabluth* is derived from *nabal*, which means *stupid, foolish*, or *arrogant*. It is logical to expect a related meaning here. There is not much evidence in the Bible to suggest a translation that denotes a particular sexual behavior or indicates the genitalia as many do. It is therefore much more obvious to think of the basic meaning—*foolishness*—as a translation.
(Andersen and Freedman, 248; Brown, 18; Gerleman, 147–58; Harper, 231; Strong's OT, words 5036, 5040; Stuart, 43; Wolff, 31)

We read: ***her foolishness before the eyes of her lovers***

Verse 9c
and-anyone not he-will-take-her from-hand-of-me
The word *natsal* means *to tear away* or *to snatch away*, both in good and bad senses. This can be *to take* but is more often translated as *to redeem* or *to save* (Genesis 32:11; 1 Samuel 4:8; Psalm 33:19). There is no compelling reason to deviate from this here, so we do not follow the NIVIHEOT translation.
(Brown, 18; Harper, 231; Strong's OT, word 5337; Wolff, 31)

We read: ***and nobody will save her from My hand***

The entire text—verse 9:
So now I will reveal her foolishness before the eyes of her lovers and nobody will save her from My hand.

Verse 11 NASB
"I will also put an end to all her gaiety, her feasts, her new moons, her sabbaths and all her festal assemblies."

Verse 11 KJV
I will also cause all her mirth to cease, her feast days, her new moons, and her sabbaths, and all her solemn feasts.

Verse 11 NIV
"I will stop all her celebrations: her yearly festivals, her New Moons, her Sabbath days—all her appointed feasts."

Verse 11 Hebrew Interlinear Text 11 (= verse 10)
and-I-will-stop all-of celebration-of-her yearly-festival-of-her New-Moon-of-her and-Sabbath-day-of-her even-all-of appointed-feast-of-her
The word *moed* means *meeting* or *assembly* (Exodus 27:21; Leviticus 1:1; Joshua 19:51; Isaiah 14:13). In Israel, these were usually also festive gatherings. However, that is no reason to translate with *feast*, as many (including the NIVIHEOT) do. It is certain that these meetings were commanded by God, so we read *[holy] meetings*.
(Born, 29; Harper, 233; Mays, 35; Strong's OT, word 4150)

We read verse 10:
Then I will stop all festivities: her annual feasts, her New Moon days and the Sabbath day, even all her [holy] meetings.

Verse 12 NASB
"I will destroy her vines and fig trees, of which she said, 'These are my wages, which my lovers have given me.' And I will make them a forest, and the beasts of the field will devour them."

Verse 12 KJV
And I will destroy her vines and her fig trees, whereof she hath said, These are my rewards that my lovers have given me: and I will make them a forest, and the beasts of the field shall eat them.

Verse 12 NIV
"I will ruin her vines and her fig trees, which she said were her pay from her lovers; I will make them a thicket and wild animals will devour them."

Verse 12 Hebrew Interlinear Text 12 (= verse 11)
and-I-will-ruin vine-of-her and-fig-tree-of-her which she-said pay they to-me that they-gave to-me ones-loving-me and-I-will-make-them into-thicket and-she-will-devour-them animal-of the-wild

Verse 11a
and-I-will-ruin vine-of-her and-fig-tree-of-her
Others read: *will lay waste, destroy,* or *ravage, exterminate.** Many interpret *vine* and *fig-tree* to represent more than one vine and fig tree.†
(*†Garrett, 84; *†Harper, 231; *Mays, 35; †Wolff, 31)

We read: *I will also destroy her vines, and her fig trees*

Verse 11b
which she-said pay they to-me that they-gave to-me ones-loving-me
The word *ethnah* (translated here as *pay*) does not occur anywhere else in the Bible. It means a kind of *gift*. It is derived from *tanah*, which means *bargain*. It has an undertone of being cheap and usually refers to forms of fornication. Some translate it with *pay for prostitution*, which reflects the correct meaning or (even better) *gratuity*.
(Born, 30; Mays, 35; Strong's OT, words 866, 8566)

We read: *of which she said, These are my gratuities given by my lovers*

Verse 11c
and-I-will-make-them into-thicket
Ya῾ar means: *a wild forest* or *thicket*. This means that the vine and the fig tree will become wild like *brushwood* or *undergrowth*. Some translate with *wood* or *forest*, but that is not the meaning here.
(Cheyne, 52; Strong's OT, word 3293)

We read: *I will turn them into undergrowth*

Verse 11d
and-she-will-devour-them animal-of the-wild
With *devour* the NIVIHEOT gives an acceptable translation here, but it does not fit the context. *Akal* can also mean eating or digesting (Kings 1:10; Nehemiah 2:13). The text speaks about shrubbery or undergrowth. When it comes to meat, *devouring* is the right translation. Here *eat it up* fits better.
(Born, 30; Strong's OT, word 398)

We read: *and the wild animals will eat them up*

The entire text—verse 11
I will also destroy her vines, as well as her fig trees; of which she said, These are my gratuities given by my lovers. I will make them into undergrowth and the wild animals will eat them up.

Verse 13 NASB
"I will punish her for the days of the Baals, when she used to offer sacrifices to them and adorn herself with her earrings and jewelry, and follow her lovers, so that she forgot Me," declares the Lord."

Verse 13 KJV
And I will visit upon her the days of Baalim, wherein she burned incense to them, and she decked herself with her earrings and her jewels, and she went after her lovers, and forgat me, saith the Lord.

Verse 13 NIV
"I will punish her for the days she burned incense to the Baals; she decked herself with rings and jewelry, and went after her lovers, but me she forgot," declares the Lord.

Verse 13 Hebrew Interlinear Text 13 (= verse 12)
and*-I-will-punish to-her . . . days-of the-Baals when she-burned-incense to-them and-she-decked-herself ring-of-her and-jewelry-of-her and-she-went after ones-loving-her but-me she-forgot declaration-of Yahweh
*The *vav* (*and*) has a broad meaning. Here it introduces an event after. We translate: *then*.

Watta ͨad means *and she adorned herself* or *she decked herself out*.
(Strong's OT, word 5710; *Studiebijbel* SBOT 12, 40)

We read verse 12:
Then I will punish her for the days when she burned incense before the Baals. Then she adorned herself with her ring and jewelry and went after her lovers. But Me she forgot, declares Yahweh.

Verse 14 NASB
"Therefore, behold, I will allure her, bring her into the wilderness and speak kindly to her."

Verse 14 KJV
Therefore, behold, I will allure her, and bring her into the wilderness, and speak comfortably unto her.

Verse 14 NIV
"Therefore I am now going to allure her; I will lead her into the wilderness and speak tenderly to her."

Verse 14 Hebrew Interlinear Text 14 (= verse 13)
therefore see! I alluring-her and-I-will-lead-her the-desert and-I-will-speak to heart-of-her

We read verse 13:
Therefore, see! I will lure her and lead her into the desert. Then I will speak to her heart.

Verse 15 NASB
"Then I will give her her vineyards from there, and the valley of Achor as a door of hope. And she will sing there as in the days of her youth, as in the day when she came up from the land of Egypt."

Verse 15 KJV
And I will give her her vineyards from thence, and the valley of Achor for a door of hope: and she shall sing there, as in the days of her youth, and as in the day when she came up out of the land of Egypt.

Verse 15 NIV
"There I will give her back her vineyards, and will make the Valley of Achor a door of hope. There she will repond as in the days of her youth, as in the day she came up out of Egypt."

Hebrew Interlinear Text 15 (= verse 14)
and-I-will-give-back to-her ... vineyards-of-her at-there and Valley-of Achor into-door-of hope and-she-will-respond at-there as-days-of youths-of-her and-as-day-of to-come-up-her from-land-of Egypt

Verse 14b
at-there and Valley-of Achor into-door-of hope
Achor means *misfortune* (Joshua 6:18; Judges 11:35; 1 Kings 18:17) or *turmoil*. If we translate the entire expression, it is *valley of misfortune* or *turmoil*.
(Mays, 45; McComiskey, 42; Strong's OT, words 5911, 5916)

We read: ***and make the Valley of Achor [turmoil] a door of hope***

Verse 14c
and-she-will-respond at-there as-days-of youths-of-her
The word *anah* means *to answer* or *to react*, often by way of a testimony. Yet the translations of many Bible scholars deviate from the Hebrew text.

Verse 14c speaks about the exodus of the people of Israel from Egypt. Many exegetes then also refer to the song of Moses (Exodus 15:1–18). From there one concludes that *anah* (*respond*) must be translated *singing*. However, this is not what the Hebrew text says. And despite the fact that this text is very popular with Bible-believing Christians and we therefore might prefer to leave the traditional translation intact, it would be incorrect. This is not about the singing of the people of Israel, but about the restoration of mutual love between God and His people.

The text speaks of answering the never-ending love that God has for Israel! That is the underlying meaning of the word *anah*. That may be a singing testimony, as in the days of Moses, but that is not what the text is about. The theme of verse 14 is that the people of Israel, as a whole, will someday answer God's love. We put the words *My love* in brackets, because they are not in the original text.
(McComiskey, 41; Strong's OT, word 6030; Wolff, 31)

The entire text—verse 14:
I will return her vineyards there and make the Valley of Achor [turmoil] a door of hope. And there she will answer [My love] as in the days of her youth, as on the day when she went out of the land of Egypt.

Verse 16 NASB
*"It will come about in that day," declares the L*ORD*, "that you will call Me Ishi and will no longer call Me Baali."*

Verse 16 KJV
*And it shall be at that day, saith the L*ORD*, that thou shalt call me Ishi; and shalt call me no more Baali.*

Verse 16 NIV
*"In that day," declares the L*ORD*, "you will call me 'my husband'; you will no longer call me 'my master.'"*

Hebrew Interlinear Text 16 (= verse 15)
and-he-will-be in-the-day the-that declaration-of Yahweh you-will-call husband-of-me and-not you-will-call to-me longer master-of-me

Verse 15a
and-he-will-be in-the-day the-that declaration-of Yahweh
Wəhāyî can mean *and-he-will-be*, but also *and it shall come to pass.** This expression is usually rendered *in that day*. This is, however, a rather weak reflection of what is written in the Hebrew text. Literally it says: *on the day, on this (or that) one*, or *on that day, the special one*. This often indicates an important moment in the history of salvation. Rabbinical writings adhere better to the Hebrew text and speak rightly of *the appointed time*, which is what we also read here.†
(†Sherman, *Daniel*, § VI; *Strong's OT, word 1961; *Studiebijbel SBOT 12, 40; †Weerd, *Daniël*, vol. 2, 7, 177)

We read: *and it shall come to pass, that at the appointed time, declares Yahweh*

Verse 15c
and-not you-will-call to-me longer master-of-me
Many exegetes and translators read *Baal*, which is the name of an idol. That is a choice that springs from their exegesis. It has certainly not that meaning here. We read *bali* (לְעַבִי) here, a word that does not appear anywhere else in the Bible. It is derived from *ba'al*, which has a varied meaning. It can mean *master* or *owner* (Exodus 21:28; 22:15), but also *man* or *men of* (Judges 9:2; 1 Samuel 23:11) and *husband* (Exodus 21:22), *bridegroom* (Joel 1:8). In this latter sense, however, it also involves *master*, in the biblical context of the man who is put over the woman.

Apart from the preceding, the word *ba'al* can also represent a proper name, namely the Baal; an idol (Judges 2:13; Jeremiah 19:5; Zephaniah 1:4). There was a whole collection of Baals: Baal Berith (lord of the covenant, the city god of Shechem), Baal Peor (the lord of Peor, a mountain top in Moab), Baal-Sephon (the lord of Sephon, a mountain north of Ugarit), and Baal-Zebub (lord of flies, the oracle god of Ekron).

The Hebrew word *bali* literally means *my master*, with the underlying meaning of *ruler*. That stands opposed to *husband-of-me*. So the prophet speaks of a changed relationship between God and His people. We will go further into this in the exegesis.
(Brown, 22; Dee and Schoneveld, vol. 1, 59; Garrett, 87, 91; Kidner, 33; Mays, 48; Strong's OT, words 1167, 1180; Wolff, 49)

The entire text—verse 15:
And it shall come to pass, that at the appointed time, declares Yahweh, you shall call Me my husband. No longer will you call Me my master.

Verse 17 NASB
"For I will remove the names of the Baals from her mouth, so that they will be mentioned by their names no more."

Verse 17 KJV
For I will take away the names of Baalim out of her mouth, and they shall no more be remembered by their name.

Verse 17 NIV
"I will remove the names of the Baals from her lips; no longer will their names be invoked."

Hebrew Interlinear Text 17 (= verse 16)
and-I-will-remove . . . names-of the-Baals from-mouth-of-her and-not they-will-be-invoked longer by-name-of-them
The word *zakar* usually means *to remember* (Genesis 9:15; Leviticus 26:42) or *to commemorate*. But also—although far less common—*to mention* or *to notice* (Genesis 40:14; Exodus 23:13). So there is very little basis for translating here (deviating from the Hebrew text) as *invoked*. We therefore do not follow the NIVIHEOT translation.
(Harper, 235; Strong's OT, word 2142; Wolff, 46)

We read verse 16:
Then I will remove the names of the Baals from her mouth, and you will no longer be reminded of their names.

Verse 18 NASB
"In that day I will also make a covenant for them; With the beasts of the field, the birds of the sky and the creeping things of the ground. And I will abolish the bow, the sword and war from the land, and will make them lie down in safety."

Verse 18 KJV
And in that day will I make a covenant for them with the beasts of the field, and with the fowls of heaven, and with the creeping things of the ground: and I will break the bow and the sword and the battle out of the earth, and will make them to lie down safely.

Verse 18 NIV
"In that day I will make a covenant for them with the beasts of the field, the birds in the sky and the creatures that move along the ground. Bow and sword and battle I will abolish from the land, so that all may lie down in safety."

Hebrew Interlinear Text 18 (= verse 17)
and-I-will-make for-them covenant in-the-day the-that with beast-of the-field and-with bird-of the-airs and-creature-of the-ground and-bow and-sword and-battle I-will-abolish from the-land so-I-may-make-lie-down-them in-safety

Verse 17b
and-creature-of the-ground
Remes (here translated *creature*) denotes reptiles and other creatures that crawl quickly over the ground. These can also be insects.
(McComiskey, 43; Strong's OT, word 7431; Wolff, 46)

We read: *and the creatures that crawl on the earth*

Verse 17c
and-bow and-sword and-battle I-will-abolish from the-land
The word *milchâmâh* is very common in the Bible and can mean *battle* or *war* or *combat* (Genesis 14:2; Judges 3:10). *War* is the logical choice here.
(Strong's OT, word 4421)

We read: *I will also abolish bow, sword, and war in the land*

The entire text—verse 17:
Then, on the appointed day, I will make a covenant for them with the wild beasts of the field, the birds of heaven, and the creatures that crawl on the earth. I will also abolish bow, sword, and war in the land; thus I will make them rest in safety.

Verse 19 NASB
"I will betroth you to Me forever; Yes, I will betroth you to Me in righteousness and in justice, in lovingkindness and in compassion."

Verse 19 KJV
And I will betroth thee unto me for ever; yea, I will betroth thee unto me in righteousness, and in judgment, and in lovingkindness, and in mercies.

Verse 19 NIV
"I will betroth you to me forever; I will betroth you in righteousness and justice, in love and compassion."

Hebrew Interlinear Text 19 (= verse 18)
and-I-will-betroth-you to-me to-forever and-I-will-betroth-you to-me in-righteousness and-in-justice and-in-love and-in-compassions

Verse 18a
and-I-will-betroth-you to-me to-forever
The word *aras* is fairly rare in the Bible and is often translated as *to engage* or *to betroth*. That is an event of limited time *before* the wedding takes place and is therefore separate from it. However that does not fit the context, because *betroth forever* is an impossible expression. The basic meaning of *aras* is *to take a wife*, or *to marry* as Deuteronomy 28:30 and 2 Samuel 3:14 clearly show and as is also the case here. We prefer *bride*, which is also a good translation and it represents the joy of this event better.
(Born, 33; Mays, 50; McComiskey, 44–45; Strong's OT, word 781)

We read: *then I will take you as My bride, forever*

Verse 18b
and-I-will-betroth-you to-me in-righteousness and-in-justice
The same expression as in verse 18a is now repeated. We therefore open with *yes*.

We read: *yes, I will take you as My bride in righteousness and justice*

Verse 18c
and-in-love and-in-compassions
The word *checed* (here translated with *love*) means *mercy* (Nehemiah 9:17) or *compassion*. And when it is addressed to God, it can mean *piety* or *faithfulness*. *Racham* is often translated in the same way (2 Samuel 24:14; Zechariah 1:16). Given the context, words like *cherishing* or *security* are better here.
(Born, 33; Cheyne, 56; Strong's OT, words 2617, 7356)

We read: *in mercy and security*

The entire text—verse 18:
Then I will take you as My bride, forever. Yes, I will take you as My bride in righteousness and justice, in mercy and security.

Verse 20 NASB
"And I will betroth you to Me in faithfulness. Then you will know the Lord."

Verse 20 KJV
I will even betroth thee unto me in faithfulness: and thou shalt know the Lord.

Verse 20 NIV
"I will betroth you in faithfulness, and you will acknowledge the Lord."

Hebrew Interlinear Text 20 (= verse 19)
and-I-will-betroth-you to-me in-faithfulness and-you-will-acknowledge . . . Yahweh

Verse 19a
and-I-will-betroth-you in-faithfulness
Again we translate: *I will take as My bride in-faithfulness* (see verse 18)

Verse 19b
and-you-will-acknowledge
The NIVIHEOT interprets here, for in the vast majority of cases yâda means to know. So we will go with that translation here also.
(Strong's OT, word 3045; Stuart, 55; Ward, 23)

We read: *and then you shall know Yahweh*

The entire text—verse 19:
I will take you as My bride in faithfulness, and then you shall know Yahweh.

Verse 21 NASB
"It will come about in that day that I will respond," declares the Lord. "I will respond to the heavens, and they will respond to the earth."

Verse 21 KJV
And it shall come to pass in that day, I will hear, saith the Lord, I will hear the heavens, and they shall hear the earth.

Verse 21 NIV
"In that day I will respond," declares the Lord—"I will respond to the skies, and they will respond to the earth."

Hebrew Interlinear Text 21 (= verse 20)
and-he-will-be in-the-day the-that I-will-respond declaration-of Yahweh I-will-respond to-the-skies and-they they-will-respond to-the-earth

We read verse 20:
And so it will be, at the appointed time, that I will give ear, thus proclaims Yahweh. I will listen to the heavens and they will listen to the earth.

Verse 22 NASB
"And the earth will respond to the grain, to the new wine and to the oil, and they will respond to Jezreel."

Verse 22 KJV
And the earth shall hear the corn, and the wine, and the oil; and they shall hear Jezreel.

Verse 22 NIV
"And the earth will respond to the grain, the new wine and the olive oil, and they will respond to Jezreel."

Hebrew Interlinear Text 22 (= verse 21)
and-the-earth she-will-respond to the-grain and-to the-new-wine and-to the-oil and-they they-will-respond to Jezreel

Verse 21a
and-the-earth she-will-respond
The word *she* is ignored by most exegetes and translators. But that directs the focus to *the earth, the grain, the new wine*, and *the oil*—so all of them!

The feminine form of *te͑ăneh*, however, points solely to *the earth*, because God will make the earth extremely fertile in the future Messianic Kingdom. Verse 22 confirms our interpretation.*
(Strong's OT, word 6030; *Wolff, 54)

We read: *and the earth, she will respond*

Verse 21b
to the-grain and-to the-new-wine and-to the-oil and-they
The NIVIHEOT has added *to*. We don't follow that.

The double use of *they* (see 21c) is ignored by most interpreters. It says something about the previous words.
(*Studiebijbel* SBOT 12, 44)

We read, first step: *the grain, the new wine, and the oil and/yes, they*

Verse 21c
they-will-respond to Jezreel
Here the NIVIHEOT renders *Jezreel* again as a name (as do many). Now the choice becomes whether it is necessary to translate the word or vocalize the Hebrew text on the basis of exegetical considerations. In this case I deviate from most exegetes and put the translation (*God's sowing*) first. Only then can this text be given logic.

With the meaning of the word Jezreel (*God's sowing*), a logical chain of events is completed. Thus the circle, which begins with the restoration of the relationship between God and His people, is completed with an abundant harvest at the right time.
(Strong's OT, word 3157)

We read: *they will respond to God's sowing (Jezreel)*

Step 2—We combine 21a, 21b, and 21c:
and the earth she will respond; yes, the grain, the new wine, and the oil, they will respond to God's sowing (Jezreel)

Step 3—The final text of verse 21:
And the earth will respond! Yes, the grain, the new wine, and the oil will respond to God's sowing [Jezreel]

Verse 23 NASB
"I will sow her for Myself in the land. I will also have compassion on her who had not obtained compassion, and I will say to those who were not My people, 'You are My people!' And they will say, 'You are my God!'"

Verse 22 KJV
And I will sow her unto me in the earth; and I will have mercy upon her that had not obtained mercy; and I will say to them which were not My people, Thou art My people; and they shall say, Thou art my God.

Verse 23 NIV
"I will plant her for myself in the land; I will show My love to the one I called 'Not My loved one.' I will say to those called 'Not My people,' 'You are My people'; and they will say, 'You are my God.'"

Hebrew Interlinear Text 23 (= verse 22)
and-I-will-plant-her for-myself in-the-land and-will-show-love to not she-is-loved and-I-will-say to-not people-of-me people-of-me you and-he he-will-say God-of-me
This is a disputed text. Very few precisely try to follow the Hebrew text. The key is in the determination that the accent lies on *in the land/earth.**

The word *zara* (NIVIHEOT: *plant*) usually means *to sow (seed)*, sometimes *to plant (seedlings)* when the context shows so. *Sowing* is the right choice here.

Literally it says: *and I will sow her for Me* (or: *because of Me*) *in the land/earth.* The KJV comes close to the literal meaning.
(Mays, 46; Strong's OT, word 2232; Stuart, 55; *Wolff, 54)

We read verse 22:
I will sow the earth for My own sake. I will show mercy to Lo-Ruchama [not loved] and I will say to Lo-Ammi [not My people]: My people [Ammi]. And they will say: my God.

Hosea 2:1–23—The corrected text:

Verse 1   *Press charges against your mother, sue her now! For she is no longer my wife, and I am no longer her husband. Let her remove that slutty finery from her face and the signs of her adultery from between her breasts,*

Verse 2   *lest I will undress her naked. I will expose her as on the day she was born. I will make her a wilderness; yes, I will turn her into a parched land. I will make her die of thirst.*

Verse 3   *Furthermore, I will not show her children compassion, for they are children from adultery,*

Verse 4   *since their mother was unfaithful and acted shamefully when she conceived them. For she said: I will go after anyone who wants to make love with me, anyone who will give me my food and my water, my wool and my linen, my oil and my drink.*

Verse 5   *Therefore: see me! Who will strew her path with thornbushes. Thus I will hedge her in with a thorn hedge, so that she can no longer find her way.*

Verse 6	*She will chase after her lovers, but not catch them. She will look for them but not find them. Then she will say: I will leave and return to my first husband, for then I was better off than now.*
Verse 7	*She did not realize that I, yes, I gave her the grain and the new wine, and also the oil and silver. Yes, I overloaded her with gold, which was used for the Baal.*
Verse 8	*Therefore I will turn away [from her] and I will take away my grain when it is ripe and the new wine when it is ready. I will also take back my wool and my linen, which should cover her nakedness.*
Verse 9	*So now I will reveal her foolishness before the eyes of her lovers and nobody will save her from My hand.*
Verse 10	*Then I will stop all festivities: her annual feasts, her New Moon days and the Sabbath day, even all her [holy] meetings.*
Verse 11	*I will also destroy her vines, as well as her fig trees; of which she said, These are my gratuities given by my lovers. I will make them into undergrowth and the wild animals will eat them up.*
Verse 12	*Then I will punish her for the days when she burned incense before the Baals. Then she adorned herself with her ring and jewelry and went after her lovers. But Me she forgot, declares Yahweh.*
Verse 13	*Therefore, see! I will lure her and lead her into the desert. Then I will speak to her heart.*
Verse 14	*I will return her vineyards there and make the Valley of Achor [turmoil] a door of hope. And there she will answer [my love] as in the days of her youth, as on the day when she went out of the land of Egypt.*
Verse 15	*And it shall come to pass, that at the appointed time, declares Yahweh, you shall call Me my husband. No longer will you call Me my master.*
Verse 16	*Then I will remove the names of the Baals from her mouth, and you will no longer be reminded of their names.*
Verse 17	*Then, on the appointed day, I will make a covenant for them with the wild beasts of the field, the birds of heaven, and the creatures that crawl on the earth. I will also abolish bow, sword, and war in the land; thus I will make them rest in safety.*
Verse 18	*Then I will take you as My bride, forever. Yes, I will take you as My bride in righteousness and justice, in mercy and security.*
Verse 19	*I will take you as My bride in faithfulness, and then you shall know Yahweh.*
Verse 20	*And so it will be, at the appointed time, that I will give ear, thus proclaims Yahweh. I will listen to the heavens and they will listen to the earth.*
Verse 21	*And the earth will respond! Yes, the grain, the new wine, and the oil will respond to God's sowing [Jezreel].*
Verse 22	*I will sow the earth for My own sake. I will show mercy to Lo-Ruchama [not loved] and I will say to Lo-Ammi [not My people]: My people [Ammi]. And they will say: my God.*

HOSEA 2
Exegesis

Introduction
Hosea 2 is among the most important prophecies in the Bible, but it is also one of the most controversial. Not surprisingly it has raised a lot of comment from theologians. This primarily concerns the reliability of the various Hebrew texts, but also its interpretation. Most of these textual criticisms concern later additions or changes which mutilated the original words of Hosea. Some scholars invest a lot of work into determining the timeline of the end time prophecies and establishing a basis for their interpretations. Others see Hosea mainly as poetry. They give up the details of the literal meaning in favor of a "reconstruction" of the "original poem." It would not be difficult to discuss all these various comments in depth, but that makes little sense, no matter how many pages we fill, though many do just that. However there is no compelling reason to deviate from the literal text, trying to find hidden meanings, or to question it. For this prophecy is clear and lucid, and Hosea's listeners have, without a doubt, understood him very well. This also means that the Hebrew text leaves the exegete and/or translator little room for speculation. Nevertheless, there is still a large difference of opinion on how this chapter is to be understood.

A. Scripture Proves Itself
This book is not written to go head-to-head with exegetes who reject the reliability of the text. We believe that there are more than enough arguments to take the Hebrew text seriously. Furthermore, there is a very simple guideline for verifying this statement. If the exegesis, which after all closely follows the Hebrew text, shows that there is logic, system, and coherence in the book of Hosea, then it is virtually impossible for the text to be unreliable. If, moreover, other books of the Bible clearly support the message of Hosea, then the hand of the Almighty becomes visible. For only He is able to make the prophets speak with unanimity throughout the ages and through each individual writer.

B. Eschatology
The book of Hosea speaks in part eschatologically (prophecies concerning the end time). Within reformational circles and in the Roman Catholic church, quite a few exegetes do not know how to handle these prophecies. They note that the literal explanation of the book of Hosea conflicts with the traditional dogmas to which the church adheres. Only a few put the authority of the Bible above that of ecclesiastical dogma in this situation. So since the book cannot be ignored, the only other option they see is to flee into allegory. Then one will be forced to replace the literal meaning with vague images and analogies, whereby the prophetic message can be adapted to one's own theology.

I pray that you will not do this but will accept the text in its literal sense. You do not have to follow me in this in all aspects. My explanation is only commentary and therefore does not have the authority of the Bible. Yet I hope that with this exegesis I will contribute to the greatness of God's name.

C. A Personal Note
Hosea 2 is a chapter in which strong emotions resonate. They do not leave an individual who loves God untouched, including me. There were times when I could not read the computer screen the text was on, because tears blurred the view. The words of the prophecy

spoke to my heart (Hosea 2:13). I was moved as I received a glimpse of the great things that are still to come.

D. Love Is a Gift from God

The best quality that a human being can show is love. We are made in God's image, the Holy Scriptures say. Genesis 1:26 gives unequivocal testimony. But it is not easy to believe that. The practice of life usually shows a completely different picture of man. Yet, if the Holy Scriptures say this, it is so. And in pure selfless love (however scarce) we see an unspoiled glimpse of God's image in our fellow humankind.

(Boice, *Minor Prophets*, 23; Bromiley, Hosea, 6)

Verse 1

Press charges against your mother, sue her now! For she is no longer my wife, and I am no longer her husband. Let her remove that slutty finery from her face and the signs of her adultery from between her breasts,

The prophecy of judgment of Hosea 1 was interrupted in verse 9 by a promise of future blessings. In Hosea 2 the judgment is continued.

Verse 1b

Press charges against your mother, sue her now!

The Hebrew text has a legal undertone. Gomer, the wife of Hosea (who is a type of the people of Israel) stands accused, not before an earthly court but before a heavenly court. The verdict is harsh: *For she is no longer my wife, and I am no longer her husband.* That was a traditional divorce formula in the ancient Middle East.

(Limburg, 10; Ward, 24)

1b.1 The prosecutors

This verse raises an important question: Who are the prosecutors? Well, that must be the children of *your mother*—that is Gomer, who typifies the people of Israel. So the prosecutors are Jezreel, Lo-Ruchama, and Lo-Ammi, because only they have a mother-child relationship with Gomer (*against your mother*). And these three again represent the individual members of the people of Israel. They characterize the deplorable condition of the people in the meaning of their names. For Israel is *sown* (Jezreel) all over the world, receives *no compassion* (Lo-Ruchama), neither from God nor from other nations, and is *no longer God's people* (Lo-Ammi).

The individual members of the people of Israel (the Ten Tribes) are therefore instructed to denounce Gomer. They must distance themselves from the behavior of the people as a whole. That starts on an individual base, so the restoration of the bond with God must come from below. In principle, the entire people of Israel must turn to God. Nationally. God's people must get rid of everything that separates them from God, from all of their *adultery*!

That will not work, you may say. Indeed, that does not work! Yet only a converted Israel will be allowed to enter the promised land. Therefore, a separation will have to take place between the believing part of Israel and the unbelieving part—on an individual basis. The prophet Ezekiel speaks about this in 20:35–38*:

35 *Then will I lead you into the wilderness of the nations, and I will judge over you there, face-to-face.*
36 *As I judged your fathers in the wilderness of the land of Egypt, so will I judge over you; speaks the sovereign Yahweh.*

37 *Then I will cause you to pass under My rod and bring you into the bond of My covenant.*
38 *And I will cleanse you from those who revolted against me and rebelled. I will lead them out of the land where they lived. Yet none of these will enter the land of Israel. Then you will know that I am Yahweh.*

It is a painful operation to *judge* and to *pass under My rod*. The prophet Zechariah talks about this in 13:8–9.[†]

8 *And it shall come to pass, says the Lord, that two parts of her inhabitants shall be put down in all the land, and they shall die. But one third will be left in her.*
9 *Then will I bring the third [part] into the fire, and I will melt them as silver is melted and purified, as gold is refined. They will call on My name. I? . . . I will answer them and say, My people. They? . . . They will say, The Lord, my God.*

Those who reject God will not survive this judgment. As stated above, *two thirds of her inhabitants* will be crushed and *they shall die*, says the prophet Zechariah. Only the chosen ones will enter the Messianic Kingdom.

([*]Andersen and Freedman, 219; Feinberg, *Minor Prophets*, 15; Pusey, 28; Stuart, 47; Walvoord and Zuck, 1295; Weerd, Hebrew text translation in *Ezechiël*, vol. 1, 532–34; [†]Weerd, Hebrew text translation in *Zacharia*, 389–90; Wood, 175)

1b.2 The divorce of Hosea and Gomer

With verse 1 the divorce between Hosea and Gomer is filed by the heavenly court. Gomer is the defendant, because she has left Hosea and retreated once again completely to her "profession" as a prostitute. She makes no effort to say good-bye to that life.

Well, you might say, maybe she could not do otherwise and was obliged to serve in the pagan temple. That could indeed be the case; however, nothing indicates that she wanted to break with her sinful life. Moreover, her life runs parallel to that of the relationship between Israel and God. In that case, there was constant sinning "with abandon," so that is likely to have been the case here as well.

See also: Exegesis of Hosea 1:3 above
(Annotation 2A; Brown, 1; Kidner, 12)

Annotation 2A: The Relationship Is Broken

2A.1 The end of the Sinaitic Covenant

The protracted and massive rebellion against God undermined the Sinaitic Covenant. This relieved the Almighty from the covenant obligation to protect Israel. Thus He became the enemy of both Israel and Judah. Not because God had changed His mind but because they had left Him and had long since turned to other gods en masse. Thus they had joined the "enemy camp." The national guilt had reached a point of no return, first in the ten-tribe kingdom of Israel, and more than a hundred years later, also in the two-tribe nation of Judah.

Due to the breach of the Sinaitic Covenant, Israel was no longer God's people. We find the formal statement with which the ten-tribe kingdom (Israel) was put out of the covenant in Hosea 2:1. The formal statement with which Judah was put out of the Sinaitic Covenant is in the book of Ezekiel, especially in chapters 4–6. However, for Judah there was a second chance when their Babylonian exile ended. That was not the case with Israel, because it disappeared into the mists of history.

2A.2 Israel becomes Ephraim

The ending of the Sinaitic Covenant also broke the bond that Israel had with the land of Canaan. However, Israel remained the bearer of the promise that the Messiah will come to unite the twelve tribes and return them to Canaan. But the fulfillment of that promise depends on strict conditions. The break between God and His people has far-reaching consequences. The Almighty gave up His rule over the land of Canaan and over Israel and left His people. And in that process of abandonment, another kind of people arose, a people who no longer belong to God. That is why the name of the people also changed. Instead of the honorific name *Israel*—that is: *God is fighting* (for them)—they were given the name *Ephraim* (the name of the largest tribe). (See Hosea 4:17.)

(See Excursus 9; "Israel and Ephraim" in the introduction to Hosea 5.)

Verse 2

lest I will undress her naked. I will expose her as on the day she was born. I will make her a wilderness; yes, I will turn her into a parched land. I will make her die of thirst.
The prophecy now focuses more exclusively on Israel (the Ten Tribes). The name Gomer is no longer mentioned, but here too, she is present in the background.

2.1 Israel got a last chance.
The charge against Gomer (Israel) is a last chance to repent, which would have averted the judgment. If Gomer (Israel) does not repent, then everything that God has given her will be taken away from her. Then she will return to the state of her birth, described in Ezekiel 16:6.* There the text speaks of a helpless baby, abandoned in the desert right after birth:

> *Then I* [God] *passed by and I saw you bathing in your blood. And I said to you, You in your blood, keep living! Yes, I spoke to you: stay alive! You in your blood!*

These words speak about the very beginning of the people of Israel, before God made a covenant with Abraham. Then He saved the helpless baby. Now, however, Hosea speaks of *dying of thirst*.
(*Weerd, Hebrew text translation in *Ezechiël*, vol. 1, 392)

2.2 Israel did not repent.
The text is clear. If Israel would not repent, the people would fall under judgment. We now know that Israel's conversion indeed did not take place. That is why the country was destroyed by the Assyrians and a large part of the population was slaughtered. The survivors were taken away and scattered among the nations. Thus the land of Canaan changed into a barren wilderness. And Israel/Canaan died because it was cut off from the water of life with which God fed it. This condition continues even to the present day. For although many of the Jews have already returned to Canaan, this is not the case with the descendants of the Ten Tribes. They live, largely anonymously, among the nations of the world.

Mind you: this *dying of thirst* (Hosea 2:2) is a metaphor. It does not look at individual Israelites but has in mind the tri-unity of God, land, and people—God, Israel, and Canaan. The term therefore refers primarily to the covenant that was broken, so that the relationship with God was ended.
(Excursuses 5; 7; Brown, 14; Reed, 35; Stuart, 48; Walvoord and Zuck, 1383; Wood, 175)

Verse 3 and 4

3   *Furthermore, I will not show her children compassion, for they are children from adultery,*

4   *since their mother was unfaithful and acted shamefully when she conceived them. For she said: I will go after anyone who wants to make love with me, anyone who will give me my food and my water, my wool and my linen, my oil and my drink.*

Gomer left her husband, the prophet Hosea. The children of the marriage with Gomer were rejected, because they were *children from adultery*. So the children became fatherless. They were not begotten by Hosea, who typifies God, but by strange men. This corelates to the great powers of that time with which Israel had made alliances: Egypt, Assyria, and Babylon. They paid for her favors with earthly goods: water, wool, linen, oil, and drink. Gomer's children were not begotten of love, but of lust and for money.

The separation of Gomer and Hosea, meant first and foremost that the people of Israel had broken with God. That is a step Gomer (Israel) made consciously. The result was that the judgment came upon the nation and with that the individual members of the people (the children) became fatherless. They therefore lost their identity.

4.1 Actually a Kind of Gentile
In their new condition the Israelites were no longer God's chosen people but had become strangers. Actually they transferred to being a kind of gentile. That has been fulfilled to the letter, for the people of Israel disappeared in the mists of history.

Verse 5
Therefore: see me! Who will strew her path with thornbushes. Thus I will hedge her in with a thorn hedge, so that she can no longer find her way.

Verse 5a
Therefore: see Me! Who will strew her path with thornbushes.
Verse 5 opens with the announcement that an important statement from God is coming. It appears to be a judgment that concerns both the short and the long term. The future of Gomer, that is to say Israel, is foretold: the Almighty God will *strew her path with thornbushes*. That does not need any further explanation, the text speaks for itself. It is an echo of Deuteronomy 28:64–65:

64 *For the Lord will disperse you and scatter you among all nations, to the farthest corners of the earth. There you will worship other gods, gods that you did not yet know nor your ancestors, gods of wood and stone.*
65 *Do not think that you can catch your breath or get a place to rest among these people. The Lord will let you live in fear there and let you lead, with dull eyes, a languishing existence.*

Verse 5b
Thus I will hedge her in with a thorn hedge, so that she can no longer find her way.
A gloomy future was foreseen for both Gomer (so Israel), and there were no points of light in the short distance. Because a *thorny hedge* blocked the view to the outside, to the future. Only their own path, the present, remained visible. The people of Israel thus lost the prospect of their future salvation, namely its destiny in the Messianic Kingdom.

5b.1 Loss of identity
With this second part of the curse, Israel lost its national identity, which distinguished it among the nations. Fragmented it lived on, hidden from humanity—but not from God. (Wood, 176)

Annotation 2B: A Different Fate

The curse of Deuteronomy is addressed to all twelve tribes of Israel. The curse seen in Hosea 2:5 (further elaborated on in Hosea 3:4–5), however, concerns the Ten Tribes exclusively and came in addition to that of curse of Deuteronomy.

The Jewish people (Judah and Benjamin) found a different fate. They first went into exile, which was a final means of moving them to repentance. They remained as the sole bearer of salvation. When that salvation came (the birth of Jesus), He was not accepted as the Messiah. Thereupon a veil was placed upon the Jewish people as an additional punishment for their unbelief, so that they could hardly recognize Jesus Christ as their Savior. It is no wonder, then, that so few Jews join the Christian faith. This is not unwillingness but impotence, the result of that veil as the following verses testify:

Romans 11:8 (NASB)
"God gave them a spirit of stupor, eyes to see not and ears to hear not, down to this very day."

Romans 11:25 (NASB)
For I do not want you, brethren, to be uninformed of this mystery—so that you will not be wise in your own estimation—that a partial hardening has happened to Israel until the fullness of the Gentiles has come in.

2 Corinthians 3:14 (NASB)
But their minds were hardened; for until this very day at the reading of the old covenant the same veil remains unlifted, because it is removed in Christ.

As said, the curse from Deuteronomy applies to all twelve tribes, including the Jews. Because after the Jewish wars (AD 66–70 and 132–136), they too were scattered, they found no peace anywhere and constantly live in fear. However they retained their identity and have been able to continue their worship of God. Their perspective on their holy destiny in the end times has not been blocked.
(See Excursuses 3; 4; 7.)

Verse 6 and 7
6 **She will chase after her lovers, but not catch them. She will look for them but not find them. Then she will say: I will leave and return to my first husband, for then I was better off than now.**
7 **She did not realize that I, yes, I gave her the grain and the new wine, and also the oil and silver. Yes, I overloaded her with gold, which was used for the Baal.**

The Ten Tribes were cut off from God. Of course, individually they can still find Him, that remains unaffected, but as a people they are God-less.

Instead of converting to God, Gomer (Israel) was looking for new lovers. In ancient times, for Israel, these were Egypt, Assyria, or Babylon, powerful neighbors, and idolatry came in with those lovers.

6/7.1 No compassion
There is always a need for safety in an uncertain world. But without God, only human or even satanic powers remain, and they offer only false security.

Over the years, the people of Israel have sought help, security, support, and affection in

all the wrong places and without success. And after many, many years—now more than twenty-five hundred years—the realization will slowly penetrate the Ten Tribes of Israel that they, as a whole, have to turn to God—*my first husband*—because *then I was better off than now*. Then Israel will recognize that God is the source of all good. That has yet to happen—the first signs of that upheaval are already visible.
(Excursus 7; Wood, 176)

Verses 8 and 9
8 *Therefore I will turn away [from her] and I will take away my grain when it is ripe and the new wine when it is ready. I will also take back my wool and my linen, which should cover her nakedness.*
9 *So now I will reveal her foolishness before the eyes of her lovers and nobody will save her from My hand.*

With verse 8 the focus of the prophecy returns to verse 5 and continues with details about the divine judgment. These concern the short term, because the *grain*, the *wine*, the *wool*, and the *linen* refer to the material prosperity of Israel. It would now taken away from her, and with that the country would lose its power and thus become an unresisting, nearly helpless prey for its attackers. This prophecy was soon fulfilled, because in 722 BC, the Northern Kingdom, Israel, was overrun by the Assyrians. A large part of its inhabitants was slaughtered and the land was completely destroyed.

Verses 10 and 11
10 *Then I will stop all festivities: her annual feasts, her New Moon days and the Sabbath day, even all her [holy] meetings.*
11 *I will also destroy her vines, as well as her fig trees; of which she said, These are my gratuities given by my lovers. I will make them into undergrowth and the wild animals will eat them up.*

With the downfall of the ten-tribe kingdom came an end to all holy festivals and to the undisturbed observance of the Sabbath. These were the characteristics that distinguished the people of Israel from the gentile nations.
(Rosenberg, vol.1, 13; Stuart, 51)

Verse 12
Then I will punish her for the days when she burned incense before the Baals. Then she adorned herself with her ring and jewelry and went after her lovers. But Me she forgot, declares Yahweh.

The conclusion is very sad indeed. The marriage relationship between God and Israel was lost. That happened here, but also again later, when the kingdom of Judah was carried away into captivity. The prophet Ezekiel reports on this. And there we learn, humanly speaking, of the emotions of God. For when Judah perished, the prophet Ezekiel, who acted in the name of the Almighty, was commanded as follows—Ezekiel 21:6 (NASB):

> *"As for you, son of man, groan with breaking heart and bitter grief, groan in their sight."*

12.1 The sorrow of God
The prophet Ezekiel speaks with the "mouth of God." So it is the Almighty Himself who laments! The grief of God is so great that the prophet must represent a broken man. Sadness over a broken love relationship. Sadness because God is hurt in the depths of His soul. Sadness, because He has been abandoned—see Ezekiel 22:30*:

"Then I sought a man among them who could build a wall and thus stand in the gap for Me on behalf of the land, so that it would not be destroyed. But I did not find one."

God was looking for someone to speak up for Him, but He did not find anyone. This is an intriguing statement, which suggests that God makes Himself dependent upon humans. Refer also to Ezekiel 23:35†:

"Because you forgot Me and cast your trust in Me careless behind your back."

(Weerd, Hebrew text translation in *Ezechiël*, vol. 1, *597, †631)

Verse 13
Therefore, see! I will lure her and lead her into the desert. Then I will speak to her heart.
In verse 13, the prophet sees into the far future, toward a moment when the fate of Israel would change radically and the salvation prophecies would come to fulfillment. This is, for us also, still unfulfilled prophecy.

Annotation 2C: The Wonder of the Love of God

Nothing has helped. Even the sending of God's prophets proved to be useless. God's laws were ignored. The punishments that were imposed to correct the people had no effect. The inevitable demise has taken place.

Then, very surprisingly, verse 13 opens with *Therefore!* Because nothing has helped, the Almighty steps over to a completely different way of acting: *I will lure her!* That is the language of lovers, as in Genesis 34:3.

If everything else fails in a relationship, pure love remains the last resort. With that, the offering party humbles itself for the sake of the other. As a Dutch hymn says, *O love of God, infinitely great, far above our understanding . . .* The prophet Zechariah also speaks of God luring His people in similar terms—see Zechariah 10:7–8*:

7   "The Ephraimites [the ten tribes of Israel] will become mighty heroes. Their hearts will be merry as from wine. Their children will see that and rejoice. Their hearts will rejoice in the Lord.
8   "I will whistle them to Me and assuredly bring them in. I will deliver them and they will become as numerous as they were."

The prophet Zechariah uses an expression that belongs to the work of a shepherd. For when he wants to lure the strayed sheep back to the flock (where they find safety), he does so by means of a whistling sound that he makes with his mouth. These prophecies are not yet fulfilled. That will only happen at the end of the great tribulation, when the Ten Tribes are also called upon to return to the land of Canaan.

Zechariah 10:9* confirms once more that it concerns the ten tribes of Israel that are lost:

"Although I sow them among the nations, yet they will remember Me in distant lands."

Sources:
(Born, 31; Stuart, 53; Walvoord and Zuck, 1385; *Weerd, Hebrew text translation in *Zacharia*, 274–75; Wood, 178–79)

2C.1 I will lure her.
This declaration of love to the people of Israel was not the first. Falling in love precedes love. We find that described in Ezekiel 16:8a*:

Then I passed you by and I looked at you. And see! The time of love had arrived.

After the love relationship between God and Israel began, a marriage was solemnized. That was the Sinaitic Covenant. It is moving to realize that the early period of the Sinaitic Covenant is called the *time of love* by the Almighty Himself. It created happiness on both sides, because all the people of Israel agreed—see Exodus 24:3 (NASB):

Then Moses came and recounted to the people all the words of the LORD and all the ordinances; and all the people answered with one voice and said, "All the words which the LORD has spoken we will do!"

(*Weerd, Hebrew text translation in *Ezechiël*, vol. 1, 393)

2C.2 Why did God wait so long?
You may wonder why God waits so long with the decision to lure Israel/Ephraim. We can only guess, and then we come to the following:

After Israel (the Ten Tribes) was rejected, the Jews (Judah and Benjamin) became the only bearers of salvation. However, when Jesus Christ came to earth and made Himself known to His people, He was not accepted as Messiah. That is why the Jewish people were temporarily set aside and salvation went to the church of Christ. But the church will be taken up into heaven (the rapture). With that, the last banner of God's holiness on earth will disappear. However, that would do too much damage to the name of the Lord. So there must be a change in the relationship between God and His people (all of His people). Only then can all prophecy be fulfilled and as a logical consequence, the Messianic Kingdom will be established. So the conclusion is that God will lure Israel, when it is the right time.

Verse 14
I will return her vineyards there and make the Valley of Achor [turmoil] a door of hope. And there she will answer [my love] as in the days of her youth; as on the day when she went out of the land of Egypt.
And when God decides to lure her (Israel, see verse 13), it appears that then His love will be answered. It will be like before, *as in the days of her youth*, when Israel *went out of the land of Egypt*. Those days were marked by a deep love relationship between God and His people. Exodus 15:1 (NASB) testifies:

Then Moses and the sons of Israel sang this song to the LORD, and said, "I will sing to the LORD, for He is highly exalted; the horse and its rider He has hurled into the sea."

And Exodus 19:5–6 (NASB):

5 *"'Now then, if you will indeed obey My voice and keep My covenant, then you shall be My own possession among all the peoples, for all the earth is Mine;*
6 *'and you shall be to Me a kingdom of priests and a holy nation.' These are the words that you shall speak to the sons of Israel."*

The period of the exodus from Egypt formed the "honeymoon" of the old Sinaitic Covenant, and that will return in the end times. It has not yet come to that point, but those who

understand the signs of the times will note that the fulfillment of the prophecy is in highest gear. It is at hand!
(See Annotation 1G.)

14.1 The Valley of Achor
This valley is found in Judah, west of the city of Jericho. There Achan was stoned to death because he took from the treasures of the defeated and destroyed city of Jericho—treasures devoted to God (Joshua 6:18–19; 7:24–26). It was a low point in the relationship between God and His people. Because of that sin the Almighty withheld His blessing and Israel was defeated by the army of the city of Ai (Joshua 7). After repentance and penance, Ai was still conquered (Joshua 8).

14.2 The great tribulation
Achor means *trouble* or *turmoil* (Joshua 6:18; Judges 11:35; 1 Kings 18:17). So if we translate the whole phrase, it says: *the valley of unhappiness* or *turmoil*. It is then only a small step to Ezekiel 37, the prophecy about the valley of the dead bones. There too is a hopeless situation for the people of Israel, just like in Hosea. There, too, the prophecy speaks of a glorious and salvific restoration of God's people. Both prophecies are therefore, largely, complementary.

The message is clear. The people of Israel must pass through the Valley of Achor—an all-time low period of misery as verses 5 and 12 also indicated. However, when that low point is reached—we speak of a period at the end of the great tribulation, in the future therefore—then God will give a door of hope and accept Israel again as His people.
(Boice, *Minor Prophets*, vol. 1, 26–27; Ironside, 23–24; Reed 40–41; Wood, 179)
(See Excursus 2: The End Time)

Verses 15 and 16
15 *And it shall come to pass, that at the appointed time, declares Yahweh, you shall call Me my husband. No longer will you call Me my master.*
16 *Then I will remove the names of the Baals from her mouth, and you will no longer be reminded of their names.*
The Almighty will purify Israel from idolatry and He will do it so thoroughly that even the memory of the idols will disappear. Zechariah prophesies about this in 13:2a*:

This says the Lord of hosts; it will happen in that day that I will drive the names of the idols out of the land, and they will be remembered no more.

The contrast that Hosea 2:16–17 evokes is great: *my man* (or husband) and *my Baal*.
(*Weerd, Hebrew text translation in *Zacharia*, 372)

15.1 My master—my husband (1)
Again, we find a beautiful wordplay. For the word Baal means master, owner, or ruler. That has a somewhat harsh undertone.

Under the Sinaitic Covenant there was a relationship between the people of Israel and God which, in addition to love and respect, also contained an element of holy fear. This will change in the future (i.e., during the Messianic Kingdom). Then there will be a much warmer relationship. The text speaks of a marriage out of love, because Israel may call God *my man* (husband).
(Andersen and Freedman, 278; Born, 32; Kidner, 33; Walvoord and Zuck, 1385–86)

15.2 My master—my husband (2)
In rabbinic writings we find a very enlightening explanation of this text. It reads as

follows: If a bride resides in the house of the father-in-law, there is a relation to that father-in-law as ba'ălîy (master). But if she stays in her father's house, she is at home. Then the bride-husband relationship comes to full bloom.
(Talmud Bavli—Pesachim 87a; Kesubos 71b)

Verse 17
Then, on the appointed day, I will make a covenant for them with the wild beasts of the field, the birds of heaven, and the creatures that crawl on the earth. I will also abolish bow, sword and war in the land; thus I will make them rest in safety.
Then, on the appointed day is a typical eschatological formula. This phrase almost always introduces a prophecy about the end times, as it does here also.

17.1 The Messianic Kingdom
All of the prophesied upheaval will find its climax in the founding of the Messianic Kingdom and the exaltation of the Messiah, Jesus Christ, as king in Jerusalem. There a new society will be established, incomparably better than the current one. This does not only apply to the relationship between God and man. Nature will also be "converted."

17.2 A garden of Eden
Eat or be eaten, natural disasters, wars—all this will be history, for God Himself will make a covenant between mankind and the animals, the birds, the fish, indeed, everything that lives.

In that covenant, the people of Israel will represent the entire population of earth as the most blessed nation in this world. Then the earth will become a paradise again, a garden of Eden, not limited to a region somewhere in the Middle East, as in the earliest time. The whole earth will share in God's rich blessing. The prophet Isaiah says about that time in Isaiah 65:25 (NASB):

> *"The wolf and the lamb will graze together, and the lion will eat straw like the ox; and dust will be the serpent's food. They will do no evil or harm in all My holy mountain,"* says the LORD.

(Andersen and Freedman, 277; Ironside, 28–29; Mays, 52; Reed, 41; Smith, 64; Walvoord and Zuck, 1386; Wood, 179)

Verses 18 and 19
18   ***Then I will take you as My bride, forever. Yes, I will take you as My bride in righteousness and justice, in mercy and security.***
19   ***I will take you as My bride in faithfulness, and then you shall know Yahweh.***
What else can we add to this prophecy? Here is a moving declaration of the love of God for the people of Israel. Here the prophet speaks about the fulfillment of the prophecy. For the marriage between God and His people will find its crowning in the establishment of the Messianic Kingdom.

Verse 20
And so it will be, at the appointed time, that I will give ear, thus proclaims Yahweh. I will listen to the heavens and they will listen to the earth.
What will God then *give ear* to? To the call for justice and the fulfillment of the prophecy. That is the call of all life that God has created, to bring it to its destination, as was once intended. That is why the apostle Paul says in Romans 8:22:

We know that all of creation is still sighing and suffering as in labor pains.

Now, in verse 20 of Hosea 2, suffering comes to an end, for it prophesies the birth of a new creation!

Verse 21
And the earth will respond! Yes, the grain, the new wine, and the oil will respond to God's sowing [Jezreel].
Can the grain, wine, and oil also "answer"? Certainly, because all those have not been created to perish, to rot, or to generate little yield. Ezekiel 36:29b (NASB) also speaks about this:

I will call for the grain and multiply it, and I will not bring a famine on you.

When God sows (Jezreel!) and blesses the crop, the yield will always be at a maximum and the quality will be higher than ever before. Because the last yield is the best. That is also a biblical principle, as shown in John 2:10b: *But you have kept the best wine until now!*
(Constable, 16; Reed, 41; Smith, 64; Walvoord and Zuck, 1386–87)

Verse 22
I will sow the earth for My own sake. I will show mercy to Lo-Ruchama [not loved] and I will say to Lo-Ammi [not My people]: My people [Ammi] and they will say: my God.
The ten lost tribes of Israel will go back to the promised land, Canaan, after many centuries. That will not be a temporary return. It will be forever, for they will be *sown in the land*! They will take root there and grow up into their destination. And the once unloved one will become the beloved of the Lord. A rejected people will become God's people again. That will not be a unilateral commitment from God, for they will unanimously confess: *my God*!
(Ironside, 27; Walvoord and Zuck, 1386–87; Wood, 180)

Annotation 2D: The Church and Israel

In Romans 9:25–26 the words of Hosea 1:10 and Hosea 2:22 are quoted. In that book the apostle Paul makes important statements about the salvation status of the people of Israel as well as of the church of Christ.

2D.1 The prophecy is broadened.
The Ten Tribes were temporarily excluded from salvation with the statement Lo-Ammi (Hosea 1). That period continues until the present day, but will once and for all end in the end time. Hosea 2:22 speaks of the ending of that period. This will happen shortly before the establishment of the Messianic Kingdom, which is also for us in the future.

The apostle Paul speaks in Romans 9 about the "chosen position" of the people of Israel. In verses 25–26 he quotes, surprisingly, Hosea 1:10 and 2:22. In doing so, he extends the scope of this ancient prophecy. There is no doubt that Hosea speaks in the first instance about the lost ten tribes of the people of Israel. However, the transformation of Lo-Ammi (not My people) to Ammi (My people) also appears to apply to converted gentiles (see also 1 Peter 2:9–10).

On the basis of the texts cited, many have come to the conclusion that the church of Christ has replaced the people of Israel. However, Paul does not say that. He expands the umbrella of salvation! Not only Israel, but also the church of Christ becomes the bearer of salvation, but in its own unique way. Paul explains this in Romans 11.

2D.2 Paul explains three lines to salvation.

If we want to understand Romans 9–11, we have to take into account that Paul speaks about salvation along three lines. One is found in the book of Hosea. It concerns the fate of the ten lost tribes of Israel. The second concerns Judah (the two-tribe nation or Jews), the only bearer of salvation after the fall of Israel. The third is that of the church of Christ, which is an independent split from the second—see Romans 11:25–26a (NASB):

> *For I do not want you, brethren, to be uninformed of this mystery—so that you will not be wise in your own estimation—that a partial hardening has happened to Israel until the fullness of the Gentiles has come in; and so all Israel will be saved.*

There is a lot in this one verse. We will walk through it briefly here.

The apostle Paul explains to the congregation in Rome (converted gentiles), how it is now with the status of Israel as the people of God. First of all, he reveals that there is a *mystery*. That means that this fact was not known before! Then he establishes that *a partial hardening* has come over Israel. With this Paul wants to say that God has imposed on the Israelites a "veil" as a punishment for rejecting Jesus Christ. This refers to a specific part of salvation, namely the recognition of Jesus Christ as Messiah and Savior. He explains this precisely in 2 Corinthians 3:15–17 (NASB):

15 *But to this day whenever Moses is read, a veil lies over their heart;*
16 *but whenever a person turns to the Lord, the veil is taken away.*
17 *Now the Lord is the Spirit, and where the Spirit of the Lord is, there is liberty.*

Paul thus declares that a Jew will be freed from the *covering* or *veil* only if he accepts Jesus Christ as his Savior. In this way he/she acquires *liberty* and thus becomes detached from that veil.

Paul continues in Romans 11:7–8 (NASB):

7 *What then? What Israel is seeking, it has not obtained, but those who were chosen obtained it, and the rest were hardened;*
8 *just as it is written, "God gave them a spirit of stupor, eyes to see not and ears to hear not, down to this very day."*

From the preceding quote it appears that only a small part of God's people will come to Christ, mainly from the firstfruits (that is the first "harvest" of converts), as described in the book of Acts. In the beginning, the church was Jewish-Christian. Later, unfortunately, deep enmity arose between the church and the Jews. They became alienated from one other. This is therefore no coincidence, because the Jewish people are being punished by God with *a spirit of stupor* or *deep sleep*.

2D.3 We continue with Romans 11:15.

> *For if their rejection is the reconciliation of the world, what will their acceptance be but life from the dead?*

The *rejection* is the rejection of Jesus Christ, by which God temporarily removes His people from their privileged status. That *rejection* then turns out to be the salvation of the nations, as appears from Romans 11:11 (NASB):

But by their transgression salvation has come to the Gentiles.

The fall of Israel leads to *salvation* for *the gentiles*. But verse 15 also speaks of their *adoption* or *acceptance*. That is the moment after their conversion when the Lo-Ammi (not My people) is revoked, which is also described in detail in the book of Zechariah. *Life from the dead* symbolizes the awakening from the *spirit of stupor* (Romans 11:8). Romans 11:23 (NASB) testifies:

And they also, if they do not continue in their unbelief, will be grafted in, for God is able to graft them in again.

Again this is a clear reference to a future restoration of the status of Israel as God's people.

Romans 11:24 (NASB) continues:

For if you were cut off from what is by nature a wild olive tree, and were grafted contrary to nature into a cultivated olive tree, how much more will these who are the natural branches be grafted into their own olive tree?

What a wonderful way of expressing it. So if we, Christ's church, are grafted into the noble olive tree as a foreign branch and already produce so much flowering, then, Paul says, how much more will God's people blossom, if they are put back into their old place!

The *hardening*, or the *spirit of stupor*, appears to be lifted only when the *fullness of the gentiles* comes (Romans 11:25). That is to say: at the moment the number of the gentiles is full. Because Paul speaks to the church of Rome, it is clear that he means converted gentiles. The number of them is full when God's goals have been achieved! That is also the time of the church of Christ, after which the great tribulation breaks out (1 Thessalonians 5).

There is thus no question of Israel being completely done as the people of God. Finding Jesus Christ has become very difficult for them. It is therefore no coincidence that Jews have gone over to Christianity with such difficulty and in such small numbers.

2D.4 Is Israel still God's people?
Paul confirms that in Romans 11:17–18 (NASB):

17 *But if some of the branches were broken off, and you, being a wild olive, were grafted in among them and became partaker with them of the rich root of the olive tree,*
18 *do not be arrogant toward the branches; but if you are arrogant, remember that it is not you who supports the root, but the root supports you.*

The broken branches represent the people of Israel. The flow of sap, that is, the food, stopped and with it the development of Israel in God's plan of salvation. The wild shoots are converted gentiles, followers of Christ. The trunk and root represent the salvation that has been promised to Israel and also that part of the counsel of God that has already been fulfilled. We, converted gentiles, may temporarily participate in this. One day, however, new branches will sprout again when God takes up the thread again with the people of Israel.

2D.5 Is the door of salvation then closed for Israel?
That is the question. The Lord Jesus says in John 14:6, *"No one comes to the Father but through Me"* (NASB). And although this is usually explained as the ultimate proof that Jesus Christ (the church) provides the only way to salvation, this is not explicitly stated. Of course it is true that Christ is the only key to salvation. That applies to Jews, gentiles, and

members of the church of Christ. However, Jews under the law were unaware of this. Yet even then people were saved (Hebrew 11: *By faith . . .*).

The relationship with the Father is an exclusive gift to the church of Christ. That relationship is not derived from the Old Testament. It is a new fact that is rooted in the person Jesus Christ. He is God's Son and is therefore entitled to address God as Father. The true Christian is part of His body, and like Christ, the relationship with the Father also applies to him or her (John 14:7; Romans 12:5; 1 Corinthians 6:15; 12:27). That is why 1 John 3:6 can make this remarkable statement: *"No one who abides in Him sins,"* and 1 John 3:9 says: *"No one who is born of God practices sin"* (NASB). The believer does not derive that exceptional salvific state from himself but from Christ who bears her or him.

In John 14 Jesus speaks to His disciples and through them to the later church of Christ. In verse 6 Jesus denies those who do not believe in Him the "Father relationship." That leaves room for the assumption that for Bible-believing Jews who do not know Christ and love God from the heart, the Old Testament dispensation remains in force. In it the blessing of the body of Christ is withheld from them, and thus the grace gifts attached to it. So a status quo has come about. The spiritual gifts, which are supplied by the trunk of the olive tree, temporarily do not benefit Israel. The church now benefits from them.

Those who follow the way of the law can, or course, accept Christ and thus join the church of Christ. For Christ is the fulfillment of the law, and thus His church is of a higher order than life under the law. Can we choose what way to go? No! A person who knows Christ belongs to Him and can no longer submit to the law (Romans 7:4; 1 Corinthians 4:1; 7:21; 2 Corinthians 1:22).
(Weerd, *Ezechiël*, vol. 2, 565–69)

2D.6 God has given gifts of grace.
Those gifts are, in principle, present in all Jews, although in a different context. After all, it cannot be a coincidence that the Jews add so much to science and culture? In Germany around 1930, for example, less than two percent of the population consisted of Jews. Yet their influence on culture and science was immense. Over thirty percent of the lawyers were Jewish, as were more than twenty percent of the scholars. And we could go on and on for some time.

This difference is, their gifts are given to each Jew at birth. It demonstrates their status as individual members of God's people. This could create an unfair advantage which might impede the advancement of the gospel. But it is the Holy Spirit who compensates for this and assigns spiritual gifts to the believer, whereby he/she becomes equal to the Jew. Here too we can see a logical continuation of the counsel of God.

The size and detail of the counsel of God is bewildering in its greatness. It leads Paul to exclaim in Romans 11:33 (NASB):

> *Oh, the depth of the riches both of the wisdom and knowledge of God! How unsearchable are His judgments and unfathomable His ways!*

Sources:
(Barnhouse, Romans 11:33; Smith, 55; Walvoord and Zuck, 1387)

HOSEA 3
Hebrew Text Translation

Introduction
This short chapter, with the exception of verse 1, hardly causes any difficulties with regard to translation. That is quite remarkable, because the prophecy itself is of great importance and usually this leads to dogmatic controversies.

Hosea 3 only contains five verses, but there is a great deal of information in them. The prophecy speaks about the return of the people of Israel (the lost Ten Tribes) in *the last days* (the end times). Many Bible scholars do not know what to do with this chapter, for it does not fit in with their dogma. An alternative translation, which fits their dogma better (the usual procedure in cases like this), does not give them a way out, because the prophecy is stated in very clear terms. Instead, they fall back on declaring verses 4 and 5 corrupt. So, based on their interpretation of Hosea 3, one might claim that these verses are not from the hand of the prophet Hosea but instead were added later to the Hebrew text by a so called "Judean redactor." But this argument would erase the prophecy or render it impotent. We, of course, do not agree with that point of view. Hosea's prophecy is clearly stated.
(Feinberg, *Minor Prophets*, 23, 26–27)

Verse 1 NASB
Then the Lord said to me, "Go again, love a woman who is loved by her husband, yet an adulteress, even as the Lord loves the sons of Israel, though they turn to other gods and love raisin cakes."

Verse 1 KJV
Then said the Lord unto me, Go yet, love a woman beloved of her friend, yet an adulteress, according to the love of the Lord toward the children of Israel, who look to other gods, and love flagons of wine.

Verse 1 NIV
The Lord said to me, "Go, show your love to your wife again, though she is loved by another man and is an adulteress. Love her as the Lord loves the Israelites, though they turn to other gods and love the sacred raisin cakes."

Verse 1 Hebrew Interlinear Text
and-he-said Yahweh to-me again go! show-love! wife one-being-loved-of another and-one-being-adulteress as-to-love Yahweh ... sons-of Israel though-they ones-turning to gods other-ones and-ones-loving-of raisin-cakes-of raisins

Verse 1c
and-ones-loving-of raisin-cakes-of raisins
This is a controversial phrase. Some try to follow the Hebrew text, however the last words are debated. In many cases this leads to a translation that seems meaningless within the context. We have studied the Hebrew text carefully and came to an unusual translation.
(See Annotation 3A below.)

We read: *and love the pressing of the grapes*

The entire sentence:
Then Yahweh said to me, Go now again! Show your love to this woman—loved by another and committing adultery—as Yahweh loves the children of Israel, though they turn to other gods and love the pressing of grapes.

Annotation 3A: *Ashishah* **and** *Enab*

3A.1 A word study
In the NIVIHEOT translation of the Hosea 3:1 we find as translation *raisin-cakes-of raisins*; so twice the word *raisin*. However, they represent two different Hebrew words: *enab* and *ashishah*. *Enab* means *grapes* (Genesis 40:10; Deuteronomy 32:14; Isaiah 5:2). Thus to translate as *raisins* is interpretation, because the translator assumes that it refers to pressed fruit cakes. These cakes cannot be made with grapes but only with the dried variety, raisins. We will always adhere strictly to the basic Hebrew text, unless there is a very good reason for switching to interpretation. That is not the case here, so we will dig deeper.

The word *ashishah* means *that which is pressed*. Many exegetes translate as *raisins* or *raisin cakes*, but that is far from certain. Others read *flagon of wine* (KJV) or *cups of the grapes* (Tenach), and some even ignore *enab* and *ashishah* altogether (NLT). Some fill in with their own composition. NKJV has: *raisin cakes of the pagans*. And Brown has: *raisins pressed together to form cakes*.

3A.2 Compare Scripture with Scripture!
The word *ashishah* occurs only four times in the Bible. Hosea 3:1 is an important text, and we would like some certainty that we have a good translation. So we will also examine the other three places it is used in Scripture to learn from their contexts.

The context of 2 Samuel 6:19 is the festive entry of the ark into Jerusalem. King David distributed a "loaf of bread, a cake of dates, and a cake of raisins" (or: the *compressed*) to the revelers (NIV).

First Chronicles 16:3 tells the same story about the entry of the ark. The NASB says David gave "to everyone a loaf of bread and a portion of meat and a raisin cake."

In both cases we are missing a drink. People who walk in a festive procession get warm and tired. They will be thirsty and desire a quick snack: so bread, a cake of dates or raisins, and something to drink. Thus the KJV translation—*a flagon of wine*—seems to fit quite well.

Song of Solomon 2:5 (NIV) reads: "Strengthen me with raisins, refresh me with apples, for I am faint with love." Here we find an extra clue, because in verse 4 it is says: "He brings me into the banquet hall," which is wrong, because *hay-yayin* means *the wine*. We prefer to read: *the best wine*, so this text would agree with the KJV translation of Hosea 3:1.

On the basis of these three Bible references it is therefore probable that these texts do indeed refer to a drink.

3A.3 Several types of wine
There are several different Hebrew words that can be translated directly or indirectly as *wine*. Some of these are very rare. A Hebrew word frequently used (134 times) is *yayin* (Hosea 4:11a). This is fermented, matured wine; so wine in the final stages of the processing of grapes to normal wine. *Yayin* can also refer to all kinds of liqueurs. *Tîrôsh* was young wine (Hosea 4:11b), perhaps even grape juice (nonalcoholic).

The basic meaning of *ashishah* is *that which is compressed*. Strong's even speaks of *something that is highly compressed*. Good wine was made from the juice of the grapes, which was obtained by bruising the grapes. In the wine industry this is called a first pressing. However, there is always a residue left over, namely the grape skins. They still contain some grape juice, because the grapes are not crushed too hard in the first pressing. By pressing this residue again, wine of a much lower quality can be obtained after fermentation. The word *ashishah* may perhaps refer to this type of wine, so "a second pressing." It was not filtered; it was diluted with water (so only slightly alcoholic); and—this is important—it was cheap.

Conclusion:
The phrase probably refers to a popular drink, a wine of lesser quality, which was prepared from a "repressing" of grapes. So we have to read: *the pressing of grapes*.

Sources:
(Brown, 28; Calvijn, *Daniël* II, *Kleine Profeten* I/II, Hosea, 80; Harper, 218; Pfeiffer, Vos, and Rea, 1812–13; Rashi, 34; Riedel, vol. 2, 1–36; Strong's OT, words 809, 3196, 6025, 8492; Ward, 48)

Verse 2 NASB
So I bought her for myself for fifteen shekels of silver and a homer and a half of barley.

Verse 2 KJV
So I bought her to me for fifteen pieces of silver, and for an homer of barley, and an half homer of barley:

Verse 2 NIV
So I bought her for fifteen shekels of silver and about a homer and a lethek of barley.

Verse 2 Hebrew Interlinear Text
so-I-bought-her for-me for-five ten silver and-homer-of barleys and-lethek-of barleys

We read:
So I bought her for fifteen pieces of silver plus a homer of barley and a lethek of barley.

Verse 3 NASB
Then I said to her, "You shall stay with me for many days. You shall not play the harlot, nor shall you have a man; so I will also be toward you."

Verse 3 KJV
And I said unto her, Thou shalt abide for me many days; thou shalt not play the harlot, and thou shalt not be for another man: so will I also be for thee.

Verse 3 NIV
Then I told her, "You are to live with me many days; you must not be a prostitute or be intimate with any man, and I will behave the same way toward you."

Verse 3 Hebrew Interlinear Text
then-I-told to-her days many-ones you-must-live with-me not you-must-be-prostitute and-not you-must-be with-man and-also I with-you

Verse 3a
then-I-told to-her days many-ones you-must-live with-me
The word *yashab* means to *stay* (Genesis 22:5; Jeremiah 42:10). In Numbers 22:5 it is

translated as *settled*, but that is also a form of residence. *Yashab* certainly does not mean *dwelling*, *living*, or *living together*, as some argue. Similar texts can be found in Genesis 22:5 (*stay here*, or *wait for me*), in Exodus 24:14 (*wait here for us*) and in Jeremiah 3:2 (*sat waiting*). Based on these, the meaning seems quite clear.
(Andersen and Freedman, 291; Buss, 10; Strong's OT, word 3427; Ward, 49–50)

We read: ***then I said to her: You will have to wait for me many days***

Verse 3b
not you-must-be-prostitute
Others read: *You shall play the harlot.*

We read: ***you will no longer be a prostitute anymore***

Verse 3c
and-not you-must-be with-man
These words make it clear that Gomer (= Israel) is to no longer have a relationship with another man. This prohibition also applies to the relationship between Gomer and Hosea (verse 3a and 3d). Their relationship will also be broken, just as the nation's relationship with God (their Husband) is broken. Wolff translates: *or belong to another man*, which is what we will follow.
(Brown, 28–29; Harper, 220; McComiskey, 52; Wolff, 56)

We read: ***or belong to another man***

Verse 3d
and-also I with-you
These words seem difficult to understand, but the context gives a clear indication as to the correct translation. To express that rightly we add *no relation*.

We read: ***and I also will have [no relation] with you***

The entire sentence:
Then I said to her: You will have to wait for me many days. You will no longer be a prostitute or belong to another man. And I also will have [no relation] with you.

Verse 4 NASB
For the sons of Israel will remain for many days without king or prince, without sacrifice or sacred pillar and without ephod or household idols.

Verse 4 KJV
For the children of Israel shall abide many days without a king, and without a prince, and without a sacrifice, and without an image, and without an ephod, and without teraphim:

Verse 4 NIV
For the Israelites will live many days without king or prince, without sacrifice or sacred stones, without ephod or household gods.

Verse 4 Hebrew Interlinear Text
for days many-ones they-will-live sons-of Israel without king or-without prince or-without sacrifice or-without sacred-stone or-without ephod or-idols

Verse 4b
without king or-without prince

The word *sar* means *leader, chieftain,* or *prince*. We find it used in the sense of a commander in Genesis 21:22 (NIV), *commander of his forces*, and in Genesis 39:1; 41:12 (NIV), *captain of the guard*. Verse 4 speaks of distinguishing marks that belong to a sovereign nation under God's rule—*king, sacrifice,* and *sacred stone* (altar). That is why the translation *army commander* fits here.
(Strong's OT, word 8269; Walvoord, 1387)

We read: ***without king or army commander***

Verse 4c
or-without sacrifice or-without sacred-stone
The word *matstsebah* means *pillar* or (erected) *sacred stone*.
(Strong's OT, word 4676; *Studiebijbel* SBOT 12, 48)
(See Annotation 3B.)

We read: ***without sacrifice, without sacred stone,***

Verse 4d
or-without ephod or-idols
The word *teraphim* often represents *idols*. It is seldom translated, but usually vocalized as *teraphim*. *Teraphim* were house gods of which man believed they could interpret the will of the gods. So here we find a play on words. To deliver that message well we read *interpreters*.
(See Annotation 3C.)

We read: ***without ephod and interpreters***

The entire sentence:
For the children of Israel will remain many days without king or army commander, without sacrifice, without sacred stone, without ephod and interpreters.

Annotation 3B: The Sacred Stone

3B.1 No pagan altar or stone
Some scholars and exegetes see in the *sacred stone* a kind of altar, or a religious object (such as a sacred pole) of a pagan religion. That certainly does not fit in the context of this chapter of Hosea. That is why we will go a little deeper into the Hebrew text.

The basic meaning of the word *matstsebah* is *something that has been erected*, for example a *column, pillar, small altar,* or *small monument*. Brown calls it *a menhir or dolmen*, or a *natural block of stone*. In a number of cases, a *matstsebah* appears to be devoted to a pagan idol. That is why many exegetes assume that there is talk of idolatry here. But there are plenty of examples where the word *matstsebah* stands for an object dedicated to God. Let's look at a few examples.
(Strong's OT, word 4676; *Studiebijbel* SBOT 12, 48)

3B.2 Compare Scripture with Scripture
In Genesis 28:18, 22 and 31:13, *matstsebah* refers to a pile of stones dedicated to God on which offerings are brought. In Genesis 31:45, 51–52 it is a memorial that seals the covenant between Jacob and Laban. We may suppose that this covenant was also entered into in the name of Yahweh.

In Genesis 35:14 the NIV translates *matstsebah* as *stone pillar*, or a stone column or small altar, perhaps one meter high, where Jacob presented a libation to God. In Genesis 35:20 it is a memorial stone at the tomb of Rachel. And, finally, in Isaiah 19:19 it is a monument to the Lord.

So we can therefore say with some certainty that, here too in Hosea, *matstsebah* is a memorial or altar. The words *sacrifice* and *sacred stone*, then, would refer to personal sanctification, by means of an offering to God.

Source:
(Walvoord and Zuck, 1388)

Annotation 3C: Teraphim—Interpreters

3C.1 Various interpretations
The NIVIHEOT translates the word *teraphim* as *idols*. Some exegetes draw the conclusion therefore that the text means that the people of Israel will no longer serve idols.* But that is not what the Hebrew text says. Other exegetes and translators regard this as a proper noun. They do not translate, but vocalize the Hebrew text to read *teraphim* as in 2 King 23:24 and Zechariah 10:2 (NASB). Generally speaking, these are viewed as household gods.

3C.2 Verse 4 points toward a transition period
The word *teraphim* embarrasses Bible scholars, for it doesn't seem to fit into the context. The preceding words of verse 4 describe the lack of external signs that represent an established nation under God's rule (as we will see in future Israel), like a king, sacrifices, an altar, and an army commander. There is no doubt that verse 5 is a prophecy of salvation. It speaks of a blessed future, where what lacks in verse 4, will definitely happen. So verse 4 seems to be the transition to that period. The last word of verse 4, *teraphim*, therefore simply does not seem to belong there. However, there must be a logical explanation for the use of the word *teraphim*. We seek this, as always, in an accurate analysis of the basic Hebrew text.

In contrast to the preceding words in verse 4 (*sacrifice* and *sacred stone*) the word *without* is missing before *idols* (or *teraphim*). The two key words are connected by a *vav* (= *and*), so we can also read *or without ephod and teraphim/idols*, in one breath. This (unusual) combination of words is also found in Judges 17:5; 18:14, 17–18, 20. In those texts an *ephod* is a priestly garment and a *teraphim* is a household god. The verses in Judges describe the beginning of a forbidden idolatry that was adhered to by the tribe of Dan (Judges 18:31). So if we take the book of Judges as a standard, then this is a (forbidden) idolatry.

3C.3 Here a translation is the key
A second possibility is that we take the meaning of *teraphim* into account, so that we simply translate as we do the rest of the sentence so that it reads *interpreters* or *explainers*. In this context the Hebrew text says that the people of Israel will be for a long time without *ephod* (high priest) and *interpreter* (of Holy Scripture or of God's will).

This second interpretation is much more convincing, for the name *ephod* also stands for the high priest's breastpiece with twelve precious stones attached to it. On each of these the name of one of the twelve tribes of Israel was engraved. This shield was called the *breastpiece of decision*. In it was a bag that contained two stones (the Urim and the Thummim), with which one could consult the will of God. This function perfectly matches the meaning of the word *teraphim* (interpreters).
(Rosenberg, vol. 1, 21, 207; Targum Jonathan, Hosea 3)

Conclusion:
The prophet Hosea thus prophesies that at some point there will be no high priest (here represented by the word *ephod*) and no one who can consult the Urim and the Thummim.

Sources:
(Brown, 32; Dee and Schoneveld, vol. 1, 153; vol. 2, 295; Edelkoort, 181n18; *Feinberg, *Minor Prophets*, 26; Garrett, 103; Mays, 59; McComiskey, 53–54; Strong's OT, word 8655; Walvoord, 1388; Wolff, 56; Wood, 183) (See Excursus 7.)

Verse 5 NASB
*Afterward the sons of Israel will return and seek the L*ORD *their God and David their king; and they will come trembling to the L*ORD *and to His goodness in the last days.*

Verse 5 KJV
*Afterward shall the children of Israel return, and seek the L*ORD *their God, and David their king; and shall fear the L*ORD *and his goodness in the latter days.*

Verse 5 NIV
*Afterward the Israelites will return and seek the L*ORD *their God and David their king. They will come trembling to the L*ORD *and to his blessings in the last days.*

Verse 5 Hebrew Interlinear Text
afterward they-will-return sons-of Israel and-they-will-seek . . . Yahweh God-of-them and David king-of-them and-they-will-come-trembling to Yahweh and-to blessing-of-him in-last-one-of the-days

Verse 5a
afterward they-will-return sons-of Israel
The basic meaning of the word *achar* is *hidden part* in the sense of what is yet to happen. It is usually translated with *after that* or *afterward*. We prefer: *after that*.
(Strong's OT, word 310)

We read: *after that the children of Israel will return*

Verse 5c
and-to blessing-of-him in-last-one-of-the-days
The word *tub* means *the good* or *best* (Genesis 45:18; Isaiah 1:19) or *goodness* (Nehemiah 9:25), or *prosperity* (Psalm 128:5). In the latter case it concerns the *prosperity* or *blessings* of the future Messianic Kingdom.
(Strong's OT, word 2898)

We read: *and to his blessings, in the last days*

The entire sentence:
After that the children of Israel will return. Then they will seek Yahweh their God and David their king. And they will come trembling to Yahweh, and to His blessings in the last days.

Hosea 3:1–5—The corrected text:

Verse 1   *Then Yahweh said to me, Go now again! Show your love to this woman— loved by another and committing adultery—as Yahweh loves the children of Israel, though they turn to other gods and love the pressing of grapes.*

Verse 2   *So I bought her for fifteen pieces of silver plus a homer of barley and a lethek of barley.*

Verse 3   *Then I said to her: You will have to wait for me many days. You will no longer be a prostitute or belong to another man. And I also will have [no relation] with you.*

Verse 4   *For the children of Israel will remain many days without king or army commander, without sacrifice, without sacred stone, without ephod and interpreters.*

Verse 5   *After that the children of Israel will return. Then they will seek Yahweh their God and David their king. And they will come trembling to Yahweh, and to His blessings, in the last days.*

HOSEA 3
Exegesis

Introduction
For the exegesis of Hosea I consulted many study books. After I had read all of them, I again read the text of Hosea and wondered at the ease with which the exegetes distort the meaning of a text, so that it fits into their own interpretation. It is alarming, that this uncontrollable tendency to adapt the text is fed by the conviction that Israel is *not* God's people. That there *cannot* be unfulfilled salvific promises for that people—once a chosen people—today nearly outcast!

Not all of the promises of salvation are so clear that they do not allow any discussion. Here in Hosea 3, however, we find a standard example of a clear divine prophecy in favor of the people of Israel, at the end time. The Almighty instructs the prophet Hosea to carry out a number of actions that model his future action with regard to the Ten Tribes of the people of Israel. In addition, for the sake of completeness, an explanation is given for these actions (verses 4–5) in order to leave no doubt whatsoever about the intention of the divine prophecy.

A. Deletions in the Original Text
If an exegete wants to explain such clear prophecies differently than the words indicated by the prophecies themselves, he must make changes to the text, which is precisely what happens. Van de Born, for example, titles chapter 3: *The Woman Bought Back and Locked Up for Improvement*. This is an explanation that, given the text, requires some imagination. Of course, Van de Born is in conflict with verse 5, where it is stated that *then they will seek Yahweh their God, and David their king* (= Jesus Christ, the Messiah). That is typical end time prophecy (yet unfulfilled prophecy). Van de Born solves it simply by saying, "David, their king is a Judean gloss"* (a later addition) which does not belong in the text. So he interprets this as not being end-time prophecy at all. Some even totally delete verses 4–5 and thus rewrite the prophecy according to their own understanding.
(Birch, 45; Born, 36)

B. The Conceit of Christianity
Many Bible scholars have a great aversion to the literal meaning of prophecy; especially where it concerns an unfulfilled future. This has lead secular and even some Bible-believing interpreters to be in an unholy agreement.

For many Bible scholars, as we have already said, it is too much to see the people of Israel as the bearers of the salvation promises of the Old Testament, thus viewing them as God's people. That is actually a very strange phenomenon, especially because the supporting argumentation is usually weak. Fortunately, there are also exegetes who notice this, such as Ward, who says: "I strongly disagree with those who deny any hopeful passage to Hosea (and ascribe it to later writers, which causes the text to lose its value)."†

In fact, this method of interpretation of Scripture, which takes away all salvation promises from Israel or the Jews, is nothing other than a shocking form of self-exaltation. All future blessings from the Holy Scriptures are then attributed to Christianity and the Jews and/or the Israelites are left with the judgments. This way of interpreting is also an important breeding ground for anti-Semitism, even in this present day. In this we recognize the hand of Satan itself.

(*Born, 36; Garrett, 97–98; Mays, 54–56; †Ward, 24)

Verse 1
Then Yahweh said to me, Go now again! Show your love to this woman—loved by another and committing adultery—as Yahweh loves the children of Israel, though they turn to other gods and love the pressing of grapes.
The text speaks, strikingly, of *this woman*. The personal name, Gomer, is thus deliberately not used by the prophet, while it is clear that she is meant. We find the explanation for this in the meaning of the name Gomer: *completion*. God's dealings with Gomer, as described in the first two chapters of Hosea, concerns the goal (completion) of the relationship between God and Israel. That is now a thing of the past. The Lo-Ammi is pronounced (Hosea 1:9). With this the name Gomer is thus done with.
(Birch, 41; Flanders, Crapps, and Smith, 348; Smith, 73)

1.1 A comforting thought
From verse 1 on, the prophecy speaks about the era after the broken marriage between God and his people (thus between Hosea and Gomer), so the period after the Sinaitic Covenant. In that era (which continues to date), Israel is typified by *a* woman with whom God no longer has a love relationship.

The description *woman* (instead of Gomer) suggests that there are several, and this is true. Ezekiel 16:46–56 speaks of Judah, Israel (Samaria), and (surprisingly) Sodom, who are called sisters of each other. From this we can in any case draw the conclusion that the word *women*, in the context of Hosea 3:1 and Ezekiel 16, refers to nations or peoples. So it seems that every nation in this world is, in principle, a natural partner for the Almighty. That is a beautiful and comforting thought.
(Jeffrey, 991; Strong's OT, word 1586; Weerd, *Ezechiël*, vol. 1, 404–8; Wood, 181–82)

1.2 Elected a second time!
With the text *show your love to this woman*, we have arrived at a beautiful piece of gospel. For the prophet Hosea represents God. And just as Hosea is told to do this, God also decides, unilaterally, to declare his love to this woman, Israel. This is in fact the same prophecy as we find in Hosea 2:13 (by our alternate numbering). And, because it is so important, we repeat the explanation.

Nothing has helped. The sending of God's prophets proved useless. God's laws were ignored. The punishments that were imposed to correct the people did not matter to them. The inevitable downfall has taken place. Then, surprisingly, Hosea says in 3:1, "*Show your love to this woman . . . as Yahweh loves the children of Israel!*"

Because nothing has helped, the Almighty will do something completely different. *I will lure her!* (Hosea 2:13). That is the language of lovers.

1.3 The great love of God
If everything fails in a relationship, pure love remains the last resort. So the offering party humbles him/herself for the sake of the other. This happens also here, however strange that may seem! O love of God, infinitely great, far above our understanding! This prophecy is yet to be fulfilled. It will only happen at the end of the great tribulation, when the Ten Tribes are also called to return to Canaan.
(Ironside, 28–29)

Verse 1b
loved by another and committing adultery
The woman (Gomer) is not an attractive party for Hosea, because she is constantly unfaithful and turns to other gods. That is also the way it was with Israel. She had turned to the idols and sought help from powerful neighbors, not from God. With that, Israel committed adultery.

Verse 1c
as Yahweh loves the children of Israel, though they turn to other gods and love the pressing of grapes
Turning to idolatry leads Israel downhill, and without God, they go from bad to worse. What is left is pure self-indulgence (*love the pressing of grapes*).

Verse 2
So I bought her for fifteen pieces of silver plus a homer of barley and a lethek of barley.
This sentence faces many exegetes and Bible scholars with insurmountable problems. Why does Gomer have to be redeemed? She was already married to Hosea, so there could no longer be a dowry that still had to be paid. The answer probably lies in Hosea 1:3. We proposed an alternative translation there. Instead of *Gomer, daughter of Diblaïm* we read: *Gomer, the daughter of two fruit cakes.*

2.1 Ransomed from paganism
In that second translation we assumed that Gomer was a prostitute in a temple or sanctuary of Ishtar. They were called *ishtarishu* (see previous commentary on the text and exegesis of Hosea 1:3). The prophet Hosea was married to her, but she simply continued with her "work," as is apparent from Hosea 1. The temple service to Ishtar was not without obligation. It usually involved women who had been sold at a young age to a temple or sanctuary. They were only allowed to leave their "duty" (in fact a kind of slavery) when the debt incurred as a result, had been settled by somebody. The prophet Hosea now buys her from her serfdom to the idolatrous sanctuary. That is, of course, a beautiful image. The people of Israel will once again be redeemed by God from paganism. That has not happened yet, but we are living in a time when we see the first signs of those great events.
(Flanders, Crapps, and Smith, 349–50; Guenther, 76; Limburg, 13)
(See Excursuses 6; 7.)

2.2 *A homer of barley and a lethek of barley*
A *lethek of barley* is, according to some exegetes, half a homer. The total involved was therefore one and a half homer of barley. That is about 546 liters.
(Edelkoort, 181)

Verse 3
Then I said to her: You will have to wait for me many days. You will no longer be a prostitute or belong to another man. And I also will have [no relation] with you.
The prophet Hosea instructs Gomer to go into seclusion. She must no longer go after strange men. Nor will the prophet Hosea have dealings (= sexual intercourse) with her. She must live in celibacy for a long time.

3.1 Nurturing care
Some exegetes suppose that Hosea locked up his wife. But that is unlikely, because in verse 1 God instructs him to show love to her. It is therefore more likely that Hosea surrounds her with nurturing care, but at the same time maintains his distance. That would

not have been a simple step for the prophet. For Gomer had loved several men in the years of their marriage, and three children had been conceived. There was certainly no basis for deep mutual affection. You cannot force love; it is not available on demand. We may therefore assume that Hosea received God's help in this.

3.2 The waiting room of history

In the context of the special relationship between God and Israel, the actions of the prophet Hosea and Gomer are not difficult to interpret. The people of Israel (the Ten Tribes) are placed in the "waiting room" of history for a long time and lose their identity. That is why they are no longer a partner for other peoples (*will no longer . . . belong to another man*). Much worse, however, is that the relationship with God is also suspended (*I also will have no relations with you*).
(Brown, 29; Ironside, 30–33; Mays, 58)

Verse 4
For the children of Israel will remain many days without king or army commander, without sacrifice, without sacred stone, without ephod and interpreters.

The prophecy of Hosea is very clear. All external signs that the people of Israel once were a holy nation, will not be there for *many days* (what means, many years): a king and an army with a general; the sacrifice in the temple and the consecrated stone (or altar); the Ephod and someone who interprets the will of God (which refers to the Urim and the Thummim as well as to the sending of God's prophets).

Thus the prophecy foretells that the people of Israel lose their identity, which was based on their service to God and was why they were called a holy nation. That has come true to the letter.

4.1 The first signs are there

Israel (the Ten Tribes) disappeared from history until the present day. It does not say how long that period will last. Even now we cannot say anything about it, but we do know that the return is near. The first signs are already there!

Sources:
(Birch, 44; Mays, 58; Rashi, cited by Rosenberg, vol. 1, 21)
(Annotations 3B; 3C; and Excursuses 7; 8.)

Excursus 8: Ephod, Urim, and Thummim

8.a The ephod
An ephod was a linen body skirt which the priests wore (1 Samuel 2:18; 22:18) that was pulled over the head. It could be used as a generic name, but the ephod of the high priest was a unique item of clothing. It contained a square breastpiece and was attached to the priest's outer garment with chains (Exodus 28:15ff). There were four rows of three gems each on the breastpiece, on which each of the names of the twelve tribes of Israel was engraved. On the left and right shoulder the bands of the breastpiece were fastened with a gemstone set in gold. On each of these the names of six tribes were engraved (Exodus 28:9–14).

The Ephod was also called the breastpiece of judgment (Exodus 28:30; Leviticus 8:8), for it contained the *Urim* and the *Thummim*.

8.b Urim and Thummim
In the ephod a small bag was incorporated, containing two stones (the Urim and the

Thummim), with which one could consult the will of God. They were called the glory of Levi. Only those of clean heart and mind had permission to use the Urim and the Thummim. King David also used them when he wanted to consult the will of God (1 Samuel 23:9; 30:7).

The word *Urim* means *lights*, or perhaps *enlightenment*, and Thummim *perfection* or *completeness* (both words are plural forms). Martin Luther translated them *light* and *justice*. However, the latter deviates from the basic meaning of the Hebrew word. In combination, we should probably think of a meaning such as *total enlightenment, the whole truth,* or *truth and clarity.* According to some ancient scrolls found in Egypt, the patriarch Abraham received the stones from God.

It is unfortunately not known how the Urim and the Thummim were used. The secret of their effect probably passed from high priest to high priest and was otherwise not known to anyone. The Bible does not make any statement about this. Some assume that they were just a kind of dice, but that opinion is based on pagan practices of oracle stones. We do not know.

After the exile, the Urim and Thummim seemed to have disappeared, although the hope remains alive that they will one day be recovered (Ezra 2:63; Nehemiah 7:65). (Read also: Numbers 27:21; Deuteronomy 33:8; 1 Samuel 28:6)

Sources:
(Brown, 30–32; Grosheide, et al., vol. 2, 45–46; vol. 5, 517–18; Dee and Schoneveld, vol. 1, 153; vol. 2, 293; Josephus, *Antiquitates Judaicæ*, vol. 3, 8–9; Pfeiffer, Vos, and Rea, 534–35, 1761; Rashi in *Talmud Bavli*, Yoma 73b)

Verse 5
After that the children of Israel will return. Then they will seek Yahweh their God, and David their king. And they will come trembling to Yahweh, and to his blessings, in the last days.
The final verse of Hosea 3 contains unmistakable messianic prophecy that has remained unfulfilled to this day. Ben Zvi speaks in this context of a promise of a messianic king *in a very distant future*. Although he draws the correct conclusion from the text, he does not share that expectation. He calls verse 5 "a typical product of that period."* Ben Zvi thus chooses the side of many exegetes who do not take the prophecies about the Messianic Kingdom seriously. For those who want to understand God's Word to the letter, the prophecy is clear. It speaks of a glorious future for the people of Israel.
(*Ben Zvi, 93–94)

5.1 The Ten Tribes rediscover Yahweh as their God
After an indefinite period, which has already lasted for more than twenty-five hundred years, the Ten Tribes will regain their identity. For some reason they will come to the conclusion that they are descended from God's people. And then they will also reclaim that position.

Impossible, you may say. Well, not with Almighty God. In Excursus 7 we show that this great miracle has already been set in motion in our time. And when Israel has regained its identity, the return of the Ten Tribes to Canaan is imminent. Then each tribe will be allowed to inhabit the piece of land originally assigned to them (Ezekiel 48). This, of course, will be preceded by a conversion. And the fruit of that conversion will be that the ten tribes of Israel will rediscover Yahweh as their God. That will cause a great shock. After so many centuries of darkness, they will be confronted again with the radiant light of Almighty God—the I-Am-Who-I-Am. Then they will also receive insight into the Scriptures. That knowledge will give them insight into the nature of God and that causes a holy fear (*trembling*).

5.2 David, their king

Some exegetes see in Hosea 3:5 an announcement of the birth of Jesus Christ, the Messiah. With that they ignore the rest of the text, which says that the Israelites then will *seek Yahweh their God*. That was certainly not the case at the time Jesus lived on earth, because the Jews rejected Jesus Christ.

5.3 To his blessings, in the last days

In the end time, Israel will again be accepted as God's people. *David* (that is the Messiah, Jesus Christ, the great Son of David) becomes *their king*. And so the lost Ten Tribes will *in the last days* fall under the *blessings* of the Messianic Kingdom. It is not that far away now, and whoever understands the signs of the times sees the first intimations of this great event.

(Boice, *Minor Prophets*, vol. 1, 81–97; Constable, 18; Feinberg, *Minor Prophets*, 27; Kidner, 43–44; Rosenberg, vol. 1, 200, 207)

(See Excursus 7.)

Excursus 9: The Messianic Kingdom in the Bible

In many places in the Bible the praises of the Messianic Kingdom are sung. We give a few examples.

Ezekiel 34:23–24*

> *And I will establish a single herdsman over them. Then He will guard them: David, My servant. He, yes, He will guard them and He, yes, He will be like a (good) shepherd to them. Then I, Yahweh, will be their God, and My servant David the prince among them. I, Yahweh, have spoken it.*

Ezekiel 37:25*

> *And they shall dwell in the land that I have given to My servant, to Jacob, in which your fathers lived. Yes, they will live in it: They and their children and their children's children forever. And David, My servant, will be their prince forever.*

Isaiah 2:2–3 KJV

> *And it shall come to pass in the last days, that the mountain of the LORD's house shall be established in the top of the mountains, and shall be exalted above the hills; and all nations shall flow unto it. And many people shall go and say, Come ye, and let us go up to the mountain of the LORD, to the house of the God of Jacob; and he will teach us of his ways, and we will walk in his paths: for out of Zion shall go forth the law, and the word of the LORD from Jerusalem.*

Isaiah 9:7 NASB

> *There will be no end to the increase of His government or of peace, on the throne of David and over his kingdom, to establish it and to uphold it with justice and righteousness from then on and forevermore.*

Isaiah 11:10 NASB

> *Then in that day the nations will resort to the root of Jesse, who will stand as a signal for the peoples; and His resting place will be glorious.*

Jeremiah 33:17–18 NASB

> *"For thus says the Lord, 'David shall never lack a man to sit on the throne of the house of Israel; and the Levitical priests shall never lack a man before Me to offer burnt offerings, to burn grain offerings and to prepare sacrifices continually.'"*

Amos 9:11 NASB

> *"In that day I will raise up the fallen booth of David, and wall up its breaches; I will also raise up its ruins and rebuild it as in the days of old."*

Micah 5:4†

> *And He shall be steadfast, and shepherd in the power of the Lord, in the majesty of the name of the Lord His God. Then they will settle, for He will be mighty to the ends of the earth.*

(Read also 2 Samuel 5:2; 7:8; Psalm 78:70–72; Amos 9:11; Hosea 3:5; Isaiah 9:6–7; 11:1; 55:3–4; Jeremiah 23:5–6; 30:9; 33:15–26; Zechariah 12:7–8; John 7:40–42)

Sources:
(Cooper, 302–3; Fairbairn, 375–81; *Weerd, Hebrew text translation in *Ezechiël*, vol. 2, 299–300, 371; †Weerd, Hebrew text translation in *Micha*, 262–66)

HOSEA 4
Hebrew Text Translation

Introduction

The fourth chapter of the book of Hosea is not easy to translate. This is mainly due to the poetic choice of words. The prophet Hosea plays with words and sounds, for example, by placing the words of the text in a rhyming cadence. To create the rhyme, the prophet uses unusual words and expressions.

Instances of such poetic license appear also in the English language. One example can be found in the following lines from the "The Star-Spangled Banner": "whose broad stripes and bright stars, through the perilous fight / O'er the ramparts we watched, were so gallantly streaming." The word *o'er* is, of course, a poetic form of *over*, but since the latter would exceed the number of syllables required here, the form of the word was adapted. Native Anglophones and those in the know will see this immediately, but for an outsider the word *o'er* remains a mystery. We encounter something similar also in the book of Hosea. That is why it is not easy to properly convey what the prophet says. So poetic language leaves extra room for interpretation.

Unfortunately, many exegetes and translators have very enthusiastically used the latitude that the Hebrew text seems to offer. As a result, considerable differences have arisen between the various translations. Most biblical scholars show little motivation to closely follow the Hebrew text, which leaves its mark. At one point, Van de Born even speaks of a *labyrinth of translations* and that is indeed the reality.
(Born, 43; Buss, 6, 12)

A. Comparing Scripture with Scripture

We are of the opinion that this chapter should be elucidated against the background of the previous three chapters. The context will therefore provide the missing data. We call this method comparing Scripture with Scripture. Unfortunately, only a few exegetes apply this method. A lot of biblical scholars are of the opinion that it is highly unlikely that Hosea is the author of this chapter, even though they concede that he is the author of the first three. Thus chapters 1–3 in many commentaries do not exert any corrective influence on the next chapters.

B. A Logical Structure and Message

As said, we do accept Hosea as the sole author of chapter 4, which relays spoken words of God Himself. So we will closely follow the Hebrew text. This leads to a pronounced logical structure of the text and an understandable message. Indirectly, this will also serve to support the reliability of the text, for it is improbable that this would happen merely by happenstance.

Verse 1 NASB
Listen to the word of the L̲ord*, O sons of Israel, for the* L̲ord *has a case against the inhabitants of the land, because there is no faithfulness or kindness or knowledge of God in the land.*

Verse 1 KJV
Hear the word of the L̲ord*, ye children of Israel: for the* L̲ord *hath a controversy with*

the inhabitants of the land, because there is no truth, nor mercy, nor knowledge of God in the land.

Verse 1 NIV
*Hear the word of the L*ORD*, you Israelites, because the L*ORD *has a charge to bring against you who live in the land: "There is no faithfulness, no love, no acknowledgment of God in the land."*

Verse 1 Hebrew Interlinear Text
hear word-of Yahweh! sons-of Israel because charge to-Yahweh against ones-living-of the-land indeed there-is-no faithfulness and-there-is-no love and-there-is-no acknowledgement-of God in-the-land

Verse 1a
hear word-of Yahweh! sons-of Israel
The word *ben* can mean *sons*, but also *children*. Most exegetes read *Israelites* here. That is of course also its meaning, but it is a bit further from the Hebrew. However, we value the familiar sound of the expression *children of Israel* and want to retain it.
(Brown, 38; Strong's OT, word 1121)

We read: *hear the word of Yahweh, you children of Israel!*

Verse 1b
because charge to-Yahweh against ones-living-of the-land
As in Hosea 2:1 (English versions: 2:2) we find a form of the Hebrew word *rib* here. There we translate it *charge*. Here is written in a substantive form, so we read *a charge*.
(Andersen and Freedman, 214, 219; Born, 27; Garrett, 75; Kidner, 46; Strong's OT, word 7378, 7379; Wolff, 30)

We read: *for Yahweh has a charge against those who live in the land*

Verse 1c
indeed there-is-no faithfulness
Certainly or *indeed* are two of the many possible translations of the word *ki*. It has a broad range of applications and usually introduces a causal link, as is also seen here. We prefer (along with many other translators) *because*.
(Strong's OT, word 3587; Stuart, 70)

We read: *because there is no faith*

Verse 1d
and-there-is-no love
We are not really happy with this translation in the Interlinear, because it is too far from the Hebrew text. The word *checed* is translated in many different ways. We found, among others, *grace*, *favors*, *mercy*, and *kindness*, but rarely *love*. The context makes clear that words like *mercy* or *grace* fit best.
(Andersen and Freedman, 336; McComiskey, 55; Strong's OT, word 2617)

We read: *and no mercy anymore*

Verse 1e
and-there-is-no acknowledgement-of God in-the-land
Daath means *knowledge* and this is how most exegetes translate it. A good example of the

meaning of this word is found in Genesis 2:9, where it says: *The tree of the knowledge of good and evil.* We follow this meaning.
(Birch, 47; Born, 37; Mays, 60; Strong's OT, word 1847)

We read: ***and there is no knowledge of God in the land***

The entire sentence:
Hear the word of Yahweh, you children of Israel! For Yahweh has a charge against those who live in the land, because there is no faith and no mercy anymore, and there is no knowledge of God in the land.

Verse 2 NASB
There is swearing, deception, murder, stealing and adultery. They employ violence, so that bloodshed follows bloodshed.

Verse 2 KJV
By swearing, and lying, and killing, and stealing, and committing adultery, they break out, and blood toucheth blood.

Verse 2 NIV
"There is only cursing, lying and murder, stealing and adultery; they break all bounds, and bloodshed follows bloodshed."

Verse 2 Hebrew Interlinear Text
to-curse and-to-lie and-to-murder and-to-steal and-to-commit-adultery they-break-bounds and-bloodsheds to-bloodsheds they-follow

Verse 2a
to-curse and-to-lie and-to-murder and-to-steal
The word *alah* means *oath* (2 Chronicles 6:22; 1 Kings 8:31) or *anathema* (they are similar in meaning). In the sense of *curse* we find it used in Numbers 5:21; Deuteronomy 29:19–21; and in Nehemiah 10:29. According to the context we chose for *curse*.

The Hebrew text suggests that there is constant swearing, lying, etc. That is why the NIV opens with: *There is only cursing . . .* etc., which we follow in terms of content.
(Strong's, word 423; Walvoord and Zuck, 1388; Ward, 75; Wolff, 65)

We read: ***constantly cursing, deceiving, murdering, and stealing***

Verse 2a
and-to-commit-adultery they-break-bounds
The basic meaning of *parats* is *to break out*. The NIVIHEOT interprets and reads: *they-break-bounds*. McComiskey translates *erupt*. Brown: *break into* (houses of neighbors).
(Brown, 39; McComiskey, 55; Strong's OT, word 6555; Stuart, 70)

The entire sentence:
Constantly cursing, deceiving, murdering, and stealing. They break out in committing adultery and bloodshed follows bloodshed.

Verse 3 NASB
Therefore the land mourns, and everyone who lives in it languishes along with the beasts of the field and the birds of the sky, and also the fish of the sea disappear.

Verse 3 KJV
Therefore shall the land mourn, and every one that dwelleth therein shall languish, with the beasts of the field, and with the fowls of heaven; yea, the fishes of the sea also shall be taken away.

Verse 3 NIV
"Because of this the land dries up, and all who live in it waste away; the beasts of the field, the birds in the sky and the fish in the sea are swept away."

Verse 3 Hebrew Interlinear Text
because-of this she-mourns the-land and-he-wastes-away all-of one-living in-her even-beast-of the-field and-even-bird-of the-airs and-also fishes-of the-sea they-die

Verse 3b
and-even-bird-of the-airs
The older translations usually speak of *heavens*. More recently *air* or *skies* has been used.

We read: *the birds in the air*

Verse 3c
and-also fishes-of the-sea they-die
The word *asaph* usually means *to remove* or *to gather*, as in the sense of being gathered to his fathers, that is why some translate *to die*. The original Hebrew has *yê'āsəpū*, that is: *will be taken away.*
(Edelkoort, 182; *Studiebijbel* SBOT 12, 50; Strong's OT, word 622)

We read: *and the fish in the sea will be taken away*

The entire sentence:
For that reason the country mourns and everything that dwells in her languishes. Even the animals of the field, the birds in the air and the fish in the sea will be taken away.

Verse 4 NASB
Yet let no one find fault, and let none offer reproof; for your people are like those who contend with the priest.

Verse 4 KJV
Yet let no man strive, nor reprove another: for thy people are as they that strive with the priest.

Verse 4 NIV
"But let no one bring a charge, let no one accuse another, for your people are like those who bring charges against a priest."

Verse 4 Hebrew Interlinear Text
but man not let-him-bring-charge and-not let-him-accuse man for-people-of-you like-ones-bringing-charges-of priest

Verse 4b
for-people-of-you like-ones-bringing-charges-of priest
Many exegetes and translators interpret this text in such a way that a charge is brought against the priest. It is an interpretation of the text that we do not follow. Verse 4b points

not to a legal case, but to harebrained accusations, thus here we have to translate with *to argue* or *to dispute*.
(Brown, 40; Gelderen, Hosea 4:4; Garrett, 113; Kidner, 49; McComiskey, 60)

We read:
However, do not let a person make a complaint, nor let anyone accuse someone else. For your people are like those who argue with a priest.

Introduction to Verse 5

This verse requires an introductory discussion, because the opinions about the possible translations vary greatly. Wolff believes that part of the sentence was added to the text later (in other words, not written by Hosea). The only part he accepts as original reads: *So that you will stumble by day and your mother will likewise*. Garrett's interpretation reads: *You stumble day and night, and the prophets stumble with you*. And Brown comments that "the text is obscure and probably corrupt." He suggests this translation: *O priest, thou dost stumble by day, and the prophet also stumbles with thee by night*. This results in a text that is difficult to understand, but we do not think that it needs to be this way. We closely follow the Hebrew text and that will lead to an understandable sentence.
(Brown, 40; Garrett, 113, 117; Wolff, 70nc)

Verse 5 NASB
So you will stumble by day, and the prophet also will stumble with you by night; and I will destroy your mother.

Verse 5 KJV
Therefore shalt thou fall in the day, and the prophet also shall fall with thee in the night, and I will destroy thy mother.

Verse 5 NIV
"You stumble day and night, and the prophets stumble with you. So I will destroy your mother—"

Verse 5 Hebrew Interlinear Text
indeed-you-stumble the-day and-he-stumbles also prophet with-you night so-I-will-destroy mother-of-you

Verse 5a
indeed-you-stumble
This verse opens with a vav (*indeed*), but we can also read *and* or *then*. Sometimes we can just leave it out, if that is the sentence structure and this has no consequences for the meaning, like here.

Kashal usually means *to fall* (also in the sense of *falling by the sword*), *to undergo* or *to stumble*. We join the majority and read *stumbles*.
(Mays, 66; Strong's OT, word 3782; Stuart, 70)

We read: ***you stumble***

Verse 5b
the-day
The Hebrew root (*hayyom*) can indeed mean the day, but also *by day*, *every day*, *day* or

today. Garrett speaks of *all of the time*. From verses 1 and 2 we know that *stumbling* (= sinning, verse 5a) happened daily. It is therefore obvious to translate here with *all days*.
(Andersen and Freedman, 351; Garrett, 117; Harper, 253; Strong's OT, word 3117; Stuart, 70)

We read: ***every day***

Verse 5c
and-he-stumbles also prophet with-you
If used after a *vav* (*and*) *gam* does not mean *also* (it would be unnecessary to say the same thing twice), but *even*.
(Brown, 169; Strong's, word 1571; *Studiebijbel* SBOT 12, 52)

We read: ***and even the prophet will stumble***

Verse 5d
with-you night
Some interpret these words to mean that the prophet will stumble with them (the people of Israel), so they will both stumble at night. An interpretation like that is meaningless. We can also read these words as: *about you [the] night*. Then the text speaks about the coming demise of Israel (later called: Ephraim).
(Calvijn, *Daniël* II, *Kleine Profeten* I/II, Hosea, 102)

We read: ***when the night comes over you***

Verse 5e
so-I-will-destroy mother-of-you
The word *damah* (here translated with *destroy*) is uncommon and means *to end, to stop, to cease*, or *to silence* (also *to perish*). It is rarely translated as *to ruin* or *to destroy* (mainly seen in the book of Hosea). This (deviant) choice is not based on the word meaning, but is nothing more than an attempt to give sense to the sentence, within one's own interpretation. We don't agree with that. The context shows another way. The northern empire of Israel was destroyed, so we believe that is what is being referred to here. Thus the *mother* (of the children of Israel = Gomer/Israel) will be silenced.

We find similar meanings in Isaiah 15:1 (KJV). And in Jeremiah 47:5 (BSB, NLT, NIV), *damah* describes the silence of a ruined city. We also found: *to be silent* (Dutch Willibrord translation), and *to silence* (CEV). We adhere to the basic meaning and read *I will silence*.
(Mays, 66; Strong's OT, word 1820; Wolff, 78)

We read: ***then I will silence your mother***

Other sources consulted:
Andersen and Freedman, 351; Born, 38; Brown, 40; Garrett, 113; Harper, 253; Mays, 66; Wolff, 70)

The entire sentence:
You stumble every day and even the prophet will stumble, when the night comes over you. Then I will silence your mother.

Verse 6 NASB
My people are destroyed for lack of knowledge. Because you have rejected knowledge, I also will reject you from being My priest. Since you have forgotten the law of your God, I also will forget your children.

Verse 6 KJV
My people are destroyed for lack of knowledge: because thou hast rejected knowledge, I will also reject thee, that thou shalt be no priest to me: seeing thou hast forgotten the law of thy God, I will also forget thy children.

Verse 6 NIV
"my people are destroyed from lack of knowledge. Because you have rejected knowledge, I also reject you as my priests; because you have ignored the law of your God, I also will ignore your children."

Verse 6 Hebrew Interlinear Text
they-are-destroyed people-from-me from-lack-of the-knowledge because you the-knowledge you-rejected so-I-reject-you from-to-be-priest to-me because-you-ignored law-of God-of-you I-will-ignore children-of-you also I

Verse 6a
they-are-destroyed people-from-me from-lack-of the-knowledge
The majority translate this with *ruin*, *perish*, or *destroy* (NASB, KJV). However, the basic meaning of *damah* is *to silence* (which can mean *to perish*) or *to make dumb** (see commentary above on verse 5e). Very few follow the Hebrew text, like the DRA does (*have been silent*) and the Dutch Willibrord translation (*My people are silenced*). The context favors a kind of silence, for Israel did not passed away. Instead they disappeared as a recognized people, so it became quiet around Israel.

Beli is a debated word. It is translated in various ways: for example *because*, *cannot*, *lack*, *unintentionally*, and *without*.† We can see it translated as *lack of* in Job 4:11 (NASB) and Isaiah 5:13. Here we are faced with a play on words with 6b/c. We prefer: *lack of*.
(Andersen and Freedman, 352; Strong's OT, words *1820, †1079)

We read: **My people have been silenced on account of lack of knowledge**

Verse 6b
because you the-knowledge
Hadda ͨat means: *the knowledge*. The definite article adds a kind of specialty or emphasis to knowledge. So usually it points to well-known or special knowledge. In this case it is the knowledge of Yahweh, what is confirmed in verse 1e. We add therefore: *godly*.
(Andersen and Freedman, 352–53; Limburg, 20; *Studiebijbel* SBOT 12, 52)

We read: ***because you . . . the godly knowledge***

Verse 6c
you-rejected
Ma'ac means *to withdraw* (Job 42:6) or *to reject* (Psalm 36:4; 78:59; 89:38). Often it is translated with *to ignore* or *despise*. However, that is somewhat further from the basic text. It is clear that Israel consciously rejected God and with that also the knowledge of God disappeared. That is why the logical choice is *to reject*.
(Andersen and Freedman, 353; Mays, 69; Strong's OT, word 3988)

We read: ***you rejected***

So now we can combine 6b and 6c. We read *you* twice here. Very few take notice of that in their translation. It is important, for it sets the sentence in the context of the broken Sinaitic Covenant.

We read: *because you, yes, you rejected the godly knowledge*

Verse 6d
so-I-reject-you from-to-be-priest to-me
The sentence opens with a *vav*. To translation as *so* is debated. We read: *then . . . also*.

Instead of *I-reject*, it would be better to read: *I will reject* (NASB). The phrase is not so difficult, but for exegetical reasons usually deviates from the Hebrew text. It can be explained a bit more clearly. It says: *I will reject you from being a priest to Me*, that is the *priesthood* that God instituted in Israel.
(Andersen and Freedman, 353; Garrett, 118; Mays, 66; Walvoord and Zuck, 1389)

We read: *then I will also reject you from being a priest to Me*

Verse 6e
because-you-ignored law-of God-of-you I-will-ignore children-of-you also I
This sentence also opens with a *vav*. A better translation would be *for*. The word *tōwraṯ* or *torah* means *teaching*. It is derived from *jarah*, that is *to say* or *to design*. If we translate here with *law*, as is usually done, we do not reflect the actual meaning of the Hebrew. We therefore read *teaching* and add *Torah* between brackets. The last words—*gam ani*—can be translated as *also I* or *even I*. It is connected with the breach in the Sinaitic Covenant and expresses astonishment or dismay. We read: *yes, I*.
(Eisemann, 675; Pfeiffer, Vos, and Rea, 1727; Strong's OT, words 3384, 8451)

We read: *because you rejected the teaching [Torah] of God, I will also reject your children, yes, I*

The entire sentence:
My people have been silenced on account of lack of knowledge, because you, yes, you rejected the godly knowledge. Then I will also reject you from being a priest to Me. Because you rejected the teaching [Torah] of God, I will also reject your children, yes, I.

Verse 7 NASB
The more they multiplied, the more they sinned against Me; I will change their glory into shame.

Verse 7 KJV
As they were increased, so they sinned against me: therefore will I change their glory into shame.

Verse 7 NIV
"The more priests there were, the more they sinned against me; they exchanged their glorious God for something disgraceful."

Verse 7 Hebrew Interlinear Text
as-to-increase-them they-sinned against-me Glory-of-them for-disgraceful-thing I-will-exchange
The word *rob* (related to *rabah*) means *to multiply* or *to increase*, but also *big* (in the sense *a lot*) or *abundance*. Most exegetes choose the first meaning. Some add the word priests, but that is not seen in the Hebrew text. Moreover, such a translation clashes with history. Nowhere does it appear that the number of priests increased significantly during the reign

of Jeroboam II or shortly thereafter. On the contrary, the service to God almost extinguished. And it is farfetched to involve the many pagan priests of that time in this text. The prophecy does not speak about that.

In our view, this text refers to the great economic prosperity during the reign of Jeroboam II. In that sense we find *rob* in Deuteronomy 28:47; Isaiah 7:22; Psalm 37:11; 52:7; and 72:7, among others. It is therefore completely logical that the same thing applies here. Literally it says: *when they got plenty* or *as abundance increased*. That is: *the more they got abundance*. (Strong's OT, words 7230, 7035; Stuart, 70)

We read:
The more they got abundance, the more they sinned against Me. I will have their glory exchanged for shame.

Verse 8 NASB
They feed on the sin of My people and direct their desire toward their iniquity.

Verse 8 KJV
They eat up the sin of my people, and they set their heart on their iniquity.

Verse 8 NIV
"They feed on the sins of my people and relish their wickedness."

Verse 8 Hebrew Interlinear Text
sin-of people-of-me they-feed-on and-on wickedness-of-them they-relish self-of-them

Introduction to Verse 8

Verse 8 is very controversial. Some translate in such a way that the priests feed on the sin (or sin offerings) of the people. Others remain closer to the Hebrew text and read: *They feed on sin* (for example: NIV, NASB and KJV). But even then, they have the priests in view. But this is not what the text says! All these translations come from the exegetes' own thoughts.

McComiskey translates: *My people feed on sin*. He comes very close to the Hebrew text. However, with this translation the priests, as addressed, are out of the picture, which of course emphatically contradicts the view of many exegetes and translators. Calvin says this about the problem:

> This verse has given occasion to many interpreters to think that all the particulars we have noticed ought to be restricted to the priests alone: but there is no sufficient reason for this. We have already said, that the Prophet is wont frequently to pass from the people to the priests, but as a heavier guilt belonged to the priests, he very often inveighs against them. For the pronoun applies to the priests as well as to the people. For he says 'jo'kelu', and then 'jis'u': "they will eat the sin" and "they lift up the soul of the sinner by iniquity."

Calvin is therefore still based on a false translation of verse 4b. For that is the only reason that he sees the priests as the ones being accused. That is not the case, according to the context of this verse. However, in terms of translation, Calvin closely follows the Hebrew text. (Calvijn, *Daniël* II, *Kleine Profeten* I/II, Hosea, 108–9)

Verse 8a
sin-of people-of-me

The word *chatta'ah* means primarily *sin*, as in Genesis 4:7; 18:20; 31:36; and Exodus 10:17. It is also translated as a *sin offering* (Exodus 29:14, 36). In those cases there is usually an animal, upon which sin is symbolically imposed and then sacrificed in the place of a human being. So the word *sin offering* is interpretation. One can just as well translate with *sin* and thus closely follow the basic text.
(Brown, 42; Strong's OT, word 2403; Ward, 75)

We read: ***the sin of My people***

Verse 8b
they-feed-on and-on
Akal is a common word and usually means *to eat*, *to consume*, or *to devour*. It is used in the negative way here, that is clear. So, *consume* (Deuteronomy 5:25; 32:22) or *devour* (Isaiah 24:6; 2 Chronicles 7:13 NASB). Given the context—a process of continuous degradation—this is also the case here. We read: *consume*.
(Strong's OT, word 398; Ward, 75)

We read: ***they consume themselves more and more***

Verse 8c
wickedness-of-them they-relish
The word *avon* (NIVIHEOT: *wickedness*) means: *iniquity*, *guilt*, or *depravity*. The meaning of the word *nasah* is *to carry* (Exodus 19:4; Judges 3:18), but also *to take along* (Exodus 10:19; 1 Chronicles 10:12; 2 Chronicles 16:6; Job 27:21; Isaiah 40:24). With the translation of *they-relish*, the NIVIHEOT gives an interpretation, which we don't share.
(Born, 39; Harper, 257–58; Owens, 767; Strong's OT, words 5375, 5771)

We read: ***their depravity takes along***

Verse 8d
self-of-them
Nephesh usually means *soul* or *life* or sometimes *heart*, if there is an inner condition as is the case here. It should be noted, however, that the words *heart* and *soul* are usually interchangeable.
(Cheyne, 66; Harper, 258; Strong's OT, word 5315)

We read: ***their heart***

The entire sentence:
Because of the sin of My people, they consume themselves more and more. Their depravity takes along their heart.

Other sources:
(Andersen and Freedman, 358–59; Calvijn, *Daniël* II, *Kleine Profeten* I/II, Hosea, 153–54; Harper, 257; McComiskey, 63; Stuart, 79; Wolff, 70, 81)

Verse 9 NASB
And it will be, like people, like priest; So I will punish them for their ways and repay them for their deeds.

Verse 9 KJV
And there shall be, like people, like priest: and I will punish them for their ways, and reward them their doings.

Verse 9 NIV
"And it will be: Like people, like priests. I will punish both of them for their ways and repay them for their deeds."

Verse 9 Hebrew Interlinear Text
and-he-will-be like-the-people like-the-priest and-I-will-punish to-him ways-of-him and-deeds-of-him I-will-repay to-him

Verse 9 begins with a standard opening phrase, which often has an eschatological nature. It serves to mark the beginning of the second part of this chapter.
(Andersen and Freedman, 359–60)

Verse 9a
and-he-will be
Many exegetes ignore the fact that the future tense is being used here. Calvin is more accurate, writing *and there shall be*. Another good translation is *and it will come to pass*.
(Andersen and Freedman, 342; Born, 40; Calvijn, *Daniël* II, *Kleine Profeten* I/II, Hosea, 153–54; Harper, 258; Stuart, 71, 79; Wolf, 71)

We read: ***and it will come to pass***

Verse 9b
like-the-people like-the-priest
Many exegetes and translators read *like people, like priest*, after a well-known expression. We rarely find this construction used that way in Scripture. Wolff emphatically takes another route and reads: *It will be for the people as for the priests*. This is already much better. The text suggests that the people and the priests have an equal status. That is indeed the fact after the break of the Sinaitic Covenant and the demise of Israel, because following verse 6e *the priesthood* was *rejected* by God—no longer existing—which is exactly what happened with Israel.
(Wolff, 82–83)

We read: ***because the priests are equal to the people***

Verse 9c
and-I-will-punish to-him ways-of-him
Most exegetes ignore the word *him* and translate *them* (plural). That is not what the text says. Hosea speaks in the singular; however *their ways* is plural. The expression *to him* has the sense of *each and every one of them*. Every priest is being punished individually as well as each and every one in the nation of Israel. The term is also used that way elsewhere in the Bible.

Derek means *way, road*, or *behavior*.
(Andersen and Freedman, 362; Brown, 43)

We read: ***yes, I will punish every one of them***

The entire sentence:
And it will come to pass, because the priests are equal to the people, that I will punish every one of them for their ways and reward them for their actions.

Verse 10 NASB
They will eat, but not have enough; they will play the harlot, but not increase, because they have stopped giving heed to the LORD.

Verse 10 KJV
For they shall eat, and not have enough: they shall commit whoredom, and shall not increase: because they have left off to take heed to the LORD.

Verse 10 NIV
"They will eat but not have enough; they will engage in prostitution but not flourish, because they have deserted the LORD to give themselves . . ."

Verse 10 Hebrew Interlinear Text
and-they-will-eat but-not they-will-have-enough they-will-engage-in-prostitution but-not they-will-increase because . . . Yahweh they-deserted to-give-to

Verse 10a
and-they-will-eat but-not they-will-have-enough
Yiśbā'ū (from *sabea*) means *they will be satisfied.*
(Brown, 43; Strong's OT, word 7646)

We read: *they will eat but not be satisfied*

Verse 10b
they-will-engage-in-prostitution but-not they-will-increase
Parats means *break through*. Sometimes one can translate with *increase*, but that needs a strong support from the context. That is missing here. According to the event prescribed in Hosea 4 we have to think of a *break through* to better times—the Messianic Kingdom.

We read: *they will commit adultery, but they will not break through*

Verse 10c
The words *because . . . Yahweh they-deserted to-give to* cannot be fit into verse 10, but undoubtedly belong to verse 11. Usually we delay the introduction of such changes until the presentation of the definitive text. Here, however, the result would be an awkward, fragmentary sentence (see NIV). This is why we are already introducing the correction here.

The entire sentence:
They will eat but not be satisfied. They will commit adultery, but they will not break through.

Verse 11 NASB
Harlotry, wine and new wine take away the understanding.

Verse 11 KJV
Whoredom and wine and new wine take away the heart.

Verse 11 NIV
"to prostitution; old wine and new wine take away their understanding."

Verse 11+10c Hebrew Interlinear Text
because . . . Yahweh they-deserted to-give-to prostitution and-old-wine and-new-wine he-takes-away understanding
The word *leb* means *heart, mind, inner man,* or *soul* but certainly not *understanding*. *Laqach* means *to take*, very seldom *to take away* which is also debated. Literally we read: *for it takes/captures their hearts* and so we translate.
(Strong's OT, word 3947, 3820; *Studiebijbel* SBOT 12, 54)

We read:
For they have deserted Yahweh to give themselves to harlotry and to old and new wine for it captures their hearts.

Verse 12 NASB
My people consult their wooden idol, and their diviner's wand informs them; for a spirit of harlotry has led them astray, and they have played the harlot, departing from their God.

Verse 12 KJV
My people ask counsel at their stocks, and their staff declareth unto them: for the spirit of whoredoms hath caused them to err, and they have gone a whoring from under their God.

Verse 12 NIV
"My people consult a wooden idol, and a diviner's rod speaks to them. A spirit of prostitution leads them astray; they are unfaithful to their God."

Verse 12 Hebrew Interlinear Text
people-of-me to-wooden-idol-of-him he-consults and-stick-of-wood-of-him he-answers to-him / indeed spirit-of prostitutions he-leads-astray and-they-are-unfaithful from-after God-of-them
The first part of verse 12 (up to the /) looks rather mysterious. The Hebrew source text reads something along the following lines: *people of Me turns to his wood and consults their rod which answers him.* Yet the mystery is solved quite readily once we realize that this verse involves irony. The people of Israel had turned to wooden idols and thought that they would answer them. Van de Born reads: *My people question their piece of wood; their rod gives them relief.* We stay a little closer to the Hebrew text.
(Born, 41)

Verse 12a
people-of-me to-wooden-idol-of-him he-consults
The word *ets* usually means *tree*, *wood*, or *piece of wood*. The NIVIHEOT therefore actually gives an interpretation of the Hebrew text. We refuse to follow in this.
(Andersen and Freedman, 365–66; Harper, 259; Owens, 767; Strong's OT, word 6086)

We read: ***My people turn to their personal piece of wood and consult that***

Verse 12b
and-stick-of-wood-of-him he-answers to-him
Maqqel means *stick*, *staff*, or *rod*. In spite of its odd appearance, we insist on a translation that closely follows the Hebrew text.

Nagad means *to be conspicuous* or *to declare*. It is a type of formal saying and is often translated with *to tell*, very seldom with *to answer*. Literally we read: *he declares for him*. It suggests that the staff speaks, so probably the staff is used as a kind of magic tool. It is commonly called *rhabdomancy*.
(Harper, 259; Reed, 48; Strong's OT, word 4731)

We read: ***and his staff makes a statement for him***

Verse 12c
indeed spirit-of prostitutions he-leads-astray
Ki means *that*, *for*, *because*, or *when*, sometimes *verily*, *indeed*, or *surely*.

We read: *surely the spirit of prostitution leads them astray*

Verse 12d
and-they-are-unfaithful from-after God-of-them
Except the NIV, very few follow the NIVIHEOT. The Hebrew text says: *and they have played the harlot.*

Tachath (NIVIHEOT) means *underneath*. We find it in Genesis 1:7 (KJV)—*under the firmament*—and Genesis 6:17—*from under heaven*. Verse 12d reads, literally, *under their God*. That suggests *under the eyes of God* or *under the rule of God*.
(Brown, 44; Harper, 260; Ogilvie, 80; Strong's OT, word 8478; *Studiebijbel* SBOT 12, 54)

We read: *and they have played the harlot under their God*

The entire sentence:
My people turn to their personal piece of wood and consult that. And his staff makes a statement for him. Surely the spirit of prostitution leads them astray and they have played the harlot under their God.

Verse 13 NASB
They offer sacrifices on the tops of the mountains and burn incense on the hills, under oak, poplar and terebinth, because their shade is pleasant. Therefore your daughters play the harlot and your brides commit adultery.

Verse 13 KJV
They sacrifice upon the tops of the mountains, and burn incense upon the hills, under oaks and poplars and elms, because the shadow thereof is good: therefore your daughters shall commit whoredom, and your spouses shall commit adultery.

Verse 13 NIV
"They sacrifice on the mountaintops and burn offerings on the hills, under oak, poplar and terebinth, where the shade is pleasant. Therefore your daughters turn to prostitution and your daughters-in-law to adultery."

Verse 13 Hebrew Interlinear Text
on tops-of the-mountains they-sacrifice and-on the-hills they-burn-offerings under oak and-poplar and-terebinth for pleasant shade-of-her for this they-turn-to-prostitution daughters-of-you and-daughters-in-law-of-you they-turn-to-adultery

Verse 13a
on tops-of the-mountains they-sacrifice and-on the-hills
The word *qatar* usually refers to the offering of *incense*, that is, a religious rite (Exodus 30:7–9; 40:27). Sometimes the term is translated as *burn/burned* (Leviticus 6:22). Its literal meaning is *to burn incense*. While this may be a form of *sacrifice*, that is not what the Hebrew text actually says.
(Born, 41; Strong's OT, word 6999)

We read: *they sacrifice on the mountaintops and burn incense upon the hills*

Verse 13b
under oak and-poplar and-terebinth for pleasant shade-of-her for this
Many translate *towb* as *agreeable* or *pleasant*.* That is probably wrong. The context places it in the field of choice between good or bad. Israel chooses the wrong direction and considers

idolatry to be good. This meaning is confirmed by ʾal†-kēn‡ = *because of that* or *rightly*.** To express this the right way, we add the words *judged* and *by them* between brackets.
(**Bulkeley, notes on Amos 5:10–13; **Finlay, 124; **Kessler, 170; **Morfix Dictionary; Strong's OT, words *2896, †5921, ‡3651; **Weerd, *Jesaja*, vol. 1, 691)

We read: *for their shade is [judged by them] to be good. Because of that*

Verse 13d
and-daughters-in-law-of-you they-turn-to-adultery
Some render *kallah* as *bride*, which is indeed one of the ways in which the term is used in Scripture. In line with the majority of biblical scholars, however, we opt for the translation *daughters-in-law* (Genesis 11:31; Ruth 1:6; 1 Samuel 4:19).
(Andersen and Freedman, 369; Strong's OT, word 3618; Wolff, 86)

We read: *and your daughters-in-law to adultery*

The entire sentence:
They sacrifice on the mountaintops and burn incense upon the hills; under oak, poplar and, terebinth, for their shade is [judged by them] to be good. Because of that your daughters turn to prostitution and your daughters-in-law to adultery.

Verse 14 NASB
I will not punish your daughters when they play the harlot or your brides when they commit adultery, for the men themselves go apart with harlots and offer sacrifices with temple prostitutes; so the people without understanding are ruined.

Verse 14 KJV
I will not punish your daughters when they commit whoredom, nor your spouses when they commit adultery: for themselves are separated with whores, and they sacrifice with harlots: therefore the people that doth not understand shall fall.

Verse 14 NIV
"I will not punish your daughters when they turn to prostitution, nor your daughters-in-law when they commit adultery, because the men themselves consort with harlots and sacrifice with shrine prostitutes—a people without understanding will come to ruin!"

Verse 14 Hebrew Interlinear Text
not I-will-punish to daughters-of-you when they-turn-to-prostitution or-to daughters-in-law-of-you when they-commit-adultery because they with the-ones-being-harlots they-consort and-with the-shrine-prostitutes they-sacrifice indeed-people not he-understands he-will-come-to-ruin
A nation that does *not understand* is a people *without insight*.
(Yee, 241)

We read:
However, I will not punish your daughters if they commit fornication, nor your daughters-in-law if they commit adultery. Because they [the men] deal with prostitutes and they sacrifice together with the whores of the sanctuary. Verily, a people without insight will be destroyed!

Verse 15 NASB
"Though you, Israel, play the harlot, do not let Judah become guilty; also do not go to Gilgal, or go up to Beth-aven and take the oath: 'As the Lord lives!'"

Verse 15 KJV
*Though thou, Israel, play the harlot, yet let not Judah offend; and come not ye unto Gilgal, neither go ye up to Bethaven, nor swear, The L*ORD *liveth.*

Verse 15 NIV
*"Though you, Israel, commit adultery, do not let Judah become guilty. Do not go to Gilgal; do not go up to Beth Aven. And do not swear, 'As surely as the L*ORD *lives!'"*

Verse 15 Hebrew Interlinear Text
though committing-adultery you Israel not let-him-become-guilty Judah and-not you-go the-Gilgal and-not you-go-up Beth Aven and-not you-swear alive Yahweh

Verse 15a
though committing-adultery <u>you</u> Israel not let-him-become-guilty Judah
This verse builds a contrast. For this reason we have added underlining to the word <u>*you*</u>.

Verse 15c
you-swear alive Yahweh
This might be translated two ways: *as sure as the Yahweh lives* or *by the living God*.
(Brown, 46; Calvijn, *Daniël* II, *Kleine Profeten* I/II, Hosea, 121–22)

We read:
Although <u>you</u> commit adultery, O Israel, do not let Judah become guilty. Do not go to Gilgal. Do not go to Beth Aven and do not swear: as sure as Yahweh lives.

Verse 16 NASB
*Since Israel is stubborn like a stubborn heifer, can the L*ORD *now pasture them like a lamb in a large field?*

Verse 16 KJV
*For Israel slideth back as a backsliding heifer: now the L*ORD *will feed them as a lamb in a large place.*

Verse 16 NIV
*"The Israelites are stubborn, like a stubborn heifer. How then can the L*ORD *pasture them like lambs in a meadow?"*

Verse 16 Hebrew Interlinear Text
indeed like-heifer being-stubborn he-is-stubborn Israel then can-he-pasture-them Yahweh like-lamb in-the-meadow
Many use *meadow* in their translations, but that is an interpretation of the Hebrew source text fueled by the use here of the word *lamb*. Yet the term *merchab* means *open space* in the widest sense of the term. Here, of course, it refers to an *open field*.
(Andersen and Freedman, 377; Strong's OT, word 4800; Stuart, 71)

We read:
Because as a one-year-old cow can be rebellious, Israel is rebellious. How then could Yahweh feed them, like a lamb in the open field?

Verse 17 NASB
Ephraim is joined to idols; let him alone.

Verse 17 KJV
Ephraim is joined to idols: let him alone.

Verse 17 NIV
"Ephraim is joined to idols; leave him alone!"

Verse 17 Hebrew Interlinear Text
one-being-joined-of idols Ephraim leave-alone! to-him
What is remarkable about the final clause here is the use of the pronoun *him* (singular). Accordingly, it is not referring back to the idols, as many exegetes would have it, but to Ephraim (that is, the ten tribes of Israel). For *leave-alone* we might also translate *to leave to*. It would seem that we ought to be interpreting the text to reflect that Ephraim is to be left to his fate due to the idolatry he is committing.
(Brown, 46; Stuart, 71; Ward, 76)

We read:
Ephraim has committed himself to the idols, leave him to his fate!

Verse 18 NASB
Their liquor gone, they play the harlot continually; their rulers dearly love shame.

Verse 18 KJV
Their drink is sour: they have committed whoredom continually: her rulers with shame do love, Give ye.

Verse 18 NIV
"Even when their drinks are gone, they continue their prostitution; their rulers dearly love shameful ways."

Verse 18 Hebrew Interlinear Text
he-is-gone drink-of-them to-commit-prostitution they-commit-prostitution they-love love! shameful-way rulers-of-her

Verse 18a
he-is-gone drink-of-them
In verse 18 many biblical scholars depart from the Hebrew source text in an effort to by-pass the unusual syntax. This is not necessary, however, since two possible solutions present themselves. The first is to translate: *their drink is lost*; the second is to read: *their drink is gone* (Brown reads: *their liquor is gone*; Buss reads: *drinking party*). The latter translation suits the theme of the present chapter better. For there was great economic prosperity under Jeroboam II. Here the end of that prosperity is being announced in poetic fashion, as we have also seen in other verses.
(Brown, 46; Buss, 12; McComiskey, 72; Ward, 81)

We read: ***their drink is gone***

Verse 18b
to-commit-prostitution they-commit-prostitution
The KJV reads: *they have committed whoredom continually*. ESV: *they give themselves to whoring*. ASV: *they play the harlot continually*. Many exegetes and translators offer a similar solution. But they are thus giving an interpretation, because it looks like the Hebrew text says the same thing twice here. Yet that is not so. The first part refers to a continuous

action, the second to the party performing that action. It is a typical Hebrew idiom that we recognize from other places in Scripture.

Stuart reads: *They really love the shame of insolence.* He therefore does take account of the repetition, but like others he also ends up just offering an interpretation. That is not necessary, since it is possible to stick closer to the source text.
(Cheyne, 70; Stuart, 71, 86)

We read: **now they commit adultery for the fornication alone**

Verse 18c
they-love love!
The NIVIHEOT gives here an interpretation. The Hebrew text says: *they play the harlot they made love* (see NASB). Andersen and Freedman speak of immoral sexual activity, thus instead of *love* we would be better to read *sex*.
(Andersen and Freedman, 379; Cheyne, 70)

We read: ***they play the harlot for sex***

Verse 18d
shameful-way rulers-of-her
Also here the NIVIHEOT interprets. It is written *hēḇū qālôwn māḡinnehā*—that is *a love that dishonors her shield*. The keyword is *qalon*—that is *to dishonor* or *to disgrace*. Again, this sentence should be read against the background of the breach in the Sinaitic Covenant. So the shameful acts of Israel took away the protection of God = *her shield*.

The *dishonor* hurts the shield of God.
(Brown, 47; Guenther, 104)

We read: ***a love that hurts her shield***

The entire sentence:
Their drink is gone. Now they commit adultery for the fornication alone. They play the harlot for sex; a love that hurts her shield.

Verse 19 NASB
The wind wraps them in its wings, and they will be ashamed because of their sacrifices.

Verse 19 KJV
The wind hath bound her up in her wings, and they shall be ashamed because of their sacrifices.

Verse 19 NIV
"A whirlwind will sweep them away, and their sacrifices will bring them shame."

Verse 19 Hebrew Interlinear Text
he-will-sweep-away whirlwind her with-wings-of-her and-they-will-bring-shame altars-of-them

Verse 19a
he-will-sweep-away
What the NIVIHEOT offers here is an interpretation; we choose not to follow it. The word *tsarar* means *to envelop* or *to wind around* (meaning a form of wrapping or binding). We likewise find the term used in the sense of *to be worried* or *anxious* or *to suffocate*. Here it

must mean *to wrap*, since Israel is being taken up (after being bound by the Assyrians) and will thereafter be scattered.
(Mays, 76; Strong's OT, word 6887; Stuart, 71)

Verse 19b
whirlwind her with-wings-of-her
The word *ruach* (NIVIHEOT: *whirlwind*) occurs often in the Bible, and most often means *spirit*, although it is also used for *wind* or *windstorm* . The translation is determined by context, which in this case leaves *storm wind* as the only possibility.

Many read: *in/with its wings*, which we follow.
(Strong's OT, word 7307; Wolff, 92)

Verse 19c
and-they-will-bring-shame altars-of-them
The word *zebach* does not mean *altars*, but *sacrifice* (here plural). However, it's clear that worship to idols is meant. So we add *to idols*.
(Strong's OT, word 2077; Brown, Driver, Briggs, 257)

The entire sentence:
A windstorm will wrap her with his wings. Then they will be brought to shame because of their sacrifices [to idols].

Hosea 4:1–19—The corrected text:

Verse 1   *Hear the word of Yahweh, you children of Israel! For Yahweh has a charge against those who live in the land, because there is no faith and no mercy anymore, and there is no knowledge of God in the land.*
Verse 2   *Constantly cursing, deceiving, murdering, and stealing. They break out in committing adultery and bloodshed follows bloodshed.*
Verse 3   *For that reason the country mourns and everything that dwells in her languishes. Even the animals of the field, the birds in the air and the fish in the sea will be taken away.*
Verse 4   *However, do not let a person make a complaint, nor let anyone accuse someone else. For your people are like those who argue with a priest.*
Verse 5   *You stumble every day and even the prophet will stumble, when the night comes over you. Then I will silence your mother.*
Verse 6   *My people have been silenced on account of lack of knowledge, because you, yes, you rejected the godly knowledge. Then I will also reject you from being a priest to Me. Because you rejected the teaching [Torah] of God, I will also reject your children, yes, I.*
Verse 7   *The more they got abundance, the more they sinned against Me. I will have their glory exchanged for shame.*
Verse 8   *Because of the sin of My people, they consume themselves more and more. Their depravity takes along their heart.*
Verse 9   *And it will come to pass, because the priests are equal to the people, that I will punish every one of them for their ways and reward them for their actions.*
Verse 10 *They will eat, but not be satisfied. They will commit adultery, but they will not break through.*
Verse 11 *For they have deserted Yahweh to give themselves to harlotry and to old and new wine, for it captures their hearts.*
Verse 12 *My people turn to their personal piece of wood and consult that. And his staff*

makes a statement for him. Surely the spirit of prostitution leads them astray and they have played the harlot under their God.

Verse 13 *They sacrifice on the mountaintops and burn incense upon the hills; under oak, poplar, and terebinth, for their shade is [judged by them] to be good. Because of that your daughters turn to prostitution and your daughters-in-law to adultery.*

Verse 14 *However, I will not punish your daughters if they commit fornication, nor your daughters-in-law if they commit adultery. Because they [the men] deal with prostitutes and they sacrifice together with the whores of the sanctuary. Verily, a people without insight will be destroyed!*

Verse 15 *Although <u>you</u> commit adultery, O Israel, do not let Judah become guilty. Do not go to Gilgal. Do not go to Beth Aven and do not swear: as sure as Yahweh lives.*

Verse 16 *Because as a one-year-old cow can be rebellious, Israel is rebellious. How then could Yahweh feed them, like a lamb in the open field?*

Verse 17 *Ephraim has committed himself to the idols, leave him to his fate!*

Verse 18 *Their drink is gone. Now they commit adultery for the fornication alone. They play the harlot for sex; a love that hurts her shield.*

Verse 19 *A windstorm will wrap her with his wings. Then they will be brought to shame because of their sacrifices [to idols].*

HOSEA 4
Exegesis

Introduction
In chapter 4 the prophet leaves the theme of the marriage between himself and Gomer, which typified the covenant breach between the people of Israel and God. Only in verse 5 do we find an allusion to his adulterous wife.

In the following verses the prophet Hosea speaks about the judgment on and the destruction of the Northern Kingdom, Israel. He does not go into any detail. Nowhere does he mention specific events like the prophet Ezekiel does (e.g., Ezekiel 8). He speaks in general terms about the coming downfall.

A. Hosea As a Unity
Many exegetes treat Hosea chapter 4 as an independent document. They assume that this part of the book is largely, or even entirely, added later. Thus the first three chapters hardly play any role in their exegesis of Hosea 4. But this largely deprives the prophecy of its strength. For Hosea 1–3 is the foundation on which the rest of this prophetic book rests. The first part of the book determines the framework within which the exegesis of the other chapters can move. McComiskey rightly says:

> Even in this section, however, we are never far from Hosea's marriage, because it is always present in the background and is the catalyst for his message to his people. (McComiskey, 56)

B. A Lawsuit against Israel
The people of Israel are being summoned before the court of God, because the Almighty has a charge against them. In Micah 6:1–16 we find God's point of view and His indictment, which leads to the sentencing. There God speaks in 6:2 (KJV) to the land and the people:

> *Hear ye, O mountains, the* LORD's *controversy, and ye strong foundations of the earth: for the* LORD *hath a controversy with his people, and he will plead with Israel.*

(Weerd, *Micha*, chap. 6, exegesis)

C. The Covenant Broken
The Almighty had made a covenant with all twelve tribes of Israel, which had lasted for centuries. When the two tribes separated from Israel and two nations emerged, Judah (= Judah and Benjamin) and Israel (= the remaining ten tribes), this covenant passed on to both nations. This was not according to God's will. The promise of salvation to Israel applied to a united nation (all twelve tribes), not just to a part of it. There was actually nothing good that could come from this split, as indeed turned out to be the case. First Israel was expelled from the Sinaitic Covenant and with this the kingdom was doomed. Judah followed well over a century later. Jerusalem was destroyed and with this came an end to God's own kingdom on earth.

The book of Hosea speaks about the breach of the Sinaitic Covenant insofar as the ten tribes are concerned. Judah was still included in the covenant. Before we go into the exegesis, we will go deeper into the nature of this covenant.
(See Excursuses 5; 6; 10.)

Excursus 10: The Three Covenants

The origin of the Hebrew word covenant (*berit*) is uncertain. It seems to be related to the word *bara*, what means *to eat*. In ancient times it represented a kind of *eating community*, which was a traditional way of fraternizing. We distinguish three covenants:

10.a The Abrahamic covenant

The covenant between God and Israel in its earliest form was a covenant between God and the patriarch of Israel, Abraham (Genesis 15:9–21; 17:7–14). In this covenant God promised, among other things, land (Genesis 15:18 NASB):

> *On that day the L*ORD *made a covenant with Abram, saying, "To your descendants I have given this land, from the river of Egypt as far as the great river, the river Euphrates."*

And see Genesis 17:7–8 (NASB):

> 7 *"I will establish My covenant between Me and you and your descendants after you throughout their generations for an everlasting covenant, to be God to you and to your descendants after you.*
> 8 *"I will give to you and to your descendants after you, the land of your sojournings, all the land of Canaan, for an everlasting possession; and I will be their God."*

We call this the Abrahamic covenant. This covenant was renewed to each of the patriarchs, to Isaac (Genesis 26:3–5) and to Jacob (Genesis 28:13–14). The covenant was confirmed with a divine oath. Thus it was a one-sided covenant, originating with God and guaranteed by Him. On his deathbed, Jacob—who then also bore the name Israel (Genesis 32:28)—transferred this blessing to the two sons of Joseph (Genesis 48:13–20) and to the other eleven brothers of Joseph (Genesis 49:28).

The Abrahamic covenant did *not* depend on the goodwill of two parties. It was a *one-sided promise* from God that *could not be undone*.

10.b The Sinaitic Covenant

The Abrahamic covenant was given a constitution by the law that was given to Moses on Mount Sinai (also called Horeb; Exodus 20–23) and officially ratified there (Exodus 24). We call that the Sinaitic Covenant. It was a commitment that had been ratified with an oath by two parties, God and Israel. So it could not be revoked unilaterally. It contained rights, obligations, and blessings. The duties consisted in keeping God's laws and completely renouncing foreign gods. In addition, Israel was to maintain the service of God in the tabernacle, later the temple service (Exodus 25–30), and to govern the land allotted to them according to God's directives (Leviticus 25).

The Sinaitic Covenant did not apply only to the people of Israel but also to the land of Canaan, which in fact became God's property. This created the relationship of landowner and tenants, as is clear from Matthew 20:1–16 and 21:33–41 for example. As a kind of holy landowner, the Almighty made sure that the land was blessed. He was more powerful than any hostile army and guaranteed fertility. So Israel had nothing to fear, provided they obeyed God and faithfully served Him (Leviticus 25).

The holy landowner let the country be governed through a council of elders, judges, and prophets. Later the kings were added, but they were in fact also like judges who acted in God's name.

In addition, there was also God's special connection with Jerusalem, the city which He had chosen as His residence. The presence of the Shekhina of God (the glory of the Lord) in the temple was a guarantee of this. The special status of Jerusalem was an important component of the Sinaitic Covenant. When that covenant was broken unilaterally by Israel, the special status of Jerusalem came to an end and both the city and the temple were destroyed. (Read also: Deuteronomy 12:5, 11; 1 Kings 8:12–21; Psalms 46, 48, 76; 78:68–69; 132:12–18; Isaiah 2:2–4; 14:32.)

10.c The Davidic covenant
And finally there was the covenant with king David. This too was a one-sided covenant. The Almighty had promised that king David and his descendants would have eternal rights to the throne of Israel. Even if a king was subject to a foreign power, such as Assyria or Babylon, the promise remained. That subordination was not a violation of the covenant but a temporary punishment for a period in which the people of Israel had left their God.

When the Sinaitic Covenant ended and Judah perished, the royal house of David also disappeared from the stage. This was and is a temporary interruption. The promise that a king from the house of David will once again rule over Israel in Canaan remains unchanged. It is yet to be fulfilled in the future, even today. So the Davidic covenant was not abolished but suspended! (Read also: 2 Samuel 7:12–17; Isaiah 9:6; 7:13–14; 11:9–10; Ezekiel 34:23–25; 37:24–26; Amos 9:11–15.)

10.d The Messianic Kingdom postponed
According to Jeremiah, the exile in Babylon (which was the second punishment God imposed in addition to the destruction of the land of Judah and the city of Jerusalem) would last seventy years.* The return afterward was in principle intended to restore the original kingdom of King Solomon.† Unfortunately, only a small part of the people of Judah responded to the call of God to return—according to Ezra 2:64 and Nehemiah 7:66 no more than 42,360 persons.‡

The mass refusal to return to Canaan nullified, at least for the moment, the promise of full restoration. It was moved to the future.** The prophet Daniel then received the prophecy of the seventy weeks of years, in which the death of the Messiah, Jesus Christ, is also foretold.

The coming of the Messiah was the next opportunity for the restoration of the Messianic Kingdom.†† Unfortunately, the Jews rejected Jesus. Then He turned to converted Gentiles and thus established the church of Christ. With that, the arrival of the Messianic Kingdom was postponed again, now until the end time.
(Weerd, *Daniël*, vol. 1, 393–94; vol. 2, †7–12, ††234–46, 247; Weerd, *Zacharia*, ‡22–23, **103)
(See also *Jeremiah 25:11b–12; 27:7; 29:10.)

10.e A new covenant: The Messianic Kingdom
The promises of salvation to the house of David did not lapse with the temporary breaking of the Davidic covenant. The Abrahamic covenant also remained in force; it will be valid forever (Genesis 17:7). They are both postponed to a future date. This is why believing Jews still look forward to the coming of the Messiah and the establishment of the Messianic Kingdom. Then a new covenant will replace the old Sinaitic Covenant, and this new covenant will never be broken again.

10.f Two covenants remain
There were three covenants: one is now abolished; two remain as promises for the future. However, two important conditions must be fulfilled before these promises can be fulfilled.
1. A future repentance and conversion of the people of Israel (Leviticus 26:40, 45; Deuteronomy 30:3–5).

2. The Messiah must come to claim His kingship (Zechariah 14:4).
(Read also: Isaiah 2:2–4; 9:6; 11:9; Jeremiah 23:3–6; 30:9; 31:33; Ezekiel 37:19–28; 45; Luke 1:32–33)
(See Annotations 1D; 2A; Excursuses 7; 9; 13.)

Verse 1
Hear the word of Yahweh, you children of Israel! For Yahweh has a charge against those who live in the land, because there is no faith and no mercy anymore, and there is no knowledge of God in the land.
This prophecy does not address the nation as a whole. It is a personal message for all inhabitants of the Northern Kingdom, Israel.

1.1 Basic concepts in Hosea
Three concepts, as we find also in the other prophetic books, play a central role in this verse and in the book of Hosea:

 a. Faithfulness—By this the prophet means faithfulness to the Sinaitic Covenant with God. By turning to idols, Israel has broken this covenant.

 b. Mercy—This concept refers to the distorted relationships among people in Israel. The kingdom of the Ten Tribes had become a very hard, capitalistic society. The country knew great prosperity, but at the same time there was great poverty. A large number of people had hardly any food. Capriciousness and abuse of power ran rampant. Justice was for sale and had therefore degenerated into injustice. In practice it was only available to the rich.

 c. Knowledge of God—The people of Israel were no longer obedient to God's laws (the Torah). They had brought in other gods. With this, completely different rules entered society. The result was a profound moral lawlessness. There was no mechanism left that could stop the decay. Israel had strayed so far away that the knowledge of God had disappeared.

1.2 A lawsuit with a predictable verdict
Verse 1 shows in a few words how far the people of Israel had gone downhill. The tone is that of an indictment in a lawsuit in which the verdict is already certain. We find this in Micah 1:6–7 (NASB):

6 *For I will make Samaria a heap of ruins in the open country, planting places for a vineyard. I will pour her stones down into the valley and will lay bare her foundations.*
7 *All of her idols will be smashed, all of her earnings will be burned with fire, and all of her images I will make desolate. For she collected them from a harlot's earnings, and to the earnings of a harlot they will return.*

When the Almighty speaks, it is in very clear language. The prophecy of Micah was fulfilled to the letter.
(Kidner, 46–47; Limburg, 15–16; Smith, 83)

Verse 2
Constantly cursing, deceiving, murdering, and stealing. They break out in committing adultery and bloodshed follows bloodshed.
At the time of Jeroboam II, society experienced great economic prosperity. Unfortunately, this did not benefit the entire population. There were many poor people. The great contrasts between rich and poor caused great tensions in Israel. The upper class of the population,

however, pretended to be deaf, and overindulged in violence, immorality, and alcoholism. Typically this society was morally debauched, although they were outwardly very rich. Such a society usually stands at the edge of the abyss and this was indeed the case here. (Flanders, Crapps, and Smith, 350–51; Guenther, 92)

2.1 The prophets' warning
We find similar prophecies in the books of Amos and Micah.

Amos 3:10 (NASB)
"But they do not know how to do what is right," declares the LORD, *"these who hoard up violence and devastation in their citadels."*

Amos 4:1 (NASB)
Hear this word, you cows of Bashan who are on the mountain of Samaria, who oppress the poor, who crush the needy, who say to your husbands, "Bring now, that we may drink!"

Micah 2:1–2 (NASB)
1 *Woe to those who scheme iniquity, who work out evil on their beds! When morning comes, they do it, for it is in the power of their hands.*
2 *They covet fields and then seize them, and houses, and take them away. They rob a man and his house, a man and his inheritance.*

(Dee and Schoneveld, vol. 2, 316; Weerd, *Micha*, 125–26)

Verse 3
For that reason the country mourns and everything that dwells in her languishes. Even the animals of the field, the birds in the air and the fish in the sea will be taken away.
The prophet describes poetically a state of general upheaval.

3.1 A warning for the present
We can also take this text to heart in our own society. There is *cursing, deceiving, murdering,* and *stealing* in our country also. People *indulge in adultery* (v. 2) and animals, birds and fish die in a heavily stressed environment. We may be slowly but surely making improvements toward recovery of the environment. However, this only applies to a limited number of countries. In the majority of the world, nature is still sacrificed on the altar of economic progress.

3.2 The prophecy of Moses
When the blessing was withheld from Israel and the people of Israel went into exile, the land pined away and became a waste. This was the fulfillment of the prophecy of Moses in Deuteronomy 28:15–20 (NASB):

15 *"But it shall come about, if you do not obey the* LORD *your God, to observe to do all His commandments and His statutes with which I charge you today, that all these curses will come upon you and overtake you:*
16 *"Cursed shall you be in the city, and cursed shall you be in the country.*
17 *"Cursed shall be your basket and your kneading bowl.*
18 *"Cursed shall be the offspring of your body and the produce of your ground, the increase of your herd and the young of your flock.*
19 *"Cursed shall you be when you come in, and cursed shall you be when you go out.*
20 *"The* LORD *will send upon you curses, confusion, and rebuke, in all you undertake to do, until you are destroyed and until you perish quickly, on account of the evil of your deeds, because you have forsaken Me."*

Verse 4a
However, do not let a person make a complaint, nor let anyone accuse someone else.
There is no excuse for the people of Israel to be falling into sin. Nobody can or may say: That person or this person is at fault; anybody else but me. All are declared guilty. An entire people stand accused in the dock.
(Rosenberg, vol. 1, 208)

Verse 4b
For your people are like those who argue with a priest.
The true priests of God had no authority anymore. They no longer stood above the people but had become vulnerable. A true priest was a servant of God who carried out His commandments. Bringing charges against a priest was therefore an accusation addressed to God. Deuteronomy 17:12 (NASB) says:

> *"The man who acts presumptuously by not listening to the priest who stands there to serve the LORD your God, nor to the judge, that man shall die; thus you shall purge the evil from Israel."*

(Calvijn, *Daniël* II, *Kleine Profeten* I/II, Hosea, 101–2; Reed, 47)

Verse 5a
You stumble every day
The sad conclusion is that the people of Israel are continually sinning heavily. It has become their daily practice.

Verse 5b
and even the prophet will stumble, when the night comes over you
It is not immediately clear what the prophet Hosea means here. The prophecy probably looks at the coming demise of Israel, described here as *night*. With the fall of Israel as an independent nation, the service of God, as maintained and promoted by the priests, the Levites (see verse 6) and the prophets, also disappeared. Thus from a spiritual perspective it became *night*!

Verse 5c
Then I will silence your mother.
The use of *mother* here refers to the united nation of Israel—Judah and the kingdom of the Ten Tribes or Israel—as does Ezekiel 19:2; 23:2–4 (two daughters of the same mother). Other theologians speak of Gomer, the wife of Hosea. But that leads us to the same meaning, because Gomer represents godless Israel. This is an example of how Hosea's prophecy is very precise, as the ten-tribe nation of Israel did disappear into the mist of history—they have indeed been silenced.
(McComiskey, 60; Reed, 48)

Verse 6a
My people have been silenced on account of lack of knowledge,
This is a familiar text that often resounds from pulpits all over the world. It is also very true and is constantly confirmed, even in our time.

Knowledge of the Bible gives knowledge of God. It is only through this that individual faith in God can be rightly formed. And this knowledge will always leads to a better society. Of course, not everyone is able to take in that knowledge, but for that reason spiritual leaders have been given to us. They can and must take the hands those who are not able to study the Bible or lack the mental ability to do so and lead them to God.

In the time of the prophet Hosea those leaders were no longer there, or they themselves had abandoned God. Thus the teaching (*torah*) of the people of God disappeared and thereby also the corrective mechanism that guarded the moral state of God's people. When the inhibitions disappeared, the arbitrariness of human self-indulgence came to the surface—hedonism is what we call it—which is also the disease of our time. As a result, society quickly decayed and corrupt pagan religions took the empty place left by the abandoned service to God.
(Ironside, 35; Rosenberg, vol. 1, 24)

Verse 6b
because you, yes, you rejected the godly knowledge. Then I will also reject you from being a priest to Me. Because you rejected the teaching [Torah] of God,
Some assume that only the priestly class is addressed here. That explanation, however, is based on a faulty interpretation of verse 4b. Hosea 4 is entirely dedicated to the judgment on the people of Israel, and thus here also.

In Hosea's time, the vast majority of the priestly class in Israel was in the service of the state. Their highest chief was therefore the king. This is in contrast to the priestly service in Judah and Jerusalem, which was independent. The cult in the Northern Kingdom was concentrated around the shrines at Bethel and Gilgal, where the bull calves stood. From the beginning the prophets saw this as idolatry and therefore strongly condemned it. Moreover, the priests at these shrines were appointed by King Jeroboam I (not by God), so they did not come from the tribe of Levi (except perhaps for some defectors). It is very likely that the true priests of God, after a while, went to Judah/Jerusalem and virtually disappeared from the Northern Kingdom. (Read also: 1 Kings 12:25–33; 13:33–34; 2 Chronicles 11:13–15)
(See Excursus 11.)

6.1 Israel as a priestly kingdom
Israel had made an agreement with the Almighty God, called the Sinaitic Covenant. That is why this people was different from the gentile people and why they were called God's people. Exodus 19:6 (NASB) says it like this:

> *"'And you shall be to Me a kingdom of priests and a holy nation.' These are the words that you shall speak to the sons of Israel."*

Israel rejected the knowledge of God and turned to the idols. With that they broke the covenant. Then the Almighty put an end to the priesthood that served Him and turned away from His children—the people of Israel.
(Andersen and Freedman, 350; McComiskey, 61)
(See Annotations 1G; 2A; Excursus 9.)

Verse 6c
I will also reject your children, yes, I.
The prophet is still speaking to Gomer/Israel. *Your children* are therefore all members of the people of Israel. The people as a whole are being rejected. The importance of the moment is accentuated by the repetition of *I—yes, I—*Yahweh.
(Andersen and Freedman, 354; McComiskey, 61)

Verse 7a
The more they got abundance, the more they sinned against Me.
This verse outlines a familiar image. Increasing prosperity does not lead to God, but most often away from God. For it suggests man-made success, in the material sense, and with that the "omnipotence" of man. This was also the case in Israel. If God's laws are ignored, the inhibitions with respect to a sinful way of life will fade away. Then moral decay will strike.

Verse 7b
I will have their glory exchanged for shame.
The *glory* of Israel was based on the Sinaitic Covenant. The temple (also called *glory*) was the visible part of it. These distinguished the people of Israel as a whole (all twelve tribes) from the surrounding gentile nations. The *shame* refers to the breach of the Sinaitic Covenant. The fact that this breach resulted in the destruction of Israel by Assyria, the destruction of Judah by Babylon, and was followed by the devastation of the temple (*the glory*), was only a consequence.

Verse 8
Because of the sin of My people, they consume themselves more and more. Their depravity takes along their heart.
Some explain this text to mean that sin has gotten such a strong grip on the people that they actually enjoy it. This is nothing new; we also see it in our society. A well-known Dutch poet recently said*: *I love black, because it symbolizes the dark side of our society. And that's the only interesting thing, isn't it?* This poet meant what he said. I feel sorry for him, because, clearly, he does not know any better. He has no knowledge of real love and happiness.

When a sense of sin disappears and God is discarded, only raw and hollow forms of happiness remain—the gratification of the self (in whatever form), power, and lust. We also know that severe forms of sin always lead to destruction. And if depravity dwells in the heart of man, it also leads to the loss of the soul. This is, in essence, the message we encounter here.
(*Quoting Jules Deelder, Rotterdam, 2017; Kidner, 50; Limburg, 20)

Verse 9
And it will come to pass, because the priests are equal to the people, that I will punish every one of them for their ways and reward them for their actions.
The general view is that this points to abuses among the priests and the Levites, that is, the servants of God. That is unlikely, however, because the priests who served at Gilgal and Bethel, were not real priests of God. They were not even Levites (1 Kings 12:31). It is therefore much more logical to assume that the prophet is emphasizing that there is no difference between the priests and the people of Israel, that they are both judged by the same criteria.

Referring to Leviticus 21–22, as many do, is therefore unjustified. It appears from that text that the priests and Levites were subject to different laws than the people. But those were real priests, from the tribe of Levi. Here we have lay priests, neither appointed nor recognized by God.
(See Excursus 6.)

9.1 Eschatology
Andersen and Freedman call the opening of verse 9 (as well as vv. 10–11!) eschatological. And we agree with that. The prophet prophesies about the future. That future starts with the downfall of Israel and lasts until the present day. During this entire period, the people of Israel (the Ten Tribes) are judged by the same criteria.
(Andersen and Freedman, 359–60; Calvijn, *Daniël* II, *Kleine Profeten* I/II, Hosea, 111–12; Harper, 258; Mays, 71; McComiskey, 63–64; Reed, 48)

Verse 10
They will eat, but not be satisfied. They will commit adultery, but they will not break through.
It is clear that the prophet Hosea expresses himself here in poetic terms. The tenor of

prophecy is that no progress whatsoever can be expected. The people will lead a dormant existence in the centuries ahead and that blocks a future salvation. And the fate of Israel can only be changed by a radical event—a real *breakthrough*. That will be the second coming of Jesus Christ.

Verse 11
For they have deserted Yahweh to give themselves to harlotry and to old and new wine, for it captures their hearts.
There is no reservation in the judgment on Israel. The prophet speaks about what is to come and looks back from there: *For they have deserted Yahweh*.

Verse 11 sketches once again the social relations in Israel that led to the downfall. The pursuit of self-interest and pleasure was the ultimate motive. Love is hard to find in such a society. This is why, with drink (and in our time also drugs) and numbing noise, we try to avoid really thinking about and thus becoming aware of our miserable state.

11.1 The road to Satan
Verse 11 is, in fact, a very penetrating prophecy. The purpose of eating and drinking is maintaining the body. That this also leads to a form of pleasure is clear and there is, in itself, nothing wrong with that, unless food and drink only serve to caress the senses. Then pleasure has become an end in itself, and one never becomes sated again.

The same applies to sexuality. The Almighty gave marriage for that, and the sexual act itself must, in essence, always be connected with love for one another. The crowning of the act is the birth of children. Here, however, we see sexuality without love. The only motive is the stimulation of senses, the pursuit of short-lived pleasure. But that is a sliding boundary line that goes further and further down to the extreme. And at the end of that road we encounter Satan.

Verse 12
My people turn to their personal piece of wood and consult that. And his staff makes a statement for him. Surely the spirit of prostitution leads them astray and they have played the harlot under their God.
With verse 12 the prophet returns to the reality of his own time. At first glance verse 12a seems strange. However, we must take into consideration that pagan idols, especially house gods, were mostly made of wood. Van de Born therefore supposes that the expression *piece of wood* was a nickname for the Asheras or for any idols. The prophet speaks disdainfully about these pieces of wood—the dead idols.
(Birch, 55; Born, 41; McComiskey, 66)

Verse 12b
And his staff makes a statement for him
This is called *rhabdomancy*. It was a pagan practice to read the will of the gods from the pattern in which rods or sticks fell (a bit similar to the famous game of Mikado, however with larger sticks).
(Edelkoort, 183; Rosenberg, vol. 1, 210; Wood, 187)

Verse 13
They sacrifice on the mountaintops and burn incense upon the hills; under oak, poplar, and terebinth, for their shade is [judged by them] to be good. Because of that your daughters turn to prostitution and your daughters-in-law to adultery.

Pagan shrines and altars were usually built on the tops of hills and mountains in Israel. It was assumed that people could thus come closer to the gods, which, it was thought, increased the chance that the sacrifices would be accepted.

The idolatry of that time was strongly interwoven with sexual acts. When the service to God was replaced by idolatry, it became quite normal that the daughters and the daughters-in-law surrendered themselves to fornication and adultery. It was a substitute for a whorehouse—a free ticket to sexual immorality.
(Birch, 56–57; McComiskey, 67; Walvoord and Zuck, 1390)

Verse 14
However, I will not punish your daughters if they commit fornication, nor your daughters-in-law if they commit adultery. Because they [the men] deal with prostitutes and they sacrifice together with the whores of the sanctuary. Verily, a people without insight will be destroyed!
Cultic prostitution was a very common phenomenon among the pagan nations. It was not limited to temple prostitutes. Men and women from the people also took part in the rites. According to pagan standards, however, this was not fornication, but part of their religion. At the time of King Jeroboam II, it had found general acceptance in Israel.

14.1 Lack of knowledge
The daughters and daughters-in-law are not punished for their lewd acts. They do not know better because they do not know God anymore. They are not to blame, but rather the leaders of the people who failed in their task.
(Edelkoort, 183n51; Rosenberg, vol. 1, 210; Walvoord and Zuck, 1390)

Verse 15
Although you commit adultery, O Israel, do not let Judah become guilty. Do not go to Gilgal. Do not go to Beth Aven and do not swear: as sure as Yahweh lives.
Gilgal and Beth Aven refer to Gilgal and Bethel. These two cities were in the north and south of Israel respectively. Originally, important schools of the prophets were established there (2 Kings 2:1–2; 4:38).

Gilgal and Bethel were also the cities where King Jeroboam I founded a surrogate temple service. He tried to keep his subjects from going to Jerusalem every year to pay homage to God in the temple. He formed two golden calves as seen here in 1 Kings 12:25–28 (NASB):

25 *Then Jeroboam built Shechem in the hill country of Ephraim, and lived there. And he went out from there and built Penuel.*
26 *Jeroboam said in his heart, "Now the kingdom will return to the house of David.*
27 *"If this people go up to offer sacrifices in the house of the* LORD *at Jerusalem, then the heart of this people will return to their lord, even to Rehoboam king of Judah; and they will kill me and return to Rehoboam king of Judah."*
28 *So the king consulted, and made two golden calves, and he said to them, "It is too much for you to go up to Jerusalem; behold your gods, O Israel, that brought you up from the land of Egypt."*

King Jeroboam built two shrines, one at Bethel and the other at Dan, in Gilgal (1 Kings 12:28–32). The prophets have always condemned this idolatry and called it *the sin of Jeroboam*.

Bethel was the more important of the two cities. This is called *Beth Aven* in verse 15 (what means: *house of the idol*). So within the name lies the judgment of God.

(King, 97; McComiskey, 70; Pfeiffer, Vos, and Rea, 221–23 and 684; Rosenberg, vol. 1, 28; Wood, 188) (See Excursus 11.)

Verse 15b
do not let Judah become guilty
It is not really clear what these words mean. Rabbinical writings suggest that the city of Bethel exercised a great attraction to the Judean population (it was on the border) and that this warning is against those of Judah who were venturing into Israel in Bethel. The Bible does not say any more about it.

A second possibility is that this prophecy sees into the future, when Judah would also be in captivity (in Babylon). Zechariah 7:2–3 speaks about a delegation from Bethel, which came to consult the priests and prophets in Jerusalem about theological issues. In Zechariah's time there was still a sanctuary in Bethel, the image of the calf had been removed. So the people of Judah were somehow involved with the worship practices in Bethel.
(King, 40–41)

Excursus 11: The Sin of Jeroboam

11.a The temple in Jerusalem was a threat.
King Jeroboam was the first king of the ten-tribe kingdom, Israel. He feared the attraction of the temple in Jerusalem, which was in Judah. That was the country where his rival king, Rehoboam, reigned, who would like to recapture Israel in order to restore the kingdom of his father Solomon.

To keep his subjects from visiting the temple (which Jeroboam saw as a threat to his position) he built two sanctuaries, at Bethel and Gilgal. In each a golden bull calf was placed, which the people had to worship. In name he claimed to serve God, but in fact it was idolatry. This cunning combination of service to God mixed with pagan idolatry had been condemned sharply by the prophets right from the start. It is known in the Bible as *the sin of Jeroboam* (1 Kings 12:28–29).

Under King Ahab and Queen Jezebel, the idolatry of Jeroboam was mixed with the Baal cult, which was even more detestable in God's eyes. Even the appearance of service to the true God was no longer upheld.

After the downfall of the kingdom of the Ten Tribes, the idolatry with the bull calves continued to exist. Only under King Josiah were the idolatrous idols destroyed in the southern priestly city of Bethel, as were the shrines in Samaria (2 Kings 23:15, 19–20). Yet the cult was not eradicated. In Bethel there was still a kind of sanctuary of idolatry—a residue of what was—along with an (official) service to God. It remained in function into the time of Ezra and Nehemiah. The sanctuary in Dan remained unharmed. This was presumably destroyed only during the campaign of King Nebuchadnezzar against Judah, in 587/586 BC.

11.b The priest were not Levites.
King Jeroboam did not appoint priests from the tribe of Levi, as God had commanded, but from all layers of the population (1 Kings 12:31). The service to God was rendered impossible for the true priests and Levites (2 Chronicles 11:14). So they left Israel. They gave up

their houses and possessions and went to live in Judah, where they could serve Yahweh properly (2 Chronicles 11:13–16).

11.c The nation rebelled against God.
The division of Solomon's kingdom into two kingdoms, one with two tribes, the other with ten, was unnatural. Although politically speaking there were two countries, Israel and Judah, there was initially only one spiritual center, Jerusalem. The temple was meant for all twelve tribes. In that way, they were still one people. They were divided into two by the construction of the shrines with the bull calves at Dan and Bethel. This idolatry was the true rebellion against God, and when the Almighty was actually renounced by the Ten Tribes.

Verse 16
Because as a one-year-cow can be rebellious, Israel is rebellious. How then could Yahweh feed them, like a lamb in the open field?
With verse 16, God lays down the purpose of His dealings with Israel. Yahweh wants to pasture them, to lead them. Only then can His people come to their destiny. That did not happen. Israel is *rebellious* and has turned to idols (verse 17).

Excursus 12: Israel Becomes Ephraim

12.a A turning point in history
With verse 17 we have arrived at a turning point in the history between God and the Ten Tribes. The kingdom of the Ten Tribes has turned away from Yahweh and has definitively turned to the idols. This led to the breaking of the Sinaitic Covenant and therefore it says in verse 17: *leave him to his fate!*

Some exegetes consider verse 17 to have been corrupted. The problem is not the Hebrew text, which is not difficult to translate, but the exegesis. They cannot fit the text into their own viewpoints. Others gloss over verse 17 almost without comment. That too is, in my view, incorrect. Verse 17 marks a very important moment in the history of salvation. (Ward, 80–81)

12.b No longer worthy of the name of honor
With verse 17 we move, theologically speaking, to a new situation. In Hosea 1–3 the Ten Tribes were still called Israel, but now that name is replaced with that of the largest tribe of the Northern Kingdom: Ephraim. There is a reason for this. With the breaking of the Sinaitic Covenant between God and the Ten Tribes, this people lost their special status as God's people. The Almighty was, after all, their great King and He was the source of all blessings. When the people of Israel served God, it knew prosperity and God fought for them when it was threatened. We see this in the name Israel (= *God battles back*, or others translate *God stands firm* or *God gets the upper hand*).

With the statement Lo-Ammi (*not My people*, Hosea 1:9) the Sinaitic Covenant was broken. With this the Almighty distanced Himself from the ten tribes of Israel. They are no longer worthy of the honorary name *Israel*, for they have attached themselves to the idols (verse 17). God no longer fights for the people of the Ten Tribes, but leaves them to their fate. From now on they are called Ephraim.

Sources:
(Calvijn, *Daniel* II, *Kleine Profeten* I/II, Hosea, 128–29; Ironside, 40–41; Pfeiffer, Vos, Rea, 863; Strong's OT, words 410, 3478, 8280; Stuart, 85)
(See Annotation 2A.)

Verse 17
Ephraim has committed himself to the idols, leave him to his fate!
The Almighty now takes His hands off that part of Israel. He no longer battles for them. Henceforth the Northern Kingdom is called Ephraim, and in the order of salvation it is no different than any nation from the gentiles. With that conclusion God leaves this people to their fate.
(Ironside, 39; Rosenberg, vol. 1, 29, 211)
(See Excursus 12.)

17.1 An irrevocable judgment
The people of Israel no longer have a possibility of conversion. The judgment is final and is carried out by powerful Assyria.

The two-tribe kingdom, Judah, got a second chance. It was allowed to return to Canaan after the Babylonian exile. The people of Israel, however, disappeared into the mists of history.
(McComiskey, 71–72)

Verse 18
The drink is gone. Now they commit adultery for the fornication alone. They play the harlot for sex; a love that hurts her shield.
Here too we have to take into account the poetic undertone of Hosea 4. Because with the expression *the drink is gone*, the prophet renders a judgment on the prosperity of Israel. It is now coming to an end; the riotous party is over.

The decline of Israel began in the wake of Jeroboam II. When he died, he was succeeded by King Zechariah, who ruled for only six months and was then assassinated. From that time on, the Northern Kingdom quickly fell into decline. Only thirty-one years after the death of Jeroboam II, in 722 BC, the kingdom perished when Samaria was taken by the Assyrians.
(Hosea 1:1b, Exegesis)

18.1 Nothing has changed
The words of God, spoken by His prophet Hosea, have apparently left little impression on His people. The warning and the spreading decay were ignored. The upper class of the population could afford a few financially bad years. So they happily continued their debauched way of life. But they were dancing on a volcano.

Verse 19a
A windstorm will wrap her up with his wings.
The announced judgment is executed. A *windstorm* comes, the Assyrians, who wipe Israel (*her*) off the map.

The Assyrians were an exceptionally cruel people. Being defeated by them usually brought a bloodbath among the population; so also here. Those who survived the war were taken captive (Hosea describes this poetically with the expression *wrap her with her wings*). Thus Israel/Ephraim perished and disappeared from sacred history.
(Wood, 187–88)

Verse 19b
Then they will be brought to shame because of their sacrifices [to idols].
It seems obvious to think here first of the altars of the shrines in Gilgal and Bethel, where the golden bull calves stood. A second explanation is that it pointed to the horrible idolatrous practice in Israel of sacrificing living children.
(See Annotation 5A; Excursus 11.)

Annotation 4A: Hosea in Our Time

During the study of the book of Hosea, and especially of those verses that deal with the sins of the people of Israel, I regularly got the impression that the prophet is not only talking about his own time, but also about our present society. There are very striking similarities. We will mention several here.

In our society fornication also plays an increasingly prominent role. There are no moral obstacles anymore when it comes to the satisfaction of sexual desire (see Hosea 4:11):

> For they have deserted Yahweh to give themselves to harlotry and to old and new wine, for they take the heart.

Judicial courts are still fairly reliable, but it does matter greatly whether you have enough money for a good lawyer and sometimes the law is even for sale.

In a moral and religious respect, the judges constantly broaden their standards. Once it was forbidden to mock the Christian faith and/or insult God. Today it seems to be a popular pastime, and swearing has become a socially accepted weakness, or a colorful habit (see Hosea 4:2a):

> *Constantly cursing, deceiving, murdering, and stealing.*

The protection of life no longer depends on God's Word but on what we judge as right. That appears to be a sliding scale without a limit. Abortion has become very common and euthanasia is only a variant option on various forms of the termination of life. In this we recognize the service to the idol of Moloch, in which people (especially children) were sacrificed (see Hosea 5:2):

> *The apostates have sunk deep in their bloodbaths*

And—worst of all—the knowledge of God disappears, and with it the dam that protects us from further degradation (see Hosea 4:6):

> *My people have been silenced on account of lack of knowledge, because you, yes, you rejected the godly knowledge. Then I will also reject you and your priesthood to Me. Because you rejected the teaching [Torah] of God, I will also reject your children, yes, I.*

Today it is hardly possible for a Christian to avoid evil influences. Garish sultry advertising decorates bus shelters and billboards. You cannot ignore them even if you want to. And every time we drive past, it suggests to us that these images show the "normal" world. Turning on a television often means an unwanted confrontation with pornography. There are always stations that broadcast that kind of entertainment, sometimes even early in the evening. Game shows are made exciting by separating partners and allowing them to be tempted: provoked adultery as a spectacle for millions. And ingenious computer games train our children to kill people (see Hosea 4:2b):

> *They break out in committing adultery and bloodshed follows bloodshed.*

There is only one satisfactory solution—Hosea 6:1:

> *Come and let us turn to Yahweh!*

(Boice, *The Minor Prophets*, 14–15)

HOSEA 5
Hebrew Text Translation

Introduction

For this chapter we could use the same foreword included with Hosea 4 Hebrew Text Translation, since the translation problems are similar.

In chapter 4 the prophet Hosea speaks about a lawsuit of the heavenly court against the people of the Northern Kingdom, Israel. He continues in the present chapter, albeit in this case more generally. For Hosea prophesies about the destiny of the entire people of Israel (in the old sense of the term, referring to all twelve tribes). The chapter closes with an open ending, since the prophesy of verse 15 has certainly not been fulfilled to this very day.

A. Textual Corruption

Translators and exegetes tend to doubt the reliability of the various source texts for Hosea. Five or six decades ago there would have been good reason for this, given the considerable divergences and obscure passages in various source texts. Today, however, there is much less reason to doubt the Hebrew text.

These days we can say with a certain degree of certainty—thanks in part to the discovery of ancient scrolls near the Dead Sea—that we have come very close to the original Hebrew text. And we have also learned that the Leningrad codex is the most important of the source texts.

The new developments have mainly influenced the way we translate the Old Testament. Our base is no longer a compilation of source texts. But we still need to be careful how we translate the Hebrew text—therein lies the key to a good translation. Few Bible scholars, however, have imprinted this on their minds. That is not because they are unaware of the new developments in this field, but because the latest results of scholarship mainly serve to increase the divine aura of biblical prophecy—and they can't stand that.

A careful, literal translation offers many details (which find confirmation in other prophetic books of the Bible). Therefore it is very unlikely that it is human product; there must be a godly source.

However, if this thesis is to serve as the basis for an explanation of the book of Hosea, it necessarily implies that human interference must take a big step back. We may no longer just delete, change, or add to the Hebrew source text. As such, Bible scholars become no more than modest listeners, who hear the sacred words of God. No longer can they rewrite parts of the Bible to fit their own theology or proposed story. It is no longer "Once upon a time . . ." but "What precisely does the prophet say?" (or in other words, "What does the Almighty God say?"!). Few are content with such a position, and so they *still* do not hesitate to change the Hebrew source text to support their own exegesis.

B. There Is Logic in Godly Prophecy!

In this commentary the source text is followed closely. See what happens then! The resulting text will show itself to have both structure and logic! As we have noted elsewhere, seeing the logic of the text is an indication that we are nearing the true meaning of the Hebrew text.

C. Israel and Ephraim

One of the most intriguing aspects of Hosea 5 is the parallel use of the names Israel and Ephraim. In chapter 1 the name of Israel was used for the Ten Tribes (with the exception of verse 10). Yet there is no doubt that the name Ephraim also occurs as a reference to the Ten Tribes. Most exegetes explain this phenomenon as poetic license, but that is a solution of desperation. For there is a good reason why Hosea use both names. In cases where Ephraim occurs besides Israel, Israel no longer refers to the Ten Tribes but to the entire nation, albeit always in the context of the future fulfillment of the prophesy. So the use of Ephraim is in fact a degradation; it shows that God does not defend the Ten Tribes anymore.*

Our exegesis puts us at odds with the majority of biblical scholars. This is not something we do lightly. Therefore, to bolster our position, we will be delving more deeply into the Hebrew text. For a careful translation represents both the solution and the justification of the exegesis we defend. Here too the maxim applies: Scripture is its own interpreter!

Sources:
(Flanders, Crapps, and Smith, 347–48)
(See Excursus 12; introduction to Hosea 1 Exegesis; *Hosea 5:3.1 Exegesis.)

Verse 1 NASB
Hear this, O priests! Give heed, O house of Israel! Listen, O house of the king! For the judgment applies to you, for you have been a snare at Mizpah and a net spread out on Tabor.

Verse 1 KJV
Hear ye this, O priests; and hearken, ye house of Israel; and give ye ear, O house of the king; for judgment is toward you, because ye have been a snare on Mizpah, and a net spread upon Tabor.

Verse 1 NIV
"Hear this, you priests! Pay attention, you Israelites! Listen, royal house! This judgment is against you: You have been a snare at Mizpah, a net spread out on Tabor."

Verse 1 Hebrew Interlinear Text
hear! this the-priests and-pay-attention! house-of Israel and-house-of-the-royalty listen! indeed against-you the-judgment indeed snare you-were at-Mizpah and-net being-spread-out on Tabor

The word *zoth* generally has the sense of *this, for this reason, therefore, similarly*, or *thus*. In this verse it is paired with *hear!* It is a traditional way to give greater emphasis to the word of Hosea. The prophet is therefore emphatically calling his audience to attention for an important prophesy. We read: *Hear, o priests!*
(McComiskey 75; Strong's OT, word 2063; Wolff, 97)

We read:
Hear, o priests! Give attention, you house of Israel! Listen, you royal house! Because the judgment is against you. For you were a trap in Mizpah and a net that was spread out on Tabor.

Verse 2 NASB
The revolters have gone deep in depravity, but I will chastise all of them.

Verse 2 KJV
And the revolters are profound to make slaughter, though I have been a rebuker of them all.

Verse 2 NIV
"The rebels are knee-deep in slaughter. I will discipline all of them."

Verse 2 Hebrew Interlinear Text
and-slaughter rebels they-are-deep and-I discipline to-all-of-them

Introduction to Verse 2
This is a very difficult passage, which has been translated in various ways. Many exegetes change the Hebrew source text to arrive at a meaning that suits their own purposes. Accordingly, the NRSV reads: *a pit dug deep in Shittim*, and the theologian Garrett translates: *The rebels are deep in slaughter.* The differences between these two renderings are sufficient to raise anyone's eyebrows.

As always, we have chosen to respect the authority of the Hebrew source text and seek our solution in a better translation. For this reason we will go through the text word-for-word and then see what happens.
(Born, 44; Brown, 49; Harper, 269)

Verse 2a
and-slaughter
The term *shachat* could also be translated *to slaughter* or *to kill*. It is often connected to human sacrifices offered in pagan rituals. We also find the term used in that sense in Ezekiel 16:21; 23:39, and it points us in the right direction.
(Andersen and Freedman, 386; Garrett, 140, 142; Kidner, 57; Strong's OT, word 7819)

We read: *in their bloodbaths*

Verse 2b
rebels
The NIVIHEOT translates the Hebrew word *set* as *rebels*, but a much better translation can be found. The word *set* does not occur anywhere else in the Bible. It is derived from *sut*, a word found in Psalm 40:4, where NASB translates *lapse*, KJV/NIV *turn aside* and Dutch NBG *to go astray*. The second place we find *sut* is in Psalm 101:3, where the KJV reads *turn aside*, the NLT *crookedly*, CSB *transgression*, and NBG *apostates*.

In its basic meaning, the term *set* refers to someone who departs from the straight path. This is why Calvin is correct to translate it as *turning aside*. The word therefore refers to someone who has *strayed*, thus an *apostate*. In this verse the word occurs in its plural form (*setîm*), which makes it natural to translate here as *apostates*.
(Brown, 49; Calvijn, *Daniel* II, *Kleine Profeten* I/II, Hosea, 184; Garrett, 140, 142; Mays, 79; Strong's OT, words 7846, 7750; Ward, 94)

We read: *the apostates*

Verse 2c
they-are-deep
The word *amoq* means *deep* or *to be deep*, and can be used both literally (Isaiah 30:33) and abstractly (Psalm 92:5). A related expression is found in Hosea 9:9 (*They sank deep and became as corrupt as in the days of Gibeah.*) It therefore seems natural to translate accordingly here.
(Andersen and Freedman, 386; Strong's OT, word 6009; Ward, 94)

We read: *have sunk deep*

Verse 2d
and-I discipline to-all-of-them
It is not entirely clear how the Hebrew text is to be translated here. Many read *musar* to mean *to discipline* or *to scourge*, but in the sense of correctively raising, as in a family (Wolff). This is why Harper translates: *There is no correction* . . . Others read *moser/ meserah*, which means *to chain*, *to bind*, or *to constrain*.

When in doubt, we always turn to the context. The theme of this chapter is the judgment upon Israel. Nothing in the text seems to point to the possibility of a conversion to avert the wrath of God. This means that a translation along the lines of *discipline* (in the sense of corrective punishment) is unlikely. The other option is that Israel will be constrained (that is, put in chains), fits very well, since the nation was taken captive by the Assyrians and taken away into exile.
(Brown, 50; Garrett, 143; Harper, 269; Strong's OT, words 4147, 4148; Stuart, 88–89; Wolff, 94)

We read: ***but I will put them all in chains***

The entire sentence:
The apostates have sunk deep in their bloodbaths, but I will put them all in chains.

Verse 3 NASB
I know Ephraim, and Israel is not hidden from Me; For now, O Ephraim, you have played the harlot, Israel has defiled itself.

Verse 3 KJV
I know Ephraim, and Israel is not hid from me: for now, O Ephraim, thou committest whoredom, and Israel is defiled.

Verse 3 NIV
"I know all about Ephraim; Israel is not hidden from me. Ephraim, you have now turned to prostitution; Israel is corrupt."

Verse 3 Hebrew Interlinear Text
I I-know Ephraim and-Israel not he-is-hidden from-me indeed now you-turned-to-prostitution Ephraim he-is-corrupt Israel

Israel Becomes Ephraim
In verse 3 we find both words used in a single sentence, as in verse 5. By far the greatest majority of biblical scholars give the names Ephraim and Israel the same meaning, and identify them as the kingdom of the Ten Tribes. They explain this phenomenon as poetic license, which they assume Hosea to be applying here. This is a very lazy solution. Up to now the book of Hosea has not exactly given the impression of being just any old text. The words are always profound and chosen with care, and we may assume the same to be true here. There must therefore be a reason for the use of two distinct names.

There is no doubt that in Hosea 1 and 2 the name Israel applies to the Ten Tribes of the Northern Kingdom. Beginning with chapter 4, we find ourselves dealing with the Ten Tribes after the verdict *Lo-Ammi* (= not My people). By that time, the people of Israel have been removed from the Sinaitic Covenant. Now Hosea is drawing a distinction between the people of Israel from the recent past (when it still was the people of God) and the status following their rejection (Lo-Ammi = not My people). This distinction is depicted in the name change to Ephraim.

In verse 3c the name Israel finally reoccurs. This does not conflict with what we have just argued. In verse 3c Hosea is speaking about the future and the renewed covenantal relationship. That always relates to the entire nation (all twelve tribes), since it is the whole people of Israel that bears the promise. This is why we, in our translation have added the word *all* (in brackets) to the word *Israel*.
(Gordis, 79; McComiskey, 76–78; Stuart, 85)
(See Excursuses 6, 12; introduction to Hosea 1 Exegesis; Hosea 4:17 exegesis.)

Verse 3a
I I-know Ephraim
The word *I*, referring to God, is used two times here. Unfortunately, it is only seldom that translations reflect that repetition. Van de Born is an exception, translating: *I, I know Ephraim*. Brown reads: *It is I who know Ephraim*, which we have chosen to follow here.
(Born, 44; Brown, 50; Harper, 270–71; Wolff, 94)

We read: ***It is I who know Ephraim***

Verse 3b
and-Israel not he-is-hidden from-me
Kachad means *hidden, secret,* or *keep secret*, in the sense of not saying something or keeping it a secret from others (Genesis 47:18; Joshua 7:19; Jeremiah 38:14).

We read, first step: ***and Israel is no secret to Me***.
This translation doesn't really capture the sense of the original. But we do have a phrase in English that will work better.
(Garrett, 144; Strong's OT, word 3582)

We read, second step: ***and Israel is an open book to Me***.

The whole text:
It is I who knows Ephraim, and Israel is an open book to Me. Because you, Ephraim, have turned to fornication, [all] Israel is defiled.

Verse 4 NASB
Their deeds will not allow them to return to their God. For a spirit of harlotry is within them, and they do not know the LORD.

Verse 4 KJV
They will not frame their doings to turn unto their God: for the spirit of whoredoms is in the midst of them, and they have not known the LORD.

Verse 4 NIV
"Their deeds do not permit them to return to their God. A spirit of prostitution is in their heart; they do not acknowledge the LORD.***"***

Verse 4 Hebrew Interlinear Text
not they-permit deeds-of-them to-return to God-of-them indeed spirit-of prostitutions in-heart-of-them and Yahweh not they-acknowledge
The Hebrew word *ki* is usually used to introduce a causal relationship. It occurs frequently and has a very wide range of meaning. This is why the context is largely determinative for the specific sense in which it is used. The NIVIHEOT reads *indeed* here. This is an interpretation, and as such the NIVIHEOT deviates from the great majority of biblical scholars

on this point. Generally the term is translated as *for, because, due to, while, although*, and *given that*. In this context we prefer to translate: *for*.
(Strong's OT, word 3588; Wolff, 95)

We read:
Their deeds prevented them from turning back to their God, for there is a spirit of fornication in their hearts and they do not know Yahweh.

Verse 5 NASB
Moreover, the pride of Israel testifies against him, and Israel and Ephraim stumble in their iniquity; Judah also has stumbled with them.

Verse 5 KJV
And the pride of Israel doth testify to his face: therefore shall Israel and Ephraim fall in their iniquity; Judah also shall fall with them.

Verse 5 NIV
"Israel's arrogance testifies against them; the Israelites, even Ephraim, stumble in their sin; Judah also stumbles with them."

Verse 5 Hebrew Interlinear Text
and-he-testifies arrogance-of Israel against-faces-of-him and-Israel even-Ephraim they-stumble in-sin-of-them he-stumbles also Judah with-them

Verse 5a
and-he-testifies arrogance-of Israel
Verse 5 begins with a *vav*, which we translate as: *and*. This serves to connect verse 5 to verses 3 and 4, which speaks about a *spirit of fornication*.

The basic meaning of *anah* is *to answer* or *to respond*. A translation as *testifies* is only possible with strong textual support, what is not the case here. Garrett says, "It does not strictly connote legal proceedings."
(Brown, Driver, Briggs, BHI 6030; Garrett, 145; Strong's OT, word 6030)

The Hebrew term *ga'own* is translated by many as *arrogance*. That is a possibility when the context calls for it, but that is not the case here. Here Israel—the "good" nation—stands in contrast with the failing nations of Ephraim and Judah. In the Bible there are a number of passages in which *ga'own* has the sense of *majesty, magnificence,* or *luster*. Examples can be found in the following verses: Exodus 15:7; Job 37:4; 40:10; Isaiah 2:10; 4:2.

The rendering in other passages, like Job 38:11; Psalm 59:12; and Isaiah 13:11, where translations have opted for *pride*, is also disputable. There too *majesty* is most likely the correct meaning. This translation is supported by rabbinic sources, which speak of the *pride* or *glory of Israel* (Rashi), which usually points to the presence of God in the temple of Jerusalem. Owens speaks about *the exaltation of Israel*. CEV: *Israel, your pride*. ASV, ESV, and DRA: *the pride of Israel*.

Conclusion:
Since in this part of Hosea the name Israel[*] conceptually contrasts with the apostate Ephraim,[†] the present context favors the interpretation *all Israel* in its messianic significance, or points to the past when the twelve tribes where still united. For this reason, *majesty* is the correct translation.
([*]This means *God struggles*. So at that time Israel was still the people of God.)

(†With the name *Ephraim*, they were no longer the people of God. Since the covenant of Sinai has been broken, they have lost their honorific title *Israel*.)

Sources:
(McComiskey, 109; Owens, 769; Rosenberg, vol. 1, 32, 45; Strong's OT, word 1347; Targum Jonathan on Hosea, Hosea 5:5)
(See Excursus 12; and section above under verse 3 titled "Israel Becomes Ephraim.")

We read: *and the majesty of Israel responds*

Verse 5b
against-faces-of-him
The word *against* seems to suggest that a testimony is being delivered against the people of Israel. However, this is not what is meant here. It is rather a spatial locator, so that the term is better translated as *in*, *to*, or *before*. Instead of *faces* we can read *presence*, what fits the context better. The *pride* or *glory of Israel* is most likely the temple, so we read His presence.
(Andersen and Freedman, 392; Brown, 51; Calvijn, *Daniël* II, *Kleine Profeten* I/II, Hosea, 191; McComiskey, 77; Owens, 769)

We read: *to His presence*

Verse 5c
and-Israel even-Ephraim they-stumble in-sin-of-them
Twice a *vav* (*and-Israel and-Ephraim*). So they both *stumble*.

We read: *Israel will stumble with Ephraim over their sins*

Verse 5d
he-stumbles also Judah with-them
The word *also* indicates that the stumbling of Israel (old name) *and* of Ephraim (the name of the Lo-Ammi people) at the same time has consequences for the southern kingdom of Judah. There are no problems in the remaining text.
(Calvijn, *Daniël* II, *Kleine Profeten* I/II, Hosea, 191–92; Kohlenberger, vol. 4, 488; Mays, 82; Wolff, 95)
(See section above under verse 3 titled "Israel Becomes Ephraim.")

We read: *also Judah will stumble with them*

The whole sentence:
And the majesty of Israel responds to His presence. Israel will stumble with Ephraim over their sins; also Judah will stumble with them.

Verse 6 NASB
*They will go with their flocks and herds to seek the L*ORD*, but they will not find Him; He has withdrawn from them.*

Verse 6 KJV
*They shall go with their flocks and with their herds to seek the L*ORD*; but they shall not find him; he hath withdrawn himself from them.*

Verse 6 NIV
*"When they go with their flocks and herds to seek the L*ORD*, they will not find him; he has withdrawn himself from them."*

Verse 6 Hebrew Interlinear Text
with-flock-of-them and-with-herd-of-them they-go to-seek ... Yahweh but-not they-will-find he-withdrew from-them
The word *tson* means *small cattle* or usually sheep and goats. The word *baqar* means *cattle* and often *an ox* or a *herd of oxen*.
(Strong's OT, words 6629, 1241)

We read:
They will go to seek Yahweh with their small cattle and their oxen, but they will not find Him. He has withdrawn from them.

Verse 7 NASB
They have dealt treacherously against the Lord, for they have borne illegitimate children. Now the new moon will devour them with their land.

Verse 7 KJV
They have dealt treacherously against the Lord: for they have begotten strange children: now shall a month devour them with their portions.

Verse 7 NIV
"They are unfaithful to the Lord; they give birth to illegitimate children. When they celebrate their New Moon feasts, he will devour their fields."

Verse 7 Hebrew Interlinear Text
to-Yahweh they-are-unfaithful indeed children ones-being-illegitimate they-give-birth now he-will-devour-them New-Moon-festival with fields-of-them

Introduction to Verse 7
Verse 7 is another one that is not easy to translate. And once again we reject a change in the Hebrew source text, although the majority of exegetes propose new readings. For this reason we will walk through the Hebrew text word-by-word, in the hopes that this process will yield a logical sentence.

Verse 7a
to-Yahweh they-are-unfaithful
Many exegetes/translators translate here using the present perfect (*have acted faithlessly*). They assume that the verse only looks back to the past. This is not what the text says, however. Thankfully there are also biblical scholars who listen more carefully to the source text. The Dutch Willibrord Bible reads: *They have become faithless to the Lord*. The WEB even uses the present tense, and that is indeed what we find in the Hebrew text. We can therefore simply stick to our source text.
(Walvoord and Zuck, 1391; World English Bible)

We read: ***they are unfaithful to Yahweh***

Verse 7b
indeed children ones-being-illegitimate
This clause begins with *ki*, which typically introduces a causal relationship. Sometimes this term is more accurately translated *indeed* or *certainly*. In this case *for* is a better translation, in which we follow the great majority of translators.
(Strong's OT, word 3588; Owens, 769)

The word *zuwr* (translated here as *illegitimate*) most often has the sense of *strange* or *stranger*, primarily in the sense of: *not sacred to* or *unauthorized before* God (Exodus 30:9; Leviticus 10:1; Numbers 26:61). Given the context, there are three options here.

1. The most common interpretation understands the text to be referring to illegitimate children, as in Hosea 1:2.
2. A second exegesis assumes that the children born out of wedlock were not circumcised and thus not included in the covenant. They are thus strangers to the people of Israel.*
3. A third exegesis recognizes that, in practice, circumcision was much less common than one might think. For this reason Brown writes: *A generation has grown up who are strangers to Jahveh*. Cheyne speaks of *strange children* (in the sense of *not sanctified* by circumcision).

When we obey the context (that the people of Israel/Ephraim are estranged from Yahweh and no longer know Him), the third interpretation must be the correct one.

(*Andersen and Freedman, 395, 397–98; Brown, 51; Cheyne, 73; Harper, 271; Strong's OT, word 2114)

We read: ***for they have given birth to children who became strangers***

Verse 7c1
he-will-devour-them
The word *akal* normally means *to eat*, and occurs frequently in Scripture. If required by context, it can also mean *devour* or *consume* (as food, a prey, or by fire).

In the present context, the prophet Hosea is speaking about the powerful nation of the Assyrians, which devours *its portion* (verse 7c3; i.e., the territory of the Ten Tribes). Assyria was the superpower in Hosea's days, becoming increasingly powerful at that time and pushing its way down to the south. It occupied Syria, and thereafter Israel (the Ten Tribes) was conquered and its territory annexed. Those who survived that bloody war were taken into captivity. It is not the people of Israel but Assyria that enjoyed the fruit of the land. The land was managed poorly, however, for it was soon reduced to a wilderness. This process took many years. That also explains our choice for the term *digest* here, since it is suggestive of a passage of time.

(Born, 45; Edelkoort, 185; Kidner, 58; Strong's OT, word 398; Ward, 95)

Verse 7c2
he-will-devour-them New-Moon-festival with fields-of-them
Normally *hds* is vocalized as *hodes* (Andersen; others write *chodesh*), that is, *moon*, *month*, or *new moon*. The NIVIHEOT translators have interpreted it as *New Moon Festival*. However, this leaves us with a strange passage, for how can a New Moon Festival devour fields? It is no wonder that many exegetes favor another translation. Some emend the Hebrew source text and read *heres* (*drought*). This leads Van de Born to translate: *through the desert wind their fields*. However, this represents a very loose interpretation of the source text. Others prefer to read *destroyer* (Kidner). NET and WEB: *devour*.

Our solution to the problem is to take the same basic root (*hds*) and to vocalize it *hadas* (*the other* or *someone else*), which is also possible. This translation brings verse 7 back within the exegesis of this chapter, namely the announcement of the judgment of God.

(Andersen and Freedman, 397; Born, 45; Brown, 51; Kidner, 59; Strong's OT, word 2320; Ward, 95)

We read: ***now someone else will digest***

Verse 7c3
fields-of-them

The word *cheleq* means a *part* or *portion of,* having a *share* in something or someone. It is often used in the context of the allocation of an inheritance, like a piece of land. A translation that includes the word *fields*, as it is found in the NIVIHEOT, is for that reason an interpretation and thus not a good translation.

Cheleq commonly means *share* (Genesis 14:24; Leviticus 6:17), and sometimes *inheritance* (Deuteronomy 18:1). Here there is no compelling reason to depart from the Hebrew text, and therefore we retain the basic meaning *share*.
(Cheyne, 73; Harper, 271; Owens, 769; Strong's OT, word 2506; Ward, 92)

We read: *their share*

The whole sentence:
They are unfaithful to Yahweh, for they have given birth to children who became strangers. Now someone else will digest their share.

Verse 8 NASB
Blow the horn in Gibeah, the trumpet in Ramah. Sound an alarm at Beth-aven: "Behind you, Benjamin!"

Verse 8 KJV
Blow ye the cornet in Gibeah, and the trumpet in Ramah: cry aloud at Bethaven, after thee, O Benjamin.

Verse 8 NIV
"Sound the trumpet in Gibeah, the horn in Ramah. Raise the battle cry in Beth Aven; lead on, Benjamin."

Verse 8 Hebrew Interlinear Text
sound trumpet in-the-Gibeah horn in-the-Ramah raise-battle-cry Beth Aven after-you Benjamin

Verse 8a
sound trumpet in-the-Gibeah
The *shophar* is a wind instrument that was made from the horn of a wild billy goat. It is an iconic instrument that played an important role in the rituals of the cultic service in Israel. This is one of the reasons why we have chosen to transliterate the word as *shofar*.
(See the Hebrew text translation of Hosea 8:1.)

We read: *sound the shofar in Gibeah*

Verse 8b
horn in-the-Ramah
The *chatsotsrah* is a trumpet-like instrument that produces high, rather piercing notes. One of its uses was to gain the audience's attention at an important event. We translate: *trumpet*.
(Strong's OT, word 2698)

We read: *and the trumpet in Rama*

Verse 8d
raise-battle-cry! Beth Aven after-you Benjamin
The word *achar* means *back part, behind, thereafter, after, follow,* or *afterward*. Most exegetes assume that it is a warning cry to announce the arrival of the enemy. This is why

Mays reads: *Put Benjamin on guard!* In the translations listed above, the clause remains unconnected to the surrounding passage on the substantive level, and there is no logic to it. For that reason we continue our search.

The KJV and NASB translate *achar* in many places as *after*, and sometimes as *following* or *behind*.

Our next step is to consider the context. The threat that Assyria represented for Judah (for that is what this is actually about) took place under King Hezekiah (2 Chronicles 32). At a certain point in time, the Assyrian king Sennacherib invaded Judah. His power was so superior that Hezekiah withdrew to Jerusalem and the surrounding area, where his defense was concentrated (cf. 2 Chronicles 32:1: *the fortified cities*). It could be that Benjamin is being urged here to withdraw to Jerusalem or, as another possibility, to fall in line behind Judah in the war. Since there are no further indications available to us, we retain the most common significance of the word and translate as: *Go after them*.
(May, 85; McComiskey, 80–81; Owens, vol. 4, 769; Strong's OT, word 310)

We read: ***let the battle cry be heard in Beth Aven. Go after them, Benjamin!***

The whole sentence:
Sound the shofar in Gibeah and the trumpet in Rama. Let the battle cry be heard in Beth Aven. Go after them, Benjamin!

Verse 9 NASB
Ephraim will become a desolation in the day of rebuke; Among the tribes of Israel I declare what is sure.

Verse 9 KJV
Ephraim shall be desolate in the day of rebuke: among the tribes of Israel have I made known that which shall surely be.

Verse 9 NIV
"Ephraim will be laid waste on the day of reckoning. Among the tribes of Israel I proclaim what is certain."

Verse 9 Hebrew Interlinear Text
Ephraim to-waste she-will-be on-day-of reckoning among-tribes-of Israel I-proclaim one-being-certain
In our translation we largely follow the translations of the Dutch NBG and NIV.

We read, first step: ***Ephraim will become a desolation on the day of judgment. Over the tribes of Israel I proclaimed what has been decided.***

This translation is not very smooth, but does capture the sense of the Hebrew text well. All that remains for us is to connect verse 9b more closely to verse 9a, since 9b says something about 9a.

We read, second step: ***Ephraim will become a desolation on the day of judgment, [because] I have proclaimed what has been decided concerning the tribes of Israel.***

Verse 10 NASB
The princes of Judah have become like those who move a boundary; On them I will pour out My wrath like water.

Verse 10 KJV
The princes of Judah were like them that remove the bound: therefore I will pour out my wrath upon them like water.

Verse 10 NIV
"Judah's leaders are like those who move boundary stones. I will pour out my wrath on them like a flood of water."

Verse 10 Hebrew Interlinear Text
they-are leaders-of Judah like-ones-moving-of boundary-stone on-them I-will-pour-out like-the-waters wrath-of-me
The word *sar* occurs very frequently in the Bible and could be translated as *leaders*, *princes*, or *sovereign*. Our preference is *princes*.

We read, first step: ***The princes of Judah will be like those that move the boundary stones. I will pour My vengeance upon them like a flood.***

It is clear that the word *be* is used here in the sense of *acting* or *doing*.
(Owens, 769; Strong's OT, word 8269)

We read, second step: ***The princes of Judah will act as those who move the boundary stones. I will pour My vengeance upon them like a flood.***

Verse 11 NASB
Ephraim is oppressed, crushed in judgment, because he was determined to follow man's command.

Verse 11 KJV
Ephraim is oppressed and broken in judgment, because he willingly walked after the commandment.

Verse 11 NIV
"Ephraim is oppressed, trampled in judgment, intent on pursuing idols."

Verse 11 Hebrew Interlinear Text
being-oppressed Ephraim being-trampled-of judgment indeed he-is-intent he-pursues after idol

Verse 11a
being-oppressed Ephraim being-trampled-of judgment
Harper translates here: *Ephraim practices oppression! he breaks down right*. This is a typical translation of desperation, since that is not what the Hebrew source text says.

Here we find *'āšūq*. Some see this as related to *ashaq*,* which means *oppressed* (Deuteronomy 24:14; 1 Chronicles 16:21; Job 10:3); others see it as related to *ashuqim*† (*oppression* or *extortion*). Sometimes it can also mean *to cheat* or *defraud* (Leviticus 19:13 KJV), but even there it would be better to translate with *oppress*.

The word *râtsats*‡ means *to break in pieces* or *to snap* (Ezekiel 29:7) or *broken, snapped, crushed* (Ecclesiastes 12:6; Isaiah 36:6). According to the context that can be interpreted as *crushed* or *trampled*.

The final word, *judgment* (*mishpât*),** is indeed an acceptable rendering of the Hebrew text, however *rightful judgment* would be better.

Some exegetes, like Mays, read verse 11a in the perfect tense, but that is not what we find in the text. On this point, the NIVIHEOT offers an accurate translation.
(Strong's OT, words *6231, †6217, ‡7533, and **4941)

The Coming Judgment
The verbal forms (*being-oppressed being-trampled*) suggest a continuing process in the future, that is, something that is yet to happen (which is as such logical, given that the judgment over Israel/Ephraim is forthcoming). However, Andersen and Freedman have trouble following the Hebrew source text literally, since, so they say, there is (in the context) no mark of future reference. But the fact of the matter is that the Hebrew source text does suggest that very thing! After all, it announces a judgment from God that is yet to come.

When that judgment has been fully executed, the conversion described in verse 11b/c will come. This is the result of the complete absence among many exegetes of a biblically sound notion of a future eschaton. For Hosea 5:11 is a soteriological, rich promise, and it fits seamlessly with our concept of the eschaton.
(Andersen and Freedman, 408–9; Harper, 275; Mays, 85)

We read: ***when Ephraim has been oppressed and trampled in rightful judgment***

Verse 11b
indeed he-is-intent
The translation offered by the NIVIHEOT is not the most natural choice. The text reads *ki* here, which normally introduces a causal relationship. For that reason, we are better off to translate it as *when* or *then*. Both fit the context well.
(Strong's OT, word 3588)

The word *yaal* refers to an act of the will, as in Exodus 2:21 (*willing, agreed*), but also in Judges 17:11 (*agreed, content*) and 1 Samuel 12:22 (*has been pleased*; others: *chosen*).
(Cheyne, 75; Strong's OT, word 2974; Ward, 102)

We read: ***then they will decide***

Verse 11c1
he-pursues
Halak means *to walk* or *to go*. It is also used in the sense of *walking in the fear of the* Lord, that is, serving God and following Him.

The word *'achar* means *back part, behind, after, follow,* or *afterward*. Here we opt for *follow* (see also verse 8).
(Strong's OT, words 310, 1980)

Verse 11c2
he-pursues after idol
The text does not read *idols*; with this translation the NIVIHEOT has given its own interpretation of the Hebrew text. Actually, this too is a desperation translation. What it says is *tsav*, which means *command, precept,* or *law* (Isaiah 28:10, 13).
(Andersen and Freedman, 409; Brown, 53–54; Harper, 276; McComiskey, 82–83; Strong's OT, word 6673; Walvoord and Zuck, 1392)

We read: ***to follow the precepts***

The whole sentence:
When Ephraim has been oppressed and trampled in rightful judgment, then they will decide to follow the precepts.

Verse 12 NASB
Therefore I am like a moth to Ephraim and like rottenness to the house of Judah.

Verse 12 KJV
Therefore will I be unto Ephraim as a moth, and to the house of Judah as rottenness.

Verse 12 NIV
"I am like a moth to Ephraim, like rot to the people of Judah."

Verse 12 Hebrew Interlinear Text
and-I like-the-moth to-Ephraim and-like-the-rot to-house-of Judah
The sudden appearance of the word *moth* seems rather strange given the context of the Hebrew text. Here too another translation option offers a better solution.

The word *ash* is very rare in the Bible, and its meaning is not certain. It is derived from *ashesh*, which probably means *being diminished* or *digested*. This is why some translate the term as *rot* or *rottenness*, which suits the context much better.
(Andersen and Freedman, 412; Driver, Hosea 5:12; Kidner, 61; Strong's OT, words 6211, 6244)

What Tense?
Hosea 5:12 could be written in either the present or the future tense. The context suggests the latter. We have chosen to follow the KJV, GNT, DRA (and many others) and use the future tense.
(Brown, Driver, Briggs, BHI Hosea 5:12)

We read:
So I will be like rot to Ephraim and decay to the house of Judah.

Verse 13 NASB
When Ephraim saw his sickness, and Judah his wound, then Ephraim went to Assyria and sent to King Jareb. But he is unable to heal you, or to cure you of your wound.

Verse 13 KJV
When Ephraim saw his sickness, and Judah saw his wound, then went Ephraim to the Assyrian, and sent to king Jareb: yet could he not heal you, nor cure you of your wound.

Verse 13 NIV
"When Ephraim saw his sickness, and Judah his sores, then Ephraim turned to Assyria, and sent to the great king for help. But he is not able to cure you, not able to heal your sores."

Verse 13 Hebrew Interlinear Text
when-he-saw Ephraim ... sickness-of-him and-Judah ... sore-of-him then-he-turned Ephraim to Assyria and-he-sent to king great but-he not he-is-able-to-cure to-you and-not he-can-heal of-you sore
The Hebrew source text for verse 13, as given by the NIVIHEOT, seems to show little logic and coherence. Yet a careful analysis of the Hebrew offers a better translation. That solution even fits seamlessly with the proposed exegesis!

Verse 13a
when-he-saw Ephraim ... sickness-of-him

The word *raah* means *to appear* (Genesis 1:9; Leviticus 16:2), but also *to see* (Deuteronomy 1:8). The underlying thought is always that something is going to happen. By far the greatest majority of exegetes and translators choose to read *Ephraim saw* here. Yet this is way too static, and hardly in agreement with the way in which *raah* is typically used in the Bible. The Dutch NBV does manage to approach the sense of the source text closely when it read: *When Ephraim saw how sick he was . . .* We can do a little better, however. We opt for a synonym of *appear*, namely *saw come up*.

The translation *sickness* is too general, since that could refer also to a simple flu. We might also follow many others who translate *illness*. Yet we prefer *torment*, since it is a grueling sickness that Israel is suffering.
(Cheyne, 75; Strong's OT, word 7200)

We read: *for Ephraim saw his torment come up*

Verse 13b
and-Judah . . . sore-of-him
The word *mazor** occurs three times in the Bible: twice in the book of Hosea and another time in Jeremiah 30:13. There the KJV translates the term as *bound up*. However, others translate the word as *lesion*, *bruise*, or *injury*. After all, we do not know exactly what *mazor* means. Andersen and Freedman call it an oozing or running infection. Strong's concordance offers the basic meaning of *binding up* or *bandage*.

The word *mazor** is related to *zur*,† which means *to press together*, *to pinch together*, or *to compress*. For this reason, *bruise* or *injury* are better choices.
(Andersen and Freedman, 413; Owens, 770; Strong's OT, words *4205, †2115)

We read: ***and Judah his injury***

Verse 13c
then-he-turned Ephraim to Assyria
This clause begins with a *vav*, which we can translate as either *and* or *then*.
(See one of the final sections of the introduction to this book titled, "The Letter Vav.")

We read: ***Then Ephraim turned to Assyria***

Verse 13d
and-he-sent
Shalach normally means *to go* or *to bring*, but it can also mean *to send (for)*. Here we retain the basic meaning and read: *He went to*.
(Strong's OT, word 7971)

Some exegetes and translators have identified a proper name here and therefore read: *king Jareb*. This name is not found anywhere else in Holy Scripture, but they assume that it references the Assyrian king and represents his family name. In support of their translation, they offer a number of examples of Assyrian kings for whom both a court title and family name are known. This seems rather farfetched, however.

The word *yareb* occurs in Hosea 5:13 and 10:6, but nowhere else in Scripture. According to Strong's, it is derived from *rib*, which most often has the meaning *to contend* or *strive (with)*, as in Judges 6:31 and Job 23:6.

There seem to be two options. We could read: *and he went to the king to contend* or *s*t*rive*. A more natural option would be to use a derivative of *rib* (*to content/strive*) in its nominal

form, namely *suppliant*. Regardless, both translations suit the context perfectly.
(Owens, 770, 779; Strong's OT, words 3377, 7378; Wood, 193)

We read: *and went to the king as a suppliant*

Verse 13e
but-he not he-is-able to-cure to-you and-not he-can-heal of-you sore
Here too we find the word *mazor* (NIVIHEOT: *sore*), which we will translate as in verse 13b with the word *injury*.
(Strong's OT, word 4205; *Studiebijbel* SBOT 12, 66)

We read: *but he is unable to give you healing, he cannot heal your injury.*

The whole sentence:
For Ephraim saw his torment come up and Judah his injury. Then Ephraim turned to Assyria and went to the king as a suppliant. But he is unable to give you healing, he cannot heal your injury.

Verse 14 NASB
For I will be like a lion to Ephraim and like a young lion to the house of Judah. I, even I, will tear to pieces and go away, I will carry away, and there will be none to deliver.

Verse 14 KJV
For I will be unto Ephraim as a lion, and as a young lion to the house of Judah: I, even I, will tear and go away; I will take away, and none shall rescue him.

Verse 14 NIV
"For I will be like a lion to Ephraim, like a great lion to Judah. I will tear them to pieces and go away; I will carry them off, with no one to rescue them."

Verse 14 Hebrew Interlinear Text
for I like-the-lion to-Ephraim and-like-the-great-lion to-house-of Judah I I-will-tear-to-pieces and-I-will-go-away I-will-carry-off and-there-will-be-no one-rescuing
In the Hebrew text of verse 14 two different words for *lion* are used. *Shachal* means *to roar*. The other word, *kephir*, means *covered* or *covering* (probably in the sense of: *covered with a mane*). The latter term is thus suggestive of pride and nobility. These days, however, both words are generally translated simply as *lion*. To distinguish them, some translate *kephir* as *young lion*, *noble lion*, or even *cub* (however the last option is rather improbable).

The term *shachal* probably refers to an old male lion. Such lions were often excluded from the pack and lived a solitary life. Since lions typically hunt together, an old lion living solitarily had a hard time capturing his prey. Moreover, generally the lionesses are the ones to initiate the hunt, while male lions are responsible for protecting their territory and for breeding.

An excluded male lion often goes hungry and therefore roars more often than other lions do. He is unpredictable and because of his hunger often comes close to inhabited places to rob cattle or even to attack people. Such a renegade lion also tends to kill more than he needs.

The text therefore depicts a savage animal that kills needlessly. So this lion is contrasted with the proud young or *great lion* that protects his group. Since the context suggests a contrast, we have chosen to add the word *old* to verse 14a.
(Born, 47; Brown, 54; Strong's OT, word 7826 and 3715; Stuart, 105)

We read:
However I will be like an [old] lion for Ephraim. But I will be to the house of Judah as a young lion. I, yes, I will tear to pieces and then leave. I will take away and there will be no one who saves.

Verse 15 NASB
I will go away and return to My place until they acknowledge their guilt and seek My face; In their affliction they will earnestly seek Me.

Verse 15 KJV
I will go and return to my place, till they acknowledge their offence, and seek my face: in their affliction they will seek me early.

Verse 15 NIV
"Then I will return to my lair until they have borne their guilt and seek my face—in their misery they will earnestly seek me."

Verse 15 Hebrew Interlinear Text
I-will-go I-will-go-back to place-of-me until when they-admit-guilt and-they-will-seek faces-of-me in-the-misery of-them they-will-earnestly-seek-me

Verse 15a
I-will-go I-will-go-back to place-of-me until when they-admit-guilt
The word *maqom* normally means *place* or *spot*, in the sense of a specific location. Whenever the text is referring to the place where God is staying, we need to translate the term as *station* or *place* (*of residence*; Ezekiel 3:12).
(Strong's OT, word 4725; Weerd, *Ezechiël*, vol. 1, 78)

We read: ***I will go and return to My residence until they recognize their guilt***

Verse 15b
and-they-will-seek faces-of-me in-the-misery of-them
Literally one ought indeed to translate *faces*, but in general the term is translated as *face*, singular.
(Garrett, 148; Kidner, 63; Mays, 86)

We read: ***then they will seek My face in their affliction***

Verse 15c
they-will-earnestly-seek-me
The word *shachar* means *timely*, *on time*, or *early* (with the underlying notion of *being on time*). Yet some, including the NIVIHEOT, translate this word as *earnestly*, *insistently*, or *seriously*. However, these translations of the Hebrew text are too free.
(Garrett, 148; Strong's OT, word 7836)

We read: ***they will seek Me in time***

The whole sentence:
I will go and return to My residence until they recognize their guilt. Then they will seek My face in their affliction; they will seek Me in time.

Hosea 5:1–15—The corrected text:

Verse 1   ***Hear, o priests! Give attention, you house of Israel! Listen, you royal house!***

	Because the judgment is against you. For you were a trap in Mizpah and a net that was spread out on Tabor.
Verse 2	*The apostates have sunk deep in their bloodbaths, but I will put them all in chains.*
Verse 3	*It is I who knows Ephraim, and Israel is an open book to Me. Because you, Ephraim, have turned to fornication, [all] Israel is defiled.*
Verse 4	*Their deeds prevented them from turning back to their God, for there is a spirit of fornication in their hearts and they do not know Yahweh.*
Verse 5	*And the majesty of Israel responds to His presence. Israel will stumble with Ephraim over their sins; also Judah will stumble with them.*
Verse 6	*They will go to seek Yahweh with their small cattle and their oxen, but they will not find Him. He has withdrawn from them.*
Verse 7	*They are unfaithful to Yahweh, for they have given birth to children who became strangers. Now someone else will digest their share.*
Verse 8	*Sound the shofar in Gibeah and the trumpet in Rama. Let the battle cry be heard in Beth Aven. Go after them, Benjamin!*
Verse 9	*Ephraim will become a desolation on the day of judgment, [because] I have proclaimed what has been decided concerning the tribes of Israel.*
Verse 10	*The princes of Judah will act as those who move the boundary stones. I will pour My vengeance upon them like a flood.*
Verse 11	*When Ephraim has been oppressed and trampled in rightful judgment, then they will decide to follow the precepts.*
Verse 12	*So I will be like rot to Ephraim and decay to the house of Judah.*
Verse 13	*For Ephraim saw his torment come up and Judah his injury. Then Ephraim turned to Assyria and went to the king as a suppliant. But he is unable to give you healing, he cannot heal your injury.*
Verse 14	*However I will be like an [old] lion for Ephraim. But I will be to the house of Judah as a young lion. I, yes, I will tear to pieces and then leave. I will take away and there will be no one who saves.*
Verse 15	*I will go and return to My residence until they recognize their guilt. Then they will seek My face in their affliction; they will seek Me in time.*

HOSEA 5

Exegesis

Introduction
Hosea 5 fits seamlessly with the content of Hosea 4 and thus continues with the judgment on the Ten Tribes (formerly called Israel, now Ephraim). In Hosea 4 the prophet spoke to the whole people of Israel. In Hosea 5 the prophet addresses the leaders of the Ten Tribes. They are held responsible for the sad spiritual state of God's people.

The prophecy of Hosea 5 speaks to a larger context than the preceding chapters did. It is pointing out that the downfall of the Ten Tribes affects the salvation of the entire nation of Israel. For the prophecies that speak of a blessed future—the Messianic Kingdom—do not focus on just one part of God's people. They concern a united people, thus all twelve tribes of Israel. The judgment on the ten-tribe kingdom, which temporarily excludes them from the blessing of God, blocks the full fulfillment of the divine prophecies for a long time.

A. Ephraim and Israel
These are key words in prophecy. We find both words in verses 3 and 5, each time used together in one sentence. That must have a meaning. In general there are three opinion about this:

A1. Most biblical scholars by far associate one and the same meaning to the names Ephraim and Israel. In both they see the kingdom of the Ten Tribes. As an explanation for this phenomenon they speak of the poetic freedom that Hosea supposedly applies.
A2. Others point out that Ephraim, as the largest tribe, had become dominant and was therefore seen as representative of the ten-tribe nation (Wood).
A3. A third opinion is that, after the invasion of the Assyrians in 733 BC, the land area of Israel had shrunk to a much smaller size and was therefore called Ephraim (Wolff).

All three proposed exegeses do not do the text justice and are weakly supported.

The use of two separate names must have a more significant reason. There is no doubt that in Hosea 1–3, except in Hosea 1:10–11, the name Israel refers to the Ten Tribes. In Hosea 1:10–11 the prophet speaks about the distant future, where the entire people (so all twelve tribes) is in view. Only the entire people of Israel bear the promise of the future Messianic Kingdom.

In Hosea 5 the blessed future of the Ten Tribes is set over against the hopeless situation of that moment. The people of Israel have been dismissed from the Sinaitic Covenant and have turned to idols. For that reason it loses the name of honor—*Israel*—and Hosea now introduces the name Ephraim. That is why we add for clarification, in Hosea 5:3, the word *all* (in brackets) to *Israel*.

B. God No Longer Fights for Israel
Israel means *God is fighting/struggling* (for His chosen people, of course). But that is no longer the case after the breaking of the Sinaitic Covenant. Thus, the covenantal name Israel expires and Hosea continues with Ephraim as the name for the kingdom or people of the Ten Tribes. The name of honor—*Israel*—is now only applied when the distant future

is in view, when Israel and Judah will be reunited in the Messianic Kingdom, and also when the past is in view, when it still bore that name.

Sources:
(Wolff, 91; Wood, 188)
(See Excursuses 3; 12; Hosea 1, Exegesis, Introduction, The People of Israel.)

Verse 1a
Hear, o priests! Give attention, you house of Israel! Listen, you royal house! Because the judgment is against you.
Verse 1 of chapter 5 introduces an important prophecy. It focuses on the leadership of the people of Israel. The priestly class (*priests*), the tribal chiefs (*house of Israel*), and the *royal house* are all being addressed.
(Born, 43–44; Ward, 93; Walvoord and Zuck, 1391)

Verse 1b
For you were a trap in Mizpah and a net that was spread out on Tabor.
It is not certain what the reason is that the names Mizpah and Tabor are mentioned here. Mizpah was a mountain in Gilead east of the Jordan river, Tabor a mountain in the valley of Jezreel. We give the following for consideration:

> In the autumn large numbers of migratory birds fly from Europe and Asia to Africa, from north to south, and in the spring from south to north. Since most species of birds do not want to or cannot fly across the Mediterranean, the ocean and the desert, many of their routes run across the land of Canaan. When the birds arrive there, they are often tired and rest on the mountains. It was therefore not difficult to catch large numbers of birds in the fall and spring with bird traps and/or nets. It was a cheap source of tasty food.*

Thus Hosea uses a very familiar image in Israel to make clear that the priests and leaders of Israel have seduced the people to sin. The leaders of Israel are designated as the main culprits.
(*Studiebijbel SBOT 1, 707)

1.1 Jewish interpretations
Rabbinical writings (from, among others, Rashi, Ibn Ezra, Kara, and RaDak) explain verse 1 very differently. They speak of sentries on the two mountains, which were meant to prevent the Israelites from going to Jerusalem for pilgrimage. But that explanation seems very farfetched.
(Garrett, 143; Harper, 269; King, 48–49; Rosenberg, vol. 1, 30; Walvoord and Zuck, 1391; Wolff, 98)

Verse 2a
The apostates have sunk deep in their bloodbaths
The prophecy speaks of *bloodbaths* by *apostates*. This points to the horrifying custom of offering small children to pagan idols—to the Moloch. The prophet Ezekiel speaks about this in 16:21 (NASB):

> "You slaughtered My children and offered them up to idols by causing them to pass through the fire."

Human sacrifices were found in several religions among the pagans. The Bible speaks of this in 2 Kings 17:17, when Hoshea was king. It is assumed that it also took place under Jeroboam II. (Read also: 2 Kings 16:3; 21:6; 23:10; Jeremiah 32:35.)
(Cooper, 172; Rosenberg, vol. 1, 30; Targum Jonathan on Hosea, Hosea 5:2; Wood, 813)

Verse 2b
but I will put them all in chains.
The prophet Hosea uses a poetic way of expressing himself. God will put Israel *in chains* or under arrest and in custody. That is exactly what happened, because after the defeat against Assyria the survivors were taken away in exile.

Annotation 5A: Child Sacrifices

One of the most horrific sins that the people of Israel committed was bringing human and/or child sacrifices. This occurred in several religions among the gentile nations surrounding Israel, but for Israel it was, of course, forbidden (Leviticus 18:21; 20:1–5; Deuteronomy 12:30–32). Yet this form of idolatry took place under, among others, Hoshea, the king of Israel (2 Kings 17:17). In this case it concerned the Baal worship that had been taken over from the city-state of Tyre. It is likely that this practice was also occurred under King Jeroboam II.

5A.1 The worship of Moloch
In the two-tribe kingdom of Judah an idolatrous worship of Moloch took place. This gruesome practice was introduced under King Ahaz, who even sacrificed one of his own sons. Melech (*melek*) was the god of the underworld. The Masoretes vocalized the word melek with the vowels of bōšet (that is: *shame, disgrace*), and so the name *Molek* arose, which became corrupted to Moloch.

The Moloch worship was practiced by the offering of young children to this idol, usually firstborn children. The idol was a large, hollow metal construction with movable, outstretched arms. In the bottom of the statue a large fire was lit, until the flames came out of the open mouth of the statue. The victim was bound and placed into the spread hands of the image. Then the arms were lifted up until the victim rolled down the arms into the open mouth.

The worship of Moloch took place both in the Northern and the Southern Kingdom. The Ben-hinnom valley (= Topheth, Jeremiah 19:6) was the most notorious place of sacrifice. The worst thing was that people did not shy away from calling upon the name of Yahweh during the sacrifices. (Read also: Leviticus 20:2–5; Jeremiah 7:31; 19:5; 32:35; 2 Kings 16:3; 21:6; 23:10; 17:17, 31; 23:10; 2 Chronicles 33:6.)

Verse 3
It is I who knows Ephraim, and Israel is an open book to Me. Because you, Ephraim, have turned to fornication, [all] Israel is defiled.
The prophecy now focuses on the consequences of the judgment of God on the ten tribes of Israel. Those consequences, surprisingly, turn out to affect all of Israel, so all twelve tribes.

The prophet makes a clear distinction between the Ten Tribes before the break in the Sinaitic Covenant and their status afterwards (Lo-Ammi = not My people, Hosea 1). The moment of transition is described in Hosea 4:17 (*Ephraim has committed himself to the idols*). That covenant with the idols replaces the Sinaitic Covenant. The transition to the new and actually pagan status is marked with a new name: *Ephraim*. From that moment on the name *Israel* refers to all twelve tribes (including Judah and Benjamin) in the messianic sense.
(Garrett, 144; McComiskey, 76)
(See Excursus 12; and exegesis of Hosea 4:17.)

3.1 The protection of the covenant
In spite of all the disciplinary measures that God brought down upon Israel every time they left Him, Israel still felt under God's protection. That continued as long as the Sinaitic Covenant was in effect. The judgment on the Ten Tribes (still called Israel under God's covenant) broke the Sinaitic Covenant. That is why the Ten Tribes lost the name *Israel* and now continue under the name *Ephraim*.

As Ephraim, the Ten Tribes have become vulnerable and as descendants of Abraham they always have to deal with the undivided enmity of Satan, who sends the army of Assyria to put an end to the nation. It does not matter to him that he is so unwittingly the executor of the judgment of God. Here too the goal justifies the means.
(See Annotations 1G; 2A; Excursuses 10; 12.)

3.2 Israel desecrated
With the downfall of Ephraim the Ten Tribes disappear into anonymity within the mists of history. However, they are an indispensable element in the future fulfillment of the prophecies of salvation. Without them the Messianic Kingdom cannot come into being. So now *[all] Israel is defiled* or has become unholy.
(McComiskey, 76)
(See Excursuses 1; 9.)

Verse 4
Their deeds prevented them from turning back to their God, for there is a spirit of fornication in their hearts and they do not know Yahweh.
The Ten Tribes have strayed so far from God, that there is no way back. For how can they find Yahweh, now that they do not know Him anymore? (See verse 4c.) Ephraim is no longer a nation that occasionally deviates from God's paths, only to come to repentance when God's prophets exhort the people. There is now *a spirit of fornication in their hearts*. With that they have separated themselves from God and are no longer God's people.

Verse 5a
And the majesty of Israel responds to His presence.
The prophecy points here to the glory that once belonged to the united people of Israel, when, thanks to God's blessings, it had become prosperous and rich under King David and King Solomon. But it looks not only to the past but also refers to the high destination of Israel in the far future. For many prophecies testify that blessing will once again come to the people of Israel. This will happen when the prophecies regarding the second coming of Jesus Christ and the Messianic Kingdom come to fulfillment.

The *majesty* of the glorious past and of the foretold future, however, was far removed from the reality of that time. Because in that present time they lacked God. Therefore it testified against the ten tribes of Ephraim in the eyes of God (*to His presence*).
(Rosenberg, vol. 1, 32)
(See Excursus 9.)

Verse 5b
Israel will stumble with Ephraim over their sins; also Judah will stumble with them.
With the downfall of Ephraim (the Ten Tribes) an indispensable part of God's people (all twelve tribes) is taken away. Thus the option disappeared that both parts of the nation could be reunited in the short term. Therefore, through the fall of Ephraim the entire people stumble, and thus also Judah (with Benjamin).
(McComiskey, 78)

Verse 6
They will go to seek Yahweh with their small cattle and their oxen, but they will not find Him. He has withdrawn from them.
The judgment had been announced but not yet executed. Meanwhile, the sacrifices at Dan and Bethel—a surrogate religion that was in fact idol worship—simply continued. People sought Yahweh with sacrifices of *sheep and oxen*, but did not find Him. The Sinaitic Covenant had been broken; *they will not find Him*. Yahweh *has withdrawn from them*.

Hosea 5:6 is the fulfillment of an ancient prophecy found in Deuteronomy 32:20 (NASB):

> *Then He said, "I will hide My face from them, I will see what their end shall be; for they are a perverse generation, sons in whom is no faithfulness."*

The first part of verse 6 is a standard expression indicating the sacrifice of cattle. That happened at Gilgal and Bethel, at the northern and southern borders of the kingdom of Israel. There, King Jeroboam I established two shrines and had golden bull calves made for them. These were worshiped in the name of Yahweh. This perversion of the temple worship in Jerusalem was heavily counted against him. In name it was a service to God. In reality it was idolatry, which was sharply condemned by the prophets. It is known as *the sin of Jeroboam*.
(Brown, 51; Ironside, 43–44; McComiskey, 78; Wolff, 100)
(See Excursus 11.)

Verse 7
They are unfaithful to Yahweh, for they have given birth to children who became strangers. Now someone else will digest their share.
It is unlikely that this is referring to children stemming from a relationship with pagans. Hosea does not speak of this. The option that remains is that the children were no longer included in the covenant. This would be the case if the male children were no longer circumcised. The knowledge of God had receded so far that even circumcision was being neglected.
(Wood, 190)

Verse 8
Sound the shofar in Gibeah and the trumpet in Rama. Let the battle cry be heard in Beth Aven. Go after them, Benjamin!
In the prophetic books, blowing on the shofar is often connected with the day of Yahweh. In the larger perspective it is the day when Yahweh will defeat all Israel's enemies and reveal Himself as the only God to the whole earth.

The judgment is spoken as if to one of God's enemies. This is how far Israel (the Ten Tribes, now called *Ephraim*) has come. It turned away from God and turned so explicitly to idols that the people became God's enemy.

The name Beth Aven is most likely a synonym for the city of Bethel. It means *house of unworthiness*, usually translated *house of the idol* or *house of evil*. In this name the judgment on the calf worship is implicit (see verse 6a).
(Ward, 103)

8.1 Hostile Assyria
The cities of Gibeah, Rama, and Bethel lay around Jerusalem. It is assumed that these were garrison cities, which formed part of the defense of Jerusalem. In this context, the

tribe of Benjamin is urged to withdraw behind the defense line around Jerusalem.

If the preceding explanation is correct, it could indirectly indicate the siege of Jerusalem as it took place under the kingship of Hezekiah. For only ten years after the fall of Samaria (the capital of Israel/Ephraim) the Assyrian king Sennacherib entered Judah with a huge army. The supremacy was so great that King Hezekiah did not let it come to a confrontation but first tried to buy off the Assyrians. In doing so he lost the favor of God and the Assyrians conquered Judah and came to the gates of Jerusalem.

Only when King Hezekiah humbled himself before God, did the Almighty One intervene. The angel of the Lord descended and killed 185,000 Assyrians in one night (2 Kings 19:35–36). It therefore would appear that the prophet Hosea warns the Southern Kingdom (Judah and Benjamin) of the impending invasion.
(Andersen and Freedman, 406–7; Born, 42; Edelkoort, 183; Ward, 103)

Verse 9
Ephraim will become a desolation on the day of judgment, [because] I have proclaimed what has been decided concerning the tribes of Israel.
This prophecy was fulfilled to the letter. For the Assyrians left behind a completely devastated country after the fall of Samaria, where few people still lived. 2 Kings 18:11–12 says about this (NASB):

11 *Then the king of Assyria carried Israel away into exile to Assyria, and put them in Halah and on the Habor, the river of Gozan, and in the cities of the Medes,*
12 *because they did not obey the voice of the LORD their God, but transgressed His covenant, even all that Moses the servant of the LORD commanded; they would neither listen nor do it.*

Also from 2 Kings 17 it appears that the country of the northern kingdom had become a wasteland. Verses 25–26 speak of freely roaming lions who often attacked and killed some of the few surviving residents.

9.1 Samaritans
Because of the war with Assyria and the subsequent deportation of the inhabitants, the northern part of Canaan had become depopulated. The few Israelites who had escaped the soldiers of the Assyrians and still lived there, mingled with strangers who had been "imported" by the Assyrians (2 Kings 17:24–41). Samaritans were the offspring of this forbidden mixture of Israelites with gentiles.

Verse 10a
The princes of Judah will act as those who move the boundary stones.
In Old Testament times there was no land registry in which the boundaries of properties were recorded. The owner of a piece of land in Canaan indicated the boundaries by means of boundary posts or boundary stones. It often happened that a landowner moved the boundary stones to enlarge his piece of land. Clearly, this was strictly forbidden.

It appears from the text that the kingdom of Judah annexed areas of the former kingdom of Israel and thus enlarged its territory. We might not have anything against that and might even find it to be a sensible policy. However, in light of the prophecies about the future salvation of Israel—the Messianic Kingdom, where every tribe gets a selected area (see Ezekiel 48)—this was an infraction on God's promises. Moving boundary stones was against God's laws and God's ways.

Vers 10b
I will pour My vengeance upon them like a flood.
This prophecy sees further into the future, when Judah's downfall would take place. Also Judah sinned heavily against God. Moving the *boundary stones* was probably not their biggest sin, however it was added to the guilt-load.
(Garrett, 151; Mays, 89; Wolff, 114)

Verse 11
When Ephraim has been oppressed and trampled in rightful judgment, then they will decide to follow the precepts.
The text speaks of a time when Ephraim would be *oppressed* and *trampled in rightful judgment*. This, of course, refers to the period that began with the captivity by the Assyrians and continues to the present day. It is striking that Hosea speaks of *rightful judgment* (*mishpât*). It was not a coincidence that Israel went down. It was a righteous punishment.

Verse 11 is a sentence that contains various subtle details. First, the name *Ephraim* is used. It tells us that the Ten Tribes in the period in question are no longer God's people, because the name *Israel* is withheld from them.

The second is that verse 11 predicts the end of that period. For the decision to *follow* God's *precepts* cannot be defined other than as a national conversion, as it will take place in the end times. That has not happened so far, and thus the period in question continues, even today—more than twenty-five hundred years later.
(See Excursus 12.)

Verse 12
So I will be like rot to Ephraim and decay to the house of Judah.
Until a nationwide conversion takes place, God will not help Ephraim. On the contrary, He is like a *rot*. All godly protection against enemy forces is gone. This had immediate consequences, because Satan has a deep hatred of Israel and Judah. He will seize every opportunity to harm them, even if it means that in doing so he executes God's counsel. Under God's permission, it is going badly with Ephraim.

It does not stop there, because this prophecy also predicts the downfall of Judah. In this context it does not matter whether the Babylonian exile is in view here or the wars between the Jews and the Romans, in 67–70 BC or 132–35 BC. Both were a punishment from God because they rejected Him so He did not protect them (see verse 13).
(Calvijn, *Daniel* II, *Kleine Profeten* I/II, Hosea, 156; McComiskey, 83)

Annotation 5B: A God of Revenge

5B.1 Two different Gods? No!
Christians often have trouble with a vengeful God. And if one cannot ignore it in the Old Testament, it is usually stated that the God of the New Testament is different. This creates a contrast of *vengeful* and *loving*, as if there are two different gods.

We cannot model the Almighty after our taste. He is a God of love, certainly, more than we can even imagine. However, He is also a God of vengeance. Herein the New Testament is no different than the Old. Hebrews 10:30–31 (NASB) makes a clear statement about this:

30 *For we know Him who said, "Vengeance is Mine, I will repay." And again, "The Lord will judge His people."*
31 *It is a terrifying thing to fall into the hands of the living God.*

Yet in our time we do not see a tit-for-tat policy any more like we find it in the book of Hosea and in many other places in the Old Testament. God no longer punishes immediately, except in special cases. However, that has nothing to do with a changed God. For the directness in His actions was connected to His covenant relationship with Israel and the land of Canaan. They were His people and it was His land. The Almighty Himself ruled over them, so His acts of government were directly applicable in society, not only for good, but also in case of punishment.

We, however, live in the age of the church of Christ, the age of grace—*You are not under law, but under grace* (Romans 6:14 NASB). This grace is accessible to everyone. In that context there is no longer any question of direct interference from God by sending great judgments, except perhaps in extreme cases. For us, Matthew 5:44–45 (KJV) applies:

44 *But I say unto you, Love your enemies, bless them that curse you, do good to them that hate you, and pray for them which despitefully use you, and persecute you;*
45 *That ye may be the children of your Father which is in heaven: for he maketh his sun to rise on the evil and on the good, and sendeth rain on the just and on the unjust.*

5B.2 The salvation postponed
With the breach of the Sinaitic Covenant started an era in which the individual was addressed. That is the reason Matthew 5:45 (KJV) says:

for he maketh his sun to rise on the evil and on the good, and sendeth rain on the just and on the unjust.

So Matthew speaks of an era that had already started in the day of Hosea. Since then, there is no longer an Israelite state in God's own land, Canaan, where He rules. That does not mean, however, a cancellation but a postponement of the great promises of salvation.

5B.3 Looking into the dark?
However, looking toward this future salvation is sometimes like looking into the dark. The Scriptures testify about the judgments (birth pangs) that precedes it, as described in both the Old and the New Testaments (especially in Revelation). The apostle Peter also wrote about this in 2 Peter 3:7 (KJV):

7 *But the heavens and the earth, which are now, by the same word are kept in store, reserved unto fire against the day of judgment and perdition of ungodly men.*

Well, that is not an attractive future. But 2 Peter continues in verse 9:

9 *The Lord is not slack concerning his promise, as some men count slackness; but is longsuffering to us-ward, not willing that any should perish, but that all should come to repentance.*

Peter called for repentance and with reason, because all who choose Christ as their savior will be saved by the rapture before the judgments start.
(See Excursus 2.)

Verse 13
For Ephraim saw his torment come up and Judah his injury. Then Ephraim turned to

Assyria and went to the king as a suppliant. But he is unable to give you healing, he cannot heal your injury.
Ephraim was condemned, because they gave their fate into the hand of Assyria and that excluded God as their potential savior. Judah got a second chance.

The decay, that is, the increasing sin, was not an accident that overtook the people. It was a conscious choice. When Ephraim realized that they were in trouble, they did not call out to God but invoked the help of the enemy, Assyria. That did not help, of course. It even aggravated the ailment, because with this rapprochement the Assyrian idols also played a greater role in Israel.

Sin is not a natural process, but a conscious choice of man against his Creator. The remedy is repentance, no more and no less. That was true for Ephraim, for Judah, and for us today.
(Calvijn, *Daniël* II, *Kleine Profeten* I/II, Hosea, 157–59; Stuart, 105)

Verse 14
However I will be like an [old] lion for Ephraim. But I will be to the house of Judah as a young lion. I, yes, I will tear to pieces and then leave. I will take away and there will be no one who saves.
An old lion is a renegade and kills more than he needs for food. A young lion defends his territory and family.
(See verse 14 in Hebrew Interlinear Text)

14.1 Cruel Assyria
With the image of a savage lion who kills without necessity, the prophecy paints the role of superstate, Assyria. And the image suits Assyria, which had a reputation of acting with great cruelty. There were far more deaths than were necessary for their purposes. In the war with Israel it was no different and it is likely that more than half (the estimates even go to 70 percent) of the population was slaughtered.

Unlike Israel, Judah did come to repentance (2 Kings 18:1–7). The kingdom of Judah was therefore spared, for a young, noble lion is a lion who defends his group. God fought for Judah (2 Kings 19:28–37).
(Malbim, cited by Rosenberg, vol. 1, 36)
(See also the section above: 8.1 Hostile Assyria.)

Verse 15
I will go and return to My residence until they recognize their guilt. Then they will seek My face in their affliction; they will seek Me in time.
God withdrew; the sky closed for Ephraim. This period continues until the present day. But it will come to an end, for if they *recognize their guilt*, they will seek and find God's *face*. That has yet to happen, but the first signs of the turnaround are already visible.
(See Excursus 7.)

15.1 They will seek Me in time.
The words *in time* has the connotation of being *on time*. For what? Apparently, the prophecy points to an important event, which is crucial for the Ten Tribes. That must be the establishment of the Messianic Kingdom. For the kingdom of God is not complete if all twelve tribes of Israel are not a part of it.

In our time we are seeing the Jews going back to the promised land. Many see in it a fulfillment of the biblical prophecies we find in Scripture. However, the Ten Tribes must also

return. Time is running out, because the end time is near. It is therefore not surprising that it is precisely during this time that the lost tribes of Israel are being rediscovered.
(Constable, 26; Feinberg, *Minor Prophets*, 27; Wood, 192)
(See Excursus 7.)

Excursus 13: Israel's Blessed Future

In many places in the Bible, the Holy Scriptures speak about the future salvation/blessing of Judah and Israel. This thus concerns all twelve tribes of Israel, including the priestly tribe of Levi. We have made a more or less arbitrary choice of supporting verses. (There are many more!) They are placed under headings, according to the nature of the events being foretold.

13.a Future blessings

13.a1   The Holy Bible speaks of a restoration of Judah (the southern kingdom) and Jerusalem:
Jeremiah 30:18; 33:26; Ezekiel 39:25; Joel 3:1; Amos 9:11; 9:14; Micah 2:12; 4:6, 8; 7:7–8, 11, 20; Zephaniah 3:19–20; Zechariah 8:15; 10:6, 8; 10:10

13.a2   God Himself will intervene by sending terrible judgments to punish the godless humanity that will serve Satan at that time.
Isaiah 2:10, 19; 13:9; 24:6; 66:15; Jeremiah 30:23–24; Ezekiel 38:19; Joel 2:30–31; 3:14, 16; Amos 8:9–10; Micah 1:3–4; Zephaniah 3:8; Haggai 2:7–8; Malachi 4:3; Matthew 24:29; Revelation 6:12; 11:13; 16:18

13.a3   God's spirit will be poured out on everything that lives.
Ezekiel 39:29; Joel 2:28–29; Zechariah 12:10

13.a4   The people of Israel and Judah will come to repentance at the end of time, when they find Jesus Christ, the Messiah.
Isaiah 10:21; Jeremiah 31:9; Zephaniah 3:9; Zechariah 12:11; 13:9

13.a5   All nations who endanger Israel will be punished by God Himself.
Ezekiel 39:6; Joel 3:2; Amos 5:18; Micah 4:12; 5:8, 10, 14; 7:17; Zephaniah 2:3; 3:19; Zechariah 12:3, 9; 14:3; Malachi 3:2; 4:1, 3; Revelation 16:16; 19:15, 20

13.a6   God Himself will fight for and with Israel.
Isaiah 66:15; Jeremiah 30:7; Ezekiel 38:16, 22–23; 39:6, 11; Daniel 12:1; Joel 3:1–2, 12, 16; Micah 2:13; 4:12–13; 5:9–10; 7:15–16; Zechariah 9:14–15; 12:5–6; 14:3, 6; Revelation 19:15–16

13.a7   The land of Canaan will be given back to Israel.
Isaiah 61:5–6; Jeremiah 23:6; 31:31; Ezekiel 37:22, 26; 45:1; Amos 9:11, 14–15; Micah 4:7; Zechariah 2:12; 8:8

13.a8   The promised land will be rebuilt and come to great fertility and prosperity.
Isaiah 9:6; 11:10; 27:6; 61:5–6, 11; Jeremiah 31:5; 33:17; Ezekiel 47:8–9; Joel 3:18; Amos 9:13–15; Zechariah 8:12; 14:8–9

13.a9   Israel will become a glory among the nations.
Isaiah 4:3; 11:10; 12:5–6; 62:12; Jeremiah 31:7; Micah 5:6; Zephaniah 3:19–20; Zechariah 8:13, 23; 14:11, 16, 21

13.a10   Israel will become a mighty nation and live in peace.
Ezekiel 37:22, 24–25; Micah 4:7; 5:3, 7–8; 7:14; Zechariah 8:21–23; 9:8

13.a11   The Davidic royal house will be restored.
Isaiah 11:10; Jeremiah 23:5; 30:9; 33:15, 17; Ezekiel 37:24; Amos 9:11; Micah 5:1–2; Zechariah 12:8

13.a12   God will come to live on Zion, His holy mountain, in a newly built temple.

Isaiah 2:2–3; 12:5–6; Ezekiel 37:27–28; 43:4, 7; Joel 3:21; Micah 4:1–3, 7; Zechariah 2:4–5, 10; 6:13; 8:3

13.b Just a selection out of many
This listing of Bible texts is far from complete. The number could easily be greatly expanded. For example, there are many references to the end time in the psalms and in the books of Moses. But message and purport are clear.

Point 13.a1 and points 13.a5 and 13.a6 can, with some imagination, be placed somewhere in the past. However, all others certainly cannot, not even point 13.a3, because the outpouring of the Holy Spirit on the day of Pentecost involved only a limited group of people. That was a far smaller number than Joel 2:28 predicts, unless the texts quoted are largely spiritualized and the literal meaning is strongly violated. (The day of Pentecost is, of course, a prefulfillment of this prophecy.)

13.c What is certainly not fulfilled
The predicted natural disasters have certainly not yet taken place, nor a mass conversion of Israel and/or Judah. And Judah, that is the Jews, is certainly no glory among the nations today. And God does not yet live in Zion (Jerusalem).

13.d What may have been fulfilled
Since 1948, there has again been a Jewish nation, so points 13.a7 and 13.a8 may be partly fulfilled. May? Yes, because clearly the nation of Israel has not converted, so we can speak here at best of a precursor to the final fulfillment. A second point is that the land of Canaan during the Messianic Kingdom will be much bigger than Israel is today.

There is also clearly no state of lasting peace, let alone of the restoration of the Davidic royal house, both of which are inextricably bound up with the promises of the return of Israel. So, very far-reaching events still have to take place before the prophecies about Israel will be fully fulfilled.

HOSEA 6
Hebrew Text Translation

Introduction
Some exegetes remove this chapter from the book of Hosea, and consider it a separate prophecy of an unknown writer. They call it a *song of repentance*,* sung by priests in hard times. (Other scholars identify only verses 1–3 as a song.) As such chapter 6 is separated from the rest of the book and given a universal significance. Consequently, it leaves the prophet's message obscured.

The reader should not be surprised to learn that we do not follow this thinking. We believe this chapter is also an essential part of the book of Hosea. We do, however, recognize the need to examine the Hebrew text carefully. For in the details we find what connects this chapter to the book as a whole. There we will find the building blocks that anchor this prophesy to the whole counsel of God.

Many biblical scholars have not bothered to study the book of Hosea in depth. They do not recognize it as divine prophesy, nor do they see how chapter 6 is integrated with the first chapters of the book. In their minds Hosea, starting with chapter 4, is a fragmentary work put together into a single book by an editor who compiled texts from different authors. It should come as no surprise that these exegetes and/or translators focus primarily on the poetic qualities of the text, at the cost of all the other riches offered.
(Andersen and Freedman, 417–18; *Limburg, 27)

A. A Messy Prophecy?
The theologians Andersen and Freedman offer an illustrative example of the way in which many biblical scholars treat Hosea 6. In reading only a few lines of their commentary, I found eight difficult words or expressions, which proves that the writers are highly educated. But they leave most of their readers empty-handed.

In a detached manner Andersen and Freedman dissect the contents of Hosea, which they assign to various classes and categories using stately technical terms. In this context they speak of a highly rhythmic piece and use such terms as "unframed speech" and "condensation" of the contents. As a result, the reader gets the impression that the text is messy, without substance, and stripped of its prophetic power.

Andersen and Freedman also devote considerable effort to recovering *four stanzas* of a *poem* of Hosea, which they try to reconstruct. From there, they go on to change what in their minds are illogical and/or corrupted texts. While their efforts may sound impressive, they are actually just rewriting parts of the Hebrew text and adjusting it to their own interpretation. As a result, many of the details offered in the original text disappear. Since many exegetes and/or translators have followed such an approach, we see vast differences between their translations. The predictable consequence is that Hosea 6 has come to be viewed as messy, both in meaning and in structure. Brown* therefore offers this unsurprising conclusion: "The text is corrupt, and it is impossible to say exactly what the prophet wrote."

B. A Powerful Prophetic Text!
In this commentary we emphatically distance ourselves from the above position. Hosea 6 is in fact a powerful prophetic text. Regardless of the text's poetic structure, the prophet

uses clear expressions when he speaks. The preceding chapters have already shown how Hosea forms a textual unity. This finds further confirmation in Hosea 6.

In contrast with the majority of interpreters, we will delve deeply into the original Hebrew text. When we adhere to and examine it carefully, a clear prophesy will unfold itself before our eyes, pertaining both to the past (the "now" of that time) and to the distant future (the eschaton). The latter is the main reason that this part of Hosea has been criticized.

C. Poetic Language

Hosea 6 is written in poetic style, to an even greater degree than the preceding chapters. This makes the process of translation more difficult than normal. But if we stick to the theme of Hosea's prophesy as it has emerged from the preceding chapters and also compare Scripture with Scripture, we can manage. This method will allow us to offer a translation that may not be perfect, but still comes close to the true sense of the Hebrew source text that the prophet wrote so many ages ago.

Sources:
(Andersen and Freedman, 415, 417–19, 421; *Brown, 61; Schmidt, 111)

Verse 1 NASB
"Come, let us return to the LORD. For He has torn us, but He will heal us; He has wounded us, but He will bandage us."

Verse 1 KJV
Come, and let us return unto the LORD: for he hath torn, and he will heal us; he hath smitten, and he will bind us up.

Verse 1 NIV
"Come, let us return to the LORD. He has torn us to pieces but he will heal us; he has injured us but he will bind up our wounds."

Verse 1 Hebrew Interlinear Text
come! and-let-us-return to Yahweh for he he-tore-to-pieces but-he-will-heal-us he-injured but-he-will-bind-wounds-of-us

Verse 1b
for he he-tore-to-pieces
In the considerations leading to our translation, we need to pay attention to both the poetic language of Hosea and to the context. Israel has been condemned by God. The Sinaitic Covenant has been abrogated, and that is why the nation is now called Ephraim. Thereafter it is sent into exile and scattered. Poetically, therefore, the people of Israel have been torn to pieces.

The word *taraph* means *to tear, to tear in pieces*, or *to pull apart*. In this case, however, the passage does not concern an animal and its prey, but a nation that has been *pulled apart* by God.
(Andersen and Freedman, 419; Brown, 55; Garrett, 155; Strong's OT, word 2963)

We read: *because He who pulled us apart*

Verse 1c
but-he-will-heal-us
Rapha means *to heal, to make whole*, or *to repair* (Numbers 12:13; Leviticus 13:18). In

combination with the expression *to pull apart*, the matching translation is *to make whole again*.
(Garrett, 155; Harper, 283; Strong's OT, word 7495; Ward, 114)

We read: *will also make us whole again*

Verse 1d
he-injured but-he-will-bind-wounds-of-us
The word *nakah* (here translated as *injured*) has a wide application in the biblical text. Among the translations, we found *beat* (Deuteronomy 25:3), *killed, slain* (Numbers 25:14), *defeated*, but also *inflict wounds* (2 Kings 8:29; 9:15). Since verse 1d also goes on to speak of *binding*, here *injured* seems the most suitable translation.
(Harper, 283; McComiskey, 88; Strong's OT, word 5221; Wolff, 105)

We read: ***He injured us, but will also bind up our wounds***

The whole sentence:
Come and let us turn to Yahweh! Because He who pulled us apart will also make us whole again. He injured us, but will also bind up our wounds.

Annotation 6A: Two Days and the Third

6A.1 The Jewish interpretation
In Hosea 6:2 we find these very intriguing words—*he-will-revive-us after-two-days on-the-day the-third*—which are explained in a variety of ways. For some it is a strange poetic way to express a short time; for others an important divine prophecy. Rabbi Rashi is representative of the view of our Jewish brothers. He explains the text as follows:

> He will strengthen us from the two retributions which have passed over us from the two sanctuaries that were destroyed. . . . With the construction of the third temple, He (Yahweh) will set us up.

Rashi explains the *two-days* and *the third* as a future prophesy, seen from the perspective of the time of prophet Hosea. In each of the three days he identifies an important event. Rashi links the first day to the destruction of Jerusalem and the first temple (by King Nebuchadnezzar). This is an event that took place long after the death of Hosea. In the second day he sees the destruction of the second temple (by the Romans), some eight centuries after Hosea. The third day he places in the eschaton, when the third and final temple will be built.
(Rosenberg, vol. 1, 37)

6A.2 The orthodox Christian interpretation
On the third day He will raise us up. This expression of course makes us think of the resurrection of Jesus Christ, and indeed the text has been explained that way by many. This already happened in the early church. The church father Tertullian (ca. 160–230 AD) was one of those who interpreted Hosea 6:2 that way, as did the Reformer Martin Luther many centuries later. In spite of this, most exegetes reject this link to the New Testament. In our discussion of the exegesis, we will return to this question.
(Reed, 54)

6A.3 Exegesis from a liberal perspective
There are very few exegetes who understand the expression *after-two-days on-the-day the-third* as a reference to a time span or even an era. This is strange, since that is indeed what the Hebrew text says. That fact, however, appears to play virtually no role in the

debates over this verse. Here exegesis has assumed a decisive role in translation and that blocks any interpretation that refers to the future. The basic assumption of that exegesis is that the prophet (or any prophet) is not able to see the future. It is the view of the unbelieving exegete that has set the tone, and liberal exegetes have followed him. There are only a few Bible-believing theologians who resist, but their voices can hardly be heard.

The above considerations led Harper to offer the following translation: *He will revive us after two or three days*—a strange expression without any logic. Andersen and Freedman speak of "an artistic turn, not a time schedule." Thereafter, they get caught up in all kinds of reflections on a pagan superstition according to which the soul needs two or three days after death to leave the body. This discussion has nothing to offer us, but only serves to fill the pages. Ward too draws a line to pagan idol worship, but reaches no coherent conclusion. He does, however, pose a crucial question: "Why are the people so sure that their healing will be accomplished on the third day?"† Wolff similarly sees no specific temporal marker there, and rather speaks of *a short time*. In support he refers to a lengthy list of rabbinic writings in which that view can likewise be found.

6A.4 The literal method

John Calvin is one of the few interpreters who understands the term *two days* as a very long period, although he does not explain himself in greater detail. The remarkable thing about all of this is that the Hebrew text itself does speak in very clear terms. For that reason, we will first analyze it, to see what happens. The real (literal) meaning of the Hebrew words will be leading the way.

Sources:
(*Andersen and Freedman, 420; Calvijn, *Daniël* II, *Kleine Profeten* I/II, Hosea, 217–20; Harper, 283; Reed, 54; †Ward, 117–21; Wolff, 117; Wood, 193)
(See Annotation 6A.)

Verse 2 NASB
"He will revive us after two days; He will raise us up on the third day, that we may live before Him."

Verse 2 KJV
After two days will he revive us: in the third day he will raise us up, and we shall live in his sight.

Verse 2 NIV
"After two days he will revive us; on the third day he will restore us, that we may live in his presence."

Verse 2 Hebrew Interlinear Text
he-will-revive-us after-two-days on-the-day the-third he-will-restore-us that-we-may-live in-presences-of-him

Verse 2a
he-will-revive-us after-two-days
The primary meaning of *chayah* is *to receive life* or *to be alive*. Sometimes it can also mean *to keep alive* (Genesis 6:19), as well as *to bring to life*, in the sense of *to revive* (Isaiah 57:15). As in verse 1, *He* refers to God Himself, so that we translate it as *He*.
(Andersen and Freedman, 421; Born, 48; Brown, 56; Calvijn, *Daniël* II, *Kleine Profeten* I/II, Hosea, 217–18; Garrett, 155; Strong's OT, word 2421; Ward, 114)

We read: *He will revive us after two days*

Verse 2b
on-the-day the-third he-will-restore-us
A translation that uses the term *renew* or *restore* is an interpretation. That is not what the Hebrew text says. The word *qum* means *to stand (up), to arise* (Genesis 13:17; Judges 7:15; Psalm 88:10) or *to raise up* (Deuteronomy 29:12).
(Andersen and Freedman, 421; Born, 48; Brown, 56; McComiskey, 87; Strong's OT, word 6965; Wolff, 105; Ward, 114)

We read: *on the third day He will raise us up*

Verse 2c
that-we-may-live
The word *chayah* reoccurs here (see verse 2a).
(Born, 48; Wolff, 105)

We read: *that we may live*

Verse 2d
in-presences-of-him
The primary meaning of the word *panim* is *faces* (plural), although it is commonly translated *face* (singular) or *presence*.

It thus says: *in/before-face-of-him*, that is, *before His face* or *in His presence*. We read *His* capitalized, since there is no doubt that it is the face or presence of God.
(Andersen and Freedman, 422; Born, 48; Strong's OT, word 6440)

We read: *in His presence*

The whole sentence:
He will revive us after two days. On the third day He will raise us up, that we may live in His presence.
In the definitive text, we will add verse 3a to verse 2.

Verse 3 NASB
"So let us know, let us press on to know the LORD. His going forth is as certain as the dawn; And He will come to us like the rain, like the spring rain watering the earth."

Verse 3 KJV
Then shall we know, if we follow on to know the LORD: his going forth is prepared as the morning; and he shall come unto us as the rain, as the latter and former rain unto the earth.

Verse 3 NIV
"Let us acknowledge the LORD; let us press on to acknowledge him. As surely as the sun rises, he will appear; he will come to us like the winter rains, like the spring rains that water the earth."

Verse 3 Hebrew Interlinear Text
so-let-us-acknowledge let-us-press-on to-acknowledge . . . Yahweh as-sunrise he-will-appear coming-of-him and-he-will-come like-the-winter-rain to-us like-spring-rain he-waters earth

Verse 3a
so-let-us-acknowledge
The sentence begins with a *vav*, which we translate here as *so*, since its function is to connect a cause (verse 2b/c/d) and an effect (verse 3).

Yada' in most cases means *to acquire knowledge* (Genesis 3:7; Exodus 1:8; Proverbs 3:6). In some cases it also has the sense of *to recognize* or *to acknowledge* (Isaiah 33:13). Here we have chosen to retain the most common meaning.
(Brown, 56; Harper, 283; Strong's OT, word 3045)
(See one of the final sections of the introduction to this book titled "The Letter Vav.")

We read: ***so let us acquire knowledge***

Verse 3b
let-us-press-on to-acknowledge . . . Yahweh
The word *radaph* means *to run after*, *to pursue*, *to chase*, or *to persecute*. Harper translates this term with the word *zealous*. Although this does capture the overall sense well, as a translation it is too far removed from the Hebrew source text.

The second word is once again derived from *yada* (see verse 3a). The text thus says: *let us pursue knowledge*.
(Andersen and Freedman, 422; Harper, 283; Kidner, 63; Strong's OT, word 7291)

We read: ***let us pursue the knowledge of Yahweh***

Verse 3c
as-sunrise
The basic meaning of *motsa* is *a place of rising* for all kinds of things (so water that rises up or world empires or people). In Psalm 19:6 NASB translates *its rising* and in 2 Kings 2:21 with *spring*. So the context decides, and here it is: *sunrise*.
(Andersen and Freedman, 423; Brown, 56; Garrett, 156; Mays, 95–96; Strong's OT, word 4151; Ward, 114)

We initially read: ***as a sunrise***

Verse 3d
he-will-appear
Kun means *to determine* (Genesis 41:32) or *to establish, to be done* (Deuteronomy 13:14, 17:4; 1 Samuel 13:13; 1 Kings 2:12; 1 Chronicles 17:14). Calvin uses the term *prepared* in this context.

In following the NIVIHEOT, we use the future tense.
(Brown, 56; Calvijn, *Daniel* II, *Kleine Profeten* I/II, Hosea, 220; Strong's OT, word 3559; Ward, 114)

We read: ***it will be established***

Verse 3e
coming-of-him
Shachar usually means *dawn* or *daybreak* (Genesis 19:15; 32:24, 26; Joshua 6:15; Nehemiah 4:21; Job 38:12), but only seldom *coming*. We have good reason, therefore, to depart from the NIVIHEOT here.
(Calvijn, *Daniel* II, *Kleine Profeten* I/II, Hosea, 222; Strong's OT, word 7837; Wolf, 105)

We read: ***His dawn will be***

Verse 3c/d/e
If we combine verse 3c, 3d, and 3e, we get something along the lines of: *as established as a sunrise is, so His dawn will be*. Garrett reads: *As surely as the sun rises, he will appear*. This is an excellent translation, which we would like to follow closely. We have, however, chosen to replace the word *appear* with *dawn*, because it is closer to the Hebrew text.
(Brown, 56; Garrett, 159)

We finally read: ***As sure as the sun rises, His dawn will be***

Verse 3f/g/h
and-he-will-come like-the-winter-rain to-us like-spring-rain he-waters earth
This passage presents us with a problem. Most exegetes suggest in their translation that there is only one kind of rain. So too Van de Born reads: *He will come to us as the rain, as spring showers that water the earth*. If we follow the Hebrew source text carefully, however, there is no doubt that it refers to two kinds of rain (the winter and spring rains), as reflected in the KJV (*the latter and former rain*). To establish more support to our translation, we will delve even deeper into the Hebrew text.
(Andersen and Freedman, 424–25; Born, 49; Mays, 96; McComiskey, 89; Walvoord and Zuck, 1393)

Verse 3f
and-he-will-come like-the-winter-rain to-us
The word *geshem* usually means *rain* or sometimes *downpour* (Genesis 7:12; 8:2). In combination with *malqosh* (verse 3g) the text refers to lengthy and rather heavy winter showers. This is also what we find in Zechariah 10:1.

Each of the three passages refers to a downpour or torrential rain, which at the same time serves to depict a judgment from God. That holds true for the present passage as well.
(Andersen and Freedman, 424–25; Garrett, 156; Harper, 283–84; Reed, 55; Strong's OT, word 1653)

We read: ***to us like torrential rain***

Verse 3g
like-spring-rain
The word *malqosh* is rare in the Bible. From the passages in which it does occur, it appears that the word is always used for *mild rain* that comes as a blessing (Deuteronomy 11:14; Job 29:23; Proverbs 16:15; Zechariah 10:1).
(Andersen and Freedman, 424–25; Garrett, 156; Strong's OT, word 4456; Wolff, 105)

We read: ***but as a mild rain***

Verse 3h
he-waters earth
This translation is an interpretation of the Hebrew source text, for which reason we choose not to adopt it. The word *yarah* means *to teach*, as in Exodus 4:12, 15; Leviticus 10:11; and Judges 13:8. Moreover, in all four passages the teaching is from God, which is something we certainly need to take into account. The word *He* therefore does not refer back to the rain, but to God Himself, for which reason we have chosen to capitalize it.
(Anderson and Freedman, 425; Strong's OT, word 3384)

We read: ***He will teach the earth***

The whole sentence:
So let us acquire knowledge; let us pursue the knowledge of Yahweh. # As sure as the

sun rises, His dawn will be. Then He will come to us like torrential rain, but as a mild rain He will teach the earth.

The first part of verse 3 (up to the #) does not connect very well to the rest of verse 3. It fits much better with verse 2 (see the discussion of verse 3a). In the definitive text, this correction will be applied.

Verse 4 NASB
What shall I do with you, O Ephraim? What shall I do with you, O Judah? For your loyalty is like a morning cloud and like the dew which goes away early.

Verse 4 KJV
O Ephraim, what shall I do unto thee? O Judah, what shall I do unto thee? for your goodness is as a morning cloud, and as the early dew it goeth away.

Verse 4 NIV
"What can I do with you, Ephraim? What can I do with you, Judah? Your love is like the morning mist, like the early dew that disappears."

Verse 4 Hebrew Interlinear Text
what? can-I-do with-you Ephraim what? can-I-do with-you Judah indeed-love-of-you like-mist-of morning and-like-the-dew one-being-early one-disappearing
The word *anan* usually means *clouds* or *cloud mass*. The NIVIHEOT translation *mist* is an interpretation, since that is not what the Hebrew text says. The verse refers to a thin cloud covering, which would have appeared in Canaan during the night and typically dissipated quickly again at dawn. (See Job 7:9.)

Wood refers to a *morning mist*. Van de Born and Calvin translate the term as *morning cloud*, but that is a little minimalist. Our preference is: *a thin cloud cover in the morning*. (Born, 49; Calvijn, *Daniel* II, *Kleine Profeten* I/II, Hosea, 223; Chaplin, 19; Harper, 285; Strong's OT, word 6051; Wood, 195)

We read:
What should I do with you, O Ephraim? What should I do with you, O Judah? For your love is like a thin cloud in the morning, like the early dew that vanishes.

Verse 5 NASB
Therefore I have hewn them in pieces by the prophets; I have slain them by the words of My mouth; And the judgments on you are like the light that goes forth.

Verse 5 KJV
Therefore have I hewed them by the prophets; I have slain them by the words of my mouth: and thy judgments are as the light that goeth forth.

Verse 5 NIV
"Therefore I cut you in pieces with my prophets, I killed you with the words of my mouth—then my judgments go forth like the sun."

Verse 5 Hebrew Interlinear Text
for this I-cut-to-pieces with-the-prophets I-killed-them with-words-of mouth-of-me and-judgments-of-you lightning he/it-flashed

Verse 5a
for this I-cut-to-pieces with-the-prophets
The word *chatseb* means *to cut, to carve,* or *to engrave.* In many cases the term is used for work on wood or stone. In those situations it is rendered as *to hew, to cleave* (1 Kings 5:15; 1 Chronicles 22:2), or *to chop.*

Rosenberg follows the Hebrew source text very closely when he translates: *Because I have hewed by the prophets.* It is his translation we are largely following here.
(Andersen and Freedman, 428; Owens, vol. 4, 771; Rosenberg, vol. 1, 38; Strong's OT, word 2672; Ward, 116)

We read: ***For this reason I have hewed them by the prophets***

Verse 5b
I-killed-them with-words-of mouth-of-me
This clause involves no difficulties.

We read: ***I killed them with the words of my mouth***

Verse 5c
and-judgments-of-you lightning
The word *or* generally means *light.* The NIVIHEOT has opted for the translation *lightning*, but this reading only finds support in a single text (Job 37:3). However, even there the translation is contested, and it therefore cannot be adduced as evidence for the present verse. Once again, we choose to follow the Hebrew text closely.
(Calvijn, *Daniel* II, *Kleine Profeten* I/II, Hosea, 229; Garrett, 160–61; Reed, 55; Strong's OT, word 216; Wolff, 105)

We read: ***and the judgments about you were like a light***

Verse 5d
he/it-flashed
Yatsa means *to go, to produce, to bring forth* (Genesis 1:12, 24), *to go out, to bring out,* or *cause to go out* (Genesis 8:16–17; Exodus 3:10). In Genesis 2:10, for example, it is sometimes translated as *sprang.* Here the text thus reads: *what causes to go out or break through.*

Linking verse 5c and 5d
We are quite likely dealing with poetic language here. Harper offers the following description: *And my judgment is like the light which goes forth.* That light was announced in verse 3 as that which emerges from God Himself—the *light breaking through* of the justice of God.
(Andersen and Freedman, 429; Calvijn, *Daniël* II, *Kleine Profeten* I/II, Hosea, 229; Garrett, 160–61; Harper, 286; Strong's OT, word 3318; Wolff, 105)

We read: ***and the judgments about you were like a light breaking through***

The whole sentence:
For this reason I have hewed them by the prophets. I killed them with the words of My mouth, and the judgments about you were like a light breaking through.

Verse 6 NASB
For I delight in loyalty rather than sacrifice, and in the knowledge of God rather than burnt offerings.

Verse 6 KJV
For I desired mercy, and not sacrifice; and the knowledge of God more than burnt offerings.

Verse 6 NIV
"For I desire mercy, not sacrifice, and acknowledgment of God rather than burnt offerings."

Verse 6 Hebrew Interlinear Text
for mercy I-desire and-not sacrifice and-acknowledgement-of God rather-than-burnt-offerings
In verse 3a we already encountered the word *yada* (which means: *to acquire knowledge*). Here we find a related word, *daath*. This word in itself already refers to acquired *knowledge*. Normally it is translated *knowledge* or *understanding* (Genesis 2:17; Exodus 31:3; Numbers 24:16).
(Brown, 57; Calvijn, *Daniel* II, *Kleine Profeten* I/II, Hosea, 230; Harper, 286; Strong's OT, word 1847)

We read:
For I desire mercy and no sacrifice; and knowledge of God, more than burnt offerings.

Verse 7 NASB
But like Adam they have transgressed the covenant; There they have dealt treacherously against Me.

Verse 7 KJV
But they like men have transgressed the covenant: there have they dealt treacherously against me.

Verse 7 NIV
"As at Adam they have broken the covenant; they were unfaithful to me there."

Verse 7 Hebrew Interlinear Text
but-they like-Adam they-broke covenant there they-were-unfaithful to-me

Verse 7a
but-they like-Adam
Some understand the word *Adam* as a place name, but there is no ground for this at all. The word *adam* occurs very frequently in the Bible, and most often means *person*, *someone*, or *human race*. At times it is used as a personal name, and then it is vocalized as *Adam*. Such a reading must, however, always be supported by the context. Since in this case it is not entirely clear, we have decided to include both in the definitive text.
(Brown, 61; Calvijn, *Daniel* II, *Kleine Profeten* I/II, Hosea, 234–35; Harper, 288; Henderson, 35; Knight, Hosea 6:7; Strong's OT, word 120)

We read: *but they are like Adam (man)*

Verse 7b
they-broke covenant
The word *abar* means *to pass by* or *to pass*. In this case it is the covenant that is bypassed. That is *to neglect* or *to break with*.
(Strong's OT, word 5674; Ward, 127; Wolff, 105)

We read: *they broke the covenant*

Verse 7c
there they-were-unfaithful to-me
The word *sham* refers to a specific time or place. Here one could read *there*, as many exegetes and/or translators indeed do. However, in the present context that is not a logical choice. It is not a place but behavior. We solve the problem when we see that *sham* refers to *Adam*. To maintain this meaning we add *likewise* to the text (it is a repetition of 7a). (Calvijn, *Daniel* II, *Kleine Profeten* I/II, Hosea, 233–34; Strong's OT, word 8033; Stuart, 111)

We read: ***and likewise they became unfaithful to Me***

The whole sentence:
But they are like Adam (man). They broke the covenant and likewise they became unfaithful to Me.

Verse 8 NASB
Gilead is a city of wrongdoers, tracked with bloody footprints.

Verse 8 KJV
Gilead is a city of them that work iniquity, and is polluted with blood.

Verse 8 NIV
"Gilead is a city of evildoers, stained with footprints of blood."

Verse 8 Hebrew Interlinear Text
Gilead city-of men-doing-of wickedness stained-with-footprint of-blood

Verse 8a
Gilead city-of men-doing-of wickedness
Gilead is certainly no city, as many translations suggest. It is a region east of the Jordan river, which belonged to the kingdom of Jeroboam II. Nevertheless, most biblical scholars still read *Gilead, city of*. In support of their translation, they claim that Hosea is referring to the city Jabesh-Gilead. This, however, is to read something into the Hebrew text that is not actually there. This is why Constable proposes to read: *Gilead is like a city*. This is an acceptable translation, and we have adopted it here.
(Constable, 28; Harper, 288; McComiskey, 95–96)

We read: ***Gilead is as a city of people who do evil***

Verse 8b NASB: rugged terrain / KJV: rough places.
stained-with-footprint of-blood
Some translate the word *aqob* as *footprints* or *trails of blood*. The term is related to the well-known personal name y*a'aqob* (Jakob), whose etymological meaning is understood by many to be *he who grasps the heal*. This is why the NIVIHEOT translates with *footprint* (*of blood*).

According to Strong's, *aqob* can also be used as an adjective meaning *insidious*, *deceitful*, or *tracked by footprints* (disputed). There are only two other occurrences of this word in the Bible. In Isaiah 40:4 the NASB translates as *rugged terrain* and the KJV as *rough places*. In Jeremiah 17:9 (NASB, KJV) we find the translation *deceitful (is the heart)*. That too is a form of injustice.

When we turn to the context, we see that Hosea is speaking of a land (Israel) that is plagued by intrigues, deception, extortion, debauchery, and murder. A literal translation

would then read: *infected with deceitful blood*, or *infected with blood of betrayal*. Rosenberg translates: *who lurk to shed blood*. This may be interpretation, but it does breathe the same spirit of the source text.
(Rosenberg, vol. 1, 39; Strong's OT, word 6121)

We read: *infected with blood of betrayal*

The entire sentence:
Gilead is as a city of people who do evil; infected with blood of betrayal.

Verse 9 NASB
And as raiders wait for a man, so a band of priests murder on the way to Shechem; Surely they have committed crime.

Verse 9 KJV
And as troops of robbers wait for a man, so the company of priests murder in the way by consent: for they commit lewdness.

Verse 9 NIV
"As marauders lie in ambush for a victim, so do bands of priests; they murder on the road to Shechem, carrying out their wicked schemes."

Verse 9 Hebrew Interlinear Text
and-as-ones-lying-in-ambush-of man marauders band-of priests road they-murder to-Shechem indeed shameful-crime they-commit

Verse 9a
and-as-ones-lying-in-ambush-of man marauders
Gedud means *a band* or *troop* or sometimes *marauder* when the context supports that.
(Strong's OT, word 1416; *Studiebijbel* SBOT 12, 74)

We read: *as marauders lie in ambush for people*

Verse 9b
band-of priests road
What the NIVIHEOT offers here is an interpretation of the Hebrew text, reading *band*. However, the basic meaning of the word *cheber* is *association*, *company*, or *spell* (Deuteronomy 18:11). In Psalm 58:5 we do find the term translated as *caster of spells*, *enchanter*, or *charming* (KJV), but there too the underlying meaning is *community* (in reference to the evil spirits consulted by the enchanter or the spirits with which he cooperates or has community).

The word *derek* can indeed be translated as *road* but also as *path in life* or *way of life* (Genesis 18:19; 24:40), which is the correct rendering here. What it thus says in verse 9b is: *(the) community of priests (is the) way of life.*
(Calvijn, *Daniel* II, *Kleine Profeten* I/II, Hosea, 237–38; Harper, 289; Strong's OT, word 2267 and 1810)

We read: *so is the way of life of the community of priests*

Verse 9c/d
they-murder to-Shechem
The word *râtsach* means *to dash in pieces* or *to crush*. It is also translated as *to slay*, *to kill*, or *to murder*.

The word *shekem* refers to the neck between the shoulders, that is, where heavy loads are placed. It is most commonly translated as *shoulder* (Genesis 21:14; 24:15, 45), but also as *back* (1 Samuel 10:9; Psalm 21:12). The word can also be a place name, however: *Shechem*.

In our choice of translation, we need to take into account the context. Hosea 6 speaks of Israel's sins that turned fatal for the nation. One of the greatest sins was *the sin of Jeroboam*. As the first king of Israel (the Ten Tribes), Jeroboam erected two sanctuaries, one in the north and another in the south, establishing two surrogate cults to God. It was in the city of Shechem that he was crowned (1 Kings 12:1–20). It was with King Jeroboam that the division between Judah and Israel was sealed, cutting off the covenant between God and Israel at its very roots. In that context, the word *manslaughter* is very fitting.

On the basis of the context, the choice is easily made: *Shechem*.
(Calvijn, *Daniel* II, *Kleine Profeten* I/II, Hosea, 237–38; Strong's OT, words 7523, 7926, 7927; Stuart, 111)

We read: ***they committed manslaughter in Shechem***

Verse 9e/f
indeed shameful-crime they-commit
The Hebrew word *ki* usually introduces a causal relationship, as is the case here. It is commonly translated *because* or *since*.

The term *zimmah* is almost always connected to some form of *fornication*. It is sometimes also translated as *unchaste*, *lewd*, or *shameless lewdness*. That is how it is used in Ezekiel 16:43, 58; 22:9.

Many exegetes, including Andersen and Freedman, Born, and Brown, use the past or present perfect tense, which we follow here.
(Andersen and Freedman, 440; Born, 51; Brown, 62–63; Strong's OT, words 2154, 3588; Ward, 130)
(See also commentary on Hosea 5:4.)

We read: ***for they have committed shameless abuses***

We read:
As marauders lie in ambush for people, so is the way of life of the community of priests. They committed manslaughter in Shechem, for they have committed shameless abuses.

Verse 10 NASB
In the house of Israel I have seen a horrible thing; Ephraim's harlotry is there, Israel has defiled itself.

Verse 10 KJV
I have seen an horrible thing in the house of Israel: there is the whoredom of Ephraim, Israel is defiled.

Verse 10 NIV
"I have seen a horrible thing in Israel: There Ephraim is given to prostitution, Israel is defiled."

Verse 10 Hebrew Interlinear Text
in-house-of Israel I-saw horrible-thing there prostitution to-Ephraim he-is-defiled Israel

The expression **ša'ărûrîyāh** means *horrible things, something horrible, most appalling* (Jeremiah 18:13; 23:14). Calvin translates the term as *outrage*, but that is somewhat further removed from the Hebrew source text.
(Andersen and Freedman, 442; Calvijn, *Daniel* II, *Kleine Profeten* I/II, Hosea, 238; Strong's OT, word 8186; Ward, 127)

We read:
I saw horrible things in the house of Israel, for there, Ephraim committed fornication and Israel was defiled.

Verse 11 NASB
Also, O Judah, there is a harvest appointed for you, when I restore the fortunes of My people.

Verse 11 KJV
Also, O Judah, he hath set an harvest for thee, when I returned the captivity of my people.

Verse 11 NIV
"Also for you, Judah, a harvest is appointed. Whenever I would restore the fortunes of my people,"

Verse 11 Hebrew Interlinear Text
also Judah he-appointed harvest for-you when-to-restore-me fortune-of people-of-me

Verse 11a
also Judah he-appointed harvest for-you
The word *shith* means *to put, to determine, to set*, or *to appoint*. Ward places brackets around this entire clause in verse 11, seeing it as a later addition from a Judaic author and foreign to the original text. We, however, choose to follow the Hebrew source text closely.

Some exegetes explain verse 11 as a judgment. From that perspective, the *harvest* would refer to a future judgment. However, the word is used very rarely in that sense in the Scriptures.
(Calvijn, *Daniel* II, *Kleine Profeten* I/II, Hosea, 240; Strong's OT, word 7896; Wolff, 106; Ward, 127, 130)

We read: *yet there is a harvest set apart for Judah*

Verse 11b
when-to-restore-me
The word *shub* occurs very frequently in the Bible. It is usually translated with *again, to turn, to turn back*, or *to return*.
(Smith, 117; Strong's OT, word 7725; Stuart, 112; Wolff, 106)

We read: *when I will turn*

Verse 11c
fortune-of people-of-me
The basic meaning of the word *shebuth* is *captivity*. Often it is related to the *fortune* of the people of God, and yet such a translation is interpretation. It is therefore better translated as *fate* or *destiny*.
(Andersen and Freedman, 443; Harper, 292; Stuart, 112; Wolff, 106)

We read: *the fate of My people*

The whole sentence:
Yet there is a harvest set apart for Judah, when I will turn the fate of My people.

Hosea 6:1–11—The corrected text:

Verse 1 *Come and let us turn to Yahweh! Because He who pulled us apart will also make us whole again. He injured us, but will also bind up our wounds.*
Verse 2 *He will revive us after two days. On the third day He will raise us up, that we may live in His presence. So let us acquire knowledge; let us pursue the knowledge of Yahweh.*
Verse 3 *As sure as the sun rises, His dawn will be. Then He will come to us like torrential rain, but as a mild rain He will teach the earth.*
Verse 4 *What should I do with you, O Ephraim? What should I do with you, O Judah? For your love is like a thin cloud in the morning; like the early dew that vanishes.*
Verse 5 *For this reason I have hewed them by the prophets. I killed them with the words of My mouth, and the judgments about you were like a light breaking through.*
Verse 6 *For I desire mercy and no victim; and knowledge of God, more than burnt offerings.*
Verse 7 *But they are like Adam (man). They broke the covenant and likewise they became unfaithful to Me.*
Verse 8 *Gilead is as a city of people who do evil; infected with blood of betrayal.*
Verse 9 *As marauders lie in ambush for people, so is the way of life of the community of priests. They committed manslaughter in Shechem, for they have committed shameless abuses.*
Verse 10 *I saw horrible things in the house of Israel, for there, Ephraim committed fornication and Israel was defiled.*
Verse 11 *Yet there is a harvest set apart for Judah, when I will turn the fate of My people.*

HOSEA 6
Exegesis

Introduction

With the definitive translation that has arisen in the discussion of the text of Hosea 6, we distance ourselves, in terms of textual content, from many existing translations. That will automatically lead to a very simple question that you may be asking: How do you come to these conclusions? First of all, I study the Hebrew source text very carefully. If you have already studied the preceding chapter on Hosea 6, it will become clear that my translation is not built on quicksand. That is why we keep going back to the pure meaning of the words as we find them in authoritative references like Strong's; Brown, Driver, and Briggs; and Botterweck, Ringgren, and Fabry. Then, I faithfully reference reputable, biblical scholars, especially when the meaning of a word is under discussion.

Another influence on our translation and exegesis is the coherence of this chapter with the rest of the book of Hosea and with other Bible books. This will have a strong corrective effect, and it is called comparing Scripture with Scripture.

This in turn leads to the question (and here I quote a well-known sportsman in the Netherlands), Are they so stupid or am I so smart? Neither. Many exegetes or translators are very intelligent people and I am not exceptionally smart (but persistent). But why then are there vast differences in translation and exegesis? Because most exegetes by far do not allow for predictive prophecy, let alone such a thing as the counsel of God (God's plan for humanity). They simply do not believe that God is the author, or they at least have strong doubts in that respect.

A. The modern exegete sets the tone.

Of course there are also exegetes who take God's Word seriously. However, in practice it is very difficult for them to go against the tide of more liberal exegetes, because the liberal opinion has become normative and almost universally accepted!

Of course not all Bible scholars agree. But the protests from Bible-believing circles are rarely voiced. So their silence suggests consent. So a way of explaining the Bible has developed, which is, above all, based on the historical-critical method—also called: higher criticism (an expression that sets the tone!)—and exegesis has suffered greatly from secular influences. In their critical attitude, many of these modern commentaries show a disconcerting mutual similarity and lack of argumentation and depth. And if the original text is looked at in more depth, the exegesis is rarely well founded. Instead, we find all sorts of hollow cries and platitudes and jargon, such as: generally accepted; cultural anthropology approach; Jewish interpretative traditions (also called, outburst of Jewish national feelings); narrative analysis; Jewish ritualism; socio-historical criticism (and I will save you from the really difficult ones). Then a flood of references is added—from like-minded Bible scholars, of course—lending extra weight to the opinion of the exegete in question.

Sadly, there are few exegetes left who openly and candidly focus on the Hebrew text. Thus a cause-and-effect cycle came about. The first critic was followed by the second, the third, the fourth, and so on. They all referred to each other and less and less to the Bible. This is how the "evidence" swelled to a backbreaking mountain of writings. In addition, the volume, not the depth, came to be of greater value. And so a proper perspective on God's Word gradually became obscured.

B. The true exegete is a seeker of God!
With the method described above, the tone of exegesis has also changed. For the older exegetes it was still entirely normal for their own spiritual life to shine through or even dominate in their writings. That is the case, for example, with the great church reformer John Calvin (his deep-rooted devotion is a joy to read).

However, the modern exegete (also unfortunately increasingly within Bible-believing circles) has become a clinical reviewer. His comments reflect, above all, the tone of textual criticism. Nonbiblical writings have been upgraded to the authority of God's Word. Pagan customs and idolatry have also become criteria of weight in the explanation or serve to "correct" the original Hebrew text. Thus the worship of the only God was downgraded to one cult among many—no more than *a* religion.

Only rarely does a Bible commentary still reveal the emotion of one seeking after God, someone who has begun a holy quest for the fingerprint of God. One who seeks after God will also deal differently with the text. He will place the most important influence on the speaker, which is where it belongs, because that is God Himself.

In our translation we have tried to respect the Hebrew text to the letter. See what happens! A prophecy has emerged that contains logic and connects with the exegesis of the previous chapters. This is very significant.

C. Eschatology
The theme of Hosea 6 is, above all, prophecy about the end times. In verses 1–3 the prophet speaks about a blessed future. Against this background, the prophet looks back at the demise of the people of Israel/Ephraim. He does this in the form of a lament and in words that make clear that the judgments have already taken place. The prophecy thus looks back to a point in the past, which for the prophet is still in the (near) future.

The chapter closes in a special way, for it ends with promises of blessing for the remaining part of "the Israel of the twelve tribes"—Judah.

Verse 1a
Come and let us turn to Yahweh!
The first verse of Hosea 6 contains clear prophecy. It is a compelling call to the ten tribes of Israel to return to Yahweh—a call to repentance. But in previous chapters it has become abundantly clear that the judgment on Israel could no longer be avoided. The logical conclusion is that this call is not addressed to the people of Israel of the time of Jeroboam II, but sounds over their heads to a scattered people in the future.

It is clear that the call of verse 1a, in the period after the downfall of Israel, did not lead to the desired effect. That means that this call still stands and now—after more than twenty-five hundred years—still sounds for the people of Israel. So will there ever be an answer to this call? Yes, and Hosea informs us when and how. In verse 2 the prophet tells us the counsel of God regarding this.

Verse 1b
Because He who pulled us apart will also make us whole again. He injured us, but will also bind up our wounds.
The prophet Hosea uses poetic, but nevertheless very clear language. Yahweh pulled Israel apart, that is, called down a judgment upon His people that was executed by the Assyrians, and sent Israel into exile. Yahweh injured them, taking away Israel's special status as God's people.

The call to repentance has a clearly defined purpose: that He may *make us* (Israel) whole again—restore us as a people—and that He may *bind up our wounds*. That has not yet happened!

Annotation 6B: The Wounds of Israel

The worship of God distinguished the people of Israel from the gentile nations. Only Israel was chosen and ranked above all other nations on earth. The outward features were the holy temple and the worship of God, the Sabbath, the high holy days, *brit milah* (the rite of circumcision), and the land allocated to them, Canaan. Because of the Assyrian conquest and the subsequent deportation and dispersion, all of this was taken away from them, like an amputation. These are the wounds that this text speaks about! So everything that was taken from the people of Israel God will give back to them if they *return to Yahweh*! (Hosea 1:1)

The great importance of the Sabbath and the high holy days in the relationship between God and Israel is evident from Ezekiel 20:12 (NASB):

> *"Also I gave them My sabbaths to be a sign between Me and them, that they might know that I am the LORD who sanctifies them."*

The word *sabbaths* is rarely found in the plural in the Bible. It therefore not only refers to the Sabbath, but to all holy days or periods—the holy feasts, the sabbatical years, and the years of jubilee.

Keeping the Sabbath is addressed in the fourth commandment in Exodus 20:8–11; 31:13. It is also called a sign that sanctified the nation of Israel. What the rainbow is for the Noahite Covenant, the Sabbath was for the Sinaitic Covenant.

Sources:
(Block, vol. 1, 632; Weerd, *Ezechiël*, vol. 1, 524–26)
(See Excursuses 14, 20, 21.)

Excursus 14: He Will Revive Us

14.a Striking prophecy
Hosea 6:2 is a striking prophecy. Garrett says: "It is impossible for the Christian to read this text and not wonder if it foreshadows Christ's resurrection on the third day." Some exegetes explain therefore this verse as having been fulfilled in Jesus Christ. Such an interpretation, however, conflicts with the Hebrew text which speaks of "us" (verse 2). Thus in its original context verse 2 speaks of the restoration of Israel and does that very precisely. Hosea speaks primarily of three future ages (called days) in which the prophecies about Israel will be fulfilled.

14.b Typology concerning Christ
Does verse 2 have no connection at all with the death and resurrection of Jesus? Certainly it does; it is also a messianic prophecy. 1 Corinthians 15:3b–4 sets the tone here (NASB):

> *Christ died for our sins according to the Scriptures, and that He was buried, and that He was raised on the third day <u>according to the Scriptures</u>.*

By "the Scriptures" the apostle Paul means the Old Testament. And Hosea 6:2 is *the only place* where a resurrection on the third day is spoken of. (Others point to Matthew 12:40

and 16:4, where Jesus refers to Jonah 1:17, but it does not speak of a resurrection.) There is typology here. Just as the people of Israel (the Ten Tribes) are paying for their sins until the present day, and on the third day will rise again, so our Savior preceded them, for the salvation of the church, of Judah, *and* of Israel.
(Garrett, 158–59; Heyer, vol. 2, 232; Heyer, vol. 3, 52–55; Kidner, 66; Oden, 26–27)

14.c Messianic prophecy
Because He (God) *who pulled us apart will also make us whole again*, says Hosea 6:1. It also tells us when this will take place. That is what verse 2a speaks about, because this is (in contrast to the opinion of most biblical scholars) definitely a stipulation as to time. And one with a messianic connotation, because it points to the Messianic Kingdom, when Israel will be revived and reunited with Judah.
(Jamieson, 655; Reed, 54)

14.d Two days and the third day
The word *yom* literally means *day* or *daytime*. However, that does not have to be a twenty-four-hour period. It can also mean a longer period or even an era. In that latter sense we find it in Jeremiah 23:20; 30:24; 48:47; 49:39, where we read: *in-coming-of the-days*; in Isaiah 2:2 *in-last-of the-days* and in Daniel 10:14 *in-future-of the-days*. Also in this case the prophet speaks about three distinct ages; called days.

14.e The seven dispensations
In the Bible we distinguish certain ages, which derive their characteristic from the way in which God deals with mankind. We also call these ages dispensations. There are many schemes in this area. One of the most applied speaks of seven dispensations, which are described as follows:

1. Dispensation of innocence (from the garden of Eden to the fall)
2. Dispensation of conscience (from the fall to the flood)
3. Dispensation of human rule (from the flood to the Babylonian confusion of tongues)
4. Dispensation of promise (from Abraham to the exodus from Egypt)
5. Dispensation of law (from the exodus to the crucifixion of Christ)
6. Dispensation of grace (from the day of Pentecost to the rapture of the church of Christ)
7. Dispensation of the kingdom of Christ (from the second coming of Christ until the last judgment)

Hosea 6:2 speaks of the last three dispensations. So it points to the Messianic Age.

Sources:
(Garrett, 158–59; Ironside, 46–47; Rashi, cited by Rosenberg, vol. 1, 37; Strong's OT, word 3117)
(See Annotation 6A; Excursuses 1, 2.)

Verse 2
He will revive us after two days. On the third day He will raise us up, that we may live in His presence. So let us acquire knowledge; let us pursue the knowledge of Yahweh.

Verse 2a/b
He will revive us after two days. On the third day He will raise us up,
When verse 2 speaks of two days, it looks at two distinct ages, namely, the fifth and sixth dispensations.* The fifth dispensation is that of the law (= the era in which the prophet

Hosea lived). The sixth dispensation is that of grace (= the age of the church of Christ that continues to this day) and ends with the rapture of the church of Christ.

The prophet Hosea thus explains that after dispensations five and six (thus at the end of the dispensation of grace / the end of the second day), a *third day* (age) will dawn. That will be the Messianic Kingdom in which all twelve tribes of Israel will find a place. To make Israel complete, the people of Israel (the Ten Tribes) will be brought to life by God Himself (*He*). This is therefore an initiative of God, not of Israel/Ephraim, and thus this prophecy connects with Hosea 2:13 and Zechariah 10:8:

> *"I will whistle for them to gather them together, for I have redeemed them; and they will be as numerous as they were before."*

That great moment of God's grace is, even for us, still in the future; it will take place in the coming end time.
(*See Excursus 14.e.)

2a/b.1 The third day
Andersen and Freedman call this *the language of the resurrection*. They hit the nail on the head, but unfortunately don't see a future fulfillment. This is about the future resurrection of the nation of Israel!

The revival of the ten tribes of Israel will be a chain of events that will take time. Once that process is completed, *He* (God) *will revive us* on *the third day*. That will be the beginning of the seventh dispensation—the kingdom of Christ, the Messianic Kingdom. That corresponds exactly with prophecies in Isaiah, Ezekiel, Daniel, Micah, and Zechariah.
(Andersen and Freedman, 419)
(See Excursuses 1, 2, 7, 13, 14.)

Verse 2c
that we may live in His presence.
In the future age of the Messianic Kingdom, the ten tribes of Israel will take their rightful place in the land of Canaan, and be reunited with the other two tribes (Judah and Benjamin). Then there will be again a temple in Jerusalem and the glory of the Lord (the Shekinah of Yahweh) will return to Jerusalem (Ezekiel 43). So the people of Israel will then indeed *live in His presence*.

Verse 2d
So let us acquire knowledge; let us pursue the knowledge of Yahweh.
How does the nation of Israel acquire these blessings? Simply by turning to God. This is not a turning from a state of wickedness to that of godliness, as a traditional conversion is. The people of Israel are no longer in that situation. Today they are scattered all over the earth and hardly know their identity. They also do not know Yahweh any more, or only very poorly. The great turnaround of the ten tribes of Israel will therefore hinge on their knowledge of Yahweh! That will give them the key with which the door of the Messianic Kingdom can be opened.

When they gain the breakthrough to the light of the knowledge of God, then the *dawn* (Hosea 6:3) of the Lord will break through, as Isaiah 58:8 (NIV) also prophesies:

> *"Then your light will break forth like the dawn and your healing will quickly appear; then your righteousness will go before you, and the glory of the LORD will be your rear guard."*

In that time the Messianic Kingdom will be established, also called *the favorable year of the LORD* (Isaiah 61:1–2 NASB; Luke 4:19 NASB) and everyone will pursue and acquire the knowledge of God as Habakkuk 2:14 (NASB) says:

> *"For the earth will be filled with the knowledge of the glory of the LORD, as the waters cover the sea."*

(Weerd, *Ezechiël*, vol. 2, 562–70)
(See Excursus 7; exegesis of Hosea 3:5.)

Verse 3a
As sure as the sun rises, His dawn will be.
The future return of God to the temple in Jerusalem (*His dawn*) is certain. The prophet Zechariah speaks about it in clear terms:

> *Thus says the LORD, "I will return to Zion and will dwell in the midst of Jerusalem. Then Jerusalem will be called the City of Truth, and the mountain of the LORD of hosts will be called the Holy Mountain."* (Zechariah 8:3 NASB)

The *dawn* comes after the night—the night of the great tribulation. Zechariah prophesies about this (we give a direct translation of the Hebrew text*):

> *And in that day, it shall come to pass that no daylight shall dawn again, but cold and frost. It will be a unique day, known to the LORD, without distinction from day or night. But at the end of it, it will happen: Let there be light!* (Zechariah 14:6–7, see also Genesis 1:3)

(*Weerd, *Zacharia*, 417–19)

This unnatural night is also described in John 9:4 (NASB):

> *"We must work the works of Him who sent Me as long as it is day; night is coming when no one can work."*

And in Isaiah 8:22 (NASB) we read:

> *Then they will look to the earth, and behold, distress and darkness, the gloom of anguish; and they will be driven away into darkness.*

In this period the last bowls of God's wrath will be poured out over mankind. But that will come to an end, and then the Messianic Kingdom will come under the governance of Jesus Christ.

3a.1 A day known to the Lord (Zechariah 14:6–7)
God Himself determines the duration and outcome, as the Lord Jesus Himself has foretold in Matthew 24:36, which we repeat again:

> *"But of that day and hour no one knows, not even the angels of heaven, nor the Son, but the Father alone."*

And when God decides that the moment has come, He will send Jesus Christ. And when Jesus Christ arrives on the Mount of Olives (Zechariah 14:4) the light of God's Shalom will break through: *Let there be light!* (Zechariah 14:7*).

Before that happens, apocalyptic catastrophes on a large-scale and the violence of war will darken the heavens with dust and smoke. It will become dark, *without distinction from day or night* (Zechariah 14:7a*). The great tribulation ends with a new beginning, the dawn of the worldwide Sabbath, the Messianic Kingdom. With this the second world begins in the same way as the first one started.

> *Then God said, "Let there be light"; and there was light. God saw that the light was good; and God separated the light from the darkness.* (Genesis 1:3–4 NASB)

Unlike the first world, the second world will reach its destination.
(*Weerd, Hebrew text translation in *Zacharia*, 417–19)

Verse 3b/c
Then He will come to us like torrential rain, but as a mild rain He will teach the earth.
Yahweh, however, will not come to bring just blessing. When He comes, it will be both for judgment (*like torrential rain*) and in blessing (*as a mild rain*). The prophet uses beautiful images. For this world is corrupted by evil, by sin. On earth it is said: eat or be eaten. We see that all around us. But that is not normal! That is a distorted picture of what God once intended. The Almighty must therefore *teach* the earth to achieve His ultimate goal and to make the earth ready to receive Him.

The Almighty God is going to live again in Jerusalem, in a new temple that will be built. Then a period of unmixed blessings will come. That means that the earth, as we know it, will change drastically. So much has been tainted, so much broken down. But God promises us to *teach* the earth! And if the good God teaches the earth, it will have immediate consequences. The earth will also respond, as we learn from Hosea 2:21:

> *And the earth will respond! Yes, the grain, the new wine, and the oil will respond to God's sowing (Jezreel).*

Excursus 15: Judgment and Blessing at the End Time

The prophets speak in many places about the day of the Lord—the day of Judgment—also called the great tribulation, which is the door to the Messianic Kingdom and the final promised redemption. Isaiah speaks about this future (which contains both judgment and blessing), in Isaiah 61:1–2 (NASB):

1   *The Spirit of the Lord GOD is upon me, because the LORD has anointed me to bring good news to the afflicted; He has sent me to bind up the brokenhearted, to proclaim liberty to captives and freedom to prisoners;*
2   *To proclaim the favorable year of the LORD and the day of vengeance of our God; to comfort all who mourn.*

And Isaiah 61:4–6 confirms once again that the people of Israel will then be placed above all other nations:

4   *Then they will rebuild the ancient ruins, they will raise up the former devastations; and they will repair the ruined cities, the desolations of many generations.*
5   *Strangers will stand and pasture your flocks, and foreigners will be your farmers and your vinedressers.*
6   *But you will be called the priests of the LORD; You will be spoken of as ministers of our God. You will eat the wealth of nations, and in their riches you will boast.*

Again from Hosea 6:3b: *Then He will come to us like torrential rain*

The coming of God, in judgment, is foretold in many places in the Bible. We quote a few:

Isaiah 2:10 (NASB)
Enter the rock and hide in the dust from the terror of the LORD and from the splendor of His majesty.

Isaiah 24:6 (NASB)
Therefore, a curse devours the earth, and those who live in it are held guilty. Therefore, the inhabitants of the earth are burned, and few men are left.

Jeremiah 30:23 (NASB)
Behold, the tempest of the LORD! Wrath has gone forth, a sweeping tempest; it will burst on the head of the wicked.

Joel 3:12 (NASB)
Let the nations be aroused and come up to the valley of Jehoshaphat, for there I will sit to judge all the surrounding nations.

Malachi 3:2 (NASB)
"But who can endure the day of His coming? And who can stand when He appears? For He is like a refiner's fire and like fullers' soap."

Malachi 4:1 (NASB)
"For behold, the day is coming, burning like a furnace; and all the arrogant and every evildoer will be chaff; and the day that is coming will set them ablaze," says the LORD of hosts, "so that it will leave them neither root nor branch."

The blessings are as abundant as the wrath of the Lord is harsh—Ezekiel 36:29 (NASB):
"Moreover, I will save you from all your uncleanness; and I will call for the grain and multiply it, and I will not bring a famine on you."

These godly deeds are part of the foundation of the Messianic Kingdom—Ezekiel 34:25–26 (NASB):

25 *"I will make a covenant of peace with them and eliminate harmful beasts from the land so that they may live securely in the wilderness and sleep in the woods.*
26 *"I will make them and the places around My hill a blessing. And I will cause showers to come down in their season; they will be showers of blessing."*

Isaiah 41:18–20 (NASB):

18 *"I will open rivers on the bare heights and springs in the midst of the valleys; I will make the wilderness a pool of water and the dry land fountains of water.*
19 *"I will put the cedar in the wilderness, the acacia and the myrtle and the olive tree; I will place the juniper in the desert together with the box tree and the cypress,*
20 *"that they may see and recognize, and consider and gain insight as well, that the hand of the LORD has done this, and the Holy One of Israel has created it."*

Thus the blessed state of the garden of Eden returns in the Messianic Kingdom (see Genesis 2:8–25) as Ezekiel 36:35 (NASB) prophecies:

They will say, "This desolate land has become like the garden of Eden; and the waste, desolate and ruined cities are fortified and inhabited."

Introduction to Verses 4–11

Verses 1–3 are promises of salvation that speak of a distant future, the end time. In the next verses, the prophet Hosea looks back at the near past, at his present, and even at what is from his perspective the near future.

Verses 5, 9, and 10, all speak of the past. Hosea prophesies about the ten tribes of Israel as if that nation is no longer there. It is clear that the prophet does not do that on his own initiative. He was not able to do that; he had no knowledge about that. It is God Himself who looks back from a moment in the near future, and Hosea speaks with God's mouth. This is a kind of looking back in sadness, which stands in stark contrast to the promises of salvation for the distant future.

Verse 4
What should I do with you, O Ephraim? What should I do with you, O Judah? For your love is like a thin cloud in the morning, like the early dew that vanishes.
The desperate condition of Israel and Judah touches the Almighty greatly. His reaction is a cry of deep grief. (See Excursus 16.)

From the perspective of the prophet Hosea there is no reason yet to think of a blessed future. The status of both Ephraim (previously called Israel, see Excursus 12) and Judah is sad. All that remains of the love for God is only a thin veneer. It is like *a thin cloud in the morning, the same as the early dew that vanishes.* What still exists of service to God is some beautiful outward appearance. There is hardly any godliness left.

Excursus 16: The Sorrow of God

Sadness appears to be not just a human emotion, but also a godly one. Is the Almighty God vulnerable like we humans are? It seems so; we call it the sorrow of God. For in Hosea 6:4 the Lord God utters a complaint:

> ***What should I do with you, O Ephraim? What should I do with you, O Judah?***

In this text sounds, humanly speaking, a tone of hopelessness, a cry of deep sorrow. For God is greatly distressed over the fall of Israel (all twelve tribes). Because of His love for Israel, the judgment was postponed again and again. Even now that the people of Israel are turning away from God, His love continues to exist. Ezekiel 18:23 (KJV) testifies:

> *Have I any pleasure at all that the wicked should die? saith the Lord GOD: and not that he should return from his ways, and live?*

And Ezekiel 18:31b–32 (KJV):

> *For why will ye die, O house of Israel? For I have no pleasure in the death of him that dieth, saith the Lord GOD: wherefore turn yourselves, and live ye.*

The Almighty grieves over the broken relationship and is hurt in the depths of His soul. He has been abandoned—Ezekiel 22:30 (NASB):

> *"I searched for a man among them who would build up the wall and stand in the gap before Me for the land, so that I would not destroy it; but I found no one."*

This is a profoundly sad statement. And who is not touched by such intense grief? God has such sorrow over everyone who strays from Him. Like the father in the parable of the prodigal son, God is eagerly looking forward to the return of each sinner (Luke 15:7):

> *"So he got up and came to his father. But while he was still a long way off, his father saw him and felt compassion for him, and ran and embraced him and kissed him."* (Luke 15:20 NASB)

And when the sinner comes to God, it is a feast, as we see in Luke 15:10 (NASB):

> *"In the same way, I tell you, there is joy in the presence of the angels of God over one sinner who repents."*

Verse 5a
For this reason I have hewed them by the prophets. I killed them with the words of My mouth,
The Israelites' love for God (verse 4) did not in fact have any substance and (at least) disappeared completely. Therefore God chastised them by *the words* of *the prophets*. When that did not help, He *killed them with the words of* His *mouth*.

Thus *I have hewed* refers first to the separation between Israel and Judah, as happened after the death of King Solomon (see Excursus 5), but also to the separation between God and His people (Lo-Ammi, Hosea 1). For the prophets foretold the judgments that would first lead Israel and later Judah into exile. In the end, it was the Assyrians who executed the sentence on Israel, pulling apart God's people by force.

Yet it says: *I (God) killed them with the words of My mouth*. This is indirectly correct, for with the breaking of the Sinaitic Covenant, the God's protection of Israel was lifted. Then Satan did not lose a moment to attack God's chosen people. The hatred of Satan toward Israel is so great that he always responds when there is a chance to harm Israel. That was the case back then, and in the last world war it was no different with the Holocaust. When God lifted His protection off Israel, it was Satan who moved the Assyrians to execute judgment.

Verse 5b
and the judgments about you were like a light breaking through.
With the judgments on the ten tribes of Israel, God made the new relationships between Himself and Israel clear. God does not allow Himself to be trifled with. No one can challenge God with impunity. Thus the judgments shed light on God's sovereign power and righteousness.

Verse 6
For I desire mercy and no victim; and knowledge of God, more than burnt offerings.
The Bible is not a "wind of doctrine" (Ephesians 4:14) but a constant factor throughout the ages. Centuries later Jesus Christ uses virtually the same words in Matthew 9:13 (NASB):

> *"But go and learn what this means: 'I desire compassion, and not sacrifice,' for I did not come to call the righteous, but sinners."*

So also, here in Hosea 6:6, God calls sinners, namely, His straying people of Israel. (Heyer, vol. 3, 194)

Verse 7
But they are like Adam (man). They broke the covenant and likewise they became unfaithful to Me.
In the word *Adam (man)* all humanity is included. So we are talking about the moment when man listened to Satan and broke with God. In that context, Eve was the first to believe the whisperings of Satan. And then seduced Adam to sin with her. Thus they broke *the covenant* between them and God. However this prophecy looks further, because here Adam means *Israel*.
(Ironside, 49; Ward, 129; Wood, 145)
(See Annotation 6C.)

Annotation 6C: Israel and Adam

In the Jerusalem Talmud, Yevamos 61a, it is written:

> *You* (Israel) *are called Adam, but the nations of the world are not called Adam.*

This statement is based, among other things, on Ezekiel 34:31 (NASB), which states:

> *"As for you, My sheep, the sheep of My pasture, you are men* (Hebrew: *Adam*), *and I am your God," declares the Lord* GOD.

On the basis of this text from Ezekiel, rabbinic literature draws the conclusion that the people of Israel are *Adam*. That is to say, the God-chosen representative of the nations on earth. But that is an objective that has never been achieved. In practice, that status was limited to the faithful among God's people. They are those who believe and serve or have served God faithfully. Only in the Messianic Kingdom will Israel really become Adam.

Adam represents Israel
In Ezekiel 34:31, the Hebrew words are *'āḏām 'attem*. We can translate: *you human* (which does not fit in the context, as it clearly concerns the people of Israel), or *you Adam* (that is only one person, so also unlikely). Much better is: *you are Adam* or *you are from Adam*. The latter two are the most obvious choices. We prefer *you are Adam*, even as most rabbinic sources, but in the sense that they are true representatives. That has a certain similarity with: *My servant David* (Ezekiel 34:23). There too the real David (who failed) is not what is being referred to but his descendant, his greatest son, Jesus Christ, the Messiah. He was perfect and fulfilled the divine expectations. In this way of thinking, the people of Israel are the successful final stage of *'āḏām* at the end time. However, then, they will be a people connected with the true Adam, Jesus Christ. That will be the purified Israel, the true Israel.

Conclusion:
Based on this we might consider applying in Hosea 6:7 the name Adam as the correct translation. This text then, perhaps, has only the nation of Israel in view.

Sources:
(Hirsch, 31–32; Kaplan, vol. 1; Sherman, *Ezekiel*, xxx; Snijders, 11; Strong's OT, word 120; Talmud Yerushalmi, 61)

Introduction to Verses 8 and 9

Verses 8 and 9 are not easy to explain. The problems are concentrated around the names Gilead and Shechem. Exegetes have come up with all kinds of solutions, but none is satisfactory. We will not try to go into this in more detail, since we have not been able to find an adequate explanation either.

Fortunately, these verses do not contain key texts. Even if we do not know exactly what the two names suggest, the scope of the prophecy is still quite clear: The prophecy of Hosea focuses on two regions in Israel. These are Gilead (the part of Israel east of the Jordan) and Shechem (the part of Israel located west of the Jordan). The ten-tribe kingdom was established in Shechem, which was its first capital. Both regions represented the wealth of the northern kingdom when Jeroboam II reigned.

Verse 8
Gilead is as a city of people who do evil; infected with blood of betrayal.
The land of Gilead was a region in the Transjordan (east of the Jordan). This area's northern boundary was the Jarmuk River, and the boundary in the south was the Dead Sea.

The Gilead area was constantly fought over. Sometimes it belonged to Israel, then it was more or less independent. Gilead is described in the same vein as the cities of Sodom and Gomorrah once were. And there also fell the judgment of God.
(Ward, 129)

Verse 9a/b
As marauders lie in ambush for people, so is the way of life of the community of priests. They committed manslaughter in Shechem,

9a/b.1 *Manslaughter in Shechem* (1)
There is a wordplay here. For there is a subtle reference to Genesis 34, where the name Shechem also occurs, in the narrative of the betrayal of the two sons of Jacob, Simeon and Levi. To avenge their sister, the men of Shechem were deceived and then slaughtered. Then the city was plundered by the sons of Jacob.

9a/b.2 *Manslaughter in Shechem* (2)
The second instance of betrayal was the division of the kingdom of David and Solomon into two separate countries, Judah and Israel. After the death of King Solomon, Israel turned away from his son, King Rehoboam, in the city of Shechem. Then all the tribes of Israel (including Judah and Benjamin) chose Jeroboam as king (1 Kings 12:1).

After having been rejected, King Rehoboam fled back to Jerusalem. Thanks to the strong professional army that supported him, he retained the territories of Judah and Benjamin. This situation stabilized and therefore two kingdoms emerged—Judah and Israel. With this split a heavy blow was inflicted on the unity of Israel, God, and the land of Canaan. Probably the term *manslaughter* also refers to this event.
(*Talmud Bavli,* Makkos 10a)
(See Excursuses 3, 5.)

Verse 9c
for they have committed shameless abuses.
The *abuses* concern primarily the sin of Jeroboam, because this king had two idolatrous shrines built, one in the north of Israel, in Gilgal, the other in the south, at Bethel, where he set up temples with golden bull calves. Thus, instead of serving God in the temple of Jerusalem (in Judah), a surrogate religion was instituted. Soon it became idolatry, with an appearance of being spiritual, like today's New Age movement.

King Jeroboam also appointed priests on his own authority, not from the tribe of Levi, as God had commanded. See 1 Kings 12:31 (NASB):

> *And he made houses on high places, and made priests from among all the people who were not of the sons of Levi.*

It is the worship of the bull calves, administered by these priests, that is meant by *shameless abuses*.
(See Excursus 11.)

Verse 10a
I saw horrible things in the house of Israel,
While Hosea spoke in verse 9 about the sin of Jeroboam, here he speaks about the serious sins that were later committed by Israel. The prophet is also speaking about other forms of idolatry, like the cult of Baal (sacred prostitution), or even worse, the child sacrifices in the cult of Moloch.*
(See *Annotation 5A, 188.)

Verse 10b
for there, Ephraim committed fornication and Israel was defiled.
With this sentence the lament over the ten tribes of Israel ends. For when Ephraim (formerly called Israel) rejected God and replaced Him with idols, the people committed fornication. Israel sinned so heavily that the Sinaitic Covenant was broken, which is why the name *Ephraim* is now used. But the idolatry of Israel did not just affect the Northern Kingdom. The whole of *Israel was defiled*, because Ephraim, in the context of the promise of salvation, is an indispensable part of God's people.

Verse 11
Yet there is a harvest set apart for Judah, when I will turn the fate of My people.
Hosea 6 closes with a somewhat mysterious text. For the prophecy predicts that Judah will bring forth *a harvest* in the future. Some then point to the birth of Jesus Christ and we join in with that view. But it does not stop there. Because the *turn* of *the fate of My people* (the Jews) did not take place when the Messiah came the first time; they rejected Jesus.

So verse 11b is still unfulfilled prophecy. Somewhere in the future this prophecy will be fully fulfilled when Jesus Christ takes the throne of His father David and becomes king in Jerusalem over the Messianic Kingdom. Only then, so many ages later than necessary, will God *turn the fate* of His people. This unfulfilled prophecy is also for us, as we are talking here about the end time.

11.1 Rabbinical sources
Some, including rabbinical sources, see verse 11 fulfilled in Judah's return from exile. But the kingdom of God was not established then as the prophets foretold. With regard to this return, we can at most speak of a (weak) prefulfillment. Other exegetes even interpret the prophecy negatively and see a judgment in the *harvest*. However, verse 11b makes it clear that this meaning certainly does not hold true here.
(Brown, 63; Ironside, 50; Rashi, cited by Rosenberg, vol. 1, 40)

Excursus 17: A Heavenly and an Earthly Kingdom

There is a striking distinction between the idea of kingdom in the Old Testament and that in the New Testament. The first is obviously an earthly kingdom, the second a heavenly one. Of both kingdoms, Jesus Christ is the prophesied Lord and King. However, up until now, He has only become Lord of the church. From this we can make the logical conclusion that His earthly kingship is still unfulfilled prophecy. Christendom is unmistakably divided on this matter. For many, the Old Testament also speaks of a heavenly kingdom, though in earthly national terms. As proof, statements of Jesus Christ Himself are used to support this.

Others see two kingdoms and the author joins them. To support this view, therefore, we will take a brief overview of texts that relate to this. We find these especially in the gospel according to Matthew.

17.a The kingdom in Matthew
The evangelist Matthew wrote his book primarily for Jews. The tenor of his message is that the coming of the Messiah fulfilled many prophecies of the Old Testament and was foretold long ago. He also shows that Jesus Christ is a descendant of Abraham as well as of King David. When we carefully read the gospel to Matthew, we find much more information, also, about the coming Messianic Kingdom. Feinberg rightly says: "From the standpoint of a study of the Kingdom there is probably no book in the entire revelation of God, that is of more importance and more decisive than the gospel of Matthew."
(Feinberg, *Millennialism*, 129)

17.b A well-known message
The message of John the Baptist and that of Jesus Christ were identical: *The kingdom of heaven is at hand* (Matthew 3:1–2; 4:17). We might expect that they would then explain this concept to their listeners. But that does not happen because it was not necessary at all! This message was generally known in Israel. The prophets of the Old Testament had spoken about this frequently. They foretold the restoration of the glorious kingdom of King David and King Solomon, but even greater and above all, more perfect, was the theocracy—the Messianic Kingdom. Every true Jew looked forward to that and still does to this present day.

17.c An earthly kingdom with heavenly traits
The *kingdom of heaven* that Jesus and John the Baptist speak of is a Hebraism, from *malkhuth shamayim*, which means *heavenly kingdom* and points to *the law of heaven on earth*. We find it explained in this way in almost all rabbinical literature on this subject. It is not a kingdom situated in heaven, but an earthly kingdom with heavenly traits. This is why it is no longer proffered after Pentecost. Since then the gospel is concentrated on another kingdom, because Jesus said: *My kingdom is not of this world* (John 18:36 NASB). It is a spiritual kingdom.

17.d A well-known issue
The royal claims of Jesus Christ are all interwoven with prophecies in the Old Testament and they speak with a clear voice. The general view in that time, both among believing Jews and among the apostles of Jesus, was that an earthly kingdom was imminent. John the Baptist and Jesus Christ *never* contradict this. On the contrary, when Jesus Christ entered into Jerusalem, He chose a young donkey to ride on, as foretold in Zechariah 9:9–10. And every faithful Jew knew that this was the prelude to the coming of the kingdom of God. Also by doing this, Jesus Christ claimed to be the promised Messiah who would, according to the prophets, become king in Jerusalem, on the throne of David.

17.e The constitution of the Messianic Kingdom
When Jesus Christ delivered His famous Sermon on the Mount (Matthew 5), He was not simply talking about a number of general rules of life. He offered His people the Messianic Kingdom with its *constitution*! Therefore, no message of future blessings is given in the Sermon on the Mount as a kind of reward in the hereafter. That does not play into this

sermon. Here the law of Moses reverberates in the highest degree; for the *here and now* of that moment! The message was therefore exclusively addressed to God's people. Evangelists were not sent to the gentiles (Matthew 10:5–6 NASB) yet, as would happen later.

> *"Do not go in the way of the Gentiles, and do not enter any city of the Samaritans; but rather go to the lost sheep of the house of Israel."*

Jesus Christ never did correct His disciples and the Pharisees on their understanding of the kingdom of heaven. Why not? Because He proclaimed an earthly kingdom just as the prophets had done before Him. Only after John the Baptist was put in prison did clouds appear on the horizon of the future earthly kingdom. The herald was not understood and his message was not accepted. And the Lord Jesus responded by pronouncing curses (Matthew 11:16–24). (See Excursus 13.)

17.f The message of Jesus changes
After Matthew 10 Jesus's message changed and became, increasingly, an individual appeal to the oppressed (Matthew 11:28–29), who are offered redemption, rest, and peace in heaven *after* their earthly life, but no earthly kingdom.

In Matthew 12:40, Jesus Christ speaks for the first time of His death and again pronounces a curse in Matthew 12:41–45, where He condemns the generation then living in harsh terms.

In Matthew 12:46–50 the message changes again. Now, however, there is no question of an earthly relationship, but the heavenly is propagated. *The king was rejected!* His attitude toward the leaders of the Jews also changes. In Matthew 12:1–8, He still addressed them lovingly, in Matthew 15:1–9, however, Jesus Christ pronounced a bitter condemnation upon them and thus in fact broke with them. For the first time there was also room for non-Jews, the gentiles (Matthew 15:21–28).

17.g The church of Christ
It is not until Matthew 16:18, when it is clear that the Messiah was rejected by His own people, that Jesus speaks of a future congregation. A new phenomenon that, according to the apostle Paul (Romans 16:25–26), had been *concealed for centuries*. He therefore calls it a *mystery* (Ephesians 3:1–12). With this a third kind of people came into the world (1 Corinthians 10:32). Where there were, from a biblical point of view, only Jews and gentiles (non-Jews), now the church of Christ has been added. A new branch on the tree of salvation (Romans 11:17–24).

17.h Are just a few chosen?
The breach between Jesus Christ and His people (Judah, the Jews) is very clearly depicted in Matthew 22:1–14, in the parable of the royal wedding supper. The king is God Himself. His son is Jesus Christ, and the guests are the people of Israel. Unfortunately, the guests stay away. Thereupon the king gathers people from the crossroads and all who pass by are invited—the gentiles, the non-Jews, those who come into contact with the gospel.

The text even says that both bad and good are invited to the wedding (verse 10). Only on the wedding day (preceded by the day of judgment = the night) the good are separated from the bad. So the call to repentance applies from that time to everyone! The chapter has a significant ending (Matthew 22:14 NASB): *"For many are called, but few chosen."*

Many refers to all Israelites. *Few* does not refer to the elect in general, as if only very few could attain salvation. It refers to the limited number of Jews who then accepted Jesus Christ as their Savior and were admitted to the wedding banquet of the Lamb.

17.i The Messianic empire postponed

The new situation was no longer as the prophets had foretold. The promises of salvation were not, however, undone. They remained valid, but the fulfillment of the prophecy concerning the Messianic Kingdom shifted to the distant future.

In the parables that follow, the Lord Jesus speaks exclusively to His twelve disciples and through them to the later church of Christ. And if one of His disciples asks Him why that message is only directed to them, He answers (Matthew 13:11):

> *Because it is given to you to know the secrets of the kingdom, but it is not given to them* (= the Jews who rejected Him).

The earthly kingdom of heaven was not a secret. That was and is known in detail. The heavenly kingdom is secret. That secret belongs to the church of Christ! Those who are on the outside will never fully understand that.

17.j Exclusively for the church of Christ

The offer of the kingdom now appears to be limited to the followers of Jesus Christ. It is no longer made to the entire people of God, as a chosen nation. From the words that Jesus speaks to Pilate, the change in the status of the Jewish people is clear (John 18:36):

> *Jesus answered, "My kingdom is not of this world. If My kingdom were of this world,* then My servants would be fighting† so that I would not be handed over to the Jews‡; but as it is,** My kingdom is not of this realm.††"*

*That is, if Jesus Christ had been accepted as Messiah.
†In that case He would have become king over Israel and then the Jews would have defended Him against the Romans.
‡The Sanhedrin, the government that represented the Jewish people and Him rejected.
**The offer has changed.
††It has now become a spiritual kingdom, the church of Christ.

17.k A new message: Salvation and grace

It will be clear that the Lord Jesus has said much more than the Gospels relate. He would have, in the beginning of His ministry, certainly offered the Messianic Kingdom many more times than is recorded. However, when the evangelists put their memories in writing, the church of Christ was already a fact and people were no longer focused on the proclamation of the kingdom. Then it was the message of salvation and grace and the testimony about the suffering and dying of Jesus Christ that had made it possible. That first message was no longer so relevant. Did the Jews not have Moses and the prophets? (See Luke 16:31.) That was sufficient.

17.l The promise remains!

Was the promise concerning the Messianic Kingdom then dead? Definitely not. In Acts 1:6 the message about the coming of the Messianic Kingdom returns:

> *So when they had come together, they were asking Him, saying, "Lord, is it at this time You are restoring the kingdom to Israel?"*

Jesus's answer is not saying that His disciples have asked a wrong question, but that it is not their business to know the answer (Acts 1:7).

17.m No stupid questions

Many Christians see Acts 1:6, in fact, as a stupid question. But that cannot be the case.

For the evangelist Luke, who wrote both the gospel of Luke and Acts, makes an important statement about this in Luke 24:45 (NASB):

Then He opened their minds to understand the Scriptures.

The text tells us that the disciples, shortly before they asked the so-called stupid question, received insight into the Scriptures. This makes it quite unlikely that the question they asked shortly afterward was a stupid question. They did not ask themselves *whether* (they did not doubt this) but *when* the earthly kingdom would come! This is confirmed by Acts 1:7, which states:

He said to them, "It is not for you to know times or epochs which the Father has fixed by His own authority."

And Matthew 24:36:

"But of that day and hour no one knows, not even the angels of heaven, nor the Son, but the Father alone."

17.n Jesus did not correct His disciples.
The *day* and the *hour* are coming, that is certain. But the knowledge as to when is kept from everyone. Even from Jesus Christ. Only *the Father*, God Himself, knows this. Shortly after they asked this question, the Lord Jesus would ascend into heaven. But He did not correct His disciples, which He would certainly have done if the question had been incorrect.

HOSEA 7
Hebrew Text Translation

Introduction
Hosea 7 poses less problems for translation than the previous chapters do. Largely due to the fact that it does not clearly present us with unfulfilled prophecies about the far future or the end time (usually the main source of differences in opinion). Secondly, Hosea 7 does not address any major theological issues. Consequently, we notice a growing consensus among translators and exegetes on this chapter of Hosea. (Of course, this is most likely due to the absence of exegetical "obstacles.") This has not, however, had the positive effect one might expect for an accurate translation. Scholars have shown themselves ready to add to, delete from, or change the Hebrew text at will to suit their own interpretation. This is true especially for verses 4, 5, 6, and 16. We, of course, will do our best to stick close to the Hebrew source text.

Verse 1 NASB
When I would heal Israel, the iniquity of Ephraim is uncovered, and the evil deeds of Samaria, for they deal falsely; the thief enters in, bandits raid outside,

Verse 1 KJV
When I would have healed Israel, then the iniquity of Ephraim was discovered, and the wickedness of Samaria: for they commit falsehood; and the thief cometh in, and the troop of robbers spoileth without.

Verse 1 NIV
"whenever I would heal Israel, the sins of Ephraim are exposed and the crimes of Samaria revealed. They practice deceit, thieves break into houses, bandits rob in the streets;"

Verse 1 Hebrew Interlinear Text
when-to-heal-me to-Israel then-he-is-exposed sin-of Ephraim and-crimes-of Samaria indeed they-practice deceit and-thief he-breaks-in he-robs bandit in-the-street

Verse 1a
when-to-heal-me to-Israel
The text describes God's determination as seen in the NIV and NET translations.

We read: *every time I wanted to heal Israel*

Verse 1b
then-he-is-exposed sin-of Ephraim and-crimes-of Samaria
This clause begins with a *vav*. The KJV and NKJV translate the *vav* as *then*, but there are many translations that regrettably leave it out. The CEV reads *but then*, indicating that the *vav* serves to connect cause and effect, which is indeed the case.

The meaning is clear. Every time God wanted to heal Ephraim, sins were unveiled. It goes without saying that these are not the old sins that had already been unveiled, but new sins committed thereafter. For greater clarity, we have chosen to render it as: *new sins were revealed.*

We read: *new sins of Ephraim and crimes of Samaria were revealed*

Verse 1c
indeed they-practice deceit

The word *ki* usually introduces a causal relationship. It occurs very frequently and has a wide range of meaning. By far the greatest number of exegetes and translators render the term here as *for* or *because*, which we follow.

The Hebrew text says, *they have committed* (see also ASV), which we follow. *Sheqer* means *deception* or *falsehood*, though *deceit* is seldom used.
(Strong's OT, word 3588; *Studiebijbel* SBOT 12, 76)

We read: ***for they have committed deception***

Verse 1d
and-thief he-breaks-in
Van de Born, like others, adds the word *house* and thus reads, *and the thief enters the house*. That is not, however, what the text actually says. Verse 1d refers to a thief, breaking in randomly wherever and whenever he wants. Thus Hosea speaks about a society of lawlessness, as is confirmed in verse 1e.
(Born, 51; Harper, 293)

We read: ***the thief just breaks in***

Verse 1e
he-robs bandit in-the-street
The word *pashat* means *to strip off*, as in to strip off or take off clothes (Leviticus 6:11; 16:23). It can also mean *to pull off* or *to skin*, as in Leviticus 1:6; 2 Chronicles 29:34; Micah 3:3. Elsewhere, as in 1 Samuel 23:27 and 2 Chronicles 28:18, the verb means *to make a raid on* or *to invade* (a land).

Each of these meanings represents an alternative for the verb *to take away* (in the sense of robbing or stealing), which is also the sense the word has here. For that reason, *scour* seems to be a good translation.

Some translators have chosen to use *without* or *outside* instead of *street*. While that is an option, the passage itself is clearly referring to the *streets*.
(Born, 51; Mays, 99; Rosenberg, vol. 1, 41; Strong's OT, word 6584)

We read: ***and criminals scour the streets***

The entire sentence:
Every time I wanted to heal Israel, new sins of Ephraim and crimes of Samaria were revealed, for they have committed deception. The thief just breaks in, and criminals scour the streets.

Verse 2 NASB
And they do not consider in their hearts that I remember all their wickedness. Now their deeds are all around them; They are before My face.

Verse 2 KJV
And they consider not in their hearts that I remember all their wickedness: now their own doings have beset them about; they are before my face.

Verse 2 NIV
"But they do not realize that I remember all their evil deeds. Their sins engulf them; they are always before me."

Verse 2 Hebrew Interlinear Text
but-not they-realize in-heart-of-them all-of evil-of-them I-remember now they-engulf-them sins-of-them before faces-of-me they-are

Verse 2a
but-not they-realize in-heart-of-them all-of evil-of-them I-remember
The Hebrew word *ra'* usually means *bad, evil,* or *wrong*. In the Bible it points mostly to severe forms of sin.
(Harper, 293; Strong's OT, word 7451)

We read: *yet it does not occur to them in their hearts that I remember all their evil*

Verse 2b
now they-engulf-them
The NIVIHEOT's translation *engulf* is an unnecessary interpretation. We can adhere more closely to the Hebrew text.

The basic sense of the verb *sabab* is *to turn about, to go around,* or *to surround.** We have found the term translated in the NASB as *to gather around* (Genesis 37:7), *to turn away* (Genesis 42:24), *to lead around* (Exodus 13:18), and sometimes it refers to boundary lines (Joshua 16:6). In the present context *to surround* represents the best option, since the guilt of Israel for its sins had risen so high that it had come to stand like a wall between God and His people. That is why they were cut off from Him. Here is written: *səbāḇūm*; that is: *they have surrounded them* (BHI).
(Brown, 65; Rosenberg, vol. 1, 41; *Strong's OT, word 5437)

We read: *now they have surround them*

Verse 2c
sins-of-them before faces-of-me they-are
The word *maalal* does not mean *sin* (as in the NIVIHEOT), but *deed, conduct,* or *behavior*. Of course, these acts may be sins, but that is an interpretation by the NIVIHEOT and it is not what the text actually says. Here too, we have chosen to stick closer to the Hebrew text.
(Brown, 64; Strong's OT, word 4611; Wolff, 106)

We read: *their deeds, as they stand before Me*

The entire sentence:
Yet it does not occur to them in their hearts that I remember all their evil. Now their deeds have surrounded them as they stand before Me.

Verse 3 NASB
With their wickedness they make the king glad, and the princes with their lies.

Verse 3 KJV
They make the king glad with their wickedness, and the princes with their lies.

Verse 3 NIV
"They delight the king with their wickedness, the princes with their lies."

Verse 3 Hebrew Interlinear Text
with-wickedness-of-them they-delight king and-with-lies-of-them princes

We read:
They delight the king with their wickedness and the princes with their lies.

Verse 4 NASB
They are all adulterers, like an oven heated by the baker who ceases to stir up the fire; from the kneading of the dough until it is leavened.

Verse 4 KJV
They are all adulterers, as an oven heated by the baker, who ceaseth from raising after he hath kneaded the dough, until it be leavened.

Verse 4 NIV
"They are all adulterers, burning like an oven whose fire the baker need not stir from the kneading of the dough till it rises."

Verse 4 Hebrew Interlinear Text
all-of-them ones-committing-adultery like oven burning from-one-baking he-stops from-to-stir from-to-knead dough till to-rise-him
Hosea 7:4 seems to be a very difficult verse, as translators and exegetes have made changes, deletions, and/or additions to the Hebrew text to their hearts' content. Reed says, "The text of verse 4 is believed by many to have been miscopied, yet it reveals the abject corruption of the age." We very much disagree with that. Context and Hebrew source text together offer sufficiently solid footing for a good translation.
(Reed, 57)

Verse 4a
all-of-them ones-committing-adultery
Here we simply follow the translation in NIVIHEOT.

We read: ***all who commit adultery***

Verse 4b
like oven burning
The word *ba'ar* means *to kindle*, *to ignite*, or *to consume*. It can be applied both to a fire (Leviticus 6:12) and to a kindled emotion (Psalms 79:5; 89:46); it is thus a kind of ignited passion.
(Harper, 295; Strong's OT, word 1197; Wolff, 107)

We read: ***are like a burning oven***

Verse 4c/d/e/f
from-one-baking he-stops from-to-stir from-to-knead dough till to-rise-him
This part of verse 4 brings us to a much more difficult clause. For now we will not try to form a sentence, but attempt first of all to get as close as possible to the Hebrew text. Only then can we move on to a definitive text.

Verse 4c
from-one-baking
This is not difficult.

We read: ***of the baker***

Verse 4d
he-stops

The verb *shâbath* means *to put to rest* (usually after some form of exertion), *to cause to stop* (Joshua 22:25; Nehemiah 4:11), *to rest*, or *to cease* (Exodus 5:5; 23:12; Leviticus 26:34).

The word *shâbath* is related to *shabbath* (Exodus 16:23). This is, of course, the Sabbath or day of rest that God instituted on the seventh day of the week.
(Brown, 65; Mays, 103; Strong's OT, words 7673, 7676)

We read: ***he rests***

Verse 4e
from-to-stir
The basic sense of *ur* is *to get up*, *to stand up*, or *to arouse/awaken* (Ezra 1:5; Job 14:12). Rashi and the Targum Jonathan similarly use *awaken*. To translate as *to stir* or *to poke awake* (as many translate) is a matter of interpretation, since that is not what the Hebrew text says.
(Andersen and Freedman, 457; Mays, 103; Rosenberg, vol. 1, 42; Strong's OT, word 5782)

We read: ***from awakening***

Verse 4f
from-to-knead dough till to-rise-him
The word *chamets* means *fermented* or *leavened* (Exodus 34:25; Leviticus 2:11). Although it can be translated as *to rise*, we prefer to stick closer to the Hebrew text.
(Brown, 65; McComiskey, 103; Strong's OT, word 2556)

We read: ***from/after kneading leaving the dough to leaven him/it***

Verse 4c/d/e/f: Definitive text, first step:
he rests from awakening after kneading the dough to leaven it
The sense of the clause has become much clearer now. It describes acts performed by a baker when baking bread.

Verse 4c/d/e/f: Definitive text, second step:
when he awakens from his rest, after the dough has been kneaded so that it be leavened

Now the entire sentence:
All who commit adultery are like a burning oven of the baker, when he awakens from his rest, after the dough has been kneaded so as to be leavened.

Verse 5 NASB
On the day of our king, the princes became sick with the heat of wine; he stretched out his hand with scoffers,

Verse 5 KJV
In the day of our king the princes have made him sick with bottles of wine; he stretched out his hand with scorners.

Verse 5 NIV
"On the day of the festival of our king the princes become inflamed with wine, and he joins hands with the mockers."

Verse 5 Hebrew Interlinear Text
day-of king-of-us they-become-inflamed princes heat-of from-wine he-joins hand-of-him with ones-mocking

Verse 5a
day-of king-of-us they-become-inflamed princes
The NIVIHEOT's translation *inflamed* is an interpretation, which we have chosen to not follow. The word *chalah* can be translated in different ways. We have found it translated in the NASB as *to be diseased* (1 Kings 15:23); *sick/sickly* (Ezekiel 34:4); *weak* (Ezekiel 34:21); and *to be wearied/faint* (Isaiah 57:10). All these translations are, however, also interpretations. Garrett translates: *incapacitated*. The *Studiebijbel*: *make ill*. Rosenberg: *became ill*. Sweeney: *are sick*.

The root meaning of *chalah* means in fact *to be weak* or *powerless*. This sense of the term emerges very clearly from Judges 16:7, 11, 17 and Isaiah 14:10. Although many translators and exegetes may read *injured* or *wounded* in Chronicles, the word actually means *powerless*.
(Garrett, 167; Rosenberg, vol. 1, 43; Strong's OT, word 2470; *Studiebijbel* SBOT 12, 78; Sweeney, vol. 1, 79–80)

We read: ***on the day of our king, the princes will become powerless***

Verse 5b
heat-of from-wine
Chemah means *heat* and can also be figurative, as in *anger*, *fury*, or *starkness*. Genesis 27:44; Leviticus 26:28; and Numbers 25:11 all offer the translation *fury* or *wrath*.

The root meaning of *chemah* is *poisoned with rage*. This explains why some translations use the term *venom* (Psalm 58:4) and *poison* (Job 6:4). In the present context, the poison is that of the alcohol in the wine—the *fury*, *wrath*, or *venom of the wine*. Literally the text here could therefore be translated as *fury of the wine out of it*. Harper tends in the same direction when he translates *fever from wine*.
(Andersen and Freedman, 458; Harper, 296; Strong's OT, words 2534, 2573; Stuart, 114)

We read: ***as the fury leaves the wine***

Verse 5c
he-joins hand-of-him
The term *mashak* has a broad meaning, but basically, *to pull*, *to draw* (a bow when shooting an arrow), *to pull off*, or *to remove*. The NASB translation includes the following: *to pull out* (Genesis 37:28), *to take with* (Judges 4:6), *to deploy* (Judges 20:37), *to continue* (Psalm 36:10), *to lead* or *to draw out* (Judges 4:7), and *to drag away* (Psalm 28:3).

Yad is a frequently occurring term in the Bible and usually means *hand* (Genesis 3:22; 4:11). It can also mean *through* or *by means of* (Exodus 9:35; 1 Samuel 16:20).
(Garrett, 167; McComiskey, 105; Strong's OT, words 3027, 4900)

We read: ***His hand causes to pull out***

Verse 5d
with ones-mocking
According to Strong's concordance, the word *latsats* means *to mock*, *to scorn*, or *to despise*. It does not appear anywhere else in the Bible, and we do not actually know what it means. In nonbiblical wisdom literature the word is also scarcely used. The context there reveals, however, that it refers to proud scoffers. Harper thus chooses to translate as *loose fellow*, while Andersen and Freedman use *depraved*, which we have chosen to follow here.
(Andersen and Freedman, 459; Brown, 65; Harper, 296; Strong's OT, word 3945)

We read: ***with the depraved***

We first combine verse 5b/c/d:
as the fury/wine leaves the wine does His hand cause to pull out the depraved
As such, we see a certain logic emerge from the structure of the sentence. The preceding verse mentioned an ignited passion. The present verse now speaks of the *fury* (or *the venom*) of *the wine*, which has similar associations. The choice of terms calls to mind the well-known saying: When the wine is in, the wit is out. Here, it seems, the same thing is meant.

Verse 5b/c/d, second step: *As the fury leaves the wine, so does His hand pull out the depraved*

Now the entire sentence:
On the day of our king, the princes will become powerless. As the fury leaves the wine, so does His hand pull out the depraved.

Verse 6 NASB
For their hearts are like an oven as they approach their plotting; Their anger smolders all night, in the morning it burns like a flaming fire.

Verse 6 KJV
For they have made ready their heart like an oven, whiles they lie in wait: their baker sleepeth all the night; in the morning it burneth as a flaming fire.

Verse 6 NIV
"Their hearts are like an oven; they approach him with intrigue. Their passion smolders all night; in the morning it blazes like a flaming fire."

Verse 6 Hebrew Interlinear Text
indeed they-approach like-the-oven heart-of-them with-intrigue-of-them all-of-the-night smoldering one-baking-of-them morning he blazing like-fire-of flame

Verse 6a
indeed
The word *ki* occurs very frequently and has a wide range of meaning. It usually introduces a causal relationship, as is true here. By far most exegetes and translators render the word here as *for* or *because*.
(Strong's OT, word 3588)

We read: *because*

Verse 6b
they-approach
Qarab means *to approach*, *to be nearby*, or *to come close by*. One of its uses is for "approaching God" as part of a sacred ceremony. Such cases usually concern sacrifices (Leviticus 1:2, 5; 2:4; Exodus 12:48). However, the word is also used in the sense of "approaching" for sexual contact (Leviticus 18:6, 14, 19; 20:16). This is indeed the case in the present context.
(Andersen and Freedman, 459; Garrett, 167, 205; Strong's OT, word 7126)

We read: *they seek sexual contact*

Verse 6c
like-the-oven heart-of-them
This is simple.

We read: ***their heart burns like an oven***

Verse 6d
with-intrigue-of-them all-of the-night
The NIVIHEOT actually interprets when it offers the translation *intrigue*. What the text says is *arab*, meaning *to ambush* (Joshua 8:4; Judges 9:25), *to lie in wait* (Deuteronomy 19:11), or *to waylay*.
(Andersen and Freedman, 459; Garrett, 168; Strong's OT, word 693)

We read: ***with their lying in wait all night long***

Verse 6e
smoldering one-baking-of-them
These words are deserving of special attention, since the NIVIHEOT departs from the Hebrew source text, which actually reads: *sleeping one-baking-of-them*. In the eyes of many, this does not fit the context, for which reason they have chosen to interpret *yashen* as *smoldering*. The NIV offers an even broader interpretation, reading *their passion smolders all night*, which is almost the exact same phrase found in the NRSV. However, like the KJV, NKJV, NBG, and DRA, we prefer to adhere more closely to the original Hebrew source text. *Yashen* means *to sleep*, *to be sleepy*, or *to slumber*.

The word *aphah* does indeed mean *to cook* or *to bake*. In its nominal form, *baker* is a logical choice for translation.
(Mays, 104; McComiskey, 105; Strong's OT, words 644, 3463; Stuart, 116; Wolff, 107)

We read: ***like their baker sleeps***

Verse 6f
morning he blazing like-fire-of flame
The word *ba'ar* can signify *burning* but also *to ignite*, *to flare up* (or *to cause to flare up*), or *to kindle* (Exodus 22:6; 2 Samuel 22:9; Psalms 2:12; 18:8).
(Mays, 104; McComiskey, 105; Strong's OT, word 1197; Wolff, 107)

We read: ***in the morning it flares up like a flaming fire***

The whole sentence, first step:
Because they seek sexual contact, their heart burns like an oven, with their lying in wait all night long. Like their baker sleeps/slumbers and flares it up in the morning like a flaming fire.

Now we can move ahead and try to formulate a readable sentence.

We read, second step:
They seek sexual contact. Their heart burns like an oven. They lie in wait all night long. Like their baker slumbers and flares it up in the morning like a flaming fire.
For the sake of clarity, we add the term *the oven*, as in several translations, such as the NBG.
(Rosenberg, vol. 1, 43)

We read, third step:
They seek sexual contact, because their heart burns like an oven. They lie in wait all night long, like the baker who slumbers and flares up [the oven] in the morning like a flaming fire.

Verse 7 NASB
All of them are hot like an oven, and they consume their rulers; all their kings have fallen. None of them calls on Me.

Verse 7 KJV
They are all hot as an oven, and have devoured their judges; all their kings are fallen: there is none among them that calleth unto me.

Verse 7 NIV
"All of them are hot as an oven; they devour their rulers. All their kings fall, and none of them calls on me."

Verse 7 Hebrew Interlinear Text
all-of-them they-are-hot as-the-oven and-they-devour . . . ones-ruling-them all-of kings-of-them they-fall there-is-no one-calling of-them on-me

Verse 7a
all-of-them they-are-hot as-the-oven
Chamam means *to be/become warm*. In Isaiah 57:5 it is translated as *to burn* (with lust). In the present verse, the verb is used in a similar sense. Given the poetic undertone of this passage, *hot* is the best translation here.
(Brown, 66; Harper, 298; Mays, 104; Strong's OT, word 2552; Wolff, 107)

We read: ***they are all hot like an oven***

Verse 7b
and-they-devour . . . ones-ruling-them
The word *shaphat* means *judge* (Genesis 18:25), or *to judge* (Genesis 16:5), but also *judges* (in the sense of leaders, see Judges 2:18). In this final sense of the word, the term includes the notions of a magistrate, a ruler (the judges ruled Israel), and that of a judge; this meaning best suits the present context.

7b.1 Who are *they*?
To shed greater light on this prophecy, we first need to determine what it is that the pronoun *they* refers to. On the face of it, there appears to be only two options: (a) the entire nation of Israel (vv. 1–3), or (b) the king and the rulers (vv. 5–7). Neither of these options, however, fits the context here.

7b.2 The context reveals option c
History tells us that there were seven kings who ruled Israel between the time of Jeroboam II and the fall of the kingdom. Four of them were killed in palace revolutions. Such revolutions, however, were rulers fighting amongst themselves. For that reason we can exclude the nation of Israel (option a).

Others have connected the death of the four kings with verse 7c (more on this below in the exegesis). Option b would mean, however, that all magistrates (*judges*) were killed (*and-they-devour*). No such event has been recorded for us, however, meaning that option b is also excluded.

The only remaining solution (which will be option c) would be to place the word *devour* in the context of passion. This also implies that the pronoun *they* is to be connected to *their smoldering passion* (verse 6) which consumes them. Such an interpretation is in full agreement with the entire purport of the chapter. For that reason, we have chosen to translate the pronoun as *that* instead of *they*.

Exegetes and translators have really struggled with this text, which has led to a number of confusing translations. Van de Born, Brown, and Mays, for example, drop the pronoun *they*. Van de Born uses the simple past tense here, like the KJV and the Luther Bible. Brown reads, *all the kings are fallen*; Rosenberg: *all their kings have fallen*. We, however, have chosen simply to follow the Hebrew text.
(Born, 52; Brown, 66; Calvijn, *Daniël* II, *Kleine Profeten* I/II, Hosea, 253–54; Garrett, 168; Mays, 104; Rosenberg, vol 1, 44; Strong's OT, word 8199; Stuart, 116)

We read: ***which devours their judges***

Verse 7c
all-of kings-of-them they-fall
Naphal means *to fall down* (Genesis 50:18; Joshua 6:5, 20) or *to cause to fall* or *fail* (1 Samuel 3:19), but also *to fall into the hands of* (Judges 15:18).
(Strong's OT, word 5307)

We read: ***and causes all their kings to fall***

The entire sentence:
They are all hot as an oven, which devours their judges and causes all their kings to fall. There is no one who calls on Me.

Verse 8 NASB
Ephraim mixes himself with the nations; Ephraim has become a cake not turned.

Verse 8 KJV
Ephraim, he hath mixed himself among the people; Ephraim is a cake not turned.

Verse 8 NIV
"Ephraim mixes with the nations; Ephraim is a flat loaf not turned over."

Verse 8 Hebrew Interlinear Text
Ephraim with-the-nations he he-mixes Ephraim he-is flat-cake not being-turned-over he-is flat-cake
The word *uggah* refers to a *cake* or *flat cake* (Exodus 12:39; 1 Kings 17:13; 19:6).
(Brown, 67; Strong's OT, word 5692)

We read:
Ephraim will mingle with the gentile nations. Ephraim is a flat cake that is not turned.

Verse 9 NASB
Strangers devour his strength, yet he does not know it; Gray hairs also are sprinkled on him, yet he does not know it.

Verse 9 KJV
Strangers have devoured his strength, and he knoweth it not: yea, gray hairs are here and there upon him, yet he knoweth not.

Verse 9 NIV
"Foreigners sap his strength, but he does not realize it. His hair is sprinkled with gray, but he does not notice."

Verse 9 Hebrew Interlinear Text
they-sap ones-being-foreign strength-of-him but-he not he-realizes and gray-hair she-is-sprinkled on-him but-he not he-notices

Verse 9a
they-sap ones-being-foreign
The word *akal* usually means *to eat*, but also *to consume* or *to devour*. Given such shades of meaning, the word seems to imply a rapid loss of strength. For that reason we translate the verb as *exhaust*.
(Born, 53; Brown, 67; Harper, 302; Strong's OT, word 398)

We read: *foreigners exhaust*

Verse 9b
strength-of-him
Koach means *power* or *strength* (Genesis 49:3, Exodus 9:16; Numbers 14:13).
(Andersen and Freedman, 467; Harper, 302; Strong's OT, word 3581)

We read: *his strength*

Verse 9c
but-he not he-realizes
This clause is easily translated.

We read: *but he does not realize it*

Verse 9d
and gray-hair
Seybah means *gray hair* (Genesis 42:38; 44:29; Isaiah 46:4). Sometimes the term is translated as *old age* or *ripe old age* (Genesis 15:15; 25:8; Judges 8:32), but that is interpretation.
(Andersen and Freedman, 467; Köhler, 269; Strong's OT, word 7872; Wolff, 107)

We read: *and gray hair*

Verse 9e
she-is-sprinkled on-him
The word *zaraq* means *to sprinkle* (a liquid; Exodus 24:6), *to toss*, or *to throw* (Exodus 9:10).
(Harper, 302; Köhler, 269; Strong's OT, word 2236)

Verse 9d/e
When we put verse 9d and 9e together, we get: *gray hair is sprinkled on him.*

We read: *he has turned gray.*

The entire sentence:
Foreigners exhaust his strength, but he does not realize it. He has turned gray, but he does not notice it.

Verse 10 NASB
Though the pride of Israel testifies against him, yet they have not returned to the L<small>ORD</small> their God, nor have they sought Him, for all this.

Verse 10 KJV
And the pride of Israel testifieth to his face: and they do not return to the L<small>ORD</small> their God, nor seek him for all this.

Verse 10 NIV
"Israel's arrogance testifies against him, but despite all this he does not return to the Lord his God or search for him."

Verse 10 Hebrew Interlinear Text
and-he-testifies arrogance-of Israel against-faces-of-him but-not they-return to Yahweh God-of-them or-not they-search-for-him despite-all-of this

Verse 10a
and-he-testifies arrogance-of Israel
Some exegetes believe *he* refers to Yahweh. That is wrong; it points to *ga'own*. Many translate the word *ga'own* as *pride* or *arrogance*, but this is debatable. In many places in Scripture, it instead means *greatness*, *majesty*, *magnificence*, *splendor*, or *glory* (Exodus 15:7; Isaiah 2:10; 4:2). In other passages, like Psalm 47:4 and Isaiah 13:19, where the term by some has been rendered as *pride*, that translation is questionable and should probably read *majesty*. This interpretation finds further support in rabbinic writings, since they commonly speak of the pride or glory of Israel (e.g., Rashi, cited by Rosenberg).

Since Israel (= *God struggles/fights*, meaning that it is still the people of God) is contrasted in this part of Hosea with Ephraim (Lo-Ammi—not My people), the present verse must be taken to refer to all Israel in the messianic sense of the word. For that reason, *majesty* is the preferred translation.
(McComiskey, 109; Owens, 769; Rosenberg, vol. 1, 45; Strong's OT, word 1347; Sweeney, vol. 1, 80; Teshuvoth Dunash, 79; Targum Jonathan, Hosea 5:5)

We read: *the majesty of Israel also testifies*

Verse 10b
against-faces-of-him
The word *against* may at first suggest that the testimony is directed against the people of Israel. However, that is not what the text means here, since the term actually goes with *faces*. Accordingly, for *against* we should rather read *in, before*, or *to*. It simply shows a contrast between *the majesty of Israel* in the pass and their actual state. Some translate: *in His presence*. That is not likely, because than very often the name *Yahweh*/LORD is added.
(Andersen and Freedman, 392; Brown, 67; Calvijn, *Daniël* II, *Kleine Profeten* I/II, Hosea, 260; McComiskey, 107; Owens, 773)

We read: *for him*

The entire sentence:
The majesty of Israel also testifies for him. But they do not return to Yahweh, their God; in spite of all this they are not looking for Him.

Verse 11 NASB
So Ephraim has become like a silly dove, without sense; They call to Egypt, they go to Assyria.

Verse 11 KJV
Ephraim also is like a silly dove without heart: they call to Egypt, they go to Assyria.

Verse 11 NIV
"Ephraim is like a dove, easily deceived and senseless—now calling to Egypt, now turning to Assyria."

Verse 11 Hebrew Interlinear Text
and-he-is Ephraim like-dove being-easily-deceived without sense Egypt they-call-to Assyria they-turn-to

The word *leb* is usually translated as *heart*. Sometimes it refers to the *mind* or *reason* and can also be translated with *sense* (Proverbs 6:32; 7:7; Jeremiah 5:21). In the present verse we prefer *reason*. Many translations support our choice including the GNT, NASB, NBG, NKJV, NRSV, and Dutch Willibrordvertaling.
(Strong's OT, word 3820)

We read:
Thus Ephraim has become like a dove, which is easily deceived, without reason. Now they call again Egypt, then they turn again to Assyria.

Verse 12 NASB
When they go, I will spread My net over them; I will bring them down like the birds of the sky. I will chastise them in accordance with the proclamation to their assembly.

Verse 12 KJV
When they shall go, I will spread my net upon them; I will bring them down as the fowls of the heaven; I will chastise them, as their congregation hath heard.

Verse 12 NIV
"When they go, I will throw my net over them; I will pull them down like the birds in the sky. When I hear them flocking together, I will catch them."

Verse 12 Hebrew Interlinear Text
as-when they-go I-will-throw over-them net-of-me like-bird-of the-airs I-will-pull-down-them I-will-catch-them at-hearing of-flocking-together-of-them

We read:
If they go, I will throw a net over them. Like birds in the sky, I will bring them down and catch them when I hear that they are gathering.

Verse 13 NASB
Woe to them, for they have strayed from Me! Destruction is theirs, for they have rebelled against Me! I would redeem them, but they speak lies against Me.

Verse 13 KJV
Woe unto them! for they have fled from me: destruction unto them! because they have transgressed against me: though I have redeemed them, yet they have spoken lies against me.

Verse 13 NIV
"Woe to them, because they have strayed from me! Destruction to them, because they have rebelled against me! I long to redeem them but they speak about me falsely."

Verse 13 Hebrew Interlinear Text
woe! to-them because they-strayed from-me destruction to-them because they-rebelled against-me and-I I-would-redeem-them but-they they-speak against-me lies

Verse 13b
because they-rebelled against-me

Most exegetes read *risen up* or *revolted*. We, however, follow in this case the NIVIHEOT text.
(McComiskey, 110; Rosenberg, vol. 1, 46; Wolff, 108)

We read: *for they rebelled against Me*

Verse 13c
and-I I-would-redeem-them
The pronoun *I* occurs twice here. This repetition serves to heighten the tension or to create a striking contrast. For that reason, this clause is sometimes translated as: *It is I who . . .* We prefer: *And I, I.*
(Andersen and Freedman, 462; Wolff, 108)

We read: *And I, yes, I still wanted to redeem them*

Verse 13d1
but-they they-speak against-me lies
Here we find the same structure as in verse 13c. Very few exegetes and translators take into account the repetition of the word *they*. Andersen and Freedman are an exception in this. While Wolff's translation does reflect that repetition in verse 13c, he does not do so here, which seems rather inconsistent.

Instead of *against-me* we could also translate *about me*. In fact, given the context this is the preferred translation. For there was hardly any interaction between the nation of Israel and their God. They did not communicate through the prophets anymore. Knowledge of Yahweh had largely been lost in the country. The little the Israelites did still know about their God reflected powerful influences from pagan views on idolatry. The speaking they did was not *with God*, but *about God* (in an erroneous way).
(Andersen and Freedman, 462, 473; Harper, 305; Kidner, 72; Mays, 110)

Verse 13d2
but-they they-speak against-me lies
Dabar usually means *to speak*, *to say*, *to communicate*, or sometimes *to answer*. The word *kazab* means *falsity* or *deceitful*.
(Andersen and Freedman, 473; Harper, 305; Mays, 110; Strong's OT, words 1696, 3577)

We read: *they, however, they spoke falsely about Me.*

The entire sentence:
Woe to them, for they strayed from Me. Downfall to them, because they rebelled against Me. And I, yes, I still wanted to redeem them. They, however, they spoke falsely about Me.

Verse 14 NASB
And they do not cry to Me from their heart when they wail on their beds; For the sake of grain and new wine they assemble themselves, they turn away from Me.

Verse 14 KJV
And they have not cried unto me with their heart, when they howled upon their beds: they assemble themselves for corn and wine, and they rebel against me.

Verse 14 NIV
"They do not cry out to me from their hearts but wail on their beds. They slash themselves, appealing to their gods for grain and new wine, but they turn away from me."

Verse 14 Hebrew Interlinear Text
and-not they-cry-out to-me from-heart-of-them but they-wail on beds-of-them for grain and-new-wine they-gather-together they-turn-away from-me

Verse 14b
for grain and-new-wine they-gather-together
This clause has been translated in widely differing ways. The keyword is *they-gather-together*. Van de Born translates: *to wound*; Mays and Wolff: *they gash themselves*. *Studiebijbel*: *they come together*.

The word *guwr* means *to abide, to dwell, to sojourn* (Genesis 12:10; Leviticus 20:2; Isaiah 11:6), or *to live with*. Thus we can translate: *To abide in* or *live with grain and new wine*, or—even better: *to deal in grain and new wine*.
(Andersen and Freedman, 475–76; Born, 54; Mays, 110; Strong's OT, word 1481; *Studiebijbel* SBOT 12, 82; Wolff, 108)

We read:
And they do not call to Me from their hearts, but wail on their beds. They deal in grain and new wine and turn away from Me.

Verse 15 NASB
Although I trained and strengthened their arms, yet they devise evil against Me.

Verse 15 KJV
Though I have bound and strengthened their arms, yet do they imagine mischief against me.

Verse 15 NIV
"I trained them and strengthened their arms, but they plot evil against me."

Verse 15 Hebrew Interlinear Text
and-I I-trained I-strengthened arms-of-them but-against-me they-plot evil
Few biblical scholars actually take into account the repetition of the pronoun *I*, although it serves to heighten the tension (see verse 13c). We could translate as either: *It was I who . . .* or *And I, I*.

The basic meaning of *yâçar* (NIVIHEOT: *trained*) is *to teach discipline*. It is commonly translated as *to chastise* or *to discipline*. Often it has the implication of *to improve* or *to discipline in rearing*, but this actually involves interpretation. If we use the term *discipline* or *chastise* in our translation, we get: *And I? I brought them discipline and strengthened their arms*. However, this would mean that discipline and support now come to stand side-by-side within a single clause, which hardly seems likely. Calvin remarks: "The notion of 'chastising' seems not to me to be in any way suitable to the context." Calvin therefore translates *yasar* as *to bind*, but this seems like a last resort and finds no support anywhere. The solution is rather to insert the basic meaning of *yâçar* here, that is, *to give* or *teach discipline*. That does fit the context.
(Calvijn, *Daniel* II, *Kleine Profeten* I/II, Hosea, 273; Edelkoort, 189.51; Harper, 306; Strong's OT, word 3256; Stuart, 116; Wolff, 108)

The entire sentence:
And I? I taught them discipline and strengthened their arms, but they did evil against Me.

Verse 16 NASB
They turn, but not upward, they are like a deceitful bow; their princes will fall by the sword because of the insolence of their tongue. This will be their derision in the land of Egypt.

Verse 16 KJV
They return, but not to the most High: they are like a deceitful bow: their princes shall fall by the sword for the rage of their tongue: this shall be their derision in the land of Egypt.

Verse 16 NIV
"They do not turn to the Most High; they are like a faulty bow. Their leaders will fall by the sword because of their insolent words. For this they will be ridiculed in the land of Egypt."

Verse 16 Hebrew Interlinear Text
they-turn not Most-High they-are like-bow-of faultiness they-will-fall by-the-sword leaders-of-them because-of-insolence-of tongue-of-them this ridicule-of-them in-land-of Egypt

Verse 16a
they-turn not Most-High
Some read *they do not turn on high*, which is also a good translation. This does not change the exegesis, however.
(Garrett, 171)

We read: ***they do not turn to the Most High***

Verse 16b
they-are like-bow-of faultiness
The word *rmiyah* means *deceit*, *deception*, or *negligence*. A deceptive or negligent bow is *a failing bow*.
(Brown, 70; Rosenberg, vol. 1, 47; Strong's OT, word 7423)

We read: ***they are like a failing bow***

Verse 16c
they-will-fall by-the-sword leaders-of-them
The word *sar* usually means *prince* or *sovereign*, but is sometimes also translated as *leader* or *chief*.
(Strong's OT, word 8269)

We read: ***their princes will fall by the sword***

Verse 16d
because-of-insolence-of tongue-of-them
The root meaning of *zaam* is *to foam at the mouth*. Most translations render this phrase as *wrath* or *ire* (Psalms 69:24; 102:10 NIV). Others translate it as *indignation* (Isaiah 10:5 NASB). None of these translations, however, cover the true meaning of the term. Strong's says: *Strictly froth at the mouth*. Thus, *fury* or *angry indignation* would be better. As such, it refers to a kind of *uncontrolled anger* that entices a person to all kinds of folly and *insolent talk* or *to bluster*.
(Andersen and Freedman, 479; Strong's OT, word 2195)

We read: ***for the insolence of their tongue***

Verse 16e
this ridicule-of-them in-land-of Egypt
This clause is generally considered to be corrupt. We do not share this opinion, however. The Hebrew word *zw* is usually vowel-pointed to read *zo* or *zôw*. As such, it would mean *this* or *that*, which is indeed how most Bible scholars translate it. Wolff interprets the text and thus reads: *it will bring*. However, *zw* can also be vowel-pointed as *zu* (commonly translated as *this, that, in which,* or *which*), or (as a third option) as *ziv*. This final option seems to offer the right solution.

According to Strong's Concordance, the basic meaning of *ziv* is *prominent* or *renowned*. It is also the name of a month in the Jewish calendar. It is derived from *ziv*, meaning *brightness* or *splendor*. The context suggests that it must refer to something commonly known (= placed in the light). The people of Israel therefore *stood out* for their insolent talk.

The word *laag* means *mocking, derision, scoffing,* or *slander* (Psalm 44:13; Ezekiel 23:32; 36:4).
(Born, 54; Joüon, § 36a; Strong's OT, words 2097, 2098, 2099, 2122, 3933; Stuart, 116; Wolff, 108)

We read: **stood out—as mockery of them in the land of Egypt**

Verse 16 d/e, therefore literally reads:
For the insolence of their tongue stood out—their mockery in the land of Egypt

We read, first step:
Because of their insolent talk, they stood out. That will be their mockery in the land of Egypt.

We read, second step:
They stood out because of their insolent talk. That will be their mockery in the land of Egypt.

Now the entire sentence:
They do not turn to the Most High, they are like a failing bow. Their princes will fall by the sword. They stood out because of their insolent talk. That will be their mockery in the land of Egypt.

Hosea 7:1–16—The corrected text:

Verse 1   *Every time I wanted to heal Israel, new sins of Ephraim and crimes of Samaria were revealed, for they have committed deception. The thief just breaks in, and criminals scour the streets.*
Verse 2   *Yet it does not occur to them in their hearts that I remember all their evil. Now their deeds have surrounded them as they stand before Me.*
Verse 3   *They delight the king with their wickedness and the princes with their lies.*
Verse 4   *All who commit adultery are like a burning oven of the baker, when he awakens from his rest, after the dough has been kneaded so as to be leavened.*
Verse 5   *On the day of our king, the princes will become powerless. As the fury leaves the wine, so does His hand pull out the depraved.*
Verse 6   *They seek sexual contact, because their heart burns like an oven. They lie in wait all night long, like the baker who slumbers and flares up [the oven] in the morning like a flaming fire.*
Verse 7   *They are all hot as an oven, which devours their judges and causes all their kings to fall. There is no one who calls on Me.*

Verse 8   *Ephraim will mingle with the gentile nations. Ephraim is a flat cake that is not turned.*

Verse 9   *Foreigners exhaust his strength, but he does not realize it. He has turned gray, but he does not notice it.*

Verse 10 *The majesty of Israel also testifies for him. But they do not return to Yahweh, their God; in spite of all this they are not looking for Him.*

Verse 11 *Thus Ephraim has become like a dove, which is easily deceived, without reason. Now they call again Egypt, then they turn again to Assyria.*

Verse 12 *If they go, I will throw a net over them. Like birds in the sky, I will bring them down and catch them when I hear that they are gathering.*

Verse 13 *Woe to them, for they strayed from Me. Downfall to them, because they rebelled against Me. And I, yes, I still wanted to redeem them. They, however, they spoke false about Me.*

Verse 14 *And they do not call to Me from their hearts, but wail on their beds. They deal in grain and new wine and turn away from Me.*

Verse 15 *And I? I taught them discipline and strengthened their arms, but they did evil against Me.*

Verse 16 *They do not turn to the Most High, they are like a failing bow. Their princes will fall by the sword. They stood out because of their insolent talk. That will be their mockery in the land of Egypt.*

HOSEA 7
Exegesis

Introduction
This section of Hosea 7 is primarily about the divine judgment on the ten-tribe kingdom (Ephraim). However, it lacks the message of hope that we find in the other chapters. The chapter contains a series of accusations and a sad enumeration of (sometimes) extreme sins. Reed rightly names them in his heading, *Seeds of Destruction*.

In God's eyes the people of Ephraim are sick. So sick that the question is whether healing is possible. That is the core message of Hosea 7. The heavenly physician mentions all the diseases His people suffer from. From this list it appears that the break between God and His people was an inevitable development.
(Reed, 57; Smith, 121)

A. Ephraim versus Israel
The name Ephraim plays a crucial role in salvation history until the end of time. And the prophecy of Hosea 7 outlines the role of Ephraim within Israel—the name of the bearer of future salvation. Because salvation is promised only to Israel—all twelve tribes in the messianic sense. After the breach of the Sinaitic Covenant, the Ten Tribes are excluded from salvation promises, and therefore called Ephraim. However they also included, because without Ephraim (the Ten Tribes) the messianic prophecy cannot be completely fulfilled. So we should call this a conditional blessing or a blessing in disguise.
(See Annotation 1D.)

B. The Soul Pain of God
Hosea 7 is also a divine lamentation, in which God's grief resounds. The bond between God and His people is described as a marriage. That is now broken, and in a divorce, there are always two who suffer. We have a tendency to focus on the suffering of Israel because we deem God above such ordinary human feelings. That appears to be incorrect. For here we hear the "soul pain of God" in the enumeration of Ephraim's misdeeds.
(Calvijn, *Daniel* II, *Kleine Profeten* I/II, Hosea, 188)
(See Excursus 16.)

Verse 1
Every time I wanted to heal Israel, new sins of Ephraim and crimes of Samaria were revealed, for they have committed deception. The thief just breaks in, and criminals scour the streets.
The decision to execute judgment on Ephraim has already been made. The events of verse 1, however, describe the beginning of the execution, which is for Hosea still in the future. So he looks back from a moment in the future as if it was history. That's not unusual in biblical prophecy; it is distinctive and we call it Perfectum Propheticum—the past tense of the prophets.

The prophetic perfect tense is a literary technique used in the Bible that describes future events that are so certain to happen that they are referred to in the past tense as if they have already happened. It serves to confirm the irrevocability of divine prophecy.

In order to fulfill the prophecies about the blessed future of Israel, both nations (Ephraim and Judah) would have to turn to Yahweh. The unity of the people also had to be restored. Only then would God heal (all of) Israel and the theocracy (the kingdom of God) would be restored. In Hosea's day, it was too late and the prophet (speaking on God's behalf) looks at it in sadness.
(See Excursuses 5, 12, 13, and the exegesis of Hosea 1.)

Verse 1b
sins of Ephraim and crimes of Samaria
The first verse outlines the sad state of the people of Ephraim/Israel toward the end of the reign of King Jeroboam II and the years thereafter. God sent prophets among them to denounce their sins. He punished them, so as to induce them to give up their evil way of life. God did not want the destruction of Ephraim, but He wanted them to repent! However, it was to no avail. The society of Ephraim was developing, irresistibly, toward a catastrophe. The moral degeneration and wickedness were constantly increasing.
(Harper, 292–93; McComiskey, 100–101; Ward, 131)

1b.1 Another translation?
Perhaps the Hebrew text should be translated as a question. Then it could mean something like: *Is it not true that every time I wanted to heal Israel, (even more) sin of Ephraim and crimes/misdeeds of Samaria were revealed?* But this hardly changes the meaning.
(Garrett, 166; Walvoord and Zuck, 1394)

Verse 2a
Yet it does not occur to them in their hearts that I remember all their evil.
The worship of God was displaced by idolatry, especially through Queen Jezebel (1 Kings 16:31; 18:12–13). After the death of King Ahab and Queen Jezebel, there was some short-lived improvement, especially under the reign of King Jehu. But that was only temporary. The images of the Baals had disappeared, but the bull calves at Gilgal and Bethel were left standing. That form of idolatry was maintained. And under Jeroboam II Israel again became infested with idolatrous shrines. During his government, the worship of God was almost extinguished. By the continual and increasing sin of Ephraim/Israel the debt of sin increased. It accumulated, because God does not forget them.
(Stuart, 118)

Verse 2b
Now their deeds have surrounded them as they stand before Me.
The debt of the sin of Israel had finally risen so high that the way back was cut off. The Ten Tribes were put before God's court (*now . . . as they stand before Me*; see also Hosea 4:1). There it appears that the accumulated burden of sin caused a separation between them and God (*their deeds . . . surrounded them*). That is characteristic of broken relationships between God and man—not that God turns away from us but that we prevent God from reaching us. By severing their relationship with Yahweh, the Ten Tribes lost their name *Israel*. They are henceforth called *Ephraim*.
(Born, 51; Calvijn, *Daniel* II, *Kleine Profeten* I/II, Hosea, 191; Garrett, 166; Rosenberg, vol. 1, 41)
(See Annotation 2A; Excursus 12.)

Verse 3
They delight the king with their wickedness and the princes with their lies.
There was no one who intervened. The king and his princes (rulers and magistrates) did not appear to be acting as judges in God's service. They preceded their people in a debauched

way of life and enjoyed every further deepening of their wickedness. In fact, they surrendered themselves to Satan. But that was a way which held no possibility of return.
(Born, 51–52; McComiskey, 101–02; Reed, 57)

3.1 Jewish interpretations
Rabbinical writings show us a different meaning. They see in *the king*, referred to in this verse, Jeroboam I, who set up the bull calves in Gilgal and Bethel. By that act, he prevented his people from going to Jerusalem to visit the temple. We do not share that opinion.
(RaDak, cited by Rosenberg, vol. 1, 42)

Verse 4
All who commit adultery are like a burning oven of the baker, when he awakens from his rest, after the dough has been kneaded so as to be leavened.
Apparently, this is a saying or a proverb, which was then generally known. For us, this verse is a bit more difficult to understand and that applies to both translation and exegesis. And yet the explanation seems obvious.

Just as the baker's oven smoldered and was stoked up when the bread was about to be baked, the desires of the king and princes smoldered—until they erupted. In staggeringly clear language, the moral degeneration of the king and his princes is described. They burned with desire and completely surrendered themselves to perverted forms of sexual degeneration.
(Garrett, 169; McComiskey, 104; Wood, 196)

Verse 5
On the day of our king, the princes will become powerless. As the fury leaves the wine, so does His hand pull out the depraved.
This is a wonderful text, which probably has a first and a second fulfillment. In the first instance, the prophecy may have looked forward to the day that the last king of Israel would be taken prisoner by the Assyrians, in 722 BC. With this the nation lost its leadership (*the princes will become powerless*).

The second part of verse 4 seems to be a saying or proverb. Wine was stored in leather bags and jugs. In early times one was not able to close them airtight, so over time the alcohol evaporated and the taste deteriorated considerably. So the strength or fury of the wine disappeared.

The word *depraved* is probably a typification of the godless people of Ephraim/Israel. The text thus expresses a form of slow purification resulting from the judgment of God (*His hand*). In this we recognize the centuries-old exile and even up to the present day.

5.1 Messianic prophecy
The preceding interpretation resolves it. Or does it? For the expression *the day of our king* is a term that usually indicates the king's coronation day. Some therefore suppose that the day of our king represents the birthday of Jeroboam II. However, that is an untenable position in light of the context. Hosea speaks nowhere about the coronation of one of the kings of Israel. Hosea 8:4 even questions their legitimacy! The prophet, however, speaks of the great judgments of God in the end times and the coming of the Messianic Kingdom.

The term *the day of our king* has strong messianic features. And there we might find the real fulfillment of this prophecy. In that view, the king is the Messiah, Jesus Christ. When the day of the Messiah comes, the degenerate will be removed from God's people. Then the Almighty will separate the goats from the sheep (as the fury leaves the wine) and the judgment of God will strike His enemies. That moment is described very clearly in Ezekiel 20:34–38:*

34 *Then will I bring you out of the peoples and gather you from the countries where you were scattered among them; with a mighty hand and an outstretched arm, but also with revenge that will be poured out.*
35 *Then will I lead you into the wilderness of the nations, and I will judge over you there, face to face.*
36 *As I judged your fathers in the wilderness of the land of Egypt, so will I judge over you; speaks the Sovereign Yahweh.*
37 *Then I will cause you to pass under my rod and bring you into the bond of My covenant.*
38 *And I will cleanse you from those who rebelled against Me. I will lead them out of the land where they lived. Yet none of these will enter the land of Israel. Then you will know that I am Yahweh.*

(Garrett, 167; Harper, 296; Beaugency, Hosea 7:5; Reed, 57; Rosenberg, vol. 1, 42; Ward, 131; *Weerd, Hebrew text translation in *Ezechiël*, vol. 1, 532–34)

Verses 6 and 7
6 **They seek sexual contact, because their heart burns like an oven. They lie in wait all night long, like the baker who slumbers and flares up [the oven] in the morning like a flaming fire.**
7 **They are all hot as an oven, which devours their judges and causes all their kings to fall. There is no one who calls on Me.**

Again the baker and his oven are put down as a type in this prophecy (see verse 4). Depravity can be a degenerate passion. However, *the* hallmark of major sins is that it becomes a self-reinforcing process. Living in sin is not a constant way of life. It is a slippery surface, where a constant need for more stimulus is the motivation to push the boundaries even further. Thus passion becomes obsession and obsession becomes surrendering to Satan, who devours them! Calvin says: "The Israelites burn so much from desire that their madness cannot be restored or brought to a standstill." The only salvation for their madness lies with God. This requires a radical conversion from their sins. But *there is no one who calls on Me*. The people of Israel have completely lost God.
(Calvijn, *Daniel* II, *Kleine Profeten* I/II, Hosea, 199; McComiskey, 106; Rosenberg, vol. 1, 42; Targum Jonathan, Hosea 7:7)

7.1 All their kings fall
Some of the exegetes see verse 7c fulfilled in the murdered kings (four out of six) who came after Jeroboam II. They were Zechariah, Shallum, Pekahiah, and Pekah. Perhaps we can see that as a second fulfillment. There is no doubt, however, that Hosea is talking about the degeneration of Israel and its rulers, above all.
(Born, 51; Walvoord and Zuck, 1395)
(See exegesis of Hosea 1:1b.)

Verse 8
Ephraim will mingle with the gentile nations. Ephraim is a flat cake that is not turned.
Verse 8 speaks of the future, when Ephraim will disappear among the gentile nations. However, some relate the text to the present day of that time. They place the prophecy before the fall of Israel/Ephraim and see in the word *mingling* the changing alliances of

Israel with Egypt and Assyria. However, that is too farfetched. Others assume that pagans increasingly mingled with the Israelites through marriage.

8.1 Deportation
After the decline of the ten-tribe kingdom, the survivors were sent into exile by the Assyrians and scattered across their great empire.

With the disappearance of the Ten Tribes, the plan of salvation for Israel is interrupted. For it is not Israel's destiny to disappear among the nations. The ultimate goal of the prophecy is to proclaim the Messianic Kingdom. Then the Messiah, Jesus Christ, will become king in Jerusalem over a united people.

Only part of the plan of salvation has been carried out—the first coming of Jesus Christ and the return of the Jews to Canaan—which is still in process. The cake of God's salvation is only baked on one side, so only half finished. The other side remains invisible, because it concerns the future and its development is now stalled. But, one day, the fate of Ephraim will also be *turned* and take up its assigned role in salvation again.
(Walvoord and Zuck, 1395; Wood, 198)

Verse 9
Foreigners exhaust his strength, but he does not realize it. He has turned gray, but he does not notice it.
In poetic language Hosea sketches the coming demise of Ephraim (the Ten Tribes). The country ages (*has turned gray*) and becomes powerless, but *does not notice it.* A metaphor of an aging man is presented. When he sees his end approaching, he should settle accounts with God—that's what people say. However, in this case the man does not even notice that his end is approaching.

A second explanation is that the gray-headedness is caused by the debauched way of life and the calamity that Ephraim suffers. This is also a possibility.
(Calvijn, *Daniel* II, *Kleine Profeten* I/II, Hosea, 203–04; Walvoord and Zuck, 1395; Wood, 198)

9.1 The end was coming fast
The empire of the ten tribes had become old, powerless, and nearing its end. The once thriving Northern Kingdom was rapidly decaying. Only thirty-one years after the death of King Jeroboam II, Israel perished.
(Rosenberg, vol. 1, 45; Stuart, 121; Targum Jonathan, Hosea 7:8)

9.2 Foreigners exhaust his strength
Ephraim paid heavy tributes several times, to Egypt as well as to Assyria. This impoverished the country and its people.
(Born, 53; Harper, 302)

Verse 10
The majesty of Israel also testifies for him. But they do not return to Yahweh, their God; in spite of all this they are not looking for Him.
This *majesty* looks back at the glory of old, under King David and Solomon; but also on the future salvation, when the Messianic Kingdom will be established. Israel/Ephraim had completely lost sight of that great goal and with this they are doing a great injustice to God. For the counsel of God wanted all prophecy to come to fulfillment, and in this Israel is a vehicle of salvation. That development is now brutally interrupted. Ten of the twelve

tribes (Ephraim) now fall. This means that all Israel is no more. And only in a united people can the prophecy be fulfilled.

Verse 11
Thus Ephraim has become like a dove, which is easily deceived, without reason. Now they call again Egypt, then they turn again to Assyria.
Ephraim did not appeal to God in its need, but tried to play the great powers of that time, Assyria and Egypt, off against one another. The rulers of Ephraim really believed they could manipulate the great powers. That was stupid; Assyria was too cruel-minded to offer fair agreements and Egypt was never strong enough to send real help. Even as an unsuspecting dove is easily confused (Matthew 10:16), so Ephraim fluttered from one alliance to another.
(Born, 53; Stuart, 122)

Verse 12
If they go, I will throw a net over them. Like birds in the sky, I will bring them down and catch them when I hear that they are gathering.
Rabbinical writings see here a judgment, namely the downfall of Ephraim. We agree with this. But we should perhaps also dig a little deeper.

The words *if they go* give an impression that here the deportation of the ten tribes of Israel is in view. Verse 12c also does this (*when I hear that they are gathering*). In this interpretation it could be meant that only a few birds (= Israelites) will escape the deportation by Assyria (by the hand of God).
(Teshuvoth Dunash, 34)

Verses 13 and 14
13 *Woe to them, for they strayed from Me. Downfall to them, because they rebelled against Me. And I, yes, I still wanted to redeem them. They, however, they spoke false about Me.*
14 *And they do not call to Me from their hearts, but wail on their beds. They deal in grain and new wine and turn away from Me.*
In these verses the sorrow of God is heard. He mourns for His people and their coming demise. Sadly the words resound: *And I, yes, I still wanted to redeem them!*

13–14.1 Wail on their beds
Some argue that the prophet Hosea is giving a poetic description of calling on the idols. However, we do not find a scriptural basis for this explanation, so we reject it.

The Assyrians' campaign against Ephraim was, in fact, a gruesome slaughter, a terrible bloodbath. But the mourning was limited to a wailing on their beds, it did not lead them to God.
(Born, 54; Calvijn, *Daniël* II, *Kleine Profeten* I/II, Hosea, 213)

Verse 14b
They deal in grain and new wine and turn away from Me.
If God is renounced, all that remains is only materialism. That is then the most successful instrument of Satan to pry us loose from God.
(Walvoord and Zuck, 1396)

Verse 15
And I? I taught them discipline and strengthened their arms, but they did evil against Me.

The Almighty gave Israel His commandments, enabling them to develop a well-regulated, just society. He *strengthened their arms*—gave them strength to maintain themselves in the world. But as a thanks, *they did evil against* Him.
(Calvijn, *Daniel* II, *Kleine Profeten* I/II, Hosea, 215)

Verse 16a
They do not turn to the Most High, they are like a failing bow. Their princes will fall by the sword.
The end of Hosea 7 comes again an inevitable conclusion, which is also an irrevocable verdict—*their princes will fall by the sword*. The expression *a failing bow* points perhaps to the dwindling military power of Ephraim, which was not at all equal to that of the Assyrians.
(Garrett, 175)

Verse 16b
They stood out because of their insolent talk. That will be their mockery in the land of Egypt.
Ephraim thought of itself as an important power in the region. In their pride they thought they could afford to switch allies at will. It now appears that it was too small for the great powers of that time. Their former friendship with Egypt proved to be of worth little, because the downfall of Israel only brought Egypt great delight.
(Stuart, 124)

HOSEA 8
Hebrew Text Translation

Introduction
Hosea 8 continues with the theme of Hosea 7. What does change is the primary focus, which now switches to the entire nation of Israel (all twelve tribes) since Judah too has sinned. As opposed to the content of Hosea 7, this prophecy speaks also about the far future, when the fate of Israel will turn into blessing. Scholars do not show any intention of following the Hebrew texts precisely. It is our desire to do that as well as possible.

Verse 1 NASB
Put the trumpet to your lips! Like an eagle the enemy comes against the house of the LORD, because they have transgressed My covenant and rebelled against My law.

Verse 1 KJV
Set the trumpet to thy mouth. He shall come as an eagle against the house of the LORD, because they have transgressed my covenant, and trespassed against my law.

Verse 1 NIV
"Put the trumpet to your lips! An eagle is over the house of the LORD because the people have broken my covenant and rebelled against my law."

Verse 1 Hebrew Interlinear Text
lip-of-you trumpet like-the-eagle over house-of Israel because they-broke covenant-of-me and-against law-of-me they-rebelled

Verse 1b
trumpet
The *shophar* is a wind instrument made from the horn of a wild billy goat. In the prophets, the sounding of the *shophar* is often connected to the day of Yahweh. In its wider significance, this phrase refers to the day on which Yahweh will destroy all of His enemies and those of true Israel and make Himself known to all the earth as the only God. At this time, the Messianic Kingdom will also be ushered in. That day will therefore mean blessings for those who love God, but judgment for His enemies.

Here in this verse, the day of Yahweh represents a judgment for the enemies of God. Israel (the Ten Tribes, here called Ephraim) has fallen this far. The nation has turned en masse from God to idols, and as such, become the enemies of God.

Trumpet is a reasonable choice, in translating from the Hebrew text, as NIVIHEOT has done. However, since the *shophar* is such a characteristic instrument, we prefer to retain the term in transliterated form.
(Andersen and Freedman, 485; Dee and Schoneveld, vol. 2, 80–81; Stuart, 131; Strong's OT, word 7782) (See Excursus 19.)

Verse 1a/b
lip-of-you trumpet/shofar
By far most translators and exegetes translate the Hebrew text as: *Put the trumpet/horn/ shofar to your mouth* or *lips*. This does not appear to be correct, however, since any translation using the word *lip* is actually an interpretation. For that is not what it says in the Hebrew source text.

The word *chek* is rare in the Hebrew Bible. The NASB translates it as *palate* (Job 6:30; 12:11; 29:10), *roof of the mouth* (Psalm 137:6), and as *mouth* (Job 20:13; Songs 7:9). Strong's concordance speaks of *palate*, *roof of the mouth*, and *gums*.

1a/b.1 Comparing Scripture with Scripture
The only verb Scripture uses in combination with *shophar* is *taqa*, meaning *to sound*. An example is Hosea 5:8 (*Sound the shofar*). There and in other places we read of someone blowing the shofar, which is therefore the meaning you should expect here as well.

The basic sense of the word *chek* is probably *mouth*, or the *innermost part of the mouth* that we use for tasting and speaking. Literally translated the Hebrew text therefore reads: *your mouth of (a) shofar*. This might be understood as: *your mouth is a shofar*, or else: *let your mouth be a shofar*. The latter option would form a command given by God to the prophet Hosea. That actually suits the present context, since here (in contrast with what we read in Hosea 5:8) the command is given to a single person.
(Andersen and Freedman, 485–86; Cheyne, 86; Garrett, 180; Mays, 115; Strong's OT, word 2441, 6310 and 7782; Wolff, 131)

We read: **let your mouth be a shofar**

Verse 1c
like-the-eagle
Instead of *like*, it would be better to read *with* or *there is*.

The basic meaning of the word *nesher* is *bird of prey*. Usually it is translated as *eagle*, although the translation *vulture* can also be found. These two renderings differ widely in terms of their significance. In our society, an eagle is typically considered a majestic bird; this does not fit the context, however. A vulture, on the other hand, is a filthy animal that eats rotting cadavers and that does fit the context here. Nevertheless, according to Mosaic law, all scavengers are unclean (Deuteronomy 14:12–17), including birds of prey and thus also the eagle.

If we were to use the word *eagle* in our translation, it would have regal connotations in English. Yet that would be out of line with the purport of the Hebrew text. For this reason we have chosen to translate the term as *vulture*.
(Cheyne, 86; Eidevall, 127; Oden, 33; Owens, 774; Wolff, 131)

We read: **there is a vulture**

Verse 1d
over house-of Yahweh
The preposition *al* has a very wide range of possible meanings, including *above*, *unto*, *against*, *over*, *through*, and *concerning*. In its basic significance, it always includes an element of "from top to bottom." In Genesis 18:5 some exegetes translate the word as *along*, although it would also be possible to use *unto* or even *descended* (which would suit the context there very well, since it concerns angels). In Genesis 27:39 and 49:25 it means (coming) *from above*. Genesis 1:2 may be the most reflective use of the term. There it means *over* or *above*, and relates to the Spirit of God hovering over the waters, or as some translate it, *incubating the waters*.

The Message Bible translates this phrase in Hosea 8 as *vultures circle above*, which is an accurate reflection of the sense of the text. We, however, have decided to stick closer to the Hebrew text.
(Strong's OT, words 5920, 5921; Rosenberg, vol. 1, 148; Stuart, 308)

We read: *above the house of Yahweh*

Verse 1e
because they-broke covenant-of-me and-against law-of-me they-rebelled
The basic sense of *torah* is *teaching* or *instruction*. If we were to follow the NIVIHEOT and translate *torah* here as *law*, we would miss out on important nuances. Some read *torah* here; we chose *teaching*.
(Strong's OT, word 8451)

We read: *for they broke My covenant and rebelled against My teaching*

The first clause actually looks like a heading to introduce the chapter. For this reason, we have chosen to set the text of that clause apart.

We read:
Let your mouth be a shofar.
There is a vulture above the house of Yahweh. For they broke My covenant and rebelled against My teaching.

Verse 2 NASB
They cry out to Me, "My God, we of Israel know You!"

Verse 2 KJV
Israel shall cry unto me, My God, we know thee.

Verse 2 NIV
"Israel cries out to me, 'Our God, we acknowledge you!'"

Verse 2 Hebrew Interlinear Text
to-me they-cry-out God-of-me we-acknowledge-you Israel

Verse 2b
God-of-me we-acknowledge-you Israel
The word *yada* almost always means *to know* or *to have knowledge of*, and sometimes also *recognize* if that is what the context requires. That is not the case here, however.

If we follow the Hebrew text literally, we get something along the lines of: *My God, we, Israel, know you*. The context indicates that these words bear the character of an excuse or protest. The people of Israel (the Ten Tribes) does not understand why the judgment is coming over them and turns to God to complain. To reflect this, we have added the words *don't we* in brackets.
(Andersen and Freedman, 490; Harper, 309; Strong's OT, word 3045; Ward, 141)

We read:
They cry out to Me: O my God, we, in Israel, know You, [don't we]?

Verse 3 NASB
Israel has rejected the good; The enemy will pursue him.

Verse 3 KJV
Israel hath cast off the thing that is good: the enemy shall pursue him.

Verse 3 NIV
"But Israel has rejected what is good; an enemy will pursue him."

Verse 3 Hebrew Interlinear Text
he-rejected Israel good one-being-enemy he-will-pursue-him
The term *radaph* (NIVIHEOT: *pursue*) means *to hunt for* something or someone, but also *to pursue, to put to flight*, or *to chase*.
(Strong's OT, word 7291; Ward, 141; Wolff, 131)

We read:
Israel refused what is good. His enemy will hunt for him.

Verse 4 NASB
They have set up kings, but not by Me; They have appointed princes, but I did not know it. With their silver and gold they have made idols for themselves, that they might be cut off.

Verse 4 KJV
They have set up kings, but not by me: they have made princes, and I knew it not: of their silver and their gold have they made them idols, that they may be cut off.

Verse 4 NIV
"They set up kings without my consent; they choose princes without my approval. With their silver and gold they make idols for themselves to their own destruction."

Verse 4 Hebrew Interlinear Text
they they-set-up-kings but-not from-me they-choose-princes but-not I-approve silver-of-them and-gold-of-them they-make for-them idols so-that he-might-be-destroyed

Verse 4a
they they-set-up-kings but-not from-me
The pronoun *they* appears twice here. Very few exegetes reflect this, however. This repetition functions as a kind of superlative and adds emphasis to the clause. We might therefore translate: *they, yea they*, or: *they however!*

We read: *they, however, appoint kings, but not through Me*

Verse 4b
they-choose-princes but-not I-approve
If we translate with *princes*, verse 4a and 4b say more or less the same thing, what makes no sense and therefore is unlikely.

The word *hêśîrū* comes from the root *sur** (*have power, make princes, to reign*) or *sarar*† (*to act like a prince, to rule*). It is translated *they-choose-princes* but that is debated. The words *sur* or *sarar* appear only very rarely in the Bible. It means something along the lines of *to be strong, to exercise power/might*, or *to reign (*by brute power*)*. Outside Hosea, the word is used only in Judges 9:22. There the NBG reads *governs* (= exercises power) and BHI, *had reigned*. Mays reads *officials*, while also Stuart offers *to rule* as a possible translation. The word *hêśîrū* reflects something like *to practice might* or even *to practice brute might*, so it tells us something about the behavior of the kings and that suits the context very well. We prefer: *ruthless leaders*.

Yada means *to know*‡ or *to acknowledge***. So the text says something like this: *It fits not My given knowledge*, so it is against God's rules. We read: *but against My rules*.
(Mays, 113; Strong's OT, words *7786, †8323, ‡3045; Stuart, 128; *Studiebijbel* SBOT 12, **86; Wolff, 132)

We read: *they chose ruthless leaders, but against My rules*

Verse 4c
silver-of-them and-gold-of-them they-make for-them idols
Literally it says *images*, but the word is generally translated as *idols*.
(Strong's OT, word 6091)

We read: *they use their silver and gold to make idols for themselves*

Verse 4d
so-that he-might-be-destroyed
With this translation, the NIVIHEOT actually interprets the Hebrew source text. We refuse to follow in this.

The word *karath* means *to cut off* or *to split*, in the sense of using a knife to separate two things from each other. In many cases, the word also means *to make a covenant*. While this may seem somewhat strange, a covenant was, as a matter of fact, originally contracted between two parties by having them swear an oath, after which the respective leaders or tribal heads passed between the pieces of the slaughtered animals in order to seal that covenant (Genesis 15:9–19).

In later times, circumcision was the sign of the covenant in Israel—once again a form of cutting off (in this case the foreskin; Exodus 4:25). Negatively, *karath* means to be cut off, in the sense of being cut off from one's salvation, relatives, or nation. It can also mean *to cut down*, in the sense of destroying (high places for the worship of idols, for example), or putting an end to life, or even simply felling a tree. Many offer a translation using the word *destroy*. However, this fails to do justice to the Hebrew text. After all, the prophet Hosea is speaking about the end of the Sinaitic Covenant. That is what Israel is being *cut off* from.

The text therefore has an allusive character here. The word *karath*, which elicits associations of covenant making, is now used also for the end of the covenant.
(Andersen and Freedman, 493; Owens, 774; Rosenberg, vol. 1, 47; Strong's OT, word 3772)

We read: *as a result, they will be cut off*

The entire sentence:
They, however, they appoint kings, but not through Me. They chose ruthless leaders, but against My rules. They use their silver and gold to make idols for themselves. As a result, they will be cut off.

Verse 5 NASB
He has rejected your calf, O Samaria, saying, "My anger burns against them!" How long will they be incapable of innocence?

Verse 5 KJV
Thy calf, O Samaria, hath cast thee off; mine anger is kindled against them: how long will it be ere they attain to innocency?

Verse 5 NIV
"Samaria, throw out your calf-idol! My anger burns against them. How long will they be incapable of purity?"

Verse 5 Hebrew Interlinear Text
let-him-throw-out calf-idol Samaria he-burns anger-of-me against-them until when? not they-will-be-capable purity

Verse 5a
let-him-throw-out
Many translators and exegetes depart from the Hebrew source text here. But there is no pressing reason to do so. *Zanach* means *to reject, to spurn,* or *to banish* (as we find in 1 Chronicles 28:9; Psalms 43:2; 44:9; 60:1). Here we find the word *zānaḥ*, which means, *is rejected*. The prophecy is looking back on when the calf idols were built, so we read: *have been*.
(Owens, vol. IV, 774; Strong's OT, word 2186; Stuart, 128; Wolff, 132)

We read: *have been rejected*

Verse 5b
calf-idol Samaria
The word *egel* means *calf*. It indeed refers to an idolatrous image here, as many state.
(Owens, 774; Strong's OT, word 5695; Ward, 141)

We read: *your calf, Samaria*

Now we combine 5a and 5b

We read: *your calf has been rejected, O Samaria!*

Verse 5c
he-burns anger-of-me against-them
This is not difficult.

We read: *My anger is kindled against them*

Verse 5d
until when? not they-will-be-capable purity
We have already encountered this short word *lo* in *Lo-Ruchama* and *Lo-Ammi* (Hosea 1). It means *not, cannot, never,* or *ever*. The context (together with the interrogative form of the clause) suggests that the last meaning listed is correct here.
(Andersen and Freedman, 494; Bright, 94–95; Strong's OT, word 3808)

We read: *will they ever succeed in becoming clean?*

Verse 6a
indeed from-Israel
The NIVIHEOT sees these words as a part of verse 6. We add it to verse 5. The word *ki* usually introduces a causal relationship, as here. The NIVIHEOT translates it as *indeed*. However, that is an interpretation, and furthermore places one at odds with the majority of biblical scholars. Usually the word is translated as *for, because, due to, while, although,* and *since*. Here we prefer *because* and *therefore*.
(Strong's OT, word 3588)

We read: *and therefore become Israel?*

The entire sentence:
Your calf has been rejected, o Samaria! My anger is kindled against them. Will they ever succeed in becoming clean and therefore become Israel?

Verse 6 NASB
For from Israel is even this! A craftsman made it, so it is not God; surely the calf of Samaria will be broken to pieces.

Verse 6 KJV
For from Israel was it also: the workman made it; therefore it is not God: but the calf of Samaria shall be broken in pieces.

Verse 6 NIV
"They are from Israel! This calf—a metalworker has made it; it is not God. It will be broken in pieces, that calf of Samaria."

Verse 6 Hebrew Interlinear Text
indeed from-Israel and-he craftsman he-made-him and-not God he indeed pieces he-will-be calf-idol-of Samaria

Verse 6a
indeed from-Israel
We are adding these words to the end of verse 5.

Verse 6b
and-he craftsman he-made-him and-not God
The word *wə·hū* means: and *himself/itself/that*, or *even this/that* (NASB). The sentence seems to be connected with verse 5b and should also be interpreted interrogatively.

The word *charash* means *carpenter* or *craftsman*. Since Scripture does not clearly indicate whether the images of the calves were made from wood (and then plated with gold) or stone, we have opted for *craftsman*.

This part of verse 6 creates a sharp contrast between idols made by people and holy objects of God. For this reason, we have added an exclamation mark to the text.
(Strong's OT, word 2796; Stuart, 126; Wolff, 132)

We read: *was it not made by a craftsman? God did not do that!*

Verse 6c
he indeed pieces he-will-be calf-idol-of Samaria
Instead of *indeed* we read *therefore* (See verse 6a).

The word *shebabim* (which is translated here as *pieces*) means *to fragment, to break to pieces*, or *to splinter*. We prefer *to pulverize*, since the prophecy here was fulfilled during the reign of King Josiah. In 2 Kings 23:15 it says:

> *Even the altar at Bethel—that high place he demolished; he burned the high place and ground it to powder.*

(Owens, 775; Reed, 61; Strong's OT, word 7616; Stuart, 128)

We read: *therefore the calf of Samaria will be pulverized*

The entire sentence:
Was it not made by a craftsman? God did not do that! Therefore the calf of Samaria will be pulverized.

Verse 7 NASB
For they sow the wind and they reap the whirlwind. The standing grain has no heads; It yields no grain. Should it yield, strangers would swallow it up.

Verse 7 KJV
For they have sown the wind, and they shall reap the whirlwind: it hath no stalk: the bud shall yield no meal: if so be it yield, the strangers shall swallow it up.

Verse 7 NIV
"They sow the wind and reap the whirlwind. The stalk has no head; it will produce no flour. Were it to yield grain, foreigners would swallow it up."

Verse 7 Hebrew Interlinear Text
indeed wind they-sow and-to-whirlwind they-reap stalk there-is-not to-him head not he-will-produce flour if he-would-yield ones-being-foreign they-would-swallow-him

Verse 7a
indeed wind they-sow
The word *ki* means *for*. (See verse 6)

We read: *for they sow wind*

Verse 7b
and-to-whirlwind they-reap
The word *cuwphah* means *high winds* or *storm* (Job 37:9; Proverbs 1:27). Some translate it as *tornado*. However, this rendering is characteristic of translations and exegeses with US origins. While tornadoes do touch down frequently in the US, this is not so in Canaan.
(Andersen and Freedman, 481; Owens, 775; Strong's OT, word 5492)

We read: *and will reap a storm*

Verse 7c
stalk there-is-not to-him
Qamah can mean both *stalk* or more generally (*standing*) *grain* (NASB), which is preferable here (Exodus 22:6; Deuteronomy 16:9; 23:25).
(Harper, 317; Mays, 113; Rosenberg, vol. 1, 50; Smith, 130; Strong's OT, word 7054; Wolff, 132)

We read: *there is no more standing grain for them*

Verse 7d
head
The above translation from the NIVIHEOT is actually an interpretation, which we will not follow. The word *tsemach* occurs rarely in Scripture. It means *bud, germ, fruit* (Isaiah 4:2), or *sprout, raise up* (Jeremiah 23:5; 33:15; Zechariah 3:8). Here the text envisions germinating grain, so that *sprout* is an accurate translation.
(Andersen and Freedman, 481; Mays, 113; Strong's OT, word 6780)

Verse 7d/e
head not he-will-produce
The verb *asah* means *to bear (fruit)* (Genesis 1:11; Ezekiel 17:23), *to do* (in the sense of *to commit*; Leviticus 5:17; 20:13), or *to perform*. In Scripture the word is used very frequently in this final sense.
(Harper, 317; Smith, 130; Strong's OT, word 6213)

We read: *no sprout will still yield flour*

Verse 7f
if he-would-yield ones-being-foreign they-would-swallow-him
The rest of verse 8 presents no difficulties.

We read: *if that were to happen, strangers would swallow it up*

The entire sentence:
For they sow wind and will reap a storm. There is no more standing grain for them. No sprout will still yield flour, and if that were to happen, strangers would swallow it up.

Verse 8 NASB
Israel is swallowed up; They are now among the nations like a vessel in which no one delights.

Verse 8 KJV
Israel is swallowed up: now shall they be among the Gentiles as a vessel wherein is no pleasure.

Verse 8 NIV
"Israel is swallowed up; now she is among the nations like something no one wants."

Verse 8 Hebrew Interlinear Text
he-is-swallowed-up Israel now they-are among-the-nations like-thing there-is-no worth to-him

Verse 8a
he-is-swallowed-up Israel
The basic meaning of *bala* is *to swallow* or *to swallow down*. It is commonly translated as *to engulf*, *to consume*, or *to swallow up*, and sometimes *to destroy*.
(Strong's OT, word 1104; Wolff, 132)

We read: *if Israel is swallowed up*

Verse 8b
now they-are among-the-nations
In the Hebrew text, verse 8a first refers to Israel (one nation; singular). Here, however, it transitions to plural forms. This can be readily explained. After the fall of the Ten Tribes, there was no longer a political unity. For this reason, the word of God then came to individual Israelites. That is why the pronoun *they* was used. It refers to the individual exiles.
(*Studiebijbel* SBOT 12, 88)

We read: *then they will be among the gentile nations*

Verse 8c
like-thing there-is-no worth to-him
The word *keli* (here translated as *thing*) has a wide application in the Hebrew Bible. Its basic meaning is *artifact* or *product*. When it has the latter significance, it usually refers to something made by a craftsman. This could be a *vehicle*, *weapon*, *vessel*, *jewels*, *instrument*, or *tool*.

Keli always has the underlying significance of a useful and/or precious object or product. It is something that helps a person and/or has great value for him (Genesis 24:53, *jewelry*; Exodus 3:22).

In the context of the book of Hosea, Israel (i.e., the Ten Tribes) is described as the bearer of salvation, together with the southern kingdom of Judah. This made Israel into a nation of great value for the human race. That lofty character, however, had been lost. Judah alone remained as the unique bearer of salvation. This was manifest in that the Messiah would later be born from Judah.
(Harper, 317; Rosenberg, vol. 1, 50; Strong's OT, word 3627; Ward, 141; Wolff, 132)

We read: *as a precious artifact that has no value anymore*

The entire text:
If Israel is swallowed up, then they will be among the gentile nations as a precious artifact that has no value anymore.

Verse 9 NASB
For they have gone up to Assyria, like a wild donkey all alone; Ephraim has hired lovers.

Verse 9 KJV
For they are gone up to Assyria, a wild ass alone by himself: Ephraim hath hired lovers.
Verse 9 NIV

"For they have gone up to Assyria like a wild donkey wandering alone. Ephraim has sold herself to lovers."

Verse 9 Hebrew Interlinear Text
for they they-went-up Assyria wild-donkey wandering-alone for-him Ephraim they-sold-themselves lovers

Verse 9a
for they they-went-up Assyria wild-donkey wandering-alone for-him
Twice the word *they* is used. Very few reflect that in their translations.

We read: *for they, they went up to Assyria like a wild donkey, wandering alone*

Verse 9b
Ephraim they-sold-themselves lovers
The word *tanah* means *to give a gift*, albeit with an unmistakably negative undertone. It refers, for example, to bribes, kickbacks, or money given to a prostitute. The NIV reflects this sense clearly in its translation.
(Harper, 318; Mays, 114; Rosenberg, vol. 1, 51; Strong's OT, word 8566)

We read: *Ephraim sold itself to lovers*

The entire sentence
For they, they went up to Assyria like a wild donkey, wandering alone. Ephraim sold itself to lovers.

Verse 10 NASB
Even though they hire allies among the nations, now I will gather them up; and they will begin to diminish because of the burden of the king of princes.

Verse 10 KJV
Yea, though they have hired among the nations, now will I gather them, and they shall sorrow a little for the burden of the king of princes.

Verse 10 NIV
"Although they have sold themselves among the nations, I will now gather them together. They will begin to waste away under the oppression of the mighty king."

Verse 10 Hebrew Interlinear Text
but although they-sold-themselves among-the-nations now I-will-gather-them and-they-will-begin wasting-away under-oppression-of king-of mighty-ones

Verse 10b
now I-will-gather-them
The word *attah* literally means *at this time* or *at this moment*. Often it is translated with *now*, but that does not suit the present context that well.
(Andersen and Freedman, 506; Cheyne, 89; Owens, 775; Strong's OT, word 6258)

We read: *I will gather them in this time*

Verse 10c
and-they-will-begin
Many change the Hebrew text here. There are three possible translations: *begin*, *decrease*, and *suffer* or *writhe in pain*. The last is preferable and works well in the context.
(Born, 57; Harper, 319; McComiskey, 130; Mays, 114; Wolff, 144)

We read: *they will writhe in pain*

Verse 10d
wasting-away under-oppression-of king-of mighty-ones
The Hebrew word *meat* means *a little* or *some*. The NIVIHEOT translators have interpreted it as a verb meaning *to decrease*. From there, they opted for the translation *wasting away*. We do not follow them, however. *Meat* can also mean *a short time*, *quickly*, or *soon* (Job 32:22; Psalm 81:14). That fits perfectly in the present context.
(Andersen and Freedman, 507–8; Harper, 319; Owens, 775; Strong's OT, word 4592; Stuart, 135; Wolff, 144)

We read: *soon under the pressure of mighty kings*

The entire sentence:
But, despite them being sold among the nations, I will gather them in this time. Soon they will writhe in pain under the pressure of mighty kings.

Verse 11 NASB
Since Ephraim has multiplied altars for sin, they have become altars of sinning for him.

Verse 11 KJV
Because Ephraim hath made many altars to sin, altars shall be unto him to sin.

Verse 11 NIV
"Though Ephraim built many altars for sin offerings, these have become altars for sinning."

Verse 11 Hebrew Interlinear Text
though he-built-many Ephraim altars to-sin they-became for-him altars to-sin
What the NIVIHEOT offers here is actually an interpretation. The word *rabah* (NIVIHEOT: *many*) means *to increase greatly*, *to multiply*, or *to make large* (Genesis

16:10; Deuteronomy 6:3; 1 Chronicles 4:10). It can also mean *much*, albeit always in the sense of increase or growth. Our preference is for the translation *multiply*.
(Born, 57; Harper, 320; Mays, 114; Strong's OT, word 7235; Ward, 142; Wolff, 133)

We read:
Ephraim sinned because it multiplied the altars. And the altars made him sin.

Verse 12 NASB
Though I wrote for him ten thousand precepts of My law, they are regarded as a strange thing.

Verse 12 KJV
I have written to him the great things of my law, but they were counted as a strange thing.

Verse 12 NIV
"I wrote for them the many things of my law, but they regarded them as something foreign."

Verse 12 Hebrew Interlinear Text
I-wrote for-him many-things-of law-of-me as one-being-alien they-were-regarded

Verse 12a
I-wrote for-him many-things-of
The basic sense of *rob* is *plenty/plentiful*. Translations include *multitude*, *plenty*, *much*, *abundance*, and *greatness*. Others translate ten thousand, but that does not change the meaning significantly. In both cases it is a form of abundance. Rosenberg reads here *great things*, and that points us in the right direction. There is no doubt that the text intends to use the word in a positive sense, for which reason we translate it as *abundance*. Wolff reads: *multitude*.
(Andersen and Freedman, 509; Rosenberg, vol. 1, 52; Strong's OT, word 7230; Wolff, 133)

We read: *I wrote to them the abundance*

Verse 12b
law-of-me
Tôwrâh or *torah* means *instruction* or *teaching*. It is derived from *jarah*, meaning *to subject* or *to point out*. If we follow the common translation of the term as *law* here, we will fail to do justice to the actual sense of the Hebrew text. This is why we translate as *teaching*, but also insert the word *Torah* in brackets.
(Allen, 243; Eisemann, 675; Mays, 114; Strong's OT, words 3384, 8451; Ward, 142)

We read: *of my teaching [Torah]*

Verse 12c
as one-being-alien they-were-regarded
The basic meaning of *zuwr* is *turned aside*, *estranged*, or *foreign*. It is often used in the sense of a *foreigner*.
(Mays, 114; Owens, 775; Strong's OT, word 2114; Ward, 142)

We read: *but they regarded it as something strange*

The entire sentence:
I wrote to them the abundance of my teaching [Torah], but they regarded it as something strange.

Verse 13 NASB
*As for My sacrificial gifts, they sacrifice the flesh and eat it, but the L*ORD *has taken no delight in them. Now He will remember their iniquity, and punish them for their sins; they will return to Egypt.*

Verse 13 KJV
*They sacrifice flesh for the sacrifices of mine offerings, and eat it; but the L*ORD *accepteth them not; now will he remember their iniquity, and visit their sins: they shall return to Egypt.*

Verse 13 NIV
*"Though they offer sacrifices as gifts to me, and though they eat the meat, the L*ORD *is not pleased with them. Now he will remember their wickedness and punish their sins: They will return to Egypt."*

Verse 13 Hebrew Interlinear Text
sacrifices-of gifts-of-me they-offer-sacrifices meat and-they-eat Yahweh not he-is-pleased-with-them now he-will-remember wickedness-of-them and-he-will-punish sins-of-them they Egypt they-will-return

Verse 13a
sacrifices-of gifts-of-me they-offer-sacrifices meat and-they-eat
There are three keywords here. The first is *zabach*, meaning *to slaughter* or *the slaughtered*, always in reference to sacrifice. For that reason, it is often translated as *to sacrifice*, *offering*, or *sacrificial victim*.

The second is *habhab* (which means *sacrifice* or *gift*), but surely in the holy context. So we add therefore the word *holy*.

The third keyword is *zebach*. It refers to the slaughtered (prepared) meat of an animal that is to be sacrificed. Usually this term is translated as *offer*, *offering*, or *sacrifice*.
(Andersen and Freedman, 510; Harper, 323; Strong's OT, words 1890, 2076, 2077; Ward, 142)

We read: *they offer the slaughter of My holy offerings as a sacrifice of meat, but they eat it themselves*

Verse 13b
Yahweh not he-is-pleased-with-them
This clause presents no difficulties.

We read: *Yahweh is not pleased with them*

Verse 13c
now he-will-remember wickedness-of-them
The word *attah* literally means *at this time* or *at this moment*. Often it is translated as *now*.
(Andersen and Freedman, 506, 510; McComiskey, 133; Owens, 775; Strong's OT, word 6258)

We read: *in this time, He will remember their wickedness*

Verse 13d
and-he-will-punish sins-of-them they Egypt they-will-return
Some scholars consider the second part of verse 13d a later addition to the Hebrew source text since they fail to see how it fits the context of the entire book of Hosea. Many exegetes and/or translators "solve" the problem by replacing the name of Egypt with Assyria.

However, that is not what the text says, and it then becomes a case of *eis*-egesis. Once again, a careful rendering of the source text offers us the right solution.

The second occurrence of the word *they* in 13d is a personal pronoun; it has been properly translated. However, the source text behind the first occurrence of the word *they* is actually *hêmmâh*. While it can indeed be used in the sense of *they*, it also means *which*, *the same*, or *similar*. One such example of its use is found in Genesis 6:4: *the same* (KJV). In 2 Samuel 24:3 (*hêm*) the KJV reads *how many soever* and in Jeremiah 36:32 it means *like* (also in the sense of *similar*).

So the second part of verse 13d—*they Egypt they-will-return*—could also be read as: *the same as Egypt they will return* or: *similar to Egypt they will return*. These translations offer greater clarity. As such, it gains a significance that actually suits the present context very well, because Hosea points to the Exodus in the context of future salvation. In Zechariah 10:10 we find a similar construction. There, too, we should probably translate: *as once from Egypt*.
(Garrett, 188; Strong's OT, word 1992; Weerd, *Zacharia*, 277–78; Wood, 202)

We read: ***then He will punish their sins. But, as once from Egypt, they will return.***

The entire sentence:
They offer the slaughter of My holy offerings as a sacrifice of meat, but they eat it themselves. Yahweh is not pleased with them, and in this time, He will remember their wickedness. Then He will punish their sins. But, as once from Egypt, they will return.

Verse 14 NASB
For Israel has forgotten his Maker and built palaces; and Judah has multiplied fortified cities, but I will send a fire on its cities that it may consume its palatial dwellings.

Verse 14 KJV
For Israel hath forgotten his Maker, and buildeth temples; and Judah hath multiplied fenced cities: but I will send a fire upon his cities, and it shall devour the palaces thereof.

Verse 14 NIV
"Israel has forgotten their Maker and built palaces; Judah has fortified many towns. But I will send fire on their cities that will consume their fortresses."

Verse 14 Hebrew Interlinear Text
and-he-forgot Israel . . . one-making-him and-he-built palaces and-Judah he-made-many towns ones-being-fortified but-I-will-send fire upon-cities-of-him and-she-will-consume fortresses-of-her

We read:
Israel has forgotten his Maker and built palaces. And Judah strengthened many cities. But I will send a fire over those cities, and that will consume its fortresses.

Hosea 8:1–14—The corrected text:

Verse 1   *Let your mouth be a shofar.*
There is a vulture above the house of Yahweh. For they broke My covenant and rebelled against My teaching.
Verse 2   *They cry out to Me: O my God, we, in Israel, know You, [don't we]?*
Verse 3   *Israel refused what is good. His enemy will hunt for him.*

Verse 4	*They, however, they appoint kings, but not through Me. They chose ruthless leaders, but against My rules. They use their silver and gold to make idols for themselves. As a result, they will be cut off.*
Verse 5	*Your calf has been rejected, O Samaria! My anger is kindled against them. Will they ever succeed in becoming clean and therefore become Israel?*
Verse 6	*Was it not made by a craftsman? God did not do that! Therefore the calf of Samaria will be pulverized.*
Verse 7	*For they sow wind and will reap a storm. There is no more standing grain for them. No sprout will still yield flour, and if that were to happen, strangers would swallow it up.*
Verse 8	*If Israel is swallowed up, then they will be among the gentile nations as a precious artifact that has no value anymore.*
Verse 9	*For they, they went up to Assyria like a wild donkey, wandering alone. Ephraim sold itself to lovers.*
Verse 10	*But, despite them being sold among the nations, I will gather them in this time. Soon they will writhe in pain under the pressure of mighty kings.*
Verse 11	*Ephraim sinned because it multiplied the altars. And the altars made him sin.*
Verse 12	*I wrote to them the abundance of my teaching [Torah], but they regarded it as something strange.*
Verse 13	*They offer the slaughter of My holy offerings as a sacrifice of meat, but they eat it themselves. Yahweh is not pleased with them, and in this time, He will remember their wickedness. Then He will punish their sins. But, as once from Egypt, they will return.*
Verse 14	*Israel has forgotten his Maker and built palaces. And Judah strengthened many cities. But I will send a fire over those cities, and that will consume its fortresses.*

HOSEA 8
Exegesis

Introduction
This chapter continues the theme of the prophecy of Hosea 7, however now in a wider perspective.

A. Again: Israel and Ephraim
Also in this section, the names *Israel* and *Ephraim* appear next to each other. The meaning is clear, however, and is in line with the previous chapters. If the people of Israel are spoken of prior to the breaking of the Sinaitic Covenant (but after the division under King Rehoboam and King Jeroboam), then the name *Israel* refers to the Northern Kingdom. After the break in the Sinaitic Covenant, that kingdom no longer appears to be worthy of the name and the Ten Tribes are designated *Ephraim*. So *Ephraim* is actually the name of the downfall!

The meaning of the name *Israel* after the downfall always refers to all Israel (all twelve tribes). This usually concerns salvation promises and/or end-time prophecy. But it could also be reflecting back on the past, before the split of the nation.
(See Excursuses 3, 4, 5, 12; introduction to Hosea 5 exegesis.)

Verse 1a
Let your mouth be a shofar.
The prophet Hosea is the herald of God's judgment, which is strikingly typified by the words of verse 1a. The prophecy of Hosea 8 is of far-reaching significance. Israel and Judah deviated many times from God, but never so far as during the time of King Ahaz and King Manasseh in Judah, as well as King Ahab and King Jeroboam II and his successors in Israel. God cannot accept that. Therefore, they had never been as close to their doom as now. There is no way back and that is why the mouth of Hosea is a *shofar*, which is preeminently the instrument to announce the judgments of God.

Verse 1b
There is a vulture above the house of Yahweh.
The house of Yahweh is a standard expression. It does not point to the people of Israel as some explain. The saying always means the tabernacle or the temple, which was the visible representation of God and the basis of the existence of Israel and Judah.

The *vulture* represents, in the first place, mighty Assyria, for the growing military power of that country threatened both kingdoms, Judah and Israel. But behind this, we recognize the hand of Satan who, like no other, is motivated to harm God's people. Satan would certainly have known that he was also carrying out the judgments of God. But his aversion to this was far less than his hatred of the people of Israel.

Verse 1c
For they broke My covenant
Some exegetes assume that the prophet opens this chapter with a prophecy about Judah *and* Israel and then moves on to the ten-tribe kingdom of Israel. They see in *the house of Yahweh* the whole Israel, but that is not the usual meaning in the Scriptures. *The house of Yahweh* is always the tabernacle or the temple. The Sinaitic Covenant is primarily at stake

here and the prophecy applies to both countries, Judah and Israel. The temple was given to all the people; not just to Judah.
(Mays, 115)

Verse 1d
and rebelled against My teaching
Because the people of Israel/Ephraim were rebelling against God's teachings (no longer allowed themselves to be corrected by God), they placed themselves under judgment. That judgment had been announced a long time ago, as uttered by Moses, and was coming true in their day, to the letter.

Deuteronomy 28:47–52 (NASB):
47 *"Because you did not serve the LORD your God with joy and a glad heart, for the abundance of all things;*
48 *"therefore you shall serve your enemies whom the LORD will send against you, in hunger, in thirst, in nakedness, and in the lack of all things; and He will put an iron yoke on your neck until He has destroyed you.*
49 *"The LORD will bring a nation against you from afar, from the end of the earth, as the eagle swoops down, a nation whose language you shall not understand,*
50 *"a nation of fierce countenance who will have no respect for the old, nor show favor to the young.*
51 *"Moreover, it shall eat the offspring of your herd and the produce of your ground until you are destroyed, who also leaves you no grain, new wine, or oil, nor the increase of your herd or the young of your flock until they have caused you to perish.*
52 *"It shall besiege you in all your towns until your high and fortified walls in which you trusted come down throughout your land, and it shall besiege you in all your towns throughout your land which the LORD your God has given you."*

This judgment not only affected the Northern Kingdom of Israel (the Ten Tribes). Judah (the two tribes) also sinned heavy (especially under the reign of King Ahaz and Manasseh). The terrible behavior of Israel *and* Judah broke the Sinaitic Covenant. As a consequence God is going to leave the temple, as reported in Ezekiel 10:18–22, for God cannot dwell among a people who have turned away from Him.

With the departure of Yahweh, there is no reason to protect Jerusalem and the temple anymore. The fury of Satan against all that is sacred and godly was a guarantee that destruction would follow.

1.1 The judgment on Judah was postponed
We, who look back, know that Judah turned back to God under King Hezekiah and that God turned His judgment away (2 Kings 19:35–36; 2 Chronicles 32:21–22). That turned out to be a temporary postponement. For under King Manasseh the people fell so deeply into idolatry that even the reforms of King Josiah could no longer extinguish the guilt of Judah.
(Wood, 201)
(See Excursus 4; exegesis of Hosea 10:11c.)

Verse 2a
They cry out to Me: O my God,
Some consider this verse as being fulfilled in the distant future, in the end time. They see it as a cry to God with which the restoration of the people of Israel is initiated. However, the context does not give any reason for this. The whole prophecy speaks about Hosea's present.

Verse 2b
we, in Israel, know You, [don't we]?
Among the people of the northern kingdom of Israel, the knowledge of Yahweh had largely disappeared (Hosea 4:1, 6). People no longer knew who Yahweh was and how He wanted to be worshiped. In their ignorance they thought that God was properly served with the idolatry surrounding the bull calves at Gilgal and Bethel. So they wondered: Why then these judgments, God; what do You want!

The people of Israel thus completely ignored the pagan character of the cult associated with the bull calves, and they ignored the fact that God does not tolerate other gods besides Himself. And there were plenty of other gods, for in Israel the Baals and Asherahs were also worshiped.
(Calvijn, *Daniel* II, *Kleine Profeten* I/II, Hosea, 223; Ironside, 62; Wood, 201)

Verse 3a
Israel refused what is good.
The *good* are the blessings of God. They fell to Israel, provided God was being served. Deuteronomy 26:11 (NASB) speaks about this:

> *"You and the Levite and the alien who is among you shall rejoice in all the good which the* Lord *your God has given you and your household."*

And Deuteronomy 28:11–12 also speaks to this:

> 11 *"The* Lord *will make you abound in prosperity, in the offspring of your body and in the offspring of your beast and in the produce of your ground, in the land which the* Lord *swore to your fathers to give you.*
> 12 *"The* Lord *will open for you His good storehouse, the heavens, to give rain to your land in its season and to bless all the work of your hand; and you shall lend to many nations, but you shall not borrow."*

Because Israel preferred the idols over the true God, the people forfeited the blessing associated with the holy nation. With that Israel lost also the protection provided by God Himself against hostile nations like Assyria, Babylon, and Egypt.

Verse 3b
His enemy will hunt for him.
That *enemy* was Assyria, which attacked Israel and thoroughly destroyed the country as told in 2 Kings 17:6 (NASB):

> *In the ninth year of Hoshea, the king of Assyria captured Samaria and carried Israel away into exile to Assyria, and settled them in Halah and Habor, on the river of Gozan, and in the cities of the Medes.*

Verse 4a/b
They, however, they appoint kings, but not through Me. They chose ruthless leaders, but against My rules. They use their silver and gold to make idols for themselves.
King Jehu was appointed by God's order and anointed by a prophet to be king (2 Kings 9:1–15). He put an end to the government of the wicked Ahab and his wife Jezebel. That is why his descendants were also rightful kings over the people of Israel. These were Jehoahaz (the son of Jehu, 2 Kings 13:1); Joash (2 Kings 13:10), Jeroboam II (2 Kings 14:23) and Zechariah (2 Kings 15:8).

Zechariah was the last king from the house of Jehu. He was murdered by Shallum, who became king in his place. However, Shallum was not appointed by God (*but not through Me*). He therefore had no right to the kingship, nor did any of the kings after him, namely Menahem, Pekahiah, Pekah, and Hoshea. Those kings and with them the appointed leaders constituted an illegal government. Israel/Ephraim was not entitled to chose their own king (*but against My rules*).
(Jeffrey, 994)
(See exegesis of Hosea 1.)

Verse 4c
As a result, they will be cut off.
This is a phrase with heavy overtones. What are the ten tribes of Israel cut off from?
1. The Sinaitic Covenant—the covenant with God.
2. The land of Canaan—because the triangular relationship between God, land, and people was the basis of the Sinaitic Covenant.
3. Their identity—for the people of Israel (as opposed to Judah) disappeared namelessly among the gentile nations.

(See Annotation 1G; Excursus 10.)

Verse 5
Your calf has been rejected, O Samaria! My anger is kindled against them. Will they ever succeed in becoming clean and therefore become Israel?
Though there was no calf set up in Samaria for idol worship, there were two golden calves, one in the south at Bethel, the other in the north at Gilgal, in the territory of Dan. The responsible authority—that is the government of the ten-tribe kingdom, referred to by the name of their capital, *Samaria*—is being held responsible here. The worship of golden bull calves was cursed idolatry. In name, it was a service to Yahweh, but it was mingled with idolatry and God condemns this. The conclusion is that Ephraim could never again *become Israel*—a blessed people of God—like before.
(Mays, 118)
(See Excursus 11.)

Verse 6a
Was it not made by a craftsman? God did not do that!
The cult of the bull calves did not come from an outside nation. It was not pagan worship, but was developed within Israel itself, under King Jeroboam I. It was a surrogate for the worship of God and in fact barred access to the temple in Jerusalem. God was not the one who had made the bull calves. These gods were conceived and manufactured by people with their own ungodly agenda.
(See Excursus 11.)

Verse 6b
Therefore the calf of Samaria will be pulverized.
This prophecy was fulfilled under King Josiah.

2 Kings 23:15 (NASB):
> *Furthermore, the altar that was at Bethel and the high place which Jeroboam the son of Nebat, who made Israel sin, had made, even that altar and the high place he* (= King Josiah) *broke down. Then he demolished its stones, ground them to dust, and burned the Asherah.*

Verse 7
For they sow wind and will reap a storm. There is no more standing grain for them. No sprout will still yield flour, and if that were to happen, strangers would swallow it up.
The coming judgment was the inevitable punishment of the heavy sins committed by (once) God's people. This punishment was executed by cruel Assyria, which destroyed the country and plundered it completely. Proverbs 22:8 (NASB): *"He who sows iniquity will reap vanity, and the rod of his fury will perish."*
(See Excursus 3.)

Verse 8
If Israel is swallowed up, then they will be among the gentile nations as a precious artifact that has no value anymore.
The people of Israel were the only ones chosen by God among all nations on earth. He forged them into a holy nation and gave them a land, Canaan, and a temple, where He Himself went to live. The Almighty was the source of all blessing and formed their protection against enemy forces. When the Sinaitic Covenant was broken, that protection for Israel/Ephraim ended. Thus they were no longer Ammi (My people) but became Lo-Ammi (not My people, Hosea 1:9). And with that, the enemy powers (prompted by Satan) were given free rein.

The downfall of the kingdom of the Ten Tribes was radical. The Assyrians killed the upper layer of the population. With that, the people were deprived of their leaders. By that the identity of Israel, what could have been saved by educated individuals and clericals (as happened in Judah), was lost. Also, the survivors were spread out over the great Assyrian empire, not concentrated on a few places, as happened with the Jews.

8.1 Precious in God's eyes
Are the people of Israel finished after this? Certainly not; they remain *precious* in God's eyes. In the eyes of the pagan peoples, however, their role had played out. For them, this people had no value any longer.
(Ironside, 61; Mays, 120)

Verse 9
For they, they went up to Assyria like a wild donkey, wandering alone. Ephraim sold itself to lovers.
In Jeremiah 2:24 (NASB) we find the explanation for verse 9:

> *"A wild donkey accustomed to the wilderness, that sniffs the wind in her passion. In the time of her heat who can turn her away? All who seek her will not become weary; In her month they will find her."*

The above text speaks for itself and only confirms the prophecy of previous chapters.

Verse 10
But, despite them being sold among the nations, I will gather them in this time. Soon they will writhe in pain under the pressure of mighty kings.
Under Jeroboam II the power of Israel had continually expanded. After his death, things went quickly downhill. A few years later, under King Menahem, it began paying tribute to Assyria.

Under King Pekah, Israel made a covenant with Syria against Assyria. Then Tiglath-pileser III marched against the coalition. This campaign took a disastrous course for both nations. In 732 BC Damascus, the capital of Syria, fell. Then Tiglath-pileser III marched against Israel and annexed part of the kingdom. Hoshea became king, as a vassal of Assyria, over what remained.

King Hoshea, however, rebelled against Assyria and joined Egypt in a coalition against Assyria. Shalmaneser V mobilized a large army and marched against Israel, which was crushingly defeated. King Hoshea was captured and the Assyrians laid siege to Samaria, which lasted no fewer than three years. In the meantime, Sargon II had become king over Assyria. In 721 BC the city of Samaria fell and was utterly destroyed. So their one-time ally, Assyria, was instrumental in their demise.

Both campaigns had cost enormous numbers of lives on the side of Israel, for the Assyrians were a very cruel and vindictive people. The upper layer of the population was virtually exterminated. Some believe Israel lost 60 to 70 percent of its population in this war. The survivors were gathered and lead in exile (*I will gather them in this time*).

10.1 No leadership—no identity!
After the fall of Samaria the remaining population was taken away and spread out over the Assyrian empire. The people of Israel were almost completely deprived of their leaders. The priests and Levites had left the country long before and had fled to Judah. So there was no intelligentsia to lead the people, nor priests and Levites who kept the worship of God alive. Thus the foundation that guaranteed the identity of the Ten Tribes, was lost. The exiles disappeared among the nations and lost their identity.
(Grosheide, et al., vol. 3, 96; Pfeiffer, Vos and Rea, 868)

Verse 11
Ephraim sinned because it multiplied the altars. And the altars made him sin.
This is a play on words like Hosea so often uses. The words speak for themselves.

Verse 12
I wrote to them the abundance of my teaching [Torah], but they regarded it as something strange.
Here we hear the echo of Deuteronomy 4:8 (NASB):

> *"Or what great nation is there that has statutes and judgments as righteous as this whole law which I am setting before you today?"*

Ephraim (the Ten Tribes) was no longer God's people. It saw God's law as something *strange*; something that did not belong to them.

This alienation from God was the result of their lack of knowledge of God (Hosea 4:1). And because of the lack of knowledge they no longer saw the blessings of God's law. For Ephraim, the one and only, true God had become like all gods—one god among many. But the Almighty does not tolerate any contenders besides Himself. He wants to be worshiped as the only one. Thus Israel's rejection of God led to their destruction.

Verse 13
They offer the slaughter of My holy offerings as a sacrifice of meat, but they eat it themselves. Yahweh is not pleased with them, and in this time, He will remember their wickedness. Then He will punish their sins. But, as once from Egypt, they will return.

The lack of knowledge of God caused Israel/Ephraim to stray more and more. It led to a distorted worship that had nothing to do with the worship of Yahweh—the worship of the golden calves at Bethel and Gilgal. With that, Israel lost the favor of God—the basis of the existence of the Sinaitic Covenant.

Although the Sinaitic Covenant has now become defunct, two more covenants remain: the Abrahamic covenant and the Davidic covenant. The first promises a blessed future in a home land, Canaan. The second promises a king, namely a descendant of King David.

The prophecies that look forward to the final fulfillments these covenants have not yet been fulfilled. But that is going to happen. The people of Israel (the Ten Tribes) failed and are back where they started. They are in exile again, like they were in Egypt a long time ago (Exodus 1–13). But, *as once from Egypt*, they will return to the promised land.
(Weerd, *Zacharia*, 277–81)
(See Annotation 1G; Excursuses 10, 13.)

Verse 14
Israel has forgotten his Maker and built palaces. And Judah strengthened many cities. But I will send a fire over those cities, and that will consume its fortresses.
Both Israel and Judah turned away from God. Both are covered by the judgment. The judgment of the Southern Kingdom, Judah, is being postponed for a number of years, but more than a hundred years later, the curtain fell for them as well. The land of Judah was also destroyed, the temple burned down, and the people led into captivity (Jeremiah 17:27 NASB):

> *"But if you do not listen to Me to keep the sabbath day holy by not carrying a load and coming in through the gates of Jerusalem on the sabbath day, then I will kindle a fire in its gates and it will devour the palaces of Jerusalem and not be quenched."*

HOSEA 9
Hebrew Text Translation

Introduction

Hosea 9 reports the downfall of the ten tribes of Israel (also called Ephraim). It speaks about the deportation of the land's inhabitants and their lot in a hostile world. But it also mentions a remnant that manages to escape to Egypt.

The prophet received this prophecy long before it became reality. The Word of God that came to him is therefore about the future.
(Reed, 64)

Verse 1 NASB
Do not rejoice, O Israel, with exultation like the nations! For you have played the harlot, forsaking your God. You have loved harlots' earnings on every threshing floor.

Verse 1 KJV
Rejoice not, O Israel, for joy, as other people: for thou hast gone a whoring from thy God, thou hast loved a reward upon every cornfloor.

Verse 1 NIV
Do not rejoice, Israel; do not be jubilant like the other nations. For you have been unfaithful to your God; you love the wages of a prostitute at every threshing floor.

Verse 1 Hebrew Interlinear Text
not you-rejoice Israel to jubilation like-the-nations for you-were-unfaithful from-with God-of-you you-love wage-of-prostitute at every-of threshing-floors-of grain

Verse 1a
not you-rejoice Israel to jubilation like-the-nations
The word *giyl* expresses here a form of rejoicing. Rosenberg translates: *joyous occasions*. Wolff: *exult*. Harper: *too loudly*. Literally, *el giyl* probably means *exceedinly*,* so a form of overreacting or *levity*.
(Harper, 326; Rosenberg, vol. 1, 53; *Strong's OT, word 1524; Wolff, 149)

We read: *do not rejoice with levity like the other nations, O Israel*

Verse 1b
for you-were-unfaithful from-with God-of-you
Many translate these words as *you have been unfaithful*, or something along those lines. But that is interpretation. Literally it says: *you have played the harlot from with your God*.
(Andersen and Freedman, 523; Owens, 776; Rosenberg, vol. 1, 53)

We read: *for you committed adultery, forsaking your God*

The entire sentence:
Do not rejoice with levity, like the other nations, o Israel. For you committed adultery, forsaking your God. On every threshing floor for the corn you love the wages of fornication.

Verse 2 NASB
Threshing floor and wine press will not feed them, and the new wine will fail them.

Verse 2 KJV
The floor and the winepress shall not feed them, and the new wine shall fail in her.

Verse 2 NIV
Threshing floors and winepresses will not feed the people; the new wine will fail them.

Verse 2 Hebrew Interlinear Text
threshing-floor and-winepress not they-will-feed-them and-new-wine he-will-fail to-her

Verse 2a
threshing-floor and-winepress not
The contents of verse 2 form a contrast with verse 1.

We read: *threshing floor nor winepress*

Verse 2b
they-will-feed-them / to-her
The Hebrew of verse 1 speaks of Israel (one nation, singular). Here, however, the text transitions to a plural form: *they*. Exegetes disagree about the pronouns *them* and *her*. The biggest reason is their common assumption that the prophecy is directed to a single nation (Israel). As such, the pronoun *them* does not fit in their exegesis. This is why some replace the word *them* with *the nation*. Others do retain *them*, but are at a loss to account for the plural form. The plural form does fit the context, however, assuming the prophecy concerns the individual exiles of Israel (thus plural). (See also Hosea 8:8b, where the same thing happens.) The word *her* refers back to *wine*. We can either translate the word as *it* or simply drop it.
(Andersen and Freedman, 516; Brown, 77; Harper, 327–28; McComiskey, 135; Stuart, 139)

We read: *will feed them*

Verse 2c
and-new-wine he-will-fail to-her
The *winepress* produces no wine because the wine harvest will fail. Here *new wine* stands for the harvest of grapes, not the wine itself. Wolff reads: *wine vat*, but that is too far from the Hebrew text. When the *new wine fails*, we say of course: *the new wine will be lacking*.
(Andersen and Freedman, 524; Owens, 776; Stuart, 142)

We read: *and the new wine will be lacking*

The entire sentence:
Threshing floor nor winepress will feed them and the new wine will be lacking.

Verse 3 NASB
They will not remain in the LORD's land, but Ephraim will return to Egypt, and in Assyria they will eat unclean food.

Verse 3 KJV
They shall not dwell in the LORD's land; but Ephraim shall return to Egypt, and they shall eat unclean things in Assyria.

Verse 3 NIV
They will not remain in the LORD's land; Ephraim will return to Egypt and eat unclean food in Assyria.

Verse 3 Hebrew Interlinear Text
not they-will-remain in-land-of Yahweh and-he-will-return Ephraim Egypt # and-in-Assyria unclean they-will-eat

This verse brings us to an important exegetical problem. By far most exegetes blindly connect verse 3 to Israel's exodus from exile in Egypt (Exodus 1–14). Accordingly, they read *Ephraim will return to Egypt* or something similar, thus splitting the sentence at the number sign (#). They object to any other translation in order to bring it into line with Hosea 8:13d (according to their translations; see the exegesis there). Since a careful analysis of the Hebrew text led us to a different translation, that objection is no longer valid.* To this we should add that the rendering in the NIVIHEOT is hardly the most natural translation of the Hebrew source text, which could rather read *and Ephraim will return*. As such, we join *Egypt* and *Assyria* together, leaving us with the following clause: *They will eat the unclean in Egypt and Assyria*. This interpretation also fits the context much better.

In light of the above translation, the words *but Ephraim will return* has a messianic meaning. For there are multiple prophecies in Scripture announcing the return of Ephraim (i.e., the Ten Tribes) at the end times. This is a theme repeatedly found in Hosea as well.
(See Excursuses 7, 13; *text translation for Hosea 8:13d; *Hosea 8:13, exegesis.)

We read:
They will not remain in the land of Yahweh, but Ephraim will return. They will eat the unclean in Egypt and Assyria.

Excursus 18: The Fraternal War

18.a An unholy coalition
History lends support to our alternative translation of verse 3. King Rezin of Syria (or Aram) and King Menahem of Israel had joined hands in a coalition against that rising world power Assyria. Judah too had been asked to join the coalition, but refused. To avenge this treachery (as Syria and Israel saw it), the armies of Syria and Israel invaded Judah (2 Chronicles 28:5–8) and committed atrocities there. Meanwhile, King Ahaz of Judah appealed to the king of Assyria for help (2 Chronicles 28:16), paying an enormous tribute to Tiglath-pileser, who invaded Syria and brought it a crushing defeat.

Israel too was trampled underfoot, as large parts of the land were annexed by Assyria. What remained became a vassal state to Assyria. Israel, however, refused to accept its subordination, as several years later King Hoshea rose up in rebellion against Assyria and made an alliance with Egypt. Under King Shalmaneser V (726–722 BC) a great army pulled out for battle against Israel. This time too, Israel was quickly defeated.

The war ended with the fall of Samaria, the capital of Israel (under the Assyrian King Sargon II). The two wars had caused enormous casualties and the land was left in ruins. Not one city had escaped the destruction. The Assyrians drove the surviving inhabitants together and carried them off into exile. The exiles were scattered throughout the great kingdom of Assyria and no longer had a distinguishable identity.

18.b Deep hostilities between Israel and Judah
A small part of Israel's population managed to flee the country, escaping deportation by the Assyrian army. It is very unlikely that they looked for a safe haven among their neighbors in Judah. The fraternal war between Israel and Judah had been bloody and bitter and had left deep hostilities between them. What we do know is that the refugees traveled

south along the coast (through Philistia) to Egypt, which had been Israel's ally in the war against Assyria.

18.c Estranged from their religion

Neither refugees nor exiles had the chance to follow the purity laws, as they were forced to eat unclean food in order to survive. Moreover, the Israelites were largely estranged from their religion, as the priests and Levites had already fled to Judah (2 Chronicles 11:13–14) prior to these events. There was no longer a spiritual class to provide leadership. This was one reason that little knowledge of the laws remained, including the purity laws that God had given to Israel (Hosea 4:6).

Sources:
(Dee and Schoneveld, vol. 1, 52; Pfeiffer, Vos, and Rea, 167–69; Reed, 63)
(See Hosea 8:13.)

Verse 4 NASB
They will not pour out drink offerings of wine to the LORD, their sacrifices will not please Him. Their bread will be like mourners' bread; All who eat of it will be defiled, for their bread will be for themselves alone; It will not enter the house of the LORD.

Verse 4 KJV
They shall not offer wine offerings to the LORD, neither shall they be pleasing unto him: their sacrifices shall be unto them as the bread of mourners; all that eat thereof shall be polluted: for their bread for their soul shall not come into the house of the LORD.

Verse 4 NIV
They will not pour out wine offerings to the LORD, nor will their sacrifices please him. Such sacrifices will be to them like the bread of mourners; all who eat them will be unclean. This food will be for themselves; it will not come into the temple of the LORD.

Verse 4 Hebrew Interlinear Text
not they-will-pour-out to-Yahweh wine or-not they-will-be-pleasing to-him sacrifices-of-them like-bread-of mourners to-him all-of ones-eating-him they-will-be-unclean indeed food-of-them for-self-of-them not he-will-come-into temple-of Yahweh

Verse 4a
not they-will-pour-out to-Yahweh wine
The word *nacak* is often used in the context of a wine offering (Genesis 35:14; Numbers 28:7; 2 Kings 16:13; Jeremiah 7:18). The more appropriate terminology for this is *to pour out libations*. This serves to reflect something of the sanctity conveyed by the original Hebrew word.
(Born, 59; Edelkoort, 192; Strong's OT, word 5258)

We read: *they will no longer pour out wine libations for Yahweh*

Verse 4b
or-not they-will-be-pleasing to-him sacrifices-of-them
The word *zebach* means *slaughter* or *the slaughtered*. Often it is translated as *sacrifice* (Genesis 31:54; Exodus 23:18; Leviticus 7:11–12; Numbers 15:8). Here that is the best option as well.
(Born, 59; Strong's OT, word 2077)

We read: *nor will their sacrifices be pleasing to Him*

Verse 4c
like-bread-of mourners to-him
The NIVIHEOT translation *mourners* is an interpretation. Scholars differ on the meaning of the word *'ōwnîm*. Most exegetes and biblical scholars understand it as being derived from *'ny* (*to mourn*) and accordingly translate as *mourners*. That sense does not suit the present context, however, and so we continue our search. The BBE refers here to *worries* or *problems*. Owens leaves the choice to the reader, offering the following translation: *mourning* or *trouble*. Rashi translates *like bread of robbery*. However, this is an interpretation of the kind that Jewish exegetes more commonly practice and yet it does suit the context here.

Strong was one who saw in the word a derivative of *aven*, and we fully agree with him. Nevertheless, the word itself remains difficult to translate. The word *'ōwnîm* in fact reflects the state of humankind (from God's perspective) in its earthly existence. This means a life contrasting starkly with the state of bliss in the garden of Eden (Genesis 2), as God intended it. That state is expressed with such words as *evil*, *worry*, *sinfulness*, *hardship*, and *misery*, all resulting from the fall into sin. This finds clear expression in Psalm 90:10, which speaks of *trouble* or *sorrow*. That helps to set us on the right path. Often *aven* is translated as *iniquity* (Job 11:14; 4:8; Psalms 5:5; 6:8), but also as *misfortune* (Numbers 23:21) or *wicked* (Job 22:15). We prefer to stick close to the Hebrew text and therefore read *iniquity*.

Many Bible scholars render the final word, *(to)-him*, as *their*. As such, they exclude God from being the referent here, since that to their mind does not fit the context. However, their reasoning is based only on their previous translation of *mourn* or *mourners*. Since we have discarded such translations, we can simply follow the Hebrew source text.
(Andersen and Freedman, 526; McComiskey, 140; Reed, 64; Owens, vol. IV, 776; Rosenberg, vol. 1, 54; Strong's OT, word 205)

We read: ***for to Him it is the food of iniquity***

Verse 4d
all-of ones-eating-him they-will-be-unclean
This is not difficult. Instead of *him* we can also read *it*.

We read: ***anyone who eats of it will become unclean***

Verse 4e
indeed food-of-them for-self-of-them
The word *nephesh* means *life* or *soul*, but it often also has a reflexive sense (himself or herself), as is the case here.
(Strong's OT, word 5315)

We read: ***because their food is for themselves***

Verse 4f
not he-will-come-into temple-of Yahweh
Many translate here with *it* instead of *he*. This reading departs from the assumption that the pronoun refers back to *the food of iniquity*. This is not likely, however. It is much more logical to take it as referring to the unclean (*anyone who eats of it*), as is most often done. The word *bo* can mean *to enter*, *to bring*, *to go*, *to come*, and *to enter into*. *Bayith* means *house*. The translation *temple* is an interpretation; it is not what the text actually says.
(Andersen and Freedman, 516; Owens, vol. IV, 776; Strong's OT, word 935 and 1004)

We read: ***he will not enter the house of Yahweh***

The entire sentence:
They will no longer pour out wine libations for Yahweh, nor will their sacrifices be pleasing to Him. For to Him it is the food of iniquity. Anyone who eats of it will become unclean because their food is for themselves. He will not enter the house of Yahweh.

Verse 5 NASB
What will you do on the day of the appointed festival and on the day of the feast of the LORD?

Verse 5 KJV
What will ye do in the solemn day, and in the day of the feast of the LORD?

Verse 5 NIV
What will you do on the day of your appointed festivals, on the feast days of the LORD?

Verse 5 Hebrew Interlinear Text
what? will-you-do on-day-of appointed-feast and-on-day-of festival-of Yahweh
The Hebrew word *moed* means *assembly* or *meeting*. It is sometimes used in the well-known biblical term *tent of meeting* or the tabernacle (Exodus 27:21; 28:43). *Moed* is typically used for a national, solemn religious assembly in Israel. The NIVIHEOT calls it a *feast*. That is indeed the significance the term has in many cases, but not in all. That is why the KJV has opted to translate as *solemn day* and the Dutch Statenvertaling as *appointed solemn day*, which is the right translation. We have adopted it with a slight modification: *fixed solemn day*.
(Born, 59; Brown, 79; Calvijn, *Daniel* II, *Kleine Profeten* I/II, Hosea, 318–19; McComiskey, 141; Strong's OT, word 4150)

We read:
What will you do on a fixed solemn day or on a feast day of Yahweh?

Verse 6 NASB
For behold, they will go because of destruction; Egypt will gather them up, Memphis will bury them. Weeds will take over their treasures of silver; thorns will be in their tents.

Verse 6 KJV
For, lo, they are gone because of destruction: Egypt shall gather them up, Memphis shall bury them: the pleasant places for their silver, nettles shall possess them: thorns shall be in their tabernacles.

Verse 6 NIV
Even if they escape from destruction, Egypt will gather them, and Memphis will bury them. Their treasures of silver will be taken over by briers, and thorns will overrun their tents.

Verse 6 Hebrew Interlinear Text
if see! they-escape from-destruction Egypt she-will-gather-them Memphis she-will-bury-them treasure of-silver-of-them brier he-will-take-over-them thorn in-tents-of-them

Verse 6a
if see! they-escape from-destruction
This verse opens with the word *ki-hinneh*. This is an exclamation of surprise (*!*), and at the same time introduces a causal relationship.
(Andersen and Freedman, 529; Born, 59; Mays, 125)

We read: ***for behold! those who escape the destruction***

Verse 6b
Egypt she-will-gather-them
Qabats means *to collect* or *to gather* (Genesis 41:35; Deuteronomy 13:16).
(Mays, 125; Strong's OT, word 6908; Ward, 157)

We read: ***Egypt will gather them***

Verse 6c
Memphis she-will-bury-them
The Hebrew word *moph* refers to the capital of Lower Egypt called *Memphis*. Some scholars transliterate the word as *Mof*. This is not necessary, however, since there is no reason to doubt the reference to Memphis.
(Calvijn, *Daniël* II, *Kleine Profeten* I/II, Hosea, 321; Owens, 777; Reed, 64; Rosenberg, vol. 1, 55; Strong's OT, word 4644)

We read: ***Memphis will bury them***

Verse 6d
treasure of-silver-of-them
The NIVIHEOT translation *treasure* is an interpretation, which is used by many others. What the text actually says is *machmad*, that is, *what is desirable* (1 Kings 20:6), or *the delight of* (Ezekiel 24:16, 21, 25). But it is also clear that the text is creating a contrast between silver, which is a precious metal, and thistles and thorns, which is worthless.
(Garrett, 189; McComiskey, 139, 141–42; Strong's OT, word 261; Wolff, 150)

We read: ***they desire their silver***

Verse 6e
brier he-will-take-over-them thorn in-tents-of-them
Outside the book of Hosea, the word *qimmos* occurs only in Isaiah 34:13. The NASB there translates with *nettles*; in Hosea 9:6 with *weeds*. The text in Hosea seems to be referring to a wild, desert-like area. Stinging nettles are rare there, but large and small *thistles* are common. Strong's is not sure and says: *perhaps thistles*. The basic meaning of *qimmos* is *spikes*, that is, a plant with spines. This is why we prefer the translation *thistles*.

The basic meaning of *choach* relates to piercing. This is why some translate *thornbushes*, others *thistles*. We prefer *thorns*.
(Born, 59; Brown, 80; Harper, 331; Owens, 777; Reed, 64; Strong's OT, words 2336, 7057)

We read: ***their property will be taken over by thistles; thorns will overgrow their tents***

The entire sentence:
For behold! those who escape the destruction will be gathered by Egypt. Memphis will bury them. They covet silver. Their property will be taken over by thistles; thorns will overgrow their tents.

Verse 7 NASB
The days of punishment have come, the days of retribution have come; Let Israel know this! The prophet is a fool, the inspired man is demented, because of the grossness of your iniquity, and because your hostility is so great.

Verse 7 KJV
The days of visitation are come, the days of recompence are come; Israel shall know it:

the prophet is a fool, the spiritual man is mad, for the multitude of thine iniquity, and the great hatred.

Verse 7 NIV
The days of punishment are coming, the days of reckoning are at hand. Let Israel know this. Because your sins are so many and your hostility so great, the prophet is considered a fool, the inspired person a maniac.

Verse 7 Hebrew Interlinear Text
they-come days-of the-punishment they-come days-of the-reckoning let-them-know Israel foolish the-prophet one-being-maniac man-of the-inspiration because-of many-of sin-of-you and-great hostility

Verse 7a
they-come days-of the-punishment
The word *pequddah* is commonly translated as *visitation* (Numbers 16:29; Isaiah 10:3; Jeremiah 8:12 all KJV), *fate* (Numbers 16:29 NASB), and *reckoning* (1 Chronicles 23:11 KJV). Others read: *responsibility, office, punishment,* or *muster*. The NIVIHEOT reads *punishment*, but this rendering doesn't really get at the significance of the source text. In its most basic sense, the term refers to the settlement of a balance (of accumulated sin) or *the reckoning of.*
(Brown, 80; McComiskey, 144; Owens, 777; Strong's OT, word 6486)

We read: *the days of reckoning have come*

Verse 7b
they-come days-of the-reckoning
Shillum is difficult to translate with a single word. It means something like *to settle the account, to compensate debt, to pay back,* or *to pay off*. Conceptually, it goes with the *pequddah* in verse 7a: the reckoning of the bill (verse 7a) and the paying of that bill (7b).
(Brown, 80; Calvijn, *Daniël* II, *Kleine Profeten* I/II, Hosea, 321–23; Strong's OT, word 7966; Stuart, 145)

We read: *the days of retribution are imminent*

Verse 7c
let-them-know Israel
Like many other exegetes, we consider verse 7c to be a separate clause.
(Garrett, 189; Rosenberg, vol. 1, 155; Ward, 157)

We read: *let Israel know*

Verse 7d
foolish the-prophet one-being-maniac
This is not difficult. Literally the text reads: *the prophet is a fool, someone who is mad*. However, this can be rendered a bit better. Some connect the final word (*one-being-maniac*) to verse 7e. This is much less logical, however.
(Harper, 331; Owens, 777; Stuart, 139)

We read: *the prophet is considered a fool, a maniac*

Verse 7e
man-of the-inspiration
The expression *'îš-hārūaḥ* means *man, person,* or *someone of spirit* or *wind*. The context makes it clear that the text must be referring to a person who is considered a fool, a

maniac. We could therefore say *a man/someone of spirit*, or *a man/someone of wind* (*who chases after wind*).
(Andersen and Freedman, 532; Reed, 64; Strong's OT, words 376, 7307; Wolff, 150)

We read: ***someone who chases after wind***

Now the entire sentence:
The days of reckoning have come; the days of retribution are imminent. Let Israel know that! The prophet is considered a fool, a maniac, who chases after wind. For your sins are many and your enmity is great.

Introduction to Verse 8

This verse is translated in very different ways, which we are not going to bother listing here since they add little to our understanding of the text. Moreover, the Hebrew source text is not as difficult as some suggest.

The key to the translation is found in the contrast between *God-of-me* and *God-of-him*. The NIVIHEOT uses a capital letter for both. However, both uses of the word *elohim* can refer to the true God and to gods in general (including idols). Here the true meaning is found in both; God and god.

The second key is in the expression *on all his paths*. This raises the question, *whose* paths are they on? . . . Those of Ephraim/Israel, of course. For like the prophet Ezekiel, the prophet Hosea has become a "watchman of Israel" now that the Sinaitic Covenant has met its end. He watches the people of Ephraim (the Ten Tribes) and looks in expectation for signs of a glorious future when the salvific prophecies about Ephraim reach their fulfillment. That is the final goal.
(See Annotation 9A.)

Conclusion:
Hosea faced a people that had abandoned God and were now serving idols. As "watchman of God" he hated those idols. For that reason, the contrast in this verse must be one between *God-of-me* (= Yahweh) and *god-of-him* (= the idol gods of Ephraim).
(Andersen and Freedman, 515; Brown, 81)
(See Annotation 9A.)

Verse 8 NASB
Ephraim was a watchman with my God, a prophet; Yet the snare of a bird catcher is in all his ways, and there is only hostility in the house of his God.

Verse 8 KJV
The watchman of Ephraim was with my God: but the prophet is a snare of a fowler in all his ways, and hatred in the house of his God.

Verse 8 NIV
The prophet, along with my God, is the watchman over Ephraim, yet snares await him on all his paths, and hostility in the house of his God.

Verse 8 Hebrew Interlinear Text
man-watching-over Ephraim with God-of-me prophet snare-of fowler on all-of paths-of-him hostility in-house-of God-of-him

Verse 8a
man-watching-over Ephraim with God-of-me prophet snare-of fowler on all-of paths-of-him
The word יהלא, vocalized as *'ĕlōhê* or *'ĕlōhāy* is often translated with *God-of-me*, but (*his*) *own God* is also possible and that fits here.
(Strong's OT, word 430; Weerd, Jesaja, vol. 2, 171–72)

We read: ***The watchman over Ephraim is with his own God. The prophet is a snare of the fowler on all his paths.***

Verse 8b
hostility in-house-of God-of-him
The word *mastemah* occurs only in the book of Hosea. It is probably derived from *shotet*, whose basic meaning is *to stir up*, *to pierce*, or *to puncture*. *Hostility* is an excessively general and weak word to use for the translation here. Preferable terms include *hate*, *deep-seated hate*, *rancor*, or *revulsion*. CEV: *hatred*. The text therefore reads something like this: *a hate* (or *revulsion*) *in* (or *of*) *the house of his god*. The NET reads *animosity rages against*, which is close to the Hebrew.
(Read, 64; Strong's OT, words 4895, 7850)

We read: ***his animosity rages against the house of his god***

The entire sentence:
The watchman over Ephraim is with his own God. The prophet is a snare of the fowler on all his paths. His animosity rages against the house of his god.

Verse 9 NASB
They have gone deep in depravity as in the days of Gibeah; He will remember their iniquity, He will punish their sins.

Verse 9 KJV
They have deeply corrupted themselves, as in the days of Gibeah: therefore he will remember their iniquity, he will visit their sins.

Verse 9 NIV
They have sunk deep into corruption, as in the days of Gibeah. God will remember their wickedness and punish them for their sins.

Verse 9 Hebrew Interlinear Text
they-sank-deep they-became-corrupt as-days-of the-Gibeah he-will-remember wickedness-of-them he-will-punish sins-of-them
The word *yizkār* (from: *zakar*) means: *he will remember*. Besides the basic meaning it is also used as a form of reclamation, which can turn out as a delayed form of punishment.
(Strong's OT, word 2142; Wolff, 151)

We read:
They sank deep and became as corrupt as in the days of Gibeah. He will be mindful of their wickedness and punish their sins.

Verse 10 NASB
I found Israel like grapes in the wilderness; I saw your forefathers as the earliest fruit on the fig tree in its first season. But they came to Baal-peor and devoted themselves to shame, and they became as detestable as that which they loved.

Verse 10 KJV
I found Israel like grapes in the wilderness; I saw your fathers as the firstripe in the fig tree at her first time: but they went to Baalpeor, and separated themselves unto that shame; and their abominations were according as they loved.

Verse 10 NIV
"When I found Israel, it was like finding grapes in the desert; when I saw your ancestors, it was like seeing the early fruit on the fig tree. But when they came to Baal Peor, they consecrated themselves to that shameful idol and became as vile as the thing they loved."

Verse 10 Hebrew Interlinear Text
like-grapes in-the-desert I-found Israel like-early-fruit on-fig-tree at-beginning-of-her I-saw fathers-of-you they they-came Baal Peor and-they-consecrated-themselves to-the-shameful-thing and-they-became vile-ones as-thing-loved-of-them

Verse 10b
at-beginning-of-her
The word *reshith* means *firstfruits* (Leviticus 2:12; Numbers 18:12; Nehemiah 10:37). It refers to the first yield of the harvest which was consecrated to God.
(Andersen and Freedman, 540; Born, 51; Mays, 131; Strong's OT, word 7225; Stuart, 148–49)

We read:
I found Israel as if it were grapes in the desert. Like the first fruits on the fig tree, her firstfruits, so I saw your fathers. But they, yes, they came to Baal Peor and they devoted themselves to this shameful object. Thus they became as horrible as the object of their devotion.

Verse 11 NASB
As for Ephraim, their glory will fly away like a bird—No birth, no pregnancy and no conception!

Verse 11 KJV
As for Ephraim, their glory shall fly away like a bird, from the birth, and from the womb, and from the conception.

Verse 11 NIV
"Ephraim's glory will fly away like a bird—no birth, no pregnancy, no conception."

Verse 11 Hebrew Interlinear Text
Ephraim like-the-bird he-will-fly-away glory-of-them from-to-bear and-from-pregnancy and-from-conception

Verse 11a
Ephraim like-the-bird he-will-fly-away glory-of-them
The KJV begins its translation of this verse with: *as for Ephraim*. This indicates that the text is now transitioning to another topic. While Hosea was first speaking about the nation of Israel (i.e., the twelve tribes), here verse 11 opens with the name of Ephraim to draw attention to this change. That should be reflected in the translation as well, so we read: *as far as Ephraim is concerned*.
(Calvijn, *Daniel* II, *Kleine Profeten* I/II, Hosea, 336)

We read: *as far as Ephraim is concerned: as a bird, its glory will fly away*

Verse 11b
from-to-bear and-from-pregnancy
Yalad means *to yield* or *to produce*. One of the ways in which it is used is in the biblical genealogies. There the context is that of *birth*, of course.
(Mays, 131; Strong's OT, word 3205; Stuart, 148)

We read: ***no birth, no pregnancy***

Verse 11c
and-from-conception
Others render this *or even be conceived* (NLT).

We read: ***and no more conception***

The entire sentence:
As far as Ephraim is concerned: as a bird, its glory will fly away. No birth, no pregnancy, and no more conception.

Verse 12 NASB
Though they bring up their children, yet I will bereave them until not a man is left. Yes, woe to them indeed when I depart from them!

Verse 12 KJV
Though they bring up their children, yet will I bereave them, that there shall not be a man left: yea, woe also to them when I depart from them!

Verse 12 NIV
"Even if they rear children, I will bereave them of every one. Woe to them when I turn away from them!"

Verse 12 Hebrew Interlinear Text
even if they-rear . . . children-of-them then-I-will-bereave-them of-everyone indeed also woe! to-them when-to-turn-away-me from-them

Verse 12b
them then-I-will-bereave-them of-everyone indeed
The word *shakol* can indeed be translated as *to bereave*, as in the NIVIHEOT. It does, however, have the sense of *to make childless, to be bereaved of children,* or *to suffer a miscarriage*.

The NIVIHEOT also reads here *everyone*. That is an uncommon interpretation. For the word *adam* means *someone, man, person,* or even *human race* (and sometimes it is the personal name *Adam*). Harper offers the translation *that there be no man*. Stuart, however, reads *without a human/man* and that fits the context much better. Such a translation is reflective of growth to maturity* which is a view that finds support in many exegetes.
(*Andersen and Freedman, 543; Harper, 338; Strong's OT, word 120; Stuart, 148–49)

We read, first step: ***then I will bereave them of every one without (becoming) man.***

We read, second step: ***I will bereave them of every one; they will not grow up.***

The entire sentence:
Even if they raise their children, I will bereave them of every one; they will not grow up. Woe to them when I turn away from them.

Verse 13 NASB
Ephraim, as I have seen, is planted in a pleasant meadow like Tyre; But Ephraim will bring out his children for slaughter.

Verse 13 KJV
Ephraim, as I saw Tyrus, is planted in a pleasant place: but Ephraim shall bring forth his children to the murderer.

Verse 13 NIV
"I have seen Ephraim, like Tyre, planted in a pleasant place. But Ephraim will bring out their children to the slayer."

Verse 13 Hebrew Interlinear Text
Ephraim like-that I-saw to-Tyre one-being-planted in-pleasant-place but-Ephraim to-bring-out to one-slaying children-of-him
The expression *to-bring-out* points to a resolve or obligation.
(Born, 62; Ward, 158)

We read:
I looked at Ephraim as I once did Tyre, which was planted in a pleasant place. But Ephraim has to hand over his children to the manslayer.

Verse 14 NASB
Give them, O Lord—what will You give? Give them a miscarrying womb and dry breasts.

Verse 14 KJV
Give them, O Lord: what wilt thou give? give them a miscarrying womb and dry breasts.

Verse 14 NIV
Give them, Lord—what will you give them? Give them wombs that miscarry and breasts that are dry.

Verse 14 Hebrew Interlinear Text
give! to-them Yahweh what? will-you-give give! to-them womb one-miscarrying and-breasts ones-being-dry
Hosea is unable to consent to the will of God without petitioning Him. It is clear that the prophet is not pleading for the announced punishment to be turned aside. That is no longer an option. God was very clear in His announcement of judgment. Consequently Hosea understands what will happen with Ephraim and expresses a state of shock; he is filled with terror concerning the coming judgment. Maybe he is even pleading for a softening of the judgment.
(Wolff, 166)

Verse 14 contains a play on words around the word *nathan*, a primitive root, used with great latitude of application, for example: *to give, to put, to place, to make, to institute, to deliver,* or *to grant*. The form of the word used here is *tēn* (NIVIHEOT: *give!*). It introduces an emotional sentence that resounds as a plea for mercy. The poetry does not allow us to translate to the letter, but we will attempt to convey the message.
(Botterweck, Ringgren, and Fabry, vol. 10, 90–108; Strong's OT, word 5414)

We read:
To what do You deliver them, O Yahweh? Would You give them wombs that miscarry and breasts that remain dry?

Verse 15 NASB
All their evil is at Gilgal; Indeed, I came to hate them there! Because of the wickedness of their deeds I will drive them out of My house! I will love them no more; All their princes are rebels.

Verse 15 KJV
All their wickedness is in Gilgal: for there I hated them: for the wickedness of their doings I will drive them out of mine house, I will love them no more: all their princes are revolters.

Verse 15 NIV
"Because of all their wickedness in Gilgal, I hated them there. Because of their sinful deeds, I will drive them out of my house. I will no longer love them; all their leaders are rebellious."

Verse 15 Hebrew Interlinear Text
all-of wickedness-of-them in-the-Gilgal indeed there I-hated-them because-of sinfulness-of deeds-of-them from-house-of-me I-will-drive-them not I-will-do-longer to-love-them all-of leaders-of-them ones-being-rebellious

Verse 15a
all-of wickedness-of-them in-the-Gilgal
Of course, it is not as if the corruption of Ephraim (the Ten Tribes) was found in the city of Gilgal alone. The entire nation (Israel *and* Judah) had departed from God and made itself guilty of idolatry. Gilgal and Bethel were the places where the golden calves were worshiped. Ephraim, however, is singled out as the center of this evil as the longest standing center of idolatry. After all, Bethel was completely destroyed during the reign of King Josiah (2 Kings 23:15). Such cleansing never did take place in Gilgal, making it a type for Ephraim's idolatry. The Hebrew text should probably be interpreted as: *Their whole corruption is evident from Gilgal.*
(McComiskey, 155; Reed, 66; Weerd, *Ezechiël*, vol. 1, 118)

We read: *their whole corruption is evident from Gilgal*

Verse 15b
indeed there I-hated-them because-of sinfulness-of deeds-of-them
Ki is translated here by *indeed*. Most exegetes have: *for.*
(Strong's OT, word 3588)

We read: *For there I hated them because of their sinful deeds*

Verse 15d
leaders-of-them ones-being-rebellious
The word *sar* does indeed mean *leaders*, but it can also mean *princes*. On this point we follow the majority of exegetes.
(Born, 62; Strong's OT, word 8269)

We read: *for all their princes are rebellious*

The entire sentence:
Their whole corruption is evident from Gilgal. For there I hated them because of their

sinful deeds. I will drive them out of My house. I will no longer exert Myself to love them, for all their princes are rebellious.

Verse 16 NASB
Ephraim is stricken, their root is dried up, they will bear no fruit. Even though they bear children, I will slay the precious ones of their womb.

Verse 16 KJV
Ephraim is smitten, their root is dried up, they shall bear no fruit: yea, though they bring forth, yet will I slay even the beloved fruit of their womb.

Verse 16 NIV
"Ephraim is blighted, their root is withered, they yield no fruit. Even if they bear children, I will slay their cherished offspring."

Verse 16 Hebrew Interlinear Text
he-is-blighted Ephraim root-of-them he-is-withered fruit not they-yield even if they-bear-children then-I-will-slay cherished-ones-of womb-of-them
Hukkā (from *nakah*) means *smitten* or *been hit*; surely not *blighted*.
(Rosenberg, vol. 1, 59; Strong's OT, word 5221)

We read:
Ephraim is smitten; his root is withered. They will not bear fruit. Even if they will produce children, I will kill the cherished of their womb.

Verse 17 NASB
My God will cast them away because they have not listened to Him; and they will be wanderers among the nations.

Verse 17 KJV
My God will cast them away, because they did not hearken unto him: and they shall be wanderers among the nations.

Verse 17 NIV

My God will reject them because they have not obeyed him; they will be wanderers among the nations.

Verse 17 Hebrew Interlinear Text
he-will-reject-them God-of-me because not they-obeyed to-him and-they-will-be ones-wandering among-the-nations
Nadad means *to wander*, *to flutter*, or *to roam*. Here we translate: *tramps*.
(Strong's OT, word 5074)

We read:
My God will reject them because they did not obey Him. So they will be tramps among the nations.

Hosea 9:1–17—The corrected text:

Verse 1   *Do not rejoice with levity, like the other nations, O Israel. For you committed adultery, forsaking your God. On every threshing floor for the corn you love the wages of fornication.*

Verse 2	*Threshing floor nor winepress will feed them and the new wine will be lacking.*
Verse 3	*They will not remain in the land of Yahweh, but Ephraim will return. They will eat the unclean in Egypt and Assyria.*
Verse 4	*They will no longer pour out wine libations for Yahweh, nor will their sacrifices be pleasing to Him. For to Him it is the food of iniquity. Anyone who eats of it will become unclean because their food is for themselves. He will not enter the house of Yahweh.*
Verse 5	*What will you do on a fixed solemn day or on a feast day of Yahweh?*
Verse 6	*For behold! those who escape the destruction will be gathered by Egypt. Memphis will bury them. They covet silver. Their property will be taken over by thistles; thorns will overgrow their tents.*
Verse 7	*The days of reckoning have come; the days of retribution are imminent. Let Israel know that! The prophet is considered a fool, a maniac, who chases after wind. For your sins are many and your enmity is great.*
Verse 8	*The watchman over Ephraim is with his own God. The prophet is a snare of the fowler on all his paths. His animosity rages against the house of his god.*
Verse 9	*They sank deep and became as corrupt as in the days of Gibeah. He will be mindful of their wickedness and punish their sins.*
Verse 10	*I found Israel as if it were grapes in the desert. Like the first fruits on the fig tree, her firstfruits, so I saw your fathers. But they, yes, they came to Baal Peor and they devoted themselves to this shameful object. Thus they became as horrible as the object of their devotion.*
Verse 11	*As far as Ephraim is concerned: as a bird, its glory will fly away. No birth, no pregnancy, and no more conception.*
Verse 12	*Even if they raise their children, I will bereave them of every one; they will not grow up. Woe to them when I turn away from them.*
Verse 13	*I looked at Ephraim as I once did Tyre, which was planted in a pleasant place. But Ephraim has to hand over his children to the manslayer.*
Verse 14	*To what do You deliver them, O Yahweh? Would You give them wombs that miscarry and breasts that remain dry?*
Verse 15	*Their whole corruption is evident from Gilgal. For there I hated them because of their sinful deeds. I will drive them out of My house. I will no longer exert Myself to love them, for all their princes are rebellious.*
Verse 16	*Ephraim is smitten; his root is withered. They will not bear fruit. Even if they will produce children, I will kill the cherished of their womb.*
Verse 17	*My God will reject them because they did not obey Him. So they will be tramps among the nations.*

HOSEA 9
Exegesis

Introduction

The preceding chapters speak about God's judgment on Israel and the end of the Sinaitic Covenant. They also give a summary of the sins that led to that break. Hosea 9 speaks of the catastrophe itself and the first years thereafter.

The hallmark of the people of Israel in their high status as God's people was their covenant with Yahweh. That high position became visible in worship and in the holy temple. With the breaking of the Sinaitic Covenant, the name Israel was taken away from them. Under the name Ephraim, they lost definitive divine protection and that led to the downfall of the ten-tribe kingdom. The breaking of the covenant did not lead to repentance and conversion. On the contrary, the worship of Yahweh was no longer just flawed, but it totally disappeared from the Northern Kingdom. Assyria was the executor of God's judgment, and they did it thorough.

Hosea 9 bears witness to the deportation of the surviving population to Assyria. The text also speaks of refugees who escaped to Egypt but were received there with hostility. It tells (although in guarded terms) of the harsh conditions during the long journey to the places to where they were exiled in the Assyrian Empire and of the difficult time thereafter, when many Israelites lived in slavery.

The prophecy is left open-ended and calls the descendants of the Ten Tribes *tramps among the* gentile *nations* (verse 17). Actually, they are some kind of gypsies; nowhere wanted and nowhere loved, waiting for the great day when Yahweh will call them to return to the land of their fathers, Canaan.

A Different Fate

The fate of Israel/Ephraim differed greatly from that of Judah. With the fall of Jerusalem in 587 BC, that nation also perished. The population of Judah, like that of Israel, was deported. But that is where the comparison ends. The cruel Assyrians killed the leading class of Israel and forced the people to give up their identity. The Babylonians acted much more wisely. They saved the upper class of the people of Judah. The deported population was allowed to live together in large groups. They retained their leaders and were allowed to maintain their religion and cultural practices. Especially the priests and Levites played a key role in this.

In contrast to Judah, the people of Israel lost their leaders. Moreover, there were no more priests and Levites of God, who could have formed a cultural and religious base giving them cohesion. The priests and Levites had long ago moved away to Judah (2 Chronicles 11:13–14). With the loss of anything that could bind them to their roots, the survivors of the people of Israel/Ephraim lost their identity and were totally absorbed into the gentile peoples. Despite all this, the prophets speak about the restoration of the Ten Tribes in the end times. For many centuries this was considered impossible. In our time, however, a start has been made with the discovery and recognition of the lost tribes of Israel. That is a great miracle and a proof that the end time is near.
(See Excursus 7.)

Verse 1a
Do not rejoice with levity, like the other nations, O Israel. For you committed adultery, forsaking your God.
The text reads *do not rejoice with levity*. That is still somewhat weak, because we should actually have used a stronger expression. In fact, a sort of wild excitement is meant. In everyday language we would say: go crazy, uninhibited fun, with a strong negative undertone. For the prophet here refers to pagan sacrificial festivals in which alcohol abuse and sexual licentiousness played a dominant role. In this Israel had become equal to the gentile nations.
(Mays, 125–26; Wolff, 153; Wood, 204)

Verse 1b
On every threshing floor for the corn you love the wages of fornication.
The threshing floor was the place where the corn was threshed. In mountainous regions this usually involved a flat rock plateau and in the lowlands a floor of tamped-down loam. When the harvest was inside and processed, it was time for a feast that was usually held there. In Ruth 3 such a feast is described.

In villages, a threshing floor was usually common property and also the central place for all festive gatherings. As is often the case on an occasion where alcohol is used, things sometimes get out of hand. The threshing floor was in fact also the meeting point for short-lived love affairs or one-time hookups. In the degenerate society of Israel it had probably also become the place where prostitutes offered their services. This seems to be what verse 1b is referring to and a well-known expression used to describe it.

The text thus gives a picture of a festive gathering (ideally, a type of the wedding celebration between God and Israel) and then the abuse of that relationship through the fornication of Israel (= Gomer, Hosea 1–2).
(Stuart, 142)

Verse 2
Threshing floor nor winepress will feed them and the new wine will be lacking.
The prophet now deals in a poetic way with the subject of abuse. On the one hand Hosea speaks of a threshing floor that is abused for fornication. On the other hand, there will not be any more threshing, because there will be no more harvest. It is a poetic way of saying that daily life will disappear. No festivals, no threshing of grain or grapes, no new wine.

With this prophecy, Hosea speaks in an allegorical way about the years in which Israel (the ten-tribe kingdom) perished, when the Assyrian army marched through the country marauding and burning. Perhaps the text also speaks of the period thereafter, when the people of Israel were already taken into exile. That was a fulfillment of the judgmental prophecy of Deuteronomy 28:47–51 (NASB):

47 *"Because you did not serve the* LORD *your God with joy and a glad heart, for the abundance of all things;*
48 *"therefore you shall serve your enemies whom the* LORD *will send against you, in hunger, in thirst, in nakedness, and in the lack of all things; and He will put an iron yoke on your neck until He has destroyed you.*
49 *"The* LORD *will bring a nation against you from afar, from the end of the earth, as the eagle swoops down, a nation whose language you shall not understand,*
50 *"a nation of fierce countenance who will have no respect for the old, nor show favor to the young.*
51 *"Moreover, it shall eat the offspring of your herd and the produce of your ground until*

you are destroyed, who also leaves you no grain, new wine, or oil, nor the increase of your herd or the young of your flock until they have caused you to perish."

(Calvijn, *Daniel* II, *Kleine Profeten* I/II, Hosea, 250–51)

Verse 3a
They will not remain in the land of Yahweh,
No one has any right to property in Jerusalem or in the land of Canaan except God alone. All claims then, but also now—not only of Palestinians, Egypt and/or Jordan, but also of church denominations—are worthless and irrelevant. Yahweh has predetermined to live in the land of Canaan Himself. There His temple stood, and there it will stand again, in the end time.

Does God then no longer live in this world? He does, not in the temple, but in the church of Christ. That will come to an end when the church is raptured. Then a world without God comes into being, that will be the great tribulation, a terrible time, which will last seven years. That is why the temple *must* be rebuilt. The world cannot exist without God. (See Excursus 2.)

3a.1 Promised to all twelve tribes of Israel!
Canaan was and is the promised land. Promised to a chosen people: Israel. Not to a part of it (the two tribes or the Jews), but to all twelve tribes. Israel/Ephraim (the Ten Tribes) was being removed from the land because they have broken the Sinaitic Covenant.
(Mays, 126)

Verse 3b
but Ephraim will return.
The exile of the Ten Tribes is not a final station. One day they will *return* and reenter the promised land again. The prophet Ezekiel speaks of this in 37:16, 19; 48, as does the prophet Jeremiah in very clear terms in chapter 31 (NASB).

6 *"For there will be a day when watchmen on the hills of Ephraim call out, 'Arise, and let us go up to Zion, to the L*ORD *our God.'"*
8 *"Behold, I am bringing them from the north country, and I will gather them from the remote parts of the earth. Among them the blind and the lame, the woman with child and she who is in labor with child, together; A great company, they will return here.*
9 *"With weeping they will come, and by supplication I will lead them; I will make them walk by streams of waters, on a straight path in which they will not stumble; For I am a father to Israel, and Ephraim is My firstborn."*
10 *Hear the word of the L*ORD*, O nations, and declare in the coastlands afar off, and say, "He who scattered Israel will gather him and keep him as a shepherd keeps his flock."*
20 *"Is Ephraim My dear son? Is he a delightful child? Indeed, as often as I have spoken against him, I certainly still remember him; Therefore My heart yearns for him; I will surely have mercy on him," declares the L*ORD.

It is almost incomprehensible that this prophecy is still being spiritualized by some, or even completely ignored. God speaks so clearly and not only here. Zechariah 10:7–10* also does not leave any doubt about the blessed future of the ten tribes of Ephraim/Israel.

7 *"The Ephraimites will become mighty heroes. Their hearts will be merry as wine. Their children will see that and rejoice. Their hearts will rejoice in the L*ORD.
8 *"I will whistle them to me and secure them. I will redeem them, and they will become as numerous as they were.*
9 *"Though I sow them among the nations, yet they will remember Me in distant lands. Then they will be kept, their children with them. Then they will return.*

10 *For I will bring them back as from the land of Egypt, and gather them out of Assyria, and bring them into the land of Gilead and Lebanon,† but this shall not be sufficient."*

(†Ezekiel 48:1–7; *Weerd, Hebrew text translation in *Zacharia*, 272–75)

Verse 3c
They will eat the unclean in Egypt and Assyria.
The people of Israel (Ephraim) have lost the knowledge of God (Hosea 4:1, 6). The priests (descendants of Aaron), who served Yahweh, had left the land (2 Chronicles 11:13–14). When the Assyrians deported the people, their cultural and religious heritage was largely lost. They no longer ate kosher food. Circumcision was only sporadically applied and they no longer paid homage to the true God. This also applied to the refugees who had escaped to Egypt.

Here also the name change—Israel became Ephraim—reflects the sad state of the Ten Tribes. It not only looks at the broken Sinaitic Covenant, but also at their identity. They have lost their roots (verse 16a).
(Yee, 265)

Verse 4
They will no longer pour out wine libations for Yahweh, nor will their sacrifices be pleasing to Him. For to Him it is the food of iniquity. Anyone who eats of it will become unclean because their food is for themselves. He will not enter the house of Yahweh.
There is a major difference of opinion on the meaning of this verse. Three possible interpretations are given:
4.1a It speaks of the idolatry at Bethel and Gilgal (the bull calves). Attending sacrificial services, that is, eating sacrificial meat, appears to be *the food of iniquity* for Israel (Ephraim).
4.1b According to Calvin, the prophet is speaking about the time after the deportation. He states that the exiles were then no longer able to visit the temple.
4.1c Or, the prophecy refers to verse 3, which talks about eating unclean food. Everyone who ate it became unclean, and thus was *not allowed to enter the house of Yahweh* (the temple in Jerusalem).

The Holy Scriptures themselves speak to this issue, so we can choose the right explanation from there.
4.2a Nowhere in the Bible is idol worship at Bethel and Gilgal described as a service to Yahweh. Verse 4a, however, does speak of worshiping *Yahweh* (*pleasing to Him*). So interpretation 1a would be invalid.
4.2b There was indeed a considerable number of Israelites who escaped to Egypt. However, they were, theoretically, still able to visit the temple in Jerusalem. Point 1b therefore does not hold true.
4.2c That leaves interpretation 1c, which also provides us with a logical explanation. If anyone ate unclean food, he was not allowed to enter the temple of God. It placed her or him on the same level as pagan people. With this same proposition the expression *food of iniquity* can also be explained. For the judgment on Ephraim was the result of severe sins (*iniquity*). The unclean food that the people of Ephraim had to eat in captivity, because of the harsh conditions, was therefore the recompense (in a bitter way) for their *iniquity*.

Conclusion:
The preceding arguments lead us to decisively choose interpretation 4.2c.
(Calvijn, *Daniel* II, *Kleine Profeten* I/II, Hosea, 253; Mays, 127)

Verse 5
What will you do on a fixed solemn day or on a feast day of Yahweh?
Since the people of Israel/Ephraim have become unclean, they can no longer participate in religious festivals and feast days. Moreover, they have lost knowledge of Yahweh and His service (Hosea 4:6). So they lose, also for that reason, the high holy days.

In a poetic way, the prophet Hosea speaks about "the time after." That is the period that began with the deportation of the ten tribes of Israel by Assyria. For the people of Israel lost their holiness and became like all other nations, like the gentiles. High holy days, the Sabbath, circumcision, purity commandments, and service to God were all part of what characterized the people of Israel and gave it its elect place in the world. All this is lost now.
(Stuart, 144)

Verse 6
For behold! those who escape the destruction will be gathered by Egypt. Memphis will bury them. They covet silver. Their property will be taken over by thistles; thorns will overgrow their tents.
The text contains a poetic play on words, namely the words *qabats* (*gathered*) and *qabar* (*bury*). This already indicates that we have to allocate a negative connotation to the verse. The refugees were apparently not welcomed as allies in Egypt, but perhaps interned in camps. This is confirmed in the second part of verse 6, where it speaks of dwelling in *tents*, in a dry and deserted region (of Egypt).
(Calvijn, *Daniel* II, *Kleine Profeten* I/II, Hosea, 258–59; Wolff, 156)

Verse 7a
The days of reckoning have come; the days of retribution are imminent. Let Israel know that!
Reckoning refers to the total of outstanding accounts—the accumulation of sins. The word *retribution* for the liquidation thereof, in terms of judgment. In its most basic sense, the sentence refers to the settlement of a balance (of accumulated sin). God's justice demands that satisfaction be given.

Verse 7b
The prophet is considered a fool, a maniac, who chases after wind.
The gulf between the people of Ephraim (the Ten Tribes) and God is made painfully clear in verse 7. The prophet Hosea prophesies at God's command about the approaching judgment. However, his hearers (the people of Israel) do not recognize him as a true prophet of God. They regard him as a fool, a *grinding person*, chasing after *chimeras*.

Verse 7c
For your sins are many and your enmity is great.
The cause of the judgment is clear: the multitude of sins and (what is perhaps the worst) the *enmity* of Israel toward the Most High.
(Brown, 80; Mays, 129; Stuart, 145–46; Wood, 204)

Verse 8
The watchman over Ephraim is with his own God. The prophet is a snare of the fowler on all his paths. His animosity rages against the house of his god.
The enmity of Ephraim toward the Almighty (verse 7c) naturally also applies to the relationship between the prophet Hosea (as God's emissary) and the people of Ephraim/Israel.

By virtue of his function, Hosea is *the snare of the bird catcher*, for he announced the judgments on Ephraim/Israel in God's name. But Hosea also has the attitudes of God. That is why he is driven by a deep aversion to the house of *his* (= Ephraim's) *god* (the idolatry of the bull calves).
(Brown, 81)

8.1 The Watchman, the petrel of salvation history
Israel's prophets were mouthpieces of God, ambassadors of a sort, who were given to God's people. When Israel/Ephraim perished, the ministry of the prophets became superfluous. But now a new task awaited them—that of Watchmen of Israel. In that function the prophet looks forward to the future; he looks forward eagerly to the fulfillment of the divine prophecies. Fisch therefore calls them: "the petrels of world history".

We may also know watchmen like this today. These are people who understand the prophecies and always keep an eye on their fulfillment. For them the dawn of God's salvation is always near. Listen to them, for they are mouthpieces of God!
(Fisch, xiv; Mays, 130)
(See Annotation 9A.)

Annotation 9A: The Watchman of Israel

On Sinai God Almighty gave the Ten Commandments to Moses (Exodus 20). They were the first lines of a number of ad itional commandments that set regulations for the people of Israel. Those laws were aimed at a secluded society, a holy nation under God's direction. In it the individual was subordinate to the collective.

Looking for the Messiah
In the era of the divine nation or theocracy, the prophets were in service of the people of Israel as a whole. They therefore focused primarily on the leaders of the country. They were, together with the high priest, God's governors on earth. When Ephraim/Israel (the northern kingdom of the Ten Tribes) perished and later the last remnant of the kingdom of God (the two-tribe kingdom of Judah) disappeared, the old task of the prophets was also lifted. A new kind of prophet now arose, the *watchman over the house of Israel** (Ezekiel 33:16–24†). He no longer supervised the functioning of the theocracy. It was no more. He looked to the future; to the coming of the Messiah and the foundation of the Messianic Kingdom under His rule. That was the next station of salvation in the counsel of Yahweh.

As the watchman on the wall looked for changes that were important to the city, the *watchman over the house of Israel** looks for the signs that announce salvation (in whatever form). Then, according to God's promise, what has gone wrong in the past will yet succeed.
(Weerd, *Ezechiël*, vol. 2, *261–62, †296–300)
(See Excursus 9.)

Verse 9
They sank deep and became as corrupt as in the days of Gibeah. He will be mindful of their wickedness and punish their sins.
The location of Gibeah is uncertain. Probably it is in the Central Benjamin Plateau, where Jacob and his family lived for some years. North of it we find the town of Shechem.

Exegetes differ in opinion as to what is meant by the expression *days of Gibeah*. There are two possible explanations. Some point to Judges 19 and 20. That could be, were it not that the same expression reoccurs in Hosea 10:9. And there we get more information, because the text speaks about the early days when Israel (Jacob and his descendants) *started to sin*.

Based on that we have to look to older sins. And the first collective sins of Israel are found in Genesis 34. It is the sad story of Dinah, the daughter of Leah and Jacob, who was raped by Shechem, the son of a local prince. The sons of Jacob demanded satisfaction. After negotiations, an agreement was made that should have brought both nations together. As part of the covenant, the prince agreed with the sons of Jacob that his people would be circumcised. When the men of Shechem had been circumcised, the male population became powerless. Two of Jacob's sons, Simeon and Levi (brothers of Dinah), raided the unsuspecting city population and killed all male inhabitants. Then they plundered the city.

Whatever *the days of Gibeah* represent, it is clear that it functions as an example of the corruption of Israel, as in the time of King Jeroboam II, and thus recalls Hosea 4:2.
(See exegeses of Hosea 4:2; 10:9.)

Verse 10a
I found Israel as if it were grapes in the desert. Like the first fruits on the fig tree, her firstfruits, so I saw your fathers.
We spoke about the sorrow of God before. This also comes to the surface in verse 10. For the Almighty looks back on the past in sadness. In His review, He begins at the very beginning of His relationship with Israel when the future was full of promises.

The *desert* typifies the earth which, since the fall, is a spiritually barren place. The patriarchs of Israel are typified by the *grapes* which you would not expect in such a barren place.

God also calls the patriarchs *firstfruits*. The first and best fruits of the first harvest (a delicacy) of the *fig tree* (which represents all Israel).
(Brown, 82; Mays, 132; Rosenberg, vol. 1, 57)

Like the first fruits . . . I saw your fathers
During the festival of weeks (Shavuot), which formed the conclusion of Pesach, the Israelites brought offerings from the first fruits of the new harvest, but also from the newborn cattle. That was the best from the harvest and from the young cattle.

Firstfruits is a term used by God to refer to the progenitors of the Israelites—the best of the harvest among mankind. That is a moving thought.

Verse 10b
But they, yes, they came to Baal Peor and they devoted themselves to this shameful object.
We should probably read here *went into to Baal Peor* (in the sense of sexual contact). That is also a good translation and fits the context better, because in Baal-Peor it was about committing fornication. And that is also the theme of the book of Hosea (see also discussions about Gomer in Hosea 1).

Peor was a peak in Moab, near the mouth of the Jordan, where the sanctuary of the god of Moab was situated, called the Baal (of) Peor.

Numbers 25 describes the Israelites carrying out fornication with Moabite girls. They seduced many of the people of Israel to join in their idol worship. This sin was heavily charged to Israel and God killed twenty-four thousand of them (Numbers 25:9). This was also the first time that the Israelites served the Baals.
(Brown, 82–83; Calvijn, *Daniël* II, *Kleine Profeten* I/II, Hosea, 270)

Verse 10c
Thus they became as horrible as the object of their devotion.
Under Jeroboam II and the kings after him, Israel fell into such a heavy idolatry that they became identified with this horrible idol worship.

Verse 11a
As far as Ephraim is concerned: as a bird, its glory will fly away.
The text does not speak about Israel, but about Ephraim (Lo-Ammi*; pagans in God's eyes). So the prophecy speaks of earthly matters that have nothing to do with the future salvation of Israel.

A second fact to note is that the name change—from *Israel* to *Ephraim*—is of recent date. So we must understand *glory* to refer to events before the death of Jeroboam II. Under Jeroboam II the northern kingdom of Israel had become powerful. After his death, in 753 BC, it went quickly downhill, and in 722 the country went under. Thus the glory of Ephraim evaporated in just thirty-one years.
(Brown, 83)

Verse 11b
No birth, no pregnancy, and no more conception.
The Assyrians were a cruel people. Insurgent peoples were suppressed bloodily and treated cruelly afterward. The goal was to exterminated the rebelling nation in such a way that they disappeared as an ethnic identity. The deportation of Israel was not a peaceful journey to a new country where better times would come. It was a tough journey that led to slavery. There is no doubt that the deportation to faraway Assyria demanded many lives—pregnant women and small children would have been among the first.

Verse 12
Even if they raise their children, I will bereave them of every one; they will not grow up. Woe to them when I turn away from them.
The text seems to suggest that God Himself kills *their children*. This was not the case. The Almighty gave up His protection over the people of Israel. The Assyrians from then on had to deal with Ephraim, no longer with Israel (which means: God fights for them). And Ephraim had become a land like all the others—no longer connected to Yahweh. This is the only reason why the Assyrians were able to slaughter the population and deport those who remained.

The Almighty reveals Himself to be the first instigator (*I*) in this chain of disastrous events. However, He is not the one who executes the judgment. That, as we know, is Satan. For he will not leave any occasion unused to harm God's people, even though in doing so he indirectly carries out a judgment from God.

Incidentally, the text, *I will bereave them of every one*, does not mean that the *children* of Ephraim were killed. In the old days it was perfectly normal to sell defeated enemies as slaves, which may also be intended here.
(Wood, 206)

Verse 13a
I looked at Ephraim as I once did Tyre, which was planted in a pleasant place.
This sentence is not easy to explain. It seems that the prophet speaks about the origin of

Tyre. This brings us to the book of Ezekiel, which connects the name Tyre with the person of Satan (Lucifer) and describes his fall. God watched Lucifer with pleasure, when he had not yet fallen into sin. He rebelled against God and was therefore called Satan. In the same way, Israel fell into sin and became Ephraim.
(Weerd, *Ezechiël*, vol. 2, chap. 28)

Verse 13b
But Ephraim has to hand over his children to the manslayer.
The murderer is of course the king of Assyria. But behind him is Satan, who urges him to do his gruesome work. That is the real *manslayer*.

Verse 14
To what do You deliver them, O Yahweh? Would You give them wombs that miscarry and breasts that remain dry?
Hosea understands what will happen with Ephraim and expresses a state of shock; he is filled with terror concerning the coming judgment. Maybe he is even pleading for God to soften the judgment. Brown calls it rightly: *The prophet's prayer on behalf of the people*.
(Brown, 84; Wolff, 166–67)

Verse 15
Their whole corruption is evident from Gilgal. For there I hated them because of their sinful deeds. I will drive them out of My house. I will no longer exert Myself to love them, for all their princes are rebellious.
Gilgal was one of the two cities where the bull calves were sacrificed. It was idolatry with a pious overtones, as if it were the worship of God.
(Wood, 207)
(See Excursus 11.)

Verse 16a
Ephraim is smitten; his root is withered. They will not bear fruit.
The prophet Hosea speaks in great detail. The ten tribes of Israel are temporarily cut off from God's salvation and are now called Ephraim. That people will no longer *bear fruit*, for the living water of God's salvation has been taken away from them. That is why the root that drew its nourishment from that salvation, is *withered*.

Verse 16b
Even if they will produce children, I will kill the cherished of their womb.
Here, too, there is a poetic play on words. For the prophecy proceeds from universal salvation—the blessing of God—to personal salvation in the form of descendants.

The Almighty does not kill the children Himself. The harsh conditions in which the survivors had to live after the fall of Israel do so. God, however, emphasizes that He Himself is responsible for this. For He withholds the protection that would have saved His people from the Assyrians.

Verse 17
My God will reject them because they did not obey Him. So they will be tramps among the nations.
Verse 17 is the fulfillment of the prophecy of Leviticus 26:31–33 (NASB):

31 *"I will lay waste your cities as well and will make your sanctuaries desolate, and I will not smell your soothing aromas.*

32 *"I will make the land desolate so that your enemies who settle in it will be appalled over it.*

33 *"You, however, I will scatter among the nations and will draw out a sword after you, as your land becomes desolate and your cities become waste."*

The curse of Hosea 9:17 is still in effect to this present day. Light dawns on the horizon, however, because in our time we see that the lost tribes of Israel are being found. (See Excursus 7.)

HOSEA 10
Hebrew Text Translation

Introduction
In Hosea 10:1, 5–7, and 9–13, this chapter presents us with a number of verses that are not easy to translate. Usually, the meaning of certain words or phrases in the text are the difficulties we face. But here the problems are different.

Until several decades ago, the basic cause for textual issues was the variety of source texts. Since choices simply have to be made, different translators will choose from different options. This results in various translations and, of course, therefore, divergent commentary on those translations.

If we continue with the above line of thought and also assume the existence of a single original source text, the only logical conclusion can be that errors were made in the process of translating and/or copying. These may be incidental in nature (resulting from sloppiness, etc.), but errors may also have their origin in the specific exegesis maintained by a copyist or translator (who edited the text to give it greater clarity). Some copyists may also say that they changed the text in an attempt to restore the original. This, by the way, is a claim I have never been able to wrap my head around.

A. The Leningrad Codex
Some seventy years ago, there was no consensus on one preferred source text over the other. As such, the text that each translator or exegete preferred was decisive for his work. The existing differences between various source texts were, sadly, also understood by many translators and exegetes as an open invitation to "edit" the text themselves, which only added to the confusion.

Over the course of time, however, an increasing number of biblical scholars and theologians have abandoned such approaches. One factor that has allowed us to be more selective in choosing our source text is the discovery of ancient scrolls, particularly the so-called Dead Sea Scrolls. As a result of this shift, the authority of the Jewish Masoretic text (and in particular that of the Leningrad Codex) has increased.
(See the section titled, Which Text?, in the introduction to this book.)

B. Comparing Scripture with Scripture
The greater certainty that has been achieved with regard to the preferred source text has also opened the road for better translations. This has led to a growing consensus that the translation issues in Hosea 10 must rather be ascribed to the poetic structure of the Hebrew text. Many books on Hosea are therefore outdated in that they still follow the old view on the text.

This conclusion has significance not only for the translation of the biblical text, but also for exegesis. According to the new view, we can no longer simply add to or change words in the text, let alone reconstruct entire sentences, as scholars once did. By now it is the surrounding context that has come to be recognized as the most important factor for interpretation. Furthermore, the method of comparing Scripture with Scripture must be applied as an important tool of study. The Bible must therefore be allowed to correct itself. This is the only way to correct our translations in an authoritative manner when the poetic language of the book of Hosea surpasses our understanding.

C. Random Source Texts
In Hosea 10 we face greater differences between translations than normal. The Septuagint* and Peshitta† (both translations of disputed quality) in particular have often been used as alternative translations. This route has, unfortunately, also been followed by the NIVIHEOT. As a result, we will be paying closer attention to the translation of the Hebrew source text than we normally do.
(*The Septuagint, also known as the LXX, is a Greek translation of the Jewish Bible, the Tanakh. It dates from 250 to 100 BC.)
(†The Peshitta is a Syriac translation of the Bible. The Syriac language is a dialect of the Aramaic language, which was probably also spoken in the time of Jesus.)
(See the section titled, Which Text?, in the introduction to this book.)

D. Lofty Poetic Language
As noted, Hosea 10 is written in poetic language. For this reason, Stuart describes it as *elegantly structured*. This feature is often lost in translation. Here we seek to retain some of that poetic structure.
(Born, 63; Stuart, 158)

Verse 1 NASB
Israel is a luxuriant vine; he produces fruit for himself. The more his fruit, the more altars he made; The richer his land, the better he made the sacred pillars.

Verse 1 KJV
Israel is an empty vine, he bringeth forth fruit unto himself: according to the multitude of his fruit he hath increased the altars; according to the goodness of his land they have made goodly images.

Verse 1 NIV
Israel was a spreading vine; he brought forth fruit for himself. As his fruit increased, he built more altars; as his land prospered, he adorned his sacred stones.

Verse 1 Hebrew Interlinear Text
vine spreading Israel fruit he-brought-forth for-himself as-to-increase to-fruit-of-him he-built-more to-the-altars as-to-prosper to-land-of-him they-adorned sacred-stones

Verse 1a
vine spreading Israel
The meaning of the word *gephen* is debated. Strong reads *vine*. BHI: *empty*. Brown, Driver, and Briggs: *luxuriant* or *profuse*. The root is probably *baqaq*.* In nearly all its occurrences it has to do with *emptiness* or *to be made empty*. The KJV translates the Hebrew source text in a negative sense. This contrasts sharply with the NASB which translates in a positive sense. These differences are reflected in other translations as well.

The word *baqaq* is rare in Scripture. The translations we found include *laid waste* and/or *spoiled* (Isaiah 24:1, 3), *emptied, ruined, destroyed* (Nahum 2:2), *winnow, devastate* (Jeremiah 51:2), *empty, pour out*, and *make void* (Jeremiah 19:7). While the NIV, NASB, and Dutch NBG suggest a positive sense for Hosea 10:1, the preceding texts all have a negative sense. This was decisive for our choice. We see it as a form of *to be made empty*. That is

supported also by textual reasons. Israel was fruitful in the pass, but does not bear fruit anymore. The vine has been made empty or, to add a more violent sense, has been shaken out.
(Andersen and Freedman, 549; Rosenberg, vol. 1, 60; Reed, 67; Strong's OT, word 1238; Stuart, 156; Ward, 174)

We read: ***the vine has been shaken out***

Verse 1b
Israel fruit he-brought-forth for-himself
Shavah means *to equate, to liken, to compare* (Lamentations 2:13), *to be equal* (Isaiah 40:25), *to be alike* (Proverbs 27:15), or *to satisfy* (Esther 5:13). Here the verb means *to destine*.
(Harper, 343; McComiskey, 158–59; Strong's OT, words 7230, 7737)

We read: ***Israel destined the fruit for itself***

Verse 1c
as-to-increase to-fruit-of-him
The word *rob* can mean *increase*. A better translation is *great multitude* or *abundance* (Deuteronomy 28:47; 1 Kings 1:19).
(Garrett, 203; Mays, 137; Rosenberg, vol. 1, 60)

We read: ***when the abundance of his produce increased***

Verse 1d
he-built-more to-the-altars
The meaning of the term *rabah* is close to that of *rob* (verse 1c). The basis meaning is *to increase*. It is distinguished from *rob* by its reference to a process of change. We find the word used in the sense of *great amount, enlarge* (1 Chronicles 4:10), *abundant*, or *abundantly* (2 Chronicles 31:5, Isaiah 55:7). Here too we have a pun (*increase/abundance* versus *more/added*), which we will include in our translation.
(Mays, 137; Owens, 778; Strong's OT, word 7235)

We read: ***he added altars***

Verse 1e
as-to-prosper to-land-of-him
The verb *tob* means *to be good* or *to do good* (Numbers 10:29), *goodness*, or *well-being*, but also *to please* (Nehemiah 2:5).
(Andersen and Freedman, 547; Owens, 778; Strong's OT, word 2895)

We read: ***when his land prospered***

Verse 1f
they-adorned sacred-stones
The meaning of the term *towb* is close to that of *tob* (verse 1e). It is conditional, as emerges from Exodus 14:12 and Genesis 1:4 (*God saw that the light was good*). This applies also when it concerns a deliberation, as in Genesis 29:19 (*It is better that . . .*), or a royal order, as in Nehemiah 2:5 (*If it please the king*). The text literally means something like: *they pleased the sacred stones*. Of course, this is not a good English translation and can be improved.
(Harper, 343; Strong's OT, word 2896; Wolff, 170)

We read, second step: ***they cherished the sacred stones***

The entire sentence:
The vine has been shaken out; Israel destined the fruit for itself. When the abundance of his produce increased, he added altars. When his land prospered, they cherished the sacred stones.

Verse 2 NASB
Their heart is faithless; now they must bear their guilt. The LORD will break down their altars and destroy their sacred pillars.

Verse 2 KJV
Their heart is divided; now shall they be found faulty: he shall break down their altars, he shall spoil their images.

Verse 2 NIV
Their heart is deceitful, and now they must bear their guilt. The LORD will demolish their altars and destroy their sacred stones.

Verse 2 Hebrew Interlinear Text
he-is-deceitful heart-of-them now they-must-bear-guilt he he-will-demolish altars-of-them he-will-destroy sacred-stones-of-them

Verse 2a
he-is-deceitful heart-of-them
Here the NIVIHEOT offers an interpretation of the Hebrew text. What the text says is *chalaq*, which means *to divide* or *to be divided* (Genesis 14:15; Exodus 15:9; Joshua 13:7).
(Brown, 88; Ironside, 78; Reed, 67; Rosenberg, vol. 1, 60; Strong's OT, word 2505)

We read: *their heart is divided*

Verse 2b
now they-must-bear-guilt
This translation is just one of the available options. But the word *asham* can also mean *to be guilty* (Leviticus 4:13, 22, 27).
(Garrett, 203; Mays, 137; Strong's OT, word 816)

We read: *now they have been found guilty*

Verse 2c
he he-will-demolish altars-of-them he-will-destroy sacred-stones-of-them
Here the pronoun *he* occurs twice. Few Bible scholars reflect this in their translation, however. It is a standard construction in Hebrew for emphasizing the *He* (that is, God). There are several different options for translation here: *He, however*, or: *it is He who*, or: *He, yea, He*. We chose: *it is He* and add *yes* to *He will destroy*.
(Mays, 137; Stuart, 156; Wolff, 170)

We read: *It is He who will destroy their altars. Yes, He will destroy their holy stones*

The entire sentence:
Their heart is divided, now they have been found guilty. It is He who will destroy their altars. Yes, He will destroy their holy stones.

Verse 3 NASB
Surely now they will say, "We have no king, for we do not revere the LORD. As for the king, what can he do for us?"

Verse 3 KJV
For now they shall say, We have no king, because we feared not the LORD; what then should a king do to us?

Verse 3 NIV
Then they will say, "We have no king because we did not revere the LORD. But even if we had a king, what could he do for us?"

Verse 3 Hebrew Interlinear Text
indeed then they-will-say there-is-no king to-us because not we-revered... Yahweh but-the-king what? could-he-do for-us

Verse 3a
indeed ... because
The NIVIHEOT translates Hebrew *ki* with *indeed* and *because*. It usually introduces a causal relationship, as is the case here. By far the greatest majority of exegetes first read *for* and then *because*, which we have chosen to follow here.
(Strong's OT, word 3588)

We read: *for then they will say: there is no king given to us because*

Verse 3b
not we-revered... Yahweh
The word *yare* means *to fear, to be afraid* (Genesis 3:10; Exodus 3:6; Joshua 9:24). If we translate the term as *revered*, we fail to do full justice to the Hebrew text. Whenever the context concerns Yahweh, there is always this element of sacred fear. His greatness far surpasses our human intellectual capacities and that must be reflected in translation.
(Born, 63; Strong's OT, word 3372; Ward, 172)

We read: *we have not feared Yahweh*

The entire sentence:
For then they will say, there is no king given to us because we have not feared Yahweh. But what could a king have done for us?

Verse 4 NASB
They speak mere words, with worthless oaths they make covenants; and judgment sprouts like poisonous weeds in the furrows of the field.

Verse 4 KJV
They have spoken words, swearing falsely in making a covenant: thus judgment springeth up as hemlock in the furrows of the field.

Verse 4 NIV
They make many promises, take false oaths and make agreements; therefore lawsuits spring up like poisonous weeds in a plowed field.

Verse 4 Hebrew Interlinear Text
they-promise promises to-take-oath falsehood to-make agreement so-he-springs-up like-the-poison lawsuit in plowed-parts-of field

Verse 4a
they-promise promises

Here *dabar* is translated as *promise*, but this is an interpretation by the NIVIHEOT. The word means *to speak*, usually with a certain degree of authority. It occurs very frequently in the Bible. The basic meaning of *dabar* is *deeds* or *acts* (1 Kings 14:19, 29; 15:7). Often it has the underlying significance of issuing assignments, commands. A related concept is that of *dâbâr* (*promises*), which is translated as *commands* (Joshua 8:8), *instructions* (1 Samuel 15:13; Esther 1:12). Literally: *they command to give commands*. That is: *they issue commands by the dozens*.
(Andersen and Freedman, 547; Strong's OT, words 1696, 1697; Ward, 172; Wolff, 170)

We read: ***they issue commands by the dozens***

Verse 4b
to-take-oath falsehood to-make agreement
The underlying sense of the Hebrew here is: *they just go ahead and do whatever pleases them*. This is why we add the word *just*.

The text reads *berith*, which almost always means *covenant* (Genesis 6:18; Exodus 6:4; Leviticus 2:13). The translation *agreement* is too weak.
(Born, 64; Kidner, 93; Strong's OT, word 1285)

We read: ***swear false oaths and [just] make covenants***

The entire sentence:
They issue commands by the dozens, swear false oaths, and [just] make covenants. That is why lawsuits appear as poisonous weeds in a plowed field.

Verse 5 NASB
The inhabitants of Samaria will fear for the calf of Beth-aven. Indeed, its people will mourn for it, and its idolatrous priests will cry out over it, over its glory, since it has departed from it.

Verse 5 KJV
The inhabitants of Samaria shall fear because of the calves of Bethaven: for the people thereof shall mourn over it, and the priests thereof that rejoiced on it, for the glory thereof, because it is departed from it.

Verse 5 NIV
The people who live in Samaria fear for the calf-idol of Beth Aven. Its people will mourn over it, and so will its idolatrous priests, those who had rejoiced over its splendor, because it is taken from them into exile.

Verse 5 Hebrew Interlinear Text
for-calf-idols-of Beth Aven they-fear people-of Samaria indeed he-mourns over-him people-of-him and-idolatrous-priests-of-him over-him they-rejoiced over splendor-of-him because he-is-taken-into-exile from-him

Introduction to Verse 5a/b
The clause at the beginning of this verse is debated. Many attribute greater significance to their exegesis than they do to the literal meaning of the Hebrew source text. For that reason, they do not adopt the text as received. Unfortunately, the NIVIHEOT does this as well. Their main reason for departing from the Hebrew text is that it yields a literal translation along the lines of: *For the calf-idols hide (or dwell) among the residents (or*

inhabitants) of Samaria. Many exegetes have found such a reading unacceptable, leading them to emend the text to achieve their own aims (See NASB, KJV, and NLT: *The people of Samaria tremble in fear for their calf idol at Beth-aven, and they mourn for it*). We refuse to follow them in this.

This verse actually presents us with an example of divine irony. We will develop this in greater detail in the exegesis. For now, we will delve deeper into the Hebrew text.

Verse 5a
for-calf-idols-of Beth Aven they-fear
To translate as *they-fear* deviates from the Hebrew source text, as *guwr* means *to reside, to stay* (Leviticus 19:34; Isaiah 16:4), *to live with, to dwell* (Isaiah 11:6; 33:14; Psalms 15:1; 61:4), or *to abide*. The underlying sense of the term always has to do with sheltering or finding safe refuge. Few exegetes, however, retain the Hebrew source text. Wolff does stay quite close when he mentions *worship* as an alternative form of accompanying or dwelling with. That would be an option, even though it is not necessary here. There is no reason to not retain the Hebrew source text.
(McComiskey, 165; Strong's OT, word 1481; Wolff, 171)

We read: *for the calf-idols of Beth-Aven shelter among*

Verse 5b
people-of Samaria
The NIVIHEOT's translation is an act of desperation. The Hebrew word *shaken* does not mean *people*, but is usually translated *inhabitant, neighbor,* or *nearest neighbor*. We find the term used in that sense in Exodus 12:4; 2 Kings 4:3; Psalm 31:11; and Jeremiah 6:21.

Some translate *shaken* as *residents* (Isaiah 33:24). We prefer to adhere more closely to the Hebrew text and therefore read *inhabitants*. This does not settle the matter altogether, however. For who are those *inhabitants of Samaria*? We have found four interpretations:

1. Some (e.g., Rosenberg) think in this context of the surrounding nations. That is *an* option, but hardly the most logical one given the context.
2. A second option is to understand the word as a reference to the foreigners living in the Northern Kingdom.
3. The third option is to see in the word a reference only to the Israelites who participated in the idolatry of Gilgal and Bethel (for there were still true followers of Yahweh).
4. The fourth option is to see in this term a reference by the prophet to those "who belong to Samaria." This would make the term a poetic way to refer to the entire nation.

Explanation 4 seems the most likely choice, suiting both text and context, as well as Hosea's poetic language throughout the chapter.
(Andersen and Freedman, 555; Rosenberg, vol. 1, 61; Strong's OT, word 7934; Wolff, 171)

We read: *the inhabitants of Samaria*

Verse 5c
indeed he-mourns over-him people-of-him
Ki usually introduces a causal relationship, as is the case here. By far the greatest majority of exegetes and translators read *because, that,* or *therefore*, which is reflected in our translation as well.
(Strong's OT, word 3588)

We read: *that is why the people mourn over him*

Verse 5d
and-idolatrous-priests-of-him over-him
The content of verse 5e follows on the heels of verse 5c. Given the structure, it seems logical to assume that verse 5c (*he-mourns over-him*) is not just saying something about *people-of-him*, but pertains also to the *idolatrous priests*. For this reason, it is better to render the *vav* (NIVIHEOT: *and*) here as *just as*.
(Mays, 138)

We read: *just as his idolatrous priests do*

Verse 5e
they-rejoiced over splendor-of-him
The word *gil* is most commonly translated as *to rejoice* (1 Chronicles 16:31; Psalm 2:11). The tone it reflects is one of greater exuberance. So we prefer *to exult in*.
(Strong's OT, word 1523; Stuart, 156; Ward, 172)

We read: *they have exulted in his glory*

Verse 5f
because he-is-taken-into-exile from-him
The final two words are all too often dropped in translation. This is regrettable, since they refer back to *Samaria* (verse 5b) and as such serve to emphasize Ephraim's greatest sin. Israel's government bore responsibility for that sin, which must be reflected in our translation. We have decided to add the words *Ephraim* and *Samaria* in brackets to make the text easier to understand.
(Born, 64; Harper, 315–16; Mays, 138)

We read: *that is why he [Ephraim] is taken into exile, because of him [Samaria]*

Now the entire sentence:
For the calf-idols of Beth-Aven shelter among the inhabitants of Samaria. That is why the people mourn over him, just as his idolatrous priests do. They have exulted in his glory. That is why he [Ephraim] is taken into exile, because of him [Samaria].

Verse 6 NASB
The thing itself will be carried to Assyria as tribute to King Jareb; Ephraim will be seized with shame and Israel will be ashamed of its own counsel.

Verse 6 KJV
It shall be also carried unto Assyria for a present to king Jareb: Ephraim shall receive shame, and Israel shall be ashamed of his own counsel.

Verse 6 NIV
It will be carried to Assyria as tribute for the great king. Ephraim will be disgraced; Israel will be ashamed of its foreign alliances.

Verse 6 Hebrew Interlinear Text
also him to-Assyria he-will-be-carried tribute for-king great disgrace Ephraim he-will-take and-he-will-be-ashamed Israel of-counsel-of-him

Verse 6a
also him to-Assyria

In our estimation, verse 6a represents a separate clause. The word *to* must be interpreted in the sense of *toward (Assyria)*. Some biblical scholars read *it* for *he,* assuming the pronoun refers to the tribute. Neither syntax nor context offer compelling reasons for this reading, however.
(Born, 64; Ward, 172; Wolff, 171)

We read: *he will also go to Assyria*

Verse 6b.1
he-will-be-carried tribute for-king great
The word *yabal* means *to bring, to offer,* or *to carry off.* It rarely occurs in the Bible and often carries overtones of consecration. An example is its use in the context of offering a gift to the Most High (Psalms 68:29; 76:11) or bringing a sacrifice (Zephaniah 3:10). It is also used in the sense of bringing a person before a judge or ruler (Psalm 45:14; that too is a form of offering). In verse 6b we find the verb used in the sense of *offering* or *bringing a tribute* to favor a king. So it seems logical to translate here *offer tribute*. Interestingly, this translation finds unmistakable support in the historical facts.
(Strong's OT, word 2986)

Verse 6b.2
he-will-be-carried tribute for-king great
Yareb is often translated here as *great,* however without any proof. It nicely fits the context, which is a striking example of wishful thinking. Some understand it to be a proper name, transliterating it in their translation as *Jareb.* In support of this strange interpretation, its proponents suggest that Jareb was the family name of a renowned Assyrian king. Neither of these interpretations, however, find any support in Scripture.

The word *yareb* is found Hosea 5:13 and 10:6, but appears nowhere else in the Bible. According to Strong, it derives from *rib,* which usually means *to plead* or *to strive with,* also in that same sense of pleading (Judges 6:31; Job 23:6). Owens translates: *one who contends.* We prefer to emphasize the notion of *pleading.* As a logical consequence we have chosen to read *suppliant* instead of *great,* just as we did in Hosea 5.*
(Owens, 770, 779; Strong's OT, words 3377, 7378)
(See text translation of *Hosea 5:13d.)

We read: *he will offer tribute as a suppliant to the king*

The entire sentence:
He will also go to Assyria. He will offer tribute as a suppliant to the king and bring shame on Ephraim. Thus Israel will be ashamed of his counsel.

Verse 7 NASB
Samaria will be cut off with her king, like a stick on the surface of the water.

Verse 7 KJV
As for Samaria, her king is cut off as the foam upon the water.

Verse 7 NIV
Samaria's king will be destroyed, swept away like a twig on the surface of the waters.

Verse 7 Hebrew Interlinear Text
he-will-float-away Samaria king-of-her like-twig on surfaces-of waters
Here the NIVIHEOT departs from the Hebrew source text, but we refuse to follow. The word *qetseph* means *to foam at the mouth,* which is usually understood as *wrath* or *ire.*

Hosea draws here on the image of a waterfall. The violence of the crashing waters (= an image of the war between Israel and Assyria) produces foam (= a poetic metaphor for Israel and its king, the victims of Assyria). However, the foam breaks loose and dissolves, while the river continues unimpeded on its way (the nation of Israel "dissolves," that is, disappears, and Assyria continues on as if nothing has happened).
(Brown, 90–91; Calvijn, *Daniel* II, *Kleine Profeten* I/II, Hosea, 363–64; Rosenberg, vol. 1, 62; Strong's OT, word 7110)
(See also text translation of Hosea 7:16d.)

We read, first step:
Samaria and his king will float away like bubbling foam on the surface of the water.
The meaning of verse 7 has now become clear, although the resulting phrase sounds somewhat odd. We have therefore opted for an English expression that nicely captures the sense of the Hebrew.

We read, second step:
Samaria and his king will perish as chaff blown away by the wind.

Verse 8 NASB
Also the high places of Aven, the sin of Israel, will be destroyed; thorn and thistle will grow on their altars; then they will say to the mountains, "Cover us!" And to the hills, "Fall on us!"

Verse 8 KJV
The high places also of Aven, the sin of Israel, shall be destroyed: the thorn and the thistle shall come up on their altars; and they shall say to the mountains, Cover us; and to the hills, Fall on us.

Verse 8 NIV
The high places of wickedness will be destroyed—it is the sin of Israel. Thorns and thistles will grow up and cover their altars. Then they will say to the mountains, "Cover us!" and to the hills, "Fall on us!"

Verse 8 Hebrew Interlinear Text
and-they-will-be-destroyed high-places-of wickedness sin-of Israel thorn and-thistle he-will-grow-up over altars-of-them then-they-will-say to-the-mountains cover-us! and-to-the-hills fall! on-us

Verse 8a
and-they-will-be-destroyed high-places-of wickedness
The word *bamah* does indeed mean *high place*. This is not what we are challenging. However, it is not entirely clear whether the Hebrew source term should actually be translated. After all, it seems to be used here as a generic or placeholder name. In Ezekiel 20:29 the same thing happens. There, many translators (NIV, NASB, KJV, NRSV) and exegetes transliterate the term as *Bamah*. We, too, opt for this solution here as well.
(Strong's OT, word 1116; Ward, 174)

We read: ***the Bamahs of wickedness***

Verse 8b
sin-of Israel
This qualifier indicates that the *bamahs of wickedness* represent the greatest sin of Israel

(now called Ephraim). This is an unmistakable reference to the two sanctuaries for the worship of the golden calves in Bethel and Gilgal. Thus we read: the *sin of Israel*.

We read:
The Bamahs of wickedness*, the *sin of Israel*, will also be destroyed. Thorns and thistles will overgrow their altars. Then they will say to the mountains: Cover us! and to the hills: Fall on us!

Verse 9 NASB
From the days of Gibeah you have sinned, O Israel; there they stand! Will not the battle against the sons of iniquity overtake them in Gibeah?

Verse 9 KJV
O Israel, thou hast sinned from the days of Gibeah: there they stood: the battle in Gibeah against the children of iniquity did not overtake them.

Verse 9 NIV
"Since the days of Gibeah, you have sinned, Israel, and there you have remained. Will not war again overtake the evildoers in Gibeah?"

Verse 9 Hebrew Interlinear Text
since-days-of the-Gibeah you-sinned Israel there they-remained not she-overtook-them in-the-Gibeah war to peoples-of evil

Verse 9b
there they-remained
The word *amad* means *to stand* or *to remain standing* and has a wide application. It can also mean *to stay on* (Psalm 119:9 NIV), or *to stay forever*, in the sense of *steadfast* or *firm* (Jeremiah 46:21). It is in this final sense that the term is being used here.

This passage is probably a case of divine irony. Steadfastness is normally a positive attribute. In the present context, that would be a code of conduct for the relationship between God and His people. Here, however, it is in his sin that Israel is steadfast. For that reason, we have added the words *in that sin* in brackets.
(Mays, 142; Harper, 351–52; Strong's OT, word 5975; Ward, 174)

We read: ***they were steadfast** [in that sin]*

Verse 9c
not she-overtook-them in-the-Gibeah war to peoples-of evil
There is much debate about this part of the verse. Many consider the Hebrew source text here impossible to translate, but we do not agree. We will treat several key words and from there go on to build a sentence.

Verse 9c.1
she-overtook-them
The word *nasag* means *to surprise*. The NASB translates *nasag* in Genesis 44:4; Exodus 15:9; and Deuteronomy 19:6 as *to overtake*. However, that term also has an underlying sense of *surprise*. The present context concerns a surprise attack, as emerges also from Genesis 34:25–26 (which describes the event alluded to here). Given that the word *to ambush* captures this element of surprise well, it is the right choice.
(Garrett, 212; McComiskey, 171; Strong's OT, word 5381)

Verse 9c.2
to peoples-of evil
The word *to* can also be understood as *because of* (Stuart, et al.). Given the context, that seems like the right translation. What the NIVIHEOT offers here is actually an interpretation of the Hebrew. The text does not say *peoples-of*. The word *bənê* means *descendants, sons,* or *children*. Here the final sense applies.
(Mays, 143; McComiskey, 171; Strong's OT, word 1121; Stuart, 165; Ward, 173; Wolff, 178)

Verse 9c.1 + 9c.2
Now we combine both parts of the source text from above in a revised form:
not she-overtook-them in-the-Gibeah war because of children-of evil
The key to a proper interpretation is the Hebrew word לא, which the NIVIHEOT rightly translates as *not*. It is more or less a solemn way to introduce a rhetorical question based on a comparison with events from the past. Harper reads: *Shall not war overtake them in Gibeah?* His rendering sets us in the right direction.
(Birch, 93; Gordon, 181–83; Harper, 351–52; Kidner, 103–5; Owens, 780; Smith, 150; Strong's OT, word 3808; Stuart, 165; Wolff, 178)

We read, first step:
Will they not be ambushed as in Gibeah, a war because of the children of evil.

We read, second step:
Will they not be ambushed, as happened in Gibeah: a war because of the children of evil?

The entire sentence:
Since the days of Gibeah you have sinned, O Israel. They were steadfast [in that sin]. Will they not be ambushed, as happened in Gibeah: a war because of the children of evil?

Verse 10 NASB
When it is My desire, I will chastise them; and the peoples will be gathered against them, when they are bound for their double guilt.

Verse 10 KJV
It is in my desire that I should chastise them; and the people shall be gathered against them, when they shall bind themselves in their two furrows.

Verse 10 NIV
"When I please, I will punish them; nations will be gathered against them to put them in bonds for their double sin."

Verse 10 Hebrew Interlinear Text
when-to-please-me then-I-will-punish-them and-they-will-be-gathered against-them nations when-to-bind-them for-double-of sins-of-them

Verse 10a
when-to-please-me then-I-will-punish-them
Avvah means *desire* or *will*, not *to please*. Rosenberg reads: *with My will* or *by My will*. The *vav* introduces a causal relationship, therefore it would be better to read *so* instead of *then*.
(BHI, Hosea 10:10; Rosenberg, vol. 1, 63; Strong's OT, word 185)

We read: *It is My will, so I will punish them*

Verse 10c
when-to-bind-them
Instead of *when* we could also read *if* or drop it; it does not change the meaning.
(Garrett, 212; Mays, 143; Ward, 175)

We read: *to bind them*

Verse 10d
for-double-of
The word *shenayim* can be translated with *both* (Genesis 2:25; 3:7) or *two* (Genesis 1:16). In 2 Kings 6:10, however, it means *time and again* or *more than once or twice* (NASB), and in Nehemiah 13:20, *once or twice*.
(Strong's OT, word 8147; Ward, 173)

Verse 10e
sins-of-them
The NIVIHEOT translation *sins* actually represents an interpretation, stemming from, among other reasons, the way it emends the Hebrew source text here (McComiskey). We choose not to follow in this course, and instead stick close to the Hebrew.

The word *'ayin* means *eyes* or *sight of* (Genesis 30:41; Judges 16:28), which is also how it is translated in the Targum Jonathan and by Rashi.
(Andersen and Freedman, 566; Brown, 92; McComiskey, 173–74; Rosenberg, vol. 1, 64; Strong's OT, word 5869; Stuart, 166)

Verse 10d + 10e (as revised)
for-both-of eyes-of-them

We read: *before both their eyes*.

The entire sentence:
It is My will, so I will punish them. Then nations will be gathered against them to bind them before both their eyes.

Verse 11 NASB
Ephraim is a trained heifer that loves to thresh, but I will come over her fair neck with a yoke; I will harness Ephraim, Judah will plow, Jacob will harrow for himself.

Verse 11 KJV
And Ephraim is as an heifer that is taught, and loveth to tread out the corn; but I passed over upon her fair neck: I will make Ephraim to ride; Judah shall plow, and Jacob shall break his clods.

Verse 11 NIV
"Ephraim is a trained heifer that loves to thresh; so I will put a yoke on her fair neck. I will drive Ephraim, Judah must plow, and Jacob must break up the ground."

Verse 11 Hebrew Interlinear Text
now-Ephraim heifer one-being-trained one-loving-of to-thresh so-I I-will-put-yoke on fairness-of neck-of-her I-will-drive Ephraim he-must-plow Judah he-must-break-up-ground for-him Jacob

Verse 11a
now-Ephraim heifer (= a young cow) one-being-trained one-loving-of to-thresh
The NIVIHEOT translates *lâmad* as *trained*. This is an interpretation and goes a little too far from the Hebrew text. This root word *lâmad* means *being taught*. The form used here is *məlummāḏāh* or *must be taught*, thus referring to a certain process of teaching or instruction. Other uses of this word (Deuteronomy 4:10; Psalm 119:71, 73; Isaiah 1:17) make it clear that the instruction in question must yet take place. This process at the same time represents a binding condition for acquiring future salvation.

If we adhere closely to the Hebrew source text, we should be translating verse 11a along the following lines: *now-Ephraim heifer one-in-the-process-of-being-trained* (or: *taught*).
(Andersen and Freedman, 567; Harper, 353; Owens, 780; Strong's OT, words 157, 3925)

We read: **now Ephraim is a heifer who must be trained to like threshing.**

Verse 11b.1
so-I I-will-put-yoke on fairness-of neck-of-her
The translation here does not follow the Hebrew source text, but is an interpretation of it. We refuse to follow in this. The word *abar* means *to cross* or *to pass*. The word has a wide application in Scripture. We found it used as *to expel, to take away*, or *to banish* (1 Kings 15:12), *to pass, to proceed*, or *to go up* or *along* (Joshua 15:3; 19:12), *to pass by* (Genesis 18:3; 37:28), and also in the sense of *to put away sin*, that is, *to forgive* (2 Samuel 12:13).

For *tub* the NIVIHEOT translation *fairness* should be replaced with *the good* (Ezra 9:12) or *the best* (Genesis 45:18).

Verse 11b.2
The corrected translation of the Hebrew source text thus reads:
and I, I will pass by [or *cause to bypass*] ***the good of/for her neck***
Now it is no longer difficult to offer a more elegant translation.
(Harper, 354; McComiskey, 176; Owens, 780; Rosenberg, vol. 1, 64; Strong's OT, words 2898, 5674)

We read: **but I, yes, I will cause the good to bypass her neck**

Introduction to Verse 11c/d
I-will-drive # Ephraim he-must-plow # Judah
The most important issue for verse 11 c/d concerns the way the words *Ephraim* and *Judah* fit in with the rest. Do these names of nations go with what comes before or with what comes after? The form of the Hebrew source text suggests the latter, as in Hosea 5:9 (*Ephraim to-waste she-will-be = Ephraim will become a desolation*). The same sentence structure recurs in many other places in Scripture.

Most biblical scholars adjust the Hebrew text to suit their own exegesis. The NKJV, for instance, "solves the problem" by replacing *drive* with *plow*, which it then relates to both Judah and Ephraim. The NRSV reads: *Ephraim [will] break the ground; Judah must plow*. However, this is not translation but eisegese, and simply bypasses the actual problem. Stuart is at least consistent, both here and elsewhere. He makes a break in the text at the number sign # and like us considers *Ephraim he-must-plow* as one unit (verse 11d).
(Andersen and Freedman, 568; Born, 66; Owens, 780; Stuart, 165)

Verse 11c
I-will-drive
A translation with *drive* is interpretation. The word *rakab* usually means *to ride* or *to ride*

on (Genesis 41:43; Deuteronomy 32:13). Some read: *I will put the yoke on* or *harness them* or *put a harness on them*. Even though this is an appealing option, we found insufficient support for it.
(Calvijn, *Daniel* II, *Kleine Profeten* I/II, Hosea, 375–76; Ward, 173)

We read: ***I will drive***

Verse 11d
Ephraim he-must-plow
Charash usually means *to be silent* (Genesis 24:21; 34:5; Numbers 30:4; Judges 18:19). Sometimes it means *to plow* (Deuteronomy 22:10; Job 4:8). These are two totally unrelated definitions. The text gains in clarity when we translate the term *charash* as *to plow under*. This also has the underlying sense of *to cover* or *to make invisible*. We can also understand this word as *to plow the truth under*. Strong's concordance comments: "Figuratively, it means to make a division." From that notion (thus *secrecy* or *stealth*) came the translation *to be silent* or *mute* (this latter option in the sense of *to isolate* or *to bring to silence*). This suits the present context very well, so we have opted for it.
(Andersen and Freedman, 560; Harper, 354; McComiskey, 175; Strong's OT, words 2790, 7392; Wolff, 179)

We read: ***Ephraim will be silenced***

Verse 11e
Judah he-must-break-up-ground
The NIVIHEOT offers an interpretation of the Hebrew source text here, but that is not what the text actually says. The word *sadad* means *to plane*. Outside Hosea, it occurs only in Job 39:10 and Isaiah 28:24. It is commonly defined as *to harrow*. However, *planing* is done to something when it is uneven. *Harrowing*, on the contrary, is what you do to break up lumps with the plow. For that reason, it seems more reasonable to translate the term here as *to level*, *to even*, or *to till*. The word *harrow* does, however, adequately get at the basic significance of the Hebrew. Since the prophet is still speaking poetically and since turning to God (i.e., conversion) is a key topic in the prophetic books, we prefer the term: *to level* a debt or (in better English) *to settle* (a debt) for our translation.
(Brown, 93; Rosenberg, vol. 1, 65; Strong's OT, word 7702)

We read: ***Judah will [now] settle***

Verse 11f
for-him Jacob
Many link these words to the preceding clause, leaving us with the following translation: *Jacob will harrow for himself*. That is not what the Hebrew text says, however. Others, including Wolff, rightly understand it as a supplemental clause, but they also go on to change the source text. We refuse to do that.
(Owens, 780; Stuart, 165; Ward, 173; Wolff, 180)

We read: ***for him Jacob***

The entire sentence:
Now Ephraim is a heifer who must be trained to like threshing. But I, yes, I will cause the good to bypass her neck: I will drive [him], Ephraim will be silenced. Judah will [now] settle for him, that is Jacob.

Verse 12 NASB
Sow with a view to righteousness, reap in accordance with kindness; break up your

fallow ground, for it is time to seek the LORD until He comes to rain righteousness on you.

Verse 12 KJV
Sow to yourselves in righteousness, reap in mercy; break up your fallow ground: for it is time to seek the LORD, till he come and rain righteousness upon you.

Verse 12 NIV
"Sow righteousness for yourselves, reap the fruit of unfailing love, and break up your unplowed ground; for it is time to seek the LORD, until he comes and showers his righteousness on you."

Verse 12 Hebrew Interlinear Text
sow! for-yourselves to-righteousness reap! to-mouth-of unfailing-love break-up! of-you unplowed-ground for-time-of to-seek . . . Yahweh until he-comes and-he-showers righteousness on-you

Verse 12a
sow! for-yourselves to-righteousness reap!
These are two imperatives.
(Born, 66; McComiskey, 175; Stuart, 165)

We read: *sow in righteousness for yourself! Reap!*

Verse 12b
to-mouth-of unfailing-love
The word *peh* is debated. Strong's translates is as *mouth*. Others translate it as *wishes* (Genesis 24:57), *take into consideration, according to* (Exodus 12:5; Numbers 7:5, 7–8), or *proportional to the needs of* (Leviticus 25:16).

Checed does not mean *love*, but is indicative of forms of *goodness*. We found *pious acts, deeds of devotion* (2 Chronicles 32:32), *goodness, acts of love* or *favor, kindness* (Genesis 20:13), *favors*, and *lovingkindness* (Psalms 17:7; 33:5). Literally the text therefore reads: *according to/after the need for goodness/lovingkindness*.
(Mays, 144; Reed, 69; Rosenberg, vol. 1, 65; Strong's OT, words 2617, 6310; Wolff, 180)

We read: *according to the need of goodness*

Verse 12c
break-up! of-you unplowed-ground
Here too we have an imperative. We have chosen to follow the NIV.

We read: *break up the unplowed ground!*

Verse 12d
for-time-of to-seek . . . Yahweh
This clause does not begin with the word *for* (an interpretation, though a legitimate option) but with a *vav* (= *and*). The text thus says something like: *and time to seek Yahweh*. Often *vav* is used to introduce a subsequent event. That holds true also in this case, so we read *then*.
(Anderson and Freedman, 560; Garrett, 213; Stuart, 165–66; Wolff, 180)

We read, first step: *then time to find Yahweh*
The text is now a lot more comprehensible. Thus, in verse 12a/b/c, we find the conditions

that precede the present clause. It is strongly suggestive of a certain state of holiness that must be achieved. If that state is attained, then . . .

We read, second step: ***then comes the time to seek Yahweh***

Verse 12e
until he-comes
Owens and others use the future tense here. *Will come* and *may come* are both possible. (Brown, 94; NRSV; NTL; Owens, 780)

We read: ***that He may come***

Verse 12f
and-he-showers righteousness on-you
The final words of verse 12 present no further difficulties.

We read: ***and pour righteousness upon you***

The entire sentence:
Sow in righteousness for yourself! Reap according to the need of goodness! Break up the unplowed ground! Then comes the time to seek Yahweh, that He may come and pour righteousness upon you.

Verse 13 NASB
You have plowed wickedness, you have reaped injustice, you have eaten the fruit of lies. Because you have trusted in your way, in your numerous warriors,

Verse 13 KJV
Ye have plowed wickedness, ye have reaped iniquity; ye have eaten the fruit of lies: because thou didst trust in thy way, in the multitude of thy mighty men.

Verse 13 NIV
"But you have planted wickedness, you have reaped evil, you have eaten the fruit of deception. Because you have depended on your own strength and on your many warriors,"

Verse 13 Hebrew Interlinear Text
you-planted wickedness to-evil you-reaped you-ate fruit-of deception because you-depended on-strength-of-you on-many-of warriors-of-you

Verse 13a
you-planted wickedness to-evil you-reaped
Again we have the word *charash* (which the NIVIHEOT erroneously translates *planted*). It means *to be silent* (Genesis 24:21; Judges 18:19) or *to plow under* (Deuteronomy 22:10; Jeremiah 26:18). Yet *charash* can also mean *to cover*, in the sense of *covering up* or *concealing, keep silent* (2 Samuel 13:20; it ought to read *secretly*). Also here the meaning is *to cover sins*. Hosea uses the term poetically, making *to plow under* the right translation. (Strong's OT, word 2790)
(See also discussion above with verse 11d.)

We read: ***you plowed the wickedness under and have harvested evil***

Verse 13b
you-ate fruit-of deception

Together with the great majority of exegetes and translators we use the present perfect tense here.
(BHI, Hosea 10:13)

We read: *you have eaten the fruit of your deceit*

Verse 13c
because you-depended on-strength-of-you on-many-of warriors-of-you
The KJV here reads *way-of-you* instead of *strength-of-you*, following the Masoretic text. We opt for this reading as well. After all, the word *derek* means *way* or *path*, also in a figurative sense.

Rob means *multitude* and *gibbor* means *mighty man*. We translate: *your multitude of warriors*.
(Brown, 94; Jeffrey, 995; McComiskey, 180; Rosenberg, vol. 1, 66; Strong's OT, word 1870; Wolff, 181)

We read: *because you trusted your own way and your multitude of warriors*

The entire sentence:
You plowed the wickedness under and have harvested evil. You have eaten the fruit of your deceit, because you trusted your own way and your multitude of warriors.

Verse 14 NASB
Therefore a tumult will arise among your people, and all your fortresses will be destroyed, as Shalman destroyed Beth-arbel on the day of battle, when mothers were dashed in pieces with their children.

Verse 14 KJV
Therefore shall a tumult arise among thy people, and all thy fortresses shall be spoiled, as Shalman spoiled Betharbel in the day of battle: the mother was dashed in pieces upon her children.

Verse 14 NIV
"the roar of battle will rise against your people, so that all your fortresses will be devastated—as Shalman devastated Beth Arbel on the day of battle, when mothers were dashed to the ground with their children."

Verse 14 Hebrew Interlinear Text
and-he-will-rise battle-roar against-people-of-you and-all-of fortresses-of-you he-will-be-devastated as-to-devastate Shalman Beth Arbel on-day-of battle mother with children she-was-dashed-to-ground

Verse 14a
and-he-will-rise battle-roar
Shaon means *tumult* or *roar*. The translation *battle-roar* is therefore interpretation, even if it does come close to the actual sense of the Hebrew text. We found it translated as *roaring* (of the sea, Psalm 65:7), *noise* (Isaiah 24:8), *reveling*, *turmoil of war*, or *uproar* (Isaiah 66:6). We prefer: *turmoil of war*.
(Born, 67; Harper, 357; Owens, 780; Wolff, 181)

We read:
And there will be turmoil of war against your people, and all your fortresses will be destroyed; just as Shalman destroyed Beth-Arbel and mothers with children were dashed to the ground on the day of the battle.

Verse 15 NASB
Thus it will be done to you at Bethel because of your great wickedness. At dawn the king of Israel will be completely cut off.

Verse 15 KJV
So shall Bethel do unto you because of your great wickedness: in a morning shall the king of Israel utterly be cut off.

Verse 15 NIV
"So will it happen to you, Bethel, because your wickedness is great. When that day dawns, the king of Israel will be completely destroyed."

Verse 15 Hebrew Interlinear Text
thus he-will-happen to-you Beth El because-of wickedness-of wickedness-of-you when-the-dawn to-be-destroyed he-will-be-destroyed king-of Israel

Verse 15b
to-be-destroyed he-will-be-destroyed
This is a typical construction used for added emphasis. Mays adds *surely*, and Harper *utterly*. We prefer *surely*.

Damah means *to cease* or *to cut off*. Here we find the word twice. *Melek* (NIVIHEOT: *king*) can also be mean *kingship*.* Literally: *cease to cease kingship of Israel.* That is: *The kingship of Israel will surely cease to exist.*
(*Andersen and Freedman, 572; Harper, 359; Mays, 148; Strong's OT, words 1820, 4428)

We read:
Thus it will happen to you, O Bethel, because of your continuing wickedness. And then when the dawn comes, the kingship of Israel will surely cease to exist.

Verse 15a goes better with verse 14 than it does with verse 15b. In the definitive text we will apply this change.

Hosea 10:1–15—The corrected text:

Verse 1   *The vine has been shaken out; Israel destined the fruit for itself. When the abundance of his produce increased, he added altars. When his land prospered, they cherished the sacred stones.*

Verse 2   *Their heart is divided, now they have been found guilty. It is He who will destroy their altars. Yes, He will destroy their holy stones.*

Verse 3   *For then they will say, there is no king given to us because we have not feared Yahweh. But what could a king have done for us?*

Verse 4   *They issue commands by the dozens, swear false oaths, and [just] make covenants. That is why lawsuits appear as poisonous weeds in a plowed field.*

Verse 5   *For the calf-idols of Beth-Aven shelter among the inhabitants of Samaria. That is why the people mourn over him, just as his idolatrous priests do. They have exulted in his glory. That is why he [Ephraim] is taken into exile, because of him [Samaria].*

Verse 6   *He will also go to Assyria. He will offer tribute as a suppliant to the king and bring shame on Ephraim. Thus Israel will be ashamed of his counsel.*

Verse 7   *Samaria and his king will perish as chaff blown away by the wind.*

Verse 8   *The Bamahs of wickedness,* **the** *sin of Israel, will also be destroyed. Thorns*

	and thistles will overgrow their altars. Then they will say to the mountains: Cover us! and to the hills: Fall on us!
Verse 9	*Since the days of Gibeah you have sinned, O Israel. They were steadfast [in that sin]. Will they not be ambushed, as happened in Gibeah: a war because of the children of evil?*
Verse 10	*It is My will, so I will punish them. Then nations will be gathered against them, to bind them before both their eyes.*
Verse 11	*Now Ephraim is a heifer who must be trained to like threshing. But I, yes, I will cause the good to bypass her neck: I will drive [him], Ephraim will be silenced. Judah will [now] settle; for him, that is Jacob.*
Verse 12	*Sow in righteousness for yourself! Reap according to the need of goodness! Break up the unplowed ground! Then comes the time to seek Yahweh, that He may come and pour righteousness upon you.*
Verse 13	*You plowed the wickedness under and have harvested evil. You have eaten the fruit of your deceit, because you trusted your own way and your multitude of warriors.*
Verse 14	*There will be turmoil of war against your people, and all your fortresses will be destroyed; just as Shalman destroyed Beth-Arbel and mothers with children were dashed to the ground on the day of the battle. Thus it will happen to you, O Bethel, because of your continuing wickedness.*
Verse 15	*And then when the dawn comes, the kingship of Israel will surely cease to exist.*

HOSEA 10
Exegesis

A. Introduction
In chapter 10, we encounter few problems that could stand in the way of a clear exegesis. The translation from the Hebrew was the one thorny issue. The exegesis can therefore remain fairly limited.

This section of Hosea has been written in highly poetic language. It has the character of a lament. Hosea used quite a few unusual concepts and words to achieve his effect. We will point these out when we come across them.

The lament of chapter 10 is a sort of inventory of events. It is as if Almighty God shakes His head in bewilderment that it has come to this point with the people of Israel, which leads Him to sum up the main issues that led to the downfall of the kingdom of the Ten Tribes. This list is not presented in order to lead to correction, nor does it call for conversion so that the disaster could be averted. It is already too late for that.

The prophecy is to be viewed from the perspective of the time after the reign of Jeroboam II, thus around 755 BC (see below, verse 1b/c). Viewed from that time frame, it is on the one hand a looking back in sadness on the past. And on the other hand, the prophecy gives a view into the future (see verses 2b, 3, 6, 7). That view, however, is from a divine perspective.

B. Predictive Prophecy
Many Bible scholars do not believe in predictive prophecy. If a text clearly deals with the future, it is usually assumed that the pericope was written at a later date or that the event in question was added later by an editor. These types of exegetes are thus suggesting that these passages are frauds and deceptions. The text may give the impression that there is an unfulfilled future, but they believe that the text is merely reporting what has already happened.

In the book of Hosea we repeatedly encounter predictive prophecy. And, you guessed it, many exegetes therefore link the chapters to various, later times and periods in order to eliminate what they view as a phenomenon. They are also thus denying that the text is authentic. This gives the unsuspecting reader the impression that the book of Hosea is a fragmentary composition, a collection of writings that hang together like loose sand. Nothing could be further from the truth. The book of Hosea is a logical and ordered whole and therefore a powerful document of the counsel of God.

Disbelief in God's power and providence is not an argument that plays a decisive role in our exegesis. We can therefore simply ignore these exegetes and stick to the facts of the Hebrew original text.
(Harper, 344)

Verse 1a
The vine has been shaken out; Israel destined the fruit for itself.
The vine represents an image of God-given fertility. In this case it is an allegorical representation of the prosperity that Israel enjoyed during the reign of King Jeroboam II. However, the fruit is not intended for personal use alone. It is also given to serve fellow humans and to build God's kingdom with it.

The vine is a plant that, if there is no yield, does not serve any purpose. The wood is worthless (Ezekiel 15:2–8), only suitable for being burnt. The text in Ezekiel shows a striking parallel with the state of humanity as it must be seen through the eyes of God. We are only of value if we bear fruit. And that rule also applies to the people of Israel (John 15:5–6 NASB):

5   "I am the vine, you are the branches; he who abides in Me and I in him, he bears much fruit, for apart from Me you can do nothing.
6   "If anyone does not abide in Me, he is thrown away as a branch and dries up; and they gather them, and cast them into the fire and they are burned."

(Harper, 343; Ironside, 76–77; Kidner, 92; Smith, 148)
(See also Hosea 9:10.)

1a.1 Wine typifies blood
Pressed grapes yield wine after fermentation. The red wine refers to the (red) blood (Deuteronomy 32:14), which was offered daily in the temple (Exodus 29:40). That is why Jesus Christ uses red wine at the last supper, and we follow Him in this when we remember His death. Figuratively, the people of Israel are often represented as God's vineyard or vine (Psalm 80:8–12; Isaiah 5:1ff.). This is also very clear from Matthew 21:33–43.

1a.2 Israel no longer bears fruit
Hosea 10:1a says that the fruit of the vine has disappeared. *The vine has been shaken out*, and with it Israel/Ephraim has lost its added value, that is, its holy state. It will be clear that the text also contains a subtle reference to the new status of Israel/Ephraim, after the breaking of the Sinaitic Covenant. Ephraim/Israel is no longer bearing fruit and is therefore no longer God's people.
(Ironside, 76–77; Kidner, 92)
(See Annotation 1G; Excursus 12.)

Verse 1b/c
When the abundance of his produce increased, he added altars. When his land prospered, they cherished the sacred stones.
The prophet Hosea paints in poetic terms the time of economic prosperity during the reign of King Jeroboam II. This period is now coming to an end. We can thus conclude that the prophecy was pronounced at the end of his reign, around 755 BC, because under his son, King Zechariah, the first crises came.*

A second conclusion is that Israel had spent the fruits of its economic prosperity wrongly. The country had a large underclass that barely had any food. However, this poverty was not ended. Instead, the abundance benefited the rich and was devoted to pagan altars and gaudy buildings.
(Born, 63; Limburg, 35; Mays, 139)
(*See also verse 13b.)

Verse 2a
Their heart is divided, now they have been found guilty.
The Israelites served different idols and also, to some extent, the true God. *Their hearts* were *divided* and therefore *they* were *found guilty*. God does not tolerate rivals. He is the one and only—Yahweh.
(Ironside, 78–79; Reed, 67; Smith, 149)

Verse 2b
It is He who will destroy their altars. Yes, He will destroy their holy stones.

The judgment also comes on the *altars* and the *holy stones*. After all, these were the outward signs of idolatry in Israel. That prophecy was not fulfilled by the Assyrians, but by the pious king Josiah, as we can read in 2 Kings 23:15, 19–20 (NASB).

15 *Furthermore, the altar that was at Bethel and the high place which Jeroboam the son of Nebat, who made Israel sin, had made, even that altar and the high place he broke down. Then he demolished its stones, ground them to dust, and burned the Asherah.*
19 *Josiah also removed all the houses of the high places which were in the cities of Samaria, which the kings of Israel had made provoking the LORD; and he did to them just as he had done in Bethel.*
20 *All the priests of the high places who were there he slaughtered on the altars and burned human bones on them; then he returned to Jerusalem.*

The prophecy of Hosea 10:2 was thus fulfilled in detail.
(See Excursus 19; exegesis of verse 8a below.)

Verse 3
For then they will say, there is no king given to us because we have not feared Yahweh. But what could a king have done for us?
The opening of verse 3 speaks about something that was yet to happen. It is highly probable that this prophecy refers to the period after the downfall of Israel/Ephraim, thus after the year 722 BC, when the people no longer had a king and also no land.

The thinking of verse 3 sounds exactly like the gentiles. Collectively they believed that they had bet on the wrong horse. In retrospect, Yahweh might have been a better choice but this is immediately followed by a sigh and the thought that this choice would not have been a better solution. For who could resist the powerful Assyrians? Nobody!
(Rosenberg, vol. 1, 60; Smith, 149)

Verse 4
They issue commands by the dozens, swear false oaths, and [just] make covenants. That is why lawsuits appear as poisonous weeds in a plowed field.
The text outlines a general condition of moral degeneration, which characterized the last decades of the existence of the kingdom of Israel. The once strong government degraded to a rattlesnake's nest, where intrigues, conspiracies, and political murders made the government a lame duck with little authority. In this period the country made various alliances with Egypt or Assyria. Those were the two superpowers of that time who both set out to dominate the Middle East. Israel (the kingdom of the Ten Tribes) constantly tried to play these countries off against each other. In doing so they played a high stakes game. For oaths were sworn and broken, according to political advantage.
(Born, 64; Calvijn, *Daniel* II, *Kleine Profeten* I/II, Hosea, 292; Rashi cited by Rosenberg, vol. 1, 61)
(See Annotation 10A.)

Verse 5a
For the calf-idols of Beth-Aven shelter among the inhabitants of Samaria. That is why the people mourn over him, just as his idolatrous priests do.
The *inhabitants of Samaria* refers to all who belong to Samaria. As it was the capital of the Northern Kingdom, Israel, this refers to all inhabitants of the kingdom of the Ten Tribes.

5a.1 Sheltering the gods
This is a curious verse and, in fact, constitutes a bit of subtle irony. People shelter with

God, not the other way around. The people of Israel should have taken shelter with the true God, but they did not do so. Gentiles also assumed that they had found protection with their gods. In reality, of course, that was not the case. On the contrary, the idols depended on the people who believed in *them*. They took shelter with the people who created them. Hosea expressed this in a piece of subtle irony: *the calf-idols of Beth-Aven shelter among the inhabitants of Samaria.*

5a.2 Bethel becomes a house of evil
Bethel means *house of God*. The name *Beth-Aven* means *house of evil* or *house of idolatry*. In ancient times it was a place (probably an idolatrous sanctuary) that lay very near Bethel (Joshua 7:2). Here the same name is given to the city of Bethel, which also implies a judgment on Israel/Ephraim.

Bethel was one of the priestly cities where Jeroboam I set up images of bull calves—a self-willed religion. The people therefore *mourn* (5a) their own creations, just as the idolatrous priests did.
(Born, 64; Dee and Schoneveld, vol. 1, 84; Ward, 178)
(See Excursus 11.)

Verse 5b
They have exulted in his glory. That is why he [Ephraim] is taken into exile, because of him [Samaria].
It must have been very hurtful to the Almighty, that Israel/Ephraim left Him behind and praised the *glory* of the idols. With that the people rejected the true God and therefore the Sinaitic Covenant was broken. The direct result was the downfall of Israel/Ephraim, after which it was taken into exile.

Verse 6
He will also go to Assyria. He will offer tribute as a suppliant to the king and bring shame on Ephraim. Thus Israel will be ashamed of his counsel.
The king of Israel represented the people of Israel. That is why *he* is spoken of, while, in fact, the people are still meant, as is the case in verse 5.
(See Annotation 10A.)

Annotation 10A: The Last Kings of Israel

Hosea 10:6 speaks about the turbulent period after the reign of Jeroboam II until the downfall of Israel. During that time Israel was ravaged by bloody civil wars and conflicts with other nations. It is very likely that Hosea 10:6 refers to King Menahem. He came to power through a coup d'état, killing his predecessor king Shallum, who came to power killing king Zechariah (the last king of the house of Jehu).

To confirm his power over Israel, King Menahem bought the support of Pul, the king of Assyria, with a huge sum of money (2 Kings 15:19; *Pul* is the Babylonian name of King Tiglath-pileser III). King Menahem was a former high officer from the army of Israel and was not a king appointed by God, as was the procedure in the past. He was a criminal who threw Israel into sin and led the country to the abyss.

After Menahem died, his son Pekahiah succeeded him. He was assassinated by Pekah (a high officer from his army) who became king in his place. Pekah was assassinated by

Hoshea the son of Elah, a captain from Pekah's personal guard, who then took the throne. He was the last king of Israel.
(Born, 63; Dee and Schoneveld, vols. 1–2)

Verse 7
Samaria and his king will perish as chaff blown away by the wind.
King Menahem reigned for ten years (2 Kings 15:17). After him came Pekahiah, who was in charge for only two years (2 Kings 15:23). He was murdered by Pekah, who reigned for twenty years (2 Kings 15:27). He was followed by Hoshea, who was king for nine years (2 Kings 17:1). It was during his government that Israel perished. Nothing remained of the originally thriving kingdom—*blown away by the wind.*
(Rosenberg, vol. 1, 62)
(See Annotation 10A.)

Verse 8a
The Bamahs of wickedness, the *sin of Israel, will also be destroyed. Thorns and thistles will overgrow their altars.*
Idolatrous shrines were erected on the tops of hills and mountains. In this case the sanctuaries (called: *Bamahs of wickedness*) refer to the bull calves that Jeroboam I had built. This is evident from the description—the *sin of Israel*.

Verse 8 contains a pun. For instead of *Bamahs of wickedness*, we could transliterate the last word. Then we would read *Bamahs of Aven*. Thus this becomes a subtle reference to the idolatry of the bull calves of Bethel (verse 5a), which is therefore called Beth-Aven.
(Calvijn, *Daniel* II, *Kleine Profeten* I/II, Hosea, 296–97; Smith, 150; Wood, 209)

Verse 8b
Then they will say to the mountains: Cover us! and to the hills: Fall on us!
The prophet Hosea uses traditional words that characterize the guilt of man toward God through which he comes under judgment. For who can resist the wrath of the Almighty God? Revelation 6:16–17 (NASB) says it very clearly:

16   *And they said to the mountains and to the rocks, "Fall on us and hide us from the presence of Him who sits on the throne, and from the wrath of the Lamb;*
17   *"for the great day of their wrath has come, and who is able to stand?"*

(Calvijn, *Daniel* II, *Kleine Profeten* I/II, Hosea, 299; Ironside, 80; Reed, 69)

Excursus 19: Gilgal and Bethel

When the Assyrians entered the Northern Kingdom and destroyed it, the shrines with the golden calves in Gilgal and Bethel were spared. This was not an exceptionally friendly gesture on the part of the Assyrians but the normal course of events. It was believed at that time that gods were bound to a certain country or region. If one country defeated the other, it was thought that one's own god had won over the other. Despite the defeat, the "vanquished god" was rarely, if ever, attacked because they feared his revenge. Thus, they respected the sanctuaries of the enemy gods and rarely destroyed them.

What did happen is that people took some trophies and placed them in their own temples. The victors could then show visible proof of the superiority of their own god. In 1 Samuel 5 such an event is described.

It was not until decades later, under King Josiah of Judah, that this prophecy came to fulfillment in part. At that time, Bethel was destroyed but not Gilgal, which was probably destroyed many years later. We have no knowledge about that.
(See Excursus 11; exegesis of Hosea 9:2.)

Verse 9
Since the days of Gibeah you have sinned, O Israel. They were steadfast [in that sin]. Will they not be ambushed, as happened in Gibeah: a war because of the children of evil?
The location of *Gibeah* is uncertain. Probably it is in the Central Benjamin Plateau, where Jacob and his family lived for some years. North of it we find the town Shechem. Exegetes differ in opinion as to what is meant by the expression *days of Gibeah*. There are apparently two possibilities.

9.1 Explanation 1: Genesis 34
In this passage of the Bible we find the sad story of Dina, the daughter of Leah and Jacob, who was raped by Shechem, the son of a local prince. The sons of Jacob demanded satisfaction. After negotiations, an agreement was reached that brought both parties together. As part of the covenant, the prince agreed with the sons of Jacob that his people would be circumcised. Once the male population had been circumcised and had become defenseless, two sons of Jacob, Simeon and Levi (brothers of Dina), surprise the unsuspecting city and kill all the male inhabitants. Then they looted the city. This event is apparently seen as the first great sin of the people of Israel.

9.2 Explanation 2: Judges 19–20
These chapters also describe a rape. This time it was a concubine of a Levite who was traveling in Israel. Those found guilty of this rape came from the tribe of Benjamin. That provoked a civil war between the other eleven tribes and the tribe of Benjamin, which decimated that tribe.

9.3 The first heavy sin
Although some of exegetes quote Judges 19–20 as an explanation for verse 9, we will not go into that in any more depth. Hosea 10:9 unmistakably indicates that reference is being made to the first heavy sin in the history of the people of Israel. Based on this conclusion, Judges 19–20 would not fit. Though it was *a* big sin, earlier passages show that it certainly was not the first. So explanation 1 seems to be the logical choice. A second argument against *days of Gibeah* coming from Judges 19–20 is that this attack was not an ambush (as 20:9 testifies), but the story told in Genesis 34 does describe an ambush.

9.4 A metaphor for the downfall
In the context of the book of Hosea, the dishonorable act of Simeon and Levi, who were in this event *children of evil*, serves as a metaphor for the downfall of Israel/Ephraim. The parallels are obvious. Now Israel is the accused party and Assyria the robber. It is *a war* that is the result of the heavy sins of Israel.
(Calvijn, *Daniel* II, *Kleine Profeten* I/II, Hosea, 300–302; Mays, 143; Wood, 210)

Verse 10
It is My will, so I will punish them. Then nations will be gathered against them, to bind them before both their eyes.
The first part of verse 10 is clear. The judgment on Israel/Ephraim is fixed and executed at the time God determines.

The second part, verse 10b, is somewhat mysterious in tone. There are two options. It may be that this is just a poetic expression meaning that the people of Israel will see the judgment with their own eyes. Another explanation is that *both eyes* refers to both Judah and Israel and that they will both face their downfall. Unfortunately it is not clear which option is best.

Verse 11
Now Ephraim is a heifer who must be trained to like threshing. But I, yes, I will cause the good to bypass her neck: I will drive [him], Ephraim will be silenced. Judah will [now] settle for him, that is Jacob.
Verse 11a describes Ephraim/Israel as a stubborn heifer (a young cow) and pictures the current situation at that time. Verse 11b gives a poetic image of the learning period. Then the *good* will be *bypassed* by God (= Ephraim will cut off from salvation). In that period Ephraim will be *trained* by God—a learning time which has lasted to the present day. Verse 11c refers also to that same period in which Ephraim/Israel would disappear (*be silenced*). And verse 11c/d refers to the blessings still to come, which will be realized in the Messianic Kingdom.
(Rosenberg, vol. 1, 64; Ganah: *Sepher Haschoraschim*; Wood, 210–11)

Verse 11a
Now Ephraim is a heifer who must be trained to like threshing.
The people of *Ephraim* are typified by a rebellious heifer (see also Hosea 4:16), who must be trained to do his work. Jeremiah 31:18 (NASB) also uses the same image:

> *"I have surely heard Ephraim grieving, 'You have chastised me, and I was chastised, like an untrained calf; bring me back that I may be restored, for You are the* Lord *my God.'"*

Verse 11 is poetic in nature. A heifer is a young cow. Cows were used (in addition to the production of milk and meat) also as beast of burden and as draft animal. A young cow was often more stubborn and difficult to control than an adult animal. The prophet thus sketches an image which represents the (evil) impetuosity of Israel/Ephraim.

We should probably understand *trained* (literally *instructing*) as *to bring under the yoke* of God's law. This is further elaborated in verse 11b.

Verse 11b
But I, yes, I will cause the good to bypass her neck:
The good refers to the blessings which the Almighty had promised to the Ten Tribes (Israel/Ephraim), if they would only follow Him. In that case they would have accepted the yoke (*her neck*), namely the provisions of the covenant between God and His people. Matthew 11:29–30 (NASB) also uses the same image:

> 29 *"Take My yoke upon you and learn from Me, for I am gentle and humble in heart, and you will find rest for your souls.*
> 30 *"For My yoke is easy and My burden is light."*

Verse 11c
I will drive [him], Ephraim will be silenced.
In verse 11c God pronounces a judgment on Ephraim. The Almighty proclaims: *I will drive [him]*. That has the intent of, "I will teach you!" Ephraim (the ten tribes of the Northern Kingdom) *will* therefore *be silenced*, that is to say, disappear into oblivion, which did indeed happen. So the *teaching* has lasted now more than twenty-five hundred years.

Verse 11d
Judah will (now) settle for him,
Salvation is taken away from Ephraim (the Ten Tribes). It is now given to Judah, the remaining nation (the two tribes). It did indeed settle the debt, because under King Hezekiah the people of Judah came to repentance and the worship of God was restored (2 Chronicles 29:35c–36 NASB):

35c *Thus the service of the house of the LORD was established again.*
36 *Then Hezekiah and all the people rejoiced over what God had prepared for the people, because the thing came about suddenly.*

Thus the judgment on Judah was averted for that moment.

Verse 11d
that is Jacob.
The last words of verse 11 place this prophecy within the framework of messianic salvation. Ephraim would no longer play a role in salvation history. Jacob, the founder of the united nation of Israel, would now be represent by Judah alone. So two very different facets are at play:
1. First of all, Ephraim has to pay for his sin and in this their debt to God is being settled. After many centuries this will culminate in a future conversion. After this time, the promises of salvation will come to fulfillment.
2. The other facet of the story runs through Judah (including Benjamin), through whom would continue the progress of salvation. That would lead, centuries later, to the birth of Jesus Christ, the Messiah.

Ultimately, both lines of salvation will come together in the future Messianic Kingdom over which Jesus Christ will become king.
(Ironside, 78)

Excursus 20: No Revival in Israel

God was rejected
Under King Hezekiah a nationwide revival took place in Judah. God reacted by sending blessings to Judah and the judgment over Judah was postponed. The revival also spread to the north of Canaan by order of King Hezekiah of Judah. At that time the northern kingdom, Israel, had already gone under and most of the surviving inhabitants were sent into exile. However, a limited number of residents managed to escape the army of the Assyrians. King Hezekiah also wanted to preach the gospel to them (2 Chronicles 30:1 NASB):

1 *Now Hezekiah sent to all Israel and Judah and wrote letters also to Ephraim and Manasseh, that they should come to the house of the LORD at Jerusalem to celebrate the Passover to the LORD God of Israel.*

The objective was to bring all the people of Israel back to God (2 Chronicles 30:5–6):

5 *So they established a decree to circulate a proclamation throughout all Israel from Beersheba even to Dan, that they should come to celebrate the Passover to the LORD God of Israel at Jerusalem. For they had not celebrated it in great numbers as it was prescribed.*
6 *The couriers went throughout all Israel and Judah with the letters from the hand of the king and his princes, even according to the command of the king, saying, "O sons*

of Israel, return to the LORD *God of Abraham, Isaac and Israel, that He may return to those of you who escaped and are left from the hand of the kings of Assyria."*

But the gospel was not accepted (2 Chronicles 30:10–11):

10 *So the couriers passed from city to city through the country of Ephraim and Manasseh, and as far as Zebulun, but they laughed them to scorn and mocked them.*
11 *Nevertheless some men of Asher, Manasseh and Zebulun humbled themselves and came to Jerusalem.*

Only *some men* from the tribes of Israel humbled themselves. So the restoration of Israel did not take place. A last chance was haughtily rejected. For Israel/Ephraim now began a very long period, in which the debt to God had to be settled. That period continues until the present day and will only end when the Ten Tribes of Israel find God again.
(Calvijn, *Daniel* II, *Kleine Profeten* I/II, Hosea, 307)

Verse 12a
Sow in righteousness for yourself! Reap according to the need of goodness! Break up the unplowed ground!
With this verse, the prophecy of Hosea jumps to an indefinite future, which began after the fall of Israel/Ephraim. From that time onward, the Ten Tribes lead an invisible existence that has lasted already more than twenty-five hundred years. Hidden among the pagan peoples of this world, they are waiting for a turning of their fate.

12a.1 Guidelines for centuries of exile
For that coming period, Ephraim/Israel will be given guidelines. These form an impetus for acquiring future salvation. These counsels will accompany the Ten Tribes in the many centuries that come. In highly poetic language, the Ten Tribes are ordered to pursue *righteousness*. *Mow to the need of goodness* is an expression that refers to the harvest. It was prescribed that, when reaping, part of the harvest was to be left behind for the poor. The divine order is to no longer designate for themselves more than is necessary. The objective here is also to combat poverty. So Hosea gives basic rules for a decent society (Leviticus 19:9; 23:22; Deuteronomy 24:19, 21; Ruth 2:2).

12a.2 From purification to conversion
Verse 12a strongly gives the impression that God calls Ephraim (the ten tribes of Israel) to personal sanctification. Thus this prophecy shows strong parallels with that of Hosea 3:3 ("the waiting room of history"*) and Hosea 3:4, because those verses have the same purport. There is also a reference to a period of purification, which has already lasted more than twenty-five hundred years now.

Hosea 3 makes it unmistakably clear that there will come an end to this period of scattering. For the Ten Tribes will once again seek *Yahweh*. And when they find Him, a large part will come to repentance. Then they will return to the land of Canaan (Hosea 3:5†):

After that the children of Israel will return. Then they will seek Yahweh their God and David their king. And they will come trembling to Yahweh, and to His blessings, in the last days.

(See exegesis of *Hosea 3:3 and †Hosea 3:5.)

Verse 12b
Then comes the time to seek Yahweh,

Before the Ten Tribes may return, they will have to search for Yahweh. That is a standard expression that indicates conversion and devotion to God. It expresses a rediscovery of Yahweh, because they have lost that knowledge.
(See exegesis of Hosea 4:6.)

Verse 12c
that He may come and pour righteousness upon you.
He is Yahweh. His coming is a prophecy that will be fulfilled in the end time. At the end of the great tribulation, Yahweh will leave His heavenly temple (Isaiah 26:21) and will come back to the earth to dwell in the coming temple in Jerusalem. Ezekiel 43:2 also speaks about that time. When Yahweh arrives in Jerusalem, the Messianic Kingdom will be established—a blessed period in which God will *pour righteousness upon* Israel.

Excursus 21: The Ten Tribes Rediscovered

21.a The time to seek Yahweh
It appears that, for Ephraim, the time has come *to seek Yahweh* (Hosea 10:12b). For several decades now, tribes and peoples have been reporting that they are descendants of the ten tribes of Israel who have disappeared. And they want to go back to the promised land! Could that be coincidence? That is highly unlikely. In these events there sounds a clarion call of the Almighty, telling us that the end time is near.
(See Excursus 7; exegesis of Hosea 3:3–5.)

21.b It will happen when Yahweh returns
About the coming of Yahweh, the prophet Ezekiel writes in 43:2 (NASB):

> *And behold, the glory of the God of Israel was coming from the way of the east. And His voice was like the sound of many waters; and the earth shone with His glory.*

In Ezekiel 11:22–23 the departure of *the glory of Yahweh* (or, the glory of the Lord) is described. That prophecy was fulfilled a long time ago, shortly before the demise of the two-tribe nation of Judah. In Ezekiel 43, the prophet speaks about the glorious moment of the return of *the glory of Yahweh*. This concerns an event that has never yet taken place and will only be fulfilled in the end time. Psalm 98 (NIV) sings about that moment.

1 *Sing to the* LORD *a new song, for he has done marvelous things; his right hand and his holy arm have worked salvation for him.*
2 *The* LORD *has made his salvation known and revealed his righteousness to the nations.*
3 *He has remembered his love and his faithfulness to Israel; all the ends of the earth have seen the salvation of our God.*
4 *Shout for joy to the* LORD, *all the earth, burst into jubilant song with music;*
5 *make music to the* LORD *with the harp, with the harp and the sound of singing,*
6 *with trumpets and the blast of the ram's horn—shout for joy before the* LORD, *the King.*
7 *Let the sea resound, and everything in it, the world, and all who live in it.*
8 *Let the rivers clap their hands, let the mountains sing together for joy;*
9 *let them sing before the* LORD, *for he comes to judge the earth. He will judge the world in righteousness and the peoples with equity.*

Many exegetes believe this psalm refers to the past; however, it does not speak about Israel or just Canaan. It speaks about something happening to all the *earth* (verses 3, 4, 9), the whole *world* (verses 7, 9).

In Ezekiel 43:4–7, the prophet describes the moment when the glory of Yahweh enters the temple and fills it with its presence:

4   *And the glory of the LORD came into the house by the way of the gate facing toward the east.*
5   *And the Spirit lifted me up and brought me into the inner court; and behold, the glory of the LORD filled the house.*
6   *Then I heard one speaking to me from the house, while a man was standing beside me.*
7   *He said to me, "Son of man, this is the place of My throne and the place of the soles of My feet, where I will dwell among the sons of Israel forever."*

This passage from Ezekiel 43 is a striking example of end-time prophecy. The text can hardly be clearer, because God does not live in Israel anymore. Nowhere in the past, from the Babylonian exile to the present, has that ever been the case. Therefore, we have to read this passage as unfulfilled prophecy. With the entry of *the glory of Yahweh*, a new and blessed era begins—the Messianic Kingdom. Some call this the "world Sabbath" and that is a beautiful description. This era will, according to Revelation 20, last a thousand years. That will be a time when justice will rule on earth.
(Weerd, *Ezechiël*, vol. 1, 265–66; vol. 2, 562–63)
(See Excursus 13.)

Verse 13a
You plowed the wickedness under and have harvested evil. You have eaten the fruit of your deceit,
The prophet uses an expression reminiscent of his earlier statement: *For they sow wind and will reap a storm* (Hosea 8:7). And so it was. Society had become completely corrupt and shockingly wicked, but that was ignored: *You plowed the wickedness under.* The downfall was nothing else than *the fruit of* their own *deceit*.

Verse 13b
because you trusted your own way and your multitude of warriors.
It is certain here that the prophet Hosea has King Jeroboam II in mind. Under his rule, Israel/Ephraim became a major power in the region. After his death, it was rapidly done with the military power and greatness.

His successor, King Zechariah, reigned for only six months. In the civil war that broke out, he was murdered by Shallum (a high army officer), who was king for only one month. He too was assassinated. He was succeeded by Menahem, who had to accept submission to the Assyrian king Pul (= Tiglath-pileser III). Menahem also paid the Assyrians a great tribute to perpetuate his kingship.

Thus the military and economic power of Israel/Ephraim eroded in a very short time. From being regional powerhouse, the kingdom fell and became an insignificant factor in the region. After that, it was only a plaything of the world empires of that time—Egypt and Assyria—used to advance their aspirations.
(Dee and Schoneveld, vol. 2, 170; Mays, 148)

Verse 14a
There will be turmoil of war against your people, and all your fortresses will be destroyed; just as Shalman destroyed Beth-Arbel and mothers with children were dashed to the ground on the day of the battle.

The tenor of the text is clear. He foretells a horrible slaughter, which the Assyrians inflicted when Israel/Ephraim perished.

14a.1 Shalman Beth-Arbel
We are not sure who Shalman was or where we should look for Beth-Arbel. Some think of a Moabite king (Salamanoe), others of Shalmaneser (an Assyrian king).

Feinberg assumes that the prophecy speaks of a battle in the city of Beth-Arbel, where the army of Israel suffered the defeat of Shalmaneser V. He took on King Hoshea and captured him (2 Kings 17:3–6). In that explanation Beth-Arbel is identified with Irbid (or Irbil), a town in Galilee, which the Greeks called Arbela. However, it remains guesswork.
(Born, 67; Calvijn, *Daniel* II, *Kleine Profeten* I/II, Hosea, 312; Feinberg, *Minor Prophets*, 53; Kidner, 99; Reed, 70; Rosenberg, vol. 1, 66; Wood, 211)

Verse 14b
Thus it will happen to you, O Bethel, because of your continuing wickedness.
The ten-tribe kingdom (Israel/Ephraim) is addressed by the name of the city where its main sin was committed (the idolatry of the golden calves). Bethel means *house of God*, which was a name of honor. However, it became Beth-Aven: *house of wickedness* (verse 5a).
(Dee and Schoneveld, vol. 1, 84–85)
(See Excursus 11.)

Verse 15
And then when the dawn comes, the kingship of Israel will surely cease to exist.
The dawn is probably a poetic reference to the dawn (or coming) of God's judgment at that time: the downfall of Israel/Ephraim. That ended both the nation and the kingship.
(Reed, 70)

HOSEA 11
Hebrew Text Translation

Introduction
The eleventh chapter of Hosea unexpectedly proved to be rather difficult to translate in places, especially in verses 1, 2, 3, 4, 9, and 10. Verse 9 in particular required a lot of study and caused much headache. Given the rather unusual nature of the outcome of that study, the critical reader may be left with some questions. After all, few exegetes and translators share the view on verse 9 we propose below. It might therefore seem logical to simply follow the majority of biblical scholars as a safe and appealing choice. However, the authority of the Holy Scripture must trump such sentiments. Several key texts from other parts of Scripture offered us a clear framework that led to the following translation and exegesis. There seems to be only one good choice.

A. Not Confusing but Clear!
If we measure Hosea 11 by its many interpretations, it is a "chapter of confusion." On that one point, at least, many exegetes agree. This confusion follows first of all from the differences between the various source texts. A similarly decisive role has also been played by the exegesis defended by individual scholars. Many exegetes and translators emend the Hebrew source text at will, changing certain words or even scrapping them altogether. In some cases, this process has resulted in a totally new text.

Another way in which the text of Hosea 11 was altered is by regularly switching between different source texts. This allowed troublesome exegetical difficulties to be easily sidestepped. Even the NIVIHEOT translators (who usually base themselves on the Masoretic text) were found guilty of this. The most important factor motivating such approaches is the fact that small changes in the source text or in its interpretation can at certain points of this chapter head the exegesis in a radically different direction. With all this in mind, the role of the exegete increases in importance.

B. Read the Hebrew Text!
In our days, we can make a relatively safe choice between the various source texts. This follows from the fact that the Leningrad Codex has emerged as the most trustworthy source. The many years I have devoted to my studies have only confirmed to me this growing consensus—my confidence in the Leningrad Codex has only increased. As happens so often, a careful translation of Hosea 11 in the Leningrad text has shown the chapter to be less confusing than many claim. This is not to suggest, however, that all problems can be resolved easily. Sometimes we need to appeal to other texts in the Bible for help. This is what we call "comparing Scripture with Scripture," a long-standing and proven method that true believers use for improving their understanding of the Bible.
(See "The Literal Method" in the preface to Hosea.)

Verse 1 NASB
When Israel was a youth I loved him, and out of Egypt I called My son.

Verse 1 KJV
When Israel was a child, then I loved him, and called my son out of Egypt.

Verse 1 NIV
"When Israel was a child, I loved him, and out of Egypt I called my son."

Verse 1 Hebrew Interlinear Text
when child Israel then¹-I-loved-him and²-from-Egypt I-called to-son-of-me

Introduction to Verse 1

This sentence is not easy to translate. The unmistakable link with Matthew 2:15, which refers to the present verse, has left its mark on translation. Yet here too we must first of all allow the Hebrew source text itself to speak to us. The passage in Matthew must therefore be considered nothing more than a text referring to our verse, rather than a translation proposal in disguise.

Verse 1 begins with the word *ki* (which usually introduces a causal relationship), followed twice by a *vav* (NIVIHEOT: *then*¹ and *and*²). In this situation, the *vav* has greater significance than the word *and*, as it is usually translated. The choice we make in the translation of these words will greatly influence the interpretation. Therefore we are devoting our attention to this question in following treatment of the text.

It is clear that Hosea 11:1 relates to Hosea 9:10. There too we read about the early phase of the relationship between God and Israel. For Hosea 9:10 speaks about *the first fruits on the fig tree, her firstfruits*.

A second clue is found in Ezekiel 16. Verse 7 speaks about a passage from childhood to young womanhood (as does Hosea 11:1a). Verse 8 (NASB) then says:

> *"Then I passed by you and saw you, and behold, you were at the time for love; so I spread My skirt over you and covered your nakedness. I also swore to you and entered into a covenant with you so that you became Mine," declares the Lord* GOD.

God remembers the day of the youth of Israel, the days in Egypt—a parallel text to Hosea 11:1. So both verses have significance for our present translation, since they both refer to that early phase of the relationship between God and His people. If we therefore allow the Bible to speak for itself (comparing Scripture with Scripture), we are given clear indicators for our exegesis and translation.
(Strong's OT, word 3588; Weerd, *Ezechiël*, vol. 1, 393–94)

Verse 1a
when child Israel
The sentence thus begins with *ki*, which means *that, for, because, when*, or *then*.* The resulting causal relationship pertains to the time when Israel/Ephraim was still a youth, prior to reaching the age of maturity (maturity refers to when the nation settled in Canaan). We like to point very clear to a certain limited time and read: *at the time when*.

The Hebrew word *naar*† (translated above as *child*) has a wide range of meaning. It can mean both *child* and *young man*, albeit in the sense of the age of thirteen or so, when a child reaches puberty. That is when a boy becomes a bar mitzvah (son of the law), signifying his passage to a religious age of maturity.

Sometimes, however, the word *naar* can also mean *servant*, referring to either a young man or a young woman. Here the term clearly means *youth*.
(*Brown, Driver, and Briggs, 471; Garrett, 219; Owens, 781; Strong's OT, words *3588, †5288)

We read: ***at the time when Israel was a youth***

Verse 1b
then-I-loved-him
This clause begins with a *vav*. The *vav*'s function can simply be to connect two clauses, as is the case here. We may therefore leave it out, provided that it does not alter the meaning.
(Stuart, 173; Wolff, 190)

We read: ***I loved him***

Verse 1c
and-from-Egypt I-called
The *vav* (here translated as *and*) introduces an event following on the preceding. In such instances, we can read *then*.

The word *qara* can sometimes mean *to call*, although always with the underlying sense of *to name* (Genesis 2:19; 4:26; Ruth 1:20) or *to summon* or *convene* as in *gathering*.
(Andersen and Freedman, 577; Brown, 98; Harper, 362; Mays, 150; McComiskey, 184; Strong's OT, word 7121)

We read: ***from Egypt I called/summoned***

Verse 1d
to-son-of-me
Most exegetes read *my son*. This is not what the text says, however. For as such they forget the word *to*, which has an underlying sense of *appointing to* or *assigning* and that changes the meaning of this phrase!
(Andersen and Freedman, 577; Brown, 98; Harper, 362; Mays, 150; Wolff, 190–91)

We read: ***to be my son***

We read, first step:
When Israel was a youth, I loved him. From Egypt I called (or summoned), to be my son.
To achieve a better translation, we have replaced the comma with the pronoun *him*. We also opted for *called*, even though *summoned* likewise represents a good translation.

We read, second step:
At the time Israel was a youth, I loved him. From Egypt I called him to be my son.

Verse 2 NASB
The more they called them, the more they went from them; they kept sacrificing to the Baals and burning incense to idols.

Verse 2 KJV
As they called them, so they went from them: they sacrificed unto Baalim, and burned incense to graven images.

Verse 2 NIV
"But the more they were called, the more they went away from me. They sacrificed to the Baals and they burned incense to images."

Verse 2 Hebrew Interlinear Text
they-called to-them so they-went from-before-them to-the-Baals they-sacrificed and-to-the-images they-burned-incense

2.1 Difficult to translate?

Many biblical scholars consider verse 2 difficult or even impossible to translate. For this reason, many translators and exegetes resort to another source text for their translation. We choose not to follow them. We are convinced that the Hebrew source text offers sufficient leads for a good translation.

Verse 2a
they-called to-them
Verse 2 is usually opened with *but* or *how*. However, that is not what it says in the text. It was brought over from the Septuagint and/or the Peshitta (an ancient Syriac translation of the Bible). The opening words of verse 2 seem to be introducing a contrast or a causal relationship, since *they-called to-them* is followed by the word *ken* (*so* in verse 2b). The main question in this translation is, to whom does *them* refer. There are two parties in this verse; God and the Baals. To maintain the contrast with verse 1, it must be the Baals.
(Owens, 781; Wolff, 190–91; Wood, 213)

Verse 2b
so
The word *ken* is translated in a wide variety of ways—*so*, *thus*, *therefore*, *afterward*, and *same*. Usually it serves to introduce a cause or reason. It is used in that sense in Nehemiah 6:6 and Numbers 16:11 (NASB; KJV). We opt for *so*, but *therefore* is also a possibility. The word *them* (2a) points to the Baals. We add that between brackets for better understanding.
(Brown, 99; Owens, 781; Strong's OT, word 3651)

We read, verse 2a/b: ***they called to them*** (the Baals)***, so***

Verse 2c
they-went from-before-them
Halak means *to go* or *to walk* (also in the sense of walking in the way of the Lord; as such, it refers to a lifestyle).

What the NIVIHEOT offers here is actually an interpretation of the Hebrew source text. We do not agree. What the text literally says is: *they went/walked from their faces (countenances/presence)*. That means *away from/with their countenances*, which is another way of saying *to turn away from*. We now add *from Me* (= God), because God is still speaking and we want to maintain the true meaning of the Hebrew text.
(Andersen and Freedman, 578; Calvijn, *Daniel* II, *Kleine Profeten* I/II, Hosea, 389; Strong's OT, words 1980, 6440; Stuart, 175)

We read: ***they turned their faces away [from Me]***

Verse 2d
to-the-Baals they-sacrificed and-to-the-images they-burned-incense
This can be understood as an independent clause. We have opted to follow the NIV here. *Pasil* means *idol*, or better yet, *image* or *carved image*.
(Strong's OT, word 6456)

We read: ***They sacrificed to the Baals, and they burned incense to carved images***

The entire sentence:
They called to them (the Baals)***, so they turned their faces away [from Me]. They sacrificed to the Baals and, they burned incense to carved images.***

Verse 3 NASB
Yet it is I who taught Ephraim to walk, I took them in My arms; but they did not know that I healed them.

Verse 3 KJV
I taught Ephraim also to go, taking them by their arms; but they knew not that I healed them.

Verse 3 NIV
"It was I who taught Ephraim to walk, taking them by the arms; but they did not realize it was I who healed them."

Verse 3 Hebrew Interlinear Text
indeed-I I-taught-to-walk to-Ephraim to-take-them by arms-of-him but-not they-realized that I-healed-them

Verse 3a
indeed-I
The Hebrew source text is constructed in a way that emphasizes the *I*.
(Andersen and Freedman, 578; Stuart, 174; Wolff, 191)

We read: *it was I*

Verse 3b
I-taught-to-walk to-Ephraim
The word *ragal* does not mean *to walk* (as the NIVIHEOT reads), but *to reconnoiter* or *to spy*. This is clear from Numbers 21:32; Deuteronomy 1:24; Joshua 6:22, 25; and 14:7.

The text thus says something like: *I caused to reconnoiter*. This probably refers to a form of guidance given at a time when Israel was reaching maturity. Andersen and Freedman read: "I was a guide for," which we follow here.
(Andersen and Freedman, 579; Calvijn, *Daniel* II, *Kleine Profeten* I/II, Hosea, 391; Harper, 363; Rosenberg, vol. 1, 68; Strong's OT, word 7270)

We read: *I was a guide for Ephraim*

Verse 3c
to-take-them by arms-of-them
The first word, *laqach*, can indeed mean *to take*, although it always has the sense of *to take away* or *to deprive* (Genesis 27:35–36; 30:15; Exodus 14:11). Some translate Exodus 25:2 as *to collect*, but even there it actually means *to take away*.

Many offer the translation *to take them on my arms*, but that is not what the text actually says. The word *al* (NIVIHEOT: *by*) has a wide range of meaning. We find it used, for example, in Genesis 43:7 (*according to the tenor of these words*, KJV) and Isaiah 59:18 (*according to their deeds*, KJV). It actually carries with it the sense of *concerning* or *in accordance with*.

The word *zeroa* means *outstretched arm(s)*, almost always with an underlying significance of *power* (Exodus 6:6; 15:16; Ezekiel 20:34; 30:21), or *strength* (1 Samuel 2:31).
(Andersen and Freedman, 579; Strong's OT, words 2220, 3947, 5921; Stuart, 175; Wood, 213–13)

We read, first step: *and took away concerning arms from them*

It should now be clear that the prophet is speaking about Israel's dwindling power (in the sense of the power of its army and/or its economic power). This fits in nicely with the context, bringing some sense to the rest of verse 3.

We read, second step: *and caused their power to dwindle*

Verse 3d
but-not they-realized that I-healed-them
It seems logical to assume a link with Hosea 7:1, where the intention was announced.
(Garrett, 218; Rosenberg, vol. 1, 68; Stuart, 174)

We read: *but they did not realize that I was healing them*

The entire sentence, first step:
It was I, I was a guide for Ephraim and caused their power to dwindle. But they did not realize that I was healing them.
As said in 3a the word *'ānōkî* emphases the *I*, but also influences verse 3b and 3c, because the speaking of the Lord continues. Therefore we amend this text to come as close as possible to the source text.

The entire sentence, second step:
It was I, yes, I was a guide to Ephraim and I caused their power to dwindle. But they did not realize that I was healing them.

Verse 4 NASB
I led them with cords of a man, with bonds of love, and I became to them as one who lifts the yoke from their jaws; and I bent down and fed them.

Verse 4 KJV
I drew them with cords of a man, with bands of love: and I was to them as they that take off the yoke on their jaws, and I laid meat unto them.

Verse 4 NIV
"I led them with cords of human kindness, with ties of love. To them I was like one who lifts a little child to the cheek, and I bent down to feed them."

Verse 4 Hebrew Interlinear Text
with-cords-of human I-led-them with-ties-of love and-I-was to-them as-ones-lifting-of yoke on necks-of-them and-I-bent-down to-him I-fed

Verse 4a
with-cords-of human I-led-them
Chebel means *rope* or *cord*, and sometimes can also mean *measuring line.**
The word *adam* usually means *person* or *human*, but also *man*. Sometimes it serves as a personal name and must then be translated as *Adam*. Here *human* seems the most obvious choice.
(Strong's OT, words 120, 2256; *Stuart, 174; Wolff, 191; Wood, 213)

We read: *I led them with human cords*

Verse 4b
with-ties-of love
The word *aboth* means something along the lines of *woven*. These can be *ties* or *cords*, but also *bands*.
(Brown, 100; Strong's OT, word 5688; Wolff, 191)

We read: ***with bands of love***

Verse 4c
and-I-was to-them as-ones-lifting-of yoke
The Hebrew word *ol* is usually translated *yoke*, which immediately makes us think of a wooden beam with a curved cutout in the middle to fit the neck of an ox. This is too restrictive, however, since the word can also refer to a combination of a halter and a yoke—an oval construction to be placed over the head of an ox, resting on its neck. Attached to it is a kind of halter to guide the head. It is similar to a harness used for horses today, with a bit wedged in the animal's mouth to control it. Hosea seems to be referring to a device of this type.

A second indication is found in verse 4d, which refers to something being lifted off the head of an ox. This also points us in the direction of a harness or halter.
(Calvijn, *Daniël* II, *Kleine Profeten* I/II, Hosea, 393; Harper, 364; Rashi cited by Rosenberg, vol. 1, 69; Stuart, 174)

We read: ***I was for them as someone who the yoke***

Verse 4d
on necks-of-them
The Hebrew word *al* can be translated in widely varying ways, including *concerning*, *above*, *toward*, *from*, *above*, or *against*. Often it includes this notion of *downward*. In Genesis 7:4 the NASB translates: *I will blot out from the face of the land every living thing that I have made*. Likewise in Genesis 24:64 the NASB has: *dismounted from the camel*; others: *got down from her camel*). Here it is best translated as *to take from* (see also verse 3c).

The word *necks* is an interpretation on the part of the NIVIHEOT, because that is not what the text actually says. *Lechi* means *to be soft*. Some translators therefore opt for *cheeks*. However, from Deuteronomy 18:3; Judges 15:15–17; and 1 Kings 22:24 it is clear that it refers to both lower jaw and cheeks.
(Cheyne, 109; Kuhnigk, Hosea 11:3; Strong's OT, word 3895; Stuart, 174–75)

We read: ***takes from their lower jaw***

Verse 4e
and-I-bent-down to-him I-fed
The word *wə'aṭ* (NIVIHEOT: *and-I-bent-down*) is problematic. The Englishman's Hebrew Concordance (by Wigram) translates this as *secret*. Harper uses *gently* and suggests it meanings *to be able* or *to move softly/gentle*. Rosenberg speaks of *ability*. Buss uses *and turns to him to feed him*; Wolff, *I bent down to him to feed him*. In 1 Kings 21:27 it probably means *in penitence*. In Genesis 33:14 it is translated as *according to my gentleness* (Brown, Driver, and Briggs) or *at my leisure* (NASB). As such, it has regal overtones in the sense of showing favor.
(Buss, 22; Harper, 364; Rosenberg, vol. 1, 69; Strong's OT, word 328; Stuart, 174; Wolff, 191)

We read: ***I also inclined Myself to them and I was gentle to them***

The entire sentence:
I led them with human cords; with bands of love. I was for them as someone who takes the yoke from their lower jaw. I also inclined Myself to them and I was gentle to them.

Verse 5 NASB
They will not return to the land of Egypt; but Assyria—he will be their king because they refused to return to Me.

Verse 5 KJV
He shall not return into the land of Egypt, and the Assyrian shall be his king, because they refused to return.

Verse 5 NIV
"Will they not return to Egypt and will not Assyria rule over them because they refuse to repent?"

Verse 5 Hebrew Interlinear Text
not he-will-return to land-of Egypt and Assyria he ruler-of-him because they-refused to-repent

Verse 5a.1
not he-will-return to land-of Egypt
Lo is a key word in the prophecies of Hosea. It means *not* or *no* (as in *Lo-Ammi*, *not My people*, Hosea 1). Many exegetes and translators have problems with this reading, and prefer to follow the Septuagint which reads: *they will return to the land of Egypt.* As such, they adjust the Hebrew source text to suit their own exegesis.

Stuart proposes to read *him* instead of *not* (but that is not what it says); others read *indeed*. This latter solution seems rather odd (since the word actually has the opposite meaning!). Yet it still represents a legitimate option that we will be discussing at length in connection with verse 9. Here, however, we retain the most common meaning (*not*).

Verse 5a.2
he-will-return (*to turn to*)
The word *shuw* means *to turn to, to turn back to, to return*, and sometimes even *to reestablish*. The choice is usually determined by the context.

The first issue to consider is whether the text is referring to an actual return to the land of Egypt or a turn toward Egypt in the sense of an alliance, for example. Given the context of verse 5b, it can hardly be doubted that the prophet is referring to the subjection of Israel/Ephraim under Assyria (which also finds reflection in the rabbinic commentaries of Rosenberg and Rashi). This dependence contrasts with the preference of Israel/Ephraim for Egypt as its ally. This makes it clear that we should be translating with *turn to* here. The prophesy is pointing to former occasions when Israel made alliances with Egypt. Therefore we prefer to translate: *they will not turn again.*
(McComiskey, 188; Rosenberg, vol. 1, 69; Strong's OT, word 3808; Stuart, 174–75; Wolff, 192; Wood, 213)

We read: ***they will not turn to the land of Egypt again***

Verse 5b
and Assyria he ruler-of-him
The word *melek* is sometimes translated as *ruler*. It occurs very frequently in the Bible and almost always means *king* (Genesis 14:1; Exodus 1:8; Numbers 20:14).
(Stuart, 175; Ward, 191; Wolff, 192)

We read: ***Assyria will be their king***

Verse 5c
because they-refused to-repent
The NIVIHEOT translates *shub* as *repent*, but that is an interpretation; it is not what the text actually says. *Shub* means *to turn back* or *return* (as in verse 5a), but also *to answer*

or *react*. The text therefore says: *because they refused to turn*. The prophet Hosea uses poetic language throughout and thus establishes a linguistic connection between verse 5a and 5c. It is very likely that, what Hosea is saying, has the sense of *to repent*, which is indeed the translation some choose. We, however, prefer to adhere as closely as possible to the Hebrew source text and therefore use a synonym for *to turn*, that is, *to change*.
(Andersen and Freedman, 584–85; Born, 69; Stuart, 175)

We read: **because they refused to change**

The entire sentence, first step:
They will not turn to the land of Egypt again; Assyria will be their king, because they refused to change.
This formulation can be improved, however.

We read, second step:
They will not turn to the land of Egypt again. Because they refused to change, Assyria will be their king.

Verse 6 NASB
The sword will whirl against their cities, and will demolish their gate bars and consume them because of their counsels.

Verse 6 KJV
And the sword shall abide on his cities, and shall consume his branches, and devour them, because of their own counsels.

Verse 6 NIV
"A sword will flash in their cities; it will devour their false prophets and put an end to their plans."

Verse 6 Hebrew Interlinear Text
and-she-will-flash sword in-cities-of-him and-she-will-destroy gate-bars-of-him and-she-will-put-end to-plans-of-them

Verse 6a
and-she-will-flash sword
The word *chuwl* is difficult to translate. It means something along the lines of *to twist*, *to whirl*, or *to writhe in pain*. This gives it a rather wide range of meaning, thus the many different translations. We found *gave birth to you in pain* (Isaiah 51:2), *be in anguish* (Deuteronomy 2:25), *waited* (Judges 3:25), and *to take part in* (Judges 21:21 NASB; *to dance*, KJV). Some read *to break out*, which is also an acceptable translation. We have opted for a synonym of *to whirl/writhe*, namely *to dance about*.
(Born, 69; Brown, 101; Strong's OT, word 2342; Wolff, 192)

We read: **then shall the sword dance about in their cities**

Verse 6b
and-she-will-destroy
Kalah means *to destroy*, *to eradicate*, or *to consume* (Genesis 41:30 KJV; Exodus 32:10 KJV; Isaiah 10:18 KJV; or *waste away*, NASB).
(Strong's OT, word 3615; Stuart, 174; Ward, 191)

We read: **and shall be destroyed**

Verse 6c
gate-bars-of-them

The Hebrew word *bad* is usually translated as *poles/carriers* (Exodus 25:13–15; 25:27–28). Here the text suggests another application for the poles. One or several heavy beams were typically used for locking the great doors of the city gates when a city came under external attack. These were wedged into notches in the city walls or behind clamps, serving to barricade the gate. These beams are also referred to in Hebrew with the word *bad*. The NIVIHEOT uses the word *gate-bars*. However, this is suggestive of a metal locking mechanism, which is unlikely. For that reason, we prefer *bars* and add *of their gates* in brackets.
(Brown, 101; Owens, 781; Strong's OT, word 905; Wood, 213)

We read: **bars *[of their gates]***

Verse 6d
and-she-will-put-end to-plans-of-them

For *plans* a better translation would be *deliberations* or *counsels*, as in Psalm 5:10 (KJV).
(Rosenberg, vol. 1, 70; Strong's OT, word 4156; Stuart, 174)

We read: ***that will put an end to their deliberations***

The entire sentence:
Then shall the sword dance about in their cities, and the bars *[of their gates]* ***shall be destroyed. That will put an end to their deliberations.***

Verse 7 NASB
So My people are bent on turning from Me. Though they call them to the One on high, none at all exalts Him.

Verse 7 KJV
And my people are bent to backsliding from me: though they called them to the most High, none at all would exalt him.

Verse 7 NIV
"My people are determined to turn from me. Even though they call me God Most High, I will by no means exalt them."

Verse 7 Hebrew Interlinear Text
and-people-of-me ones-being-determined to-turning-away-from-me if-to Most-High they-call-to-him altogether not he-will-exalt-them

Verse 7a
and-people-of-me ones-being-determined

The word *tala* is very rare in the Bible. The NIVIHEOT translates it as *determined*, but we discard that as a possibility. *Tala* means something like *to put off* but also *to exclude from* in the sense of staying somewhere (*to stay with* or *reside among*). We found two texts of significance for deciding on the translation here. The first is Deuteronomy 28:66, where the NASB translates: *shall hang* (*in doubt*). The text describes a lengthy but unpleasant situation. The same is true in 2 Samuel 21:12, where NASB translates: *had hanged them*.

Here in Hosea the text refers to a kind of *residence in*, which presents a lasting state of mind. That is *to persevere in*. Stuart translates *tala'* as *to be strong* which he then interprets as *to be stubborn*. This yields almost exactly the same meaning.
(Owens, 782; Strong's OT, word 8511; Stuart, 174–75; Wolff, 192)

We read: *my people persevere in*

Verse 7b
to-turning-away-from-me
The word *meshubah* is another term that rarely occurs in the Bible. Strong lists twelve occurrences. It is found predominantly in Jeremiah (eight occurrences), where the NASB translates *faithless* and the KJV *backsliding*. Others, like the Dutch NBG translates it as *aversion*. That is also the meaning it has in Proverbs 1:32 (KJV: *turning away*; NASB: *waywardness*). *Meshubah* is related to *shuw* (verse 5a/c), which is why some opt for the translation *to turn* or *to turn away*.
(Brown, 101; Strong's OT, word 4878; Stuart, 174)

We read: *in their aversion to Me*

Verse 7c
if-to Most-High they-call-to-him
Some interpret this to read: *they call on high*. We, however, prefer to stick closer to the source text.
(Kidner, 104–6; McComiskey, 187, 189; Owens, 782)

We read: *if then they will cry to the Most High*

Verse 7d
altogether not he-will-exalt-them
Yachad means *in the same way* or *like/alike* (Deuteronomy 12:22; 15:22). In Genesis 13:6 and 22:6 (KJV) we find it translated as *together*, but also there it actually ought to be rendered as *in the same way*.

Some exegetes drop the word *not* on the grounds that it does not fit the present context. However, its inclusion need not be problematic, given that we can also construct the sentence in a question form. As such, it represents a subtle form of irony, which fits the context very well.
(Andersen and Freedman, 587; Rosenberg, vol. 1, 70; Strong's OT, words 3162. 7311; Stuart, 174)
(See "Preliminary discussion" with verse 9)

We read: *will He not raise them up in the same way?*

The entire sentence:
My people persevere in their aversion to Me. If then they will cry to the Most High, will He not raise them up in the same way?

Verse 8 NASB
How can I give you up, O Ephraim? How can I surrender you, O Israel? How can I make you like Admah? How can I treat you like Zeboiim? My heart is turned over within Me, all My compassions are kindled.

Verse 8 KJV
How shall I give thee up, Ephraim? how shall I deliver thee, Israel? how shall I make thee as Admah? how shall I set thee as Zeboim? mine heart is turned within me, my repentings are kindled together.

Verse 8 NIV
"How can I give you up, Ephraim? How can I hand you over, Israel? How can I treat

you like Admah? How can I make you like Zeboyim? My heart is changed within me; all my compassion is aroused."

Verse 8 Hebrew Interlinear Text
how? can-I-give-up-you Ephraim can-I-hand-over-you Israel how? can-I-treat-you like-Admah can-I-make-you like-Zeboiim he-is-changed within-me heart-of-me altogether they-are-aroused compassions-of-me

Verse 8a
how? can-I-give-up-you Ephraim
The word *nathan* usually means *to give to* (Genesis 3:6), *to bring to* (Genesis 42:34), *to deliver* (Exodus 5:18), or *to hand over* (Judges 15:13). These are all different forms of *passing on*. Here the text refers to God giving Israel/Ephraim into the hands of others (the enemy), that is, *to give up*.
(Born, 69; Strong's OT, word 5414; Stuart, 174; Wolff, 193)

We read: *how can I give you up, O Ephraim,*

Verse 8b
can-I-hand-over-you Israel how?
Most exegetes read *to surrender* or *to give up*, in which we follow them.
(Born, 67; Garrett, 219; Harper, 369; Mays, 150; McComiskey, 191; Ward, 191)

We read: *how can I give you up? O Israel?*

Verse 8c
can-I-treat-you like-Admah
Here once again we encounter the word *nathan*. For the sake of variety, we have chosen to translate it here as *to hand over*.
(Born, 69; Stuart, 174; Wolff, 193)

We read: *how can I hand you over like Admah*

Verse 8d
can-I-make-you like-Zeboiim
In his case we simply follow the NIVIHEOT Hebrew text.

We read: *how can I let you become as Seboim*

Verse 8e
he-is-changed within-me
Haphak means *to change* or *turned into* (Exodus 7:15) or *to turn* or *turn around* (Judges 20:41).
(Brown, 102; Born, 69; Garrett, 219; Strong's OT, word 2015)

We read: *my inside has changed*

Verse 8f
heart-of-me altogether
The NIVIHEOT reads *totally/altogether* here, but we have opted not to follow it. The word *yached* means *in the same way*, *like*, or *together* (see KJV), and only rarely *totally* or *entirely*.
(Andersen and Freedman, 574; Born, 69; Strong's OT, word 3162)

We read: *my heart like*

Verse 8g
they-are-aroused compassions-of-me

The word *kamar* has two different meanings. It can mean *to shrivel, to be grow hot*, or *to melt from the heat* (mainly from emotional heat), which confirms Lamentations 5:10, where the KJV reads *our skin was black like an oven* and the Dutch NBG has *our skin glows like an oven*. The second meaning is *to grow warm and tender* or *to be deeply stirred* (Genesis 43:30 NASB: *for he was deeply stirred over*; others: *his heart yearned for*). In 1 Kings 3:26 we find *kâmar* used in the sense of *her motherly instinct*. NASB reads there also *deeply stirred*. So, logically, the context will determine which meaning we choose. Verse 9 in the NASB opens with: *I will not execute My fierce anger*. And our translation of verse 9 is: *Shall I not carry out my burning anger?* Thus verse 8 testifies that *My* (God's) *insides have changed*; to what and how? The answer is: God's loving heart for Israel has changed to *burning anger*! The conclusion is that both His (God's) heart and His pity have shriveled. (Andersen and Freedman, 589; Harper, 369; Strong's OT, word 3648)

We read: ***my pity has shriveled***

The entire sentence:
How can I give you up, O Ephraim? How can I give you up, O Israel? How can I hand you over like Admah? How can I let you become as Seboim? My insides have changed; My heart, like My pity, has shriveled.

Verse 9 NASB
I will not execute My fierce anger; I will not destroy Ephraim again. For I am God and not man, the Holy One in your midst, and I will not come in wrath.

Verse 9 KJV
I will not execute the fierceness of mine anger, I will not return to destroy Ephraim: for I am God, and not man; the Holy One in the midst of thee: and I will not enter into the city.

Verse 9 NIV
"I will not carry out my fierce anger, nor will I devastate Ephraim again. For I am God, and not a man—the Holy One among you. I will not come against their cities."

Verse 9 Hebrew Interlinear Text
not I-will-carry-out fierceness-of anger-of-me not I-will-turn to-devastate Ephraim for God I and-not man in-among-you Holy-One and-not I-will-come in-wrath

9.1 Preliminary discussion
This verse presents us with a difficulty. While most translations reflect a reading whereby God does *not* execute His wrath, history shows that He *did*. This is something no one can contest. In 722 BC Israel/Ephraim met its downfall, and that is a simple fact. What is surprising, therefore, is how few exegetes identify this as a conundrum. And those who do, only reflect on it in passing. Among the few exceptions are Andersen and Freedman, who treat this key passage at length and also propose a defensible solution.

9.2 The consensus view
According to the consensus view, the source text must simply be read to reflect that Israel/Ephraim will not be destroyed altogether (= *rooted out*; Mays). This is why Brown observes: "Jahveh must punish, but He will not exterminate."

Some interpret the text to mean that God will not destroy Ephraim a second time (Born, Constable, Harper, McComiskey). This exegesis can also be found in several rabbinic commentaries. RaDak, for example, translates: *If I chastised them for their iniquity, I will not return upon them to destroy them completely.* As such, the prophecy would be looking into the far future, following Israel's downfall under Assyria (we have to consider that Assyria often typifies the enemy of Israel at the end time). Stuart also sees this passage in this context of eschatology.

All these interpretations, however, are forced and they do violence to the literary meaning of the Hebrew text. They also conflict with history which, at least on this point, is unequivocal.
(RaDak, 71)

9.3 A better solution

The solution to this conundrum seems to present itself in the meaning of the word לֹא (*lo = not*). If we understand the clause as a question, we get something along the lines of the following (verse 9a): *Shall I not carry out my burning wrath?* It is thus a rhetorical question, and as such it actually has an affirming significance, although still with a rather plaintive undertone. It is the expression of the divine claim: *I can do nothing else, for this is what my justice requires.* This is the road also taken by Andersen and Freedman, who express their view as follows: "A decision about this reading cannot be made with the help of grammar. The decision (leading to a choice) must be guided by the context. . . . The decision must arise from a theological expectation, and that depends on the meaning of verse 9b."
(Andersen and Freedman, 589)

In verse 9b the Almighty reminds us that he is *God and not a man*. As such, He is bound to the execution of His justice, meaning here the judgment upon Ephraim. This thesis is rooted in Numbers 23:19 (NIV), which reads:

> *God is not human, that he should lie, not a human being, that he should change his mind. Does he speak and then not act? Does he promise and not fulfill?*

(Andersen and Freedman, 590)

Also elsewhere in the Bible we also find the word *lo* used in a question form:

Amos 3:8 (NASB)
> *A lion has roared! Who will not fear? The Lord GOD has spoken! Who can but prophesy?*

Jeremiah 5:22 (NASB)
> *"'Do you not fear Me?' declares the LORD. 'Do you not tremble in My presence?'"*

Jeremiah 10:7 (NASB)
> *Who would not fear You, O King of the nations? Indeed it is Your due! For among all the wise men of the nations and in all their kingdoms, there is none like You.*

9.4 Conclusion

It therefore seems logical to conclude that we must interpret the Hebrew source text such that it confirms the judgment of God emphatically. Given the framework of God's justice, this is the only possible solution. Andersen and Freedman clearly reflect this in their translation, which reads: *I will certainly act out my burning anger. I will certainly come back to destroy Ephraim.* While this may go a little too far as an interpretation of the Hebrew, it does reflect what the text is actually getting at.
(Andersen and Freedman, 574, 589–590; Born, 69; Brown, 102; Constable, 45; Harper, 370; Holladay, Hosea 11:9; Mays, 157; McComiskey, 191–92; Rosenberg, vol. 1, 71–72; Smith, 163; Stuart, 182)

Verse 9a
not I-will-carry-out fierceness-of anger-of-me
We interpret this clause as a question (see introductory discussion to verse 9).

We read: *Shall I not carry out my burning anger?*

Verse 9b
not I-will-turn to-devastate Ephraim
Here too we interpret the clause as a question. For *turn* we could also read *turn away*, which suits the context better.
(Brown, 102; Owens, 782; Rosenberg, vol. 1, 71; Stuart, 174)
(See introductory discussion to verse 9.)

We read: *Shall I not turn away, that Ephraim may be destroyed?*

Verse 9c
for God I and-not man in-among-you Holy-One
This is simple to translate.

We read: *for I am God and not a man, the Holy One in your midst!*

Verse 9d
and-not I-will-come in-wrath
This excerpt is translated in widely different ways. The NIVIHEOT reads *wrath*, but this is probably wrong. This translation is based on only a single text, namely Jeremiah 15:8. If we were to apply the regular meaning of *wəlō'ābō bə'îr*, the text would read: *and-not I-will-come in-a-city*. However, we assume that all of verse 9 has the same grammatical structure, which is why we once again propose to read the text in question form.
(Andersen and Freedman, 591; Garrett, 228; Harper, 370; Owens, 782; McComiskey, 192–93; Rosenberg, vol. 1, 71–72; Strong's OT, words 935, 3808, and 5892; Stuart, 174–75; Wood, 215)
(See introductory discussion to verse 9.)

We read: *shall I therefore not enter a city?*

The entire sentence:
Shall I not carry out my burning anger? Shall I not turn away, that Ephraim may be destroyed? For I am God and not a man, the Holy One in your midst! Shall I therefore not enter a city?

Introduction to Verse 10

At verse 10, the Hebrew source text transitions to a new topic. It now concerns an unfulfilled future, that is, eschatology. This prophecy is about the future restoration of Israel/Ephraim, and describes events that will take place shortly before the establishment of the Messianic Kingdom.
(Harper, 371; McComiskey, 195)

Verse 10 NASB
*They will walk after the L*ORD*, He will roar like a lion; indeed He will roar and His sons will come trembling from the west.*

Verse 10 KJV
*They shall walk after the L*ORD*: he shall roar like a lion: when he shall roar, then the children shall tremble from the west.*

Verse 10 NIV
*"They will follow the L*ORD*; he will roar like a lion. When he roars, his children will come trembling from the west."*

Verse 10 Hebrew Interlinear Text
after Yahweh they-will-follow like-lion he-will-roar when he he-roars then-they-will-come-trembling children from-west

Verse 10a
after Yahweh they-will-follow
The word *'aḥărê* (NIVIHEOT: *after*; from *achar**) is related to *ochoreyn*† (as many suggest), but *ochoreyn* is quite rare in Scripture. In Daniel 2:39 and 7:6 it means *after* or *afterward*, but also *another*.‡ There it serves as a temporal indicator referring to the time after what has just been described. Also related is the Aramiac word *'āḥorên* (Daniel 4:8), which means *finally*.

The root *achar** is often translated as *after* or *afterward*. However, there are two variations on *achar*. The meaning of the second *achar* is *hind part* or *following part*.** It refers to a hidden future, that is, to subsequent developments. Many exegetes deviate from the text and read *(to go) after*. However, the term does not occur in Scripture with that meaning. Instead of *follow* we read *afterward*.
(McComiskey, 194; Rosenberg, vol. 1, 72; Strong's OT, words **310, *311, ‡312, †318)

Verse 10c
then-they-will-come-trembling children from-west
Yam means *large body of water*, *sea*, or *great sea* (Genesis 1:26, 28; Numbers 11:22) not *from-west* as the NIVIHEOT translates. The word is used frequently in the Bible. It has an underlying significance of *rushing* or *roaring*. As such, we read here a play on words between *trembling* and *like-lion he-will-roar* in verse 10b.

Usually *yam* refers to the Mediterranean Sea. Sometimes it is also translated as *west* or *westward*, but this is interpretation. The text thus speaks about a people (Ephraim) that comes from the great sea. We have chosen to translate as: *over the great sea*. In fact it could be any great sea or ocean.
(Andersen and Freedman, 592; Strong's OT, word 3220)

We read:
Afterward they will follow Yahweh. He will roar like a lion. When He roars, then the children will come trembling over the great sea.

Verse 11 NASB
They will come trembling like birds from Egypt and like doves from the land of Assyria; and I will settle them in their houses, declares the LORD.

Verse 11 KJV
They shall tremble as a bird out of Egypt, and as a dove out of the land of Assyria: and I will place them in their houses, saith the LORD.

Verse 11 NIV
"They will come from Egypt, trembling like sparrows, from Assyria, fluttering like doves. I will settle them in their homes," declares the LORD.

Verse 11 Hebrew Interlinear Text
they-will-come-trembling like-bird from-Egypt and-like-dove from-land-of Assyria and-I-will-settle-them in homes-of-them declaration-of Yahweh

We read:
They will come trembling like a bird from Egypt and like a dove from the land of Assyria. Then will I settle them in their homes; thus speaks Yahweh.

Hosea 11:1–11—The corrected text:

Verse 1   *At the time Israel was a youth, I loved him. From Egypt I called him to be my son.*

Verse 2   *They called to them, so they turned their faces away [from Me]. They sacrificed to the Baals, and they burned incense to carved images.*

Verse 3   *It was I, yes, I was a guide to Ephraim and I caused their power to dwindle. But they did not realize that I was healing them.*

Verse 4   *I led them with human cords; with bands of love. I was for them as someone who takes the yoke from their lower jaw. I also inclined Myself to them and I was gentle to them.*

Verse 5   *They will not turn to the land of Egypt again. Because they refused to change, Assyria will be their king.*

Verse 6   *Then shall the sword dance about in their cities, and the bars [of their gates] shall be destroyed. That will put an end to their deliberations.*

Verse 7   *My people persevere in their aversion to Me. If then they will cry to the Most High, will He not raise them up in the same way?*

Verse 8   *How can I give you up, O Ephraim? How can I give you up, O Israel? How can I hand you over like Admah? How can I let you become as Seboim? My insides have changed; My heart, like My pity, has shriveled.*

Verse 9   *Shall I not carry out my burning anger? Shall I not turn away, that Ephraim may be destroyed? For I am God and not a man, the Holy One in your midst! Shall I therefore not enter a city?*

Verse 10   *Afterward they will follow Yahweh. He will roar like a lion. When He roars, then the children will come trembling over the great sea.*

Verse 11   *They will come trembling like a bird from Egypt and like a dove from the land of Assyria. Then will I settle them in their homes; thus speaks Yahweh.*

HOSEA 11
Exegesis

Introduction
The book of Hosea shows that God had great sorrow over the fall of Israel and the inevitable punishment that followed. The judgment, although righteous, was postponed again and again. For a long time, God's love for His people was dominant above His righteousness. Even when it had advanced to the point that the people of Israel had turned completely away from God, His love continued. This is not only apparent from the book of Hosea. We find it on many places in the Bible, such as Ezekiel 18:23, 32 (NASB):

> *"Do I have any pleasure in the death of the wicked," declares the Lord GOD, "rather than that he should turn from his ways and live? . . . For I have no pleasure in the death of anyone who dies," declares the Lord GOD. "Therefore, repent and live."*

The kingdom of Israel/Ephraim perished. However, this was not an event that aroused God's satisfaction. It was a profoundly sad event that deeply offended God, because it affected the progress of salvation *and* damaged His love for the people of Israel.

A. The Sorrow of God
The eleventh chapter contains a lament. It is a lamentation of someone who sits beside the wreckage of a lost marriage. The bride, Israel/Ephraim, has not only run away, but is also badly tattered. Not much of her personality is left. The special thing about this lament is that the mourner is the Almighty Himself. It is the sorrow of God.
(See Excursus 16.)

B. Woman or Son?
It is striking that Israel/Ephraim is first typified as a woman: Gomer (Hosea 1:3) and also: *this woman* (Hosea 3:1) and *your mother* (Hosea 2:1; 4:5). Now the prophecy speaks of a *youth*, *him*, and *son* (not a natural son, but in the sense of a builder of a family name or of a people; see verse 1). This transition from the female to the male form runs parallel to the transition from the status of the Ten Tribes. The people first bore the name Israel, now they are called Ephraim. We may therefore conclude that Ephraim is no longer a candidate for marriage with God. Basically these people are no different from the gentiles. Only when Ephraim comes to repentance, as part of the whole people of God—thus all Israel—will it become God's bride again under the name of Israel. This has yet to happen, but we see the first signs that the time is coming closer.

C. Marriage Candidate
Incidentally, the previous consideration brings us to a fascinating thought. For if we apply it to all the peoples of this earth, then every nation that serves God would typify a woman and thus, by definition, be a kind of marriage candidate for God. A godless people, however, would then be seen as a man—a rival of God.

Verse 1
At the time Israel was a youth, I loved him. From Egypt I called him to be my son.
The story of the budding relationship between God and the people of Israel is the story of the patriarchs. Hosea describes that period with the term *youth*, which has something of

being unspoiled. The youth (Israel) grows up and at a certain point he is called to a task—Exodus 4:22–23a (NASB):

22 *"Then you shall say to Pharaoh, 'Thus says the LORD, "Israel is My son, My firstborn.*
23 *"So I said to you, 'Let My son go that he may serve Me.'"'"*

It is this text that Hosea 11:1b refers to.

1.1 God's son?

It seems strange that Israel is called the son of God, but we have a play on words here. The Hebrew word *ben* has a broad meaning. It means, in fact, *builder of a family name*. And that family can be anything, including a people, which is the case here.

So the people of Israel are invited (= elected) to fulfill a mission: to be God's people in God's own land, Canaan. Israel is called out of Egypt for that sacred task. And that calling has an underlying meaning of *giving a name, naming,* or *appointing.*
(Heyer, vol. 2, 208; Strong's OT, word 1121)

And when the *youth* (Israel) leaves Egypt and begins his life task, he becomes mature. Then comes the moment when God declares His love to Israel.

At that point, it is not only a different relationship that arises, but also a different personality. Not a relationship between God and a young man, but between God and a young woman. So it seems that with the female form (as a type of Israel), the love of Israel takes shape before God. That moving moment is described in Ezekiel 16:8 (NASB):

> *"Then I passed by you and saw you, and behold, you were at the time for love; so I spread My skirt over you and covered your nakedness. I also swore to you and entered into a covenant with you so that you became Mine," declares the Lord GOD.*

This declaration of love leads to a marriage (*you became Mine*). That is the making of the Sinaitic Covenant.
(Heyer, vol. 2, 121; Wood, 212)
(See Excursuses 10, 13.)

1.2 A second fulfillment

Except for its meaning for that time, as given above, there is a second fulfillment of this text. Hosea 1 is actually quoted in Matthew 2:15. In this second fulfillment, the prophecy refers to Jesus Christ and to His exile in Egypt, where He stayed as a child when His parents fled from King Herod. We quote Matthew 2:13–15 (NASB) in full:

13 *Now when they had gone, behold, an angel of the Lord appeared to Joseph in a dream and said, "Get up! Take the Child and His mother and flee to Egypt, and remain there until I tell you; for Herod is going to search for the Child to destroy Him."*
14 *So Joseph got up and took the Child and His mother while it was still night, and left for Egypt.*
15 *He remained there until the death of Herod. This was to fulfill what had been spoken by the Lord through the prophet: "Out of Egypt I called My Son."*

The parallels are clear. First, the people of Israel were called to be the vehicle of God's salvation. For Ezekiel 34:31 (NASB) says:

> *"As for you, My sheep, the sheep of My pasture, you are men, and I am your God," declares the Lord GOD.*

Israel was given a sacred task, but failed. Then a second Son (now with a capital S) was called—Jesus Christ, the Messiah.

As in the parable of the vineyard, someone new is called (Matthew 21:33–44) who is of a higher order than his predecessor. First the owner of the vineyard sent *slaves* (or *servants*, which is a much better translation), and in the end he sent his son. We know the fatal outcome. He was killed (as was Jesus Christ). That is why God chose a new people, which became the church of Christ.

The people of Israel could not meet God's conditions. Therefore a second Adam (= man, human) arrived—Jesus Christ. He too was called from Egypt and in this way was appointed as the new bearer of salvation. In Him God's promises of salvation would indeed come to fruition, as Paul confirms in 1 Corinthians 15:45–47 (NASB):

45 *So also it is written, "The first man, Adam, became a living soul." The last Adam became a life-giving spirit.*
46 *However, the spiritual is not first, but the natural; then the spiritual.*
47 *The first man is from the earth, earthy; the second man is from heaven.*

(Heyer, vol. 3, 105; Kidner, 92; Sherman, Ezekiel, xxx–xxxvii; Strong's NT, word 1401; Strong's OT, word 1121)
(See exegesis of Hosea 10:1.)

Verse 2a
They called to them (the Baals)***, so they turned their faces away [from Me]***.
The word *them* refers, of course, to the Baal idols. We also find a significant wordplay in this. For the true God is known as Yahweh; the *I AM WHO I AM*; the *only* true God. Pious Jews have professed this for many centuries in their morning and evening prayers. That is *the* central theme of their worship: *Shema Yisrael, Adonai Eloheinu, Adonai Echad*. We find the basis for this in Deuteronomy 6:4 (NASB): *Hear, Israel! the* LORD *is our God, the* LORD *is one!*

When *them* is then spoken of, the plural form—typifying the quantity of the many idols that Israel served—automatically stands in contrast to the *I AM*—Yahweh, the one and only!

Verse 2b
They sacrificed to the Baals, and they burned incense to carved images.
The honeymoon of the marriage between God and His people lasted only for a short time. Judges 2:10–14a (NIV) addresses this:

10 *After that [Joshua's] whole generation had been gathered to their ancestors, another generation grew up who knew neither the* LORD *nor what he had done for Israel.*
11 *Then the Israelites did evil in the eyes of the* LORD *and served the Baals.*
12 *They forsook the* LORD*, the God of their ancestors, who had brought them out of Egypt. They followed and worshiped various gods of the peoples around them. They aroused the* LORD*'s anger*
13 *because they forsook him and served Baal and the Ashtoreths.*
14 *In his anger against Israel the* LORD *gave them into the hands of raiders who plundered them.*

Nothing damages a relationship as much as the rejection of love. This theme also plays out here. The people of Israel were called to a high purpose. Yet they turned away from God

and preferred idols rather than a relationship with the Almighty. Humanly speaking, the people of Israel thus grieved Yahweh to the depths of His soul.
(Heyer, vol. 1, 70)

Verse 3a
It was I, yes, I was a guide to Ephraim
The Almighty was *a guide to Ephraim*. During their journey through the wilderness, a column of cloud or of fire went before them. Then He gave them judges and prophets to help His people stay on the right path (Hosea 7:1*):

> *Every time I wanted to heal Israel, new sins of Ephraim and crimes of Samaria were revealed.*

(Calvijn, *Daniel* II, *Kleine Profeten* I/II, Hosea, 319)
(*See exegesis of Hosea 7:1.)

Verse 3b
and I caused their power to dwindle.
The Almighty could not ignore the sinful way of life in Israel/Ephraim. It affronted His justice and therefore He had to intervene. The word *power* typifies the might of the kingdom of Jeroboam II, which had also been given by God. But Israel/Ephraim had misused that power.

During the reign of Jeroboam II, Israel became a semisuperpower in the region. The economy flourished, the army was strong, and the influence of Israel was extended far beyond its borders. With the increase of power and prosperity, sin also increased greatly. Therefore God took that power away from them. His purpose was to encourage them to repent. To teach them not to put their trust in an army or in the power of money, but in the true God of Israel.

Verse 3c
But they did not realize that I was healing them.
Israel/Ephraim, however, had strayed so far from God that they did not even understand that it was God who was punishing them. Nor that the punishment was necessary to get them back on the right path.

Verse 4
I led them with human cords; with bands of love. I was for them as someone who takes the yoke from their lower jaw. I also inclined Myself to them and I was gentle to them.
Verse 4 presents an overview of the entire history of God's people. In all those centuries past, God always tried to bind His people to Himself, to keep them on track. He did not put too heavy a yoke on His people. He took it off, as in Egypt when He liberated them from slavery. He fed His people with manna in the desert.

There is a nurturing, protective tone in Hosea 11:4. It is the love of God for His people that we get a taste of here. Verse 4 echoes Deuteronomy 30:11–20 (NIV):

11 *Now what I am commanding you today is not too difficult for you or beyond your reach.*
12 *It is not up in heaven, so that you have to ask, "Who will ascend into heaven to get it and proclaim it to us so we may obey it?"*
13 *Nor is it beyond the sea, so that you have to ask, "Who will cross the sea to get it and proclaim it to us so we may obey it?"*
14 *No, the word is very near you; it is in your mouth and in your heart so you may obey it.*

15 *See, I set before you today life and prosperity, death and destruction.*
16 *For I command you today to love the LORD your God, to walk in obedience to him, and to keep his commands, decrees and laws; then you will live and increase, and the LORD your God will bless you in the land you are entering to possess.*
17 *But if your heart turns away and you are not obedient, and if you are drawn away to bow down to other gods and worship them,*
18 *I declare to you this day that you will certainly be destroyed. You will not live long in the land you are crossing the Jordan to enter and possess.*
19 *This day I call the heavens and the earth as witnesses against you that I have set before you life and death, blessings and curses. Now choose life, so that you and your children may live*
20 *and that you may love the LORD your God, listen to his voice, and hold fast to him. For the LORD is your life, and he will give you many years in the land he swore to give to your fathers, Abraham, Isaac and Jacob.*

This song is about the rules God gave them, to help them know how to live with the Him, rules of salvation which are not given exclusive to Israel. It calls to Christians as well. However, our promise is a heavenly land. In that sense we are descendants of Abraham too, a branch grafted into the tree of salvation (Romans 11).
(Calvijn, *Daniel* II, *Kleine Profeten* I/II, Hosea, 320–22; Heyer, vol. 1, 70)

Verse 5
They will not turn to the land of Egypt again. Because they refused to change, Assyria will be their king.
After King Jeroboam II, Israel's power quickly vanished. Already, under Menahem, they paid tribute to Assyria (2 Kings 15:19). In the time that was left until the judgment fell, Israel/Ephraim did not come to repentance. Therefore, they were given into the hands of the king of Assyria.

Israel/Ephraim constantly tried to play the great powers of that time, Egypt and Assyria, against one another. Assyria was the more powerful one, so they sought support from Egypt in an attempt to prevent the upper hand in the region to pass entirely over to Assyria. But that opportunity came to an end. Egypt was no longer an option; *Assyria will be their king.*

Verse 6
Then shall the sword dance about in their cities, and the bars [of their gates] **shall be destroyed. That will put an end to their deliberations.**
This verse speaks for itself. It is a reference to the terrible way in which the Assyrians wreaked havoc in Israel/Ephraim, as has already been discussed extensively.
(Calvijn, *Daniel* II, *Kleine Profeten* I/II, Hosea, 322–23)

Verse 7
My people persevere in their aversion to Me. If then they will cry to the Most High, will He not raise them up in the same way?
Here we find a piece of divine irony.* For with the coming of the divine judgment, which was performed by the Assyrians, Israel/Ephraim called (at their wits' end) upon the true God. However, it was too late, and so God did to them according to their behavior; in accordance with *their aversion to Me.*
(Calvijn, *Daniel* II, *Kleine Profeten* I/II, Hosea, 325–27)
(*See also Genesis 40:13, where *lift up/raise up* is used in the same sense.)

Verse 8a

How can I give you up, O Ephraim? How can I give you up, O Israel? How can I hand you over like Admah? How can I let you become as Seboim?

Admah and Seboim were two cities who perished in the destruction of Sodom and Gomorrah (Genesis 19). They are mentioned in Deuteronomy 29:22–24 (NIV):

22 *Your children who follow you in later generations and foreigners who come from distant lands will see the calamities that have fallen on the land and the diseases with which the LORD has afflicted it.*
23 *The whole land will be a burning waste of salt and sulfur—nothing planted, nothing sprouting, no vegetation growing on it. It will be like the destruction of Sodom and Gomorrah, Admah and Zeboyim, which the LORD overthrew in fierce anger.*
24 *All the nations will ask: "Why has the LORD done this to this land? Why this fierce, burning anger?"*

8a.1 Covenant versus justice, a quandary!
God has an obligation to Himself to give up Ephraim. That demands His justice, but with that He also gives up Israel (as a whole). For without Ephraim (the Ten Tribes) the prophecies about the Messianic Kingdom cannot be fulfilled. For that, it takes all twelve tribes.

So here the covenant that God made with Abraham stands, in terms of purpose, diametrically opposed to the demand for righteousness. The covenant promise can be fulfilled only if Ephraim becomes God's people again, since all twelve tribes are needed for that. However, divine justice demands judgment. This is a dilemma that must have given the Eternal great sorrow.

Verse 8b

My insides have changed; My heart, like My pity, has shriveled.

The love that Almighty God has for Israel/Ephraim *has shriveled*. His mind has *changed*. He has now become a God of vengeance. That is what His justice requires, but He does so with a bleeding heart. This is evident from the tone of Hosea 11. That emotion is also evident from the book of Jeremiah where it is confirmed again that the story of Ephraim is not finished yet. There is still an unfulfilled future and great promises of salvation—Jeremiah 31:20 (NASB):

"Is Ephraim My dear son? Is he a delightful child? Indeed, as often as I have spoken against him, I certainly still remember him; therefore My heart yearns for him; I will surely have mercy on him," declares the LORD.

(Heyer, vol. 1, 74)

Verse 9

Shall I not carry out my burning anger? Shall I not turn away, that Ephraim may be destroyed? For I am God and not a man, the Holy One in your midst! Shall I therefore not enter a city?

The lament about Ephraim/Israel is continued in verse 9. Here too it is apparent how much God grieves about the coming judgment; about the inevitable fall of the kingdom of the Ten Tribes. And again the Almighty points to His own divinity. It demands justice, because God is a law unto Himself. That is why the judgment on the people of Ephraim can no longer be averted.

Introduction to verses 10 and 11

The last two verses of Hosea 11 contain promises of salvation. However, these have a sad undertone. It starts with the word *afterward* (verse 10), with which the prophecy takes a big step toward the future. This means that there will be no turn for the better in the prophet Hosea's time. There would come a long period of time when Israel/Ephraim, as a people, would separated from God. That period has already lasted more than twenty-five hundred years today. There will be a moment however, perhaps not so far from now, when Israel/Ephraim will come to know Yahweh again—Ephraim will rediscover Him.

The lack of knowledge causes fear
When the future salvation arrives (also for us still future), there will be no great jubilation. The miracle of the return, the renewed acquaintance with Yahweh as their God, will put a spirit of great fear on Israel/Ephraim, because the text speaks of *trembling*. We also read this in Jeremiah 31:9 (NASB):

> *"With weeping they will come, and by supplication I will lead them; I will make them walk by streams of waters, on a straight path in which they will not stumble; For I am a father to Israel, and Ephraim is My firstborn."*

The texts from Hosea and Jeremiah make it clear that those future events will take the exiles by surprise. They will certainly not be prepared, when in the end time the Almighty will roar like a lion (Hosea 11:10), when the Holy One of Israel will deal with His enemies. Only later, when the vanished Ten Tribes are also incorporated into the Messianic Kingdom and are fighting alongside the Messiah, will the joy of meeting with God sound again—Zechariah 10:7–9 (NASB):

7   *"Ephraim will be like a mighty man, and their heart will be glad as if from wine; Indeed, their children will see it and be glad, their heart will rejoice in the LORD.*
8   *"I will whistle for them to gather them together, for I have redeemed them; and they will be as numerous as they were before.*
9   *"When I scatter them among the peoples, they will remember Me in far countries, and they with their children will live and come back."*

Verse 10a
Afterward they will follow Yahweh. He will roar like a lion.
With the word *afterward*, the prophecy takes a huge step forward in time. Because we now end up in an unfulfilled future, also for us, in the end time. For the world has not yet come to know Yahweh as a roaring lion. It is going to happen, because it is foretold by the prophets. It will occur shortly before the establishment of the Messianic Kingdom, when the Almighty God deals with His enemies. Amos 1:2 speaks about this, as well as Joel 3:16 (NASB):

14 *Multitudes, multitudes in the valley of decision!* For the day of the LORD is near in the valley of decision.*
15 *The sun and moon grow dark and the stars lose their brightness.[†]*
16 *The LORD roars from Zion and utters His voice from Jerusalem, and the heavens and the earth tremble. But the LORD is a refuge for His people and a stronghold to the sons of Israel.[‡]*
17 *Then you will know that I am the LORD your God, dwelling in Zion, My holy mountain.** So Jerusalem will be holy, and strangers will pass through it no more.[††]*

*See also Ezekiel 38–39; Zechariah 14 on the battle of Armageddon.
†A clear picture of God's judgment in the great tribulation
‡See Isaiah 4:5–6: *for over all the glory* [Jerusalem] *will be a canopy* [a protective shield]
**The Lord will dwell on Zion, in the temple in Jerusalem.
††Never again will the people of Israel have to face enemies. It will be peace for a thousand years—the Messianic Kingdom (Revelation 20:1–6).

Jeremiah 25:30–31 (NASB):
30 *"Therefore you shall prophesy against them all these words, and you shall say to them, 'The* LORD *will roar from on high and utter His voice from His holy habitation; He will roar mightily against His fold. He will shout like those who tread the grapes, against all the inhabitants of the earth.*
31 *"'A clamor has come to the end of the earth, because the* LORD *has a controversy with the nations. He is entering into judgment with all flesh;* as for the wicked, He has given them to the sword,†' declares the* LORD*."*

*All inhabitants of the earth will fall under God's judgment.
†For those who will remain evil and wicked there will be no mercy.

Luke 23:29–31 (NASB) also prophesies about the roar of Yahweh. Although this text looks initially at the Jewish war in 67–70 AD, this prophecy also reaches forward to its final fulfillment at the end of time.

29 *"For behold, the days are coming when they will say, 'Blessed are the barren, and the wombs that never bore, and the breasts that never nursed.'*
30 *"Then they will begin to say to the mountains, 'Fall on us,' and to the hills, 'Cover us.'*
31 *"For if they do these things when the tree is green, what will happen when it is dry?"*

Verse 10b
When He roars, then the children will come trembling over the great sea.
The foretold vengeance of our God is still unfulfilled prophecy, yet to happen in the end time. We also receive here an introduction to the definitive return of the lost ten tribes of Israel.

Isaiah 43:5 (NASB)
"Do not fear, for I am with you; I will bring your offspring from the east, and gather you from the west."

Isaiah 49:12 (NASB)
"Behold, these will come from afar; and lo, these will come from the north and from the west, and these from the land of Sinim [= China]*."*

The last words of verse 10 lift a tip of the veil of the future. The descendants (*children* of Ephraim/Israel) will come *over the great sea* to Canaan.
(See Excursuses 7, 13.)

Verse 11a
They will come trembling like a bird from Egypt and like a dove from the land of Assyria.
The land of Canaan was on the route that migratory birds took when they went from the north to the south or from the south to the north. It was precisely there that they rested from their long journey, hence the word *trembling* (from fatigue).

The parallel is clear. Israel/Ephraim is also engaged in a long trek through history. Like the migratory birds, they are on their way to a better country (the prosperous future). They too will tremble; not only from fatigue, but also because they will know Yahweh again. That will be an acquaintance that does not just happen automatically. Because they cannot just undo their centuries-long isolation from God. To approach God is to taste His holiness. That will be both a joyful and an awe-inspiring reunion—far beyond our understanding.

Verse 11b
Then will I make them settle in their houses; thus speaks Yahweh.
Chapter 11 closes with the promise that once again Israel will settle in the land of Canaan. Reed rightly calls it *the day of the messianic promise*. The prophet Jeremiah speaks about this in chapter 32:37–42 (NASB):

37 *"Behold, I will gather them out of all the lands to which I have driven them in My anger, in My wrath and in great indignation; and I will bring them back to this place and make them dwell in safety.*
38 *"They shall be My people, and I will be their God;*
39 *"and I will give them one heart and one way, that they may fear Me always, for their own good and for the good of their children after them.*
40 *"I will make an everlasting covenant with them that I will not turn away from them, to do them good; and I will put the fear of Me in their hearts so that they will not turn away from Me.*
41 *"I will rejoice over them to do them good and will faithfully plant them in this land with all My heart and with all My soul.*
42 *"For thus says the* LORD, *'Just as I brought all this great disaster on this people, so I am going to bring on them all the good that I am promising them.'"*

(Reed, 73)

HOSEA 12
Hebrew Text Translation

Introduction
The introduction to chapter 11 could also serve as an introduction to Hosea 12. For if we were to set various translations alongside each other and to consult a number of commentaries, we would find ourselves in a state of total confusion. This has led some exegetes to devote very little attention to this chapter. Others, like Wolff, follow a very different approach. They simply rewrite large portions of the Hebrew source text and fashion it after their own theology. This shows how little faith they have in the Word of God as it has come to us. It should come as no surprise that we will have nothing to do with such an approach. (Wolff, 205–7)

A. Poetic Language
Hosea 12 contains a variety of unusual syntactical constructions. This results from the poetic structure of the book. The prophet repeatedly plays on words. To that end, he sometimes makes use of uncommon words or verbal forms so as to achieve rhyme in certain passages. It goes without saying that this makes the translation more difficult. But yet again we will see that the Hebrew source text itself offers us the answer. If we follow it closely and let ourselves be guided by context, we will find clarity and logic.

B. Versification
The NASB, KJV, and NIV number the verses differently than we do. We believe our approach is correct, based on the context. Hosea 11:10–11 contains a message of salvation. Hosea 11:12 (according to the numbering in other translations), however, is a complaint about the bad behavior of Israel and Judah. That would make for an abrupt change of subject between verses 11 and 12. But if we renumber Hosea 11:12 to become Hosea 12:1 it fits well with the following verse. In doing this, we follow the Dutch Statenvertaling, NBG, the NIVIHEOT, and some German and French translations.

Chapter 11:12 NASB
Ephraim surrounds Me with lies and the house of Israel with deceit; Judah is also unruly against God, even against the Holy One who is faithful.

Chapter 11:12 KJV
Ephraim compasseth me about with lies, and the house of Israel with deceit: but Judah yet ruleth with God, and is faithful with the saints.

Chapter 11:12 NIV
Ephraim has surrounded me with lies, Israel with deceit. And Judah is unruly against God, even against the faithful Holy One.

Verse 1 Hebrew Interlinear Text (= chapter 11:12)
they-surrounded-me with-lie Ephraim and-with-deceit house-of Israel and-Judah still he-is-unruly against God even-against Holy-Ones one-being-faithful

Verse 1a
they-surrounded-me with-lie Ephraim and-with-deceit house-of Israel

Sabab means *to circle around* but also *to surround* or *to bind*.
(Mays, 159; McComiskey, 197; Strong's OT, word 5437)

We read: ***Ephraim has surrounded me with lies, the house of Israel with deceit.***

Verse 1b.1
and-Judah still
The *vav* introduces an explanation as to why the name Israel is used in verse 1a. Both parts of Israel are being referred to—the twelve tribes of Israel. We therefore read *also*.

The term *od** means *continuously* or *again* (Genesis 4:25). In Deuteronomy 13:16 we find it translated as *rebuilt*, but we might also render the term as *built again*, while in Esther 9:12 we find the translation *further* (again with the sense of *again* or *anew*).
(Andersen and Freedman, 593, 602; Owens, 782; Strong's OT, word *5750)

We read: ***also Judah constantly***

Verse 1b.2
he-is-unruly
The word *rud* occurs very rarely in the Bible. Many exegetes/interpreters give it a positive significance, as in: *Judah yet ruleth with God* (KJV), or *Judah still walks with God* (NRSV). As such, these translators have opted to follow rabbinic commentators (like Rashi and David Kimhi). Increased knowledge of biblical Hebrew has taught us that *rud* has a negative sense, meaning *to roam*, *to wander*, or *to err*, perhaps even *to stray from*. We found *restless* (Psalm 55:2) and *roam* (Jeremiah 2:31; however, *strayed from* would have been a more accurate translation). We opted for *strayed* in the sense of *to wander*, especially from the right path.
(Andersen and Freedman, 601–2; Brown, 105; Garrett, 219; McComiskey, 198; Strong's OT, words 5750, 7300; Stuart, 185–86; Talmud Bavli, *Taanith*, 5a; Wood, 218)

We read (1b.1 + 1b.2): ***also Judah constantly strayed***

Verse 1c
against God
The word *im* can mean *again*, but also *at*, *with*, *to*, or *from*. Here we opt for the translation *from*.

The word *el*, which is translated as God, could also be translated *the mighty one*. It is used for pagan gods in general and for God Himself; thus we have written it with an uppercase G.
(Brown, 105; Mays, 160; Strong's OT, words 5973, 410)

We read: ***from God***

Verse 1d
even-against Holy-Ones one-being-faithful
The NIVIHEOT translation *even-against* is an interpretation; that is not what the text says. The clause opens with a *vav*, followed by *im* (that is *from* or *with*; see verse 1c). It would therefore be better to start with *and-from* or *yes-from*.

The word *aman* often means *to believe* (Exodus 4:1; Isaiah 7:9), but also *to trust* (Numbers 14:11; 1 Samuel 27:12 MSG). Both have this underlying significance of something or someone *being dependable* or *faithful*.
(Strong's OT, word 5973)

We read: ***yes, from the Holy One who is faithful***

The entire text—verse 1:
With lies Ephraim has surrounded Me, with deceit the house of Israel. For also Judah constantly strayed from God; yes, from the Holy One who is faithful.

Verse 1 NASB
Ephraim feeds on wind, and pursues the east wind continually; he multiplies lies and violence. Moreover, he makes a covenant with Assyria, and oil is carried to Egypt.

Verse 1 KJV
Ephraim feedeth on wind, and followeth after the east wind: he daily increaseth lies and desolation; and they do make a covenant with the Assyrians, and oil is carried into Egypt.

Verse 1 NIV
Ephraim feeds on the wind; he pursues the east wind all day and multiplies lies and violence. He makes a treaty with Assyria and sends olive oil to Egypt.

Verse 2 Hebrew Interlinear Text
Ephraim feeding-on wind and-pursuing east-wind all-of the-day lie and-violence he-multiplies and-treaty with Assyria they-make and-oil to-Egypt he-is-sent
The root meaning of *ra'ah* (NIVIHEOT: *feeding*) is *to pasture (a herd)* (Genesis 29:7); *graze* (Exodus 34:3); *shepherd* (Genesis 46:34); and *shepherds* (Exodus 2:17). *To feed on wind* or *to graze on wind* is probably an expression, however with negative connotations. In English we would say something like: *to go where the wind blows*.
(Garrett, 235; Mays, 159; McComiskey, 196; Strong's OT, word 7462; Wolff, 206)

We read—verse 2:

Ephraim goes where the wind blows and also chases the east wind. Day after day he piles lies on top of violence. They made a covenant with Assyria, while olive oil was sent to Egypt.

Verse 2 NASB
The Lord also has a dispute with Judah, and will punish Jacob according to his ways; He will repay him according to his deeds.

Verse 2 KJV
The Lord hath also a controversy with Judah, and will punish Jacob according to his ways; according to his doings will he recompense him.

Verse 2 NIV
The Lord has a charge to bring against Judah; he will punish Jacob according to his ways and repay him according to his deeds.

Verse 3 Hebrew Interlinear Text
indeed-charge to-Yahweh against Judah and-to-punish to Jacob according-to-ways-of-him according-to-deeds-of-him he-will-repay to-him

Verse 3a
indeed-charge to-Yahweh against Judah
The sentence opens with a *vav*. It is connecting the event of verse 3a to verse 2 and subsequently leads to a conclusion—verse 3b. We read *also*.

Some choose to translate the word *rib* (here rendered as *charge*) as *controversy* or similar

terms. This is suggestive of a difference of opinion between two equal parties. However, that is not what the text has in view. A court case has been launched *against* Judah. A charge is brought by God and cannot be defended. Thus the NIVIHEOT translation is correct (see also NRSV). The word *lawsuit* brings us closer to the sense of the Hebrew text.
(Brown, 106; Garrett, 236; Strong's OT, word 7379)

We read: *there is also a lawsuit of Yahweh against Judah*

Verse 3b
and-to-punish to Jacob according-to-ways-of-him according-to-deeds-of-him he-will-repay to-him
In the name Jacob, of course, all the tribes are included.
The letter *vav* (*and*) has a wide meaning. In this case the *vav* leads to a conclusion that both are guilty. We read: *thus*.

We read: *thus He will punish Jacob according to his ways; He will reward him according to his deeds*

The entire text—verse 3:
There is also a lawsuit of Yahweh against Judah. Thus He will punish Jacob according to his ways. He will reward him according to his deeds.

Verse 3 NASB
In the womb he took his brother by the heel, and in his maturity he contended with God.

Verse 3 KJV
He took his brother by the heel in the womb, and by his strength he had power with God:

Verse 3 NIV
In the womb he grasped his brother's heel; as a man he struggled with God.

Verse 4 Hebrew Interlinear Text
in-the-womb he-grasped-heel . . . brother-of-him and-in-manhood-of-him he-struggled with God

Verse 4a
in-the-womb he-grasped-heel . . . brother-of-him
The first part of verse 4 is simple to translate.

We read: *in the womb he grasped the heel of his brother*

Verse 4b
and-in-manhood-of-him
The meaning of Hebrew *on* is not easy to reflect using a single word or concept. It actually depicts a person with a powerful demeanor or personality. In Job 18:7 NASB translates it as *vigorous*; in Job 18:12 as *strength* and in Psalm 78:51 with *virility*, which comes close. We prefer: *manly strength*.
(Andersen and Freedman, 607; Mays, 161; McComiskey, 199; Owens, 783; Strong's OT, word 202; Stuart, 185–86)

We read: *and in his manly strength*

Verse 4c
he-struggled

The word *sarah* (or śry) occurs only twice in Scripture. Apart from this use, it is also found in Genesis 32:28, to which our text is referring. The word śry is probably related to the name *Israel* (= wrestles God). Some exegetes and translators render the word as *wrestled*, while others use *to gain the upper hand* or *to overcome*. Owens opts for *he persevered* and Andersen and Freedman suggest it means something along the lines of *be correct* or *just*.

Nowhere in Genesis 32 do we find any suggestion that Jacob won. For that reason, a rendering like *to overcome* or something similar (as in many other translations) must be rejected. It seems more logical to assume that Jacob's achievement was his ability to *resist* the heavenly being. He had the courage to measure himself against him. Perhaps there are even macho overtones here (see 4b).
(Andersen and Freedman, 607; Brown, 106–7; Garrett, 236; Mays, 163; Owens, 783; Smith, 173; Strong's OT, words 430, 8280)

We read: ***he measured himself***

Verse 4d
with God
The word *elohim* has the root meaning of *gods* or *deities*. When it is preceded by a definite article, it often means God Himself (as in *the only* God) which is how it is usually translated here in Hosea 12:4. Some scholars are rather quick in applying the latter translation. This holds true also for the story of Jacob wrestling, as it is described for us in Genesis 32 and alluded to here. Nowhere do we find the name *Yahweh* there; it is always *elohim*. While *divine* is another option, that word is all too readily associated with the one true God. A much better option is therefore to retain the original term *Elohim*. The word is a plural form; nevertheless, Jacob only wrestled a single person (more on this in the exegesis). We have therefore decided to reflect both aspects at once.
(Andersen and Freedman, 607; Calvijn, *Daniel* II, *Kleine Profeten* I/II, Hosea, 420–21; Garrett, 236; Strong's OT, word 430)
(See Excursus 22.)

We read: ***with one from the Elohim***

The entire text—verse 4:
In the womb he grasped the heel of his brother and in his manly strength he measured himself with one from the Elohim.

Excursus 22: Did Jacob Struggle with God?

In Hosea 12:4 we find an allusion to the patriarch Jacob wrestling with an unknown being at the crossing of the Jabbok river (Genesis 32:24). In Genesis 32:25 many translations describe this being as *a man*. The Hebrew word, however—*'îysh*—can also mean *someone*. That does not necessarily refer to a human being. This is clear from Hosea 12:4, which teaches us that it is *one from the Elohim*. In Hosea 12:5 this unknown being is defined more clearly using the word *mal'âk*, meaning *messenger* or *runner* (Genesis 32:3; Judges 6:35). Context often shows the messenger in question to have come from God, for which reason it is then translated as *angel* (Genesis 16:7; Exodus 3:2; Numbers 20:16).

22.a It was an archangel
The word *elohim* is the plural of *eloah*, meaning *divinity* (singular) or *divinities* or *divines* (plural). Some exegetes erroneously consider *elohim* to be the plural form of ĕl (which is the name generally applied to God, even in the context of a heathen god). Synonyms of ĕl

in other Semitic languages are: *elah* (Aramaic), *ilah* (Arabic), and *ilu* (Akkadian). It probably means *strong* or *powerful one*.

In Genesis 35:2, Exodus 12:12; Deuteronomy 29:18; and 32:17 the word *elohim* means *gods*. In Psalm 8:5 it means *divine* (where the text is probably referring to the status of the exalted angels), and in Psalm 82:1 we find *elohim* first translated as *God* and second as *the gods* (KJV). Many believe, as I do, that it refers to exalted heavenly spirits (probably archangels). In that context we find many supernatural or heavenly spirits and identities, among them both Satan (Lucifer) and the archangels. All of them are included among the *elohim*.

If the word *elohim* is accompanied by a definite article, it usually means God (with an uppercase G). In Hebrew, the definite article is more expressive than it is in English. For that reason, we could render it as *the one* or *that one from the Elohim*, which is, of course, Yahweh. Since Hosea 12:4 does not use the definite article, it probably refers to an archangel.

22.b God is spirit not man

Some exegetes are of the view that Jacob wrestled with God, but Hosea 12:5 suggests that this interpretation must be discarded. When we are dealing with biblical passages that speak of a higher power, but without explicitly referring to Yahweh, the context must be used to decide on the specific translation. From Genesis 32 there is no clear indication that the person with whom Jacob wrestled was God. The Bible itself teaches us how we are to understand this passage. In Exodus 33:20 (NIV) it says:

> *[God] said, "you cannot see my face, for no one may see me and live."*

Other textual proofs include Deuteronomy 4:12; Judges 13:22; Isaiah 6:5; John 1:18; 1 John 4:12. Moreover, in Hosea 12:5, the text speaks of *an angel*. Together these two texts unequivocally indicate that Jacob *could* not have wrestled with Yahweh. It must therefore have been a higher, unspecified heavenly power—an archangel.

Sources:
(Dee and Schoneveld, vol. 1, 164, 168; Grosheide, et al., vol. 2, 60; NIV Bible Dictionary, 298, 309; Pfeiffer, Vos, and Rea, 506, 523; Strong's OT, words 430, 433)
(See Excursus 12.)

Verse 4 NASB
Yes, he wrestled with the angel and prevailed; he wept and sought His favor. He found Him at Bethel and there He spoke with us,

Verse 4 KJV
Yea, he had power over the angel, and prevailed: he wept, and made supplication unto him: he found him in Bethel, and there he spake with us;

Verse 4 NIV
He struggled with the angel and overcame him; he wept and begged for his favor. He found him at Bethel and talked with him there—

Verse 5 Hebrew Interlinear Text
and-he-struggled with angel and-he-overcame he-wept and-he-begged-favor of-him Beth El he-found-him and-there he-talked with-him

Verse 5a
and-he-struggled with angel
The word *sur* is very rare in Scripture and means *to be powerful*, *to exercise power*, or *to*

dominate. In Hosea 8:4 we rendered the word as *leaders* (NASB: *princes*), while in Judges 9:22 the NASB translates *ruled* (others: *to govern*). Owens reads: *and he persevered*, which succeeds in reflecting something of the sense of the Hebrew text.

Malak means *messenger, emissary*, or *angel*. The final option here has been adopted almost universally for verse 5.
(Brown, 107; Owens, 783; Strong's OT, words 4397, 7786; Stuart, 128)

We read: ***then he persevered against the angel***

Verse 5b
and-he-overcame
Yakol is often translated as *overcame*, but this seems doubtful. Its basic meaning is *to be able* or *capable of* (Genesis 13:6; 15:5; Exodus 10:5; Numbers 11:14). The term thus refers to a capacity, ability, or a certain mindset or passion. Stuart's translation follows along these same lines: *so that he might win*. Our translation largely follows his.
(Strong's OT, word 3201; Stuart, 186)

We read: ***to gain the upper hand***

Verse 5c
he-wept and-he-begged-favor of-him
Bakah means *to mourn, to bewail*, or *to lament* (Genesis 21:16; Leviticus 10:6), or can even refer to a baby crying (Exodus 2:6).
(Garrett, 238–40; Mays, 161, 164; Strong's OT, word 1058)

We read: ***he cried and begged him for a favor.***

Verse 5d
Beth El he-found-him and-there he-talked with-him
Verse 5d has little connection to verse 5a/b/c. It does go well with verse 6, so we have located it there.

The entire text—verse 5:
Then he persevered against the angel to gain the upper hand. He cried and begged him for a favor.

Verse 5 NASB
Even the Lord, the God of hosts, the Lord is His name.

Verse 5 KJV
Even the Lord God of hosts; the Lord is his memorial.

Verse 5 NIV
the Lord God Almighty, the Lord is his name!

Verse 5d + 6 Hebrew Interlinear Text
Beth El he-found-him and-there he-talked with-him indeed-Yahweh God-of the-Hosts Yahweh name-of-renown-of-him

Verse 5d/6a
Beth El he-found-him and-there he-talked with-him
The word *'immānū* means *with us*, not *with him* as many translate. It is connected with and points to Genesis 35:6–15, where Jacob spoke with God.

At Pniel Jakob got a new name—Israel—from an angel (Genesis 32:27–30). In Genesis 38:10 Yahweh Himself confirmed this name change. Thus here we find a play on words. Hosea links this event to the people of Israel (*us*), because since then God has spoken many times with them.
(BHI, Hosea 12:4; *Studiebijbel* SBOT 12, 114)

We read: *he found Him in Bethel, there He spoke with us*

Verse 6b
indeed-Yahweh God-of the-Hosts Yahweh name-of-renown-of-him
Stuart reads *It was Yahweh*, although one might just as well use the present tense. Harper translates: *as truly as*. If we follow the Hebrew text very carefully, we see that it says *and-Yahweh*. The *vav* (*and*) can introduce a later event, but also an added explanation. This is why some have opted to begin the sentence with *namely*, which we will follow.
(Brown, 107; Harper, 382; Stuart, 187)

The entire text—verse 6:
He found Him in Bethel. There He spoke with us; namely Yahweh, the Lord of Hosts. Yahweh is His glorious Name.

Verse 6 NASB
Therefore, return to your God, observe kindness and justice, and wait for your God continually.

Verse 6 KJV
Therefore turn thou to thy God: keep mercy and judgment and wait on thy God continually.

Verse 6 NIV
But you must return to your God; maintain love and justice, and wait for your God always.

Verse 7 Hebrew Interlinear Text
but-you to-God-of-you you-must-return love and-justice maintain! and-wait! for God-of-you always
The word *elohim* occurs twice here. It is commonly translated as *God*, as we have done here also, although one could also read *the divine*.
(Strong's OT, word 430)

Verse 7a
but-you to-God-of-you you-must-return
By opening with *but-you*, it indicates that there is a change in subject. Others have translated as *and you* or *therefore you*. We opt for *as for you* as does the NRSV.
(Garrett, 233; Mays, 161)

We read: *as for you, you must return to your God*

Verse 7b
love and-justice maintain!
The significance of the word *cheçed* extends further than *love*. It is better translated as *kindness* or *lovingkindness* (Genesis 19:19 NASB), or *mercy* (Exodus 15:13 KJV).
(Brown, 108; McComiskey, 202; Strong's OT, word 6960)

We read: *maintain mercy and righteousness*

Verse 7c
and-wait! for God-of-you always
When the NIVIHEOT renders this *wait!*, it is an interpretation that is somewhat too ambiguous. The word *qavah* can indeed mean *to wait* but also *to look out for* or *to await* (Job 3:9; Psalm 40:1; 69:20; 130:5).

The word *tamid* means *continually* (Leviticus 24:2), *constantly*, *daily*, or *continual* (Exodus 29:42; Numbers 4:7; 28:10).
(Brown, 108; Mays, 161; Strong's OT, words 6960, 8548)

We read: *and constantly look out for your God!*

The entire text—verse 7:
As for you, you must return to your God. Therefore maintain mercy and righteousness and constantly look out for your God!

Verse 7 NASB
A merchant, in whose hands are false balances, he loves to oppress.

Verse 7 KJV
He is a merchant, the balances of deceit are in his hand: he loveth to oppress.

Verse 7 NIV
The merchant uses dishonest scales and loves to defraud.

Verse 8 Hebrew Interlinear Text
merchant in-hand-of-him scales-of dishonesty to-defraud he-loves

Verse 8a
merchant in-hand-of-him
Here we find the word *kna'an*, meaning *Canaan*, that is, a geographical region (Genesis 9:18; 50:13; Exodus 15:15). People from Canaan were often traveling merchants. Over the years the name Canaanite became a substitute for *merchant* and that is why the NIVIHEOT translates *merchant*. However, the context would need to support that translation but it does not in this case.

The word *bəyāḏōw* is derived from *yad* (*hand*) and means *in his hand*. However, the expression *in the hand of* can also mean *in the power of something* or *someone* (Judges 3:10; 1 Samuel 4:8; 1 Kings 11:12; 1 Chronicles 22:18). Here the text is referring to a situation in Canaan, when the people were intoxicated with dishonesty.
(Andersen and Freedman, 615; Mays, 165–66; McComiskey, 205; Strong's OT, word 3027)

We read: *Canaan smitten with*

Verse 8b
scales-of dishonesty
Mirmah means *dishonesty*, *treacherous*, or *deceit*.
(Brown, 108; Garrett, 233; Strong's OT, word 4820)

We read: *scales of deceit*

Verse 8c
to-defraud he-loves

The term *ashaq* means *to oppress* or *to subjugate* (Deuteronomy 28:29; Job 10:3; Psalm 146:7).

The pronoun *he* refers to *Canaan*; for that reason we render it as *it*.
(Garrett, 233; McComiskey, 204)

We read: *it loves oppression*

The entire text—verse 8:
Canaan smitten with scales of deceit. It loves oppression.

Verse 8 NASB
And Ephraim said, "Surely I have become rich, I have found wealth for myself; in all my labors they will find in me no iniquity, which would be sin."

Verse 8 KJV
And Ephraim said, Yet I am become rich, I have found me out substance: in all my labours they shall find none iniquity in me that were sin.

Verse 8 NIV
Ephraim boasts, "I am very rich; I have become wealthy. With all my wealth they will not find in me any iniquity or sin."

Verse 9 Hebrew Interlinear Text
and-he-boasts Ephraim very I-am-rich I-found wealth for-myself all-of wealths-of-me not they-will-find in-me iniquity that sin

Verse 9a
and-he-boasts Ephraim
The NIVIHEOT translates *boasts*, but this is an interpretation based on context. A number of other translators do the same. We prefer to stick closer to the Hebrew text. The word *amar* occurs very frequently in Scripture and just means *to say*.
(Mays, 165; McComiskey, 204; Strong's OT, word 559)

We read: ***Ephraim says***

Verse 9b
very I-am-rich
Ak can mean *very*, but could also be rendered as *surely*, *nevertheless*, or *yet*.
(Brown, 109; Strong's OT, word 389)

We read: ***yet I have become rich***

Verse 9c
I-found wealth for-myself
Here the NIVIHEOT translation is actually an interpretation. The Hebrew word *on* means *achievement*, *ability*, or *power* (in the sense of *ability/capacity for*; Job 40:16), *wealth* (Job 20:10), *strength*, or *might* (which is likewise a kind of *ability* or *capacity*; Isaiah 40:26, 29). Mays uses *fortune* here, which is likewise an option.
(Mays, 166; McComiskey, 204; Strong's OT, word 202)

We read: ***I found the power in myself***

Verse 9d
all-of wealths-of-me

Ygiya' is translated here as *wealths*. We will not follow in this. The basic meaning of the term is *work*, *labor*, *toil* (Genesis 31:42), *possession* (Nehemiah 5:13; although there too it concerns the fruit of one's labor).
(Brown, 109; Mays, 166; McComiskey, 204; Strong's OT, word 3018; Wolff, 207)

We read: *in all my labor*

Verse 9e
not they-will-find in-me iniquity
The word *they* is used impersonally here (NBG; NIV) (i.e., *one*).
(Brown, 109)

We read: *one will not find in me any injustice*

Verse 9f
that sin
Asher (*which*) is a concept that is difficult to define. It means something along the lines of *to head a course* or *to guide that course*. Accordingly, we found *guide* (BHI), *direct* (Proverbs 23:19); *proceed* (which is likewise a kind of directing toward; Proverbs 4:14; 9:6).
(Strong's OT, word 833; Wolff, 207)

We read: *that leads to sin*

The entire text—verse 9:
Ephraim says, yet I have become rich. I found the power in myself. In all my labor one will not find in me any injustice that leads to sin.

Verse 9 NASB
But I have been the L<small>ORD</small> your God since the land of Egypt; I will make you live in tents again, as in the days of the appointed festival.

Verse 9 KJV
And I that am the L<small>ORD</small> thy God from the land of Egypt will yet make thee to dwell in tabernacles, as in the days of the solemn feast.

Verse 9 NIV
"I have been the L<small>ORD</small> your God ever since you came out of Egypt; I will make you live in tents again, as in the days of your appointed festivals."

Verse 10 Hebrew Interlinear Text
indeed-I Yahweh God-of-you from-land-of Egypt again I-will-make-live-you in-tents as-days-of appointed-feasts

Verse 10a
indeed-I Yahweh God-of-you from-land-of Egypt
We find these same words in Hosea 13:4. There it is an unmistakable reference to the exodus from Egypt; the same applies here.
(McComiskey, 204; Wolff, 207)

We read: *But I am Yahweh, your God, who brought you out of Egypt*

Verse 10b
again I-will-make-live-you in-tents
We prefer *again* over *yet again* or *anew* as some do.
(Brown, 109; Mays, 166; McComiskey, 204)

We read: *again, I will make you dwell in tents*

Verse 10c
as-days-of appointed-feasts
The Hebrew word *moed* means *meeting* or *assembly* (Exodus 27:21; Leviticus 1:1; Numbers 18:31). In Exodus 23:15 we may find it translated as *appointed* (time), but there too it actually means the *time of meeting*. Often it is used in the context of a religious ceremony. This is why Brown has chosen to render the term as *solemn feast*. However, that rendering would place us a little further from the Hebrew source text.
(Brown, 109; Strong's OT, word 4150; Wolff, 207)

We read: *as in the days of the meeting*

The entire text—verse 10:
But I am Yahweh, your God, who brought you out of Egypt. Again, I will make you dwell in tents, as in the days of the meeting.

Verse 10 NASB
I have also spoken to the prophets, and I gave numerous visions, and through the prophets I gave parables.

Verse 10 KJV
I have also spoken by the prophets, and I have multiplied visions, and used similitudes, by the ministry of the prophets.

Verse 10 NIV
"I spoke to the prophets, gave them many visions and told parables through them."

Verse 11 Hebrew Interlinear Text
and-I-spoke to the-prophets and-I vision I-gave-many and-through-hand-of the-prophets I-told-parables
The *vav* (*and*) serves to introduce an explanation of what preceded it. That is why we read *for*.

We read—verse 11:
For I spoke to the prophets and gave them many visions. I also told parables by the hand of the prophets.

Verse 11 NASB
Is there iniquity in Gilead? Surely they are worthless. In Gilgal they sacrifice bulls, yes, their altars are like the stone heaps beside the furrows of the field.

Verse 11 KJV
Is there iniquity in Gilead? surely they are vanity: they sacrifice bullocks in Gilgal; yea, their altars are as heaps in the furrows of the fields.

Verse 11 NIV
Is Gilead wicked? Its people are worthless! Do they sacrifice bulls in Gilgal? Their altars will be like piles of stones on a plowed field.

Verse 12 Hebrew Interlinear Text
if Gilead wickedness surely worthlessness they-are in-the-Gilgal bulls they-sacrifice also altars-of-them like-piles-of-stones on plowed-parts-of field

Verse 12a
if Gilead wickedness
This clause begins with *'îm*. It often means: *if, except, though, or surely*. It is sometimes used as a hypothetical particle or interrogative particle as in the following examples (where the underlined parts indicate the use of *'îm*: Joshua 5:13 (NASB)—*"Are you for us or for our adversaries?"*); Judges 9:2 (NASB)—*or that one man rule over you?*; Genesis 24:21 (NASB)—*whether the LORD had made his journey successful or not?*; and 2 Chronicles 2:6 (NASB)—*except to burn incense before Him?*. Thus, when a verse begins with *'îm*, the clause it introduces can take the form of a question* that actually has a confirming significance. The same applies here.
(*Brown, 110; Garrett, 244; McComiskey, 209; Strong's OT, word 518)

We read: *is not Gilead's wickedness*

Verse 12b
surely worthlessness
The word *ak* means *surely, albeit,* or *only*.* Brown, Driver, and Briggs† says it indicates "a contrast to what precedes." Together with the Dutch Statenvertaling we read: *only*.

The word *šāw* (from *shaw*) means emptiness or vanity (Strong's). The NIVIHEOT translates *šāw* here as *worthlessness*. This is interpretation, however, since it takes us a little too far from the source text. The word *šāw* is usually translated as *vain* or *vanity* (Exodus 20:7; Psalms 89:47; 108:12). At times it is also translated as *deception* or *falsehood* (Psalm 12:2; Isaiah 5:18), although there too the word has the underlying significance of *vanity*.
(Calvijn, *Daniël* II, *Kleine Profeten* I/II, Hosea, 441; †Brown, Driver, Briggs, word 389; Brown, 110; *NAS Exhaustive Concordance, word 389; Strong's OT, word 7723)

We read: *only vanity?*

Verse 12c
they-are in-the-Gilgal bulls they-sacrifice
This is not difficult.

We read: *so they are in Gilgal! they sacrifice bulls!*

Verse 12d
also altars-of-them like-piles-of-stones on plowed-parts-of-field
The word *gallîm* is a play on words with *Gilead and Gilgal*. Instead of *piles of stones* we could also read *ruins*.
(Brown, 110; Strong's OT, word 1530)

We read: *their altars too will become piles of stones on a plowed field*

The entire text—verse 12:
Is not Gilead's wickedness only vanity? So they are in Gilgal! They sacrifice bulls! Their altars too will become piles of stones on a plowed field.

Verse 12 NASB
Now Jacob fled to the land of Aram, and Israel worked for a wife, and for a wife he kept sheep.

Verse 12 KJV
And Jacob fled into the country of Syria, and Israel served for a wife, and for a wife he kept sheep.

Verse 12 NIV
Jacob fled to the country of Aram; Israel served to get a wife, and to pay for her he tended sheep.

Verse 13 Hebrew Interlinear Text
and-he-fled Jacob country-of Aram and-he-served Israel for-wife and-for-wife he-tended

Verse 13a
and-he-fled Jacob country-of Aram
The NIVIHEOT gives its own interpretation of the Hebrew source text here. For *sadeh* actually means *fields* not *country*, as we saw in verse 12.
(Mays, 169; McComiskey, 208; Strong's OT, word 7704)

We read: **Jacob fled to the fields of Aram**

Verse 13b
and-he-served Israel for-wife and-for-wife he-tended
The word *shamar* is translated in a variety of ways. It can mean *to see to, to observe* (Exodus 12:25), *to watch out for, to take heed*, or *to beware* (Genesis 31:24; Exodus 19:12). Context suggests that *tended* is the correct translation here.

One should note that *he-tended* alludes to the labor Jacob performed for Laban. He served Laban as a shepherd to pay the dowry for Leah and Rachel. Jacob tended sheep and goats (Genesis 29), therefore we add *livestock* in brackets.
(Brown, 110; Mays, 169; Strong's OT, word 8104)

We read: *and Israel served for a wife and for a woman he tended [livestock]*

We read, verse 13:
Jacob fled to the fields of Aram, and Israel served for a wife and for a woman he tended [livestock].

Verse 13 NASB
But by a prophet the L<small>ORD</small> brought Israel from Egypt, and by a prophet he was kept.

Verse 13 KJV
And by a prophet the L<small>ORD</small> brought Israel out of Egypt, and by a prophet was he preserved.

Verse 13 NIV
The L<small>ORD</small> used a prophet to bring Israel up from Egypt, by a prophet he cared for him.

Verse 14 Hebrew Interlinear Text
and-by-prophet he-brought-up Yahweh . . . Israel from-Egypt and-by-prophet he-took-care

Verse 14a
and-by-prophet he-brought-up Yahweh
The word *alah* means *to go up, to rise, to ascend* (Genesis 2:6; 17:22), or *to depart* (= to go up from; Exodus 1:10).
(Brown, 110; Mays, 169; Strong's OT, word 5927; Wolff, 207)

We read: **through a prophet Yahweh brought Israel up from Egypt**

Verse 14b
Israel from-Egypt and-by-prophet he-took-care
Both in verse 13 and here the term *shamar* means *to guard*. It is a poetic play on words involving the preceding verse. For the sake of clarity, we have added the pronoun *them* in brackets.
(Brown, 110; Strong's OT, word 8104; Wolff, 207)

We read: ***and through a prophet He tended [them]***

The entire text—verse 13:
Through a prophet Yahweh brought Israel up from Egypt. And through a prophet He tended [them].

Verse 14 NASB
Ephraim has provoked to bitter anger; so his Lord will leave his bloodguilt on him and bring back his reproach to him.

Verse 14 KJV
Ephraim provoked him to anger most bitterly: therefore shall he leave his blood upon him, and his reproach shall his LORD*** return unto him.***

Verse 14 NIV
But Ephraim has aroused his bitter anger; his Lord will leave on him the guilt of his bloodshed and will repay him for his contempt.

Verse 15 Hebrew Interlinear Text
he-provoked-to-anger Ephraim bitter and-bloods-of-him upon-him he-will-leave and-contempt-of-him he-will-repay to-him Lord-of-him

Lord-of-him
The word *adonay* can mean *lord* (Genesis 18:12; Ruth 2:13), but also *Lord* (= God; Exodus 23:17), *master/lord* (Genesis 24:9), or *owner/ruler* (1 Kings 16:24). One must therefore examine the context to determine whether the word refers to God or to someone else (e.g., a lord or ruler, or a pagan deity). Here it refers unmistakably to the one who executes the judgment upon the nation of Israel/Ephraim—the king or *ruler* of Assyria.
(Garrett, 247; Strong's OT, word 136; Wolff, 217)

We read, verse 15:
Ephraim provoked bitter anger and his blood will rest on himself. Then his contempt will be repaid to him by his ruler.

Hosea 12:1–15—The corrected text:

Verse 1   ***With lies Ephraim has surrounded Me, with deceit the house of Israel. For also Judah constantly strayed from God; yes, from the Holy One who is faithful.***
Verse 2   ***Ephraim goes where the wind blows and also chases the east wind. Day after day he piles lies on top of violence. They made a covenant with Assyria, while olive oil was sent to Egypt.***
Verse 3   ***There is also a lawsuit of Yahweh against Judah. Thus He will punish Jacob according to his ways. He will reward him according to his deeds.***
Verse 4   ***In the womb he grasped the heel of his brother, and in his manly strength he measured himself with one from the Elohim.***

Verse 5	*Then he persevered against the angel to gain the upper hand. He cried and begged him for a favor.*
Verse 6	*He found Him in Bethel. There He spoke with us; namely Yahweh, the Lord of Hosts. Yahweh is His glorious Name.*
Verse 7	*As for you, you must return to your God. Therefore maintain mercy and righteousness and constantly look out for your God!*
Verse 8	*Canaan smitten with scales of deceit. It loves oppression.*
Verse 9	*Ephraim says, Yet I have become rich. I found the power in myself. In all my labor one will not find in me any injustice that leads to sin.*
Verse 10	*But I am Yahweh, your God, who brought you out of Egypt. Again, I will make you dwell in tents, as in the days of the meeting.*
Verse 11	*For I spoke to the prophets and gave them many visions. I also told parables by the hand of the prophets.*
Verse 12	*Is not Gilead's wickedness only vanity? So they are in Gilgal! They sacrifice bulls! Their altars too will become piles of stones on a plowed field.*
Verse 13	*Jacob fled to the fields of Aram, and Israel served for a wife and for a woman he tended [livestock].*
Verse 14	*Through a prophet Yahweh brought Israel up from Egypt. And through a prophet He tended [them].*
Verse 15	*Ephraim provoked bitter anger and his blood will rest on himself. Then his contempt will be repaid to him by his ruler.*

HOSEA 12
Exegesis

Introduction
Although chapter 12 unmistakably continues the prophecy of the previous chapter, there is nevertheless a striking difference in tone. It almost seems that the mood of the Almighty has changed. Hosea 11 still reflected the grief of God, but here we find a very different emotion. A tone of bitterness has crept into the prophecy. The Almighty surveys history and comes to the conclusion that Ephraim is a hopeless case. He mentions some incidents in the history of salvation which serve as illustrations of the fall of Ephraim.

Verse 1
With lies Ephraim has surrounded Me, with deceit the house of Israel. For also Judah constantly strayed from God; yes, from the Holy One who is faithful.
Hosea sketched the distorted relationship between God and Israel/Ephraim in a striking, poetic way. The Almighty is *surrounded* by *lies* and *deceit* and can therefore no longer reach His people. It is another poetic way of giving shape to the Lo-Ammi of Hosea 1:9. As has become apparent several times in the prophecy of Hosea, the sinful way of life of Ephraim (the Ten Tribes) has consequences for the entire people of Israel. But Judah's behavior does not seem to be much better. The two tribes are also guilty because they continually stray from God.

In verse 1 we find a play on words again. It contains the concepts of *lies* and *deceit*, the characteristics of Israel and Judah, in poignant contrast to the words *Holy* and *faithful*, the characteristics of God.
(Reed, 74; Wood, 216)

Verse 2a
Ephraim goes where the wind blows
Here is another poetic description, this time of the political situation of that time. For Ephraim/Israel indeed went where the wind blew. For from the reign of King Menahem to the downfall of the nation, coalitions were constantly being forged and alliances made for political gain. Conspiracy and rebellion caused chaos in Israel/Ephraim and so it turned into what we call a banana republic.
(Wood, 216)
(See Annotation 10A.)

Verse 2b
and also chases the east wind.
The sirocco from the east was notorious for its devastating power. With this the prophet presents a striking picture of the brutal world power of Assyria. Ephraim entered into an alliance with Assyria (*the east wind*), which was asking for trouble. Assyria was the superpower of that time. A covenant with that country degraded any ally to a vassal.

Verse 2c
Day after day he piles lies on top of violence. They made a covenant with Assyria, while olive oil was sent to Egypt.
It is very likely that the *he* in verse 2c refers to King Menahem. He came to power through a coup d'etat and killed his predecessor, King Shallum. To secure his throne he bought the

support of Pul, the king of Assyria, with a huge sum of money (2 Kings 15:19). (Pul is the Babylonian name of King Tiglath-pileser III.)

The covenant that Menahem made with Assyria naturally tied him to that land, and thus his independence was at stake. Behind the back of the Assyrians, the ties with Egypt were then cited as a counterweight. That was a dangerous game for Israel/Ephraim which went very wrong.
(Calvijn, *Daniel* II, *Kleine Profeten* I/II, Hosea, 339–41; Ironside, 89; McComiskey, 198)

Verse 3
There is also a lawsuit of Yahweh against Judah. Thus He will punish Jacob according to his ways. He will reward him according to his deeds.
It is not only the people of Israel/Ephraim that are placed under judgment. Judah has also left God. Both nations are summed up in the name of the patriarch Jacob, who stands for the entire people of Israel.
(Reed, 74)

Annotation 12A: The Patriarch Jacob

Hosea focuses in verses 3–6 on the patriarch Jacob. These verses cause confusion in both translation and exegesis. Most exegetes see Hosea 12:4a in a negative sense. In many languages Jacob is called a heel-grabber (which strongly points to sneaky behavior) and this also colors the exegesis. Does the text say all this? No! This meaning is a traditional conclusion made based on the story of Jacob who, by means of an elaborate double deception, managed to obtain his older brother's birthright from their father, Isaac (Genesis 25:23–34). But such meaning finds no grounds in the Scriptures.

The real problem focuses on the question, why is the person of Jacob brought onto the stage here? Is it because Jacob also sinned and thus the behavior of Ephraim is typified? Not very likely, because the story in Genesis does not make a weighty point of it. Or is the patriarch Jacob presented as an example? We think the latter and on that basis we now continue.
(Ironside, 90; Kidner, 109)

Verse 4
In the womb he grasped the heel of his brother, and in his manly strength he measured himself with one from the Elohim.
This verse refers to the story about the birth of Jacob and Esau (Genesis 25:19–26). From this text in Hosea we get the impression that God is much more positive about Jacob's action than we might be. Verse 4a suggests something like: already as an unborn baby he showed courage and initiative.* Verse 4b also gives that impression. To stand up against an Elohim† (a nonhuman, heavenly identity) requires courage, determination, and perseverance.
(Feinberg, *Minor Prophets*, 59)
(See Annotation 12A; Excursuses 22, †24; *see text translation of v. 4.)

Verse 4b
one from the Elohim
We do not know who that heavenly opponent was. He is called *malâk* (what means: messenger). This is translated almost universally as *angel*. It is certain that it could not have

been God Himself, as so many assume. No one can meet the Almighty face-to-face and survive, according to the Holy Scriptures (Exodus 33:20, John 1:18; 1 John 4:12). It is very likely that this heavenly identity was sent from God, for in Genesis 32:28 Jacob receives a new name: Israel. This means *God fights* or perhaps even *divine battle*.
(Ironside, 90; Kidner, 108–9; Reed, 74; Strong's OT, word 4397)
(See Excursus 22.)

Verse 5a
Then he persevered against the angel to gain the upper hand.
Jacob was a born winner. He did not give up, although he probably knew he could not win against the angel. Ironside calls that *the irresistible power of weakness* and so it was. In fact, Jacob offered the angel a choice: Either I die or you bless me! The important role that Jacob has in salvation history left the angel no choice and forced him take the second option.
(Ironside, 90)

Verse 5b
He cried and begged him for a favor.
The battle was difficult for Jacob and his strength was failing. This is evident from the fact that he was disabled from then on (Genesis 32:31–32). If winning was not possible, all that remained was to beg *for a favor*, for mercy. That favor was granted, along with a new name—Israel. The fact that the heavenly being allowed him to pass was a recognition of Jacob's superiority.
(McComiskey, 201)

Verse 6
He found Him in Bethel. There He spoke with us; namely Yahweh, the Lord of Hosts. Yahweh is His glorious Name.
If a man wants to serve God, it is not something that accidentally happens to him. It is a personal decision, an act. Every person who gets to know God reaches a moment in her or his life when they must make that decision. In addition, the initiative can also come (and sometimes very clearly) from God Himself. That is also the case here. For Jacob found Yahweh, his God, in Bethel (Genesis 28:10–22). He dreamed that Yahweh appeared to him. In that dream God renewed the Abrahamic covenant, just as He had done with Jacob's father Isaac. There he *spoke with Yahweh*. There God made Himself known under His *glorious Name*, as the I-am-that-I-am: *Yahweh, the Lord of Hosts* (Lord of the heavenly hosts).
(Calvijn, *Daniel* II, *Kleine Profeten* I/II, Hosea, 353; Rosenberg, vol. 1, 75; Wood, 216–17)

Verse 7a
As for you, you must return to your God.
The patriarch Jacob set the example. He chose Yahweh as his God. That is the message here. This also indicates the way Israel/Ephraim must take—turning to God. This is a completely new way of life that will have to be totally different from the wicked behavior of Israel during the reign of King Jeroboam II and after.

Verse 7b
Therefore maintain mercy and righteousness and constantly look out for your God!
The people of Israel/Ephraim have lost God (Lo-Ammi; Hosea 1:9). A new attitude must pave the way for a new and blessed future in which *mercy* and *justice* are the key words. If that will be put into practice, Israel/Ephraim may look forward to God, because then He

will come. That has not happened thus far. Although, maybe we are now at the beginning of that process.
(McComiskey, 202–3; Rosenberg, vol. 1, 75)
(See Excursus 7.)

Verse 8 and 9a
Canaan smitten with scales of deceit. It loves oppression. Ephraim says, Yet I have become rich. I found the power in myself.
The Bible teaches us that the land of Canaan is God's. Any discussion about the rights of other peoples to the land of Canaan is futile. God is very clear in His prophecies. He has promised it to the people of Israel. With this, it is, by definition, a holy country. *Deceit* and *oppression* do not belong there, and the fact that it happens without restraint affects the holiness of God. Unfortunately, these two sins are at the root of the wealth of Ephraim/Israel. This kind of prosperity was not from God. That is why Ephraim says, *I found the power in myself.* The people sees no sin in its detestable way of life and thus show that the knowledge of Yahweh has virtually disappeared (Hosea 4:6).

Verse 9b
In all my labor one will not find in me any injustice that leads to sin.
Society at the time of Jeroboam II experienced great economic prosperity. But this only benefited a small part of the population. There were many poor people. The poignant contrast between rich and poor caused great tension in Israel. The rich upper class of the population, however, pretended not to notice and surrendered to violence, impurity, and alcoholism. Proudly Ephraim states that no *injustice* is found in him, of course, measured by their own ungodly laws. The people have strayed so far from Yahweh that it no longer recognizes *sin*.
(Ironside, 91; Rosenberg, vol. 1, 76)

Verse 10
But I am Yahweh, your God, who brought you out of Egypt. Again, I will make you dwell in tents, as in the days of the meeting.
Verse 10a is also called the *declaration of the sovereignty of Yahweh*. With these words, God opened His proclamation to the people of Israel when it received the Torah. These holy words sounded from Mount Sinai when the covenant with the people of Israel was made (Exodus 20:2). That covenant has now been broken and therefore this part of the people of Israel was returning to the state of the days of the exodus. Then the people of Israel left the land of Egypt and went into the wilderness. Now it is scattered among the gentile nations; it is now in the *wilderness of the nations*. However there is hope, because Ezekiel 20:33–38 (NASB) speaks about a blessed future at the end time.

33 *"As I live," declares the Lord G*OD*, "surely with a mighty hand and with an outstretched arm and with wrath poured out, I shall be king over you.*
34 *"I will bring you out from the peoples and gather you from the lands where you are scattered, with a mighty hand and with an outstretched arm and with wrath poured out;*
35 *"and I will bring you into the wilderness of the peoples, and there I will enter into judgment with you face to face.*
36 *"As I entered into judgment with your fathers in the wilderness of the land of Egypt, so I will enter into judgment with you," declares the Lord G*OD*.*
37 *"I will make you pass under the rod, and I will bring you into the bond of the covenant;*
38 *"and I will purge from you the rebels and those who transgress against Me; I will*

bring them out of the land where they sojourn, but they will not enter the land of Israel. Thus you will know that I am the LORD."

Israel/Ephraim is expelled and will *dwell in tents* again. Nevertheless, the *I am Yahweh, your God* (Hosea 12:10a) is like a beckoning perspective on the horizon of time. The Almighty wants to become their God again, if they repent. That will not happen without a struggle. For in the end times the Israelites will have to *pass under the rod* of God (Ezekiel 20:37). Then unbelievers and believers will be separated from each other. The unbelievers and the wicked will fall under judgment, but God's children will then be brought within the *bond* of a new *covenant*. And that new covenant will become visible within the Messianic Kingdom, where peace and justice will dwell.

(Calvijn, *Daniel* II, *Kleine Profeten* I/II, Hosea, 362; Ironside, 91–92; Wood, 217)

Verse 11
For I spoke to the prophets and gave them many visions. I also told parables by the hand of the prophets.
The judgment on the ten tribes of Israel/Ephraim came as a surprise. Yet the Israelites should have known what the consequence of their sinful way of life was. God had always spoken clearly to His people and held the blessing and the curse before them. The choice was theirs. The blessing is laid down in Deuteronomy 26:17–19 (NASB):

17 *"You have today declared the LORD to be your God, and that you would walk in His ways and keep His statutes, His commandments and His ordinances, and listen to His voice.*
18 *"The LORD has today declared you to be His people, a treasured possession, as He promised you, and that you should keep all His commandments;*
19 *"and that He will set you high above all nations which He has made, for praise, fame, and honor; and that you shall be a consecrated people to the LORD your God, as He has spoken."*

The curses are described in Deuteronomy 28:15ff, of which we quote select verses:

25 *"The LORD shall cause you to be defeated before your enemies; you will go out one way against them, but you will flee seven ways before them, and you will be an example of terror to all the kingdoms of the earth.*
36 *"The LORD will bring you and your king, whom you set over you, to a nation which neither you nor your fathers have known, and there you shall serve other gods, wood and stone.*
37 *"You shall become a horror, a proverb, and a taunt among all the people where the LORD drives you.*
49 *"The LORD will bring a nation against you from afar, from the end of the earth, as the eagle swoops down, a nation whose language you shall not understand,*
50 *"a nation of fierce countenance who will have no respect for the old, nor show favor to the young.*
62 *"Then you shall be left few in number, whereas you were as numerous as the stars of heaven, because you did not obey the LORD your God.*
63 *"It shall come about that as the LORD delighted over you to prosper you, and multiply you, so the LORD will delight over you to make you perish and destroy you; and you will be torn from the land where you are entering to possess it.*
64 *"Moreover, the LORD will scatter you among all peoples, from one end of the earth to the other end of the earth; and there you shall serve other gods, wood and stone, which you or your fathers have not known.*

65 "Among those nations you shall find no rest, and there will be no resting place for the sole of your foot; but there the LORD will give you a trembling heart, failing of eyes, and despair of soul."

Verse 12
Is not Gilead's wickedness only vanity? So they are in Gilgal! They sacrifice bulls! Their altars too will become piles of stones on a plowed field.

The region of Gilead was located east of the Jordan. It was the first area that Israel/Ephraim lost to Assyria. That too was a punishment for their depraved way of life. But it was not seen by the people of Ephraim. For the remaining territory of the once mighty nation of Jeroboam II (here typified in the name Gilgal) simply continued to sin. The judgment was now to fall on them as well.
(See Excursuses 3, 19.)

Verse 13
Jacob fled to the fields of Aram, and Israel served for a wife and for a woman he tended [livestock].

This verse again contains a poetic wordplay. The patriarch Jacob went away from Canaan as a young man and *fled to the fields of Aram* (Assyria), where his uncle Laban lived (Genesis 27:43; 29:1-14). He left with the name Jacob and returned as Israel, his new name (Genesis 32:28). In the period in between, he tended livestock for his uncle Laban to pay the dowry for his two wives, Rachel and Leah (Genesis 29:15-30).

With this comparison Hosea expresses a remarkable prophecy. For the same will happen to the people of Ephraim/Israel. They too must escape from Canaan (the exile). The Israelites also go to Aram (Assyria). They too will return to Canaan only when they are allowed to wear the name Israel (again). That is the name of the future; that is the name of a converted people.

Verse 14a
Through a prophet Yahweh brought Israel up from Egypt.

Christians characterize Moses in general as an important leader. However, in rabbinical commentaries he is called the greatest prophet of the Old Testament. Indeed, he was the leader of the Israelites during the exodus from Egypt. But, more importantly, his ministered as mediator between God and His people. He was the receiver of the Torah and the executor of God's instructions. In this he is a type of the coming Messiah.

Verse 14b
And through a prophet He tended [them].

Verse 13 presented a contrast. The name of Jacob typifies the people of Ephraim when it goes into exile. But here the name Israel is that of the return to Canaan. This prophecy is still unfulfilled. The name change marks a turning point in the life of Jacob, who was then called Israel. The same will also be true of the people of Ephraim who will (again) be allowed to carry the name Israel, provided the people repent. Perhaps we should therefore read: *And by a prophet they* (the Israelites) *will be tended*. That prophet is Jesus Christ, their Messiah! The prophet Isaiah prophesied about that day in Isaiah 11:11-13 (NASB):

11 *Then it will happen on that day that the Lord will again recover the second time with His hand the remnant of His people, who will remain, from Assyria, Egypt, Pathros, Cush, Elam, Shinar, Hamath, and from the islands of the sea.*

12   And He will lift up a standard for the nations and assemble the banished ones of Israel, and will gather the dispersed of Judah from the four corners of the earth.
13   Then the jealousy of Ephraim will depart, and those who harass Judah will be cut off; Ephraim will not be jealous of Judah, and Judah will not harass Ephraim.

Jeremiah also speaks about the blessed future of Ephraim in chapter 31:

6   "For there will be a day when watchmen on the hills of Ephraim call out, 'Arise, and let us go up to Zion, to the LORD our God.'"
7   For thus says the LORD, "Sing aloud with gladness for Jacob, and shout among the chief of the nations; proclaim, give praise and say, 'O LORD, save Your people, the remnant of Israel.'
8   "Behold, I am bringing them from the north country, and I will gather them from the remote parts of the earth, among them the blind and the lame, the woman with child and she who is in labor with child, together; A great company, they will return here.
9   "With weeping they will come, and by supplication I will lead them; I will make them walk by streams of waters, on a straight path in which they will not stumble; for I am a father to Israel, and Ephraim is My firstborn."

Verse 15
Ephraim provoked bitter anger and his blood will rest on himself. Then his contempt will be repaid to him by his ruler.
The final conclusion is that the people of Israel/Ephraim have only themselves to blame for the judgment. God's protection has fallen away, and now it is confronted with the anger of a mighty ruler—the king of Assyria, driven by Satan. For Ephraim has violated his covenant with Assyria.

HOSEA 13
Hebrew Text Translation

Introduction
The majority of problems in chapter thirteen are concentrated around verses 14 and 15. The remaining verses hardly pose any difficulties for translation at all. The entire passage addresses the coming judgment on Ephraim/Israel.

Verse 1 NASB
When Ephraim spoke, there was trembling. He exalted himself in Israel, but through Baal he did wrong and died.

Verse 1 KJV
When Ephraim spake trembling, he exalted himself in Israel; but when he offended in Baal, he died.

Verse 1 NIV
When Ephraim spoke, people trembled; he was exalted in Israel. But he became guilty of Baal worship and died.

Verse 1 Hebrew Interlinear Text
when-to-speak Ephraim trembling he-was-exalted he in-Israel but-he-became-guilty concerning-the-Baal and-he-died

Verse 1a
when-to-speak Ephraim trembling
The word *rətêt* occurs only in this text. It is derived from *retheth*, which also occurs only a single time in Scripture, in Jeremiah 49:24, where the BHI and NLT reads *fear*, while the NASB and Dutch Willibrordvertaling render it as *panic*. The meaning of *rətêt* has long remained uncertain. Greater clarity came with the discovery of the Dead Sea Scrolls. It confirmed that it means *trembled*.
(Mansoor, 130; Strong's OT, word 7374 and 7578)

We read: *when Ephraim spoke, people trembled*

Verse 1b
he-was-exalted he in-Israel
In the Hebrew text, the second *he* differs in form from the first. The Hebrew text reads *hū*, which sometimes means *he* but more often *self* or *oneself* (Genesis 20:5 BIB*; Numbers 35:19 BIB*). This is also the meaning it has here.
(*BHI Interlinear Bible; Strong's OT, word 1931)

We read: *he raised himself up in Israel*

Verse 1c
but-he-became-guilty concerning-the-Baal
The sentence begins with a *vav*, which is here translated as *but*. We read: *and*.

The word *asham* means *to be guilty of*. It is a form of judgment, which in the Bible is usually followed by punishment.
(Burroughs, 544; Davies, 286; Mays, 171; Strong's OT, word 816; *Studiebijbel* SBOT 12, 120)

We read, first step: ***and made himself guilty of Baal***

Verse 1d
and-he-died
In many translations we read that the nation Ephraim died (referring in the book of Hosea to the Northern Kingdom). That is a most bewildering way to twist the text. For in reality Israel/Ephraim did not die, but was sent into exile. Someone who is dead no longer has a role to play on earth. The prophet, however, says that the Ten Tribes will also be a part of the future Messianic Kingdom. So this phrase cannot mean that Israel/Ephraim would die.

Some adjust the meaning of the text and read *destruction* (NLT), or *were destroyed* (CEV), but this is a translation of desperation. A better solution emerges if we interpret the Hebrew source text in a different way. *Muth* can indeed mean *to die*, but it can also mean *to kill* or *to put to death* (Genesis 26:11; Exodus 21:12; Judges 20:13). The key to the solution here is verse 2, insofar as it reveals that we are dealing with human sacrifice. Accordingly, we ought to read *and killing*.
(Cheyne, 119; Eidevall, 194; Harper, 394; Strong's OT, word 4191; Stuart, 187)

Verse 1c/d, second step:
We now join verse 1c and 1d (since both begin with a *vav*, meaning that verse 1d can also be linked to *Baal*).

We read: ***and made himself guilty of both Baal and killing***

The entire sentence:
When Ephraim spoke, people trembled. He raised himself up in Israel and was guilty of both Baal and killing.

Verse 2 NASB
And now they sin more and more, and make for themselves molten images, idols skillfully made from their silver, all of them the work of craftsmen. They say of them, "Let the men who sacrifice kiss the calves!"

Verse 2 KJV
And now they sin more and more, and have made them molten images of their silver, and idols according to their own understanding, all of it the work of the craftsmen: they say of them, Let the men that sacrifice kiss the calves.

Verse 2 NIV
Now they sin more and more; they make idols for themselves from their silver, cleverly fashioned images, all of them the work of craftsmen. It is said of these people, "They offer human sacrifices! They kiss calf-idols."

Verse 2 Hebrew Interlinear Text
and-now they-do-more to-sin and-they-make for-themselves idol from-silver-of-them according-to-cleverness-of-them images work-of craftsmen all-of-him of-them they ones-saying ones-offering-sacrifice-of human calf-idols they-kiss

Verse 2a
and-now they-do-more to-sin
Yasaph means *to add, to continue, another* (Genesis 30:24; Leviticus 6:5), or *again* (Judges 3:12; Esther 8:3).
(Cheyne, 119; Owens, 784; Strong's OT, word 3254)

We read: *even now they add sins*

Verse 2b
and-they-make for-themselves idol from-silver-of-them
The word *maccekah* means *molten* or *casting* (Exodus 32:4; Leviticus 19:4; Numbers 33:52). The KJV reads *molten images* here. The Hebrew text is singular, so we translate: *molten image*.
(Burroughs, 548; Strong's OT, word 4541)

We read: *for they make for themselves a molten image of their silver*

Verse 2c
according-to-cleverness-of-them
The word *tebunah* means *intellect* or *understanding* (Proverbs 3:13, Exodus 31:3; Job 12:13).
(Cheyne, 119; Owens, 784; Strong's OT, word 8394)

We read: *according to their own understanding*

Verse 2d
images work-of craftsmen all-of-him
The word *maaseh* is usually translated as *work* or *labor* (Exodus 18:20; Judges 19:16).
(Strong's OT, word 4639; Stuart, 198; Wolff, 219)

We read: *images that are all the work of craftsmen*

Verse 2e
of-them they ones-saying ones-offering-sacrifice-of human
Zebach actually means *to slaughter*, but it is almost always translated as *to offer* or *to sacrifice* (Genesis 31:54; Exodus 23:18; Leviticus 17:5). Here we find our text referring to human sacrifices.
(Andersen and Freedman, 624; Eidevall, 194; Garrett, 245; Strong's OT, word 2076)

We read: *it is said of them: they sacrifice people*

Verse 2f
calf-idols they-kiss
The NIVIHEOT translation *calf-idols* is an interpretation. The Hebrew word *egel* means *calf* (Exodus 32:4; Leviticus 9:8). This is an unmistakable reference to the calves of Bethel and Gilgal, which is why we read *the calves*.
(Beeby, 165; Birch, 112; Strong's OT, word 695; Wolff, 219)

We read: *and kiss the calves*

The entire text:
Even now they add sins. For they make for themselves a molten image of their silver, according to their own understanding, images that are all the work of craftsmen. It is said of them, they sacrifice people and kiss the calves.

Verse 3 NASB
Therefore they will be like the morning cloud and like dew which soon disappears, like chaff which is blown away from the threshing floor and like smoke from a chimney.

Verse 3 KJV
Therefore they shall be as the morning cloud, and as the early dew that passeth away,

as the chaff that is driven with the whirlwind out of the floor, and as the smoke out of the chimney.

Verse 3 NIV
Therefore they will be like the morning mist, like the early dew that disappears, like chaff swirling from a threshing floor, like smoke escaping through a window.

Verse 3 Hebrew Interlinear Text
therefore they-will-be like-mist-of morning and-like-the-dew one-being-early one-disappearing like-chaff he-swirls from-threshing-floor and-like-smoke through-window

Verse 3a
therefore they-will-be like-mist-of morning
Many translate the word *'anan* as *mist*. This is interpretation (even though it may be what the text is actually referring to). We, however, prefer to adhere closely to the Hebrew source text and therefore read *cloud* (Genesis 9:13; Numbers 9:19).
(Brown, 112; Burroughs, 551; Strong's OT, word 6051; Studiebijbel SBOT 12, 120)

We read: *therefore they will be like a cloud in the morning*

Verse 3c
one-disappearing like-chaff he-swirls from-threshing-floor
The word *saar* means *to storm* or *to rage*. However here it is referring to *chaff* blowing in the wind, so we follow the NIVIHEOT.

We read: *which disappears from the threshing floor like whirling chaff*

Verse 3d
and-like-smoke through-window
The meaning of *mê'ărubbāh* is uncertain. We follow the KJV and NASB: *chimney*. Others: *window*.

We read: *like smoke that leaves a chimney*

The entire sentence:
Therefore they will be like a cloud in the morning and as the early dew, which disappears from the threshing floor like whirling chaff, like smoke that leaves a chimney.

Verse 4 NASB
*Yet I have been the L*ORD *your God since the land of Egypt; and you were not to know any god except Me, for there is no savior besides Me.*

Verse 4 KJV
*Yet I am the L*ORD *thy God from the land of Egypt, and thou shalt know no god but me: for there is no saviour beside me.*

Verse 4 NIV
*"But I have been the L*ORD *your God ever since you came out of Egypt. You shall acknowledge no God but me, no Savior except me."*

Verse 4 Hebrew Interlinear Text
But*-I Yahweh God-of-you from-land-of Egypt and†-God but-me not you-shall-acknowledge and-One-Saving there-is-no except-me

Verse 4 opens with *wə·'ānōḵî Yahweh*. In some way it is a play on words: *but I, Yahweh* (I am who I am). Thus we would be better to translate, *but it was Me, Yahweh*, followed by (literally), *your God from land* (*mê·'ereṣ*) *Egypt*. LXX translates *mê·'ereṣ* as: *led you out of the land*, which we will follow.

The first *vav (NIVIHEOT: *but*) introduces an explanation of verses 4–6—why God is so angry with Israel/Ephraim. It contains a short summary of godly deeds from the past in which Yahweh proved to be Israel's God. The second †vav leads to the condition which arose from 4a. It has the function of *therefore*.
(Andersen and Freedman, 634; Garrett, 256–57; Walvoord and Zuck, 1405)

We read:
But it was Me, Yahweh, who led you out of the land Egypt, and therefore you shall not acknowledge any God beside Me, for there is no savior besides Me.

Verse 5 NASB
I cared for you in the wilderness, in the land of drought.

Verse 5 KJV
I did know thee in the wilderness, in the land of great drought.

Verse 5 NIV
"I cared for you in the wilderness, in the land of burning heat."

Verse 5 Hebrew Interlinear Text
I-cared-for-you in-the-desert in-land-of burning-heats
The word *tal'uḇōwṯ* is related to *lahab* and means *flame*. Therefore *burning heat* is the right translation.
(Brown, Driver, Briggs, 529; Koehler and Baumgartner, vol. 1, 520; Strong's OT, words 3851, 8514)

We read:
I took care of you in the desert, in the land of burning heat.

Verse 6 NASB
As they had their pasture, they became satisfied, and being satisfied, their heart became proud; therefore they forgot Me.

Verse 6 KJV
According to their pasture, so were they filled; they were filled, and their heart was exalted; therefore have they forgotten me.

Verse 6 NIV
"When I fed them, they were satisfied; when they were satisfied, they became proud; then they forgot me."

Verse 6 Hebrew Interlinear Text
when-feeding-of-them then-they-were-satisfied they-were-satisfied then-he-became-proud heart-of-them for this they-forgot-me

Verse 6a
when-feeding-of-them then-they-were-satisfied
We do not follow the NIVIHEOT in its translation of the opening word (*when*). Their use of the word *feeding* (Hebrew *marith*) is also an interpretation that we refuse to accept.

The word *marith* means *to graze* or *to pasture*. The text may indeed indicate that pasturing is going on, but that is not how the phrase has been formulated. Brown reads: *according to their pasture*. Owens: *according to the pasturage*. Since this translation comes closest to the Hebrew source text, we have adopted it.
(Brown, 113; Cheyne, 121; Eidevall, 196; McComiskey, 216; Owens, 785; Strong's OT, word 4830)

We read: *they were satisfied in accord with their pasturage*

Verse 6b
they-were-satisfied
This is easy to translate.

We read: *when they were satisfied*

Verse 6c
then-he-became-proud heart-of-them
The sentence opens with a *vav*. It can be translated as *then* or *and*, or it can also simply be dropped for the sake of readability.

Rum means *to exalt*, which could indeed be translated as *proud*, but that is interpretation.
(Harper, 398; McComiskey, 217; Strong's OT, word 7311; Wolff, 220)

We read: *their heart exalted itself*

Verse 6d
for this they-forgot-me
The word *al* (here translated as *for*) has a wide application. It can mean *above*, *in*, *on*, *through*, or *further*; often its underlying meaning is that of *lower* or *to worsen*.

Kên is translated here as *this*. However, we prefer *so* (Genesis 1:7) or its synonym *consequently*.
(Harper, 398; Mays, 173; Strong's OT, words 3652, 5920)

We read, first step: *for so they forgot me*

We read, second step: *consequently they forgot me*

The entire sentence:
They were satisfied in accord with their pasturage. When they were satisfied, their heart exalted itself; consequently they forgot Me.

Verse 7 NASB
So I will be like a lion to them; like a leopard I will lie in wait by the wayside.

Verse 7 KJV
Therefore I will be unto them as a lion: as a leopard by the way will I observe them:

Verse 7 NIV
"So I will be like a lion to them, like a leopard I will lurk by the path."

Verse 7 Hebrew Interlinear Text
so-I-will-come upon-them like lion like-leopard by path I-will-lurk

We read:
Therefore I will overtake them like a lion. Like a leopard along a path, I will lie in wait.

Verse 8 NASB
I will encounter them like a bear robbed of her cubs, and I will tear open their chests; there I will also devour them like a lioness, as a wild beast would tear them.

Verse 8 KJV
I will meet them as a bear that is bereaved of her whelps, and will rend the caul of their heart, and there will I devour them like a lion: the wild beast shall tear them.

Verse 8 NIV
"Like a bear robbed of her cubs, I will attack them and rip them open; like a lion I will devour them—a wild animal will tear them apart."

Verse 8 Hebrew Interlinear Text
I-will-attack-them like-bear robbed-of-cubs and-I-will-rip-open enclosure-of-heart-of-them and-I-will-devour-them there like-lion animal-of-the-wild she-will-tear-apart-them

Verse 8a
I-will-attack-them like-bear robbed-of-cubs
The NIVIHEOT translation *attack* is actually an interpretation, which we will not adopt. For *pagash* means *to meet, to go to, to encounter,* or *to come upon* (Genesis 32:17; Job 5:14; Proverbs 17:12).
(Cheyne, 122; Owens, 785; Strong's OT, word 6298)

We read: *I will meet you like a bear robbed of her cubs*

Verse 8b
and-I-will-rip-open enclosure-of-heart-of-them
The only other place where the word *segor* occurs is Job 28:15. Since that passage is highly debated, it is of no help to us. The form used here is *səḡōwr* which is derived from *sagar*, meaning *to shut, to close in* (Genesis 7:16; 19:6), or *to isolate* (Leviticus 13:4–5, 21).
(Harper, 398; Strong's OT, words 5458, 5462; Wolff, 220)

We read: *and I will rip open their isolated heart*

The entire sentence:
I will meet you like a bear robbed of her cubs, and I will rip open their isolated heart. Yes, I will devour them there like a lion; wild animals will tear them apart.

Verse 9 NASB
It is your destruction, O Israel, that you are against Me, against your help.

Verse 9 KJV
O Israel, thou hast destroyed thyself; but in me is thine help.

Verse 9 NIV
"You are destroyed, Israel, because you are against me, against your helper."

Verse 9 Hebrew Interlinear Text
he-will-destroy-you Israel because against-me against-help-of-you

Verse 9a
he-will-destroy-you Israel
There are very few exegetes who actually follow the Hebrew source text here. Adhering

closely to the Hebrew text leaves us with two alternatives: *He will destroy you, Israel* (which assumes that *He* refers to God); or *one/it will destroy you* (which might also be rendered: *You will be destroyed*). Given that it is God Himself who is speaking in verse 8 (*I will . . .*), a transition to the third person singular (*He*) hardly seems logical. For this reason, we have chosen to adopt the latter alternative.
(Andersen and Freedman, 636; Brown, 113–14; Harper, 399)

We read: *you will be destroyed, O Israel!*

Verse 9b
because against-me against-help-of-you
This clause is translated in a wide variety of ways. Brown and Harper both read, *Yea, who is they help?* Wolff reads, *Who will help you?* Mays translates, *Who then is your helper?* And in Owen we find, *but in me your help.*

The key to a sound translation lies in the word *bi*, which is translated here as *against-me*. It probably serves to introduce a question or request, as in Judges 13:8 (*O Lord . . .*) and in Numbers 12:11 (*Oh, my lord . . .*). Some translators use *woe*, which is also an option. The text here probably says, *for woe to help of you* or *who will be your helper then?*
(Andersen and Freedman, 636; Brown, 114; Harper, 399; Mays, 176; McComiskey, 220; Owen, 785; Wolff, 221)

We read: *who will be your helper then?*

The entire sentence:
You will be destroyed, O Israel! Who will be your helper then?

Verse 10 NASB
Where now is your king that he may save you in all your cities, and your judges of whom you requested, "Give me a king and princes"?

Verse 10 KJV
I will be thy king: where is any other that may save thee in all thy cities? and thy judges of whom thou saidst, Give me a king and princes?

Verse 10 NIV
"Where is your king, that he may save you? Where are your rulers in all your towns, of whom you said, 'Give me a king and princes'?"

Verse 10 Hebrew Interlinear Text
where? king-of-you then? that-he-may-save-you in-all-of towns-of-you and-ones-ruling-you whom you-said give! to-me king and-princes

Verse 10a
where? king-of-you
Here we encounter an important textual problem, related to the meaning of the word *ehi*, which is here translated *where?* The matter will be considered in greater detail in connection with verse 14, where we conclude there that *ehi* is related to Yahweh (= *I am*). We prefer to stick as close as possible to the source text and therefore read: *will I?*

The word *epho* is a temporal indicator. It can be translated as either *then* or *now*.
(Cheyne, 123; Eidevall, 199; Harper, 399–400; Koehler and Baumgartner, vol. 1, 18; McComiskey, 220; Owens, 785; Strong's OT, words 165, 645)
(See Excursus 12.)

We read, first step: *will I be king of you then?*

We read, second step: *should I not have been your king?*

Verse 10b
then? that-he-may-save-you in-all-of towns-of-you
The word *'êpōw* means seldom *then?* (as a question), but mostly *now* or *then*.

The pronoun *he* goes back to the word *king*. The text uses the first person singular here. If impersonal we read: *one* or simply drop the *he*. McComiskey is right to observe, "The question [verse 10a/b] is more than rhetorical. It echoes a philosophy."
(McComiskey, 221; Strong's OT, word 645; Stuart, 199; Wolff, 221)

We read: *then you might have been saved in all your cities*

Verse 10c
and-ones-ruling-you
Shaphat usually means *to sit in judgment* or *to judge* (Genesis 16:5; Exodus 5:21). In Judges 2:18 we find the translation *judges*. The latter term unites the notions of *judging* and *ruling*, and therefore represents the correct translation here. For a smoother text, we repeat the words *where is/are . . . now*.
(McComiskey, 220; Strong's OT, word 8199)

We read: *and where are your judges now*

Verse 10d
whom you-said give! to-me king and-princes
The word *asher* (NIVIHEOT: *whom*) has a wide application. Often it introduces an explanation for what precedes. For this reason we prefer *of which*.
(Harper, 400; Strong's OT, word 834; Stuart, 199)

We read: *of which you said: Give me a king and princes?*

The entire sentence:
Should I not have been your king? Then you might have been saved in all your cities. And where are your judges now of which you said: Give me a king and princes?

Verse 11 NASB
I gave you a king in My anger and took him away in My wrath.

Verse 11 KJV
I gave thee a king in mine anger, and took him away in my wrath.

Verse 11 NIV
"So in my anger I gave you a king, and in my wrath I took him away."

Verse 11 Hebrew Interlinear Text
I-gave to-you king in-anger-of-me and-I-took-away in-wrath-of-me
The word *ebrah* refers to an outburst of emotion. Some of the ways it has been translated include *grimness*, *outrage*, *vengeance*, and *wrath* (Psalm 78:49). The final option comes closest to the sense of the Hebrew source text.
(McComiskey, 221; Strong's OT, word 5678; Stuart, 199)

We read:
In my anger I gave you a king, and in my wrath I took him away.

Verse 12 NASB
The iniquity of Ephraim is bound up; his sin is stored up.

Verse 12 KJV
The iniquity of Ephraim is bound up; his sin is hid.

Verse 12 NIV
"The guilt of Ephraim is stored up, his sins are kept on record."

Verse 12 Hebrew Interlinear Text
being-stored-up guilt-of Ephraim being-recorded sin-of-him

Verse 12a
being-stored-up guilt-of Ephraim
The word *tsarar* can be found translated in many and widely varying ways. For example, it is translated as *bound up* (Exodus 12:34), *besiege* (Deuteronomy 28:52), *is bound* (1 Samuel 25:29), and *wrapped up* (Proverbs 30:4).

Until several decades ago, there was little certainty regarding the meaning of *tsarar*. Studies on the Dead Sea Scrolls (Qumran), however, suggest that *tsarar* refers to the custom of wrapping up scrolls, placing them in jars, or storing them. As such, we arrive at translations like *sealed, fastened, wrapped*, or *stored*. Accordingly, it is also possible to account for the translation in Leviticus 18:18 as *shame* (nakedness) or *what is wrapped up* (covered with clothing).
(Strong's OT, word 6887; Vuillenmier-Bessard, 281–82)

We read: *the debt of Ephraim is sealed*

Verse 12b
being-recorded sin-of-him
The definition of the word *tsaphan* is likewise debated. Its basic meaning is *to conceal, to hide*, or *to cover*. We found it translated as *to hide* (Exodus 2:2; Joshua 2:4) or *to store up* (Psalm 31:19; Proverbs 2:7).
(Andersen and Freedman, 625; McComiskey, 223; Strong's OT, word 6845)

We read: *his sin is stored away*

We read:
The debt of Ephraim is sealed; his sin is stored away.

Verse 13 NASB
The pains of childbirth come upon him; he is not a wise son, for it is not the time that he should delay at the opening of the womb.

Verse 13 KJV
The sorrows of a travailing woman shall come upon him: he is an unwise son; for he should not stay long in the place of the breaking forth of children.

Verse 13 NIV
"Pains as of a woman in childbirth come to him, but he is a child without wisdom; when the time arrives, he doesn't have the sense to come out of the womb."

Verse 13 Hebrew Interlinear Text
pains-of woman-bearing-child they-come to-him he child not wise when time not he-comes to-opening-of-womb-of children

Verse 13a
pains-of woman-bearing-child they-come to-him
Chebel means twisted. It can refer to a rope or cord (Micah 2:5 KJV), but also to the twisting of one's inner being from severe pain. It thus means writhing in pain, as in the present verse.
(Andersen and Freedman, 638; Eidevall, 200; Strong's OT, word 2256; Wolff, 221)

We read: *pains like those of a woman in labor will come over him*

Verse 13b
he child not wise when time not he-comes to-opening-of-womb-of children
We choose not to follow the translation *when*. Typically the word *ki* introduces a causal relationship, as it does here. We read: *because*.

The words *not wise* can be captured in the term *unwise*. However, we prefer *stupid* on the grounds that it better reflects the sense of the Hebrew source text.
(Cheyne, 123; Eidevall, 200; Strong's OT, word 3588)

We read: *he is a stupid child because he does not know the time when the children are born*

The entire sentence:
Pains like those of a woman in labor will come over him. He is a stupid child because he does not know the time when the children are born.

Introduction to Verse 14

This may well be the most difficult verse in all of Hosea, especially in regard to the interpretation of the Hebrew source text. Ben Zvi lists no less than nine possible translations. Not all of them are legitimate, but still the source of the difficulties lies in the complex syntax of verse 14. Many biblical scholars interpret the Hebrew text so as to give it a positive significance (NIV; Dutch Statenvertaling). This interpretation is motivated in particular by 1 Corinthians 15:55, where Hosea 14:13 is cited. In this New Testament text, our verse does indeed receive a positive sense, which has led many scholars to interpret Hosea 13:14 accordingly. We do not agree with this approach, however. After all, the apostle Paul may have intended to contrast the salvific promises for the church of Christ with the judgment of God pronounced over Ephraim/Israel.

Verse 14 NASB
Shall I ransom them from the power of Sheol? Shall I redeem them from death? O Death, where are your thorns? O Sheol, where is your sting? Compassion will be hidden from My sight.

Verse 14 KJV
I will ransom them from the power of the grave; I will redeem them from death: O death, I will be thy plagues; O grave, I will be thy destruction: repentance shall be hid from mine eyes.

Verse 14 NIV
"I will deliver this people from the power of the grave; I will redeem them from death. Where, O death, are your plagues? Where, O grave, is your destruction? I will have no compassion,"

Verse 14 Hebrew Interlinear Text
from-power-of Sheol I-will-ransom-them from-death I-will-redeem-them where?

plagues-of-you death where? destruction-of-you Sheol compassion he-will-be-hidden from-eyes-of-me

14.1 Judgment language

In any case, a positive interpretation of Hosea 13:14 clashes with the impenetrable wall of the surrounding context. Hosea 13 is in its entirety devoted to the judgment upon Ephraim/Israel. This would make it very strange for verse 14 to represent a salvific promise, especially without any textual indicators pointing in that direction. Ben Zvi observes in this regard: "In fact, even the most positive possible reading of 14a can only reinforce the sense of doom over Israel/Ephraim." We wholeheartedly agree.

14.2 Two potential solutions

As noted, the context leaves us no choice but to place verse 14 among the judgments on Ephraim. As such, two potential solutions remain.

> a. Option 1:
> The first option would be to render 14a/b in the form of a question. It would then read something along the lines of: *Will I release them from the power of Sheol? Will I deliver them from death?* As such, it represents a rhetorical question. From there, many exegetes continue reading as follows: *Where is your plague, O death? Where is your destruction, O Sheol?*; famous words strongly grounded in tradition.
>
> There are, however, two important objections to such a translation. In the first place, the book of Hosea offers no support for such an interpretation anywhere. The second objection would require a rather free rendering of the word *ehi* (NIVIHEOT: *where?*). In spite of these difficulties, many exegetes and translators have decided to take this route. They find partial support for their position in the Septuagint, Vulgate, and Targum.
> (Andersen and Freedman, 404; Ben Zvi, 274–76; Birch, 110; Born, 77; Calvijn, *Daniel* II, *Kleine Profeten* I/II, Hosea, 475–79; Cheyne, 124; Eidevall, 202; Joüon, § 161a; Mays, 178; Reed, 78; Wolff, 221)
>
> b. Option 2:
> The key to the second alternative is found in the word *ehi*. It is not entirely clear what this word means. In the Bible it occurs only here and in Hosea 13:10. Literally it means something along the lines of: *I will (be)** (this is the translation we find in the Vulgate, for example). It is related to the word Yahweh† (= *I AM, I will be*, or *He is*). A related form appears in Hosea 1:9 (*ehyeh*). There it is translated *I AM*.
>
> If we apply the meaning *will I (be)* or *I will (be)* to the Hebrew text, we get the following:
>
> *from-power-of Sheol I-will-ransom-them from-death I-will-redeem-them I-will-be (*or: exist*)? pest/plague‡-of-you death I-will-be (*or: exist*)? destruction-of-you Sheol compassion he-will-be-hidden from-eyes-of-me.*
>
> In this rendering, the ransoming and redeeming are connected to God's very essence. They are thus measured by His justice. That is indeed a familiar theme in the book of Hosea. For the judgment on Ephraim placed the Almighty (humanly speaking) in an awkward position. On the one hand is His justice (which demands satisfaction), and on the other hand is His compassion and love for the nation of Israel (which thus cries out for grace).
> ‡*Deber* is often translated *pest* but means *plague* or *pestilence*.
> (Andersen and Freedman, †639, ‡640; Eidevall, 199, 202; Garrett, 264; Johnston; ‡Mays, 178; McComiskey, 224; *Owen, 786; ‡Stuart, 199; *Wolff, 228)

Making a sentence, step 1:
From the power of Sheol shall I ransom them (?); from death shall I redeem them (?) / Shall I exist (?) / Your plague and death / Shall I exist (?) / your destruction and Sheol. Compassion will be hidden from my eyes.

As such, the text is gradually beginning to gain greater clarity. It seems indeed to represent a rhetorical question. This reading does not follow from the syntax of verse 14a/b, however, but from the meaning of the word *ehi*. As such, we arrive more or less at the same translation as with option 1, albeit via an alternate route.

Making a sentence, step 2:
It needs to be pointed out that the actual connotation of the Hebrew source text remains difficult to capture in our language. We will try to stick to it as close as possible, but still use underlining to emphasize the *I*, reflecting the fact that essential attributes of the Almighty are being called into question here. We read (close to the translations of Wolff and Stuart), verse 14a/b:

Will I ransom them from the power of Sheol? Will I redeem them from death?

The second part of the verse cannot be interpreted as *where is your plague . . . ?* as exegetes and translators commonly do. For that would require the repetition of the word *ehi*. Here too we choose to adhere closely to the Hebrew source text:

Your plague is death. Your destruction is Sheol. Pity will be hidden from my eyes.

(Stuart, 199; Wolff, 221)
(See Excursus 23.)

We read:
Will I ransom them from the power of Sheol? Will I redeem them from death? Your plague is death. Your destruction is Sheol. Pity will be hidden from my eyes.

Verse 15 NASB
Though he flourishes among the reeds, an east wind will come, the wind of the Lord coming up from the wilderness; and his fountain will become dry and his spring will be dried up; it will plunder his treasury of every precious article.

Verse 15 KJV
Though he be fruitful among his brethren, an east wind shall come, the wind of the Lord shall come up from the wilderness, and his spring shall become dry, and his fountain shall be dried up: he shall spoil the treasure of all pleasant vessels.

Verse 15 NIV
"even though he thrives among his brothers. An east wind from the Lord will come, blowing in from the desert; his spring will fail and his well dry up. His storehouse will be plundered of all its treasures."

Verse 15 Hebrew Interlinear Text
though he among brothers he-thrives he-will-come east-wind wind-of Yahweh from-desert blowing-in and-he-will-fail spring-of-him and-he-will-dry-up well-of-him he he-will-plunder storehouse all-of article-of treasure

Verse 15a
though he among brothers he-thrives

This sentence begins with *ki*, a word typically used to introduce a causal relationship. We read: *because*.

The word *para* (as the majority of exegetes read it) occurs only in this text. Many interpret it to mean *to flourish*, *to thrive*, or *to be fruitful*. However, this would conflict with the context, as Ephraim/Israel was actually passing through a period of decay.

Andersen and Freedman suggest there is a play on words involving Hosea 8:9 (*a wild donkey*). They read *pere* instead of *para* (which is also an option). According to such interpreters, the term derives from *pr'* (which means *to be wild*; see MSG). That indeed fits the present context.
(Andersen and Freedman, 640; Strong's OT, words 6500, 6501)

We read: **because he was like a wild [donkey] among his brothers**

Verse 15b
he-will-come east-wind wind-of Yahweh
Qadim means *the east*, or sometimes *east wind*. It probably refers to the (very dry) desert wind or (feared) sirocco.

The word *ruach* can mean *wind*, *spirit*, or *breath*. Here Yahweh is both speaking *and* acting. We prefer the translation *breath*.
(Brown, 116; McComiskey, 225; Strong's OT, words 6921, 7307; Wolff, 222)

We read: **the east will bring the breath of Yahweh**

Verse 15c
from-desert blowing-in
The word *alah* (here translated *blowing-in*) means *to rise* or *to ascend* (Exodus 19:18; Joshua 8:21).
(Owens, 786; Strong's OT, word 5927; Wolff, 222)

We read: **that will rise from the desert**

Verse 15d
and-he-will-fail spring-of-him and-he-will-dry-up well-of-him
When a *well* is *failing*, it of course means that it is exhausted. With our rendering, we follow the overwhelming majority of scholars.
(Burroughs, 590; Stuart, 199)

We read: **then his spring will be exhausted and his well will dry up**

Verse 15e
he he-will-plunder storehouse all-of article-of treasure
The double *he* has a reinforcing sense which adds emphasis to *He* (i.e., Yahweh). Few exegetes or translators reflect this in their work. We read: *It is He who . . .*
(Brown, 116; Wolff, 222; Stuart, 199)

We read: **it is He who will plunder his storehouse of all its treasures**

The entire sentence:
Because he was like a wild [donkey] among his brothers, the east will bring the breath of Yahweh that will rise from the desert. Then his spring will be exhausted and his well will dry up. It is He who will plunder his storehouse of all its treasures.

Some Bible translations close Hosea 13 after verse 15. The majority of exegetes and translators, however, continue with verse 16; this also holds true for most English translations. In light of both the contents of the verse and the scope of Hosea 14:2–4, the verse seems indeed to go with chapter 13.

Verse 16 NASB
Samaria will be held guilty, for she has rebelled against her God. They will fall by the sword, their little ones will be dashed in pieces, and their pregnant women will be ripped open.

Verse 16 KJV
Samaria shall become desolate; for she hath rebelled against her God: they shall fall by the sword: their infants shall be dashed in pieces, and their women with child shall be ripped up.

Verse 16 NIV
"The people of Samaria must bear their guilt, because they have rebelled against their God. They will fall by the sword; their little ones will be dashed to the ground, their pregnant women ripped open."

Verse 16 Hebrew Interlinear Text
she-must-bear-guilt Samaria because she-rebelled against-God-of-her by-the-sword they-will-fall little-ones-of-them they-will-be-dashed-to-the-ground and-pregnant-women-of-him they-will-be-ripped-open

Verse 16a
she-must-bear-guilt Samaria because she-rebelled against-God-of-her
The Hebrew source text uses the future tense here. This makes sense, given that Hosea uttered his prophecies before the fall of Israel/Ephraim, which is being described here.
(Calvijn, *Daniël* II, *Kleine Profeten* I/II, Hosea, 483; Mays, 179; McComiskey, 225; Owens, 786; Strong's, Hosea 13:16)

We read: *Samaria will have to bear his guilt because he rebelled against his God*

Verse 16b
by-the-sword they-will-fall little-ones-of-them they-will-be-dashed-to-the-ground
The word *olel* is derived from *ol*, which means *to suckle* or *to breastfeed*. However, we ought not to interpret this as *suckling*, for the Hebrew language uses the word *yanaq*. In ancient times, children were sometimes breastfed until they reached the age of five. We therefore have to think of *children* (1 Samuel 22:19, Psalm 8:2; Isaiah 13:16) between the age of two and five years, that is, *little children*. Rosenberg reads: *infants*.
(Calvijn, *Daniel* II, *Kleine Profeten* I/II, Hosea, 483; Rosenberg, vol. 1, 85; Strong's OT, words 3243, 5763, 5768)

The verb *ratash* has the basic meaning of *to dash down*. Often it is translated as *crushed*. The NIVIHEOT adds *to-the-ground*, but this is interpretation and we refuse to follow it.
(Birch, 111; Calvijn, *Daniel* II, *Kleine Profeten* I/II, Hosea, 483; Garrett, 266; McComiskey, 225; Strong's OT, word 7376)

We read: *they will fall by the sword, his little children will be crushed*

Verse 16c
and-pregnant-women-of-him they-will-be-ripped-open

The root meaning of *baqa'* is *in pieces*. It is also translated as *to break open, to burst open* (Genesis 7:11), *to divide, to break up* (Proverbs 3:20), and *to breach* (Jeremiah 39:2). Many exegetes read *ripped open* here. We prefer the basic meaning, namely *(chopped) in pieces*. (Birch, 111; Strong's OT, word 7376; Stuart, 199)

We read: *and his pregnant women will be chopped into pieces*

The entire text:
Samaria will have to bear his guilt because he rebelled against his God. They will fall by the sword. His little children will be crushed and his pregnant women will be chopped into pieces.

Hosea 13:1–16—The corrected text:

Verse 1 *When Ephraim spoke, people trembled. He raised himself up in Israel and was guilty of both Baal and killing.*

Verse 2 *Even now they add sins. For they make for themselves a molten image of their silver, according to their own understanding, images that are all the work of craftsmen. It is said of them, they sacrifice people and kiss the calves.*

Verse 3 *Therefore they will be like a cloud in the morning and as the early dew, which disappears from the threshing floor like whirling chaff, like smoke that leaves a chimney.*

Verse 4 *But it was Me, Yahweh, who let you out of the land Egypt, and therefore you shall not acknowledge any God beside Me, for there is no savior besides Me.*

Verse 5 *I took care of you in the desert, in the land of burning heat.*

Verse 6 *They were satisfied in accord with their pasturage. When they were satisfied, their heart exalted itself; consequently they forgot Me.*

Verse 7 *Therefore I will overtake them like a lion. Like a leopard along a path, I will lie in wait.*

Verse 8 *I will meet you like a bear robbed of her cubs, and I will rip open their isolated heart. Yes, I will devour them there like a lion; wild animals will tear them apart.*

Verse 9 *You will be destroyed, O Israel! Who will be your helper then?*

Verse 10 *Should I not have been your king? Then you might have been saved in all your cities. And where are your judges now of which you said: Give me a king and princes?*

Verse 11 *In my anger I gave you a king, and in my wrath I took him away.*

Verse 12 *The debt of Ephraim is sealed; his sin is stored away.*

Verse 13 *Pains like those of a woman in labor will come over him. He is a stupid child because he does not know the time when the children are born.*

Verse 14 *Will I ransom them from the power of Sheol? Will I redeem them from death? Your plague is death. Your destruction is Sheol. Pity will be hidden from my eyes.*

Verse 15 *Because he was like a wild [donkey] among his brothers, the east will bring the breath of Yahweh that will rise from the desert. Then his spring will be exhausted and his well will dry up. It is He who will plunder his storehouse of all its treasures.*

Verse 16 *Samaria will have to bear his guilt because he rebelled against his God. They will fall by the sword. His little children will be crushed and his pregnant women will be chopped into pieces.*

HOSEA 13
Exegesis

Introduction

In this chapter God speaks one more time about the fall of Israel/Ephraim through his prophet Hosea. This is done in general terms. Nowhere does the prophet go into detail about causes and/or events.

Hosea 13, like Hosea 7, is a lament in which God's grief resounds. But Hosea 7 was about the marriage bond, that is, the Sinaitic Covenant, and about the adulterous behavior of Israel, which led to the separation between God and His people.

Here the prophecy is put on the canvas in much broader strokes. In it resounds the question, why was this really necessary? God shows His sad surprise at the fact that Israel/Ephraim could stray like this and thus went toward its ruin with open eyes. The seeming incomprehensibility of this behavior is very clear from verses 4–6, which we restate in colloquial language:

> *But I am Yahweh, your God, who led you out of Egypt. I am the only God and your only savior. I took care of you and gave you everything you needed. I made you live in a land of milk and honey. And as thanks you left Me.*

(See Excursus 10.)

Verse 1a

When Ephraim spoke, people trembled. He raised himself up in Israel

Ephraim was the largest tribe of Israel. In the northern kingdom of Israel this was the dominant population group. From this text it appears that there was no natural leadership, but that the leadership was based on numerical superiority, i.e., abuse of power. (Read also: Judges 8:1–3; 12:1–6.)

Verse 1b

and was guilty of both Baal

It will be clear that we also must include in Baal the idolatry at Gilgal and Bethel.
(Calvijn, *Daniel* II, *Kleine Profeten* I/II, Hosea, 371–72)
(See Excursus 11.)

Verse 1c

and killing.

The text probably refers to the offering of human sacrifices. This was one of the most horrific sins that the people of Israel committed. The idolatry of the Baals also involved this pernicious practice. This happened especially in times of crisis and often the victims were children.
(Wood, 220)
(See Annotation 5A.)

Verse 2

Even now they add sins. For they make for themselves a molten image of their silver, according to their own understanding, images that are all the work of craftsmen. It is said of them, they sacrifice people and kiss the calves.

The first great sin of the Northern Kingdom was the establishing of calf worship at Bethel and Gilgal, under Jeroboam I. That was an abomination in God's eyes, but it did not stop there. It went from bad to worse. Under the wicked reign of King Ahab and his wife Jezebel, Israel surrendered to the Baal worship. And during the reigns of the last kings, they worshiped almost every idol from neighboring countries in their wider area.

The text says emphatically that these idols are not real, but people's inventions. Sadly the verse closes with the lament that Israel was known for sacrificing people to the idols and for the worship of calves, not as the land where Yahweh was worshiped.
(Calvijn, *Daniel* II, *Kleine Profeten* I/II, Hosea, 373)
(See Excursus 11.)

Verse 2b
they sacrifice people
This probably refers to the Molech idolatry (other names include Milcom, Malcart, and Melqart). It was the name of a Canaanite god associated with child sacrifice. Fire-gods appear to have been common to all the Canaanite, Syrian, and Arabian tribes who worshiped these destructive idols with the most inhuman rites. According to rabbinic tradition, Molech was a hollow brass image. His hands stretched forth like a man with open hands. The priests would kindle the fire and place a babe into the hands of Molech, causing it to die.

Verse 2c
and kiss the calves
The kissing of idols was a familiar form of obeisance in those days. 1 Kings 19:18 (ESV) says:

> Yet I will leave seven thousand in Israel, all the knees that have not bowed to the Baal, and every mouth that has not kissed him.

This custom has continued to exist into our time. For it is a common practice to kiss holy images in Roman Catholic churches.
(Calvijn, *Daniel* II, *Kleine Profeten* I/II, Hosea, 376; Smith, 177)

Verse 3
Therefore they will be like a cloud in the morning and as the early dew, which disappears from the threshing floor like whirling chaff, like smoke that leaves a chimney.
Verse 3 clearly indicates the proper relationship between the Almighty and man. As long as we serve God, we receive a high status in Him. If we leave Him, we are only a thin mist in the wind and as smoke that evaporates.

So it also happened to the ten tribes of Israel. They were blown away like shreds of mist in the morning and disappeared into the sea of the nations.

Verses 4–6
4   *But it was Me, Yahweh, who let you out of the land Egypt, and therefore you shall not acknowledge any God beside Me, for there is no savior besides Me.*
5   *I took care of you in the desert, in the land of burning heat.*
6   *They were satisfied in accord with their pasturage. When they were satisfied, their heart exalted itself; consequently they forgot Me.*
Verse 4 introduces a passage about God's righteousness. God is a law unto Himself and

He cannot tolerate injustice. These words therefore refer back to Exodus 20 and thus to the beginning of the Sinaitic Covenant.

Verses 4–6 are not words that recall ancient events and describe the failure of God's people. Here the Almighty speaks about the basic rights of the Sinaitic Covenant, the rights and duties that this covenant imposed upon both the people of Israel and God. Of the two parties, God has carefully observed the provisions. He cared for them during the harsh journey through the desert (verse 5); He gave them a land overflowing with milk and honey in Canaan (verse 6, *their pasturage*).

However, all those blessings did not make the people of Israel grateful. The provisions of God did not bring them to the state of holiness as was God's purpose. The opposite happened; Israel rose up (verse 6)—that is, it became haughty—and turned to the idols. Blessed prosperity was exchanged for licentious freedom. And ultimately God was forgotten. The people of Israel were warned. Deuteronomy 8:11–20 (NASB) makes a clear prophetic statement about this:

11 *"Beware that you do not forget the* LORD *your God by not keeping His commandments and His ordinances and His statutes which I am commanding you today;*
12 *"otherwise, when you have eaten and are satisfied, and have built good houses and lived in them,*
13 *"and when your herds and your flocks multiply, and your silver and gold multiply, and all that you have multiplies,*
14 *"then your heart will become proud and you will forget the* LORD *your God who brought you out from the land of Egypt, out of the house of slavery.*
15 *"He led you through the great and terrible wilderness, with its fiery serpents and scorpions and thirsty ground where there was no water; He brought water for you out of the rock of flint.*
16 *"In the wilderness He fed you manna which your fathers did not know, that He might humble you and that He might test you, to do good for you in the end.*
17 *"Otherwise, you may say in your heart, 'My power and the strength of my hand made me this wealth.'*
18 *"But you shall remember the* LORD *your God, for it is He who is giving you power to make wealth, that He may confirm His covenant which He swore to your fathers, as it is this day.*
19 *"It shall come about if you ever forget the* LORD *your God and go after other gods and serve them and worship them, I testify against you today that you will surely perish.*
20 *"Like the nations that the* LORD *makes to perish before you, so you shall perish; because you would not listen to the voice of the* LORD *your God."*

Israel forgot his God and turned to the idols. The predictable result was that the Sinaitic Covenant was terminated. The people of Israel should have known this, because God is not fickle but always the same. Even when God has to punish, it is for our good—he tries to cure us! For God's salvation is not a gift without binding consequences. James 1:17–18 (NASB):

17 *Every good thing given and every perfect gift is from above, coming down from the Father of lights, with whom there is no variation or shifting shadow.*
18 *In the exercise of His will He brought us forth by the word of truth, so that we would be a kind of first fruits among His creatures.*

Israel rejected these gifts and therefore fell under His judgment.
(Wood, 220)

Verses 7–8
7   *Therefore I will overtake them like a lion. Like a leopard along a path, I will lie in wait.*
8   *I will meet you like a bear robbed of her cubs, and I will rip open their isolated heart. Yes, I will devour them there like a lion; wild animals will tear them apart.*

The image is clear. The break with Israel has deeply hurt God. It has robbed Him of something He loved. In order to depict this, Hosea uses the image of *a bear robbed of her cubs*. That changes her into a ferocious, mauling animal, driven by the powerful emotion of injured motherly love. The Almighty reacts similarly and it is for this reason that He now opens the floodgates of His anger.
(See Hosea 5:14.)

Verse 9
You will be destroyed, O Israel! Who will be your helper then?
This verse also speaks of the hurt of the Supreme One. For He was Israel's *helper*, but His people did not want Him. Now that their protection has fallen away and the Assyrians are attacking their country, there is no one who stands up for them.

Verse 10
Should I not have been your king? Then you might have been saved in all your cities. And where are your judges now of which you said: Give me a king and princes?
The people of Israel did not rely on God, but on His king and the power of His army. The seed of this misconception was planted a long time ago, when Israel rejected the kingship of God and demanded an earthly king like those of the surrounding peoples. We find this in 1 Samuel 8:4–9 (NASB):

4   *Then all the elders of Israel gathered together and came to Samuel at Ramah;*
5   *and they said to him, "Behold, you have grown old, and your sons do not walk in your ways. Now appoint a king for us to judge us like all the nations."*
6   *But the thing was displeasing in the sight of Samuel when they said, "Give us a king to judge us." And Samuel prayed to the L*ORD*.*
7   *The L*ORD *said to Samuel, "Listen to the voice of the people in regard to all that they say to you, for they have not rejected you, but they have rejected Me from being king over them.*
8   *"Like all the deeds which they have done since the day that I brought them up from Egypt even to this day—in that they have forsaken Me and served other gods—so they are doing to you also.*
9   *"Now then, listen to their voice; however, you shall solemnly warn them and tell them of the procedure of the king who will reign over them."*

Well, Israel got his king, Saul (1 Samuel 10:1). It was against God's will. For He had given them *judges* every time His people were threatened. In those cases God intervened Himself, because He was king over Israel then. However, when a king and his princes (or magistrates) were appointed over Israel, there were no more judges to assist Israel when it was threatened.

In the time of the prophet Hosea, when the downfall of Israel was inevitable and at hand, a judge could have offered God's deliverance. But there is none.

Verse 11
In my anger I gave you a king, and in my wrath I took him away.

A king was appointed in Israel against God's will. That was an emotional decision from God, because He was in fact rejected by Israel and He had become tired of their complaining. The same emotion is now the basis of the judgment on Israel/Ephraim.

Thus the beginning and the end of the kingship over Israel/Ephraim was marked by disobedience to God—because they rejected Me!
(Calvijn, *Daniel* II, *Kleine Profeten* I/II, Hosea, 389)

Verse 12
The debt of Ephraim is sealed; his sin is stored away.
The word *sealed* carries here the connotation of being officially determined. This has the underlying meaning of a verdict. And that verdict is backed up by the recorded sins of Ephraim/Israel (*stored away*). Verse 12 then begins a closing speech, which will also signal a new period after the fall of Israel/Ephraim.

In the many centuries that followed, the Ten Tribes were paying for their sins. They had fallen deeply—from once My people (Ammi) to not My people (Lo-Ammi, Hosea 1:9); from the most blessed people on earth to a position of outcast among humanity. A deeper fall is hardly conceivable.
(Wood, 221)

Verse 13
Pains like those of a woman in labor will come over him. He is a stupid child because he does not know the time when the children are born.
There are hard times ahead for the ten tribes of Israel. They start with a bloody war against the mighty Assyria, a crushing defeat, and their subsequent exile. *Pains like those of a woman in labor* is what Hosea calls the coming judgments. This torturing pain typifies the slaughter that the Assyrians wreaked among the people of Israel. Perhaps 50 to 70 percent of the population lost their lives. What remained was deported and spread across the big empire.

13.1 Beginning anew
As in ordinary life, here too, pain usher in birth. The people of Israel/Ephraim must start all over again. The goal is to become God's people again, as Hosea 2:22 foretells. The Ten Tribes will not achieve that status according to a well-considered plan. For they have lost the knowledge of Yahweh (Hosea 4:6) and have become spiritually like a naïve child, who has no knowledge of the time or place where salvation will come to them. That salvation does not depend on themselves, but on God. He will take the initiative.

Hosea 2:13
Therefore, see! I will lure her and lead her into the desert. Then I will speak to her heart.

Zechariah 10:8 (NASB)
"I will whistle for them to gather them together, for I have redeemed them; and they will be as numerous as they were before."

Verse 14
Will I ransom them from the power of Sheol? Will I redeem them from death? Your plague is death. Your destruction is Sheol. Pity will be hidden from my eyes.
The Almighty withdrew His hands from Ephraim/Israel. Hosea described that in poetic language. There is no doubt that God could have redeemed them, but He did not. His justice demanded that judgment be meted out. Ephraim was therefore at the mercy of the power of

Sheol (the realm of the dead) and was not delivered from the coming judgments—from ruin. This was no empty prophecy, because the war against Assyria and their subsequent defeat did indeed cost Ephraim/Israel many lives, possibly 60 to 70 percent of their population. (See Excursus 23.)

Excursus 23: *Sheol*, the Hereafter?

23.a *Sheol* is surely not hell

The origin of the word *Sheol* is unknown. Some see it as a derivative of šu'āla, an Akkadian concept that signifies the mythical spiritual world. Others consider š'h as the root form, which means *being abandoned*. People then come to terms like *unland* or *unworld*, but that adds nothing to our understanding. It is certainly a world that is invisible to human beings.

Sheol is certainly not *hell* (*gehenna*) as the Dutch Statenvertaling and sometimes the KJV (add others) translate it (Job 26:6; Psalms 9:17; 16:10). Hell is the place where the divine punishment on the wicked is carried out and it is unlikely that there is anyone there already. The first to be thrown in it will be the Antichrist and the False Prophet, and then also Satan and the wicked who are resurrected from the dead (Revelation 20:10; 21:8).

Old Testament, Jewish theology saw *Sheol* as the hereafter, where all those who die find their destination. Heaven and hell were, as concepts, hardly developed at that time. People thought in levels. The heavens and God's dwelling place were above the earth and *Sheol* (the realm of the dead) was under the earth. There were also differences in degrees within *Sheol*. People spoke of honorable and dishonorable places.
(McGee, 138–39; Stuart, 295)

23.b A cautious statement

Therefore it is difficult to give a conclusive definition of the concept of *Sheol*. Opinions are therefore widely divergent. One sees it as the realm of the dead, but then another as a place where the dead "sleep" (Daniel 12:13) until they are resurrected to be judged (this author agrees with this). Another sees in *Sheol* a sort of purgatory, a portal into eternity. Still others believe that *Sheol* is a synonym for hell. Only a few come to a well-founded conclusion. We quote two of them, because they express the opinions of Bible-believing circles well. Haagen says it like this:

> Of all the dead—both believers and unbelievers—the soul goes to the realm of the dead, which is entered through gates (Isaiah 38:10 and Matthew 16:18). However, the realm of the dead is divided into two by a deep chasm (Luke 16:23), where the souls of the righteous may enjoy what no eye has seen and no ear has heard and has not entered into a human heart (1 Corinthians 2:9). On the other hand, there is a place of outer darkness, where there is weeping and gnashing of teeth (Matthew 24:51). There is the place where the souls of wicked and sinners wait for the resurrection of the dead to take place, to then be judged before the Great White Throne.

Van der Haagen thus takes the content of parables, such as those of the rich man and the poor Lazarus (Luke 16:19–31), literally. That is a very big step and certainly not in keeping with tradition. It is wiser to be more restrained on this point. For example, as Snijders describes *Sheol*:

> That is where all the dead live until the day of the resurrection (Acts 2:27, 32). Or perhaps only the wicked (Luke 16:23 and Revelation 20:13), while the righteous are then, after their death, in the house of the Lord.

The latter statement is somewhat more cautious, which appeals to me more.

23.c Conclusion

It is clear that *Sheol* indicates a place where the dead reside. Ezekiel 31 makes it clear that living beings already lived there (v. 16), although they are probably not human. It is therefore not a solution to read *realm of the dead* as many do instead of *Sheol*, because this results exegesis that cannot be substantiated.

If the prophet Daniel represents the wise and righteous among the dead (Daniel 12:2–3), then all those who have been found righteous before God, but who have not fallen asleep in Christ, are sound sleep in the realm of the dead. For those who have not been found to be righteous, the judgment applies when they appear before the great white throne. However, that judgment is executed only after the resurrection of the dead (Revelation 20:10; 21:8).

Daniel 12:2 (NASB) says:

> *"Many of those who sleep in the dust of the ground will awake, these to everlasting life, but the others to disgrace and everlasting contempt."*

Those who have fallen asleep in Christ, however, inherit the Father's house immediately after their death (1 Corinthians 15:52; 1 Thessalonians 4:13–18).

Sources:
(Baumgartner, 233–35; Blenkinsopp, 143; Block, vol. 2: 191–92, 196; Craigie, 232; Haagen, 34–35; Ouweneel, chap. 2; Weerd, *Daniël*, vol. 2, 404–6, 430–31; Weerd, *Ezechiël*, vol. 1, 50–52, 63–64)

Verse 15

Because he was like a wild [donkey] among his brothers, the east will bring the breath of Yahweh that will rise from the desert. Then his spring will be exhausted and his well will dry up. It is He who will plunder his storehouse of all its treasures.

The prophet quotes here from Hosea 8:9, where Israel is compared to a roaming wild donkey. These animals were known for their indomitable sex drive. No female donkey was safe from them. Thus the whorish behavior of the people of Israel is typified, because they committed brazen adultery.

Verse 16

Samaria will have to bear his guilt because he rebelled against his God. They will fall by the sword. His little children will be crushed and his pregnant women will be chopped into pieces.

In the name *Samaria* the northern kingdom of the Ten Tribes is summarized. The judgment has fallen. Now the debt must be paid. Israel/Ephraim stood up against God, now they would bear the terrible consequences; the text does not mask anything.

(Wood, 222)

HOSEA 14
Hebrew Text Translation

Introduction

Hosea 14 is highly debated. This can be seen in the many different translations we have come across. There are remarkable differences between a number of translations (not only those cited in the present commentary but in many more we encountered in the course of our study). The Hebrew source text is admittedly difficult. But that only accounts for a small portion of the differences in translation and their interpretation. The scholars permit themselves great freedoms to bend the translation to their own theology, as we have already seen in earlier chapters. They show little regard for the source text itself and reveal themselves rather carefree in introducing all kinds of "improvements" to the text. Moreover, for at least some exegetes, the exegesis they support plays a "strongly corrective" role or is sometimes altogether decisive.

A. New Studies Were Found

The final chapter of the book of Hosea demanded a lot of study. In the end I was still not satisfied, thus a number of additional studies were purchased and I started the study from scratch, ignoring what I had already written. Only after these new works had been examined could the process of exegesis finally reach a satisfying end. Once again, the great majority of problems were resolved by a very careful study of the Hebrew text.

B. Comparing Scripture with Scripture

Unfortunately, not every issue could be solved simply by recourse to the source text. Wherever the Hebrew text failed to offer a satisfying solution, we had to turn to context for help (comparing Scripture with Scripture). Our Bible-believing perspective was of decisive importance for verses 3, 4, and 9 in particular. These days, however, this exegetical method is uncommon, as few exegetes make use of it. Secularization has left its clear mark. It was not all that long ago that Holy Scriptures were still considered their own norm, leaving modern Scripture criticism on the fringes. Now, however, we are painfully aware that the situation has been reversed. There is only one possible remedy: *Come and let us return to Yahweh!* (Hosea 6:1).

C. Versification

Most translations begin Hosea 14 with what is identified as Hosea 14:2 in several other translations (Dutch Statenvertaling and NBG; NIVIHEOT). We have followed the majority of exegetes and English translations on this point. Thus NIVIHEOT Hosea 14:1 = our Hosea 13:16.

Verse 1 NASB
Return, O Israel, to the LORD your God, for you have stumbled because of your iniquity.

Verse 1 KJV
O Israel, return unto the LORD thy God; for thou hast fallen by thine iniquity.

Verse 1 NIV
Return, Israel, to the LORD your God. Your sins have been your downfall!

Verse 1 (2) Hebrew Interlinear Text
return! Israel to Yahweh God-of-you indeed you-fell-down because-of-sin-of-you

Verse 1b
indeed
The word *ki* usually introduces a causal relationship. It occurs very often and has a wide range of meaning. The NIVIHEOT follows its own interpretation here, which few biblical scholars support. The great majority of exegetes and translators read *for* or *because*, which we follow.
(Harper, 411; Strong's OT, word 3588)

We read: ***for***

Verse 1c
you-fell-down
The word *kashal* means something along the lines of *to fall* or *to stumble* (Leviticus 26:37; Psalm 9:3; Proverbs 4:16). Many use the present prefect tense, with which we agree.
(Andersen and Freedman, 642; Harper, 411; Strong's OT, word 3782; Wolff, 231)

We read: ***you have stumbled***

Verse 1d
because-of-sin-of-you
The word *avon* means *unrighteousness* or *iniquity* (Genesis 15:16; Leviticus 19:8). It is sometimes translated as *sin*, but that puts us a little further from the Hebrew source text.
(Andersen and Freedman, 642; Strong's OT, word 5771; Stuart, 210)

We read: ***because of your iniquity***

The entire text:
Return to Yahweh your God, O Israel, for you have stumbled because of your iniquity.

Introduction to Verse 2

This is a very important prophecy, which has had great theological significance for rabbinic teachings throughout the ages, especially after the destruction of the second temple. Verse 2 is a godly command that overcomes the loss of the holy temple in Jerusalem, the center of Jewish worship. Thanks to this command of God the rabbis institutionalized public prayer as a replacement for the temple service. A new concept was added to the life of the Jewish people: the synagogue and study hall became miniature sanctuaries. There the Jew could send his prayers to Yahweh as if they were true offerings. Thus was the synagogue made the center of Jewish communal life wherever they were in the world. To unveil this prophecy we must translate the Hebrew text to the best of our knowledge.
(Eisemann, xl)

Verse 2 NASB
Take words with you and return to the Lord. Say to Him, "Take away all iniquity and receive us graciously, that we may present the fruit of our lips."

Verse 2 KJV
Take with you words, and turn to the Lord: say unto him, Take away all iniquity, and receive us graciously: so will we render the calves of our lips.

Verse 2 NIV
Take words with you and return to the L*ORD*. Say to him: "Forgive all our sins and receive us graciously, that we may offer the fruit of our lips."

Verse 2 (3) Hebrew Interlinear Text
take! with-you words and-return! to Yahweh say! to-him all-of you-forgive sin and-receive! graciously that-we-may-offer bulls lips-of-us

Verse 2a
take! with-you words
The word *laqach* means *to take* (*with*) (Genesis 9:23; 11:29), *to take away* (Genesis 27:35), or *to get* (Judges 14:2 NASB).
(Birch, 116; Born, 78; Cheyne, 126; Strong's OT, word 3947)

We read: ***take these words with you***

Verse 2b
and-return! to Yahweh
We follow the NIVIHEOT in reading an imperative (command) here.

We read: ***then turn to Yahweh!***

Verse 2c
say! to-him all-of you-forgive sin
Few exegetes follow the NIVIHEOT in reading *sin*. *Avon* actually means *unrighteousness* or *iniquity*.

The NIVIHEOT translates the word *nasah* as *forgive*. This is interpretation, since the basic meaning of *nasah* is *to lift* or *to carry off*. In Leviticus 16 the context is that of carrying off sin (alluding to the goat of Azazel*—Leviticus 16:10 NLT, ESV, or ASV), a ceremony which is indeed a form of forgiveness. However, this may not serve as a basis for the translation here. *Nasah* is sometimes also translated as *to bear* punishment (Genesis 4:13), *to bear* iniquity (Leviticus 5:1), *to carry* (Genesis 44:1), and *to get/take* (another form of carrying, Genesis 27:3).

*Azazel is the name used in the Bible for the goat that was sent out into the wilderness on Yom Kippur. It symbolically bore the sin of the people of Israel out from the encampment, as described in Leviticus 16:8–10 (NASB):

> 8 *"Aaron shall cast lots for the two goats, one lot for the L*ORD *and the other lot for the scapegoat.*
> 9 *"Then Aaron shall offer the goat on which the lot for the L*ORD *fell, and make it a sin offering.*
> 10 *"But the goat on which the lot for the scapegoat fell shall be presented alive before the L*ORD*, to make atonement upon it, to send it into the wilderness as the scapegoat."*

(Born, 78; Calvijn, *Daniel* II, *Kleine Profeten* I/II, Hosea, 488–89; Mays, 184; Strong's OT, word 5375; Stuart, 210)

We read: ***and say to Him: remove all our iniquity***

Verse 2d
and-receive! graciously

The first word is *laqach* again (as in verse 2a), which the NIVIHEOT renders as *receive!* We opt not to follow it. We prefer to stick closer to the Hebrew and therefore read: *accept* (Psalm 6:9).

The root meaning of *towb* is *better* (Genesis 29:19; Psalm 63:3), or *the goodness* or *good* (Exodus 18:9; Numbers 10:29; Judges 9:11). Here we translate the word as *graciously* (as in the KJV, NKJV, NIV, NASB, and NLT).
(Cheyne, 126; Owens, 787; Reed, 80; Strong's OT, word 2896)

We read, first step: **and accept in graciously**
The message here is undoubtedly addressed to Israel/Ephraim. For that reason, we have repeated *us* from the preceding clause (as do many other translators.)

We read, second step: **accept us graciously**

Verse 2e
that-we-may-offer
A translation that uses the term *offer* is interpretation. *Shalam* means *to complete* or *to make good*. That is why it is also translated as *to compensate* (Exodus 21:36), *to pay* (Deuteronomy 23:21; Psalm 66:13), and *to make peace* (Deuteronomy 20:12). The final rendering may seem somewhat strange, but even there it carries this sense of *satisfaction*.
(Andersen and Freedman, 642; Born, 78; Cheyne, 126; Hubbard, 227; Mays, 184; Strong's OT, word 7999)

We read: **that we may pay**

Verse 2f
bulls lips-of-us
Here we find ourselves facing a linguistic problem. Most translators and exegetes read *pārîm* (םירפ), meaning *bulls* or, more accurately, *bullocks*.

Some are convinced that such a translation does not fit the present context. Modern exegetes therefore see in the term a derivative from *pᵉrîy* (ירפ), meaning *fruit* or *fruits*. This follows, at least in part, the Septuagint, which likewise reads *fruit*.

The scholars who support the translation *bulls/bullocks* include the following:
Brown, 119; Calvijn, *Daniel* II, *Kleine Profeten* I/II, Hosea, 488–90; Cheyne, 126–27; Garrett, 271; Guenther, 207; Keil, 163–64; Owens, 787; Rosenberg, vol. 1, 86; Sweeney, vol. 1, 138; Ward, 227; Wood, 224.

Other exegetes/translators agree that the text reads *bulls*, but they still discard this reading for exegetical reasons. Included among them are the following:
Ben Zvi, 294–95; Eidevall, 211; Harper, 411–12; Hubbard, 223; McComiskey, 229–30; Wolff, 231.

The translation *fruit of our lips* is supported by the following:
Beeby, 180; Birch, 116; Born, 78; Hubbard, 228; Mays, 184; Stuart, 210)

Conclusion:
If we wish to stick close to the Hebrew text, there is no doubt that we must read *bulls* or *bullocks*. This is what we have done. For the sake of clarity we have added the word *you* between brackets so as to indicate that the words are spoken in reference to Yahweh.

We read: **that we may pay** [You] **the young bulls with our lips**

The entire text:
Take these words with you. Then turn to Yahweh! and say to Him: Remove all our iniquity and accept us graciously, that we may pay [You] *the young bulls with our lips.*

Verse 3 NASB
"Assyria will not save us, we will not ride on horses; Nor will we say again, 'Our god,' to the work of our hands; For in You the orphan finds mercy."

Verse 3 KJV
Asshur shall not save us; we will not ride upon horses: neither will we say any more to the work of our hands, Ye are our gods: for in thee the fatherless findeth mercy.

Verse 3 NIV
"Assyria cannot save us; we will not mount warhorses. We will never again say 'Our gods' to what our own hands have made, for in you the fatherless find compassion."

Verse 3 (4) Hebrew Interlinear Text
Assyria not he-can-save-us on horse not we-will-mount and-never we-will-say again gods-of-us to-thing-made-of hands-of-us for in-you he-finds-compassion fatherless

Introduction to Verse 3

We encounter new problems in the text of verse 3a/b. If we follow the majority of exegetes in their translation, this verse would begin as follows: *Assyria cannot save us; no horse will be mounted* (or something along those lines). In the present context that does not seem to make sense, for the following two reasons:

1. Assyria never appears in Hosea as a potential savior of Israel/Ephraim; it rather represents the main threat to the nation.
2. Israel/Ephraim was not renowned for its cavalry. Of Assyria, however, we know that their cavalry and battle chariots formed the backbone to their army and also that they were greatly feared.
   (Beeby, 181; Wolff, 231)

A similar objection applies to the common translation of verse 3c. Nowhere does Hosea 14 give reason to assume that the speaker is now Israel/Ephraim. It is still the prophet who is speaking here, as in the preceding verse. As "Israel's watchman" he is the mouthpiece of the future people of God, while in the verses that follow, it is God Himself who speaks (Hosea 14:4–8). Nowhere does the nation of Israel/Ephraim speak.

The same line of reasoning has led many to suppose also that 3c does not fit in the present context. Many exegetes and translators have no problem with this supposition. This confirms once again how little respect they have for the faithfulness of the source text and for the divine authority of all prophecy (which, of course, exudes the logic and durability of the counsel of God). We, however, do hold them in esteem and therefore propose a translation that does justice to the entire chapter and also to its writer, God Himself!

Based on the reasoning of many exegetes, the first part of verse 3 is often divided as follows: a) *Assyria not he-can-save-us*; and b) *on horse not he-will-mount*. We do not follow this translation. We believe the syntax shown here matches what we find in several other passages in the Bible. For if we turn to Amos 3:8a in the Hebrew source text, we find a similar construction: *who not he-will-fear*. NASB translates there: *Who will not fear?* In Amos 3:8b the source text says: *who not he-will-prophesy*, meaning: *Who can but prophecy?*

A third expression can be found in the source text of Jeremiah 5:22, where we read: *me not should-you-fear*. There it means: *Do you not fear Me?* And, finally, a similar syntax can be found in Hosea 11:9: *Shall I not carry out my burning anger?*.

Conclusion:
On the basis of the above cross references, Hosea 14:3a/b are best interpreted as questions. (For additional and extended treatment of this textual problem, see Andersen and Freedman, 574, 589–590 and text translation of Hosea 11:9.)

Verse 3a
Assyria not he-can-save-us
We interpret the Hebrew source text here as a rhetorical question.

Yasha' is rendered in a variety of different ways, such as *to save* (Deuteronomy 22:27; Joshua 10:6) or *to deliver* (Judges 2:16; 12:2).
(Brown, 119; Mays, 184; Strong's OT, word 3467)

We read: ***would Assyria not deliver us?***

Verse 3b
on horse not we-will-mount
Here too we interpret the Hebrew source text as a rhetorical question.

A translation that uses the term *mount* is an interpretation. *Rakab* means *to ride* (Genesis 41:43; Judges 5:10; Isaiah 30:16). The word *horse* is singular, but often serves as a collective, as it does in the present context.
(Brown, 119; Hubbard, 228; Mays, 184; Strong's OT, word 7392)

We read: ***will they not ride their horses?***

Verse 3c
and-never we-will-say again gods-of-us to-thing-made-of hands-of-us
We likewise consider this clause a rhetorical question (see introduction to verse 3).

The word *elohim* means *gods*. If it is preceded by a definite article, it usually refers to God Himself (in the sense of *the* God among gods), for which we use a capital letter. In all other cases, context is decisive. The term means *gods* in, for example, Exodus 12:12; Numbers 25:2; and Joshua 24:15. Here that represents the right translation as well.
(Brown, 119; Hubbard, 228; Strong's OT, word 430)
(See Excursus 24.)

We read: ***will we ever say "our gods" to an object that our hands have made?***

Verse 3d
for in-you he-finds-compassion fatherless
The word *for* (Hebrew *asher*) is only one of several possible translations. The other variants we found include *because* (Numbers 25:13), *as* (Genesis 7:9; Ecclesiastes 9:2), *like*, *from the moment*, and *after* (Judges 16:22). This wide range of possible meanings is indicative of the trouble many exegetes/translators experience in rendering *asher*.

3.1 Another interpretation of the Hebrew source text
In Hebrew letters, the word *esher** is written the same way as the word *asher*.† That these consonants in this verse are commonly vocalized as *asher* follows the work of the Masoretes‡ (who were responsible for the pointed text = the text with the vowels and punctuation

marks added). However, the process of pointing involves interpretation, and the Masoretes were not always right. *Esher* means something along the lines of *how happy, happily,* or *blessed.* It occurs in several places in Scripture, including Psalms 1:1 and 2:12.

In Hosea 14:3 context demands the vocalization *esher.* For if we translate the term as *because* or *for (= asher),* it would mean that verse 3d has a causal relationship with what precedes. But there is just no way this can be true. However, if we read *esher*, the sentence (which looks upon the fall of Israel/Ephraim with sad irony) closes with God's offer of grace. This is entirely in line with the spirit of the prophecy of Hosea.

Yathom means *orphan.*** It is however often translated as *fatherless*, which is sometimes not a problem, but here it would be wrong. For the relationship between God and Israel is pictured as that between a man and wife. But to use the word *fatherless* would refer to God, who never is called Israel's father or the father of the land of Canaan. Neither would match the context.
(*Koehler and Baumgartner, vol. 1, 99; Strong's OT, words †834, *835, **3490; ‡*Studiebijbel* SBOT 12, 128; *Brown, Driver, Briggs, 81)

We read: ***happily the orphan finds mercy in You***

The entire text:
Would Assyria not deliver us? Will they not ride their horses? Will we ever say "our gods" to an object that our hands have made? Happily the orphan finds mercy in You.

Excursus 24: Names of the Almighty

Ancient Hebrew has different words that in one way or another include or refer to the name of God. Usually these are translated rather sloppily, with an unfortunate loss of nuance as a result. Most translations have followed tradition in this point as well.

Adon, Adonay
This term has a rather wide range of meaning. We found it rendered it as *ruler, sovereign, master,* or *owner*. When used on its own, the term is usually translated Lord or alternatively as God. If used in combination with YHWH, it is typically translated as *Lord God, Lord Jehovah,* or *Lord of Lords*. However, it is best rendered *Sovereign Yahweh*.

YHWH, YH
Usually this word is vocalized as *Yahweh* and *Yah* (a short form of Yahweh). It is not a name or personal name in the regular sense of the term, but is referred to as the tetragrammaton (the four letters). Most scholars understand it to mean something along the lines of *to be* or *to become*, which they then render as *I am* or *I am who I am* (Exodus 3:14). This is the name for God that occurs most frequently. It is used no less than 5,371 times in the Bible. Some vocalize *YHWH* as *Yahowah*. To arrive at this rendering, they insert the vowels *a, o,* and *a* from *adonay* into the basic consonantal root *YHWH*. Later on this was corrupted as Jehovah, a form that emerged in the early medieval period but has no biblical basis. The Septuagint usually translates *Yahweh* as *kyrios*, meaning *master, lord*, or sometimes just *sir*. English translations usually render this term as Lord. However, it is much better simply to read Yahweh. We find *Yah* in the word *Hallelujah*, meaning *Praise Yahweh*.

El
This is the most generally used term for God/god. It is also found in various related languages (Aramaic: *elah*; Arabic: *ilah*; Akkadian: *ilu*). The Hebrews borrowed this word

from the language of the Canaanites, who used it as the name for their most high idol. There is uncertainty surrounding its meaning. Nevertheless it appears to mean something like *leader* or *the strong one*. The plural form is *elim*, which appears in a related form in Hebrew as *Elohim*. Another derivation is the word *'eljoon*, meaning *Most High*.

Elohim, Eloah
This is another word that occurs very frequently in Scripture, for a total of more than twenty-five hundred times. Its origins go back to very ancient times. Usually it is translated as *God*. However, it is actually a plural form, and can refer to God Himself, but also to angels (Psalm 8:5; 97:7) or even pagan gods (Genesis 35:2; Exodus 18:11; 20:3). It would therefore be better translated as *divine ones* or *the divine*. Extra emphasis (e.g., *the*) could then be used to distinguish God from other divines.

Shaddai, Sadday
This term is usually translated as *almighty*; when combined with *'ēl* (God), we get *God Almighty* (Exodus 6:3). It means something along the lines of *mighty mountain* or *mountain god*. This comes from the understanding of the pagan nations, who usually conceived of tall mountains as the dwelling place of the gods.

Saba, Sebaoth
This Hebrew word is translated in a wide variety of ways. Sometimes we find *almighty* or *Almighty One*, or even *hosts*. The word occurs 486 times in Scripture, in half of these cases in combination with *Yahweh*. The NBG uses the translation L ORD *of hosts*. Literally it means something like: *The "I am" of hosts*.

Sources:
(*Encyclopedia of Bible Words*, 33–34, 44, 313, and 416; Harford, 2–4; Harris, Archer, and Waltke, 41–35, 210–12; Meister, 29, 32, 414–17, 429; *NIV Bible Dictionary*, 309–10, 393–94, 1078; Wijchers and Kat, 94, 235, 244)

Verse 4 NASB
I will heal their apostasy, I will love them freely, for My anger has turned away from them.

Verse 4 KJV
I will heal their backsliding, I will love them freely: for mine anger is turned away from him.

Verse 4 NIV
"I will heal their waywardness and love them freely, for my anger has turned away from them."

Verse 4 (5) Hebrew Interlinear Text
I-will-heal waywardness-of-them I-will-love-them freedom for he-turned-away anger-of-me from-him

Verse 4a
I-will-heal waywardness-of-them
Meshubah means *to fall back*, *to turn away*, *faithless*, *apostasy*, or *aversion* (Proverbs 1:32; Jeremiah 3:6, 8, 11). The translation *waywardness* is a little further removed from the sense of the Hebrew source text.
(Calvijn, *Daniel* II, *Kleine Profeten* I/II, Hosea, 494–95; Harper, 412–13; Strong's OT, word 4878)

We read: *I will heal their aversion*

Verse 4b
I-will-love-them freedom
Nedabah means *spontaneous*, *freewill*, or *voluntary* (Numbers 29:39; Ezra 1:4).
(Calvijn, *Daniel* II, *Kleine Profeten* I/II, Hosea, 494–95; Harper, 413; Strong's OT, word 5071)

We read: *I will love them voluntarily*

The entire text:
I will heal their aversion. I will love them voluntarily, because My anger has turned away from him.

Verse 5 NASB
I will be like the dew to Israel; he will blossom like the lily, and he will take root like the cedars of Lebanon.

Verse 5 KJV
I will be as the dew unto Israel: he shall grow as the lily, and cast forth his roots as Lebanon.

Verse 5 NIV
"I will be like the dew to Israel; he will blossom like a lily. Like a cedar of Lebanon he will send down his roots;"

Verse 5 (6) Hebrew Interlinear Text
I-will-be like-the-dew to-Israel he-will-blossom like-the-lily and-he-will-send-down roots-of-him like-the-Lebanon

Verse 5b
and-he-will-send-down roots-of-him
Nakah means *to strike*. It can be used in the sense of *to slay*, *to put to death* (Leviticus 24:17), or *to strike/send down* (Deuteronomy 27:25; Judges 1:4; 1 Samuel 15:3). We find the meaning *send down* to fit well here. Some read *to fix* or *to grasp firmly*, but that is a result of sending down roots.
(Calvijn, *Daniel* II, *Kleine Profeten* I/II, Hosea, 497; McComiskey, 233; Strong's OT, word 5221)

We read:
I will be like the dew of Israel, and he will blossom like a lily. Then he will send down his roots as the [cedars of] Lebanon.

Verse 6 NASB
His shoots will sprout, and his beauty will be like the olive tree and his fragrance like the cedars of Lebanon.

Verse 6 KJV
His branches shall spread, and his beauty shall be as the olive tree, and his smell as Lebanon.

Verse 6 NIV
"his young shoots will grow. His splendor will be like an olive tree, his fragrance like a cedar of Lebanon."

Verse 6 (7) Hebrew Interlinear Text
they-will-grow young-shoots-of-him and-he-will-be like-the-olive-tree splendor-of-him and-fragrance of-him like-the-Lebanon

Verse 6a
they-will-grow young-shoots-of-him
Yoneqeth means *sprouts* or *shoots* (Job 14:7; 15:30; Psalm 80:11), and can refer to *branches* (Job 8:16), or *twigs* (Ezekiel 17:22). Here the text no doubt envisions newly forming branches, which is why we have opted for the translation *young branches*.
(Garrett, 275; Owens, 787; Strong's OT, word 3127; Wood, 224)

We read: **his young branches will grow**

Verse 6b
and-he-will-be like-the-olive-tree splendor-of-him
The NIVIHEOT rendition using *splendor* is actually an interpretation. We will not follow it. The word *hod* means *glory*, *splendor*, or *majesty* (1 Chronicles 16:27; Psalm 45:3). Sometimes the translators and exegetes use synonyms, including *wonderful*, *beauty*, and *proud*. Rabbinic teachings sometimes translate as *abundant fruit*, expressing the fertility of Lebanon.
(Owens, 787; Strong's OT, word 935; Wolff, 232; Wood, 224)

We read: **and his majesty will be like an olive tree**

Verse 6c
and-fragrance of-him like-the-Lebanon
A forest of cedar trees releases a distinctive aroma. Therefore we add the words *cedars of* in brackets, since that is what the text is referring to.
(Eidevall, 215; Garrett, 274; Wood, 224)

We read: **and his scent as the [cedars of] Lebanon**

The entire text:
His young branches will grow and his majesty will be like an olive tree and his scent as the [cedars of] Lebanon.

Verse 7 NASB
Those who live in his shadow will again raise grain, and they will blossom like the vine. His renown will be like the wine of Lebanon.

Verse 7 KJV
They that dwell under his shadow shall return; they shall revive as the corn, and grow as the vine: the scent thereof shall be as the wine of Lebanon.

Verse 7 NIV
"People will dwell again in his shade; they will flourish like the grain, they will blossom like the vine—Israel's fame will be like the wine of Lebanon."

Verse 7 (8) Hebrew Interlinear Text
they-will-dwell men-dwelling-of in-shade-of-him they-will-flourish grain and-they-will-blossom like-the-vine fame-of-him like-wine-of Lebanon

Verse 7a
they-will-dwell men-dwelling-of in-shade-of-him
In its translation of 7a, the NIVIHEOT virtually repeats the same expression twice. This

seems to be incorrect, since the underlying Hebrew source texts differ. We do follow the NIVIHEOT for the second part, but the first part actually reads *swb* or *shub*, meaning *to turn* or *to return*.

Their use of the word *men* is an interpretation by the NIVIHEOT. It is better rendered *they who* or *those who dwell* or *live*. The text thus reads: *they-will-return they-dwelling in-shade-of-him*.
(Andersen and Freedman, 647; Brown, 121; McComiskey, 233; Owens, 787; Strong's OT, word 7725; Wolff, 232)

We read: **those who live in his shadow will return**

Verse 7b
they-will-flourish grain
The word *chayah* means *to live* (Genesis 5; 6:19; Numbers 31:15; Joshua 9:15), as well as *to come to life*, *to revive* (Psalm 80:18; 119:37), *restored*, or *recovery* (Isaiah 38:9, in the sense of raising to life). That is also the sense it has here, because the context suggests a new begin.

Garrett reads *make grain live*. He calls this "a strange way of saying *grow grain*" (as Wolff also translates). This is how many interpret it, but it is surely not what the Hebrew text says, thus we refuse to follow this reading.
(Eidevall, 216; Garrett, 275–76; Guenther, 211; Harper, 414; Strong's OT, word 2421)

We read: **they will come to life as the grain**

Verse 7c
and-they-will-blossom like-the-vine
The NIVIHEOT translation here is erroneous. Literally it may be correct, but in view of the context it is wrong. For the vine is rather *un*remarkable when it blossoms, making it unsuitable as a metaphor here.

The word *parach* means *to bud* or *to sprout*. Sometimes it can mean *to flourish* or *to blossom* (Isaiah 35:1), but that is not an option here. *Bud* does work, however, since vines produce copious new branches (Genesis 40:10; Job 14:9).
(Calvijn, *Daniel* II, *Kleine Profeten* I/II, Hosea, 498–99; Guenther, 211; Harper, 414; Strong's OT, word 6524)

We read: **then they will bud like a vine**

The entire text:
Those who live in his shadow will return. They will come to life as the grain. Then they will bud like a vine. His fame will be like the wine of Lebanon.

Verse 8 NASB
O Ephraim, what more have I to do with idols? It is I who answer and look after you. I am like a luxuriant cypress; From Me comes your fruit.

Verse 8 KJV
Ephraim shall say, What have I to do any more with idols? I have heard him, and observed him: I am like a green fir tree. From me is thy fruit found.

Verse 8 NIV
"Ephraim, what more have I to do with idols? I will answer him and care for him. I am like a flourishing juniper; your fruitfulness comes from me."

Verse 8 (9) Hebrew Interlinear Text
Ephraim what? to-me more with-the-idols I I-will-answer and-I-will-take-care-of-him I like-pine-tree green from-me fruitfulness-of-you he-is-found

Verse 8a
Ephraim what? to-me more with-the-idols
A translation with *more* is highly inadequate. The word *od* means *constantly* or describes a form of *continuity*. We found it translated as *forever* (= always or constantly; Deuteronomy 13:16); *no longer* (Ezekiel 37:22), and *as long as* (in the sense of *during my entire life*; Psalm 104:33). Some translate it as *still* or *again*, but that is likewise too limited in meaning. Others use the translation *always*, which is somewhat better.

8.1 God has nothing to do with idols!
Many read: *O Ephraim, what do I still* (or: *did I ever*) *have to do with idols?* or something similar. This is actually a rather strange interpretation, given the fact that God has never had anything to do with idols. He is exalted far above them. It was not Yahweh, but the nation of Ephraim/Israel that was bound to these idols (Wolff, 233). Some "resolve the problem" by emending the text to read: *What has Ephraim any more to do with idols?* With this reading, the clause becomes a rhetorical question from God, as a future admonition or guiding principle (Ben Zvi).

If we closely follow the Hebrew source text, it offers a ready solution by dividing this sentence into two parts. First, we read: *Ephraim, what to Me?* Then we read: *Constantly with the idols* (which is in reference to the people of Ephraim/Israel, suggesting that we should be repeating the word *Ephraim* here or inserting *you*). Now we can readily present a new translation.
(Andersen and Freedman, 642; Ben Zvi, 299; Brown, 121; McComiskey, 236; Reed, 81; Wolff, 233)

We read: ***Ephraim, what are you doing to Me? You are constantly involved with the idols!***

Verse 8b
I I-will-answer
The double occurrence of the word *I* is emphatic. Its use by the author thus serves to add extra emphasis. We can translate it as *I, yes, I* or *It is I who* . . .

We read: ***It is I who will answer***

Verse 8c
and-I-will-take-care-of-him
The word *'ă·nî* means: *I am.** Many translate as *I*, but that is not really the meaning. It expresses a kind of omnitemporal existence. We read; *It is I who*.

The word *shur*** means *to look around* or *to behold* and can be used in both a positive and a negative sense (Job 7:8; 33:14; Jeremiah 5:26 *to lurk* = to lie in wait). The *Studiebijbel* translates: *I shall guard him*. That's also a possibility, however it may be a bit too strong. So we think it's better to go with a saying like *and I am to keep an eye on him* or, even better, *look after him*.
(*Brown, Driver, Briggs, 59; Calvijn, *Daniel* II, *Kleine Profeten* I/II, Hosea, 502; Harper, 414–15;
*Harris, Archer, and Waltke, 57; Strong's OT, words *589, **7789; *Studiebijbel* SBOT 12, 130; Wood, 224)

We read: ***it is I who will look after him***

Verse 8d
I like-pine-tree green

The word *'ă·nî* means: *I am* (see verse 8c), but here it has the sense of *where I am, you will flourish like a pine tree*. We read: *As a cypress stays green in My presence*.

We find *berosh* translated as *spruce, fir, pine, cedar,* or *cypress* (2 Samuel 6:5; 1 Kings 5:10). We prefer: *cypress*.
(Beeby, 184; Eidevall, 218; Strong's OT, word 1265)

We read: *as a cypress stays green in My presence*

Verse 8e
from-me fruitfulness-of-you he-is-found
What the NIVIHEOT offers here is an interpretation of the Hebrew source text. The word *peri* means *fruit* (Genesis 1:11; Numbers 13:26).
(Beeby, 184; Calvijn, *Daniel* II, *Kleine Profeten* I/II, Hosea, 502; Harper, 415; Owens, 787; Strong's OT, word 6529)

The expression *from-me* (in verse 8e) probably goes with both clauses (verse 8d and 8e). We read: *from Me*, since it is God who is speaking.
(Guenther, 213)

We read: *from Me your fruit is found*

The entire text:
Ephraim, what are you doing to Me? You are constantly involved with the idols! It is I who will answer and it is I who will look after him. As a cypress stays green in My presence, from Me your fruit is found.

Verse 9 NASB
Whoever is wise, let him understand these things; Whoever is discerning, let him know them. For the ways of the LORD are right, and the righteous will walk in them, but transgressors will stumble in them.

Verse 9 KJV
Who is wise, and he shall understand these things? prudent, and he shall know them? for the ways of the LORD are right, and the just shall walk in them: but the transgressors shall fall therein.

Verse 9 NIV
Who is wise? Let them realize these things. Who is discerning? Let them understand. The ways of the LORD are right; the righteous walk in them, but the rebellious stumble in them.

Verse 9 (10) Hebrew Interlinear Text
who? wise indeed-he-will-realize these ones-being-discerning indeed-he-will-understand-them indeed right-ones ways-of Yahweh and-righteous-ones they-walk in-them but-ones-being-rebellious they-stumble in-them

Verse 9a
who? wise
There are two possible translations here. The most obvious one reads: *Whoever is wise . . .**
Another possibility is to read: *Who is so wise . . . ?*† We prefer the former, since it is more in line with the structure of verse 9.
*(Andersen and Freedman, 643; Ben Zvi, 313; Calvijn, *Daniel* II, *Kleine Profeten* I/II, Hosea, 503–4; Harper, 416; Mays, 190; Owens, 788)
†(Brown, 122; Cheyne, 129; Reed, 82; Wolff, 239)

We read: *whoever is wise*

Verse 9b
indeed-he-will-realize these
The word *bin* can mean *to realize*, as in the NIVIHEOT. It can also mean *to understand* (Mays, Owens, and Wolff), but an even better translation is *to discern* (McComiskey, Harper, Ben Zvi, and *Studiebijbel*). The latter is the way we find it translated in Genesis 41:33; 41:39; Deuteronomy 1:13; and 1 Kings 3:12.

We prefer the final reading because of context, among other reasons. Wisdom in the godly sense of the term is granted to those who have insight and they are therefore able to exercise discernment.

The word *these*, of course, refers to the future events of which Hosea is prophesying. This is why many translators/exegetes interpret the source text as *these things*, which we follow also.
(Ben Zvi, 313; Garrett, 281; Harper, 416; Mays, 190; McComiskey, 236; Owens, 788; *Studiebijbel* SBOT 12, 130; Wolff, 239)

We read: *will certainly discern these things*

Verse 9c
ones-being-discerning
There are few biblical scholars who follow the reading of the NIVIHEOT. Some read *ones-being-intelligent*, appealing to the word *yâbîyn* as the source for their interpretation. Others consider the source text to derive from the Hebrew root *bin*, meaning *to consider*, *to discern*, or *to be attentive* (Deuteronomy 32:7; Jeremiah 2:10). We prefer *to be alert*, since it captures both of these senses.
(Garrett, 281; Harper, 416; McComiskey, 236–37; Reed, 82; Strong's OT, words 995, 2985)

We read: *whoever is alert*

Verse 9d
indeed-he-will-understand-them
This is not difficult.

We read: *he will certainly understand them*

Verse 9e
indeed
The word *ki* usually introduces a causal relationship. Many exegetes and translators read *for* or *because*, which we follow.
(Harper, 416; Strong's OT, word 3588)

We read: *for*

Verse 9f
right-ones ways-of Yahweh
Here we depart somewhat from the reading in the NIVIHEOT. Instead of *right-ones*, we read *being right*.
(Ben Zvi, 313; Mays, 190; Owens, 788; Reed, 82; Wolff, 239)

We read: *the ways of Yahweh are right*

Verse 9g
and-righteous-ones they-walk in-them

This clause is easy to translate. The pronoun *them* obviously refers back to *ways-of* (verse 9f).

We read: ***and righteous those who walk in them***

Verse 9h
but-ones-being-rebellious they-stumble in-them
The translation *rebellious* is interpretation. The term *pasha* means *to transgress* (1 Kings 8:50; Ezra 10:13; Isaiah 43:27) or *to sin*.
(Harper, 417; McComiskey, 237; Owens, 788; Reed, 82; Strong's OT, word 6586)

We read: ***but transgressors will stumble on them***

The entire text:
Whoever is wise will certainly discern these things. Whoever is alert will certainly understand them. For the ways of Yahweh are right. Righteous are those who walk in them, but transgressors will stumble on them.

Hosea 14:1–9—The corrected text:

Verse 1   ***Return to Yahweh your God, O Israel, for you have stumbled because of your iniquity.***

Verse 2   ***Take these words with you. Then turn to Yahweh! and say to Him: Remove all our iniquity and accept us graciously, that we may pay*** [You] ***the young bulls with our lips.***

Verse 3   ***Would Assyria not deliver us? Will they not ride their horses? Will we ever say "our gods" to an object that our hands have made? Happily the orphan finds mercy in You.***

Verse 4   ***I will heal their aversion. I will love them voluntarily, because My anger has turned away from him.***

Verse 5   ***I will be like the dew of Israel, and he will blossom like a lily. Then he will send down his roots as the [cedars of] Lebanon.***

Verse 6   ***His young branches will grow and his majesty will be like an olive tree and his scent as the [cedars of] Lebanon.***

Verse 7   ***Those who live in his shadow will return. They will come to life as the grain. Then they will bud like a vine. His fame will be like the wine of Lebanon.***

Verse 8   ***Ephraim, what are you doing to Me? You are constantly involved with the idols! It is I who will answer and it is I who will look after him. As a cypress stays green in My presence, from Me your fruit is found.***

Verse 9   ***Whoever is wise will certainly discern these things. Whoever is alert will certainly understand them. For the ways of Yahweh are right. Righteous are those who walk in them, but transgressors will stumble on them.***

HOSEA 14
Exegesis

Introduction
Hosea 14 is a very controversial chapter as already mentioned in the introduction to the Hebrew text translation. This is readily apparent from the consulted translations, among other things, as they vary widely. There is no other chapter in Hosea where so many changes and additions to the text have been proposed. This shows a certain desperation on the part of the scholars as they seek a possible meaning. The simplest solution that they offer is to see Hosea 14 as having been added later—like a "happy ending," made up by a so-called "additional author," because the sad end of Hosea 13 was considered not very inspiring. That is an easy solution driven by their lack of other arguments.
(Harper, 408)
(See introduction to Hosea.)

A. The Key to the Explanation
Critical consideration and inventory of arguments reveals, that all the confusion about translation and interpretation of Hosea 14 has arisen because the biblical scholars in question miss the key to the explanation. This key lies in a certain vision of the end time. This is a scriptural position of great importance. Often, we hear the argument that "after all, it is impossible to prove prophecies about the future until they are fulfilled." But there are many prophecies that have already been fulfilled—not an unimportant given. Nevertheless many theologians ignore or even despise prophecy, hardly allowing it to play any role in their translations. We call this the text-critical approach, and this secularization has "slain its thousands."

"After all, it is impossible to prove prophecies about the future . . ." or is it? Is the long string of events in the past, that prove the fulfillment of godly prophecy, not a strong indication that biblical prophecy indeed is true foretelling? Is the given, that end-time prophecy fits into a strict schedule that finds its roots in the whole Bible, not a strong sign that God speaks? Is this system of biblical research, that leads to certain conclusions, not common sense in science? Is the process of testing a hypothesis using experimentation, direct or indirect observation, and experience not called empirical research? And is that not *the* way of gaining knowledge? So why it there so much doubt about accepting the outcome of biblical research in this field? Answer: Because of an inner instinct of human beings to rebel against the Almighty God!

If we apply the right key and we see that Hosea 14 speaks mainly about an unfulfilled future, then order and logic arise. We discover that God Himself is speaking.

B. A Vision of Hope
Hosea 14 is a very important chapter in the Old Testament. It is the final speech of the prophet, in which he says farewell to ancient Israel/Ephraim. He says farewell to the convict before he goes to his punishment. Opposite this sad point of view stands a vision of the future blessed state of the people of God. That is the purified Israel that will once again take his rightful place in salvation history. On the long road to that goal, Hosea gives them a message, an exhortation to conversion that is required to make this transformation possible. In the vision of the end time (the final stop of the people of Israel; their holy

destination) the prophet outlines the promise of salvation as we find it in the other prophets. This is a final stop that promises prosperity and happiness and a blessed companionship with the Almighty God. A blessed future for the people of Israel in the holy land—the Messianic Kingdom—is unacceptable for many exegetes.* Perhaps this is the source of confusion about the interpretation of Hosea 14 and what really drives exegetes and translators to avoid the true message of the prophet.

*This point of view is, of course, most prominent among nonbelieving and secular scholars. However, it also occurs in the Bible-believing camp. There the motives are determined by ecclesiastical dogmas which negate the authority of the Bible.

C. Who Is Speaking?
In the first three verses of this chapter the prophet Hosea speaks on behalf of God. Then the speaker is God Himself. Some therefore also include verses 1–3 (in some translations verses 2–4) in Hosea 13, but that is not necessary.

The prophecy ends with a kind of benediction—a conclusion that actually gives a summary of the entire book of Hosea.

Sources:
(Barthélemy, 620–27; Ben Zvi, 300)
(See preface to Hosea.)

Verse 1
Return to Yahweh your God, O Israel, for you have stumbled because of your iniquity.
The word *stumble* is a frequently used standard concept in the Bible. It summarizes the transgressions of Israel/Ephraim and the associated judgment (thus including the breach in the Sinaitic Covenant) in one word (see also verse 9). That stumbling is described extensively in Hosea 13 and earlier chapters. The text emphasizes that these is not mere peccadilloes, but that God's law has been trampled under their feet.

Verses 1–2 are related to Hosea 6:1. It is a call for a renewed relationship with Yahweh. This message travels with the people of Israel into the exile, which has now lasted more than twenty-five hundred years. And when the people of Israel once again respond to that call, then God will extend His hand to them again. Then the promises of salvation will become a reality for the people of Israel—Hosea 6:2c: *that we may live in His presence.**
That moment is coming when the Messianic Kingdom will be proclaimed. Then God will return to the temple in Jerusalem again, and then the twelve tribes of Israel will be able to live undisturbed *in His presence.*

The key to their re turn to Yahweh is mentioned not only here, but also in Hosea 6:2d:

So let us acquire knowledge; let us pursue the knowledge of Yahweh.†

That process may have already started in our days.
(Beeby, 178; Eidevall, 210)
(See Excursuses 7, 13; exegesis of Hosea *6:2c and †6:2d.)

Verse 2a
Take these words with you.
As luggage for the long journey in time that faces Israel/Ephraim, the people are given two urgent pieces of advice in verse 2b/c.

Verse 2b

Then turn to Yahweh! and say to Him: Remove all our iniquity and accept us graciously,

Many exegetes relate these words to the people of Israel in the time of Hosea. That is, of course, nonsense, because the judgment on Israel was fixed. There was no longer any possibility of averting it. No, this message is addressed to the people of Israel after the downfall. It belongs in their spiritual baggage for the ages to come, lasting more than twenty-five hundred years already. They *take these words with them*, and those words speak of events that will precede the prophecy of Hosea 3:5:

> *After that the children of Israel will return. Then they will seek Yahweh their God, and David their king. And they will come trembling to Yahweh and to his blessings in the last days.*

The text thus speaks of a future national conversion, of a restoration of the covenant with God. (Garrett, 271)

Verse 2c

that we may pay [You] ***the young bulls with our lips.***

Ben Zvi interprets this text as follows: *We can reward [you] with our lips as if they were young bulls*, and that is probably indeed the meaning. For on the basis of this text from Hosea, Jewish rabbis state that an end to the bringing of sacrifices in the temple never came. (Ben Zvi, 294)

(See Excursus 25.)

Excursus 25: The Sacrificial Services Were Never Discontinued

According to general opinion, with the destruction of the temple in 70 AD came an end to the sacrifices. Many Jewish rabbis think very differently about this. In their eyes—as the Talmud teaches—the sacrificial services continue uninterrupted, albeit in a different way than before.

In the Talmud we find extensive commentaries on the Bible. These are not commentaries as we know them. The Jewish theologian delves deeper into the being of the Almighty than the Christian theologian does; what is often depicted as possible conversations between key persons and God. So these statements do not come word for word from the Bible, yet they often show the fingerprint of God's Word. Rabbi Yaakov says this about the period after the destruction of the temple, when the Jews were no longer able to fulfill the legal task of the sacrificial services:

> *Abraham said: Master of the Universe, perhaps the Jews will sin before You. Will You treat them as You did the generation of the flood and the generation of the dispersion, and destroy them?*
>
> *God said to him: No.*
>
> *Abraham said before God: Master of the Universe, tell me, with what shall I inherit it? How can my descendants ensure that You will maintain the world?*
>
> *God said to Abraham: Take for Me a three-year-old heifer, and a three-year-old goat, and a three-year-old ram, and a turtledove, and a young pigeon. (God was alluding to the offerings, in whose merit the Jewish people, and through them the entire world, will be spared divine punishment.)*

Abraham said before God: Master of the Universe, this works out well when the Temple is standing, but when the Temple is not standing, what will become of them?

God said to him: I have already enacted for them the order of offerings. When they read them before Me, I will ascribe them credit as though they had sacrificed them before Me and I will pardon them for all their transgressions. Since the offerings ensure the continued existence of the Jewish people and the rest of the world, the act of Creation is read in their honor.*

Thus, in Jewish eyes, the sacrificial service has never ended, even though there is no longer a temple. For the Jews of today, the appeal of Hosea 14:2a/b applies:

Then turn to Yahweh! and say to Him: Remove all our iniquity and accept us in favor.

The national conversion of the people of Israel (words of confession) has not yet taken place. Yet the sacrifices continue, although in a completely new form, Hosea 14:2c:

that we may pay You the young bulls with our lips.

This situation continues until the present day. However, it will come to an end once God calls the lost ten tribes of Israel (*I will whistle them to Me* [Zechariah 10:8]). Then God *will redeem* them (Zechariah 10:8b) and the lost tribes of Israel will also accept Jesus Christ as their Messiah—Zechariah 12:10–11a (NASB):

10 *"I will pour out on the house of David and on the inhabitants of Jerusalem, the Spirit of grace and of supplication, so that they will look on Me whom they have pierced; and they will mourn for Him, as one mourns for an only son, and they will weep bitterly over Him like the bitter weeping over a firstborn.*
11 *"In that day there will be great mourning in Jerusalem."*

And when the people of Israel come to repentance, history will take a definitive turn and the Messiah will show His glory to the world. That will happen in the last days, when the Messianic Kingdom is established.

Sources:
(Eisemann, 604; Fisch, xviii, 265; Price, chap. 22–23; Weerd, *Zacharia*, chap. 12; *Yaakov)

Verse 3a
Would Assyria not deliver us? Will they not ride their horses? Will we ever say "our gods" to an object that our hands have made?
Almost bitterly, the prophet is pointing one more time to the coming judgment. Did Israel not seek help from the Assyrian superpower? That "help" comes in the form of a powerful army (*their horses*), however, not to redeem them, but to bring judgment.

3.1 Assur and Assyria
There is a double meaning in this text. The name Assyria usually refers to the nation. However, sometimes the Hebrew text uses Assur instead. That is, in fact, the name of the god of Assyria. And although it is usually translated as Assyria, a telling play on words arises. Sarcastically the prophet Hosea asks: *Will we ever say again "our gods"* (Assur) and worship them? Don't forget the downfall of Israel did not yet happen; Hosea looks into the future. The sarcasm is rooted in this knowledge.
(Andersen and Freedman, 645; Hubbard, 228; Ward, 227)

Verse 3b
Happily the orphan finds mercy in You.

The word *orphan* has the connotation of *without family*. It points to the broken relations between God and Israel/Ephraim, but also to the broken relations between Ephraim and Judah (the southern kingdom). But since the Lo-Ammi (= not My people; Hosea 1: 9) has sounded, Israel/Ephraim is an orphan. Yet there will also be mercy for them, provided they repent (Hosea 14:1):

Return to Yahweh your God, O Israel!

Verse 3b therefore concerns future prophecy, because up to the present day the lost Ten Tribes have not yet regained their status as God's people.

Hosea 14:4–8 Salvation Promises

The next verses are salvation promises that look forward to the blessings of the Messianic Kingdom. That will be a new era unlike any that has ever been up to this present day. It is therefore unfulfilled prophecy.
(Ironside, 108–10; Kidner, 124; Wood, 223)

Verse 4
I will heal their aversion. I will love them voluntarily, because My anger has turned away from him.
Here again we see a parallel with Hosea 6:1, because it also talks about the need to heal Israel. God's people have been severely wounded by the breaking of the Sinaitic Covenant. It has to be healed, but for to accomplish that, *their aversion* to God must first be healed. Once that happens, which is still unfulfilled prophecy, then God will be able to love the people of Ephraim for what they are. Not in the forced way of the past, when the love for His people constantly fought with God's justice for Israel/Ephraim, as they sinned again and again. But under this new Eternal Covenant (or Berit Olam), Israel will sincerely serve God and so God will *love them voluntarily*.
(See Excursus 10)

4.1 Berit Olam
This new covenant is described in Ezekiel 16:60 (NASB):

"Nevertheless, I will remember My covenant with you in the days of your youth, and I will establish an everlasting covenant with you."

Jeremiah also speaks of the new covenant (31:31–32 NASB):

31 *"Behold, days are coming," declares the* Lord, *"when I will make a new covenant with the house of Israel and with the house of Judah,*
32 *"not like the covenant which I made with their fathers in the day I took them by the hand to bring them out of the land of Egypt, My covenant which they broke, although I was a husband to them," declares the* Lord.*"*

From the preceding words it appears that the new covenant is fundamentally different from the Sinaitic Covenant, because it can no longer be broken!

Jeremiah 31:33 (NASB):
33 *"But this is the covenant which I will make with the house of Israel after those days," declares the* Lord, *"I will put My law within them and on their heart I will write it; and I will be their God, and they shall be My people.*

34 *"They will not teach again, each man his neighbor and each man his brother, saying, 'Know the LORD,' for they will all know Me, from the least of them to the greatest of them," declares the LORD, "for I will forgive their iniquity, and their sin I will remember no more."*

Verse 5a
I will be like the dew of Israel, and he will blossom like a lily.
Besides rain, the dew was indispensable for the crops in Canaan. Without the dew, which the west wind brought, the harvest failed. If it blew, it could drop a dew so heavy that it was comparable to a mild rain shower. It was the ideal way to moisten the crops. It was very different from the dreaded rain of the rainy season, which sometimes also fell during the growing season and could destroy the harvest. The dew serves here as an image of the blessing of God or the Holy Spirit.
(Ironside, 109)

Verse 5b
Then he will send down his roots as the [cedars of] Lebanon.
In a poetic way, the prophet Hosea speaks about settling in Canaan, the promised land. His way of expressing this represents, above all, permanence. And the mountains of Lebanon serve as a metaphor for a garden-of-Eden-like condition, which Hosea 2:17 also talks about:

> *Then, on the appointed day, I will make a covenant for them with the wild beasts of the field, the birds of heaven, and the creatures that crawl on the earth. I will also abolish bow, sword and war in the land; thus I will make them rest in safety.*

(Eidevall, 214; Garrett, 274)

Verse 6
His young branches will grow and his majesty will be like an olive tree and his scent as the [cedars of] Lebanon.
In a poetic manner the prophet speaks about an unfulfilled future in which Israel will flourish and shine on this earth. Ezekiel 37:26 (NASB) speaks of this:

> *"I will make a covenant of peace with them; it will be an everlasting covenant with them. And I will place them and multiply them, and will set My sanctuary in their midst forever."*

The old Sinaitic Covenant was annulled with the downfall of Israel and later Judah. But that did not erase the promise to Abraham, that Israel would become a great nation in his own country—Canaan (Genesis 17:4–8).

The return to the Holy Land and the kingship of the Messiah are sealed with a new covenant. Jeremiah 31:31–34 prophesies about this. It speaks of a covenant *after these days* (= ages), thus after the dispensation of the law (the time of Hosea) and the dispensation of grace (in which we live)—so the Messianic Kingdom.
(See Excursuses 1, 2.)

6.1 The Messianic Kingdom
That future age is referred to as the Messianic Kingdom. Jeremiah describes some characteristics of that blessed era:

Jeremiah 31:34 (NASB):
> *"They will not teach again, each man his neighbor and each man his brother, saying,*

'Know the LORD,' for they will all know Me, from the least of them to the greatest of them," declares the LORD, "for I will forgive their iniquity, and their sin I will remember no more."

Jeremiah 31:40c (NASB):
"It will not be plucked up or overthrown anymore forever."

The status of the people of Israel will then undergo a radical change, from pariah to the most honored people in this world. That will be a different kind of world than we know today.

Isaiah 62:12 (NASB):
And they will call them, "The holy people, the redeemed of the LORD"; and you will be called, "Sought out, a city not forsaken."

Isaiah 11:9 (NASB):
They will not hurt or destroy in all My holy mountain, for the earth will be full of the knowledge of the LORD as the waters cover the sea.

Verse 6b
and his majesty will be like an olive tree
The word *hod* means *glory* or *majesty* (see text translation). This often refers to the majesty of God (Job 37:22; Psalms 8:1; 104:1; 111:3; 148:13; Habakkuk 3:3). Isaiah 30:30–31 speaks of a mighty voice (= the majestic/glorious voice of God). In Psalm 45:3 and Jeremiah 22:18 it is translated as *splendor* and *majesty*. And in Zechariah 10:3 *beautiful/majestic steed* (= the majestic steed of God).

So in most cases *hod* points to the majesty of God or that of a king (who has received his majesty from God). Sometimes the majesty of the coming Messiah is mentioned, as in Zechariah 6:13. That is probably also the case here.

The prophecy looks at the end time when the people of Israel reach their destination in the Messianic Kingdom. There is no doubt that the *olive tree* is Israel (cf. Romans 11:17–24). But his *majesty* is not in his own strength. It is found in the kingship of the Messiah, Jesus Christ, and in the *majesty* of God who will then live in a newly built temple.

Isaiah 12:5–6 (NASB):
5   Praise the LORD in song, for He has done excellent things; Let this be known throughout the earth.
6   Cry aloud and shout for joy, O inhabitant of Zion, for great in your midst is the Holy One of Israel.

Verse 7a
Those who live in his shadow will return.
Those who hide in the shadow of the majesty of the olive tree are those Israelites who will accept Jesus Christ as their Messiah. Because only the true Israel will be allowed to enter the Messianic Kingdom. Ezekiel 20:37a (NASB) speaks about this:

"I will make you pass under the rod, and I will bring you into the bond of the covenant."

This refers to the counting of the sheep when the tithes were separated as an offering for God (Leviticus 27:32). Here it is meant that there will be separation between the good and the evil, as confirmed in Ezekiel 20:38 (NASB):

> *"And I will purge from you the rebels and those who transgress against Me; I will bring them out of the land where they sojourn, <u>but they will not enter the land of Israel</u>. Thus you will know that I am the LORD."*

Ezekiel 20:37–38 do not refer to the time back then but refer explicitly to the end time when the Messianic Kingdom will be established. Zechariah also speaks about the purification of Israel, which is the door to salvation, in 13:9 (NASB):

> *"And I will bring the third part through the fire, refine them as silver is refined, and test them as gold is tested. They will call on My name, and I will answer them; I will say, 'They are My people,' and they will say, 'The LORD is my God.'"*

Only those who have faithfully served God will gain access to the land of Canaan. Those are the purified, those who have not denied God and thus receive their reward. They also form the core of the future Messianic Kingdom.
(Eisemann, 336; Walvoord and Zuck, 1266; Weerd, *Zacharia*, 389–90)

Verse 7b
They will come to life as the grain.
A metaphor is used here that represents life from the dead or a kind of resurrection. The ten tribes of Israel have spread out over the world and have become invisible. But when the springtime of God's favor comes, they will sprout. And in the seemingly lifeless field (the earth after the Great Tribulation), the new life will break through, just as wheat can color a field green in a few days. The apostle Paul speaks about this in the epistle to the Romans. He typifies rejected Israel as the broken-off branches of the olive tree. But Paul also prophesies about the moment when these barren branches will be grafted in again. He describes this in Romans 11:15 (NASB):

> *For if their rejection is the reconciliation of the world, what will their acceptance be but life from the dead?*

Hosea 14:7 also speaks about the restoration of Israel. That is life from the dead, thus the coming back to life of God's people!
(Garrett, 276)
(See Excursus 2)

Verse 7c
Then they will bud like a vine.
A vine shows an exuberant outgrowth of its shoots. Hosea uses that as a metaphor with which he characterizes the blessed future of Israel. For once, that people will again fall under the blessing of God and take its allotted place in the future Messianic Kingdom. That is the transition from Lo-Ammi (not My people, Hosea 1:9) to Ammi (My people, Hosea 2:22). The apostle Paul describes that as follows in Romans 11:23–24 (NASB):

23 *And they also, if they do not continue in their unbelief, will be grafted in, for God is able to graft them in again.*
24 *For if you were cut off from what is by nature a wild olive tree, and were grafted contrary to nature into a cultivated olive tree, how much more will these who are the natural branches be grafted into their own olive tree?*

Verse 7d
His fame will be like the wine of Lebanon.
In the Messianic Kingdom the people of Israel will be praised among the nations. Then it

will take its rightful place as people of God again. That happens in Canaan, where Jesus Christ becomes King, and God Himself will dwell in a new, rebuilt temple in Jerusalem.

Annotation 14A: Songs about the Messianic Kingdom

The future Messianic Kingdom is a theme that is often praised in song in the Bible. Some examples include the following:

Zechariah 8:23 (NASB):
> "Thus says the LORD of hosts, 'In those days ten men from all the nations will grasp the garment of a Jew, saying, "Let us go with you, for we have heard that God is with you."'"

Isaiah 43:19–21 (NASB):
> 19 "Behold, I will do something new, now it will spring forth; will you not be aware of it? I will even make a roadway in the wilderness, rivers in the desert.
> 20 "The beasts of the field will glorify Me, the jackals and the ostriches, because I have given waters in the wilderness and rivers in the desert, to give drink to My chosen people.
> 21 "The people whom I formed for Myself will declare My praise."

Isaiah 61:9–11 (NASB):
> 9 Then their offspring will be known among the nations, and their descendants in the midst of the peoples. All who see them will recognize them because they are the offspring whom the LORD has blessed.
> 10 I will rejoice greatly in the LORD, my soul will exult in my God; for He has clothed me with garments of salvation, He has wrapped me with a robe of righteousness, as a bridegroom decks himself with a garland, and as a bride adorns herself with her jewels.
> 11 For as the earth brings forth its sprouts, and as a garden causes the things sown in it to spring up, so the Lord GOD will cause righteousness and praise to spring up before all the nations.

Isaiah 62:7–9 (NASB):
> 7 And give Him no rest until He establishes and makes Jerusalem a praise in the earth.
> 8 The LORD has sworn by His right hand and by His strong arm, "I will never again give your grain as food for your enemies; nor will foreigners drink your new wine for which you have labored."
> 9 But those who garner it will eat it and praise the LORD; and those who gather it will drink it in the courts of My sanctuary.

Jeremiah 33:7–9 (NASB):
> 7 "I will restore the fortunes of Judah and the fortunes of Israel and will rebuild them as they were at first.
> 8 "I will cleanse them from all their iniquity by which they have sinned against Me, and I will pardon all their iniquities by which they have sinned against Me and by which they have transgressed against Me.
> 9 "It will be to Me a name of joy, praise and glory before all the nations of the earth which will hear of all the good that I do for them, and they will fear and tremble because of all the good and all the peace that I make for it."

Excursus 26: The Purification of Israel

In Ezekiel 13:9 (NASB) we read the following:

> *"So My hand will be against the prophets who see false visions and utter lying divinations. They will have no place in the council of My people, nor will they be written down in the register of the house of Israel, nor will they enter the land of Israel, that you may know that I am the Lord God."*

This is a so-called triple curse. It involves three concepts:

1. *No place in the council of My people*
2. Not *written down in the register of the house of Israel*
3. Not entering *the house of Israel* in *the land of Israel*

26.a *No place in the council of My people*
As the text shows, this is a circle or meeting that is secret. It is not known to the people, but only to God. The prophecy in this context speaks literally about true Israel. They are those who are serving and have served God faithfully and are only known by God Himself. This can therefore refer both to living believers and to believers who have already died. Only that interpretation actually does justice to the text and the meaning of the two following concepts.

26.b Not *written down in the register of the house of Israel*
We can also translate *the registered ones*. It is therefore a register, which contains the names of the members of *the house of Israel*, with at least one exception: the false prophets that the text speaks about.

The Bible speaks in several places of heavenly books: Exodus 32:32; Daniel 12:1c; Malachi 3:16; Luke 10:20; Revelation 20:12; 21:27. This commentary is not the right place to go into this in great detail. However, it is likely that there are three books in heaven in which the names of people are recorded.

26.b1 **The Book of Life**
This book lists all the people who have ever lived and who are yet to be born. This book contains a record of their life on earth (Psalm 69:28; Revelation 20:12).

26.b2 **The Register of the House of Israel** (also called: *Those Who Fear the Lord*)
It contains the names of all true believers of the people of Israel, except for the members of the church of Christ (Ezekiel 13:9; Malachi 3:16).

26.b3 **The Book of Life of the Lamb**
In it we find all who have died and will yet die in Christ, but also those who will ascend to heaven with Him (Hebrews 12:23; Revelation 13:8).

So this passage in Ezekiel refers to the *Register of the House of Israel* (26.b2).
(Bette, Brink, and Zwiep, *Openbaring*, 413–14)

A scroll is also spoken of in Ezekiel 9:2 and that too is probably the *Register of the House of Israel*. That book probably contains the names of all Israelite believers, with the exception of the members of the church of Christ. The only alternative to our interpretation is that it lists those who returned from exile, which we find in Ezra and Nehemiah. That explanation, however, has little credibility.

Does the prophecy speak of the returned exiles? No!

It is probable that in 538 BC the first small groups of Jews returned to Canaan and that it was only toward 520 (the start of the rebuilding of the temple) that larger numbers could be spoken of. Since the prophecy of Ezekiel took place just before the destruction of Jerusalem (587 BC), certainly about sixty to seventy years had passed.

If we assume that the false prophets (Ezekiel 13:9a) were at least thirty years old at the time of the prophecy, they would have to have been between seventy-nine and one hundred years old or even older at the time of the return. By far the majority of them would already have died, so this option is highly unlikely. Moreover, in Ezra 2 and Nehemiah 7 there is no mention of persons who are excluded from the list or the *Register*.

The conclusion is therefore that Ezekiel speaks about the *Register of the House of Israel*. We also note that this prophecy is universal, so it applies to all times. So salvation is at stake for the false prophets. They are excluded from this *Register*.
(Greenhill, vol. 1, 303–5; Jagersma, vol. 1, 270–73)

26.c Not entering *the house of Israel* in *the land of Israel*
We are dealing here with a typical designation with a pronounced messianic character. The term *land of Israel* therefore also refers to that land in the future Messianic Kingdom. No prophets will be tolerated in that realm, for all prophecy will then be fulfilled. Thus, everyone who acts as a prophet is a false prophet! Zechariah 13:2–3 is very clear on this.

Thus here too there is a universal meaning. This prophecy rules out false prophets entering the Messianic Kingdom once it is established.
(See Weerd, *Zacharia*, chap. 13.)

Verse 8
Ephraim, what are you doing to Me? You are constantly involved with the idols! It is I who will answer and it is I who will look after him. As a cypress stays green in My presence, from Me your fruit is found.
Verse 8 wraps up Hosea 14. The text is reminiscent of Deuteronomy 11:26–28 (NASB):

26 *"See, I am setting before you today a blessing and a curse:*
27 *"the blessing, if you listen to the commandments of the Lord your God, which I am commanding you today;*
28 *"and the curse, if you do not listen to the commandments of the Lord your God, but turn aside from the way which I am commanding you today, by following other gods which you have not known."*

In Hosea 14:8 God also holds before the people blessing and curse. The curse is a result of Israel/Ephraim *constantly* being *involved with the idols*, which led to the breach of the Sinaitic Covenant. Thus God's protection of the nation lapsed, allowing the Assyrians to destroy the country and take the surviving population into exile. Therefore the kingdom of the Ten Tribes came to an end.

The restoration of the Ten Tribes lies in the hands of God (*from Me your fruit is found*). He is the source of all blessing. He is the eternal—the always constant. God does not change. If Israel/Ephraim repents, then that people will also become an ever-*green cypress*. This prophecy gives us a picture of continuous prosperity. This is the blessed society of the future Messianic Kingdom.
(Ironside, 111)
(See Annotation 1D, 1F; Excursus 13.)

Verse 9
Whoever is wise will certainly discern these things. Whoever is alert will certainly understand them. For the ways of Yahweh are right. Righteous are those who walk in them, but transgressors will stumble on them.

The final words of Hosea are easy to understand. *Whoever is wise* (has wisdom from God) will understand the progress of God's salvation, for he or she receives insight. *Whoever is alert* will certainly notice the signs of the times. For the wise person the dawn of God's salvation is already visible. He/she knows that the end time is near. Christ is coming, Maranatha!

BIBLIOGRAPHY

Abraham, Trommius. *Concordantie van de Bijbel, De Nederlandse*, Den Haag, Netherlands: Voorhoeve.

Allen, L. C. *Word Biblical Commentary. Ezekiel 20–48*. Dallas: Word Books, 1990.

Alt, A. *The Origins of Israelite Law*. Garden City, New York: Doubleday.

———. *The Formation of the Israelite State in Palestine*. New York: Doubleday, 1968.

(ASV) *American Standard Version*. Brunswick, ME: Bible Hub International, 1901.

Andersen, F. I., and D. N. Freedman. *Hosea: A New Translation. The Anchor Bible*. New York: Doubleday & Company, 1980.

Bacher, W. *Sefer Haschoraschim; Wurzelwörterbuch der Hebräischen Sprache von Ibn Ganâh*. Berlin, Deutschland: Meqitze Nirdamim, 1896.

Barnhouse, D. G. *Epistle to the Romans*. Philadelphia: The Bible Study Hour.

Barthélemy, D. *Critique Textuelle de l'Ancien Testament III*. Roma: Orbis biblicus et orientalis.

Baumgartner, W. *Zeitschrift für die Alttestamentliche Wissenschaft 33*. Berlin, Deutschland: Töpelmann, 1913.

Beaugency, Eliezer of. *Commentary on the Twelve Prophets and Ezekiel*. Jerusalem, Israel: Bar-Ilan University Press.

Beeby, H. D. *Hosea, Grace Abounding*. International Theological Commentary. Edinburgh, Scotland: Handsel.

Beecher, W. J. *The Prophets and the Promise*. New York: Crowell, 1905.

Beegle, D. M. *Prophecy and Prediction*. Ann Arbor, Michigan: Pryor Pettengill, 1978.

Ben Zvi, E. *Hosea*. The Forms of the Old Testament Literature. Grand Rapids: Eerdmans.

(BSB) *Berean Study Bible*.) Brunswick, ME: Bible Hub International.

Bette, J. C., G. van den Brink, and A. W. Zwiep. *Matteüs. StudieBijbel*. Soest, Netherlands: Uitgeverij In de Ruimte.

Bette, J. C., G. van den Brink, and A. W. Zwiep. *Openbaring. StudieBijbel*. Zaltbommel, Netherlands: Van de Garde.

Bette, J. C., G. van den Brink, and A. W. Zwiep. *Romeinen. StudieBijbel*. Zaltbommel, Netherlands: Van de Garde.

Bette, J. C., G. van den Brink, and A. W. Zwiep. *Thessalonicenzen. StudieBijbel*. Zaltbommel, Netherlands: Van de Garde.

(BHI) *Bible Hub Interlinear. Hebrew Text: Westminster Leningrad Codex*. Glassport, Pennsylvania: Biblehub.

(BBE) *Bible in Basic English*. Translated by S. N. Hooke, Cambridge: Cambridge Univ. Press, 1949.

Birch, B. C. *Hosea, Joel and Amos*. Louisville, KY: Westminster John Knox Press.

Blenkinsopp, J. *Ezekiel: An Interpretation*. Louisville, KY: Westminster John Knox Press.

Block, D. I. *The Book of Ezekiel, Chapters 1–24*. Grand Rapids: Eerdmans.

———. *The Book of Ezekiel, Chapters 25–48*. Grand Rapids: Eerdmans.

Boice, J. M. *The Last and Future World*. Grand Rapids: Zondervan.

———. *The Minor Prophets*. Vols. 1–2. Grand Rapids: Kregel.

Born, A. van de. *De Boeken van het Oude Testament: De Kleine Profeten*. Roermond, Netherlands: Romen.

Botterweck, G. J., H. Ringgren, and H.-J. Fabry, eds. *Theological Dictionary of the Old Testament*. 15 vols. Grand Rapids: Eerdmans, 1980.

Breuer, Rabbi Joseph. *Introduction to Rabbi Samson Raphael Hirsch's Commentary on the Torah*. Vol. 1. New York: Philipp Feldheim, 1948.

Bright, J. *The Future in the Theology of Eighth-Century Prophets*. Philadelphia: Westminster Press.

Bromiley, G. W. *International Standard Bible Encyclopedia*. Grand Rapids: Eerdmans.

Brown, F., S. Driver, and C. Briggs. *The Brown-Driver-Briggs Hebrew and English Lexicon*. Peabody, MA: Hendrickson, 2014.

Brown, S. L. *The Book of Hosea*. Westminster Commentaries. London, UK: Methuen & Co., 1932.

Bulkeley, T. *Hypertext Bible Commentary*. Notes on Amos 5:10–13. Postmodern Bible Software.

Burroughs, J. *An Exposition of the Prophecy of Hosea*. Grand Rapids: Reformation Heritage Books.

Buss, M. J. *The Prophetic Word of Hosea*. Berlin, Germany: Verlag Alfred Töpelmann, 1969.

Calvijn, J. *Verklaring van de Bijbel, Daniël II en Kleine Profeten I–II*. Kampen, Netherlands: De Groot Goudriaan.

———. *Verklaring van de Bijbel, Jesaja I–III*. Kampen, Netherlands: De Groot Goudriaan.

———. *Verklaring van de Bijbel, Kleine Profeten III–V*. Netherlands: De Groot Goudriaan.

Canisiusvertaling, Petrus. *De Heilige Schrift, Vertaling uit de Grondtekst met Aantekeningen*. Utrecht, Netherlands: Het Spectrum.

Cazelles, H. S. *The Customary Laws and the Return of the Ancient Kings*. Richmond, Virginia: John Knox.

Chaplin. *Palestina Exploration Quarterly, 1883*.

Cheyne, T. K. *The Book of Hosea*. Cambridge: Cambridge Univ. Press, 1905.

(CSB) *Christian Standard Bible*. Brunswick, ME: Bible Hub International.

Cohen, H. *The Commentary of Rabbi David Kimhi on Hosea*. New York: AMS Press.

Concordantie van de Bijbel. NBG vertaling. Kampen, Netherlands: J. H. Kok.

Constable, T. L. *Hosea*. Plano, Dallas, Texas: Plano Bible Chapel, 2020.

(CEV) *Contemporary English Version*. Philadelphia, Pensylvania: American Bible Society.

Cooper, L. E. Sr. *Ezekiel*. The New American Commentary. Nashville, Tennessee: Broadman & Holman.

Craigie, P. C. *Ezekiel*. The Daily Study Bible Series. Louisville, KY: Westminster John Knox Press.

Crosius, J. *Hypotyposes Concionum in Prophetas Minores*, 1673.

Dahood, M. *The Root GMR in the Psalms*. Theological Studies 14. Garden City, New York: Doubleday, 1953.

Davidson, B. *The Analytical Hebrew and Chaldee Lexicon*. Grand Rapids: Zondervan.

Davies, G. I. *Hosea*. Grand Rapids: Eerdmans, 1992.

Dee, S. P., and J. Schoneveld. *Encyclopedie van het Oude en Nieuwe Testament A–K*, Baarn, Netherlands: Bosch & Keuning.

———. *Encyclopedie van het Oude en Nieuwe Testament L–Z*. Baarn, Netherlands: Bosch & Keuning.

(DRA) *Douay-Rheims Bible*. Bishop Challoner Revision, 1752.

Driver, G. R. *Zeitschrift für Alttestamentliche Wissenschaft*. Oldenbourg, Deutschland: Ed Gruyter, 1953.

Easton's Bible Encyclopedia. Edenburgh, Scotland: Thomas Nelson, 1897.

Edelkoort, A. H. *Bijbel met Kanttekeningen. De Profeet Hosea*. Baarn, Netherlands: Bosch & Keuning.

Eidevall, G. *Grapes in the Desert*. Stockholm, Sweden: Almqvist & Wiksell, 1996.

Eisemann, M. *The Book of Ezekiel*. Artscroll Tanach Series. New York: Mesorah.

Encyclopedia of Bible Words. Grand Rapids: Zondervan.

Encyclopedie van Westerse Goden en Godinnen. Netherlands: De Kern.

(ESV) *English Standard Version*. Washington: Christian Education of the National Council of the Churches of Christ in the USA, 1971.

Fairbairn, P. *Exposition of Ezekiel*. Lafayette, IN: Sovereign Grace.

Feinberg, C. L. *Millennialism: The Two Major Views*. Winona Lake, IN: BMH Books.

———. *The Minor Prophets*. Chicago: Moody Press.

Finlay, D. T. *The Birth Report Genre in the Hebrew Bible*. Tübingen, Deutschland: Gulde-Druck, 2005.

Fisch, S. *Ezekiel*. Soncino Books of the Bible. London, UK: Soncino Press, 1950.

Flanders, H. J., R. W. Crapps, and D. A. Smith. *People of the Covenant*. New York: Oxford Univ. Press.

Fowler, J. A. *Commentary on the Epistle to the Hebrews. Jesus Better Than Everything.* Fallbrook, CA: CIY Publishing.

Freedman, H. and Simon, M. *Midrash Rabbah.* 10 vols. New York: The Sonico Press, 1983.

Fuchs, D. *Israel's Holy Days.* New Jersey: Loizeaux Brothers.

Garrett, D. A. *Hosea, Joel.* The New American Commentary. Nashville, Tennessee: Broadman & Holman

Gelderen, C van. *Het boek Hosea.* Kampen, Netherlands: J. H. Kok.

Gerleman, G. *Der Nicht-Mensch.* Vetus Testamentus 24. Leiden, Netherlands: Brill, 1974.

Ginzberg, L. *The Legends of the Jews.* Vols. 1–2. New York: Alef Torah Institute.

Goldwurm, Rabbi H. *Daniel.* Brooklyn, NY: Mesorah Publications, 1979.

(GNT) Good News Translation. Philadelphia: American Bible Society, 1992.

Gordis, R. *Poets, Prophets, and Sages.* Bloomington: Indiana Univ. Press, 1971.

Gordon, R. *Studies in the Relationship of Biblical and Rabbinic Hebrew.* New York: Academy for Jewish Research, 1945.

Gordon, Robert P. *Studies in the Targum to the Twelve Prophets.* New York: E. J. Brill, 1994.

Gradwohl, R. *Wat Is de Talmud? Inleiding in de mondelinge traditie van het Jodendom.* Baarn, Netherlands: Ten Have.

Greenberg, M. *The Anchor Bible. Ezekiel 1–20.* New York: Doubleday.

———. *The Anchor Bible. Ezekiel 21–37.* New York: Doubleday.

Greenhill, W. *An Exposition of Ezekiel.* Edenbergh, Scotland: The Banner of Truth.

Grosheide, F. W., J. H. Landwehr, C. Lindeboom, and J. C. Rullmann. *Christelijke Encyclopædie voor het Nederlandse Volk.* Vols. 1–6. Kampen, Netherlands: J. H. Kok.

Guenther, A. R. *Hosea & Joel.* Believers Church Bible Commentary. Waterloo, ON: Herald.

Haagen, C. van der. *Profetisch Perspectief.* Doorn, Netherlands: Het Zoeklicht.

Hakvoort, R. A. *Namen van God in het Oude Testament.* Den Haag, Netherlands: Initiaal.

Handboek van De Geschiedenis van het Christendom. The History of Christianity. Bristol, UK: Purnell and Sons.

Harford, J. B. *Studies in the Book of Ezekiel.* Cambridge: Cambridge Univ. Press, 1935.

Harper, R. W. *Amos and Hosea.* The International Critical Commentary. Edinburgh, Scotland: T & T Clark.

Harris, R. L., G. L. Archer, and B. K. Waltke. *Theological Wordbook of the Old Testament.* Chicago: Moody Publishers.

Harrison, R. K. *The Zondervan Pictorial Bible Dictionary.* Grand Rapids: Zondervan, 1963.

Henderson, E. *The Book of the Twelve Minor Prophets.* Boston: Gould & Lincoln, 1860.

Hengstenberg, E. W. *Die Christologie des Alten Testaments*, 1863.

Heschel, A. J. *God in Search of Man: A Philosophy of Judaism.* New York: Farrar, Straus and Giroux, 1980.

———. *De Profeten.* Vught, Netherlands: Scandalon, 2013.

Heyer, C. J. den. *De Messiaanse Weg.* 3 vols. Kampen, Netherlands: J. H. Kok.

Hill, D. *Greek Words and Hebrew Meanings.* Society for New Testament Studies. Monograph Series 5. Cambridge: Cambridge Univ. Press.

Holladay, W. L. *The Root šûbh in the Old Testament.* Leiden, Netherlands: Brill, 1959.

Hubbard, D. A. *Hosea. Tyndale Old Testament Commentaries.* Leicester, UK: Inter-Varsity Press.

(ISV) *International Standard Version.* Bellflower, California: The ISV Foundation, 2011.

Ironside, H. A. *Notes on the Minor Prophets.* Neptune, NJ: Loizeaux Brothers.

Jagersma, H. *Geschiedenis van Israël.* Vols. 1–2. Het Oud-Testamentische Tijdvak. Kampen, Netherlands: J. H. Kok.

Jamieson, R. *A Commentary on the Old and New Testaments.* Vol. 1. Hartford, CT: Scranton.

Jeffrey, G. R. *KJV Prophecy Marked Reference Study Bible.* Grand Rapids: Zondervan.

Johnston, P. S. *Dictionary of the Old Testament: Wisdom, Poetry and Writings.* Nottingham, England: InterVarsity Press, 2008.

Josephus, F. *Antiquitates Judaicæ*. Deel I–XX. Amsterdam, Netherlands: Ambo Klassiek.

———. *De Joodse Oorlog & Uit Mijn Leven*. Amsterdam, Netherlands: Ambo Klassiek.

Joüon, P. *Grammaire de l'Hebrew Biblique*. Italia, Roma: Pontifical Biblical Institute, 1947.

Kaplan, A. E. *Divrei Talmud*. Vols. 1–2. Jerusalem, Israel: Mossad Harav Kook Publishers.

Keck, L. E. *The New Interpreter's Bible*. A Commentary in Twelve Volumes. Vol. 1 Nashville: Abingdon Press.

Keil, C. F. *The Book of Hosea*. Grand Rapids: Eerdmans.

Keil, C. F., and F. Delitzsch. *The Twelve Minor Prophets*. 2 vols. Edinburgh, Scotland: T & T Clark, 1893.

Kessler, M. *Reading the Book of Jeremiah. A Search for Coherence*. Winona Lake, Indiana: Eisenbrauns, 2004.

Kidner, D. *The Message of Hosea*. The Bible Speaks Today. Cambridge: Inter-Varsity Press.

King, P. J. *Amos, Hosea, Micah: An Archaeological Commentary*. Philadelphia: Westminster Press.

Kittel, G. and G. Friedrich, eds. *Theological Dictionary of the Old Testament*. 10 vols. Grand Rapids: Eerdmans, 1999.

(KJV) King James Version. Grand Rapids: Zondervan.

Knight, G. A. F. *The Torch Bible Commentaries*. Louisville, Kentucky: Westminster John Knox Press, 1980.

Koehler, L., and W. Baumgartner. *The Hebrew and Aramaic Lexicon of the Old Testament*. 2 vols. Boston: Brill Publishers, 2001.

Kohlenberger, J. R. III, *The NIV Interlinear Hebrew-English Old Testament*. 4 vols. Grand Rapids: Zondervan, 1987.

Köhler, L. *Kleine Lichter; Fünfzig Bibelstellen Erklärt*. Zürich, Schweiz: Livingli, 1945.

Koekkoek, H. G. *De Geheimen van Offers*. Alphen aan den Rijn, Netherlands: Het Licht des Levens.

Krelof, S. A. *God's Plan met Israël: Een Studie over Romeinen 9–11*. Doorn, Netherlands: Uitgeverij Het Zoeklicht.

Kuhnigk, W. *Nordwestsemitische Studien zum Hoseabuch*. Italia, Roma: Pontifical Biblical Institute.

Lankester, J. and K. Lankester. *Westerse Goden en Godinnen*. Utrecht, Netherlands: Uitgeverij De Fontein.

Leeuwen, W. S. van, W. Semmelink, and J. H. Smilde. *Bijbel met Kanttekeningen, Mattheus–Johannes*. Baarn, Netherlands: Bosch & Keuning, 1955.

Leidse Vertaling. Leiden, Netherlands: Brill, 1914.

Limburg, J. *Hosea–Micah*. Interpretation, A Bible Commentary. Louisville, Kentucky: Westminster John Knox Press.

Lutherse Vertaling. Adolf Visscher. Amsterdam, Netherlands: J. Brandt en Zoon, 1896.

Mansoor, M. *The Thanksgiving Hymns*. Vol. 3 of *Studies on the Texts of the Desert of Judah*. Leiden, Netherlands: Brill, 1961.

Mays, J. L. *Hosea: A Commentary*. Philadelphia: Westminster Press.

McComiskey, T. E. *The Minor Prophets*. Vol. 1. Grand Rapids: Baker.

McGee, J. V. *Hosea and Joel*. Nashville: Thomas Nelson, 1996.

Meister, A. *Namen des Ewigen*. Frankfurt, Deutschland: Pfäffikon, 1973.

(MSG) *The Message*. Trans. by Eugene Peterson. Carol Stream, Illinois: NavPress, 2018.

Negenman, J. *Een Geografie van Palestina*. Kampen, Netherlands: J. H. Kok.

Nestle, *Zeitschrift für Alttestamentliche Wissenschaft*. Vol. XXIX, Berlin, Deutschland: De Gruyter.

Neusner, J. *Hosea in Talmud and Midrash: Studies in Judaism*. Boulder, NY: University Press of America.

(NASB) *New American Standard Bible*. La Habra, California: The Lockman Foundation, 1995.

NASB Exhaustive Concordance of the Bible. La Habra, CA: The Lockman Foundation, 1981.

(NEB) *New English Bible*. British and Foreign Bible Society. Coronet, UK: Hodder & Stoughton, 1970.

(NET) *New English Translation*. Nashville: Harper Collins Christian Publishing, 1997.

(NIV) *New International Version*. London, UK: Hodder & Stoughton.

NIV Bible Dictionary. Ed. Merrill C. Tenney. Grand Rapids: Zondervan.

NIV Study Bible. UK: Hodder & Stoughton.

NIV Topical Study Bible. Grand Rapids: Zondervan.

(NKJV) *New King James Version.* Nashville: Thomas Nelson.

(NLT) *New Living Translation.* Carol Stream, IL: Tyndale, 2015.

(NRSV) *New Revised Standard Version.* British and Foreign Bible Society. UK: Hodder & Stoughton, 1990.

(NBG) *Nieuwe Bijbelvertaling.* Amsterdam, Netherlands: Nederlands Bijbelgenootschap, 1951.

(NBV) *Nieuwe Bijbelvertaling.* Haarlem, Netherlands: Nederlands Bijbelgenootschap, 2004.

Obbinkvertaling. Leiden, Netherlands: Brill, 1937.

Oden, T. C. *The Twelve Prophets.* Vol. 14 of *Ancient Christian Commentary on Scripture.* London, England: Inter-Varsity Press.

Ogilvie, L. J. *Hosea, Joel, Amos, Obadiah, Jonah.* Vol. 20 of *Mastering the Old Testament.* Dallas: Word, 1990.

Oswalt, John N. *The Book of Isaiah, Chapters 1–39.* New International Commentary on the Old Testament. Grand Rapids: Eerdmans.

———. *The Book of Isaiah, Chapters 40–66.* New International Commentary on the Old Testament. Grand Rapids: Eerdmans.

Ouweneel, W. J. *De Negende Koning.* Vaassen, Netherlands: Medema.

Owens, J. J. *Analytical Key to the Old Testament.* Vol. 4. Grand Rapids: Baker.

Pache, R. *De Komende Christus.* Laren, Netherlands: Novapres.

Paul, M. J., G. van den Brink, and J. C. Bette. *Bijbelcommentaar, SBOT 1–12.* Veenendaal, Netherlands: Centrum voor Bijbelonderzoek.

Paul, M. J., G. van den Brink, and J. C. Bette. *Bijbelcommentaar, SBNT 1–16.* Veenendaal, Netherlands: Centrum voor Bijbelonderzoek.

Paul, M. J., G. van den Brink, and J. C. Bette. *Ezechiël en Daniël. Studiebijbel Oude Testament. Bijbelcommentaar.* Veenendaal, Netherlands: Centrum voor Bijbelonderzoek, 2014.

Paul, M. J., G. van den Brink, and J. C. Bette. *Hosea tot Maleachi. Studiebijbel Oude Testament. Bijbelcommentaar.* Veenendaal, Netherlands: Centrum voor Bijbelonderzoek, 2015.

Petuchowski, J. J. *Van Pesach tot Chanoeka.* Baarn, Netherlands: Ten Have, 1987.

Pfeiffer, C. F., H. F. Vos, and J. Rea. *Wycliffe Bible Dictionary.* Peabody, MA: Hendrickson.

Phillips, J. *Exploring the Future: A Comprehensive Guide to Bible Prophecy.* Neptune, NJ: Loizeaux Brothers.

Price, R. *The Coming Last Days Temple.* Eugene, Oregon: Harvest House Publishers, 1999.

Pusey, E. B. *The Minor Prophets.* New York: Funk and Wagnalls, 1886.

RaDaK (R. David Kimchi). *Mikraoth Gedoloth; The Book of the Twelve Prophets.* Vol. 1. New York: Judaica Press.

Reed, F. O. *Hosea through Malachi.* Vol. 5 of *Beacon Bible Commentary.* Kansas City, MS: Beacon Hill.

(REB) *Revised English Bible.* Oxford: Oxford University Press, 1990.

Riedel, W. *Alttestamentliche Untersuchungen.* Vols. 1–2. Berlin, Deutschland, De Gruyter, 1902.

Rosenberg, A. J. *The Book of the Twelve Prophets.* Vols. 1–2. New York: Judaica Press.

Rossier, R. *God's Bemoeiingen met Israël en de Volken.* Vols. 1–3. Den Haag, Netherlands: Stichting Deborah.

Rowley, H. H. *Men of God: Studies in Old Testament History and Prophecy.* London: Nelson, 1963.

Schmidt, H. *Hosea 6:1–6. Beiträge zur Religionsgeschichte und Archäologie Palästinas.* 1927.

Sherman, N. *The Book of Ezekiel.* New York: Mesorah Publications.

———. *Daniel: A Bridge to Eternity.* New York: Mesorah Publications.

Simundson, D. J. *Hosea, Joel, Amos, Obadiah, Jonah, Micah.* Nashville: Abingdon, 2005.

Singer, I. *Jewish Encyclopedia.* Jewish Encyclopedia Foundation. Skokie, Illinois: Varda Books, 1901–6.

Smith, G. V. *Hosea, Amos, Micah.* The NIV Application Commentary. Grand Rapids: Zondervan.

Snijders, L. A. *Bijbels Woordenboek*. Zutphen, Netherlands: Thieme.
Statenvertaling, MediaanBijbel. Den Haag, Netherlands: Boekencentrum, 1637.
Stone, N. J. *Names of God*. Chicago: Moody Press, 1944.
Strong, J. *Exhaustive Concordance of the Bible, Red Letter*. Tennessee: Thomas Nelson.
———. *Exhaustive Concordance of the Bible, Topical Index*. Tennessee: Thomas Nelson.
Stuart, D. *Hosea–Jonah*. Vol. 31 of *Word Biblical Commentary*. Waco, TX: Word Books.
Studiebijbel SBOT 1, Genesis–Exodus. Doorn, Netherlands: Centrum voor Bijbelonderzoek, 2004.
Studiebijbel SBOT 12, Hosea–Malachi. Doorn, Netherlands: Centrum voor Bijbelonderzoek, 2012.
Sweeney, M. A. *The Twelve Prophets*. Berit Olam Studies in Hebrew Narrative and Poetry. 2 vols. Collegeville, MN: Liturgical Press, 2000.
Talmud Bavli, The William Davidson Talmud. USA: Sefaria, American Digital Libraries.
Targum Jonathan on Hosea. Jonathan ben Uziel. USA: Sefaria; American Digital Libraries.
Trommius, Abraham. *Concordantie van de Bijbel. De Nederlandse*. Den Haag, Netherlands: Voorhoeve.
Unnik, W. C. *Bijbel met Kanttekeningen, Paulus–Openbaringen*. Baarn, Netherlands: Bosch & Keuning.
Veldkamp, H. *De Zoon van Beëri (Hosea)*. Franeker, Netherlands: T. Wever, 1938.
Vermes, G. *The Dead Sea Scrolls in English*. Boston, MA: Brill.
Vries, S. *Joodse Riten en Symbolen*. Amsterdam, Netherlands: Arbeiderspers.
Vuillenmier-Bessard, R. "Osée 13:12 et les Manuscrits." *Revue de Qumran 1 (1958)*.
Walvoord, J. F. *The Millennial Kingdom*. Grand Rapids: Zondervan.
Walvoord, J. F., and R. B. Zuck. *Bible Knowledge Commentary*. Dallas Seminary Faculty. Colorade Springs: Victor Books.
Ward, J. M. *Hosea: A Theological Commentary*. New York: Harper & Row.
Weerd, G. A. van de. *De Profeet Daniël, deel 1*. Bijbelverklaring. Ede, Netherlands: PMI, 2001
———. *De Profeet Daniël, deel 2*. Bijbelverklaring. Ede, Netherlands: PMI, 2001.
———. *De Profeet Ezechiël, deel 1*. Bijbelverklaring. Ede, Netherlands: PMI, 2004.
———. *De Profeet Ezechiël, deel 2*. Bijbelverklaring. Ede, Netherlands: PMI, 2006.
———. *De Profeet Jesaja, deel 1*. Bijbelverklaring. Ede, Netherlands: PMI, 2015.
———. *De Profeet Jesaja, deel 2*. Bijbelverklaring. Ede, Netherlands: PMI, 2018.
———. *De Profeet Micha*. Bijbelverklaring. Ede, Netherlands: PMI, 2001.
———. *De Profeet Zacharia*. Bijbelverklaring. Ede, Netherlands: PMI, 1999.
Weinfeld, M. *Deuteronomy and the Deuteronomic School*. University Park, Pennsylvania: Journal of the American Oriental Society.
Westermann, C., and E. Jenni. *Theologisches Handwörterbuch zum AT*. München, Deutschland: Kaiser, 1976.
Wiersinga, H. A. *Bijbel met Kanttekeningen, Jesaja*. Baarn, Netherlands: Bosch & Keuning.
Wigram, George V. *Englishman's Hebrew Concordance of the Old Testament*. Massachusetts: Hendrickson.
Wijchers, J. and S. Kat. *Het Bijbels Namenboek*. Den Haag, Netherlands: Thieme.
Wildschut, A. A. *Bijbel met Kanttekeningen, Jeremia*. Baarn, Netherlands: Bosch & Keuning.
Willibrordvertaling. Nederlands Bijbelgenootschap, 2004.
Wolff, H. W. *Hosea*. Hermeneia: A Critical & Historical Commentary on the Bible. Translated by G. Stansell. Philadelphia: Fortress Press.
Wood, L. J. *Hosea*. The Expositor's Bible Commentary. Grand Rapids: Zondervan.
Würthwein, E. "Der Ursprung der Prophetischen Gerichtsrede." *Zeitschrift für Theologie* 49 (1952).
Yee, G. A. "Hosea" in vol. 7 of *The New Interpreter's Bible*. Nashville: Abingdon, 1996.
Yaakov, Rav Nachman bar. *Gemara Teachings in the Talmud Bavli, Acha Ta'anit 27b*. New York: Sefaria.
Zuckerman, B. *The West Semitic Research Project*. Los Angeles: University of Southern California, School of Religion.

Other Jewish Sources:

Midrash Rabbah. Amoraic Midrash on the Torah and the Five Megillos. 10 vols. London, UK: The Soncino Press, 1983.
Midrash Tanchuma. Midrash on the Torah. By Rabbi Tanchuma. New York: Mesorah.
Talmud Yerushalmi, Schottenstein. Vol. 2. New York: Mesorah Publications.
Targum Onkelos. The Book of Deuteronomy. Israël: Church of Jerusalem.
Targum Jonathan. Aramaic Bible Series. USA: Liturgical Press.
Rashi, the Sapirstein Edition. Vols. 1–5. A Commentary on the Books of Moses by Rashi. Ed. N. Sherman and M. Zlotowitz. New York: Mesorah, 1995.
Talmud Bavli (Babylonian Talmud):

Berachos 1–2	Shabbos 1–4	Eruvin 1–2	Pesachim 1–3	Rosh Hashanah
Yoma 1–2	Succah 1–2	Beitzah	Taanis	Megillah
Moed Katan	Chagigah	Yevamos 1–2	Kesubos 1–3	Nedarim 1–2
Nazit 1–2	Sotah 1–2	Gittin 1–2	Kiddushin 1–2	Bava Kamma
Bava Metzia 1–3	Bava Basra 1–3	Sanhedrin 1–3	Shevuos	Makkos
Zevachim 1–3	Chullin	Niddah		

Uzziel, Jonathan ben. *Targum Jonathan on Hosea.* USA: Sefaria Free Library.

The Internet

Bible Hub International. Search program with Strong's Concordance. www.biblehub.com.
BijbelOnline. Bible search program. Nederlands Bijbelgenootschap. https://www.online-bijbel.nl/.
Handschriften van de Bijbel. www.godswoord.nl.
Interlinear Bible and Concordance Search Software. http://www.scripture4all.org/.
Jewish Encyclopedia. The Kopelman Foundation. www.jewishencyclopedia.com.
Mark, J. J. *Ancient History Encyclopedia.* Montréal. Canada: Ancient History Encyclopedia Foundation, 2017.
Morfix—English to Hebrew Translator & Dictionary. Tel Aviv, Israel: Melingo, 2016.
NASB Exhaustive Concordance. www.biblehub.com.
Nissaba, *Godinnen uit de Hele Wereld.* Netherlands: Els Geuzebroek. www.nissaba.nl.
Online Bible Study and Bible Dictionary. www.johnhurt.com.
Radavich, R. *Targum Jonathan to the Prophets*, 2017. https/tuxdox.com/targum-jonathan-to-the-prophets-pdf.
Strong's Concordance and Dictionary. Glassport, Pennsylvania: Bible Hub International. www.biblehun.com.
Sulam, B. *The Revelation of Godliness.* Kabbalah Education & Research Institute, http://www.kabbalah.info/eng/content/view/frame/3796?/eng/content/view/full_list/3796&main.
Talmud Bavli. "Ta'anith." www.halakhah.com.
The Unbound Bible. Biola University. www.unboundbible.org.

INDEX ANNOTATIONS AND EXCURSUS

The Seven Dispensations	Excursus 1	20
The End Time	Excursus 2	21
The Downfall of the Northern Kingdom, Israel	Excursus 3	26
The Fall of Judah	Excursus 4	27
Girl of Two Fruit Cakes	Annotation 1A	48
Temple Prostitution	Annotation 1B	63
The Bloodguilt of King Jehu	Annotation 1C	64
Conditional Prophecy	Annotation 1D	66
God's Name Was at Stake	Annotation 1E	67
Israel and Judah	Excursus 5	68
The House of Israel	Excursus 6	71
The Lost Ten Tribes of Israel	Excursus 7	75
The Messianic Kingdom	Annotation 1F	79
The End of the Sinaitic Covenant	Annotation 1G	80
The Relationship Is Broken	Annotation 2A	105
A Different Fate	Annotation 2B	108
The Wonder of the Love of God	Annotation 2C	110
The Church and Israel	Annotation 2D	114
Ashishah and *Enab*	Annotation 3A	120
The Sacred Stone	Annotation 3B	123
Teraphim—Interpreters	Annotation 3C	124
Ephod, Urim, and Thummim	Excursus 8	130
The Messianic Kingdom in the Bible	Excursus 9	132
The Three Covenants	Excursus 10	156
The Sin of Jeroboam	Excursus 11	165
Israel Becomes Ephraim	Excursus 12	166
Hosea in Our Time	Annotation 4A	168
Child Sacrifices	Annotation 5A	189
A God of Revenge	Annotation 5B	193
Israel's Blessed Future	Excursus 13	196
Two Days and the Third	Annotation 6A	201

The Wounds of Israel	Annotation 6B	217
He Will Revive Us	Excursus 14	217
Judgment and Blessing at the End Time	Excursus 15	221
The Sorrow of God	Excursus 16	223
Israel and Adam	Annotation 6C	225
A Heavenly and an Earthly Kingdom	Excursus 17	227
The Fraternal War	Excursus 18	285
The Watchman of Israel	Annotation 9A	304
The Last Kings of Israel	Annotation 10A	332
Gilgal and Bethel	Excursus 19	333
No Revival in Israel	Excursus 20	336
The Ten Tribes Rediscovered	Excursus 21	338
Did Jacob Struggle with God?	Excursus 22	373
The Patriarch Jacob	Annotation 12A	386
Sheol, the Hereafter?	Excursus 23	414
Names of the Almighty	Excursus 24	423
The Sacrificial Services Were Never Discontinued	Excursus 25	435
Songs about the Messianic Kingdom	Annotation 14A	441
The Purification of Israel	Excursus 26	442

ABOUT THE AUTHOR

Gert A. Van de Weerd was born in 1946, in Veenendaal, the Netherlands. After college he studied high-frequency technology. He is a husband and the father of four children.

In 1973 he started his professional career as a junior technician serving electronic organs for a small import company of musical instruments. In subsequent years his interests changed from the technical aspects to a business focus. In a few years he rose to the function of director. Meanwhile, he studied economics at the Institute for Social Studies in Utrecht, the Netherlands.

In 1981 he started as an independent entrepreneur and founded his own company in electronic engineering. In 1988 he acquired Johannus Orgelbouw in Ede, a well-known producer of electronic church organs. Today this company is part of the Global Organ Group, which consists of Makin Organs (UK), Copeman-Hart Church Organs (UK), Rodgers Organs (US), Monarke Organs (NL), and Johannus Organs (NL).

Despite his love for church organs, his main interest has become the Holy Bible. In 1978 he started a long quest for the general meaning of Old Testament prophecy (he calls it the prophetical backbone of the Scriptures). In 1981 he was asked by the Evangelical Alliance (a platform for cooperation between Christian churches) to give a series of lessons about the prophet Zechariah. The many inconsistencies he found in commentaries inspired him to deepen his study.

In September 1999 he issued his first book: *A Commentary on the Prophet Zechariah*. This generated many positive reactions, even among professional theologians. In 2001 a second book followed, *The Prophet Micah*; in 2001 and 2002, *The Prophet Daniel*, volumes 1 and 2; and in subsequent years, *The Prophet Amos* and *The Prophet Hosea*.

With his extended commentary on Ezekiel, volumes 1 and 2, he became well known to many Christians in the Netherlands, because he succeeded in explaining the Scriptures in everyday language.

In 2010 he started his research in Isaiah—the most discussed book of the Old Testament. After six years of intensive study, *The Prophet Isaiah*, volume 1, was brought out. With over one thousand pages, this study book has given many people new insights. The book drew attention in wide circles and, in spite of the high price, it sold surprising well. In 2018 volume 2 followed. Because of the many discussions around this book, he was asked to lead a Bible study on television for Family7. So far, he has conducted forty-three half-hour broadcasts.

His next project will be a study in the Revelation of John—about eight hundred pages. Many Christians are looking forward to its release.

www.ingramcontent.com/pod-product-compliance
Lightning Source LLC
Chambersburg PA
CBHW081005180426
43194CB00044B/2762